Second Edition

FUNDAMENTALS OF PHYSICAL GEOGRAPHY

Glenn T. Trewartha, *Professor of Geography, University of Wisconsin*

Arthur H. Robinson, *Professor of Geography, University of Wisconsin*

Edwin H. Hammond, *Professor of Geography, Syracuse University*

Cartography by **Randall D. Sale,** *Associate Professor of Geography, University of Wisconsin*

McGRAW-HILL BOOK COMPANY
New York, St. Louis, San Francisco, Toronto, London, Sydney

FUNDAMENTALS OF PHYSICAL GEOGRAPHY

Library of Congress Catalog Card Number 67-24447

65181

1 2 3 4 5 6 7 8 9 0   L K B P   7 5 4 3 2 1 0 6 9 8

Cover photograph: NASA
photograph 65-HC-789.

PREFACE

In this edition the authors have tried to build on the elements that teachers favored in the first edition of *Fundamentals of Physical Geography*. As before, the materials have been selected to fit a one-semester, one-quarter, or two-quarter, introductory college survey course. The degree of generalization has been kept at a high level, with the major focus on general world patterns and their interrelationships. On the other hand, the organization of this second edition has been changed to what seems to be a more logical way of presenting the material.

Much of the content is based upon the authors' more comprehensive text, *Physical Elements of Geography,* fifth edition; but this book has been organized and written quite independently. The illustrations, all newly prepared in two colors for *Physical Elements of Geography,* have been liberally used here, and five of the multicolored world maps have been newly compiled and modernized for both books.

All the subject matter has been brought up to date; only a few highlights can be mentioned. The opening chapter has been recast and reillustrated. The sections dealing with the elements of climate have been revised to reflect current research, and more emphasis has been placed on the role of solar radiation, energy exchange, and the weather element. The section on groups and types of climate continues to focus on the world pattern and the characteristic location of the climates. The older system of climatic classification has been modified, a change which the authors consider a marked improvement over the system used in the first edition.

The chapter on water now includes a discussion of the water balance, and more stress is placed on the role of water as a critical resource. As requested by many users, the section dealing with land-surface form has been considerably expanded. In particular the chapters concerning gradation and plains have been recast to emphasize modern geomorphological theory. In the section on soils an up-to-date classification has been added which takes into account the *7th Approximation*.

Immediately following this preface is a brief section, "Introduction to the Student," which the authors hope will provide a useful, brief orientation to the field of geography in general and the study of physical geography in particular. As in the first edition, the authors have not included chapter outlines or review questions in the belief that by refraining from doing so they have aided the instructional process. It is hoped that the student himself will prepare these aids to learning. For those who wish to range further, brief lists of selected references are provided at the ends of most chapters. Wherever such a section covers several chapters (as in the case of Chaps. 2 to 5, for example), these appear at the end of the first chapter in the sequence (i.e., Chap. 2) so that the student will take notice of it early rather than late.

The authors acknowledge a great debt to their colleagues, students, and other friends for this second edition. Their many suggestions based upon the first edition, and their assistance in ways too numerous to mention, are deeply appreciated.

Glenn T. Trewartha
Arthur H. Robinson
Edwin H. Hammond

CONTENTS

INTRODUCTION TO
THE STUDENT

Man, along with all other creatures, lives in a complex environment that is made up of such things as people, land, air, water, plants, soil, and a host of others. These phenomena are distributed in surprising complexity over the surface of the earth, and they vary not only from place to place, but from time to time. Since the days of ancient Egypt and classical Greece, man's writings have been full of his fascination with the variety of the earth's surface. He discovered early that differences in the environment are not only interesting but intricate and important. The Greeks made them the objects of a field of scholarly study, to which they gave the name "geography."

One way to learn something about the scope and objectives of physical geography and what its relationships are to the rest of geography and to other branches of earth science is to read this book; but that will take the whole term. As a kind of preliminary substitute, this introduction attempts, in broad terms, to characterize the study of geography as a whole and physical geography as a segment.

To begin, one must realize that geography, like history, is not restricted to a particular group of phenomena. Theoretically geography is concerned with all earth "things" that are spatially arrayed; its uniqueness is in the method and aim of the study. While history emphasizes time or chronology, geography emphasizes location, distribution, and place. As a "science of place," geography is concerned with how and why the various environmental differences are arranged as they are over the earth, and in what way these world patterns are themselves important.

The Study of Geography

The study of geography is based upon a set of fundamental facts that can be summarized in five remarkably simple statements:

All parts of the world are different. This statement seems rather obvious, but the task of systematically working out the ways in which the various places differ is immense. Geography is the one scientific field that has as a major goal the development of organized knowledge regarding the nature and pattern of place-to-place differences over the earth. Thus geography has an important descriptive function, which it accomplishes by statistics, by verbal characterization, and by maps. In common speech the *geography* of an area sometimes means simply this description of its environmental characteristics.

Each individual phenomenon varies from place to place. In addition to studying the complex of things that gives places their distinctive characters, we can concentrate on the differences from place to place of one set of environmental factors, such as climate, population, or the form of the land. The number of such phenomena is nearly unlimited and encompasses the range of human creation as well as the natural world. Each of these has its own pattern of occurrence and its own reasons for varying from place to place as it does.

The pattern of variation of one element is functionally related to the patterns of other elements. Individual things and processes on the earth are never independent, but are bound together in an incredibly tangled web of interrelationships. Some of the linkages are simple cause-and-effect ones, many more are indirect, and a great many involve the mind of man. All are tied to places.

For example, precipitation affects the vegetation of an area, and also the soil. Vegetation in turn affects soil development, and soil character affects vegetation. Man therefore takes precipitation, vegetation, and soil (among many other things) into account in planning his agriculture. But his agricultural practices affect the quality of the soil, and changes in soil quality may in turn affect the yields of his crops, and so on. The chain of interconnection is almost endless, and everywhere it involves place-to-place contrasts and similarities. Geography attempts to describe and explain these interconnections, particularly as they relate one distribution pattern to others.

The interrelationships among the patterns of phenomena may be studied in detail in a local area, over a larger region, on a continental level, or on a worldwide basis. This part of the study of geography has no bounds.

There is a continual interaction among areas. No area of the earth is independent in all respects. Just as heat flows from warmer to cooler bodies, places on the earth interact with one another because of their differences. Sometimes the interaction is simple, and sometimes the connections are quite indirect or dependent upon past events. An agricultural area trades with an urban center; melting snows in a high mountain region feed streams that periodically water an adjacent dry lowland; or life-giving moisture is brought to the land by air masses moving in from the oceans. The patterns of such interactions interest geographers, both as products of place-to-place differences and as spatial phenomena in their own right.

The geography of one time is not the geography of another. The world patterns of particular elements, the character of specific places, and therefore, the relationships among places and elements are continually changing. In the short run there are the changes of the seasons with their accompanying modifications of the environment, such as changes in vegetation, water storage (snow and ice), and so on. In the long run there are far-reaching changes, many of which are nonperiodic, progressive, and in some cases irreversible. In historical time, most of the rapid and obvious changes of the nonperiodic type have been initiated by man: for example, man cleared the vegetation cover for cropland; he created resources, such as atomic energy or petroleum, by technological development; he destroyed them by consumption or abuse as, for example, through promoting soil erosion; he migrated to new lands carrying his culture with him; or he altered his pattern of political and economic control through force or economic competition. Changes also occur in nature without man's aid, though most of these are slower. Mountain ranges have been formed and eroded away; immense ice sheets have grown and decayed; plant and animal species have spread from a source region into many parts of the earth.

Thus geography has a dynamic aspect not only in the place-related processes of a given time, but also in periodic and nonperiodic changes in the whole nature and pattern of place-to-place variation.

The Study of Physical Geography

Physical geography, which focuses upon those surface phenomena that are not primarily of man's making, runs parallel to *human geography* as one of the chief traditional topical subdivisions of the field. Each of the groups of phenomena it concerns—climate, land-surface form, the seas, waters of the lands, soils, vegetation, and minerals—is of basic significance to man in many ways. The distribution pattern of each of these physical elements is strongly related to patterns of many of the others; consequently, the study of physical geography is also concerned with these interrelations and their explanation.

To study the elements of the physical environment scientifically, one must consider the processes involved in their interaction in place. In this respect there is inevitably a two-way overlap between geography and the other sciences concerned, such as meteorology, geology, oceanography, hydrology, pedology (soil science), botany, or zoology. The difference lies chiefly in emphasis —in the kinds of questions each group of scientists is most inclined to ask about the phenomena. The geographer's fundamental concern is with distribution—local, regional, and worldwide—the relations between patterns, the interactions among phenomena that establish the physical character of areas, and the interactions between areas that arise from their differences.

Many scientists study the nature and behavior of particular kinds of things with no real concern about the place where they occur. A geologist or hydrologist, for example, might study the streams of northern Missouri in order to learn how water moves in natural channels; those channels just happen to serve as the "laboratory" for deducing some general laws of behavior. The nongeographer has little interest in the streams as features of the particular area or as part of a continental or worldwide pattern. The geographer, however, would study them for just these reasons. As the streams of northern Missouri, they most likely differ from the streams of adjacent Illinois or southern Missouri, or any other part of the world. Also, they are intimately related to the surface form, precipitation, surface materials, and vegetation of northern Missouri, and they are an integral, functioning part of the distinctive physical character of that part of the world. Furthermore, they form one element of the pattern of worldwide stream character, the distribution of which is related to worldwide variations in the many elements which affect stream character.

In scholarly research there are, of course, no fenced boundaries of learning fields. There are geographically minded geologists, soil scientists, and botanists, just as there are many geographers who have contributed to the other sciences of nature.

While there are traditional and practical justifications for splitting geography into physical and human sections for teaching, the practice also has its drawbacks. Geography does not readily lend itself to a clear division for however much man enjoys thinking of himself as a creature apart and as a conqueror of nature, he is nonetheless a part of nature and lives in nature. Even modern urban man expends much of his time, energy, and technological skill in coping with the nonhuman phenomena of the world. The patterns of man's many activities and even his own distribution on earth partly reflect his efforts to come to terms with a highly diverse "natural" world that simply cannot be treated as if it were everywhere the same.

Although the study of physical geography deals with phenomena of nature ranging from local variations to world patterns, it is not simply nature study. Man is always involved—as an evaluator, a user, and a modifier. When he tills the soil, irrigates a crop, extracts or fights for control of a mineral deposit, shelters himself from the cold, dams or fouls a stream, starves from drought, clears the forest from half a continent, pours noxious gases into the air, introduces crops into a new region, or avoids a huge section of the earth because it is too costly or too trying for him to handle, he is living with and is a part of physical geography. As it becomes ever more clear that the world is neither limitless nor secure against irreparable damage, it also becomes clear that man desperately needs to know far more than he does about all aspects of the natural world that sustains him, and not least its geography.

It is the purpose of this introductory book to focus attention on the areal distribution and the functional interrelationships of the elements of physical geography. There are two ways this may be done: one is by concentrating on the individual elements and their distribution and relation to other elements, and the other is by dealing with the variety of elements as they are integrated within various areas. In this book the first approach is followed, and the broad earth distributions and relationships among patterns are stressed, with less emphasis upon the mechanics of interrelation in specific places. The authors believe that this provides the most interesting and efficient way of obtaining that fundamental understanding of the earth's physical geography which in turn is prerequisite to an intelligent appreciation of the "nonphysical" earth.

1

The Earth and Its Study

The Earth in Space

The earth is a very small satellite which is in orbit around a central star, the sun. The earth would be a desolate place, rather like the moon, were it not for the fact that a number of conditions exist at the earth's surface which have allowed the development of many forms of life.

One of these conditions is that the surface of the earth is part solid and part liquid. Another is that a gaseous atmosphere has developed around the solid-liquid earth. Also, temperatures near the bottom of the atmosphere stay within a rather small range. And finally, radiant energy from the sun regularly bathes all parts of the earth's surface. The effects of radiant energy are tremendously complex, partly because there are systematic variations in the amounts received at different places and times. These variations in turn induce regular circulations in the earth's liquids and gases, as well as constant changes in its biological elements.

Because the earth's surface zone is the home of man, he is intensely curious about the character of his natural environment. And so the science of geography has grown up to study the character of this surface zone and the ways in which it differs from place to place on the sphere that is the earth.

The Earth as a Sphere

The earth is almost a true sphere, with a radius of nearly 4,000 miles and an area of about 197 million square miles. The earth rotates steadily, and the opposite, or antipodal, points of the sphere that lie in the axis of rotation are called the earth *poles.* An imaginary line encircling the surface midway between the poles is called the *equator.*

The earth departs somewhat from true sphericity because there is a slight flattening in polar areas and a correspondent bulging in equatorial regions caused by its rotation. The polar radius is about 13.5 miles shorter than an equatorial radius. Yet given the size of the earth, this spheroidal deformation is small: It would amount to less than $\frac{1}{10}$ in. on a ball 5 ft in diameter. Thus for most purposes we shall consider the earth to be a sphere.

The relative smoothness of the earth is not generally appreciated by diminutive man, to whom even the differences between uplands and lowlands seem profound. But the extreme difference in elevation between the highest mountain and the lowest ocean deep is only about 13 miles, or less than $\frac{1}{300}$ of the earth's radius. If the earth were reduced to the size of a very large globe with a diameter of 5 ft, the Rocky Mountains in the United States would be only about $\frac{1}{50}$ in. above the general surface level. On an ordinary desk globe they could hardly be felt at all.

Most of the earth's solid surface is covered

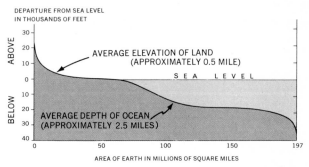

Figure 1.1   Relative amounts of water and land surface on the earth and the average elevation and depth of the solid surface in relation to sea level. Note that most of the earth's surface is water.

by water, and the 29 percent that does protrude above water does so only slightly. The average elevation of the land above sea level is about $\frac{1}{2}$ mile (Fig. 1.1). It is on this low-lying, restricted land area that man makes his home.

The distribution of the land and water surfaces is not symmetrical, especially in terms of an equatorial division. There is twice as much land in the Northern Hemisphere as in the Southern. The total area of the exposed solid surfaces is about 57 million square miles (equal to about sixteen times the area of the United States); but a considerable portion of that land is unsuitable for much human occupation at present, being too hot or cold, too wet or dry, too mountainous, too steeply sloping, or ill suited in some other way.

A large number of the variations in the earth environment are directly or indirectly related to its spherical form. For example, the differences in different parts of the earth in the duration and intensity of the sunlight received are largely a function of the curvature of the rotating surface. These differences in energy receipt affect such phenomena as air and soil temperatures and the circulation of the atmosphere and the oceans. Man's systems of specifying position, of reckoning time, of indicating direction, and many other basic operations are also founded on the earth's spherical form. It is important for students of geography to be familiar with some of the properties of the sphere, the circle, and the arc as they apply to the earth.

Great Circles. If we were to shine a flashlight on a ball in a dark room, we would demonstrate several fundamental consequences of the earth's spherical form (Fig. 1.2). First, we would be showing how the earth is lighted—that is, how it intercepts the solar energy which maintains life and drives the circulations on its surface. Second, we would exhibit the concept of a great circle, for the line separating the dark from the light (the circle of illumination) is a great circle, and it remains one no matter how we may rotate or move the ball with respect to the source of light.

A great circle, geometrically defined, is the path of the intersection of a spherical surface with any plane which includes the center of the sphere. A great circle has many important characteristics: (1) It is the largest possible circle on a sphere, (2) it divides the earth's surface into hemispheres, (3) any two points on a sphere can be "connected" by a part of a great circle, and the course along that arc is always the shortest course (Fig. 1.3), and (4) any great circle bisects any other great circle.

Of course, it is not possible for two great circles to be parallel.

The intersection of the surface of a sphere with any plane that does *not* include the center of the sphere also makes a circle, but it is called a small circle. Small circles have *none* of the characteristics of great circles listed above, and moreover, small circles can be parallel to one another. A view around the horizon, whether from fairly close to the surface or from an orbiting satellite, is a small circle.

Distance on the Earth. Because the surface of a sphere is uniformly curved, the distance from one place to another on it can be stated as the number of degrees, minutes, and seconds included in the great-circle arc that connects the two (Fig. 1.4). The arc distance can, of course, be translated into other units of measure, such as miles or kilometers, by calculating the size of the sphere. This is done by measuring a short arc distance with precision and then extending the result to the entire great circle. Such a calculation was first attempted (with

Figure 1.2 The earth ball, primarily lighted from the sun, is always half dark and half light; the division between the two, the circle of illumination, is a great circle.

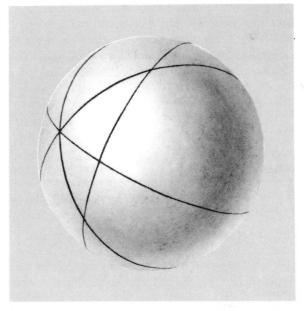

Figure 1.3 Any two points on the surface of a sphere may be "connected" by a great circle, which is the shortest possible course over the surface between the two.

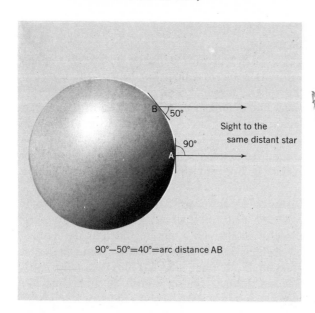

Figure 1.4 Arc distance along the great circle between two points is obtained by observing the difference in the astronomical altitude of a celestial object, real or imaginary, which lies in the plane of the great circle.

limited success) more than 2,000 years ago; today the relationships are known with considerable exactness. One minute of arc (one-sixtieth of a degree) of a great circle is practically equal to the distance recognized as the international nautical mile. The relation of the nautical mile to other standard measures is shown below.

	Feet	Meters
International nautical mile	6,076.10	1,852.00
Statute mile	5,280.00	1,609.35
Kilometer	3,280.83	1,000.00

Direction on a sphere is more difficult to specify than distance is, because direction on such a curved surface is quite arbitrary. A system that is generally useful over a good part of the earth's surface is based on the spherical coordinate referencing framework. This method of designating direction will be described later, but it is worth observing here that the only "straight line" on a sphere is actually the curve along a great circle. As previously pointed out, the shortest course—that is, the "true"

direction—from any point to any other point is always along the great-circle arc which joins the two.

The Earth as a Satellite

Since the earth is a satellite of the sun it moves systematically around it, and the two bodies maintain certain important relationships. The primary movement of the earth is termed its *revolution,* which is simply its orbit around the sun (Fig. 1.5). Note that all points of the earth's orbit lie in a plane, called the *plane of the ecliptic.* The orbiting earth has a second major movement, *rotation,* in which it spins constantly toward the east while orbiting (Fig. 1.6). Revolution and rotation are quite different motions and should not be confused.

In addition to the two primary motions, the surface of the rotating, orbiting sphere maintains some critical directional relationships with the sun. These are best summed up in the terms inclination and parallelism. *Inclination* refers to the fact that the axis of the earth has a special relationship to the plane in which it orbits, while *parallelism* refers to the fact that all the while the earth is moving, the direction of its axis is always almost exactly the same relative to the other stars, though it changes markedly with respect to the sun.

The earth revolves around the sun in a slightly elliptical orbit, and in the course of its revolution, it moves somewhat faster during the period when it is closer to the sun. The average time required for the earth to complete one circuit of its orbit is designated as a year. During this period the earth rotates in relation to the sun approximately $365\frac{1}{4}$ times, thus determining the number of days in the year. Primarily because of the variations in the speed of the earth along its annual orbit, the time interval between successive complete daily rotations relative to the sun varies slightly. The average rotational day is arbitrarily divided into 24 hr of constant duration.

The axis of the earth's rotation is inclined about $66\frac{1}{2}°$ from the plane of the ecliptic (or $23\frac{1}{2}°$ from a line perpendicular to it), and the axis at any time during its orbit is parallel to the position that it occupies at any other time. These impor-

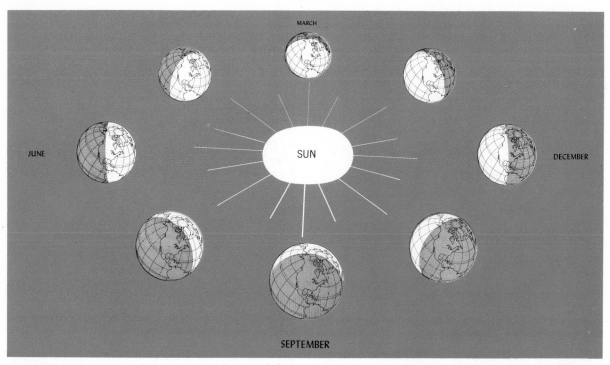

Figure 1.5   The relation of the inclination and parallelism of the earth's axis to the change of the seasons. For this drawing the observer is far outside the earth's orbit and slightly "above" the plane of the ecliptic.

tant relations or "movements" are shown diagrammatically in Fig. 1.5.

The inclination and parallelism of the earth's axis, together with the earth's shape, its rotation, and its revolution about the sun, combine to produce several earth phenomena that are of vital importance to physical geography. Some of these are (1) variations in the distribution of solar energy over the earth, (2) the changing of the seasons, (3) the variation in the lengths of day and night, and (4) the general manner in which the atmosphere and oceans circulate. These matters and other related ones will be discussed more fully in the following chapters dealing with the atmosphere and climate.

Locational Systems on the Earth

Man has developed a coordinate system based on the earth's form and its movements which enables him to determine and describe position on the earth's surface. On an ordinary sphere there is neither beginning nor end, no natural point or line of reference from which to reckon the positions of points with respect to one another. If it were not for its systematic motions and planetary relations, the earth also would have no natural point or line to use in measuring distance and direction. But the fact of rotation establishes the geographic poles of the earth, and these serve as reference points for a whole system which makes it possible to determine directions and locations.

The Spherical Coordinate System

This system consists of an arrangement of intersecting lines on the earth. It is similar to the familiar rectangular coordinates of ordinary graph paper, modified to fit the spherical earth. In the spherical coordinate system an infinite number of small circles is arranged parallel to the equator, as illustrated in Fig. 1.7. All of them, including the equa-

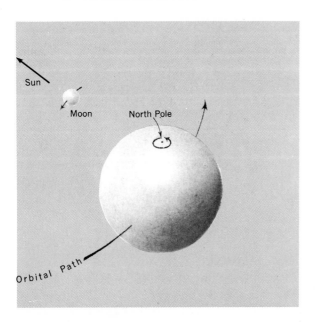

Figure 1.6 Assuming one is looking at the earth's orbit with the northern part of the earth uppermost, then it moves counterclockwise in its orbit (see Fig. 1.5) and rotates the same way. The moon also orbits the earth counterclockwise.

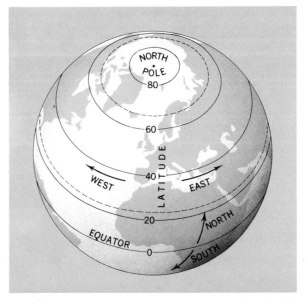

Figure 1.7 The parallels in the earth's coordinate system. Parallels coincide with the direction of east and west, and their arrangement provides a method for specifying north-south position. Only a few of the infinite number possible are shown here.

tor, are called *parallels,* and east-west direction on the earth coincides with their orientation on the surface. Since each of the small circles is parallel to the equator, every point on a given parallel will be the same distance from the equator and the same distance from the North Pole or South Pole. The distance of a point from the equator or one of the poles is called *latitude* in the earth's coordinate system. This distance, or latitude, is expressed by identifying the parallel on which the point is located.

A statement of latitude alone cannot serve to locate a point, because a parallel is a circle, and the point could be anywhere on it. Position east or west on a parallel, called *longitude,* is established by employing a different system of circles which are perpendicular to the parallels. In a plane, or flat, coordinate system these lines are also parallel to one another, but on the spherical earth they must converge and intersect at the poles. They are equally spaced on any parallel, however. These lines are arcs of great circles and are called *meridians.* The directions *north* and *south* coincide with the posi-

tions of the meridians on the surface of the earth, as shown in Fig. 1.8.

Latitude. Latitude is distance north-south. In the earth's coordinate system, the single great circle formed by a matching pair of meridians is divided into quadrants, the points of division being the two poles and the two intersections with the equator. Each meridional quadrant is thus divided into 90° of latitude, and the numbering of the latitude proceeds from the equator (0° Lat) to each pole (90° Lat), as shown in Fig. 1.9. Location along a meridian is established by noting its intersection with a particular parallel. Because latitude is reckoned from the equator toward the poles, the small- or low-numbered latitudes are near the equator, while the large- or high-numbered parallels are near the poles. Consequently it is conventional to speak of *low, middle,* and *high* latitudes. For example, Brazil lies in the low latitudes, France in the middle latitudes, and Alaska in the high latitudes.

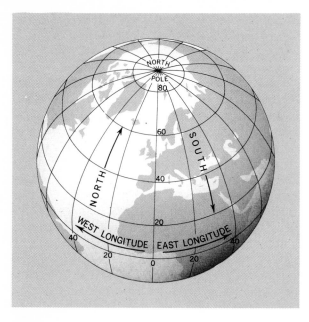

Figure 1.8 The meridians coincide with the direction of north and south, and provide a method for specifying east-west position.

The lengths of the degrees of latitude are not quite identical along a meridian. The latitude of a point is determined by observing, at the point in question, the angular difference between horizontal and the elevation of some celestial body, such as Polaris (the North Star) or the sun. A degree of latitude is, therefore, the distance one must move along a meridian in order to observe a 1° change in this angle. Because of the slight flattening of the earth in the polar regions, one must go farther along a meridian there to obtain a change of 1°. The first degree of latitude from the equator covers a distance of 68.7 miles, while the first degree away from either pole is 69.4 miles long.

Each degree of latitude is divided into 60 minutes ('), and each minute into 60 seconds ("). An average minute of latitude is about 1 nautical mile and about 1.15 statute miles, and 1 second of latitude is about 101 ft. The length of the meter (the standard of distance measurement in the metric system) is in theory one ten-millionth of the meridional quadrant—that is, one ten-millionth of the

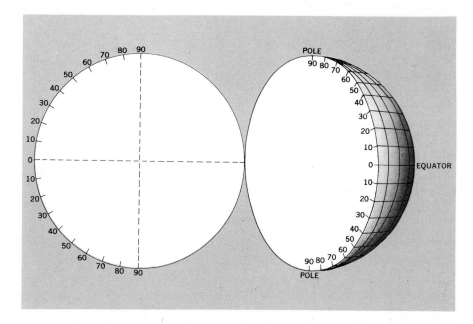

Figure 1.9 If the earth were opened along a meridian, it would show that latitudes along each north-south meridian are numbered from 0° (at the equator) north and south to 90° (at a pole).

distance along a great-circle arc from the equator to the pole.

Commonly only a few of the infinite number of meridian and parallel circles are shown on maps, such as those of the multiples of 5 or 10°. Often, however, four particular parallels in addition to the equator are emphasized. Because of the inclination and parallelism of the earth's axis with respect to the plane of the ecliptic, the sun at noon appears at different elevations above the horizon in different regions. The parallels of 23½° N and S from the equator are called the Tropics of Cancer and Capricorn, respectively. They mark the limits of the zone near the equator within which the sun ever appears directly overhead. The parallels of 66½° N and S from the equator are called the Arctic and Antarctic Circles, respectively. They mark the limits of the polar area in each hemisphere within which the sun ever appears above the horizon continuously for 24 hr or more or, at the same time in the opposite hemisphere, remains below the horizon for 24 hr or more (Fig. 1.10).

Longitude. Longitude is distance east-west, and it is reckoned in degrees, minutes, and seconds along the parallels. There is no particular meridian marked by nature from which the system of numbering longitude may be started (as the equator is for specifying latitude), since all meridians are exactly alike. In fact, for several centuries many countries designated some meridian that lay within their own borders as 0° Long. So much confusion resulted that the meridian passing through Greenwich Observatory (London, England) was chosen in 1884 by international agreement as 0° Long. It is called the prime meridian, and it intersects the equator in the Atlantic Ocean near Africa at a point which is notable for having 0°00'00" Long and 0°00'00" Lat. The degrees of longitude in each parallel are numbered to the east and to the

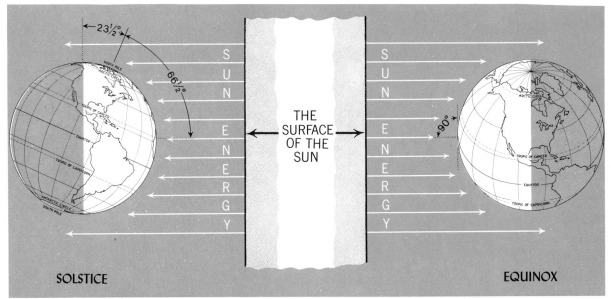

Figure 1.10 The angular relationship between the direction of the sun's energy and latitudes on the earth's surface changes during the year. The left-hand diagram of the June solstice shows that the noon sun would appear directly overhead (90°) at the Tropic of Cancer, while at the Antarctic Circle it would appear on the horizon; i.e., the rays would be tangent (0°) to the earth's surface. At the time of an equinox (March or September), the noon sun would appear directly overhead at the equator and the circle of illumination would pass through the poles. See Fig. 1.5. The segments of the sun's surface shown here to scale with the earth represent only about 1/200 part of its circumference. Consequently, for practical purposes they have almost no curvature.

west from the prime meridian to 180° (see Fig. 1.11). The prime meridian and the meridian of 180° together make a great circle.

All the parallels, except the equator, are small circles, and they become progressively smaller poleward. Each parallel, regardless of size, is divided into 360° of longitude, and consequently the length of 1° of longitude decreases with higher latitude. On the equator (which is a great circle), 1° of longitude has about the same length as an average degree of latitude. The following table shows the decreasing lengths of the degrees of longitude at various latitudes from the equator to the pole.

Latitude	Statute miles	Kilometers
0°	69.17	111.32
15°	66.83	107.56
30°	59.96	96.49
45°	49.00	78.85
60°	34.67	55.80
75°	17.96	28.90
90°	0.00	0.00

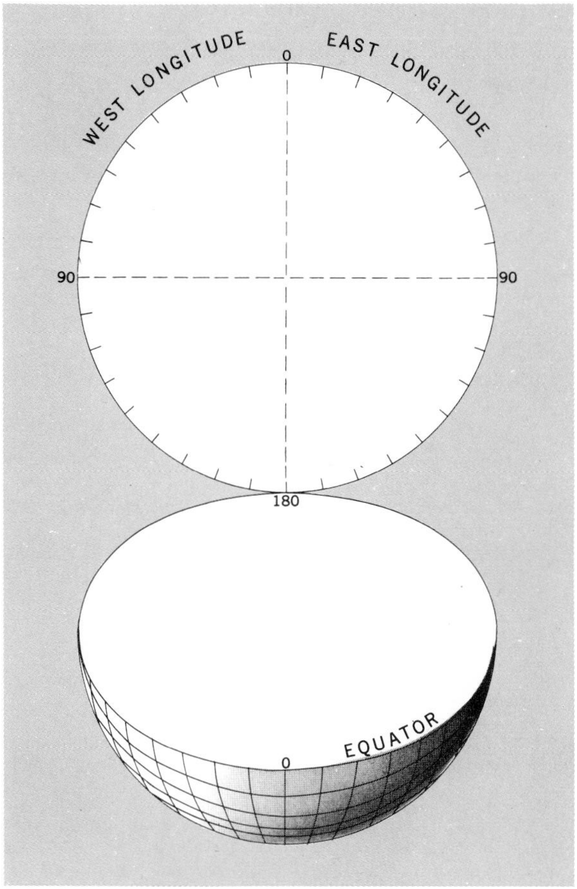

Direction on the Earth. The relative location of places on the earth's surface may be indicated in directional terms as well as by identifying their latitudes and longitudes. The expression of precise direction on the earth is more complex than most people realize, because the earth is a sphere and its coordinate system is spherical instead of rectangular.

The path along a great circle is the most direct surface course between points on the earth, and it is analogous to the straight line on a plane. Since the directions at any point on the earth are defined simply by the orientation of the parallels and the meridians, and since these are on a spherical surface, it follows that directional relationships change from place to place on the earth. Consequently, although one can easily describe the "beginning direction" of the great-circle course from one point to another, the angular relation between the coordinate system and that particular great circle will often be different along the circle's course —except, obviously, when the great circle in question is itself a meridian or the equator. The direction from one place to another is specified by stating the angle at the starting point between the meridian of that point and the great-circle arc to the other point. The statement may be given either as a bearing, e.g., NE, or as an azimuth, that is, a statement of the number of degrees in the angle between the meridian and the great circle, usually reckoned clockwise from north, such as NE = 45° azimuth. Another way of stating the same bearing would be N45°E.

Figure 1.11 If the earth were opened along the equator, it would show that the 360° of longitude in the equator (and each parallel) are counted 180° to the east and the west of the prime meridian.

When people think of bearings, they commonly think of the compass rose or card. The needle of the compass aligns itself with the forces emanating from that great magnet, the earth. Unfortunately, only in limited areas does the magnetic needle actually parallel the meridian; in most places the needle comes to rest at an angle with it. This angle varies considerably from place to place, and the magnitude of the variation at any point is called the compass declination of the point. For example, Fig. 1.12 shows the lines of equal compass declination in the United States. East of the line marked 0°, the compass has a west declination. The compass declination varies widely from place to place, and in both polar regions it is extreme.

Time on the Earth. The movements of the earth relative to the sun and other stars provide the bases for systems of reckoning time on the earth.

Clock time (mean solar time) is measured in relation to the period of average rotation of the earth relative to the sun. This period is arbitrarily designated as 24 hr. Since each point on the earth's surface (except the poles) rotates a full circle (360°) in the average 24-hr period, it follows that in 1 hr any point will traverse 15°. This relationship provides the basis for a system of standard-time zones. Until about a century ago, each place on the earth reckoned time according to the sun in relation to its own local meridian. With the growth of rapid travel in the nineteenth century, this became increasingly confusing, so that the choice of the Greenwich meridian as the prime meridian also allowed the development of a system of standard time.

The standard-time system, in theory, requires that all parts of a north-south zone 15° of longitude wide adopt the mean solar time of that

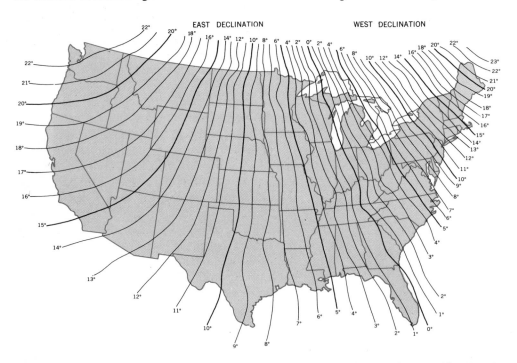

Figure 1.12 Lines of equal magnetic declination in the conterminous United States (the United States exclusive of Alaska and Hawaii) in 1965. Only at points on the line of 0° declination does the magnetic compass parallel the meridian; elsewhere a correction must be made. *(Generalized from a map by U.S. Coast and Geodetic Survey.)*

zone's central meridian. Changes of time would then be necessary only when crossing the boundary of a zone, and each change would be exactly 1 hr. The clock would be set forward (i.e., later, as from 3:00 to 4:00) by people traveling east and back (i.e., earlier, as from 3:00 to 2:00) by those traveling west. Where the system has been adopted, the zones commonly are not bounded by meridians but by irregular lines, the locations of which are subject to change and are dictated by administrative convenience (Fig. 1.13).

Although most of the world follows the standard-time plan, some countries have not yet adopted it. Also, a few employ the mean solar time of meridians that are not multiples of 15 and therefore do not differ from Greenwich time by exact hours. And many make regular or irregular use of daylight saving time (i.e., clocks ahead, as from 1:00 to 2:00). Consequently, the map of world time zones related to Greenwich time is complicated and changes frequently.

The other system of reckoning time is called calendar time. One rotation of a point on the earth relative to the sun is termed one day, and the completion of one average orbit is termed a year. Since the earth rotates relative to the sun approximately 365¼ times during one orbit, minor adjustments, such as leap years, must be made in the calendar. By international agreement, the days are specified to begin and end at the date line, a line extending from pole to pole in the area of the Pacific approximately following the 180th meridian (Fig. 1.14).[1]

Plane Coordinate Systems

On most maps used in the study of physical geography, one finds the geographical coordinate sys-

[1] If a traveler makes a complete east-west circuit of the earth, he either adds or cancels one of the earth's rotations relative to the sun, depending on which way he goes. Consequently, he will either gain or lose one day of his calendar relative to the people who remained in one place. Only when he crosses the date line, however, will he have to adjust his calendar: he must add a day—i.e., repeat a day—if he crosses it going eastward, and must drop out a day—e.g., Wednesday is followed by Friday—if he crosses it going westward.

Figure 1.13 Standard-time zones in the United States in 1965, as defined by the Interstate Commerce Commission.

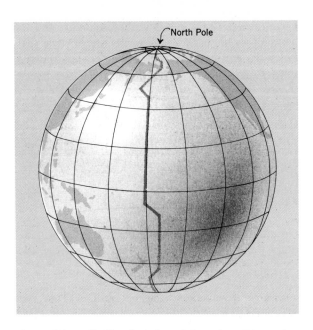

Figure 1.14 The date line deviates from the 180° meridian in order not to divide countries and island groups that lie along it inconveniently into two calendar days.

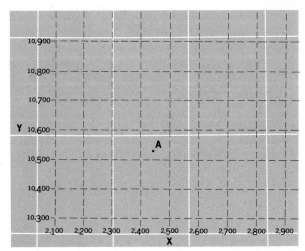

Figure 1.15 A plane coordinate grid (broken black lines) placed over the parallels and meridians of the geographical coordinate system (solid white lines). Ordinarily only the bolder digits are used to begin each half of the grid reference, so point A is at 445530 in the plane coordinate grid. Note that magnetic north, geographical north, and grid north might all be different, and consequently, bearings as related to each system could all be different. Such designations must be carefully identified.

tem; that is, a selection of parallels and meridians. In recent times, however, another type of system based on plane coordinates has come to appear frequently on detailed maps along with the geographical coordinate system. Plane coordinates are very helpful when one is concerned with limited areas or must perform trigonometric calculations having to do with localized distance and direction. In a plane coordinate system the curved surface of the earth is mapped on a plane, and then a simple rectangular coordinate system which uses decimals is placed on the map (Fig. 1.15). Such a system is much simpler than one requiring latitude and longitude to degrees, minutes, and seconds. However, a spherical surface cannot be transformed to a plane without introducing some kinds of distortion, and therefore a plane coordinate system can conveniently be extended only to a limited area.

Only the upper right-hand portion of the rectangular coordinate system is employed (positive x, positive y). The x distances are called *eastings,* and the y distances are called *northings.* The num-

bering of the map coordinates is fitted to the land distances on the individual map, so that one can designate position to the nearest 100,000, 10,000, 1,000, etc., meters or yards. In Fig. 1.15, for example, if each square formed by the broken black lines were 100,000 meters on a side, then the position of point A could be stated as having an x value of 445 and a y value of 530. This would locate it on the earth's surface within a 1,000-meter square. An additional digit added to each value would describe the position of point A within a 100-meter square. In giving such a position, one does not identify x or y; instead, the easting value is always named first and the northing value second: thus point A is at 445530. A simple rule is that to give or locate a grid reference properly, one must "read right up."

Ground Referencing Systems

The geographical coordinate system (latitude and longitude) is the fundamental basis for establishing relative location on the earth. Yet for bounding small areas or locating specific positions on the land, this system is inconveniently complicated and is subject to errors of definition and instrumentation. Consequently other methods are necessary.

Throughout the world the most widely used method of describing sections of land is known as metes and bounds. In this method an arbitrary point, such as an iron stake or other identifiable object, is designated as a point of beginning. From this point the parcel of land in question is bounded by a series of lines having given lengths and true (not magnetic) compass directions. In most parts of the world the bounding lines are more or less fortuitous. They lead to no consistent regularity in the pattern of fences, hedges, and roads which commonly separate properties. This may be seen in detailed maps of many areas, including parts of North America such as Texas or New England.

In contrast to the essentially unplanned subdivision used in most parts of the earth, some large areas have been subdivided according to a system of rectangular survey. This system has even been introduced into some long-inhabited areas of Europe by means of re-subdivision. Mostly, however, rectangular survey is found in the "newer" lands of the earth—for example, in some sections of southern Africa and Australia, and especially in parts of the United States and Canada, where rectangular subdivision was used in almost all the region lying to the west of the earlier-settled eastern seaboard (Fig. 1.16). All detailed maps of these areas of the United States carry lines and numbers referring to this rectangular survey system, which is described briefly below.

U.S. Public Land Survey System. This system employs a network of approximately north-south and east-west lines. The north-south lines are selected meridians, called *principal meridians;* the east-west ones are selected parallels, called *base lines* (Fig. 1.16). They have had the effect of dividing the land into essentially rectangular blocks called townships, which are approximately 6 miles on a side. The locations of the blocks are indicated by numbered

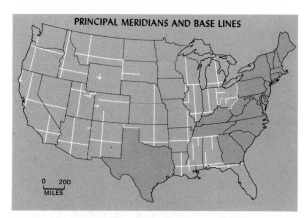

Figure 1.16 Shown in white are the *principal meridians* and *base lines* of the land survey system which was used to subdivide most of the conterminous United States, except for Texas and the Atlantic Coast states. The system is also used in Alaska.

townships (north-south) and *ranges* (east-west), as shown in Fig. 1.17.[2]

[2] But note that the civil, organized towns, townships, or incorporated municipalities into which counties in the United States are divided are units of political administration, and they may or may not coincide with government survey townships, which exist for purposes of land identification.

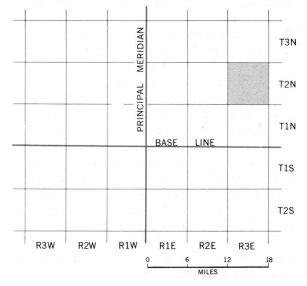

Figure. 1.17 The system of designating government survey townships by township and range numbers with respect to a principal meridian and a base line. The green-shaded township is T2N, R3E.

The ranges are 6-mile-wide strips of land running north and south, each numbered to the east or west of a particular principal meridian. Each range is divided into a tier of townships by east-west lines 6 miles apart, each township being numbered north or south from its base line. A particular township is located by reference to its township and range numbers: for example, township 2 north, range 3 east—usually written T2N, R3E (Fig. 1.17). Owing to the fact that north-south lines converge poleward, certain corrections, offsets, and allowances must be made.

The usual government township is divided into 36 sections, each approximately 1 mile square. The sections are numbered, beginning at the northeastern corner and ending at the southeastern, as shown in Fig. 1.18. The locations of the township and section corners were originally marked on the ground by a stake, stone, mound, tree, or other device.[3]

Wherever such a basic survey framework has been employed, it has left an indelible imprint on the landscape—a pattern of patchwork rectangularity easily seen from the air (Fig. 1.19). It is even reflected in road maps, since the minor roads (along with field boundaries) tend to be oriented with the cardinal directions.

Maps of the Earth

Maps allow the scientist to bring selected aspects of a large area, or even of the entire earth, into view at once. This operation is as necessary for students of earth science as microscopic enlarge-

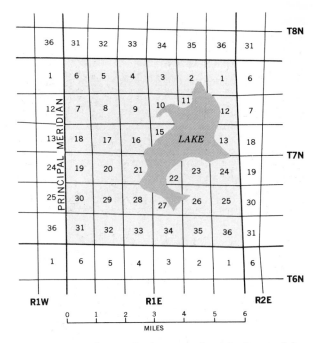

Figure 1.18 The standard system of numbering used for the sections within a township, in this case of the township T7N, R1E. Because of survey problems, sections are not always 1 sq mile.

ment is for some other scientists. With maps, the geographer may observe or record factual observations, describe how individual earth phenomena vary from place to place, develop hypotheses concerning the association of environmental factors, and, in general, study the spatial correlation and distribution of the elements and processes that characterize the earth's surface.

Maps are nearly infinite in variety but, like a written language, their construction generally conforms to basic rules. The student of geography should learn to "read" this sort of graphic language. Specifically, he should learn to analyze every map in terms of three fundamental aspects: (1) the *scale,* that is, the relation between the various dimensions on a map and the corresponding dimensions on the earth, (2) the system of *projection* employed in transforming the spherical surface of the earth to the plane surface of the map sheet, and (3) the cartographic *notation,* that is, the various

---

[3] Since each section is supposed to be 1 mile square, its area should be 640 acres. The section may be divided into quarters, each containing 160 acres, and the quarter sections may be further divided into parcels of 40 acres each. These are commonly called "forties." The quarter sections are indicated by the points of the compass, and so also are the forties. To describe and locate a given forty, therefore, one might say that it is in the NE ¼ of SW ¼ of Sec 20, T44N, R5E, of the particular principal meridian to which the range number referred. This statement would then be followed by the names of the administrative districts—for example, the town, county, and state in which the area is located.

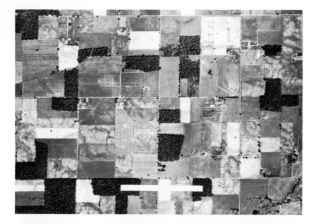

Figure 1.19 Contrasting landscapes, as seen from the air, that have resulted from rectangular and nonrectangular survey. These two areas, otherwise almost alike, are in central Ohio. *(Based upon Norman J. W. Thrower. Original Survey and Land Subdivision . . . Monograph 4, Assoc. Amer. Geographers and Rand McNally & Company, Chicago, 1966.)*

symbols and methods employed to represent the earth elements on the map.[4]

Scale

A globe represents the simplest kind of scaled reduction in size. A dimension of the globe can be

[4] *Cartography,* or map making, is a field of study in itself. Only the fundamentals necessary for using maps can be treated in a book devoted to physical geography. For the student who wishes more information, additional references on cartography are listed at the end of this chapter.

measured, and its relation to the corresponding dimension on the earth can be expressed as a ratio. This ratio will be the *scale* of the globe. For example, the earth has a diameter of about 500,-000,000 in., so that a globe with a diameter of 25 in. has a scale ratio of 25 to 500,000,000— or more simply, of 1 to 20,000,000, commonly written as a ratio or fraction: 1:20,000,000 or $\frac{1}{20,000,000}$. The statement of such a ratio is, of course, independent of any kind of unit, since it is equally applicable to inches, centimeters, feet, etc. This ratio or fractional relationship is commonly called the representative fraction, or *RF* for short.

Flat maps, like globes, always have a scale relationship to the area being portrayed. Commonly the scale is given in the form of the *RF*; occasionally it is expressed in words—for instance, "One inch represents one mile." Most often, however, it is indicated by a "graphic scale," that is, by a measured line showing the map lengths of earth distances, as in Fig. 1.18. A map may have any scale, but the convenience of using round numbers and the particular advantages of some map dimension–earth dimension relationships have given rise to a number of preferred scales. Some of the more common are these:

Map scale	1 in. represents	1 cm represents
1:10,000	0.158 mile	100 m
1:24,000	2,000 ft	0.24 km
1:50,000	0.789 mile	0.500 km
1:62,500	0.986 mile	0.625 km
1:63,360	1.000 mile	0.634 km
1:100,000	1.58 miles	1.00 km
1:500,000	7.89 miles	5.00 km
1:1,000,000	15.78 miles	10.00 km

Maps are often described as being large-, medium-, or small-scale; the distinction is important. Large-scale maps are those in which the fraction stated by the RF is relatively large: the fraction $\frac{1}{25,000}$ is twenty times larger than the fraction $\frac{1}{500,000}$, for instance. Most detailed ("topographic") survey maps are made at scales considerably larger than 1:125,000, and these maps would be classed as large-scale. Maps having scales much smaller than 1:1,000,000—a scale at which 1 km is represented by only 1 mm (or 1 mile by less than $\frac{1}{10}$ in.)—are generally called small-scale. As a rough guide, one can say that small maps of large areas (for example, the maps of the world found in the Map Section of this book) are small-scale maps, while large maps of small areas (for example, a government survey map of a township) are large-scale maps. Of course, there are always those in between which are classed as medium-scale.

The significant differences among small-, medium-, and large-scale maps are due not only to differences in the amount of information they can show, but also to the greater degree of generalization that must be used in smaller-scale maps. Small maps of states or countries, to say nothing of the world as a whole, are highly generalized and should be read as such.

The scale of a globe is the same all over, since it is just a straightforward reduction of the earth. But when the spherical surface of the earth is transformed to the plane of a flat map (map projection), the scale will be reduced unequally. Whatever the RF or graphic scale may "say" on a map, it can never be precisely that ratio everywhere on the map in every direction. The differences are generally insignificant and unnoticeable in large-scale maps, but they become very important in small-scale ones.

Map Projection

In geometric transformation, dissimilar surfaces are said to be applicable if one can be bent into another without modifying the geometric relationships among the points on the surface. Thus a cylinder or a cone may be cut and then laid out flat to form a plane, and neither distance nor directional relationships across the surface will be changed. A spherical surface and a plane surface are not applicable, however, and the bending required to transform one to the other must involve differential stretching and shrinking. Thus all map projections result in changing the scale unequally and consequently in distorting the distance and directional relationships among points on the earth. Even so, the many practical advantages of a flat map over a bulky globe usually far outweigh the disadvantages that come from differential stretching and compression.

There are an infinite number of ways one can distribute the necessary deformation which is inescapable in a flat map. (In many instances the deformation can actually be turned to advantage; for example, there are certain navigational purposes for which the "inaccurate" projection is far superior to the more "accurate" sphere.) Not very many ways of distributing the deformation are in common use, however. Map projections may be designed so as to have one or more specific useful characteristics, each of which is called a property. For example, a projection can have the property of equivalence or equal-area, which means that the map shows the relative sizes of all areas as they are on the earth. There is a variety of useful properties, and some projections can combine several of them.

Of the many kinds of properties, one projection shows all great-circle arcs as straight lines (gnomonic); another shows rhumb lines, or lines of steady and true bearing, as straight lines (Mercator); while several show east-west or north-south directions as parallel anywhere within the map. Since the properties of a projection may not be indicated in its name, sometimes the map reader must consult a treatise on cartography to find a description. The two most widely employed and important properties are those known as equivalence (or equal-area) and conformality. They are mutually exclusive; that is, they cannot exist together in the same system of projection.

Equivalence. A projection is said to be equal-area when the inescapable inequality of scale reduction is so arranged that at any point the maximum stretching in one direction is balanced by a reciprocal compression in the direction perpendicular to it. The consequence is that the area of any region on the map is shown correctly in relation to the area of any other region.

Over most of an equal-area projection the scale is different in different directions at each point, and this causes shapes of areas, even small ones, to be deformed. Indeed, equivalent projections always deform shapes, in some instances to a very large degree. Various equivalent projections arrange the scale departures in different ways so that the deformation may be concentrated in the less-used portions of the map. The map reader must be alert to make allowances for this. Figure 1.20, the equal-area map projection used for most of the world maps in this book, shows how the greatest deformation of shape has been relegated to the peripheral areas of the map.

Conformality. The property of maintaining correct directional relationships around each point, called conformality, is valuable in maps used for a variety of purposes. To obtain conformality, the inequality of scale reduction is arranged in such a way that, whatever the scale may be at any point on the projection, it is the same in all directions at that point. The consequence of this is that earth directions (the compass rose) will be truly shown. Thus conformality is helpful for maps on which directions at points are important—for example, maps used for navigation, surveying, or plotting wind directions. Although directions may be properly represented at each point on a conformal projection, the great-circle courses (and their azimuths or bearings) between places far from one another usually are somewhat deformed. Similarly, shapes of small areas are well represented on conformal projections, but the shapes of large areas are considerably deformed, as they are on all projections. Just as equivalent projections must modify angular relationships, so conformal projections must modify size relationships.

Map Symbols

Because a great many symbols are needed to identify the various distributions and correlations of geography, a large assortment of marks, colors, and

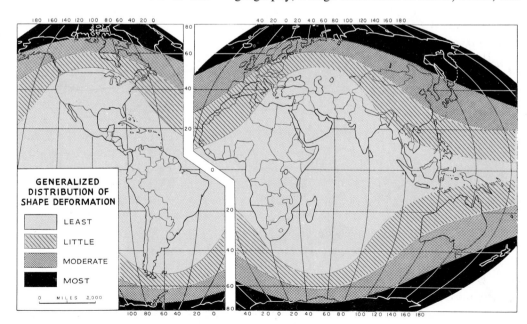

GENERALIZED DISTRIBUTION OF SHAPE DEFORMATION

LEAST

LITTLE

MODERATE

MOST

Figure 1.20 The flat polar equal-area projection used for many of the world maps in this book, showing the areas where the shape deformation has been concentrated. The darker the shading, the more the shape deformation.

shadings is employed in the graphic language of maps. These devices may be divided into four groups, though they are neither all-inclusive nor even entirely separate from one another. The groups are used to show (1) areal extent, shape, or outline; (2) various kinds of patterns; (3) relative land elevation or surface relief; and (4) areal distribution of numerical values of actual or relative quantity.

Group 1 includes all those familiar devices of line and color which mark off areas on the basis of some kind of internal unity. These may be countries or other political divisions, or they may be areas of general similarity in soil character, climatic type, population characteristics, or some other trait (Fig. 1.21).

Group 2 shows patterns—such as landform or drainage, the distribution of resources, the arrangements of weather stations or ridge lines, or the location of mining regions with respect to each other (Fig. 1.22).

Group 3 includes various graphic devices, such as shading and hachures, to produce the effect of light and shadow that would occur on a lighted three-dimensional surface like the land or the sea bottom (Fig. 1.23). Also in this group is that useful symbol the isarithm (contour line), which is discussed more fully below.

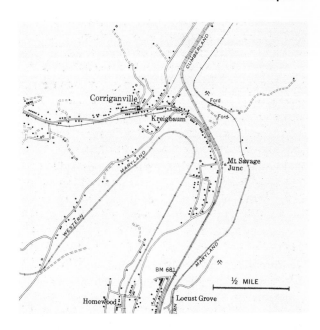

Figure 1.22 Group 2: A map showing one kind of pattern—in this instance, the pattern of settlement and transportation routes in the narrow valleys of western Maryland. *(Reduced from Cumberland quadrangle, U.S. Geological Survey, 1:24,000.)*

DISTRIBUTION OF THE DOMINANT SOIL ORDERS IN THE UNITED STATES

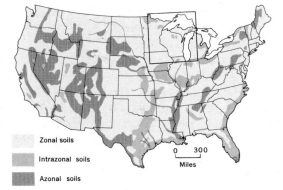

Figure 1.21 Group 1: A map showing areas classified on the basis of some characteristic of internal unity—in this instance, the dominant soil orders in the United States.

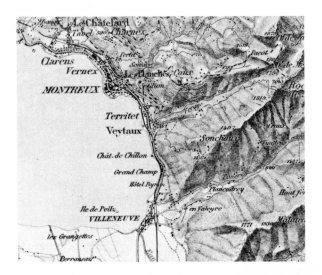

Figure 1.23 Group 3: A map simulating the appearance of the land-surface form. A portion of the famous Dufour map of Switzerland.

Group 4 contains many symbols. Prominent among them are dots of uniform size and
circles of contrasting area, used to represent magnitudes of various kinds in specific localities on the
earth's surface. The detail portrayed by such maps
varies. Sometimes there are a few circles whose
sizes show magnitudes referring to large areas (Fig.
1.24); sometimes many uniform dots represent
small units of value distributed within small units of
area (Fig. 1.25). Such symbols can depict the areal
arrangement of many kinds of phenomena, especially those that occupy a great deal of space but
not the entire area of the mapped region.

Most of these cartographic devices are self-
explanatory, or if not, they can be easily understood
by reading the legend which usually accompanies a
map.

Generalization in Maps. Much of the information
placed on a map must be generalized—that is,
selected, simplified, and graded as to the visual
emphasis it should be given relative to the other

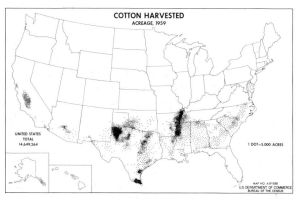

Figure 1.25 Group 4: A dot map showing considerable
detail of a distribution. *(U.S. Department of Agriculture.)*

data. Therefore the map reader must be careful not
to "read into" the map symbols a greater degree of
accuracy, precision, or prominence than is war-
ranted by their nature or by the scale of the map.
For example, many of the maps in this book indicate the distribution of things by showing abrupt
changes in coloring or shading, or merely by using
lines to separate areas. Yet such color changes and
boundaries frequently lie in transition zones and
represent only average conditions. Similarly, coastlines, boundaries, landform regions, soil areas, average rainfall amounts, and other such information
must be greatly simplified on most small-scale maps.

Isarithms. One of the frequently used, but not self-
explanatory, symbolic ways to show distributions of
quantity on maps is by means of successive lines,
each of which is drawn through all points having a
particular numerical value (Fig. 1.26). Such lines
are called isarithms (or isolines) from the Greek
isos, equal, + *arithmos,* number. When the values
represented are actual measures such as atmospheric pressure, amount of rainfall, or temperatures, the lines are sometimes called isometric lines.
When they represent relative values expressed as
ratios involving area, such as the number of persons
per square mile or the percent of land in crops, they
are commonly called isopleths. Isarithms employed
in connection with a particular class of phenomena
are frequently identified by combining the prefix *iso*

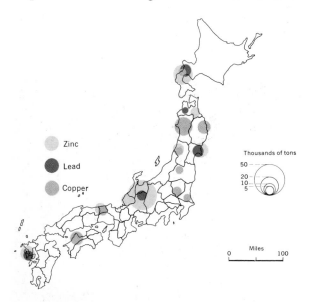

Figure 1.24 Group 4: A map showing the gross aspects of
a distribution—the production of copper, lead, and zinc in
Japan in 1960 by prefectures. *(After map in Glenn T.
Trewartha, Japan, The University of Wisconsin Press, Madison, Wis., 1965.)*

NUMBER OF DAYS WITH SNOW COVER

Figure 1.26 An isarithmic map showing the variation over the United States of the number of days with snow cover. Where the interval is 30 days, the closer together the lines are, the steeper is the gradient.

with a term derived from the type of data. Hence one speaks of isotherms (temperature) or isobars (air pressure).

Whatever the phenomenon being mapped by isarithms, the spacing of the isarithms generally shows *gradient*—that is, the change or difference per unit of distance. The closer together the lines are, the greater the rate of change per horizontal unit. Most isarithmic maps should be read in much the same way that one reads a contour map, which is a map showing variations in elevation and slope by means of isarithms.

Contours. Isarithms are more widely used than any other means for depicting the comparative elevations of the land surface above sea level on large-scale topographic maps. The term for such isarithms is isohypses (Greek *hypsos,* elevation) but they are commonly called contour lines. A particular contour line on a map passes through all points which have the same elevation above sea level.

The idea of contour lines, the significance of their comparative spacing, and their arrangements and shapes can be clarified by a simple illustration. In an open tank one may place an oval mound of modeling clay approximately 6½ in. high, steeply sloping at one end and gently sloping at the other, like a hill (Fig. 1.27). To make the

Figure 1.27 An imitation hill with two gullies, which has been modeled from clay and placed in a tank. The green lines show the successive positions of the horizontal "shorelines" if water in the tank were lowered 1 in. at a time.

hill more realistic, a pair of gullies can be added on one side like those that might result from rapid erosion by running water. If 6 in. of water is then permitted to flow into the tank, less than 1 in. of the mound will protrude. The position of the horizontal edge of the water (the shore) upon the clay can be marked with a sharp point. Next the water level can be lowered by 1-in. stages and the position of each stage similarly marked in the clay. The lowest will be everywhere 1 in. above the bottom of the tank, the next 2 in., and so on to the sixth, as shown in Fig. 1.27. These marks will appear as contour lines on the mound. If the mound is viewed from directly above, the arrangement of the contour lines will look like that shown in Fig. 1.28. On this small model, the successive water levels, and therefore the contour lines, have a vertical separation of 1 in. This is the contour interval.

The model in Fig. 1.27 and the contours in

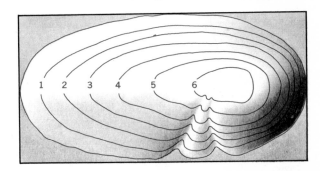

Figure 1.28 A shaded contour map of the model hill shown in Fig. 1.27. The contour interval is 1 in.

Fig. 1.28 illustrate some general rules for the interpretation of any kind of isarithmic map. The most important is that where the slope of the mound is steep—i.e., where the gradient is high—the isarithms are close together on the map, and they become more widely spaced as the slope or gradient becomes less. It will also be seen that on the mound, the contour lines follow along the side of a gully, cross its bottom, and return along its other side. One may then observe on the contour map that when isarithms cross a trough or valley, they do so by forming a bend whose closed end points in the upslope direction. Between the two gullies is a ridge. On the contour map, the lines emerge from the gullies and pass over the ridge and thus appear to loop so that their bends point in the downslope direction. Thus, contour lines bent toward the

downslope direction always indicate ridges. This principle is illustrated in Fig. 1.29.

The principles just stated—(1) the closer the isarithms, the steeper the gradient, and (2) successive bent isarithms pointing upslope indicate a trough—are applicable no matter what phenomenon is being represented (see Fig. 1.26).

Topographic Maps

For some 200 years man has been carefully surveying the land surface with its complex of natural and cultural phenomena and has been preparing detailed maps from these data. Such maps are called topographic maps. They represent the basic geographical data from which many other maps of smaller scale may be derived. Topographic maps

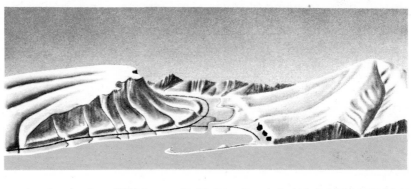

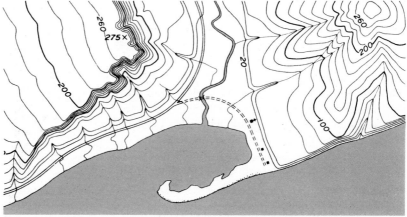

Figure 1.29 A perspective view with the corresponding topographic map below it. Note the spacings and shapes of the contours. *(Modified from U.S. Geological Survey.)*

are a prerequisite to the careful scientific study of the physical geography of an area. So far, perhaps half the land areas of the earth have been adequately mapped. Because it is a more difficult operation, the mapping of the sea areas of the earth is not nearly as far advanced.

Hundreds of series of topographic maps are produced by the national surveys of the different countries. They are made on a variety of projections, at a multitude of scales, and with somewhat different systems of symbols. Two basic observations about man's progress in mapping can be made: (1) In general, the more densely populated areas are well mapped at large scales; (2) elevational data are known in less detail than are planimetric data (horizontal position).

United States Topographic Maps. The National Map Series include seven scales, as follows:

RF	1 in. represents
1:24,000	2,000 ft
1:31,680	0.50 mile
1:62,500	0.99 mile (approx. 1 mile)
1:63,360 (Alaska)	1.00 mile
1:125,000	1.97 miles (approx. 2 miles)
1:250,000	3.95 miles (approx. 4 miles)
1:1,000,000	15.78 miles (approx. 16 miles)

The three most commonly used in the conterminous United States (that is, the United States with the exception of Alaska and Hawaii) are the 1:24,000, the 1:62,500, and the 1:250,000. The standard detailed maps are the 1:24,000 for a quadrangle of 7.5 min of latitude and longitude, and the 1:62,500.[5]

The maps are printed in colors. Black is commonly used for features classed as cultural, i.e., features which have human origin—such as roads, houses, towns, place names, boundary lines, and

[5] The Map Information Section of the U.S. Geological Survey, Washington, D.C. 20240, regularly publishes up-to-date indexes showing the status of topographic mapping and air photography and the agencies from which they are available.

parallels and meridians. All water features, both natural and man-made—such as canals, streams, marshes, lakes, and seas—are blue. Red is used for built-up areas and sometimes for survey lines and roads. The contour lines and other symbols relating to the elevation of the land surface are shown in brown, and woodlands are occasionally shown in green. In recent years shading has been applied to the maps in order to provide a realistic impression of the terrain.

Each map contains a place title, parallels and meridians, plane grid coordinates, and (where they exist) the section and township lines of the Public Land Survey. Each also gives a scale and a statement of the contour interval used on that map. The contour intervals employed usually are 10, 20, 50, or 100 ft. On maps of extremely flat land, intervals as small as 5 ft, or even 1 ft, are used; but on maps of rugged mountains, intervals are sometimes as much as 250 ft. Both the map scale and the contour interval of each map must be read and considered carefully.

Topographic maps are made by the U.S. Geological Survey in cooperation with the individual states, as well as by some other agencies. They are available for considerably more than half the area of the United States.

Selected References for Chap. 1

Birch, T. W. *Maps: Topographical and Statistical.* 2d ed. Oxford University Press, Fair Lawn, N.J., 1964.

Greenhood, D. *Mapping.* The University of Chicago Press (Phoenix Science Series), Chicago, 1964.

Harrison, L. C. *Sun, Earth, Time and Man.* Rand McNally & Company, Chicago, 1960.

Johnson, W. E. *Mathematical Geography.* American Book Company, New York, 1907.

Monkhouse, F. J., and H. R. Wilkinson. *Maps and Diagrams.* 2d ed. Methuen & Co., Ltd., London, 1963.

Pattison, W. D. "The Original Plan for an American

Rectangular Survey." *Surveying and Mapping,* Vol. 21, pp. 339–345, 1961.

Raisz, E. *General Cartography.* 2d ed. McGraw-Hill Book Company, New York, 1948.

Robinson, A. H. "An Analytical Approach to Map Projections." *Ann. Assoc. American Geographers,* Vol. 39, pp. 283–290. 1949.

———. *Elements of Cartography.* 2d ed. John Wiley & Sons, Inc., New York, 1960.

Strahler, A. N. *The Earth Sciences.* Harper & Row, Publishers, Incorporated, New York, 1963.

The Universal Grid Systems. U.S. Army TM 5-241, U.S. Air Force TO 16-1-233. U.S. Government Printing Office, Washington, D.C., 1951.

Wright, J. K. "Map Makers Are Human. . . ." *Geog. Rev.,* Vol. 32, pp. 527–544, 1942.

2

Introduction to Climate;
Solar Energy and Air Temperature

Man permanently occupies only the solid part of the earth's land-sea surface, not the ocean. Yet in a very real sense he lives always at the bottom of a great ocean—an ocean of air several thousand miles deep which surrounds the earth's solid-liquid core. Correctly speaking, the true surface of the earth is at the outer limits of its atmosphere, and man is a bottom-crawling creature. Man and all other land animals, as well as the plant life from which they ultimately draw their sustenance, are greatly influenced by their canopy of atmosphere, which varies widely in both time and place.

Except for a very small percentage of other gases, the atmosphere is a mixture of nitrogen and oxygen. Yet water vapor, one of the air's minor gases, is by far the most important in terms of weather and climate. It is the source of moisture for clouds and all forms of precipitation. It is the main absorber of solar energy and of radiated earth energy as well, so that it greatly influences the distribution of temperature over the earth.

In addition to nitrogen, oxygen, water vapor, and other minor gases, the lower air contains numerous impurities, collectively called dust. Particularly in the vicinity of cities and great industrial concentrations, air pollution has become a grave and rapidly worsening problem. Its recent increase stems from the expanding consumption of coal, petroleum, and natural gas. Many atmospheric pollutants come from factory smokestacks. The main offender lately, however, is the prodigious amount of exhaust fumes from the ever swelling tide of motor vehicles. As a consequence the poisoning of air over cities has already become a serious menace not only to comfort, but to health as well.

The condition of the atmosphere at any time or place is expressed by the terms *weather* and *climate*. Weather refers to the condition of the atmosphere during a brief period of time, such as a day or a week. In contrast, climate is a composite of day-to-day weather averaged over many years. Among the natural equipment of the earth—climate, terrain, natural vegetation, water, soils, minerals, etc.—climate ranks with the most important, especially as a cause of regional variations on an extensive scale in the land's productive capacity. In addition, climate strongly influences the character of such natural features as the vegetation cover, soil, and drainage. To a lesser degree, it even affects terrain features.

Elements of Climate. Climate, and also weather, are described in terms of several *elements*. Chief of these, as regards their effects on the earth's living things, are solar energy, temperature, and precipitation-humidity. An additional element, winds, while certainly not as important as the three mentioned above, has risen in rank since air transport has become common. These four elements are the main ingredients of climate. It is their combination in varying intensities and amounts which causes climates to differ widely over the earth, leading to striking regional diversity in human comfort, economic productivity, and man's use of the land.

Controls of Climate. But what causes the climatic elements to vary so greatly that some places and some seasons are hot while others are cold, some are wet while others are dry? The answer is found in the operation of the climatic *controls*. Each of the climatic elements named above—solar energy, temperature, precipitation-humidity, winds—also functions as a climatic control and influences each of the other elements. Indeed, winds are actually far more important as a control than as an element of climate. Other climatic controls include altitude, the distribution of land and water, terrain barriers, the vast semipermanent cells of high and low pressure, ocean currents, and a great variety of atmospheric disturbances. It is these controls, themselves acting in different combinations and with variable intensities, that cause areal and seasonal differences in temperature and precipitation—differences which in turn result in the many climates on the planet earth.

Varied though they are, these climates can be classified into a system of general types. The characteristics of the different types of climate and their world distribution are easier to understand, however, when the student knows something about the individual climatic elements and the more important climate controls. That is why the rest of this chapter and the three which follow it deal with solar energy, temperature, winds, precipitation, and atmospheric disturbances.

Solar Energy

Solar energy (solar radiation) is both an element and a control of climate. Unquestionably it is the ranking climatic control, for it is the one important source of atmospheric energy. Its influence is expressed most directly through air temperature distribution, but indirectly solar energy is the ultimate cause of nearly all changes and motions within the atmosphere.

Yet quite apart from its effects on air temperature and other climatic elements, solar radiant energy as an element of climate is a major determinant of the growth and character of terrestrial life. Sunlight intensity and the varying lengths of daylight and night markedly affect plants. These same features influence the health and comfort of human beings, as well as the nature and distribution of human diseases. For outdoor workers, sunlight is an important feature of the work environment, and for everyone it is extremely important in outdoor recreation and enjoyment. Because of its high rank as both an element and a control of climate, this discussion of climates rightly begins with a description of solar energy—how it is distributed, how it heats the atmosphere, and how it functions to produce the great variety of temperature conditions in the different latitudes and regions of the earth.

As noted above, the sun is the single important source of energy for the earth's atmosphere. From this small star, whose surface has an estimated temperature of about 10,000°F, there streams outward into space an enormous and continuous flow of radiant energy.[1] The planet earth, 93,000,000 miles distant, intercepts only an infinitesimally small fraction of the sun's energy output. Yet this minute fraction is enough to maintain the earth's atmospheric processes, and some important physical and biologic ones as well. Energy from the sun is transmitted through space in the form of very short magnetic waves. A portion of the solar spectrum can be perceived as light; there are other invisible wavelengths, some too short and others too long for humans to see.

Factors Influencing
Solar Energy Distribution

Disregarding for the moment the effects of an atmosphere and its clouds, the amount of solar energy—

[1] Except where degrees centigrade (°C) are specified, this book employs the Fahrenheit (F) scale commonly used in the United States and England to express temperature degrees.

in other words, climatic energy—that any latitude on the earth's surface receives depends largely upon two factors: (1) the *intensity* of solar radiation, or the angle at which the rays of sunlight reach the various parts of the earth's spherical surface, and (2) the *duration* of solar radiation, or length of day compared with night.

Rays of sunlight are always parallel, to be sure. But because of the earth's changing orbital positions, these rays reach different latitudes of the earth's curved surface at different angles in different seasons (refer back to Fig. 1.10). Since an oblique solar ray is spread out over a larger segment of the earth's surface than a vertical one, it delivers less energy per unit area (Fig. 2.1). (An

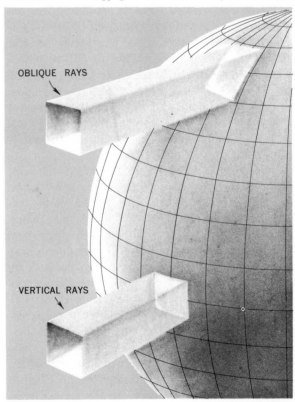

OBLIQUE RAYS

VERTICAL RAYS

Figure 2.1 Oblique rays deliver less energy at the earth's land-water surface than vertical rays, both because the energy of oblique rays is spread over a larger surface and because they must pass through a thicker layer of depleting atmosphere.

oblique ray is weaker also because it has passed through a thicker layer of scattering, absorbing, and reflecting air.) Outside the tropics, therefore, winter sunlight is much weaker than that of summer. For the same reasons, on any given day the sunlight is much more intense at noon than in the early morning or late afternoon hours.

As for the duration of solar radiation, obviously the longer the sun shines (i.e., the longer the day), the greater the amount of solar energy received, all other conditions being equal (see the following table and Fig. 2.2). Thus it is quite understandable that in the middle latitudes summer temperatures are much higher than those of winter; not only are the summer sun's rays less oblique, but summer days are much longer.

Since on any one day, both length of day and angle of the sun's rays are equal all along any parallel of latitude, it follows that all parts of a parallel receive identical amounts of solar energy both in a day and in a whole year (allowing, of course, for differences in the transparency of the atmosphere). Different parallels receive unlike amounts of solar radiation, the annual amount decreasing from equator to poles. Thus if solar energy were the only control of weather and climate, all places in the same latitude would have identical climates. Although obviously they do not, there are strong temperature resemblances within latitude belts which testify to the dominant, even though not exclusive, influence of sun control.

Earth and Sun Relations

The rotation and revolution of the earth and the inclination and parallelism of its axis were discussed in Chap. 1. The following section shows how these earth motions and axis positions produce the changing lengths of day and varying angles of the sun's rays which in turn are the causes of the seasons.

Equinoxes: Spring and Fall. Twice during the yearly period of revolution, on about March 21 and September 23, the sun's noon rays are directly overhead, or vertical, at the equator (Fig. 2.2). On these dates, therefore, the circle of illumination, marking the position of the sun's tangent rays, passes through both poles and cuts all the earth's parallels exactly in half. One-half of each parallel (180°) is in light and the other half is in darkness, and days and night are equal (12 hr each) over the entire earth. Because of this fact the two dates March 21 and September 23 are called the *equinoxes* (derived from Latin words meaning equal night). At these times the maximum solar energy is received in equatorial latitudes; it diminishes regularly toward either pole, where it becomes zero.

Solstices: Summer and Winter. On about June 22 the earth is approximately midway in its orbit between the equinoctial positions, and the North Pole is inclined 23½° toward the sun (Fig. 2.2). As a result of this axial inclination, the sun's rays are shifted northward the same number of degrees, so that the noon rays are vertical at the Tropic of Cancer (23½°N), and the tangent rays in the Northern Hemisphere pass over the pole and reach the earth 23½° of latitude beyond it, at the Arctic Circle (66½°N). In the Southern Hemisphere the tangent rays do not reach the pole but terminate at the Antarctic Circle, 23½° short of it. Thus while all parts of the earth north of the Arctic Circle are in constant daylight, similar latitudes in the Southern Hemisphere (poleward from the Antarctic Circle) are entirely without sunlight. All parallels, except

EXTREMES IN LENGTH OF DAY FOR DIFFERENT LATITUDES
IN HOURS AND MINUTES

Latitude (degrees)	0	10	20	30	40	50	60	66½
Longest day (shortest night)	12:00	12:35	13:13	13:56	14:51	16:09	18:30	24:00
Shortest day (longest night)	12:00	11:25	10:47	10:04	9:09	7:51	5:30	0:00

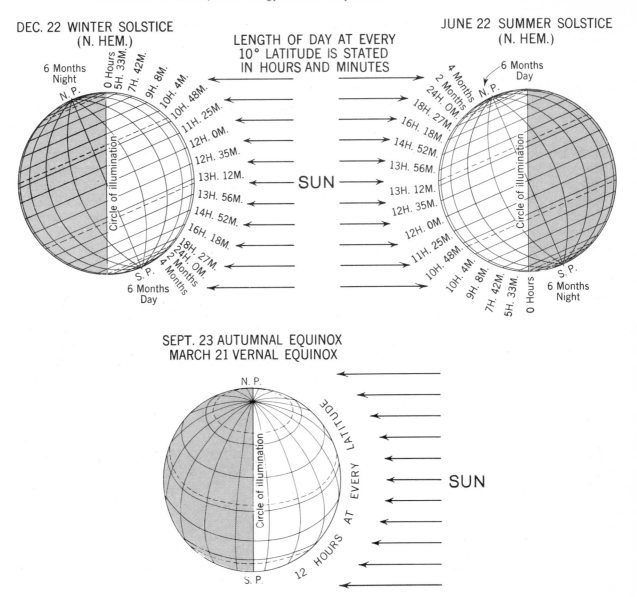

Figure 2.2 At the time of the two equinoxes, when the sun's vertical noon rays are at the equator, the circle of illumination cuts all parallels in half, so that days and nights are equal (12 hr) over the whole earth (see Fig. 1.10 in Chap. 1). At the times of the solstices, the sun's vertical noon rays have reached their greatest poleward displacement, 23½° north or south. The circle of illumination then cuts all parallels except the equator unequally, so that days and nights are unequal in length except at latitude 0°.

the equator, are cut unequally by the circle of illumination. Those in the Northern Hemisphere have the larger segments of their circumferences toward

the sun, so that days are longer than nights. Longer days, plus a greater angle of the sun's rays, make for a maximum receipt of solar energy in the Northern Hemisphere at this time. Summer, with its associated high temperatures, is the result, and north of the equator June 22 is known as the *summer solstice*. In the Southern Hemisphere all these conditions are reversed: nights are longer than days and the sun's rays are relatively oblique, so that solar radiation is at a minimum and winter conditions prevail.

On about December 22, when the earth is in the opposite position in its orbit, it is the South Pole that is inclined $23\frac{1}{2}°$ toward the sun. The noon rays are then vertical over the Tropic of Capricorn ($23\frac{1}{2}°$S), and the tangent rays pass over the South Pole to the Antarctic Circle $23\frac{1}{2}°$ beyond ($66\frac{1}{2}°$S). Consequently, south of $66\frac{1}{2}°$S there is constant light, while north of $66\frac{1}{2}°$N there is none. All parallels of the earth except the equator are cut unequally by the circle of illumination, with days longer and the sun's rays more nearly vertical in the Southern Hemisphere. This, therefore, is summer south of the equator but winter in the Northern Hemisphere (winter solstice).

Effects of Atmosphere upon Incoming Solar Energy

When solar radiation is in transit through the atmosphere, it may be *reflected, transmitted,* or *absorbed.* Only that part which is absorbed heats the air. The total effect of the atmosphere upon a beam of sunlight passing through it is to reduce its intensity by amounts varying with latitude, the season's, and the degree of cloudiness. The atmosphere weakens solar energy through (1) selective scattering, chiefly of the short waves of blue light, by very small obscuring particles, (2) diffuse reflection of all wavelengths by larger particles, such as cloud droplets, and (3) absorption of selected wavelengths, chiefly by water vapor concentrated in the lower strata of the atmosphere. The scattering and reflecting processes operate to send a part of the solar radiation they affect back to space, but some of it reaches the earth's surface as diffuse daylight.

Quantitatively, it is estimated that about 34 percent of the solar radiation reaching the outer limits of the air layer is returned to space by scattering and reflection from clouds, small dust particles, and molecules of air, as well as by direct reflection from the earth's surface (Fig. 2.3). This percentage lost by scattering and reflection, known as the earth's *albedo,* has no part in heating either the solid-liquid earth or its atmosphere. Another 19 percent of the total solar radiation acts directly to heat the air, for it is absorbed by the atmosphere, most of it by water vapor. The remaining 47 percent is transmitted to the earth's surface either as direct sunlight or as diffuse daylight. There it is absorbed by the surface, heats it, and eventually heats the atmosphere as well.

Thus only about two-thirds (66 percent) of the solar radiation (19 percent absorbed by the atmosphere directly, and 47 percent absorbed by the earth's surface) is available for heating the atmosphere. Also, and equally significant, the atmosphere receives several times as much energy from the heated earth's surface as it does from direct absorption of solar radiation by the air itself.

Distribution of Solar Radiation over the Earth's Surface

To repeat, the belt of maximum solar radiation swings back and forth across the equator during the course of a year, following the shifting rays of the sun, with two variables, the angle of the sun's rays and the length of day, largely determining the amount of solar energy received at any time or place.

Distribution from Pole to Pole. Assuming cloudless skies, solar radiation *for the year as a whole* is greatest at the equator and diminishes with regularity toward the poles; and the Northern and Southern Hemispheres share equally in the annual amounts of solar energy received (Fig. 2.4a). This distribution has important climatic consequences. Chief of these is that average air temperatures for the year are highest in the tropics, or low latitudes, and decrease toward the poles.

At the time of the *equinoxes,* disregarding

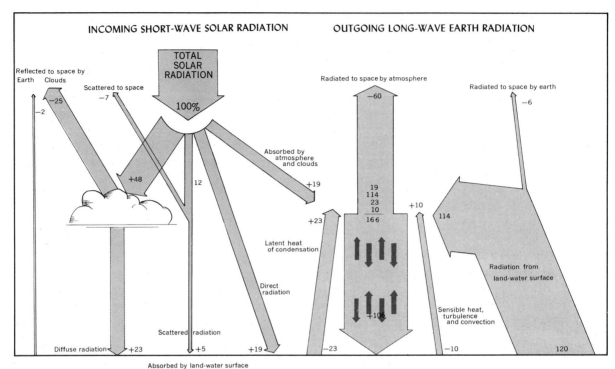

Figure 2.3 Terrestrial heat balance. Note that the number of energy units absorbed by the earth's atmosphere and land-water surface just equals the units of energy radiated by the earth to space. Only about two-thirds of the total incoming solar radiation is utilized in heating the earth, one-third being reflected and scattered back to space.

again the effects of clouds, the latitudinal distribution of solar radiation is similar to that for the year as a whole (Fig. 2.4b). There is a maximum of solar radiation at the equator and a minimum at each pole. This fact also has important climatic implications. For it is in the equinoctial seasons of spring and fall, when the Northern and Southern Hemispheres are receiving approximately equal amounts of solar energy, that temperature conditions in the two hemispheres are most nearly alike. Similarly, pressure, wind, and precipitation, and as a result the overall weather, are more in balance to the north and south of the equator than at other times. Finally, world temperature, pressure, wind, and precipitation patterns for spring and fall bear close resemblances to those for the year as a whole.

At the time of the two *solstices,* when the sun's noon rays are vertical 23½° poleward from the equator and the length of day increases toward

one pole and decreases toward the other, the latitudinal distribution of solar radiation is very asymmetrical. The summer hemisphere receives two or three times as much as the winter hemisphere (Fig. 2.4c, d).[2] Distribution of solar radiation at the surface of the earth shows a broad maximum in the belt of latitude that extends from about 30° to almost 40°, while latitude 60° receives as much as or more than the equator. It is not surprising, therefore, that the highest surface-air temperatures in summer occur over the land masses of the lower middle latitudes (30°–40°) and not at the equator.

During the course of a year, the zone of maximum solar radiation shows a total latitudinal displacement of more than 60° (Fig. 2.4c, d), which is bound to have important effects upon sea-

[2] The *summer hemisphere,* of course, is the hemisphere that has summer. In July the summer hemisphere is the Northern Hemisphere; in January it is the Southern.

sonal temperatures, rainfall, pressure, and winds. It is significant also that the latitudinal solar radiation gradient (the rate of change in solar radiation) is much steeper in the winter hemisphere than in the summer hemisphere.

The characteristics of solar radiation distribution at the times of the solstices, which are the extreme seasons of summer and winter, provide the basic explanations for many of the earth's larger features of weather and climate: (1) Marked north-south shifting of temperature, wind, and precipitation belts follows a similar migration of solar radiation belts. (2) Warm-to-hot summers occur in the lower middle latitudes, where solar radiation reaches a near maximum for the summer hemisphere. (3) There are much steeper temperature gradients in the winter hemisphere than in the summer hemisphere, the temperature gradients paralleling solar radiation gradients. (4) Greater storminess and weather variability are found in the winter hemisphere.

Annual Distribution by Latitudes. Yearly solar radiation curves for the different latitudes can be arranged in three general groups: those for low, middle, and high latitudes (Fig. 2.5).

In the *low,* or *tropical,* latitudes between the Tropics of Cancer and Capricorn, solar radiation is high and varies little throughout the year. This accounts for the constant year-round heat of the tropics. Since during the course of a year, all regions between the two tropics are passed over

Figure 2.4 Latitudinal distribution of solar energy at the earth's surface. For the year as a whole and at the two equinoxes, solar energy is symmetrically distributed in the Northern and Southern Hemispheres. There is a maximum in equatorial latitudes and minima at the North and South Poles. At the solstices, solar energy is very unequally distributed, with the summer hemisphere receiving two to three times the amount that the winter hemisphere does.

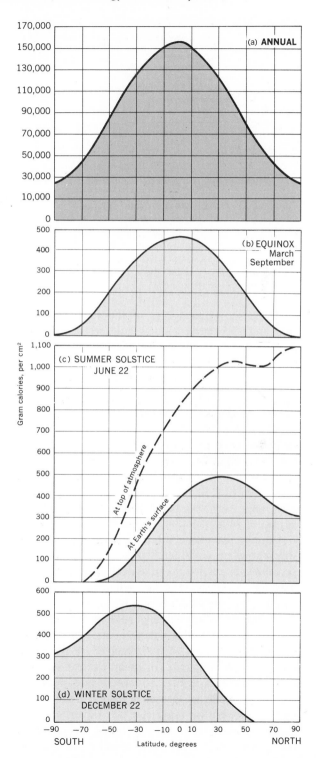

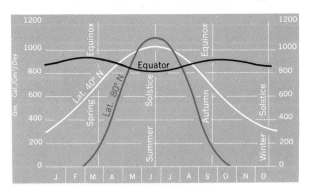

Figure 2.5 Annual march of solar radiation received at the outer limits of the earth's atmosphere at different latitudes. In the very low latitudes close to the equator, the amount of solar energy received at the top of the atmosphere is large, and varies little throughout the year. In the middle and higher latitudes, there are great seasonal differences in receipts of solar energy.

twice by the vertical rays of the sun, the annual solar radiation curve for low latitudes (black curve in Fig. 2.5) contains two weak maxima and two slight minima.

The *middle*-latitude curve (white curve in Fig. 2.5), on the other hand, has a single maximum, but as in the tropics, solar radiation at no time declines to zero. The great seasonal contrasts in solar radiation are reflected in large seasonal contrasts in temperature.

The *high* latitudes—that is, the regions poleward from the Arctic and Antarctic Circles—also have only one maximum and one minimum period of solar radiation (green curve in Fig. 2.5). But unlike the other latitudes, there is a portion of the year when direct sunlight is completely absent; i.e., the solar radiation curve declines to zero. Also, seasonal contrasts in solar radiation are marked, and temperature contrasts are strong.

For both high and middle latitudes, the annual march of solar energy at ground level corresponds fairly well to that received at the top of the earth's atmosphere. In other words, the white and green curves in Fig. 2.5 would show peaks and depths occurring at the same general times if they were replotted to represent the radiation which reaches ground level. But this would not be true of the black equatorial curve, because in the wet

tropics, cloudiness is usually at a maximum during the season of highest sun. Thus in that period proportionately less solar radiation is received at the ground than at the top of the air ocean, and the ground-level equatorial curve is often out of phase with the outer-atmosphere curve shown in Fig. 2.5.

Air Temperature

How Solar Energy Heats the Atmosphere

Solar radiation, the single important source of atmospheric energy, heats the air directly by processes involving absorption of solar energy, and indirectly by earth radiation, conduction, and condensation. The heat acquired by these processes is then transferred from one part of the atmosphere to another by vertical and horizontal currents.

Absorption of Solar Energy by the Atmosphere

Sun energy is in the form of such short wavelengths that only relatively small amounts (around 19 percent, as we have seen) can be absorbed directly by the earth's atmosphere, chiefly by the water vapor in it. Of that 19 percent, most is taken up by the comparatively humid lower atmosphere. However, since this absorption still occurs well above the immediate surface layer, it is not very effective in heating the ground-level air which is in contact with life forms. On a clear winter day, for example, the air may remain bitterly cold in spite of a bright sun.

Conduction

If two objects with quite different temperatures are in contact, by molecular conduction energy in the form of heat passes from the warmer to the colder object until both have the same temperature. In the absence of a snow cover, a land surface during daylight hours attains a higher temperature than the air above. This is because land is a more efficient absorber of solar energy than air. Then, by conduction, a thin layer of air resting on the warm land is heated. Likewise, a cold land surface on a winter night, chilled by loss of heat through outgoing earth radiation, cools a thin layer of adjacent air. But air is a very poor conductor; consequently molecular conduction alone, in the absence of vertical movement to mix the air layers, is a negligible factor in heating or cooling an appreciably thick air layer.

Earth Radiation

The earth's land-water surface is capable of absorbing short-wave sun energy much more readily than the atmosphere is. As mentioned earlier, about 47 percent of the solar radiation reaching the outer atmosphere gets through to the earth's surface, is absorbed by it, and heats it. In its turn, the heated surface becomes a radiator of energy to the atmosphere.

Because the earth's temperature is lower than that of the sun, earth radiation is composed of longer wavelengths. While the atmosphere is able to absorb only about 19 percent of the incoming short-wave radiation, it can absorb 80 to 90 percent of the outgoing long-wave earth radiation. Thus the atmosphere receives most of its heat *indirectly* from the sun and *directly* from the earth's surface. The atmosphere acts like the glass in a greenhouse or automobile, letting through much of the incoming short-wave solar energy but greatly retarding the escape of the heat, or long-wave earth radiation. This is called the *greenhouse effect* of the atmosphere (Fig. 2.6).

The total influence of the atmosphere's greenhouse effect on climate is to keep surface-air temperatures considerably higher than they otherwise would be, and also to prevent great extremes in temperature between day and night. Chiefly it is the water vapor in the air which absorbs the earth radiation. This fact is illustrated by the more rapid night cooling in deserts, where the dry air and cloudless skies permit a rapid escape to space of heat radiated from the earth.

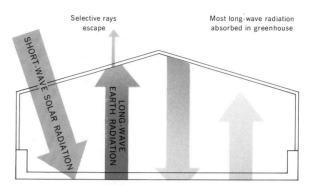

Figure 2.6 The "greenhouse effect" of the earth's atmosphere. Like the atmosphere, the glass in the roof and sides of a greenhouse is relatively transparent to short-wave solar energy, but relatively opaque to long-wave earth radiation.

Since various kinds of earth surfaces react differently to solar energy, they acquire different temperatures and so radiate somewhat differently. Land surfaces of various colors and shadings (snow, light sand, green fields, and forests) differ in temperature because they reflect and absorb solar energy differently. The greatest contrasts in temperature, however, are between land and water surfaces.

Land-Water Contrasts. For a number of reasons well known to students of elementary physics, a land surface without snow heats (and cools) more rapidly than a water surface, even when both receive similar amounts of solar energy. The most important factor is that the fluid character of water causes vertical and horizontal currents, tides, and waves to distribute the sun energy received at the sea surface throughout a large mass. Similarly, when a water surface begins to cool, the surface water becomes heavier and sinks, to be replaced by warmer, lighter water from below. Both kinds of distribution make for slower temperature change at the water surface than on the solid land surface.

A supplementary factor is that water is transparent. The sun's rays are able to penetrate a water body to considerable depths, and in this way also they distribute energy throughout a somewhat larger mass. On the other hand, the opaqueness of land concentrates the sun energy close to the surface, so that heating is comparatively rapid and intense. This concentration likewise permits a land area to cool more rapidly than a deeply warmed water body.

Also of some significance is the fact that the specific heat of water is higher than that of land. In other words, it requires only one-third to one-half as much energy to raise a given volume of dry earth by one degree as it does an equal volume of water.

As a consequence of these land and water contrasts, land-controlled, or continental, climates in general are characterized by large daily and seasonal extremes of air temperature, becoming alternately hot and cold, whereas ocean-controlled, or marine, climates are usually more moderate, with only small seasonal and daily temperature changes.

Mechanics of Earth Radiation. Radiation of heat from the earth's land-sea surface upward through the atmosphere toward space is a continuous process. During the daylight hours and up to about midafternoon, however, more energy is received from the sun than is radiated from the earth, with the result that surface-air temperatures usually continue to rise. But during the night, when receipts of solar energy cease, a continued loss of energy through earth radiation results in a cooling of the earth's land surface and a consequent drop in air temperature.

Being a better radiator than air, the ground becomes cooler than the air above it during the night. When this happens, the lower layers of atmosphere lose heat by radiation to the colder ground as well as upward toward space. This process is particularly important during the long nights of winter, when if the skies are clear and the air is dry, the loss of heat is both rapid and prolonged.

If a snow cover mantles the ground, night cooling is even more pronounced, for 50 to 80 percent of the incoming solar radiation during the short day was reflected by the snow and thus did not heat the earth's surface. At night the snow, which is a poor conductor of heat, allows little energy stored in the soil layer below to come up and replenish that lost by radiation at the top of the snow surface.

As a result, the snow surface becomes extremely cold, and then so does the air layer resting on it.

Water, like land, is a good radiator. But as described earlier, the cooled surface waters constantly sink, to be replaced by the warmer water from below. Extremely low air temperatures over a body of water are therefore impossible until it is frozen over, after which it acts like a land surface.

Water vapor is an effective absorber of some (though not all) wavelengths of earth radiation. Therefore a humid atmosphere acts to retard night cooling, because a portion of the energy selectively absorbed by the water vapor is reradiated back to lower levels. But a low-level cloud cover is a far more effective shield against loss of heat by earth radiation, for the liquid and solid particles of the cloud *completely* absorb *all* the wavelengths of earth radiation, and reradiate them back to lower levels. In short, air temperatures remain higher and frosts are less likely on humid nights, but especially so on nights when a low cloud deck is present.

Heat of Condensation

A large amount of the solar energy which reaches the earth's surface is consumed in evaporating water and changing it into a gas. This converted solar energy consequently is contained in the atmosphere's water vapor in latent or potential form. When condensation occurs and water vapor is returned to the liquid or solid state, the latent energy is again released into the atmosphere and heats it. Heat of condensation is a principal source of energy for the atmosphere.

Transfer of Heat by Air Currents

The heat acquired by the atmosphere through absorption of solar energy, conduction and radiation processes, and condensation is transferred from one part of the atmosphere to another by vertical and horizontal currents.

Vertical Transfer. Vertical transfer of heat results from thermal convection currents, mechanical turbulence, and eddy motions in the atmosphere. When surface air is heated, it expands and consequently becomes less dense and more buoyant. Hence it is forced upward by the surrounding colder, denser air, which at the surface flows toward the warm source. Such a circulation is called a *convectional system.* Vertical circulation, whether by thermal convection, turbulence induced by rough terrain, or eddy currents, is the main process by which the heat acquired at the land-sea surface is distributed through a great depth of the atmosphere.

Horizontal Transfer. Horizontal transfer of heat, which is carried out by winds, is called *advection.* For the earth as a whole this is the most important means of heat transfer. Advection by winds produces many of the earth's day-to-day weather changes, as well as causing the storminess of winter climates in the middle latitudes. For instance, in the Northern Hemisphere middle latitudes, a south wind usually means unseasonably high temperatures, as almost everyone who lives there knows. In this case the wind acts as the conveyor of heat from lower latitudes, where solar radiation is greater and higher temperatures are normal. Such an advection of southerly warmth in winter results in mild weather, with melting snow and slushy streets. In summer, several days of south wind may result in a heat wave, with maximum temperatures over 90°.

Similarly, north winds from colder, higher latitudes, or from the cold interiors of continents in winter, advect lower temperatures. These cold importations are particularly effective where there are no mountain barriers to block the wind movement. Large-scale horizontal transfer of temperature conditions likewise may result from winds moving onshore from large bodies of water.

Heat Balance in the Atmosphere

Since the mean temperature of the earth as a whole gets neither higher nor lower, it is clear that the heat lost by the earth through radiation to space is identical in amount to solar energy absorbed by the earth. But this balance does not hold for individual latitudes. In the low latitudes, equatorward from about 37°, the incoming solar energy exceeds the outgoing earth energy; whereas poleward from latitude 37°, exactly the reverse is true. If there were not a continuous transfer of energy from low to high latitudes, temperatures in low latitudes would constantly increase and temperatures in middle and higher latitudes would constantly decrease. This transfer of energy is carried out by winds and ocean currents. In fact, in the unequal latitudinal distribution of solar and terrestrial radiation is to be found the ultimate cause of the earth's atmospheric circulation and of much of its weather.

Temporal Distribution of Air Temperature

The average temperature of any month, season, year, or even long period of years is determined by using the *mean daily temperature* as a basic unit. This is the average of the highest and lowest temperatures recorded during the 24-hr period.

The *daily march of temperature,* or the rhythm of day and night temperatures, is obtained by plotting the temperature for each hour of the day. Chiefly it reflects the balance between incoming solar radiation and outgoing earth radiation (Fig. 2.7). From about sunrise until 2:00 to 4:00 P.M., energy is being supplied by incoming solar radiation faster than it is being lost by earth radiation, so that the daily temperature curve usually rises (Figs. 2.7, 2.8). Conversely, from about 3:00

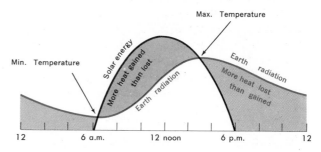

Figure 2.7 The march of incoming solar radiation and of outgoing earth radiation for a daily 24-hr period around the time of an equinox, showing their combined effects upon the times of daily maximum and minimum temperatures.

P.M. to sunrise, loss by terrestrial radiation exceeds receipt of solar energy, and the temperature curve usually falls. Often, however, clouds and advection modify this symmetrical rise and fall of the temperature curve (in the top graph of Fig. 2.8, see the white curve of December 22, when southerly winds prevented normal night cooling).

In marine locations the daily temperature curve is relatively flat, because there is only a small difference between day and night. By contrast, in continental, or land-controlled, climates the amplitude of the daily temperature curve is much greater.

The *annual march, or cycle, of temperature* is obtained by plotting the mean temperature for each month. It reflects the increase in solar energy (and hence heat accumulated in the air and ground) from midwinter to midsummer, and the corresponding decrease from midsummer to midwinter (Fig. 2.9). Over large land masses the temperature maximum (and minimum) usually lags about a month behind the period of maximum (and minimum) solar energy. This seasonal lag is even greater over oceans and along windward coasts in middle latitudes, where August may be the warmest month and February the coldest. Normally, marine locations have flatter annual temperature curves than continental locations, just as their daily temperature curves are flatter.

Geographical Distribution of Air Temperature

Vertical Distribution

Under normal conditions there is a general decrease in temperature with increasing elevation up to about 6–8 miles. The rate of decrease, called *lapse rate,* is not uniform but varies with time of day, season, and location. It generally averages about 3.6° for each 1,000-ft rise (Fig. 2.10). The fact that air temperature is usually highest close to the earth's surface and decreases with altitude bears out the point that most atmospheric heat is received directly from the earth's land-sea surface and only indirectly from the sun.

Inversions. When air temperature *increases* with altitude, it is called a *temperature inversion.* Such a reversed temperature condition can occur in the lowest layer of the atmosphere next to the land surface, or at various levels above it at altitudes of several thousand feet.

Above-surface Inversions. This type of inversion originates principally from the slow sinking or sub-

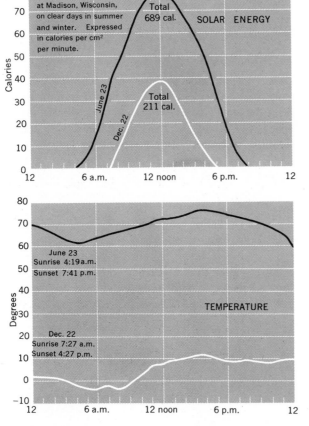

Figure 2.8   Daily march of solar radiation and temperature on cloudless days at the times of the summer and winter solstices at Madison, Wisconsin. The total solar energy recorded was 3.27 times as great on June 23 as on December 22. Note that temperature lags somewhat behind solar radiation. Advection by southerly winds prevented normal night cooling on December 22.

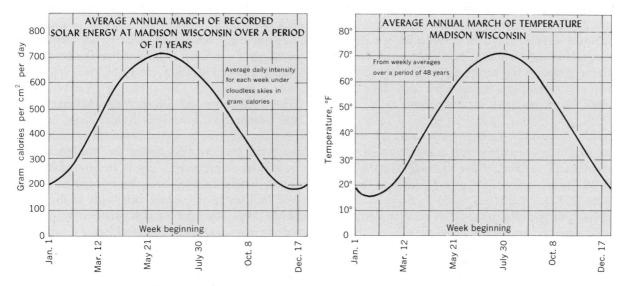

Figure 2.9 Note that temperature lags a month or more behind solar radiation. The solar radiation curve has been smoothed slightly.

sidence of an extensive and thick layer of air aloft. The sinking acts to heat the air by compression and reduce its relative humidity (Fig. 2.11). It is thereby made drier, stable, and nonbuoyant, so that it resists upward movement, which is essential for

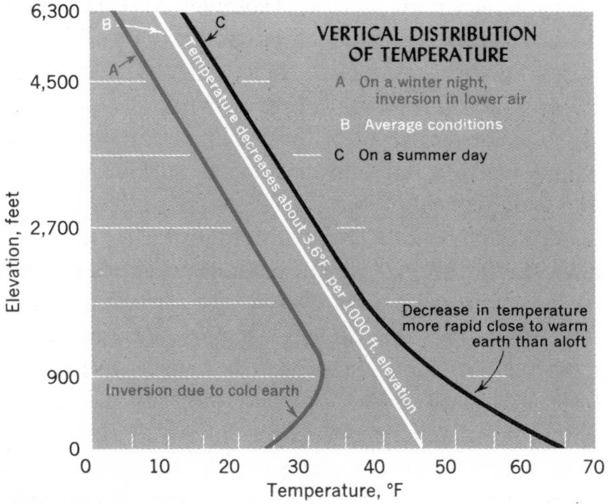

precipitation. Therefore regions with strong and relatively persistent above-surface inversions are likely to be dry.

Air subsidence (and hence above-surface

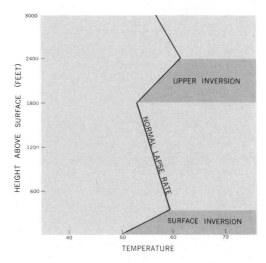

Figure 2.10

Figure 2.11 Vertical temperature profile showing two inversion layers.

inversions) is characteristic of extensive high-pressure systems or anticyclones, especially stationary or slow-moving ones. These systems, which will be described in more detail in Chapter 3, are common in many parts of the subtropics at all seasons and in the Northern Hemisphere continents in winter. Some of the earth's largest deserts coincide with the subtropical anticyclones and their trade winds where inversions are widespread.

Surface Inversions. Surface temperature inversions, one of the most common and easily observed kinds of inversion, originate from the radiational cooling of the lowest layers of air by a colder land surface. Because a land surface is a more efficient radiator of heat energy than air, it can become colder at night than the air over it. Under these conditions the coldest air is at ground level, and temperatures in the air layer at the surface increase upward. Ideal conditions for the development of surface inversions are (1) long winter nights, in which there are many hours when outgoing earth radiation exceeds incoming solar radiation, (2) a clear sky, so that loss of heat by terrestrial radiation is rapid and not retarded by a cloud cover, (3) cold, dry air that absorbs little earth radiation, (4) calm air, which prevents much mixing from taking place, so that the surface stratum becomes very cold by conduction and radiation, and (5) a snow-covered surface, which, owing to reflection of solar energy, heats little by day and, being a poor conductor, retards the upward flow of heat from the ground below the snow cover (Figs. 2.10 and 2.11 both illustrate this condition).

Surface inversions are common to all latitudes, although in the wet tropics they are weak and insignificant. Over the snow-covered polar regions, deep inversions are normal in both summer and winter, both day and night. In middle latitudes, calm, clear weather produces surface inversions in summer as well as winter, but in summer, surface heating causes them to disappear by day. They are also deeper and stronger in winter.

A close relationship exists between surface inversions on one hand and fog and frost on the other, since similar conditions are favorable for all three. The same is true of smoke-polluted fog, or smog. During a surface temperature inversion, when the coldest, densest air is at the surface, the air is stable or nonbuoyant—that is, not inclined to rise. Such a condition is opposed to the formation of cloud and precipitation.

Surface Inversions and Air Drainage. Although surface temperature inversions (green line in Fig. 2.10) are common over flattish land surfaces, they are most perfectly developed in low spots, or topographic depressions. This is because cold surface air, owing to its greater density, moves downslope into low areas, where it collects in the form of cold pools. Such gravity downslope movement of cold air is known as *air drainage*. Because of it the first frosts in fall and the last in spring occur in bottomlands, and on a clear, cold night, valleys and depressions have the lowest temperatures.

Frost and Its Distribution. Frost is an air temperature of 32° (freezing temperature) or below. The period between the last killing frost in spring and the first in fall is known as the *growing season.* Throughout the middle latitudes, frost is most serious as a menace to crops in spring and fall, or at the beginning and end of the growing season. In subtropical areas such as Florida and California, however, some sensitive crops are grown during the normally mild winters so that it is the midwinter frosts which are critical (Fig. 2.12).

Ideal conditions for a killing frost are those which favor rapid and prolonged surface cooling and the creation of surface inversions: advection of a mass of dry, cool polar air, followed by a calm, clear night during which the temperature of the surface air is brought below the freezing point through radiational cooling. If the late afternoon temperature of the cool, northerly air is not much over 40°, and skies are clear and the air calm, killing frost is likely during the following night. But even when conditions are generally favorable for a killing frost over an extensive area, destructive effects upon plant life are usually local and patchy

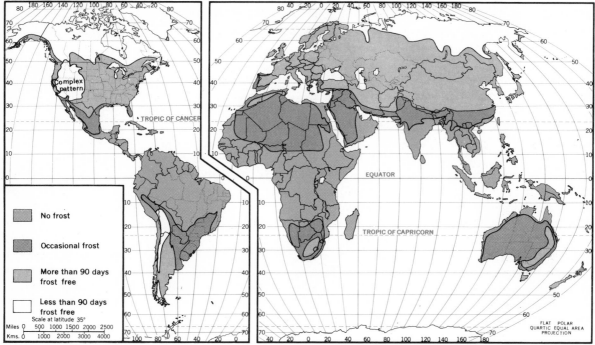

Figure 2.12   Average length of the frost-free period, or growing season, in days. The frost pattern in a great section of the highland western United States is too complex to indicate on a map of this size. *(From Great Soviet World Atlas, Vol. 1.)*

in distribution. This is chiefly a matter of terrain irregularities and air drainage, with most frost damage restricted to the lower lands. Thus sensitive crops such as fruit and vegetables are commonly planted on slopes rather than in valley bottoms.

For small-scale vegetable gardeners or fruit growers, the simplest and most effective means of protection against frost is to spread some nonmetallic covering, such as straw, paper, or cloth, over the crop. The function of the cover is not to keep the cold out but the heat in; it tends to retard heat loss by radiation from the ground and from the plants themselves. This method is not suitable for protecting extensive orchards, however. In such places as the valuable citrus groves of California and Florida, the two most common methods of frost protection are orchard heaters burning diesel fuel oil, and huge motor-driven fans which agitate the lowest 10 to 20 ft of air and thereby destroy the surface inversion.

Horizontal Distribution of Temperature

Isothermal Maps. Temperature distribution over the earth is represented on maps by *isotherms*. As Chapter 1 explained, these are lines connecting places with the same temperature (Figs. 2.13, 2.14). All points on the earth's surface through which any one isotherm passes have identical average temperatures. In Figs. 2.13 and 2.14, temperatures everywhere have been reduced to those which would prevail if all places were at sea level. This was done by means of the formula which assumes an average vertical change of about 3.6° in temperature for each 1,000-ft change in altitude. If temperatures had not been reduced to eliminate the effects of altitude, the complications in the isotherms caused by mountains and other local topography would be so confusing that general world patterns of temperature distribution would be difficult to see.

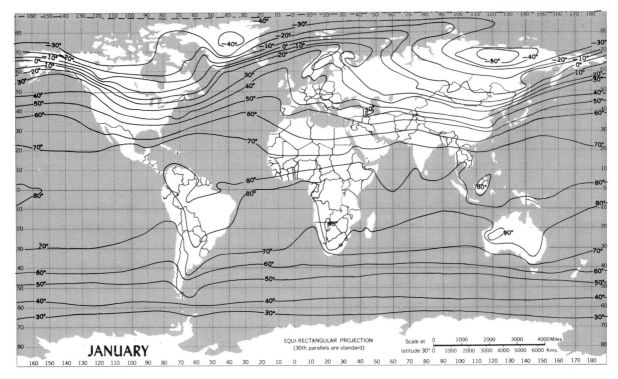

Figure 2.13 Average sea-level temperatures, January.

One conspicuous feature of these temperature maps is that the isotherms have a strong east-west alignment, roughly following the parallels of latitude. This is not surprising, since except for differences in the transparency of the atmosphere, all places in the same latitude receive the same amount of solar energy. Thus the east-west course of the isotherms simply illustrates the point made earlier in the chapter—that solar energy is the single most important control of broad-scale temperature distributions over the earth.

Notice on the temperature maps that in some parts of the world, isotherms are closely spaced, indicating rapid horizontal temperature change; in others they are far apart, signifying slight temperature differences. The rate of horizontal temperature change is called the *temperature gradient*. The gradient is steep where the isotherms are closely spaced, and weak where they are far apart.

Average annual temperatures (the mean of 12 monthly averages) are not very significant except in equatorial latitudes, for elsewhere they usually represent a mean of moderate-to-large seasonal extremes. As would be expected average annual temperatures are highest (80°±) in low latitudes, where solar energy is greatest. They are lowest in the vicinity of the poles, the regions of least annual solar energy. Within a broad tropical belt some 40° wide, annual temperature varies little. It is mainly poleward of 20°–25° N and S that average annual temperature decreases markedly toward the poles.

Isotherms tend to be straighter and also more widely spaced in the Southern Hemisphere, where oceans predominate. As can be seen from Figs. 2.13 and 2.14, the greatest deviations from east-west courses occur where isotherms pass from continents to oceans. This is caused by the contrasting heating and cooling properties of land and water surfaces, and by the effects of warm or cold ocean currents. Next to solar energy, land and

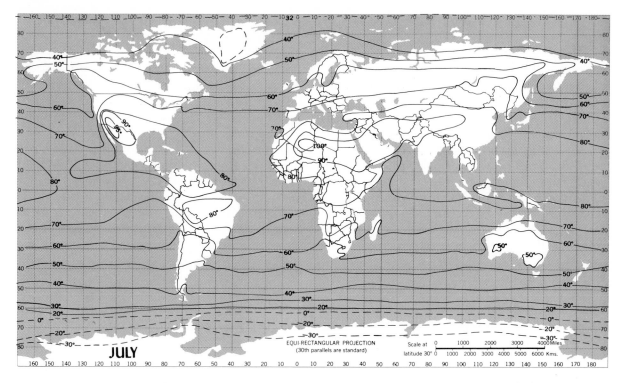

Figure 2.14   Average sea-level temperatures, July.

water distribution is the most important control of temperature distribution. Cool ocean currents off the coasts of Peru and northern Chile, southern California, and southwestern Africa cause equatorward bending of isotherms. Similarly, warm currents in higher latitudes cause isotherms to bend poleward, a condition most marked off the coast of northwestern Europe.

January and July Average Temperatures. Figures 2.13 and 2.14, the temperature maps for January and July, represent thermal conditions during the extreme seasons of winter and summer. Note these features:

1. There is a marked latitudinal shift of isotherms during the course of a year, northward between January and July and southward between July and January. This parallels a similar shift of solar energy. The shifting of isotherms is much greater over continents than over oceans because of the greater seasonal extremes of temperature over land.

2. In both January and July the highest temperatures are over land areas, and in January much the lowest temperatures are over Asia and North America, the largest land masses in the middle and higher latitudes.

3. In the Northern Hemisphere the January isotherms bend equatorward over the colder continents and poleward over the warmer oceans, whereas in July exactly the opposite happens.

4. No such seasonal temperature contrasts between land and water are to be found in the Southern Hemisphere, for it has no large land masses in the higher middle latitudes.

5. The lowest temperatures in January are over northeastern Asia, the leeward side of the largest land mass in higher middle latitudes. The next lowest temperatures are over Greenland and North America.

6. North-south temperature gradients, like solar energy gradients (Fig. 2.4), are steeper in winter than in summer. Steep gradients, represented by close spacing of isotherms, are particularly conspicuous over the Northern Hemisphere continents in January.

Annual Range. The difference between the average temperatures of the warmest and coldest months is called the *annual range of temperature*. The largest annual ranges are over the great Northern Hemisphere continents, which become unusually hot in summer and cold in winter (Fig. 2.15). Ranges are never large near the equator, where solar energy varies little. Nor are they large over extensive water bodies, which explains why ranges are small everywhere in the middle latitudes of the Southern Hemisphere. In summary, they become larger toward higher latitudes, with the increase much more marked over the continents than over the oceans.

Air Temperature and Sensible Temperature. Correct air temperature can be obtained only by an accurate thermometer *properly exposed*. It must not be set in the sun, for then it receives heat not only from the surrounding air but also from the absorption of solar energy. It should also be protected against direct radiation from sky, ground, and adjacent buildings.

Sensible temperature is the sensation of temperature that the human body feels, as distinguished from actual air temperature recorded by a thermometer. Unlike a thermometer, which has no temperature of its own, the human body is a heat engine, generating energy at a relatively fixed rate when at rest. Sensible temperature is affected by anything that affects the rate of heat loss from the body, which includes not only air temperature but also wind, humidity, and sunlight. Thus humid heat is more oppressive than dry heat because there is less cooling from evaporation. A hot day with a good breeze feels less oppressive than a hot, still day because of increased evaporation. A windy cold day feels uncomfortable because the loss of heat is speeded up by greater evaporation. A sunny day in winter feels less cold than it actually is, owing to the body's absorption of solar energy. Because of its sensitiveness to all these factors, the

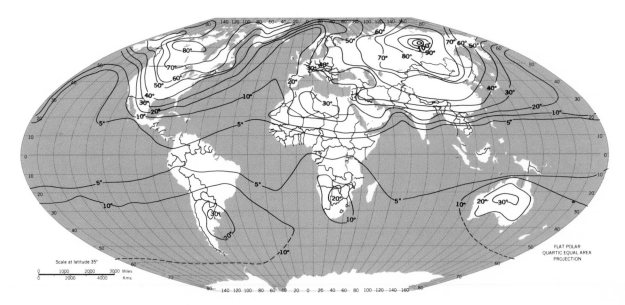

Figure 2.15 Average annual ranges of temperature.

human body is not a very accurate instrument for measuring air temperature.

Selected References
for Chaps. 2–5

Aviation Weather. U.S. Federal Aviation Agency and Department of Commerce, Washington, D.C., 1965.

Blair, Thomas A., and Robert C. Fite. *Weather Elements*. 5th ed. Prentice-Hall, Inc., Englewood Cliffs, N.J., 1965.

Blumenstock, David I. *The Ocean of Air*. Rutgers University Press, New Brunswick, N.J., 1959.

Climate and Man. Yearbook of Agriculture, 1941. U.S. Department of Agriculture, Washington, D.C. See particularly Parts 1 and 4.

Critchfield, Howard J. *General Climatology*. 2d ed. Prentice-Hall, Inc., Englewood Cliffs, N.J., 1966.

Hare, F. K. *The Restless Atmosphere*. Harper & Row, Publishers, Incorporated, New York, 1963.

Kendrew, W. G. *Climatology*. 2d ed. Oxford University Press, Fair Lawn, N.J., 1957.

Koeppe, Clarence E., and George C. De Long. *Weather and Climate*. McGraw-Hill Book Company, New York, 1958.

Miller, A. Austin. *Climatology*. 3d ed. E. P. Dutton & Co., Inc., New York, 1953.

Petterssen, Sverre. *Introduction to Meteorology*. 2d ed. McGraw-Hill Book Company, New York, 1958.

Riehl, Herbert. *Tropical Meteorology*. McGraw-Hill Book Company, New York, 1954.

————. *Introduction to the Atmosphere*. McGraw-Hill Book Company, New York, 1965.

Trewartha, Glenn T. *An Introduction to Climate*. 4th ed. McGraw-Hill Book Company, New York, 1968.

Watts, I. E. M. *Equatorial Weather*. University of London Press, Ltd., London, 1955.

3

The Circulation of the Atmosphere: Winds and Pressure

The sea of air which envelops the solid-liquid earth is in motion almost everywhere at all times. When this movement is in a direction essentially horizontal to the earth's surface, it is known as wind. Air is set in motion by differences in its density which cause variations in the weight or pressure of the atmosphere at the same altitude.

As elements of climate, atmospheric pressure and winds are modest in importance compared with temperature and precipitation. This is especially true of pressure. It is mainly as climatic *controls* that pressure and winds are considered in this book. The basic significance of atmospheric pressure is that pressure differences generate winds. And the two fundamental and crucially important climatic functions of winds are (1) the maintenance of a heat balance between the high and low latitudes, in spite of a constant low-latitude excess, and high-latitude deficiency, of radiant energy; (2) the transporting of water vapor from the oceans to the lands, where the water vapor may condense and fall as rain. Thus pressure and winds are also essential to an understanding of the spatial arrangement of temperature and precipitation on the earth.

Pressure Differences and Their Origins

The downward pressure (weight) of the air is measured by a barometer. At sea level, this weight is equal to the weight of a column of mercury 29.9 in., or 760 mm (millimeters), in length. The more air pressure, the higher the mercury rises in the tube. Until about 1914 it was customary to report pressure in units of length (inches, millimeters, or centimeters of mercury). Since then a new measuring unit, called the *millibar (mb),* has come into general use by the weather services of the world. Because $1/10$ in. of mercury is equivalent to 3.4 mb, average sea-level atmospheric pressure may be expressed as 29.9 in., 760 mm, or 1013.2 mb.

Atmospheric pressure at sea level is not uniform over the earth; it varies with latitude and also with regions within the same latitudinal belt. The variations can be classified into two general types: (1) high-pressure systems, called *anticyclones* or *highs;* (2) low-pressure systems, called *cyclones, depressions,* or *lows.*

The origins of many of these systems are still not completely understood. Some highs and lows appear to be caused in part by air temperature characteristics. Thus, some surface highs in winter are partly created by the cold, dense air which composes them, and some summer lows may result from high surface temperatures which make the air less dense. However, many more pressure systems seem to owe their origins to dynamic factors associated with air in motion. These include frictional effects, centrifugal force, and the blocking of winds by highlands.

Distribution of Atmospheric Pressure
Vertical Distribution

Since air is very compressible, there is a rapid decrease in air weight or pressure with increasing altitude. The lower layers of the atmosphere are most compressed, or densest, because the weight of all the layers above rests upon them. For the first few thousand feet above sea level the rate of pressure decrease is about 1 in., or 34 mb, of pressure for each 900 to 1,000 ft. At higher altitudes the air rapidly becomes much thinner and lighter. Thus at an elevation of 18,000 ft one-half the atmosphere by weight is below the observer, although a highly rarefied atmosphere extends to a height of several thousand miles.

Horizontal Distribution at Sea Level

Just as temperature distribution is represented by isotherms, so atmospheric pressure distribution is represented by *isobars,* that is, lines connecting places having the same atmospheric pressure at a given elevation. On the isobaric charts shown here (Figs. 3.3, 3.4), all pressure readings have been reduced to sea level to eliminate the effects of altitude on pressure. Many pressure-distribution charts do represent sea-level pressures, although the need for understanding upper-air flow has in recent years caused the development of pressure charts for higher levels, usually for about 10,000 ft (750 mb) and 18,000 ft (500 mb).

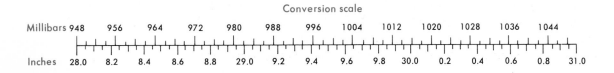

Conversion scale

| Millibars | 948 | 956 | 964 | 972 | 980 | 988 | 996 | 1004 | 1012 | 1020 | 1028 | 1036 | 1044 |

| Inches | 28.0 | 8.2 | 8.4 | 8.6 | 8.8 | 29.0 | 9.2 | 9.4 | 9.6 | 9.8 | 30.0 | 0.2 | 0.4 | 0.6 | 0.8 | 31.0 |

Where isobars are closely spaced, there is a rapid horizontal change in pressure in a direction at right angles to the isobars. The rate and direction of the change is called the *pressure gradient*. Where isobars are widely spaced, the pressure gradient is weak.

The worldwide arrangement of average sea-level pressures is reasonably well generalized and portrayed by both the idealized isobaric chart (Fig. 3.1) and the meridional profile of pressure (Fig. 3.2). Both figures suggest that pressure, when averaged for all longitudes, is arranged in zones resem-

bling belts. These so-called belts are more accurately described as centers, or cells, of pressure, which appear in latitudinal bands. The belted arrangement is more conspicuous in the relatively homogeneous Southern Hemisphere, where oceans prevail. This suggests that two features of the great Northern Hemisphere continents—their highlands which obstruct the free flow of the atmosphere, and their great seasonal temperature changes—have much to do with the origin and arrangement of pressure cells.

The most noteworthy features of the generalized world pattern of sea-level pressure can be derived from Figs. 3.1 and 3.2:

1. The dominant element is the series of high-pressure cells which form irregular belts of high pressure at about 25°–30° N and S. These are the subtropical highs. Their origin is not fully understood, but certainly it is mechanical or dynamic, not thermal.

2. Between the belts of subtropical high pressure is the equatorial trough of low pressure.

3. Poleward from the subtropical highs, pressure decreases toward either pole, with minima being reached in the vicinity of about 65° N and S. At these latitudes are the subpolar centers, or troughs, of low pressure. Their origin is not clear,

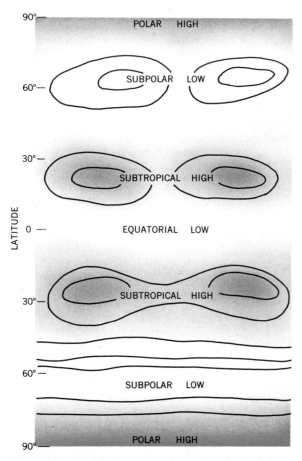

Figure 3.1 Idealized patterns of zonal sea-level pressure. Except in the higher latitudes of the Southern Hemisphere, the zonal pressure "belts" are cells of low or high pressure arranged in belts which are concentrated in particular latitudes.

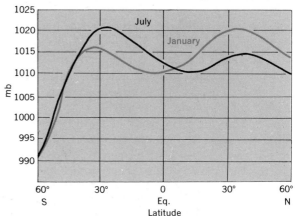

Figure 3.2 Profiles of sea-level pressure from 60°N to 60°S, averaged for all longitudes, at the time of the extreme seasons. Equatorial low, subtropical highs, and subpolar lows are conspicuous features of both profiles. Note the seasonal north-south displacements of the pressure belts following the sun.

but it is due more to mechanical than to thermal causes.

4. Poleward from about latitude 65°, data are so scanty that the pattern of pressure distribution is not well known. It is generally assumed that fairly shallow surface highs, partly of thermal origin, occupy the inner polar areas.

If one were to inspect a weather map of the earth for a single day, the arrangement of zonal surface pressure shown in Fig. 3.1 would not be so evident. This fact suggests that the generalized cells and zones of surface pressure are, partly at least, statistical averages of complicated day-to-day systems of moving highs and lows.

January and July, the Extreme Seasons. Figures 3.3 and 3.4 illustrate some important features of seasonal pressure distribution:

1. Pressure belts and cells, like those of temperature, migrate with the sun's rays—north-ward in July and southward in January. (This is most readily observed in Fig. 3.2, which shows the meridional profiles of pressure.) In general, pressure is higher in the winter, or cold, hemisphere.

2. The oceanic subtropical highs are best developed over the eastern sides of the oceans and tend to be weaker toward the western sides.

3. In the Southern Hemisphere, the sub-polar low is very deep, i.e., characterized by very low pressure, and forms a continuous circumpolar trough in both January and July. In the Northern Hemisphere, however, the subpolar low consists of individual oceanic low-pressure cells which are much more seasonal in character, being strongest in winter.

4. In January a strong thermal cell of high pressure develops over the cold continent of Eurasia, a weaker one over smaller and less frigid North America. In July these same continents, now warm, develop weaker thermal lows.

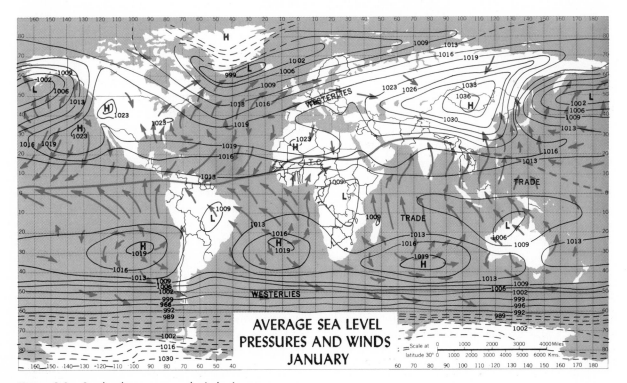

Figure 3.3 Sea-level pressures and winds, January.

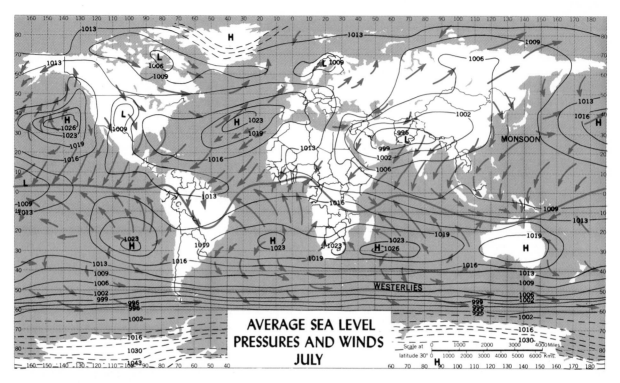

Figure 3.4   Sea-level pressures and winds, July.

Relation of Winds to Pressure

Large-scale horizontal movements of air, or winds, operate to correct latitudinal inequalities in the amounts of incoming solar energy and outgoing earth radiation.

Forces Governing Winds. It is *pressure gradient force* that sets the air in motion and causes it to move with increasing speed from high to low pressure. This force derives from differences in air density, which in turn are caused by differences in air pressure at a given altitude. Wind, therefore, represents nature's method of correcting pressure inequalities. Pressure gradient, as shown by the isobars, has both direction and magnitude. *Direction* of the gradient is indicated by an arrow drawn at right angles to the isobars, and pointing from high to low pressure (see Fig. 3.5). Thus direction of airflow is from high to low pressure, al-

though obliquely. *Magnitude* of the pressure gradient force is the steepness of the pressure gradient. It is inversely proportional to the isobar spacing— close spacing denotes a steep gradient, a strong and accelerating pressure gradient force, and high wind speeds. Weak winds are associated with widely spaced isobars (Fig. 3.5).

A second force, which affects only direction of winds (not speed), is the *deflecting force of earth rotation,* known as the *Coriolis force.* On a nonrotating earth, air set in motion by pressure differences would simply flow along the pressure gradient at right angles to the isobars. But on a rotating earth where meridians and parallels, the guidelines of direction, are themselves constantly changing direction, winds have an *apparent* deflection from the gradient direction, so that they cross the isobars at an oblique angle.

In the Northern Hemisphere, earth rotation or Coriolis force causes all winds to have an appar-

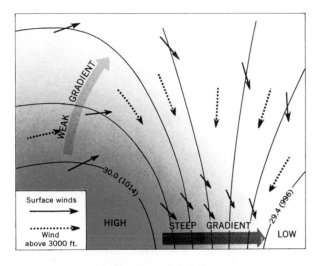

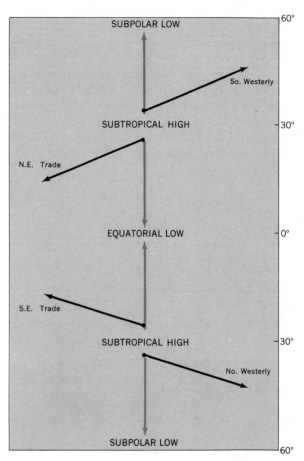

Figure 3.5 Pressure gradient is the rate and direction of pressure change. It is represented by the wide gray arrows drawn at right angles to the isobars. Gradients are steep where isobars are closely spaced and weak where they are far apart. Winds move from high to low pressure, although they do so indirectly. At the earth's surface, friction causes them to cross the isobars at an angle of 10 to 40°, but aloft they nearly parallel the isobars.

Figure 3.6 Apparent deflection of the planetary winds on a rotating earth. Green arrows indicate wind direction as it would be from pressure gradient alone. Black arrows show the actual direction of deflected winds resulting from earth rotation.

ent deflection to the right of the gradient direction; in the Southern Hemisphere, the apparent deflection is always to the left (Fig. 3.6). When tested, however, this rule will not appear to be true unless the observer faces in the direction the wind is blowing. Deflective force of earth rotation increases with increasing latitude, i.e., toward either pole; only at the equator is it absent.

A third force, which affects both direction and speed of winds, is *friction* between moving air and the land-sea surface (Fig. 3.5). Ground friction mainly affects only the lower 2,000–3,000 ft of the air ocean. It acts both to slow up the speed of the surface winds, and to cause them to cross the isobars at a wider angle than those aloft, which nearly parallel the isobars. Frictional effects are stronger over the more irregular land surface than over the ocean. Over land surfaces, for example, surface winds make an angle with the isobars of 20 to 40°. Over oceans, where friction is much less, the angle may be as low as 10°. But in the free atmosphere several thousand feet above the earth's surface, winds nearly parallel the isobars, the angle being as low as 1 to 3°.

Wind Direction Terminology. Winds are always named by the direction from which they come. Thus a wind from the south, blowing toward the north, is called a south wind. The wind vane points toward the source of the wind. But on the weather map, wind arrows fly *with* the wind. *Windward* refers to the direction from which a wind blows; *leeward* refers to the direction toward which it blows. Along a windward coast, the flow of air is onshore; on a leeward coast, it is offshore. In a closed-isobar low-pressure system, the winds have a *cyclonic* flow—an inward-curving convergent motion—counterclockwise north of the equator and clockwise to the south. In a high-pressure system, the winds have an *anticyclonic* flow—a spirally outward or divergent motion—clockwise in the Northern Hemisphere and anticlockwise in the Southern (Figs. 3.7, 5.6).

The Earth's Winds

Zonal Pattern of Surface Winds. The two main systems of surface winds in either hemisphere have their origins in the subtropical highs (Figs. 3.3, 3.4, 3.6, 3.7). From these highs, positioned at about 25°–30° N and S, surface winds flow toward the low-pressure trough near the equator. Earth rotation deflects these two airstreams into oblique easterly winds, appropriately called the *tropical easterlies.* They are also known as the *trade winds,* or *trades* for short: northeast trades north of the equator, and southeast trades to the south of it.

Poleward from the subtropical highs in each hemisphere, winds flow downgradient toward the subpolar lows. They are turned by earth rotation so that they have a general west-to-east movement. These are the middle-latitude *westerlies:* southwest in the Northern Hemisphere and northwest in the Southern. Poleward from about 65°, where weather observations are few, the nature of the surface-wind system is uncertain. It seems probable, however, that easterly winds prevail.

To summarize zonal surface winds, easterly winds predominate in the low latitudes, or tropics; westerly winds in the middle latitudes (Fig. 3.8).

Between the converging trades, in the vicinity of the equatorial trough of low pressure, is a zone of variable and weak winds. This transition belt between the two trades has several names:

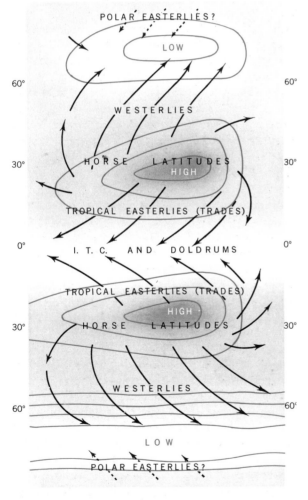

Figure 3.7 A much idealized representation of the earth's surface winds. Average airflow is predominantly from an easterly direction in most of the low latitudes and from a westerly direction in the middle latitudes.

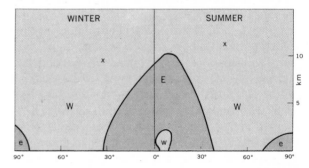

Figure 3.8 A pole-to-pole cross section of the planetary winds up to about 8 or 9 miles above the earth's surface. E = tropical easterlies or trades; W = westerlies; x = average location of the jet stream; w = the somewhat less certain belt of equatorial westerlies; e = polar easterlies *(After Flohn.)*

intertropical convergence zone (ITC), *doldrums,* and *equatorial belt of variable winds.* Here, in some seasons and over extensive longitudes, equatorial westerly winds prevail. At other times and places in this zone, winds are easterly. Upward movement of air is widespread.

Still another belt of weak and variable winds, the *horse latitudes,* is found in the intermediate area between the diverging trades and middle-latitude westerlies, fairly coincident with the crests of the subtropical highs located at about 25°–30° in each hemisphere. Here a slow settling of air prevails.

Seasonal Surface Winds. The zonal pattern of surface winds described above is a simplified model. Actual conditions are better represented by Figs. 3.3 and 3.4, which show circulations during the extreme seasons, winter and summer. On these seasonal maps a zonal belted arrangement of winds is not so conspicuous. More prominent are the spiraling circulations around individual cells of high and low pressure. Chief of these are the divergent anticyclonic circulations around the subtropical highs.

Since temperature and pressure belts shift north and south following the annual course of the sun (Fig. 3.2), it can be expected that wind systems will do likewise. Close scrutiny of Figs. 3.3 and 3.4 is required, however, to observe such a latitudinal shifting of the wind systems. It is easier seen on Fig. 4.12.

Notable features of the *January* map (Fig. 3.3) are the following: Over the oceans in the Northern Hemisphere, the subtropical warm anticyclones and their circulations are fairly weak; they are best developed in the eastern parts of these subtropical oceans. Over the Southern Hemisphere oceans, such warm anticyclones are stronger and more continuous. Circulations associated with cold anticyclones are characteristic of central eastern Asia and North America. These are the winter monsoons. Over the North Atlantic and North Pacific Oceans, deep and extensive cyclonic circulations prevail, while over summer-heated Australia, a cyclonic circulation exists.

In *July,* the cyclonic circulations over the North Atlantic and North Pacific are much weaker (Fig. 3.4). But over Asia and to a lesser degree North America, extensive cyclonic circulations with converging winds develop around low-pressure cells, which are partly of thermal origin. These are the *summer monsoons.*

Areas of Horizontal Divergence and Convergence. Where surface winds converge, the air must escape through upward movement (Fig. 3.9). This condition favors condensation and the development of storms, with their associated clouds and precipitation. By contrast, where surface winds diverge, there must be a downward movement (subsidence) of air from aloft to compensate for the divergent surface flow (Fig. 3.9). Since such subsidence heats and dries the air, causing temperature inversions, it is opposed to the development of storms and to the formation of clouds and precipitation. Best developed of the divergence-subsidence zones are those associated with the subtropical anticyclones located at about 25°–30° north and south of the equator (Figs. 3.3, 3.4). These zones are not continuous around the earth, for the oceanic cells of high pressure are strongest toward the eastern sides of the oceans. There subsidence is best developed, and deserts are conspicuous features of the adjacent lands. Toward the western sides of the oceans, where the subtropical anticyclones (and thus divergence and subsidence) are weaker, humid climates are likely to prevail. Surface divergence is likewise strong in the winter anticyclones over central and eastern Asia and over northern North America.

Most prominent of the extended lines of average surface convergence is the one located between the trades—the intertropical convergence (ITC). The surface-convergence lines of the winter cyclonic circulations over the North Pacific and North Atlantic are less continuous. There, much of the convergence appears to be concentrated in the numerous individual traveling cyclonic storms which infest these locations. In summer, convergence is associated with the seasonal cyclonic circulations over Asia and North America.

General Circulation of the Atmosphere. Certain features of the atmosphere's general circulation are important for an understanding of world climates.

The necessity for a general circulation of the atmosphere to compensate for the unequal distribution of solar energy over the earth between poles and equator has been described earlier. Winds and ocean currents are the means by which the excess of energy received in the tropics is carried to the deficit regions farther poleward. Atmospheric circulation, however, is not in the form of a gigantic convectional system with a direct meridional flow—aloft from warm equator to cold poles, and at the surface from cold poles to warm equator. On the rotating earth, with its surface composed of continents and oceans having contrasting frictional and heating properties, such a simple direct convectional circulation between equator and poles is impossible. The one that actually prevails is much more com-

plex—so much so that no acceptable unified theory of the general circulation now exists.

In its simplest form, the atmospheric circulation between equator and poles is usually represented as broken down into three smaller meridional circulations: tropical, middle-latitude, and polar (Fig. 3.9). In the low latitudes equatorward from about 30°, and also in the high latitudes poleward from about 65°, the evidence suggests circulations which resemble that of a convectional system. In both there is, on the average, an oblique movement of air equatorward at the surface and poleward aloft. The deflective force of earth rotation causes the surface winds to be easterly (trades and polar easterlies) and those at higher levels to be westerly. Such a circulation requires an upward movement of air in equatorial latitudes, and likewise in the vicinity of latitude 60°. Similarly, there is a settling of the upper air both in subtropical latitudes and near the poles.

It is principally in the middle latitudes (35°–60°) that the circulation pattern is most complex and controversial. Here, apparently, much of the necessary north-south heat exchange occurs in the form of sporadic thrusts of cold polar air moving equatorward, and warm surges of tropical air moving poleward. In these latitudes, both at the surface and aloft, the prevailing air movement is from the west. However, wind as well as weather is highly variable—a result of the frequent, alternating passage of cyclones and anticyclones, accompanied by shifts in wind direction and marked changes in temperature. These cyclones and anticyclones are thought to be closely associated with the alternating thrusts of cold and warm air which accomplish the required heat exchange. Note in Fig. 3.9 that only in the middle-latitude cell of meridional circulation do the mean surface winds flow poleward, and hence in an opposite direction from those of a convectional circulatory system (in which surface air moves from cold poles to warm equator). Because their flow is counter to the surface winds of the polar and tropical cells, there is a zone of divergence on the equatorial side of the middle-latitude westerlies, and frequent convergences in the form

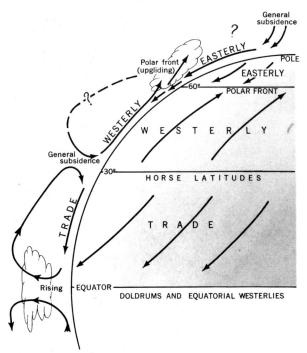

Figure 3.9 Important elements of the general circulation of the atmosphere. Some features of the upper circulation are not at present sufficiently well understood, or are too complicated, to be represented in a simple diagram.

of traveling cyclonic centers in their more poleward parts. This fact has important consequences for weather and climate.

Above-surface Circulation. At altitudes of 4 to 7 miles, features of the atmospheric circulation with strong climatic implications are the jet streams and their long meridional waves. Jet streams are violently rushing rivers of air within the high westerlies of middle latitudes. They encircle the earth in meandering courses, shifting their average latitudinal positions with the seasons. The jets and their long waves also shift in large-scale nonperiodic variations. At times the high westerlies and their jets are strongly zonal (oriented east-west), the meridional waves are short, and the polar air is restricted to high latitudes (Fig. 3.10a). These are periods of relatively mild and settled weather at the surface. At other times the whole westerly wind system goes into gigantic convolutions: the jets take very sinuous courses, waves become greatly elongated, and there are rapidly alternating thrusts of polar and tropical air in the middle latitudes. These are the stormy periods of changeable weather at the earth's surface (Fig. 3.10b).

Clearly, jet streams and long waves are intimately related to surface weather. A majority of surface cyclonic storms appear to be linked to upper-level waves and jet streams which act to steer the course of the storms. Rainfall is concentrated underneath the jet. The meanders of the jet aloft can be identified with the surface polar front, a zone of steep temperature gradients and active development of atmospheric disturbances.

Individual Surface Winds and Their Weather

Tropical Easterlies, or Trade Winds. These are the easterly surface winds which move obliquely downgradient from the subtropical anticyclones toward the equatorial trough of low pressure, roughly between latitudes 20°–25° and 5°–10° in each hemisphere over the oceans (Fig. 3.7). The tropi-

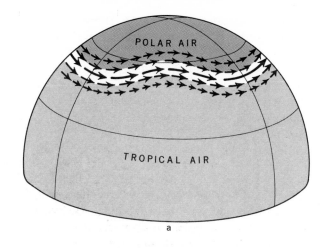

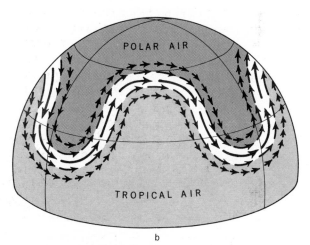

Figure 3.10 The jet stream and long waves in the upper atmosphere. In stage *a* the jet is positioned well to the north, waves are weak, and weather is relatively quiet. In stage *b* the jet has developed great oscillations in the form of waves. These waves carry polar air into low latitudes and tropical air into middle and high latitudes, creating stormy periods in the earth's weather.

cal easterlies, or trade winds, have always been renowned for their prevailing fair weather and steadiness of flow. However, the trades are now known to be neither as uniformly steady in direction and speed nor as full of fair weather as was formerly thought.

Over the central and eastern parts of the oceanic trades, where the subtropical anticyclones and their subsidence are strong, storms are few, winds steady, cloud and rainfall meager, and fair weather prevalent. But in the western parts, where the anticyclones and their accompanying subsidence are weaker, atmospheric disturbances are more numerous, the trades less constant, and cloud and rainfall more common (Fig. 3.11).

There are likewise important weather contrasts within the trade winds in a north-south direction. Toward their poleward margins, which are close to the centers of the subtropical highs where subsidence is strong, the trades are characterized by dry weather and much sunshine (Fig. 3.11). Here the air is said to be stable, for it lacks buoyancy; that is, it is disinclined to rise, and is opposed to the formation of rainbringing storms. But gradually, as the oceanic trades move equatorward, they acquire more and more moisture, and they become farther removed from a zone of subsidence and closer to one of convergence and lifting. Thus the trades are likely to be dry, fair-weather winds on their poleward sides and eastern oceanic parts, while their equatorward margins and western oceanic sections are characterized by more weather disturbances, cloud, and precipitation.

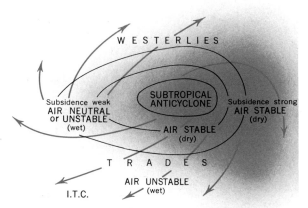

Figure 3.11 The circulation pattern around a subtropical anticyclone, with general areas of stability and instability shown. The eastern end of the cell and its trade winds are much more stable than the western end. The poleward parts of the trades are more stable than the equatorward parts. Degree of stability is suggested by the intensity of green shading.

But even in these rainier parts of the trades, the air is not usually so buoyant and unstable as it is in equatorial latitudes close to the ITC, or where equatorial westerlies prevail. As a consequence, except where highlands augment precipitation, the total annual rainfall is not excessive.

Winds of the ITC. Winds are very complex in the vicinity of the equatorial trough of low pressure, whose mean location is close to the geographic equator. In the extreme seasons, however, this trough may shift 10 to 20° to the north and south over the continents (Fig. 3.2). Air movement is usually light, and it is variable in both speed and direction. Calms are frequent. Over extensive longitudes, airflow is from the west (equatorial westerlies); at other times and places, it is from the east. The east winds are less rainy.

As a rule this ITC region between the trade winds is characterized by much horizontal convergence and associated rising air, so that the atmosphere is buoyant and unstable. Only slight lifting is required to trigger strong vertical air currents, resulting in cumulonimbus clouds of great height, capable of producing heavy, showery rains. Convergence and ascent of air cannot be continuous, however, for all days are not rainy. Probably the convergence and lifting are concentrated in the numerous weak disturbances which infest these areas close to the ITC.

Winds of the Subtropics. Close to the crests of the subtropical anticyclones (about 25 to 35° N and S), and situated between trades and middle-latitude westerlies, are the horse latitudes, a region characterized by a slow settling of the atmosphere (Fig. 3.7). This subsidence is opposed to the formation of cloud and precipitation.

Like the ITC zone, the horse latitudes are characterized by light winds coming from a variety of directions, and by frequent calms. However, the two regions are quite unlike in their general weather conditions, the ITC being a region of horizontal convergence, numerous atmospheric disturbances, and much showery rainfall, while the horse latitudes

are an area of horizontal divergence, few disturbances, and generally fair weather.

In reality the horse latitudes are not altogether similar in weather throughout (Fig. 3.11).
Toward the western margins of each oceanic anticyclone there is less atmospheric subsidence than
in the center and eastern parts, so that while the
latter are characteristically dry, the western parts
have a moderate amount of cloud and precipitation.
This is why the eastern parts of subtropical oceans
and the adjacent (western) parts of continents have
dry and subhumid climates, while the western parts
of subtropical oceans and their bordering land areas
have humid climates.

Variable Westerlies of Middle Latitudes. The
stormy westerlies (30°–35° to 60°–65° N and S,
Fig. 3.7) move obliquely downgradient from the
centers of subtropical high pressure to the subpolar
lows. Much tropical-equatorial air also feeds into
the middle-latitude westerlies through the gaps between the individual subtropical anticyclones. In this
region the airflow is highly variable, both in speed
and in direction. At times, especially, in the winter,
the westerlies blow with gale force; at other times,
mild breezes prevail. Although the west is the
direction from which the strongest and most frequent winds come, they do blow from all points of
the compass.

The variability of the winds in both direction and strength is largely the result of numerous
atmospheric disturbances—cyclones and anticyclones—which travel from west to east in these
latitudes. The disturbances, with their local systems
of converging and diverging winds, tend to disrupt
and modify the general westerly air currents. Moreover, on the eastern sides of Asia, and to a lesser
degree in the eastern part of North America, continental wind systems called monsoons tend to modify
the westerlies, especially in summer. Except in the
interiors of large continents, the stormy westerlies
are likely to produce humid climates.

The poleward margins of the westerlies
near the subpolar troughs of low pressure are particularly subject to surges of cold polar air, espe-

cially in winter. A sinuous line of discontinuity
known as the polar front separates the cold, dry
polar air from the warmer and usually more humid
airstream of the westerlies coming from the subtropics and tropics (Fig. 3.9). A great many
middle-latitude cyclones originate along the polar
front. It and its accompanying belt of storms migrate with the sun's rays, retreating poleward in
summer and advancing equatorward in winter. Consequently, aperiodic storm control of weather in
the middle latitudes is most pronounced in winter.

Terrestrial Modifications
of Surface Winds

Latitudinal Shifting of Wind Belts. Because solar
energy belts shift north and south during the course
of a year, thereby producing the march of the seasons, temperature, pressure, and wind belts do also.
But the latitudinal shifting of wind systems is by no
means simple. The amplitude of the shift is much
greater over continents, where seasonal temperature
extremes are stronger, than over the more temperate oceans. Seasonal north-south shifting of the wind
belts is especially significant in latitudes which lie
between two wind systems having unlike weather
conditions—as, for example, between a wet converging and a dry diverging system. Such latitudes
are encroached upon by one wind system and its
weather conditions at one season, and by the other
wind system and its weather at the opposite season.

For example, latitudes about *5 to 15°
north and south* of the equator lie between the wet
equatorial convergence zone (ITC and equatorial
westerlies) with its unstable air, numerous atmospheric disturbances, and abundant rainfall on one
side, and the dry subsidence and divergence zone of
the subtropical anticyclones (horse latitudes) on
the other (Fig. 4.12). These latitudes mainly get
weather associated with the ITC and its rainbringing disturbances at the time of high sun (summer).
But in low sun (winter), they are dominated by the
dry, fair weather of the subtropical anticyclones and
their trade winds. One wet season and one dry season are the result in most areas of these longitudes,

although the pattern is not found everywhere. For example, on the western sides of tropical oceans and the adjacent eastern sides of continents, the anticyclone is weaker and the air is less stable.

Likewise, latitudes about *30 to 40°* represent transition zones between the dry subtropical anticyclones, and the middle-latitude westerlies with their numerous rainbringing cyclonic storms (Fig. 4.12). Drought associated with anticyclonic subsidence and divergence is characteristic of summer, while in winter there is adequate precipitation from cyclonic storms in the westerlies. This seasonal rainfall variation in latitudes 30°–40° is confined largely to the eastern sides of oceans and the adjacent western sides of continents, where the subtropical anticyclone is well developed and the air is stable.

Monsoon Winds. These are winds that reverse their direction of flow during the course of a year. Monsoons most commonly, but not always, blow from land to sea in winter and from sea to land in summer.

In middle latitudes this seasonal wind reversal appears to be, partly at least, a consequence of the unequal heating and cooling of continents and oceans. In winter, for example, a large continent in middle latitudes is colder than the surrounding sea surface, so that the air over the land is colder and denser and the atmospheric pressure is higher (see eastern Asia in Fig. 3.3). As a result there is likely to be a flow of surface air from land to sea. Because this winter monsoon originates over a cold land mass, it is dry, cold, and stable, and therefore resists upward movement which might result in cloud and precipitation.

In summer, by contrast, the land air is warmer and less dense than that over the sea, and atmospheric pressure is lower over the land. As a consequence surface air flows from sea to land (eastern Asia, Fig. 3.4). This summer monsoon originates over the sea, and usually over relatively warm waters. Thus its humidity content is high, a condition which is favorable to the development of atmospheric disturbances capable of producing clouds and rainfall. The causation sequence of monsoon systems in middle latitudes can be summarized as follows:

Winter—land cold with high pressure—surface winds from land to sea.

Summer—land warm with low pressure—surface winds from sea to land.

In the tropics, where seasonal temperature contrasts between continent and ocean are small, the seasonal reversal of wind direction is mainly a result of the latitudinal shifting of wind belts following the course of the sun (see southern Asia in Figs. 3.3, 3.4). Thus dry easterlies or trades predominate in low sun (winter), and wet equatorial westerlies and ITC in high sun (summer).

The climatic consequences of monsoons are often striking. In the middle latitudes, they tend to produce cold, relatively dry winters and hot, wet summers. Thus seasonal extremes in both temperature and rainfall are characteristic. In the tropics, the seasonal wind reversal obviously does not produce cold winters, but it does result in dry winters and wet summers. East Asia is by far the best example of a region of middle-latitude monsoons, although central and eastern North America also have some features of them. In the tropics, monsoons are especially characteristic of southern Asia, northern Australia, and Tropical West Africa.

It should be emphasized that the winter monsoon is dry both because it originates over land and because it has its source in an anticyclonic circulation; thus it is both low in humidity and stable. By contrast, the summer monsoon is composed of tropical-subtropical air that is usually warm, humid, and buoyant or unstable. It creates an environment which favors precipitation. In this environment numerous atmospheric disturbances are capable of producing much showery convectional rainfall. Of course a winter monsoon may be wet if it is forced to ascend highlands.

Land and Sea Breezes. Like middle-latitude monsoons, land and sea breezes are wind reversals that originate from the unequal heating of land and water surfaces. But these wind reversals have a daily periodicity, not the seasonal one of the monsoons. At night the land's greater coolness results in an offshore (land to sea) breeze; by day the heated land causes wind to flow onshore (sea to land). The sea breeze is rarely felt more than a few miles inland. In the middle latitudes they occur only in the warmer seasons, but along tropical coasts the daily sea breeze is a year-round weather feature. Sea breezes may help appreciably to reduce high daytime temperatures. It is believed also that the sea breeze may have some generating effect on thunderstorm activity, thereby increasing the total precipitation along littorals.

4

Atmospheric Moisture and Precipitation

Water Vapor, or Humidity

Only in the invisible, or gas, form is water an integral part of the atmosphere; it is then referred to as water vapor or humidity. The air's water vapor varies in quantity from place to place and also from time to time, but always comprises only a small part of the total atmosphere. If all the water vapor in the air were condensed to the liquid form and evenly distributed over the earth as rain, it would form a layer only about 1 in. deep. Nevertheless, as far as weather and climate are concerned, water vapor is much the most important gas in the atmosphere, for several reasons: (1) It is the source of all forms of condensation and precipitation. (2) The more water vapor in the atmosphere, the more latent or stored-up energy is available for the development of atmospheric disturbances or storms. (3) Water vapor is the chief absorber of both solar radiation and earth radiation and therefore acts to regulate air temperature. (4) The amount of water vapor in the atmosphere affects the rate of evaporation, a process important to both plant and animal life. It also affects the human body's rate of cooling and hence its feeling of heat and cold, i.e., the sensible temperature.

Evaporation

Water vapor in the air is derived from water in the liquid or solid form through the process of *evaporation*. The rate of evaporation depends chiefly on air temperature, the aridity of the air, and the speed of the wind. On a hot, arid, windy day, evaporation is unusually rapid.

Evaporation is greater over oceans than over continents because of the unlimited supply of water at the ocean surface. It is high in the tropics-subtropics where temperatures are high, and declines poleward as temperatures drop.

Hydrologic Cycle

The atmosphere's water vapor moves through a never-ending cycle (see Fig. 11.1). Humidity is added to the air by evaporation of water from sea and land. It is lost to the air by condensation, mainly in the form of clouds, which are composed of liquid or solid particles. Coalesced cloud droplets are subsequently returned to land and sea by precipitation. Since continents have an excess of precipitation over evaporation, the surplus must be returned to the oceans—as runoff in the form of rivers and glaciers, and as water vapor gas contained in great continental air masses moving seaward.

In addition to the moisture exchange between continents and oceans, there is another exchange between latitude belts. Close to the equator, and also in the middle latitudes of each hemisphere, precipitation exceeds evaporation. In contrast, two other zones have a net deficiency of moisture. These are latitudes 10 to 30 or 40° in each hemisphere— the zones of the subtropical anticyclones and the trade winds, from which vast amounts of water vapor are advected both equatorward and poleward.

Latent Energy in Water Vapor

In the course of evaporation, liquid water and solid ice are converted into water vapor, a gas. This process consumes transformed solar energy in the form of heat. It follows that an equivalent amount of energy in the form of heat is released to the air and to the land-sea surface when condensation occurs and water vapor is changed into liquid and solid cloud particles, which fall to the land-sea surface as precipitation. To convert a gram of ice into a gram of water at freezing temperature, 79 calories of heat are required. To evaporate the gram of water at 32° and convert it into water vapor, 607 calories are required. This stored-up energy in water vapor is known as *latent heat* or *latent energy*.

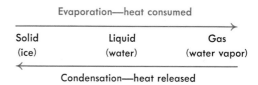

Evaporation—heat consumed →		
Solid (ice)	Liquid (water)	Gas (water vapor)
← Condensation—heat released		

Humidity Variants

The capacity of the air for water vapor depends almost entirely upon its temperature. Warm air can hold more water vapor than cold air. Moreover, the air's capacity for water vapor not only grows with increasing temperature, but increases at an increasing rate. (See Fig. 4.1 and the table showing maximum water vapor capacities.) A 10°· rise in air temperature from 90 to 100° increases the humidity capacity five times more than a similar rise from 30 to 40°. It follows that warm tropical air has a far greater capacity for water vapor than the cold air of higher latitudes, while summer air has a much greater capacity than that of winter. These facts have important climatic implications for precipitation.

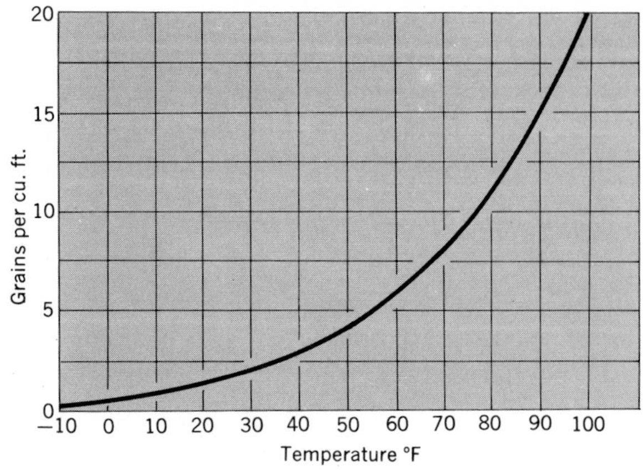

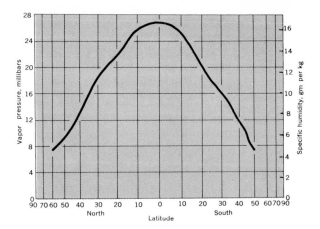

Figure 4.1 Variations in the capacity of air for water vapor at different temperatures. Not only does capacity increase as the temperature of the air rises, but equally important, it increases at an increasing rate.

Figure 4.2 Zonal distribution of the water vapor content of the air. Specific humidity is highest in the vicinity of the equator and decreases toward the poles. *(After Haurwitz and Austin.)*

When a given volume of air has all the water vapor it is capable of holding, it is said to be *saturated*. The amount of water vapor in the air can be expressed several different ways: as absolute humidity, specific humidity, or vapor pressure.[1]

Distribution of Humidity. The water vapor content of the air (if given as absolute humidity, specific humidity, or vapor pressure) normally is highest near the earth's surface and decreases rapidly upward. Such a vertical distribution is to be expected, since the earth's surface is the source of the atmosphere's humidity, and since temperatures normally are higher at low elevations. Half the water vapor in the deep air ocean lies below an altitude of 6,500 ft.

Likewise in a north-south direction, or along a meridian, water vapor distribution is associated with temperature distribution: humidity is highest in the low latitudes near the equator and decreases poleward (Fig. 4.2). As a general rule,

winds arriving from tropical latitudes, especially from oceanic and rainforest sources, contain an abundance of water vapor, and so are conducive to large-scale condensation and precipitation. By contrast, air from cold polar and continental sources is low in water vapor content and hence too dry to yield much precipitation.

As for the seasonal distribution of water vapor, humidity obviously is higher in warm summer air than in the colder air of winter. Air over the central United States in July contains three to six times as much humidity as air in January.

Relative Humidity. Relative humidity refers to the amount of water vapor actually in the air (absolute or specific humidity) compared with the greatest amount that the air could contain at the same temperature (its capacity). Relative humidity is always expressed in the form of a fraction, ratio, or percentage. For example, air at 70° has the capacity to contain 8 grains of water vapor per cu ft. If it actually does contain 6 grains, then it is only three-fourths saturated, and its relative humidity is 75 percent. When the relative humidity reaches 100 percent, the air is said to be saturated.

The relative humidity of an air mass can be altered in two ways: (1) by a change in the

[1] *Absolute humidity* is the actual mass of water vapor per unit volume of air (i.e., grams per cubic meter or cubic foot). *Specific humidity* is the mass of vapor per unit mass of air (grams per kilogram). *Vapor pressure* is that part of the total atmospheric pressure which can be attributed to the water vapor pressure.

MAXIMUM WATER-VAPOR CAPACITY OF 1 CU FT OF AIR AT VARYING TEMPERATURES

Temperature, degrees Fahrenheit	Water vapor, grains	Difference between successive 10° intervals, grains
30	1.9	
		1.0
40	2.9	
		1.2
50	4.1	
		1.6
60	5.7	
		2.3
70	8.0	
		2.9
80	10.9	
		3.8
90	14.7	
		5.0
100	19.7	

amount of water vapor in the air, or (2) by a change in the air's temperature and hence its capacity. The following table shows how air which is saturated (relative humidity 100 percent) at 40° acquires successively lower relative humidities simply by an increase in temperature, the water vapor content remaining unchanged. Various humidity relationships are also illustrated by Fig. 4.3.

Temperature, degrees Fahrenheit	Absolute humidity, grains	Relative humidity, percent saturated
40	2.9	100
50	2.9	71
60	2.9	51
70	2.9	36
80	2.9	27
90	2.9	20

Since relative humidity is a major determinant of the amount and rate of evaporation, it has an important influence on the rate of moisture and heat loss by plants and animals, including human beings. Consequently it materially affects the sensible temperature and therefore human comfort. Relative humidity is also closely related to the development of clouds and precipitation. Air that is close to the saturation stage requires only a minimum amount of cooling to bring about condensa-

SATURATED CONDITIONS
(RELATIVE HUMIDITIES 100%)

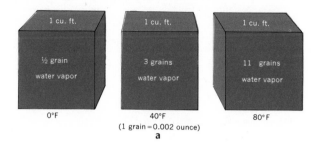

(1 grain = 0.002 ounce)

a

UNSATURATED CONDITIONS
RELATIVE HUMIDITY

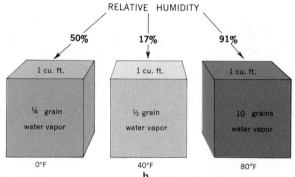

b

Figure 4.3   Each cube represents 1 cu ft of air. The top row shows the changing capacity for water vapor of a saturated cubic foot of air under three different temperature conditions. The cubic-foot samples in the bottom row have the same temperatures as those in the top, but they are unsaturated—they do not contain all the water vapor possible at those temperatures. The different amounts of water vapor which they hold at the different temperatures cause them to have different relative humidities, as represented by the variations in green shading.

tion and the formation of clouds. On the other hand, air with low relative humidity requires a large amount of cooling in order to form clouds and cause rainfall. In desert regions the relative humidity is usually so low that the air is rarely cooled enough for rain clouds to form.

Distribution of Relative Humidity.   As Fig. 4.4 shows, a strong maximum of relative humidity exists in equatorial latitudes. From there it declines both to the north and to the south, with minima at about

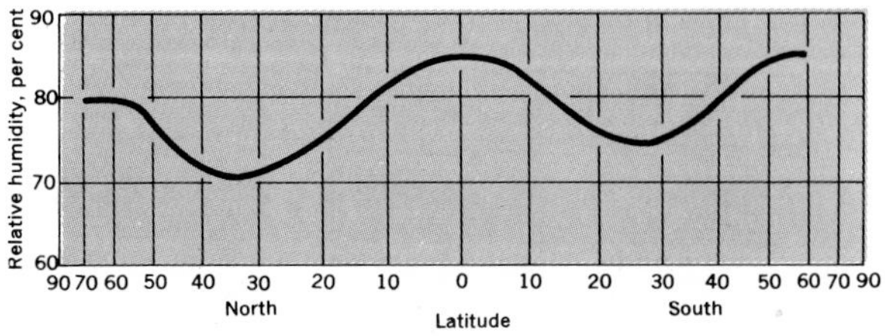

Figure 4.4 Zonal distribution of relative humidity. Note that the north-south distribution of relative humidity is quite different from that of specific humidity (Fig. 4.2).

25°–35° N and S. These are the latitudes of the subtropical anticyclones and their extensive continental deserts. Unlike specific humidity (Fig. 4.2), relative humidity increases poleward from the subtropics as temperature declines. Thus maxima are located at about 60° N and S. During the daily period of 24 hr, the relative humidity of the air near the ground is usually highest in the cool night and early morning hours, and lowest in the warm midafternoon. It is normally higher in winter than in summer.

Condensation

Origin

If nonsaturated air is subjected to progressive cooling so that its capacity for moisture is thereby reduced, a temperature is eventually reached at which the air is saturated (relative humidity 100 percent), even though the total amount of water vapor has remained unchanged. This critical temperature is called the *dew point*.

If the air is further cooled below the dew point, the excess water vapor, over and above what the air can contain at this lower temperature, forms as minute droplets of water (if the temperature is above 32°) and possibly tiny ice crystals (if below 32°). When this happens, condensation has taken place. As an example, air with a temperature of 80° and containing 8 grains of water vapor per cu ft has a relative humidity of 73 percent (see table, p. 000). If this air is gradually cooled and its capacity for water vapor thus lowered, it eventually

reaches its dew point, 70°, the temperature at which it is saturated. Further cooling results in condensation and the release of latent heat. The varying amount of condensation that occurs at the different temperatures reached reflects the changing water vapor capacity of the air.

Remember that an equivalent cooling of warm air and of cold air does not result in the same amount of condensation (table, p. 000). This is the reason why warm summer air has a greater potential for abundant condensation and precipitation than cold winter air, and tropical air usually has a greater potential than polar air.

Most large-scale condensation, including the formation of all precipitation, is a consequence of the reduction of air temperature below the dew point. It is clear that condensation depends upon two variables: the amount of cooling, and the relative humidity of the air.

Fog

Fog, dew, white frost, and rime are mostly caused by the direct cooling of shallow layers of surface air by radiation, conduction, or mixing. Of these minor types of condensation, fog alone has modest climatic importance.

A very common type of land fog known as *radiation* or *ground-inversion* fog results from the cooling by radiation and conduction of shallow layers of quiet, humid air overlying a chilled land surface. Clear nights with little or no wind favor the development of radiation fogs. They are deeper and more prevalent in valleys and depressions, where the colder, heavier air collects as a result of air drainage. Radiation fogs usually are short-lived, being characteristic of the cooler night hours.

Also common is the *advection-radiation* type of fog, which develops when mild, humid air moves over a colder surface and is chilled by radiation and conduction. Here the emphasis is on *moving*, rather than quiet, air. These fogs are very common over oceans, especially in summer; along seacoasts and the shores of large inland lakes; and over middle-latitude land surfaces in winter. They occur particularly in the vicinity of cool ocean currents. In general, advection fogs are less local than the simple radiation type, and they tend to persist for longer periods, so that days as well as nights may remain shrouded in fog.

A third fog type is associated with belts of frontal rainfall. It originates when falling rain saturates the cool surface air.

Fog Distribution. Generalizations concerning fog distribution are not easy to make. Without much doubt, fog is more common over oceans than over continents, and it is more frequent over oceans in middle and higher latitudes than over those in the tropics. On continents it is the coastal areas that have the greatest number of days with fog. Within the United States, fog days are most frequent along the Pacific Coast, along the North Atlantic seaboard, and over the Appalachian Highlands. The least foggy area is the dry interior western country.

Clouds and Precipitation

Condensation in the form of clouds is of the highest importance in weather and climate, because all precipitation originates in clouds. Clouds with enough vertical thickness to yield considerable precipitation are formed almost exclusively by one process of atmospheric cooling—that which results from expansion in deep, upward-moving air masses.

When air rises, no matter what the cause, it expands, because there is less weight of air upon it at the higher altitudes. For example, if a mass of dry air at sea level rises to an altitude of about 18,000 ft, the pressure upon it is reduced by one-half, and consequently its volume is doubled, omitting any effect of temperature change. Thus 1 cu ft of sea-level air would occupy 2 cu ft if carried to that altitude. To make room for itself as it ascends and gradually expands, this air has to displace other air. The work of displacing the surrounding air requires energy, and this necessary energy is subtracted from the rising air mass in the form of heat. As a result its temperature is lowered.

Conversely, when air descends from higher altitudes, it is compressed by the denser air at lower levels. Since this means that work is done upon it, its temperature is raised. In short, rising air cools, while descending air is warmed. This is spoken of as *adiabatic temperature change.*

The rate of cooling resulting from the ascent and expansion of dry or nonsaturated air— the *dry adiabatic rate*—is approximately $5.5°F$ per 1,000-ft change in altitude. This is considerably greater than the normal rate of vertical temperature decrease within the general atmospheric environment (about $3.6°$ per 1,000 ft), which is called the *lapse rate.* Note that these two rates, the adiabatic rate and the lapse rate, are very different things. The adiabatic rate represents the cooling of a rising and therefore moving mass of air. The lapse rate represents the change in the temperature that would be recorded by a thermometer carried up through the atmosphere in a balloon or airplane.

Keep in mind that the process of atmospheric cooling by expansion within rising air currents is the *only* one which can reduce the temperature of thick and extensive masses of air below the dew point. It is the only process, therefore, which is capable of producing condensation on such a large scale that abundant precipitation results. There is no doubt that nearly all the earth's precipitation is the result of expansion and cooling in rising air currents. The direct result of cooling due to ascent, however, is not precipitation but clouds.

Cloud Types. Clouds, which are a striking feature of the natural landscape, have been arranged in an elaborate classification by the weather analyst. For the geographer's purposes, however, it is necessary to mention only two general cloud types.

Clouds known as *cumulus* are characterized by considerable vertical thickness but rather small horizontal dimensions, a dome-shaped cauliflower top, and a flat base. They are evidence of vertical convection currents. Cumulus clouds produce a very active, even dramatic, sky. Small cumuli flecking a blue sky are fair-weather features. But when they grow to great heights and become cumulonimbus, they are awesome spectacles, capable of producing heavy showers, strong squall winds, and lightning and thunder (Fig. 4.5). Because of their limited diameters, cumulus clouds do not ordinarily cover the sky to form a complete overcast.

A second principal cloud type is the *stratus,* or sheet, cloud. Characteristically it produces a gray, solid overcast, often without much shape or form. Dull, dark weather results. If precipitation occurs, it is usually steady and long-continued.

Cloud Distribution. The world's greatest average cloudiness, most of it stratus, is in the middle and high latitudes (Fig. 4.6). A modest secondary maximum, mostly composed of cumulus clouds, occurs in equatorial latitudes. Cloudiness declines to minimum values around latitudes 20 to 30°, the zones of subtropical anticyclones and trades.

Buoyancy of Air

Since practically all precipitation results from cooling in ascending air, the conditions which promote or hinder such vertical movements are of prime importance.

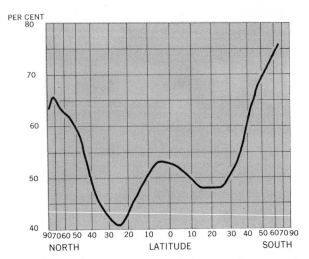

Figure 4.6 Zonal distribution of the annual means of cloudiness, in percent. Note that greatest cloudiness is not close to the equator where rainfall is highest, but in the middle and higher latitudes, where stratus clouds associated with cyclonic storms reach a maximum development. Cloudiness is least in the subtropics.

Stability. When air resists vertical movement and tends to remain in its original position, it is nonbuoyant and said to be *stable.* Normally an air mass

Figure 4.5 A cumulonimbus cloud, a type in which convective showers originate. Photographed from an airplane. *(Courtesy of T. Fujita.)*

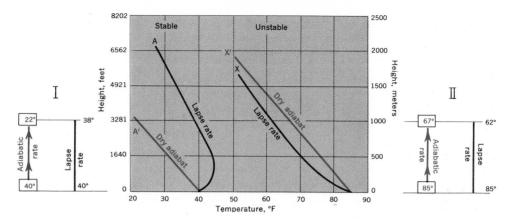

Figure 4.7 Conditions of atmospheric stability and instability. When rising air, as indicated by the dry adiabat, is cooler at any level than the atmosphere through which it is forced to ascend (lapse rate), it tends to resist vertical movement, and stability prevails. When rising air is warmer than its surrounding atmospheric environment, instability exists.

is most stable when colder air underlies warmer air —that is, when a temperature inversion exists (Fig. 4.7). The denser air below the lighter air makes upward movement difficult. Thus in very stable air abundant precipitation is less likely to occur. However, even stable, nonbuoyant air may be forced to rise, cool, and produce cloud and rainfall, as when an airstream is obstructed by mountains or hills (Fig. 4.8), or when two airstreams converge.

Atmospheric stability is promoted by at least two conditions: (1) when air is cooled at its base, and (2) when air subsides and spreads laterally (horizontal divergence). The second process occurs in high-pressure anticyclonic systems.

Instability. When air does not resist upward vertical displacement but, on the contrary, is buoyant and has a tendency to move upward from its original position, a condition of *instability* prevails. Upward vertical movement is made easy, and clouds and precipitation are likely in such buoyant air. Instability is characteristic of warm, humid air in which there is a rapid vertical decrease in temperature (a steep lapse rate) and in humidity.

Atmospheric instability is promoted (1) in air that is warmed and humidified in its lower layers, and (2) in a deep air mass that is forced

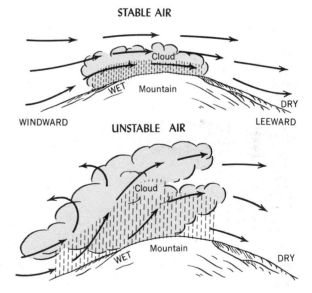

Figure 4.8 When stable or nonbuoyant air is forced upward over a terrain obstacle, the resulting clouds are more of the stratus type with less vertical thickness, so that the resulting rainfall may be fairly light. But in unstable or buoyant air, cloud forms are likely to be cumulus types with great vertical thickness, and the resulting showery rainfall will ordinarily be heavier.

to rise. Precipitation occurring in unstable, buoyant air is likely to be heavy and showery in character, and usually is associated with thick cumulus clouds (Fig. 4.8). Unstable air will continue to rise until it reaches an atmospheric environment which has a temperature and density similar to its own.

Precipitation

Forms

Although all precipitation originates in clouds, not all clouds yield precipitation. Before they can, the myriads of tiny cloud droplets must combine to produce drops of sufficient size and weight to reach the ground.

Rain, which is much the commonest and most widespread form of precipitation, results from cloud condensation in ascending air at temperatures above freezing. Some of the earth's rain, however, originates as ice and snow particles which are formed at temperatures below 32° and which subsequently melt as they fall through the warmer atmosphere closer to the earth's surface.

The most common kind of solid precipitation is snow. Its fundamental form is the intricately branched, flat six-sided crystal which occurs in an almost infinite variety of patterns. Numbers of these crystals matted together comprise a snowflake. Snow must develop from condensation taking place at temperatures below freezing. On the average it takes about 1 ft of snow to yield as much water as 1 in. of rain.

Data on the amount and distribution of snowfall are scanty for much of the earth. Snow occasionally falls near sea level in subtropical latitudes, but it does not remain on the ground. Farther equatorward, snow does not occur at low elevations. Poleward from about 40°, however, a winter snow cover durable enough to last for a month or more does exist at low elevations in the interior and eastern parts of Eurasia and North America.

In low and middle latitudes a *permanent* snow cover is characteristic only of elevated areas, with the height of the snow line, or limit of perpetual snow, declining poleward. Thus in the deep tropics, permanent snow is usually found only at elevations over 15,000 ft; but at 60° N in Norway, snow remains on the ground throughout the year at an elevation of about 3,500 ft.

Sleet and hail are other forms of solid precipitation. They occur only occasionally and usually over small areas; thus their total climatic significance is minor. Sleet consists of frozen raindrops. Hail, which falls almost exclusively in the violent thunderstorms to be described in the next chapter, is composed of ice lumps which are larger than sleet.

Precipitation Types

As discussed earlier almost all precipitation originates in ascending air which is cooled by expansion. Patterns of precipitation distribution over the earth are the result of three principal kinds of atmospheric lifting, which are described below. None of these three ordinarily exists in pure form, however; most precipitation is a consequence of the combined effects of more than one.

Orographic Precipitation. This is precipitation caused or intensified by the lifting effect of highlands on air masses (Fig. 4.8). Even a quick glance at a world rainfall map (see Plate 1 in the back of the book) shows many cases where areas of heavy rainfall coincide with highlands. Besides the forced upgliding of air that terrain obstacles cause, they induce precipitation by triggering convectional updrafts. These are partly the result of strong heating of slopes, which are inclined toward the sun's rays.

Convective Precipitation. Convection currents are local columns of unstable, buoyant air whose ascent is both rapid and truly vertical. It is not an oblique upglide movement. A convective system consists of several cells, each one a rapid vertical updraft of limited diameter, separated by broader, slower down currents. If the chimneys of ascending and cooling air rise above condensation level, each is capped by a cumulus cloud (Fig. 4.5).

Although vigorous convective overturning is fostered by warm, moist air that is buoyant and unstable, even such air probably requires some initial upward displacement to trigger its ascent. This trigger action may be provided by terrain obstacles as described above, by mechanical turbulence due to surface friction, or by convergence of airflow within an extensive atmospheric disturbance. Whether strong solar heating of a land surface can provide effective trigger action is controversial. Certainly it can make surface air more buoyant and unstable, so that convection usually reaches a maximum in the warmer hours of the day. Still, convective showers occur predominantly in organized (not random) regional patterns, and the shower regions are related to one or more of the types of trigger action mentioned above.

Convective precipitation is likely to be brief, intermittent, heavy, and localized. These features reflect the nature of the air ascent—rapid, vertical, and confined to chimneys of small diameter. Because the showers are so heavy, much of the water runs off rather than soaking into the ground. Washing and gulleying of plowed fields may be serious. Offsetting this handicap is the fact that convective rain tends to be concentrated in the warmer months, when growing crops can make full use of it.

Because it is closely associated with high temperatures, this type of rainfall is at a maximum in tropical and subtropical latitudes, and in middle latitudes in summer. It is negligible in high latitudes. In areas where convective showers occur, they normally reach a maximum in the warmer hours of afternoon and early evening.

Precipitation in Atmospheric Disturbances. Of necessity, convergence of surface airflow must result in upward movement with consequent cooling. Many types of widespread atmospheric disturbances involve convergence. In the middle latitudes, where converging airstreams are likely to differ in temperature and density, lifting of air within a disturbance usually results from an upglide of warm air over a mildly sloping surface of cold air (Fig. 4.9). Such a discontinuity surface separating unlike air masses is called a front. Frontal precipitation is very common in middle latitudes. And since fronts are a characteristic feature of cyclonic storms, most

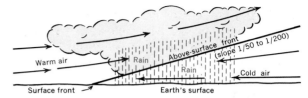

Figure 4.9 The origin of precipitation along a front. Here the warmer and less dense air cools owing to expansion as it ascends over a wedge of cooler, denser air.

frontal rainfall is also cyclonic in origin. A good part of cyclonic, or frontal, precipitation falls as steady long-continued rain from a gray overcast deck of stratus clouds.

In the tropics, where significant temperature contrasts between air masses are usually absent, fronts are rare. Instead, convergence in atmospheric disturbances leads to a more general upward movement of the air, which in turn triggers convective shower activity.

Important Features of Precipitation

At least four features are important in describing the precipitation of a region: (1) the average annual amount of precipitation, (2) the seasonal distribution of the annual total, (3) the variability of the annual total, and (4) the number of raindays.

Average Annual Rainfall. For the whole earth the annual rainfall is estimated to be about 39 in.: 26 in. over the continents, and 44 over the oceans. But such averages are not very meaningful, because annual rainfall is spread so unevenly over both land and sea—as low as 1 or 2 in. in some regions, and as high as 400 and more in a few.

Seasonal Distribution. An area's seasonal distribution of precipitation is as important as the annual amount. The fact that Omaha, Nebraska, receives 30 in. of rainfall a year is no more significant than the fact that 17 in. (58 percent of the annual total) falls during the warm months from May to August and only 3 in. (11 percent) falls during the cold period from November to February. Seasonal distribution of precipitation is of greatest importance in the middle latitudes, where winter is a dormant period and only the part of the annual precipitation which falls during the frost-free season is effective for plant growth. In the tropics, where frost is prac-tically unknown except at higher elevations, rainfall contributes to plant growth no matter what time of year it falls.

Variability. Variability (that is, dependability or reliability) of precipitation may be defined as the deviation from the mean computed from 35 years or more of observations. In humid climates the annual variability is usually not greater than 50 per-cent on either side of the mean; i.e., the driest year can be expected to have about 50 percent of the normal value, the wettest year 150 percent (Fig. 10.1). In dry climates these values vary between about 30 and 250 percent. Thus it is a general rule that variability increases as the amount of rainfall decreases.

Precipitation variability must be taken into consideration by the farmer, for he must expect that there will be many years when precipitation is less than the average. In semiarid and subhumid climates, where crop raising normally depends on a small margin of safety, rainfall variability is of utmost concern. Moreover, the negative deviations from the mean are more frequent than positive ones; that is, a greater number of dry years are compensated for by a few excessively wet ones. Variability of seasonal and monthly rainfall amounts characteristically is greater than that of annual values.

Number of Rain-days. The intensity of rainfall is judged by comparing the number of rain-days (those on which 0.01 in. or more falls) with the region's annual or monthly totals. This information also provides a general impression of the relative wetness or dryness of a climate. For example, Mar-quette, Michigan, annually receives about 33 in. of rain on 165 rain-days or, on the average, 0.2 in. per rain-day. Comparable figures for Pensacola, Florida, are 58, 114, and 0.51.

Distribution of Precipitation

Average Annual Amount. A glance at Plate 1 makes it obvious that world distribution of annual precipitation is very uneven and its patterns very complicated. There is no simple explanation for this; but fundamentally, two factors are involved: (1) the nature of the air itself, especially its vary-ing temperature, humidity, and stability; (2) the distribution over the earth of influences which affect vertical movement of air—influences such as zones of horizontal convergence and divergence, atmo-spheric disturbances, and highland barriers. As far as humidity is concerned, the nature of an air mass is chiefly determined by its place of origin: whether over ocean or continent, and whether over the tropics or the high latitudes.

Some of the most fundamental facts about world rainfall distribution may be presented in a simple meridional profile of the precipitation means by latitude belts (Fig. 4.10). It shows a strong pri-mary maximum in equatorial latitudes, or close to the ITC. Belts of lower rainfall occur in the sub-tropics, where anticyclonic diverging-wind systems and vertical subsidence are relatively strong. Pole-ward from the subtropics, Fig. 4.10 shows rainfall increasing again to secondary maxima in latitudes 40°–50° N and S. These are the middle-latitude convergences with their numerous cyclonic storms. Poleward from about 50°–55°, precipitation de-clines sharply; minima of 10 in. and less character-

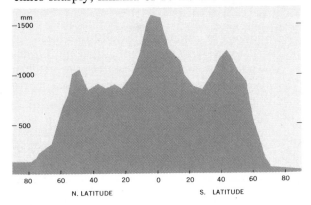

Figure 4.10 Distribution of annual precipitation amounts averaged by latitude zones. *(After Brooks and Hunt.)*

ize the very high latitudes, where low temperatures, low moisture content, and subsidence are typical.

Figure 4.11 is a highly generalized representation of annual rainfall distribution, both longitudinally and latitudinally, on a hypothetical continent. It shows a belt of heavy rainfall extending entirely across the continent in equatorial latitudes. This belt coincides with the mean position of the equatorial convergence zone. Here not only is the air warm, humid, unstable, and characterized by much upward movement, but in addition there are numerous weak atmospheric disturbances. This wet equatorial belt broadens markedly on the eastern side, which is close to the more unstable western margin of an oceanic subtropical anticyclone. The eastern side is also usually the windward side and

is paralleled by warm ocean currents. On the west side, where opposite conditions prevail, the wet belt is narrower. More restricted wet areas also occur along the windward western side in middle latitudes, both north and south of the equator.

Dry areas on the hypothetical continent form continuous bands in each hemisphere, reaching from low into middle latitudes. In the low latitudes, dry areas are skewed toward the west and thereby avoid the east side. Significantly, it is the western side of the continent that is strongly influenced by the stable eastern end of an oceanic subtropical high, where subsidence is strong and the temperature inversion low. Cool ocean water along tropical west coasts may also act to intensify their aridity. In middle latitudes, the dry areas are located toward the center of the broad land mass, a location which is farthest removed from oceanic sources of moisture. In the narrowed continent in the Southern Hemisphere, the dry belt extends almost to the east coast—as it does in middle-latitude South America, for example. The very high latitudes are not classified as dry climates even though their precipitation is meager, for their low temperatures result in such low evaporation that they have no strong and persistent moisture deficiency.

Humid (including subhumid) conditions, indicating moderate rainfall, prevail in two locations, both situated between the wet and the dry types (Fig. 4.12). One of these begins poleward of the equatorial wet belt and continues into the middle latitudes along the eastern side of the continent (Fig. 4.11). The low-latitude part is affected alternately by ITC and dry trades; the part within the middle latitudes is influenced by cyclonic storms in all seasons. The second general location of humid conditions is along the continent's western side in middle latitudes, but inland from the wet oceanic margins. Here cyclonic activity accounts for most of the precipitation. These patterns applied to a hypothetical continent should be compared with actual distributions as represented on Plate 1.

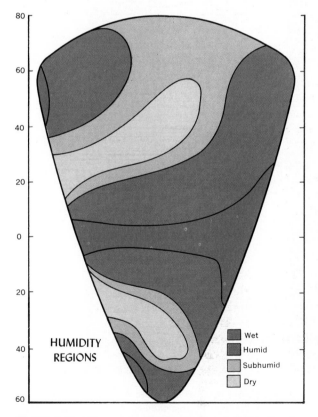

Figure 4.11 Very generalized patterns of distribution for four great annual rainfall subdivisions as they might appear on a hypothetical continent.

Seasonal Concentration (Annual March). Oceanic precipitation not only is usually greater in annual amount than continental, but is also less seasonally concentrated. Land masses, with their tendency toward strong summer heating and onshore summer winds, are likely to have more of their annual precipitation concentrated in summer. Over large land masses in middle and higher latitudes, the cold-season anticyclone with its diverging winds and temperature inversions also makes for dry winters.

In the vicinity of the equator, where the ITC prevails at all seasons, rainfall not only is abundant but also falls throughout all, or nearly all, the year; there is either no dry season or at most a very short one (Fig. 4.12, 4.13). Farther away from the equator, from about 5°–10° out to 15°–20°, rainfall becomes more seasonal as it decreases in amount, with a marked dry period in the low-

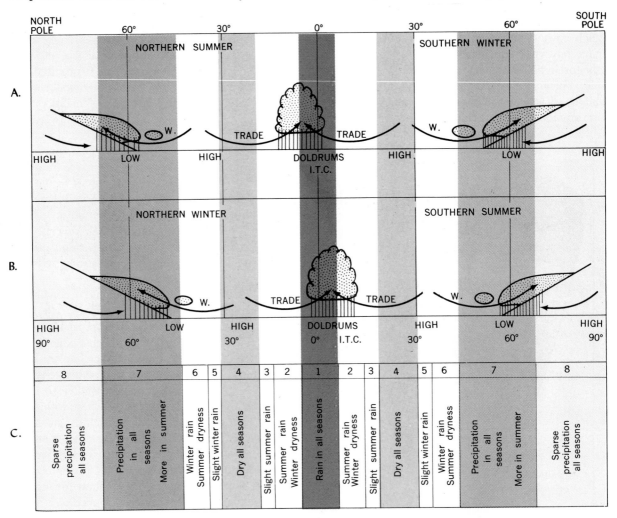

Figure 4.12   Schematic cross section through the atmosphere showing the main zones of horizontal convergence and ascent, and of divergence and subsidence, together with associated seasonal characteristics of precipitation; *A,* during the Northern Hemisphere summer; *B,* during the Northern Hemisphere winter; *C,* zones of seasonal precipitation. But remember that many nonzonal features of precipitation distribution cannot be adequately represented on this type of diagram. *(From Sverre Petterssen, Introduction to Meteorology, 2d ed., McGraw-Hill Book Company, New York, 1958.)*

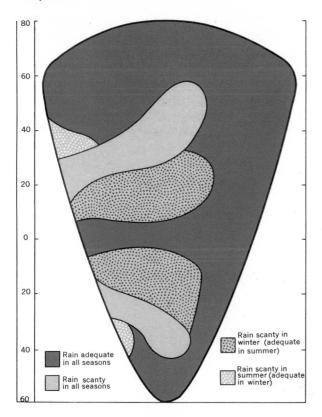

Figure 4.13 Generalized patterns of seasonal rainfall distribution as they might appear on a hypothetical continent.

sun, or winter, season, when dry trades prevail. The high-sun, or summer, period is wet, owing to the ITC. This sequence of high-sun rainfall and low-sun drought is associated with the latitudinal shifting of the zones of convergence and divergence following the sun (Figs. 4.12, 4.13). Note in Fig. 4.13 that the area of winter drought does not extend to the east side of the continent, where the subtropical anticyclone is weaker.

In the subtropical parts of the lower middle latitudes at about 30°–40°, there are areas (usually small ones restricted to the western side of continents) where summer is the season of drought and winter is wet (Fig. 4.13). Here, because of latitudinal migration of pressure and wind systems following the sun, the stable eastern limb of a subtropical anticyclone controls the weather in summer, and the cyclonic westerlies in winter (Fig. 4.12).

In the middle latitudes poleward from about 40° there is usually no dry season, since adequate precipitation falls at all times of the year (Fig. 4.13). Yet this is not to say that all seasons have equal amounts. It is in the interiors of the great continents that the seasonal precipitation maximum and minimum are most emphatic and most consistent. Here summer, with its warmer air of higher moisture content, is usually the wettest season. As explained earlier, the drier winter is related to the lower temperatures and anticyclonic wind system of that season.

5

Air Masses, Fronts, and Atmospheric Disturbances

Climate is a generalization of a region's day-to-day weather. And the weather of an area is closely identified with its prevailing air masses and with the atmospheric disturbances (to the layman, storms) which develop in connection with them.

Air Masses and Fronts

Origin and Characteristics. An air mass is an extensive portion of the air ocean whose temperature and humidity are relatively uniform in horizontal directions. Such an air mass develops whenever the atmosphere remains in contact with a large and relatively uniform land or sea surface long enough to take on the temperature and moisture characteristics of the surface. Weather properties of an air mass depend upon two basic attributes: the vertical temperature distribution, and the moisture content together with its vertical distribution.

Those extensive parts of the earth's land-sea surface where air masses develop are called *source regions*. An essential attribute of an air-mass source region is that its surface be fairly uniform. Also, its atmospheric circulation must be relatively stagnant as well as divergent in character. A convergent or cyclonic circulation is out, for it often results in sharp temperature contrasts. Weak anticyclonic circulations, therefore, provide the best source region conditions. The snow-covered arctic plains of Canada and Siberia in winter, large areas of tropical ocean in any season, and the hot, arid Sahara in summer are good examples of source regions.

As a rule air masses do not remain overly long in their source regions but move out to invade adjoining areas whose weather they then affect. In turn, they are affected by their new surface environment and change character, although this happens very slowly.

When air masses with different temperatures and humidities come together, they do not mix freely. They tend to keep separate and to maintain a fairly distinct sloping boundary surface between them, the warmer and therefore less dense air mass being forced aloft over the wedge of colder air (Fig. 5.1). This sloping surface is called a frontal surface, or a *surface of discontinuity*. Where a surface of discontinuity, or front, in the atmosphere intersects the earth's surface, a *surface front* is formed.

Surface fronts are not thin lines but rather zones varying from about 50 to 150 miles in width in which the temperature gradient is very steep. Usually they bring marked changes in temperature and humidity as they pass. The location of fronts and the nature of the contrasting air masses on either side of them are of great importance in weather forecasting, for it is along fronts that a

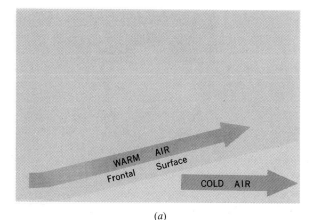

(a)

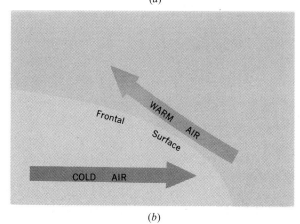

(b)

Figure 5.1 Arrangement of air masses along (a) warm front and (b) cold front.

great many storms and associated weather changes originate.

It is unusual for a front to remain very long in a stationary position. Commonly one of the unlike air masses it separates is the more active and advances into the other's domain. The position of the front then shifts. When the warmer air mass is more aggressive and advances against the cold air, the lighter warmer air upglides over the wedge of colder denser air (Fig. 5.1a). This is a *warm front*. When the colder air is the aggressor, it underruns the warmer air and forces it upward (Fig. 5.1b). This is a *cold front*. How the two differ in their effects on weather will be considered later in the section on middle-latitude cyclones.

Classification of Air Masses. Air masses are usually designated by the name or abbreviated name of their source region. Source regions fall naturally into two great groups: those of high, or *polar* (*P*), latitudes, and those of low, or *tropical* (*T*), latitudes. It is mainly in the high and the low latitudes that there are large areas with relatively homogeneous surfaces and relatively light air movement. The middle latitudes, by contrast, are the scene of intense interaction between polar and tropical air masses, so that they generally lack the uniform conditions essential to a source region (Figs. 5.2, 5.3).

The air-mass classification may be further refined by dividing both the cold polar (*P*) and warm tropical (*T*) groups on the basis of moisture and temperature characteristics, so that each contains *continental* (*c*) and *maritime* (*m*) subgroups. This results in four main types of air masses: polar continental (*cP*), polar maritime (*mP*), tropical continental (*cT*), and tropical maritime (*mT*). They are summarized in the table below, and illustrated by the North American source regions in Fig. 5.4.

All four main air-mass types may be modified as they move out from their source regions over contrasting surface environments. When an air mass is heated from below by a warm surface, it is made more buoyant and unstable. When it is chilled from below by a colder surface, it gains stability. To indicate these important modifications, two more letter symbols may be added to the classification:

K = air mass colder than underlying surface; increased surface instability

W = air mass warmer than underlying surface; increased surface stability

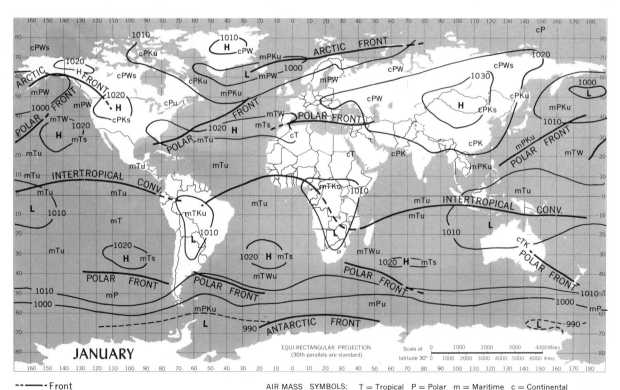

Figure 5.2 Air masses and fronts in January. (*After Haurwitz and Austin.*)

CLASSIFICATION OF AIR MASSES

Major group	Subgroup	Source region	Properties at source
Polar (including arctic)	Polar continental (cP)	Arctic Basin; northern Eurasia and northern North America; Antarctica	Cold, dry, very stable
	Polar maritime (mP)	Oceans poleward of 40 or 50°	Cool, moist, unstable
Tropical (including equatorial)	Tropical continental (cT)	Low-latitude deserts, especially Sahara and Australian Deserts	Hot, very dry, stable
	Tropical maritime (mT)	Oceans of tropics and subtropics	Warm, moist, greater instability toward west side of ocean

Air-mass modification also results from lifting or subsidence. Convergence and ascent, as in a cyclonic circulation, act to stretch an air mass vertically and so promote unstable conditions aloft. Conversely, subsidence and divergence shrink an air mass and thereby produce stability. Thus two

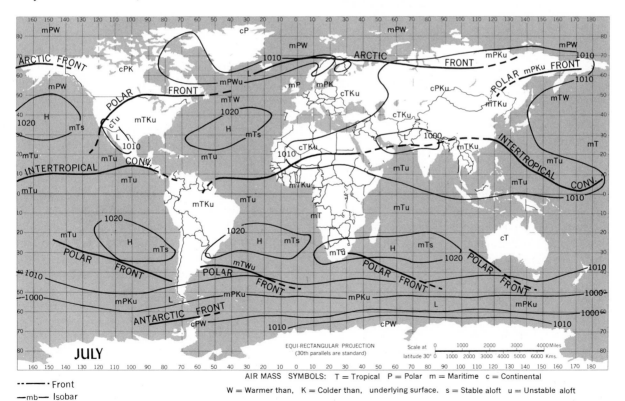

Figure 5.3   Air masses and fronts in July. *(After Haurwitz and Austin.)*

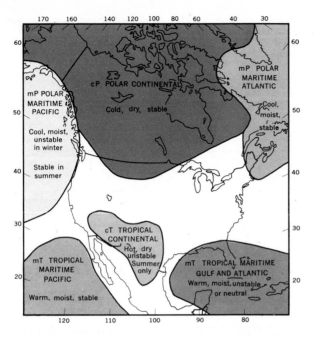

Figure 5.4   North American air masses and their source regions.

more letters may be used to indicate above-surface stability conditions (Figs. 5.2, 5.3):

s = stable air aloft
u = unstable air aloft

   When an air mass is greatly humidified from below while passing over an extensive water surface, *potential* instability is increased, because the water vapor represents a reservoir of energy. When this energy is released in the form of sensible heat during condensation, the lower air is heated and made more buoyant.

Atmospheric Disturbances

Atmospheric disturbances are extensive waves, eddies, or whirls of air which exist within the earth's great wind systems. These disturbances can be observed on a daily weather map of the earth by their pressure and wind patterns (Fig. 5.5). They are so numerous and widespread that many times

they tend to obscure the features of the general atmospheric circulation, just as the minor whirls and eddies of a river can almost conceal the flow of the main current.

   Except where highlands force air to rise, atmospheric disturbances in great variety are the principal centers of large-scale air ascent. Consequently they are the earth's main generators of clouds and precipitation. In addition, their cloud systems have important effects on both incoming solar and outgoing earth radiation, and hence on air temperature. And outside the tropics, the mass movement of air from one place to another by disturbance circulations is a principal cause of temperature changes as well.

Middle-latitude Disturbances: Traveling Cyclones and Anticyclones

In the world's middle latitudes the fickleness of the weather is proverbial. It is here that weather forecasting services are most necessary and best developed. The frequent, erratic, day-to-day weather changes in these parts are produced chiefly by the moving cyclones and anticyclones which fill the westerly wind belts.

   Chapter 3 described semipermanent stationary cyclones and anticyclones. Here the emphasis will be on traveling disturbances. But no two storms are exactly alike, and their weather may differ significantly from region to region, so that the generalizations concerning cyclones and anticyclones which follow must not be expected to fit any particular storm in all respects.

General Characteristics. Moving cyclones are low-pressure systems and commonly go by the name of lows or depressions—or troughs, if they are elongated. Anticyclones are high-pressure systems and are called highs or, if elongated, ridges. Being mainly features of the middle-latitude westerlies, they are best known between about 35 and 65° in each hemisphere. Because they are embedded in the westerly circulation, they are carried by those winds in a general west-to-east direction.

ATLANTIC SECTION
FEBRUARY 13, 1965   TIROS IX

1200 GMT   SURFACE ANALYSIS

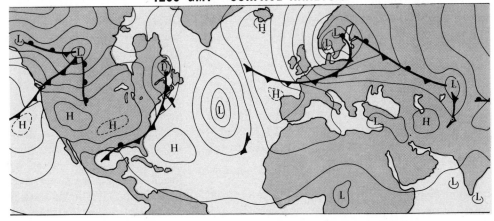

Figure 5.5 At bottom, surface weather map covering about 220° of longitude in the Northern Hemisphere on a winter day. Wave and vortex disturbances and their fronts are conspicuous. (Fronts are shown as heavy black lines bearing sharp or rounded projections.) At top, the satellite photograph of the same area on the same day clearly reveals cloud patterns associated with a number of these winter storms. See especially those over the North Atlantic and Europe, and again over the southeastern United States and northwestern North America. *(Courtesy U.S. Weather Bureau.)*

On the surface weather map these disturbances are represented by a system of closed concentric isobars varying from nearly circular to oval (Fig. 5.6). In the cyclone the lowest pressure is at the center; in the anticyclone the highest pressure is at the center. No precise amount of pressure distinguishes lows from highs; pressure difference between them is entirely a relative thing.

In a low, the pressure at the center is normally 10 to 20 mb, or several tenths of an inch, lower than the pressure at the margins. In a high as a general rule, the pressure difference between

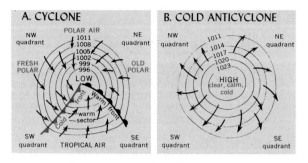

Figure 5.6 (*A*) Model cyclone (Northern Hemisphere) showing arrangement of isobars, wind system, warm and cold air masses, and surface fronts. Note the contrasting symbols for warm and cold fronts. (*B*) Model anticyclone.

center and margins does not vary so widely. Commonly both cyclones and anticyclones are less well developed in summer than in winter. Also, in summer they show smaller internal differences in pressure, have weaker pressure gradients, and travel more slowly.

There are great variations in the size of these disturbances, but as a rule they spread over huge areas. Sometimes a storm may cover a region as large as one-third of the conterminous United States, or about a million square miles, although most storms are smaller. Diameters of 500 to 1,000 miles are common. Emphatically, such storms are extensive rather than intensive.

Direction and Rate of Movement. Cyclones and anticyclones in middle latitudes are carried in a general easterly direction by the system of westerly winds in which they exist. This is not to say, however, that storms always move due east; individual storms follow different routes. Still, a general eastward progress prevails, to the extent that the weather forecaster in middle latitudes bases his prediction upon weather conditions to the west, rather than on those to the east, of his station. The storms to the east have already passed; those to the west are approaching.

Cyclones and anticyclones vary in rate of movement both with individual storms and with the season. In general, highs are somewhat slower than

lows. In the United States, cyclones move eastward across the country at velocities averaging 20 miles an hour in summer and 30 miles an hour in winter; in winter a well-developed low characteristically requires 3 to 5 days for this transcontinental journey. In summer, when the whole atmospheric circulation is slowed down and storms are more sluggish, the contrasts between cyclones and anticyclones are less pronounced. As a consequence, warm-season weather is less changeable, and atmospheric disturbances are less vigorous.

Just as temperature, pressure, and wind belts shift poleward in summer and equatorward in winter, following the seasonal movements of the sun's rays, so also do the storm tracks. This helps to explain why there are fewer and weaker storms over the lower middle latitudes in summer than in winter.

Origin. Probably most, though not all, middle-latitude cyclones begin as waves along atmospheric fronts, either near the earth's surface or high in the atmosphere. Since the cyclones which develop near the surface were studied first and are most readily observed, it is these that are analyzed in the following section. Less is known about moving anticyclones. Several types are usually recognized: (1) Cold anticyclones, which are strongest and most numerous in winter, move rapidly toward lower latitudes as masses of cold, dense polar air. (2) Warm, slow-moving anticyclones, whose origin is not well understood, are especially characteristic of the lower middle latitudes in summer. (3) Sluggish, weak anti-cyclones seem to occupy the spaces between the more vigorous moving cyclones. They bring clearing cold weather, but their temperatures are not extreme.

Structure of a Model Cyclone. On the daily weather map a cyclonic storm is often first noted as a slight indentation or wave along a surface front. It takes the form of a shallow thrust of warm air into the mass of colder air. As the incipient wave moves along the front, it deepens, and the cyclone grows in size and intensity (Fig. 5.7). A prime feature is that winds, temperature, clouds, and precipitation are not the same throughout the disturbance.

As Fig. 5.7 shows, a cyclone is normally made up of two or more contrasting air masses. To

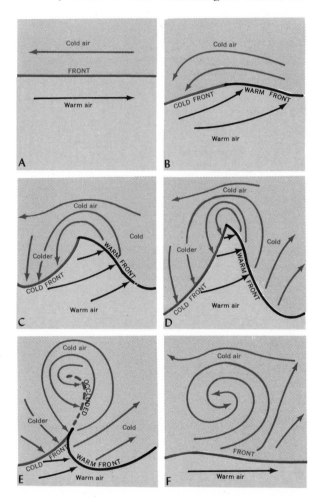

Figure 5.7 Six stages in the life of frontal cyclone. *B* shows the beginning of a small horizontal wave along the front. In *C* there is a definite cyclonic circulation with well-developed warm and cold fronts. Because of the more rapid movement of the cold front, *D* shows a narrowed warm sector as the cold front approaches the retreating warm front. In *E* the occlusion process is occurring: the cyclone has reached its maximum development, and the warm sector is being rapidly pinched off. In *F* the warm sector has been eliminated; the cyclone is in its dying stages and is represented by only a whirl of cold air. *(Courtesy U.S. Weather Bureau.)*

the south and southeast there is a poleward projection of warm, humid, southerly air which originated in lower latitudes (Fig. 5.8*b*). Enveloping this warm tongue of tropical air on its western, northern, and eastern sides are colder, drier, and denser polar air masses. The zone of conflict between the tropical and polar air is the front. Along part of this front, the less dense tropical air glides upward over a mildly inclined wedge of polar air. This lifting of the warm air is the cause of the clouds and much of the precipitation in the storm.

That part of the extended front lying *ahead,* or east, of the advancing tongue of warm air is the warm front, while that to the *rear,* or west, of the warm air is the cold front. In the later stages of the cyclone, the cold front overtakes the warm front, resulting in a narrowing, and eventually a pinching out, of the tongue of warm air at the surface. The cyclone then becomes a whirl of colder air, and the disturbance is said to be *occluded* (Fig. 5.7*E, F*).

Wind System of a Cyclone. Because the lowest pressure is at the center of a cyclone, the flow of air is obliquely from the circumference toward the center in the form of a whirl which is anticlockwise in the Northern Hemisphere (Fig. 5.6*A*). It is a converging vortex system, which of necessity requires upward movement. Much of this movement is a slow upglide, producing clouds of the extensive sheet variety. (See also Fig. 5.9.)

Because the cyclone's wind system is a converging one, the winds to the east, or front, of the storm's center must be easterly and southerly, while to the rear, or west, of the center the airflow must be from the west and north (Fig. 5.7*B, C, D*). Easterly winds in middle latitudes, therefore, often foretell the approach from the west of a cyclonic storm, with its accompanying cloud and rain. Westerly winds, by contrast, indicate the retreat of the storm center and the arrival of clearing weather.

Suppose the cyclone center passes to the north of a weather station, so that the observer is in the southern parts of the storm. Then the wind shift from easterly flow on the front to westerly on the rear will be accompanied by a southerly flow of

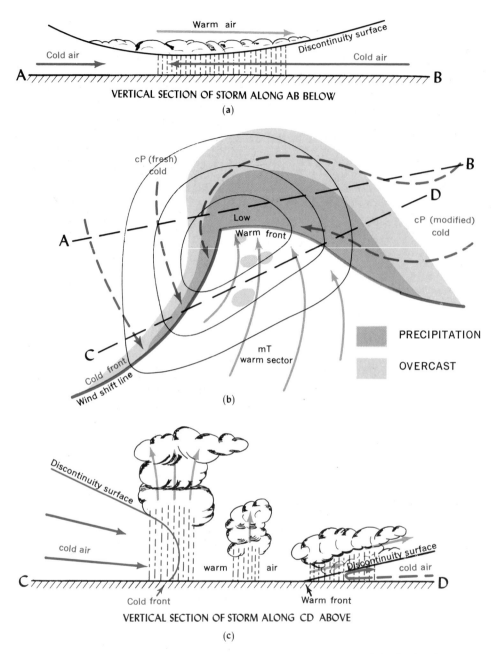

Warm air

Cold air

Discontinuity surface

Cold air

A

B

VERTICAL SECTION OF STORM ALONG AB BELOW

(a)

cP (fresh) cold

B

D

cP (modified) cold

A

Low

Warm front

C

mT warm sector

Cold front

Wind shift line

PRECIPITATION

OVERCAST

(b)

Discontinuity surface

cold air

warm air

Discontinuity surface

cold air

C

D

Cold front

Warm front

VERTICAL SECTION OF STORM ALONG CD ABOVE

(c)

Figure 5.8 A model cyclone. Ground plan (b) and vertical sections (a and c) of a Northern Hemisphere cyclone in a stage of early maturity, before occlusion has commenced.

air (Fig. 5.10). Under these conditions, weather will be relatively warm, clouds and precipitation may be less persistent, and in winter, rain is as likely as snow. But suppose the storm center travels south of the station. Then northerly winds prevail, temperatures are relatively low, the cloud cover lasts longer, and snow is more common. Thus a region which normally is situated to the south of

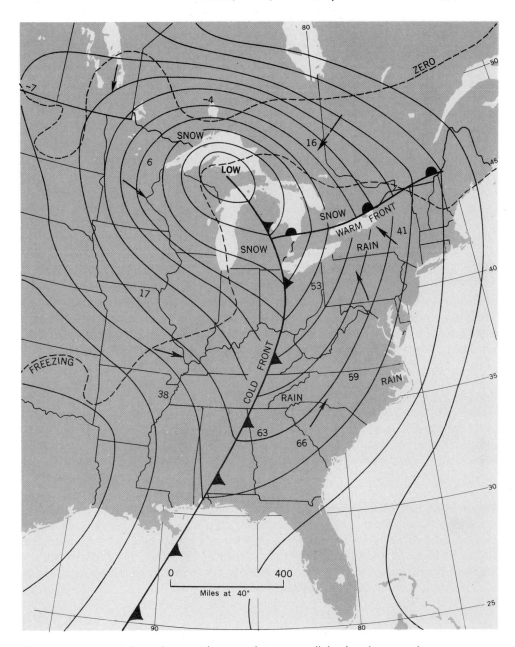

Figure 5.9 Section of a surface weather map showing a well-developed wave cyclone over eastern North America. This representation of an actual cyclone should be compared with the ground plan of the model cyclone in Fig. 5.8.

passing cyclones will have very different weather from one lying to the north (Fig. 5.9).

Wind System of an Anticyclone. An anticyclone's wind system is opposite in all respects to that of a

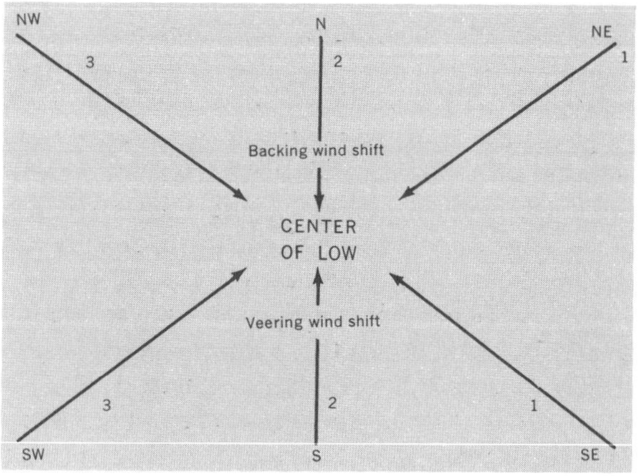

Figure 5.10 The usual shifts in wind direction when a cyclone passes poleward (veering shift) or equatorward (backing shift) of a station. Numerals 1, 2, 3 represent time.

cyclone. Pressure is highest at the center, so surface winds flow outward, or diverge, from the center, and there must be a compensating downward, or subsiding, movement of air to feed the surface flow (Fig. 5.6B). Earth rotation causes the diverging flow to develop something of a clockwise whirl in the Northern Hemisphere. Because this slow subsidence causes the anticyclone's air to be stable and nonbuoyant and because above-surface temperature inversions tend to develop, the whole environment of an anticyclone is opposed to formation of cloud and precipitation.

Precipitation in Cyclones and Anticyclones. As the preceding sections have shown, a cyclone's convergence and ascent of air favor cloud and precipitation, while the opposite is true for an anticyclone. Much of the precipitation that falls on lowlands in middle latitudes owes its origin either directly or indirectly to cyclonic storms and their fronts. In the cooler seasons, this precipitation is most commonly a result of a forced but gradual upglide of warmer, lighter air over a sloping surface of colder air. The result is an extensive cloud deck creating a gray, dull overcast, from which widespread and long-continued rain or snow usually falls. But in the warmer months, when the air is likely to be more unstable, much cyclonic precipitation is in the form

of local showers falling from cumulus clouds, although it is organized (not random) in its distribution.

Characteristically the eastern, or front, half of a cyclone, where convergence is more marked, is cloudier and rainier than the western or rear half (Fig. 5.8b). In winter lows, snow is commoner in the colder northern part, whereas rain occurs more frequently in the warmer southern sectors.

Of the several regions of precipitation within a cyclone, two are associated with fronts. Usually the most extensive area of rain occurs along the warm front. To the east and north of the storm center, warm southerly air glides upward over a gently inclined wedge of colder air (Fig. 5.8). This upglide on the warm front results in widespread clouds and precipitation, commonly in the form of rains which are light to moderate, but long-continued and soaking.

Along the cold front, usually positioned to the south and southwest of the storm center, is a second region of active air ascent with accompanying precipitation. Here cold northwesterly air underruns the warm southerly air and lifts it. But because the sloping surface of the cold air is steeper, the warm air is lifted more rapidly than it is along the warm front. As a consequence cold-front precipitation is likely to be somewhat more vigorous but briefer than precipitation along the warm front. However, where the air to the rear, or west, of the cold front is from maritime sources, as it is along west coasts in middle latitudes, showery rainfall in the cool, moist polar air may extend for some distance to the rear of the surface cold front. In the warmer months, thunderstorms may occur along both fronts, but they are more common and likely to be stronger along the cold front.

During the warmer seasons, some showery convective rain may also fall within the warm sector of southerly airflow to the south of the cyclone center, where it is not associated with any front (Fig. 5.8b).

Temperatures in Cyclones and Anticyclones. In themselves, cyclones and anticyclones are neither always warm nor always cold. Anticyclones develop in both cold polar air and warm tropical-subtropical air, so that they may bring either very cold or very hot weather. Indeed, the coldest weather in winter and the hottest in summer are usually associated with anticyclones.

Moreover, the clear skies which are characteristic of anticyclones add to their tendency to produce marked daily and seasonal temperature effects. During long winter nights in middle latitudes, the lack of clouds permits a rapid loss of heat from the earth; thus a cold anticyclone may bring subzero temperatures (Fig. 5.11). But the

same clear skies in summer, when days are long and sunlight is intense, can produce very high daytime temperatures in a warm anticyclone of subtropical origin (Figs. 5.12, 8.14). Rapid night cooling follows, however, so that diurnal ranges are usually large. Internal temperature variations are commonly smaller in anticyclones, which tend to have a fair degree of air-mass homogeneity.

Cyclones, since they are usually accompanied by cloud covers that reduce night cooling in winter and daytime heating in summer, tend to bring less extreme temperatures than anticyclones. However, since a cyclone is composed of unlike air

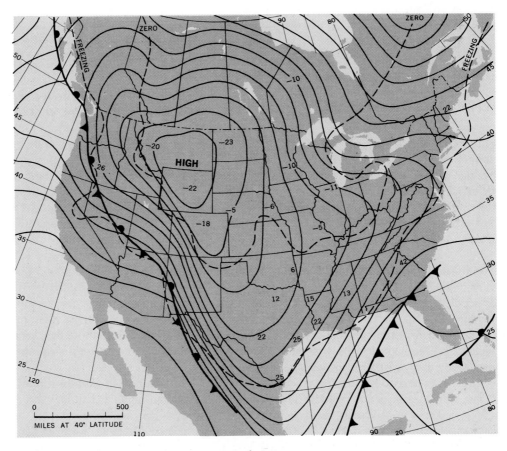

Figure 5.11 Polar-outbreak cold anticyclone advancing rapidly southward as a mass of unusually cold and stable cP air. On this occasion Minot, North Dakota, experienced a temperature of 23° below zero, Denver −18°, Jackson, Mississippi, 15°. Below-freezing temperatures were common along the margins of the Gulf of Mexico. *(From Weatherwise, June, 1962.)*

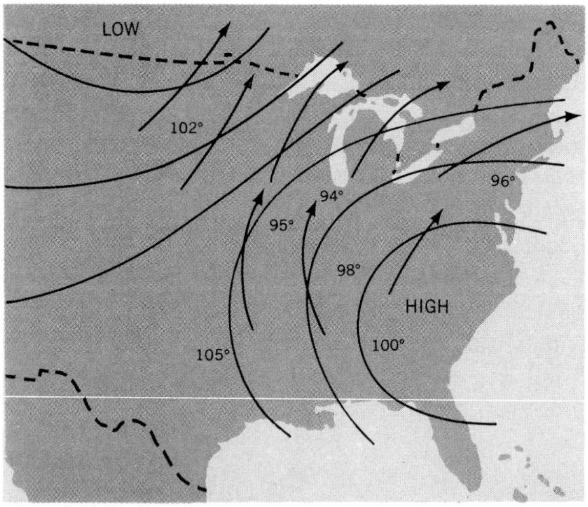

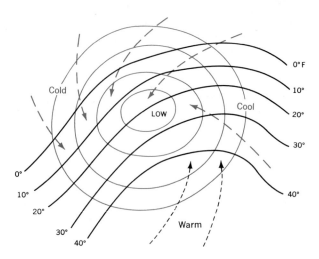

Figure 5.12 A warm anticyclone, relatively stagnant over the southeastern United States. Such an atmospheric disturbance produces unseasonably hot weather over the central and eastern parts of the country.

Figure 5.13 Characteristic arrangement of isotherms in a model cool-season cyclone over the central-eastern United States.

masses, temperatures may vary greatly in different parts of it. Where northerly winds prevail (*cP* air), as they do to the northeast, north, and west of the cyclone center, relatively low temperatures are to be expected (Fig. 5.13). Where the airflow is from the south (*cT* or *mT* air), as is commonly the case to the south of the storm center, temperatures are usually unseasonably high.

Middle-latitude Weather in General. Since the very essence of middle-latitude weather is its aperiodic changeability, the *averages* of such weather elements as temperature and precipitation for a month or a year give an atypical and lifeless picture of the climate. They should be supplemented by daily weather maps, which show the procession of eastward-moving cyclones and anticyclones that largely control middle-latitude weather (Figs. 5.9, 5.11). Weather maps in turn can be supplemented by graphs such as those in Fig. 5.14, which represent pressure and temperature tracings and wind and cloud conditions for a week of winter and a week of summer. Comparison of these weeks shows striking contrasts between the two seasons. Pressure and temperature graphs can also illustrate

the changing conditions associated with the passage of an individual storm, as in Fig. 5.15.

These methods for observing the weather element lead to the general conclusion that middle-latitude weather variability reaches its peak during the colder months. Variability is weaker in summer, when the dominant sun control produces more regular diurnal changes (Fig. 5.14). Remember, however, that the weather conditions described here and in the preceding sections are generalized ones. Individual storms vary greatly in the weather patterns they produce, and different parts of the middle latitudes tend to breed different types of storms. Within the United States, for example, cyclones produce relatively different weather patterns along the Pacific Coast from those they generate over the interior and eastern parts of the country.

Distribution of Middle-latitude Cyclones. All parts of the middle latitudes are affected by moving cyclones and anticyclones, but not to the same degree. Cyclones, for example, cross some extensive areas more frequently than others, as shown by Fig. 5.16. In the Southern Hemisphere, vigorous cyclonic activity is a feature of all seasons. But as Fig. 5.16 indicates, only the southern tips of Africa and Australia, and the part of South America which

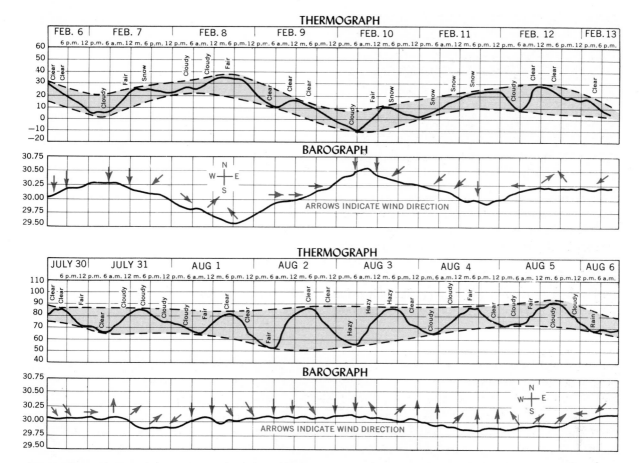

Figure 5.14 Temperature and atmospheric pressure traces (recorded by a thermograph and a barograph) for a week of winter (top) and summer (bottom) weather. Note that the barograph trace for winter shows much wider fluctuations than that for summer, indicating much stronger cyclonic-anticylonic control in the cooler months. The two temperature traces indicate a stronger diurnal sun control in the warm season, when the rise and fall in temperature is highly regular. If a temperature "belt" (indicated by shading) is created for each of the two temperature traces by connecting the diurnal crests and troughs, it will be noted that the temperature belt of winter shows wide nonperiodic oscillations and that of summer is relatively flat. The wide winter oscillations of the belt are caused by the air masses of passing cyclones and anticyclones. The flat belt of summer indicates weaker air-mass and cyclonic control in that season.

lies south of about 30° S, are strongly affected by them.

     In the Northern Hemisphere, cyclonic storms are much more numerous and vigorous in winter, when the continental cold sources are better developed than in summer. Two of the main regions of cyclone origin are the waters just east of North America and those just east of Asia. From these breeding grounds, cyclones move eastward across the northern Atlantic and Pacific Oceans, and

arrive in western Europe and western North America in the form of strongly occluded storms. A third region of vigorous cyclonic activity, but only in the cooler seasons, is the Mediterranean Basin.

     The eastern half of the United States and adjacent parts of Canada have the distinction of being the continental area with the greatest cyclonic activity. One reason may be that North America east of the Rocky Mountains is a place of numerous well-developed fronts. These result from the

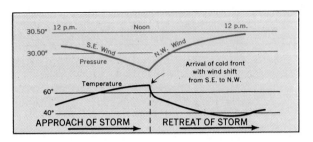

Figure 5.15 Barograph and thermograph traces registered during the approach and retreat of a middle-latitude cyclone.

clash of polar and tropical air masses, which can move freely across the region's extensive lowlands from arctic to tropical latitudes. As illustrated in Fig. 5.17, all parts of the United States east of the Rockies, except possibly peninsular Florida, have an abundance of cyclonic weather. But it is in the northeastern parts of the country, including the Great Lakes–New England region and adjacent Canada, that cyclone tracks are bunched and that changeable weather is therefore most striking.

Tropical Weather Disturbances

The Nonperiodic Weather Element. Compared with the highly variable middle latitudes, weather in the tropics is more periodic and sun-controlled. Weather observations during the past few decades have revealed, however, that the low latitudes have a greater variety of extensive weather disturbances than was suspected earlier. Unfortunately, the many kinds of disturbances which cause the modest aperiodic weather changes of the tropics are not well understood, and any discussion of them must reflect that fact. No satisfactory classification exists; here they are grouped only into two general classes —the weak and the severe.

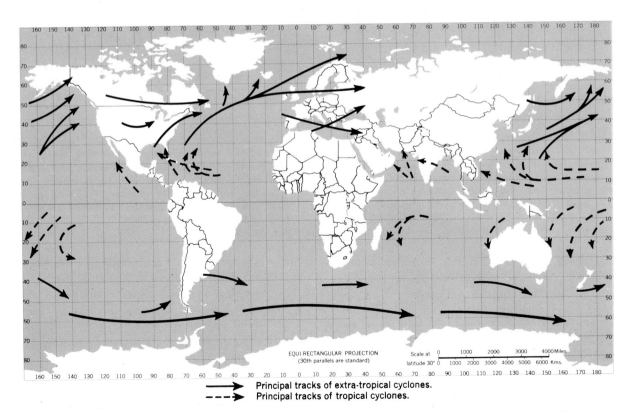

⟶ Principal tracks of extra-tropical cyclones.
- - -⟶ Principal tracks of tropical cyclones.

Figure 5.16 A greatly simplified representation of the main tracks of middle-latitude and tropical cyclones. *(After Petterssen.)*

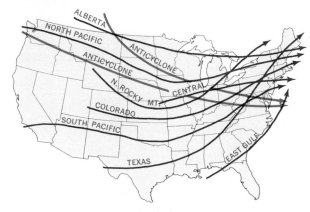

Figure 5.17 Main tracks of cyclones and anticyclones in the United States. Note how the cyclone tracks converge toward the northeastern part of the country. Cold anticyclones have a dual origin. Those which move south from northern Canada (cP air) bring severe cold in winter; those from the Pacific Northwest (modified mP air) bring only moderate cold. Many of the latter are in the nature of weak highs situated between passing cyclones. Warm anticyclones are not shown.

Weak Tropical Disturbances. Much less is known about the weak variety of tropical disturbance as a class than about the more severe and spectacular hurricane type. Yet the former is far more numerous than the better-studied severe tropical storm, and affects much larger areas and many more people.

Most of these weak disturbances have feebly developed pressure and wind systems, which makes them difficult to detect. Some are obscure because they exist only as above-surface phenomena. As a rule they become known chiefly through the spells of cloudy, rainy weather which they generate. Since advective effects are typically weak, they have relatively little influence on air temperature, though their cloud decks may somewhat meliorate daytime temperatures.

One very general type of extensive disturbance, for want of a better name, is called here a *weak tropical low.* These probably are widespread throughout the wet tropics, but appear to be most numerous in the vicinity of the ITC. On the surface weather map they can often be detected by their one or two closed isobars (Fig. 5.18). Most of their precipitation is in the form of organized convective showers. A very few weak tropical lows evolve into severe tropical storms.

Another weak tropical disturbance is in the nature of a *surge* within the equatorial westerlies. Such wind surges cause speed convergences, in which the accelerated air forces the slower-moving air ahead of it to rise. Convective showers result. A third type of tropical disturbance is the *easterly wave,* a weak trough aloft which moves slowly westward in the trades (Fig. 5.19). Convergence to the rear of the trough may cause showers. A very few easterly waves also grow into hurricanes.

Severe Tropical Disturbances; Hurricanes (Typhoons). These storms have been studied intensively because of their violence and destructive effects. Since they originate and mature only over oceans, the land areas chiefly affected by them are islands and certain restricted continental margins. In addition to being fewer and less widespread than middle-latitude cyclones, hurricanes differ from them in these respects: (1) As Fig. 5.20 shows, isobars in a hurricane are more circular and gradients are much steeper. Winds are also markedly stronger—at least 75 miles per hour in a genuine hurricane. (2) Diameter of the storm varies from 100 to 400 miles, or is roughly one-third the diameter of middle-latitude cyclones. (3) Rains are more torrential and more evenly distributed about

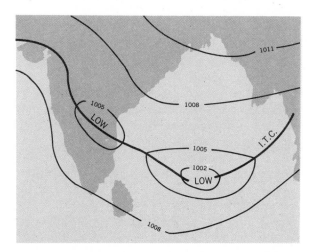

Figure 5.18 Weak tropical disturbances of the summer monsoon period over the Bay of Bengal and India. Some such monsoon lows appear to be associated with a fluctuating ITC.

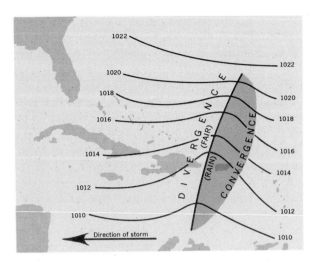

Figure 5.19 A tropical disturbance of a type known as an easterly wave. *(After Riehl.)*

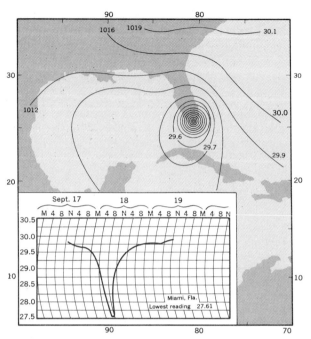

Figure 5.20 A Caribbean hurricane together with its barograph trace as recorded at Miami, Florida.

the center. (4) Temperature distribution around the center is relatively similar in every direction. There are no surface fronts, as in the middle-latitude low. (5) No sharp wind shifts occur within the violent parts of the storm. Winds develop a perfect spiral whirl, with strong vertically ascending currents around the vortex, or core. (6) Tropical cyclones are most plentiful in the warm season rather than in winter. (7) Hurricanes have relatively calm, rainless centers, 5 to 30 miles in diameter. This area of descending air is called the "eye" of the storm. (8) The tropical cyclone has no anti-cyclonic companion, because a hurricane is maintained by heat of condensation and not primarily by temperature contrasts.

There is no generally accepted theory of hurricane origin. It is clear that they develop only over warm water, probably 82° or higher. Significantly summer and fall, when they are most numerous, is the period when the ITC is farthest from the equator. Many seem to begin as weak disturbances which subsequently mushroom into the intense and dreaded hurricane.

Severe tropical cyclones appear to occur occasionally over the warmer parts of most tropical oceans, but not in close proximity to the equator, and probably nowhere in the South Atlantic. There are a number of areas of marked concentration of these storms (Fig. 5.16). These are the China Sea, whose typhoons particularly affect the Philippines, southeastern China, and southern Japan; the Arabian Sea and the Bay of Bengal, on either side of peninsular India; the Caribbean Sea, whose hurricanes reach the West Indies, Yucatan, and the southeastern United States; the eastern North Pacific in the region west of Mexico; the South Indian Ocean east of Madagascar; and the tropical waters both northeast and northwest of Australia.

Since hurricane winds may reach destructive speeds of 90 to 130 miles per hour, they cause tremendous property damage to shipping and coastal settlements, and sometimes great loss of life. Many deaths from drowning and a considerable part of the property destruction are due to great avalanches of sea water piled up and driven onshore by gale winds. Much harm is also done by the torrential rains and associated floods that accompany hurricanes.

Thunderstorms

A thunderstorm is only an intense convective shower accompanied by lightning and thunder. In its mature stage it is characterized by several chimneys of vigorously ascending warm air, each surrounded by compensating cooler downdrafts. This strong turbulence causes the seething and convulsions that can be observed in the awesome cumulonimbus cloud, or thunderhead (Fig. 5.21). A thunderstorm is a kind of machine: in it the potential energy of latent heat of condensation in warm, moist, unstable air is converted into the kinetic energy revealed in violent vertical air currents, torrential rains, squall winds, lightning, and thunder.

Among conditions favoring thunderstorm development, the most important is atmospheric instability. Such buoyancy promotes upward vertical motion. Instability in turn is fostered by high temperatures in the surface air, which produce a steep lapse rate. Consequently thunderstorms are most numerous in the warm latitudes, the warm seasons, and the warm hours of the day. But heat alone is not sufficient; the warm air must also be humid in order to provide an abundance of heat of condensation, which is the main source of storm energy. In addition, some trigger action involving an initial upward movement of air seems essential to start convection. A terrain obstacle may be the trigger; but more commonly, convection is initiated by the convergent circulation within extensive low-pressure disturbances. Thus most thunderstorm activity is organized (not random) in its distribution, shifting position with the movement of the disturbance of which it is a part.

Precipitation. The section on Precipitation Types

in Chap. 4 has already discussed the general features of convective precipitation. Besides these, violent convection in severe middle-latitude thunderstorms may produce hail, a very destructive form of solid precipitation. The original ice pellet forming a hailstone grows as a result of a long fall through the deep cumulonimbus cloud, during which it captures supercooled water droplets and snow crystals with which it collides.. Hail occurs in only a few thunderstorms and only in restricted belts of any particular storm—which is fortunate, for large hailstones are exceedingly destructive, especially to growing crops.

Hail is almost unknown in the wet tropics, where thunderstorms are most numerous, because there the atmosphere is too warm up to great altitudes for hail to persist. Within the United States hail rarely occurs in the humid subtropical parts, such as Florida and the Gulf states, which have the most thunderstorms. Distribution patterns of hail frequency and hail damage are exceedingly local, although frequency is greatest over parts of the Rocky Mountains and the Great Plains.

Lightning, Thunder, and Squall Winds. A lightning flash requires a separation of electric charges within the thunderstorm cloud, but how this separation occurs is not entirely clear. Fortunately, most lightning flashes occur within a cloud, or between two clouds; probably not more than 1 percent reach the land-water surface. Within the United States, fire losses due to lightning amount to millions of dollars annually. The greatest losses result from the kindling of forest fires.

Thunder is a result of the violent expansion of the air caused by the tremendous heat generated along the path of the lightning flash. A squall wind is a strong outrushing mass of cool air just ahead of the thunderstorm (Fig. 5.21). Sometimes thundersqualls are violent enough to do serious damage.

Types of Thunderstorms. A vast majority of the earth's thunderstorms occur in more or less distinct patterns; their distribution is not random but has an organized arrangement. *Orographic* thunderstorms are those produced or intensified by high-

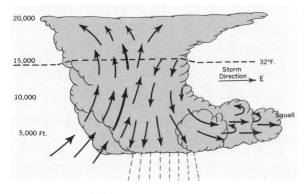

Figure 5.21 A vertical section through a thunderstorm and its cumulonimbus cloud. *(After Byers and others.)*

lands. *Air-mass* thunderstorms are those which develop within relatively homogeneous air. Usually they are found in the convergent airflow associated with a great variety of extensive disturbances, both tropical and middle-latitude. *Frontal* thunderstorms occur predominantly in middle latitudes, where temperature and density fronts are common. Here it is the lifting of air along frontal surfaces that triggers convection. While thunderstorms may develop along any and all kinds of fronts, a majority of the severe ones seem to be associated with cold fronts. Such storms are followed by a shift of wind to the northwest, accompanied by clearing and cooler weather.

Very occasionally, severe thunderstorm activity, associated with well-developed cold fronts and squall lines, may be accompanied by widely scattered *tornadoes,* the most violent and destructive of all atmospheric disturbances. But spectacular and awesome as they are, tornadoes are of minor consequence in world climates. Their distribution is limited to a few regions, their occurrence is infrequent, and the width of their destructive path usually does not exceed ½ mile.

Distribution. As shown in Fig. 5.22, thunderstorms are most numerous near the equator and decrease in frequency poleward; few occur at all beyond latitudes 60°–70°. This distribution chiefly reflects the general decline in air temperature from equator to poles. But air temperature is not the only control of the distribution of thunderstorms, for while their frequency declines sharply between latitudes 0 and 20°, temperatures drop little if at all. Thus the strong equatorial maximum is also a consequence of the convergent nature of the airflow and the high humidity near the equator. The marked falling off in thunderstorm frequency away from the equator reflects decreasing humidity and increasing subsidence, horizontal divergence, and stability owing to the subtropical anticyclones.

As indicated by the black and green lines in Fig. 5.22, thunderstorms are much more frequent over land areas than over oceans in similar latitudes. This is because summer temperatures are higher over land. Some weather stations in equatorial lands record over 100 days with thunderstorms during the year; a few places even experience 200 such days.

In the United States, the Pacific Coast states, which are dominated by cool, stable, anticyclonic air masses in summer, have the fewest thunderstorms (Fig. 5.23). There are two regions of maximum occurrence in this country: (1) the subtropical Southeast, and (2) the Rocky Mountain area in New Mexico, Colorado, and Montana. The eastern Gulf Coast region in the United States is the world's most thundery area outside of the tropics, having 70 to 80 days per year with thunderstorms.

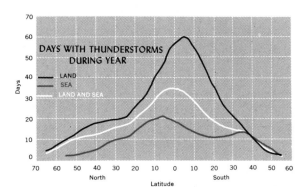

Figure 5.22   Zonal distribution by latitude belts of average number of days with thunderstorms. *(After Brooks.)*

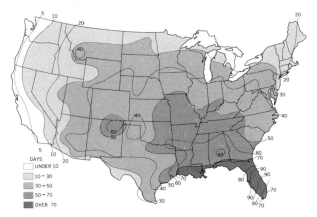

Figure 5.23   Average number of days with thunderstorms in the United States.

6

Classification of Climates;
The Tropical Humid Climates (A)

Chapters 2 to 5 have analyzed the individual elements from which climates are composed, as well as the controls affecting the distribution of these elements over the earth. Variations in the amount, intensity, and seasonal patterns of the elements, as determined by the climatic controls, create the variety of climates which will be described in Chaps. 6 to 10.[1]

In order to study general world patterns of climate, the great diversity of regional and local climates must be reduced to a few large

[1] In addition to the controls which have already been discussed, ocean currents are a climatic control of at least modest significance. But since they are not as important as the others, they are not taken up until Chap. 12, where they can be treated in connection with water and the seas. See especially Figs. 12.2 and 12.3.

groups with important characteristics in common. Essentially this reduction is accomplished through classification, a process common to all sciences.

Classification: Climatic Regions, Types and Groups

A *climatic region* is any portion of the earth's surface which has broadly similar, though not necessarily identical, climatic characteristics. Similar climatic regions are found in widely separated parts of the earth, but they commonly lie within corresponding latitudes and roughly corresponding continental locations (see Plate 2 inside the front cover). This fact suggests that there is order and system in the distribution of the climatic elements and so of the climatic regions. Indeed, their latitudinal and continental correspondence makes it possible to gather the numerous climatic regions into a few principal *climatic types*. These types can be reduced to still fewer *climatic groups*. Thus regions are combined into types and types into groups (see Figs. 6.1, 6.2, and the table following). The fact that there is a recognizable world pattern of climatic distribution is not surprising, since the greatest controls of climate—the distribution of solar energy and the general circulation of the atmosphere—themselves have distinct world patterns.

Figures 6.1 and 6.2 give the pattern of climates as they might appear on a hypothetical continent which has relatively low and uniform elevation. These two drawings indicate characteristic positions and arrangements of the climatic types and groups without the peculiarities which individual continents have because of their size, shape, and surface configurations. Throughout Chaps. 6 to 10 on climate, keep referring to Figs. 6.1 and 6.2, as well as to Plate 2.

Scheme of Climatic Classification. The system of climatic classification employed in this book recognizes six great groups of climate. Five of these—tropical, subtropical, temperate, boreal, and polar—are differentiated on the basis of temperature:

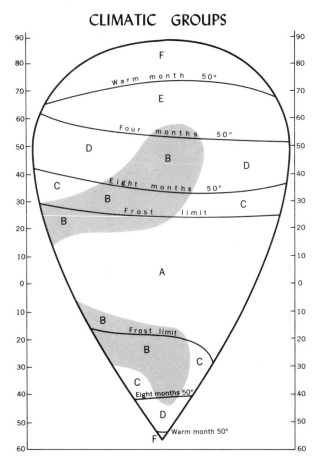

CLIMATIC GROUPS

Figure 6.1 Arrangement of the six great groups of climate on a hypothetical composite continent. The shaded areas indicate the dry-climate group, which cuts across the others.

that is, their boundaries are thermally defined. A sixth group is based on yearly precipitation and includes all the dry climates—those where potential evaporation exceeds precipitation. The five thermally defined groups are strongly zonal in arrangement, reflecting the distribution of solar energy. The dry group (shaded areas in Fig. 6.1) cuts across thermal zones and is to be found in all of them but the polar group. The six great groups of climate are further subdivided into eleven main types.

These groups and their types can be described briefly. In the low latitudes is a winterless, frostless belt with adequate rainfall. This is the tropical humid climate, or *A* group. It is subdivided

OUTLINE OF CLIMATIC CLASSIFICATION*

Groups	Types
A. Tropical humid climates	Tropical wet (Ar) Tropical wet-and-dry (Aw)
B. Dry climates	Steppe (BS, semiarid) Desert (BW, arid)
C. Subtropical climates	Subtropical dry-summer (Cs) Subtropical humid (Cf)
D. Temperate climates	Temperate oceanic (Do) Temperate continental (Dc)
E. Boreal climate	Boreal (E)
F. Polar climates (including high altitudes)	Tundra (Ft) Ice cap (Fi)

Definitions and boundaries†

A = Without frost. In marine locations, average temperatures of all months over 65°F (18°C)

B = Evaporation exceeds precipitation

  S = Steppe, or semiarid

  W = (German Wüste) Desert, or arid

C = Eight months or more over 50°F (10°C); cool month under 65°F (18°C)

D = 4 to 8 months over 50°F (18°C)

E = Up to 3 months over 50°F (18°C)

F = All months below 50°F (18°C)

r = Rainy; not more than two months dry

a = Average temperature of warmest month over 72°F (about 22°C)

b = Average temperature of warmest month under 72°F

s = Summer dry

w = Winter dry

f = No dry season

o = Oceanic

c = Continental

t = Warmest month below 50°F (10°C) but above 32°F (0°C)

i = All months below 32°F (0°C)

A/C boundary = Equatorial limits of frost; in marine locations the isotherm of 65°F (18°C) for coolest month

C/D boundary = 8 months 50°F (10°C)

D/E boundary = 4 months 50°F (10°C)

E/F boundary = 50°F (10°C) for warmest month

t/i boundary = 32°F (0°C) for warmest month

B/A, B/C, B/D, B/E boundary = Evaporation equals precipitation

BS/BW boundary = One-half the B/A, B/C, B/D, B/E boundary

h/k boundary in dry climates = same as C/D

Do/Dc boundary = 32°F (0°C) for coolest month; up to 36°F (2°C) farther inland

CLIMATIC TYPES

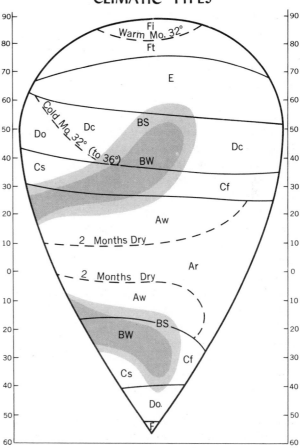

Figure 6.2 Arrangement of the principal types of climate on a hypothetical composite continent. The green-shaded area shows the arid type, the gray the semiarid.

* The earlier edition of this book employed a significantly modified form of the Köppen climatic classification. The present classification departs still farther from Köppen; so much so that in fairness to him, it should no longer be designated as even a modified Köppen scheme. It will be observed, however, that a few features of his justly renowned classification have been retained. Ideas have also been incorporated from the works of Wissmann, Creutzburg, Troll, and Paffen.
† Climatic boundaries are approximate only.

into two types: *tropical wet* (*Ar*) and *tropical wet-and-dry* (*Aw*). On the low-latitude margins of middle latitudes, where winters are mild and killing frosts only occasional, is the subtropical belt, or *C* group. Here two subdivisions are made: *subtropical dry-summer* (*Cs*) and *subtropical humid* (*Cf*). Poleward from the subtropics is the temperate belt, or *D* group. It contains two types: *temperate continental* (*Dc*) and *temperate oceanic* (*Do*). Still farther poleward is the boreal or subarctic belt, the *E* group. It has not been subdivided. In the very high latitudes lie the polar climates (*F* group), subdivided into 2 *tundra climate* (*Ft*) and *ice-cap climate* (*Fi*). The dry climates, group *B*, are subdivided into a *semiarid* or *steppe type* (*BS*) and an *arid* or *desert type* (*BW*).

The Tropical Humid Climates (Group A)

The tropical humid climates (*A*) form a somewhat interrupted belt 20 to 40° wide around the earth astride the equator (Fig. 6.1, Plate 2). This belt is distinguished from all other humid regions of the earth by the fact that it is constantly warm; in other words, it lacks a winter. Frost is absent. On its poleward margins the group of tropical humid climates may be terminated either by diminishing rainfall or by decreasing temperature. Usually it merges with dry climates in the western and central parts of continents (Fig. 6.1). On the more humid eastern sides, it extends poleward until a season of cold develops and occasional frosts occur in winter. Highlands, with their lower temperatures, are responsible for the principal interruptions in the belt of tropical humid climates over the continents.

Normally the tropical humid climates form a wider belt, and thus extend farther poleward, along the eastern side of a continent. This is the side which is dominated by the unstable or neutral air in the western end of an oceanic subtropical anticyclone (refer back to Fig. 3.11). Narrowing of the belt of *A* climates toward the center and west side of a continent reflects the greater stability of the eastern end of a subtropical oceanic anticyclone.

Rainfall is relatively abundant, most of it being of the showery, convective type. Although temperatures in *A* climates are fairly uniform over the seasons and the years, rainfall is more variable, both in annual amounts and in seasonal distribution.

The two principal climatic types within the tropical humid group are distinguished from each other on the basis of their seasonal distribution of precipitation: *tropical wet* has ample rainfall for ten or more months of the year; *tropical wet-and-dry* has a longer and more severe dry season (lasting over two months).

Tropical Wet Climate (Ar)

Location

Uniformly high temperatures and heavy precipitation distributed throughout a great share of the year are the two basic characteristics of tropical wet (*Ar*) climate. When typically located, it is found astride the equator and extending out 5 to 10° on either side. This latitudinal spread may be increased to 15 or even 25° along the eastern margin of a continent where the subtropical anticyclone is weak (Fig. 6.2). Tropical wet climate is sometimes called the *tropical rainforest* climate. This climate is closely associated with equatorial westerlies and the intertropical convergence zone (ITC), where weak rain-generating disturbances are numerous and the air is unstable (Fig. 6.3). Characteristically, tropical wet climate is bounded by the tropical wet-and-dry type on its poleward side. Along the wetter eastern margins of continents, however, it usually extends farther poleward and makes contact with the subtropical humid climate of middle latitudes (Fig. 6.2).

The Amazon Basin in northern South America and the Congo Basin in Africa are the two largest continuous areas with tropical wet climate (Plate 2). A third extensive, but not continuous, area includes much of insular and peninsular Southeast Asia. Numerous smaller areas can be identified from Plate 2.

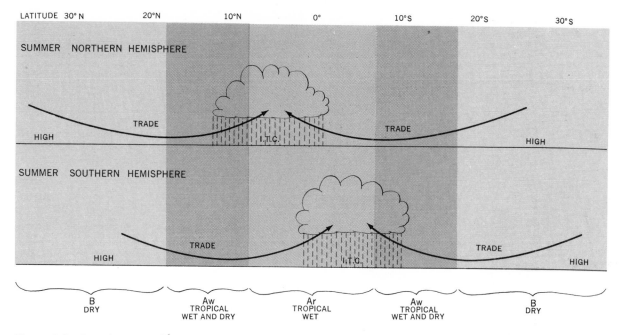

Figure 6.3 Type locations of tropical wet (Ar), tropical wet-and-dry (Aw), and dry (B) climates, as well as their locational relations to pressure and wind systems, at the times of the extreme seasons.

Temperature

Annual and Seasonal Temperatures. Because areas with the tropical wet type of climate commonly lie athwart the equator, and consequently in the belt of continuously strong solar radiation, it is logical that temperatures are uniformly high. Yearly averages, as shown in the following table, usually range between 77 and 80°. Moreover, since the sun's noon rays are never far from a vertical position, and since the length of days and nights varies only slightly from one part of the year to another, there is little seasonal variation in temperature (Fig. 6.4).

The annual temperature range, or difference between the average temperatures of the warmest and coolest months, is usually less than 5°, but it may be somewhat greater farther from the equator (see data for Belize in the following table). It is not because the average monthly temperatures are so high (indeed, average July temperatures in much of the subtropical southeastern United States are similar to the monthly averages of stations near the equator) but rather because the heat is so constant and monotonous that tropical wet climate is a forbidding one.

Daily Temperatures. The daily, or diurnal, range of temperature (difference between the warmest and coolest hours of the day) is usually 10 to 25°, several times greater than the annual range. For example, at Bolobo in the Congo, the average daily range is 16°, while the annual range is only 2°. During the afternoons the thermometer ordinarily rises to temperatures varying from 85 to 93° and at night sinks to 70 or 75°. It is commonly said that night is the winter of the tropics.

During the day the heat, even though not extremely high, combines with intense light, quiet air, and high relative humidity to produce an atmospheric condition with low cooling power. It is oppressive and sultry; the sensible temperature is very high.

Even the nights give little relief from the oppressive heat. Rapid nocturnal cooling is not to

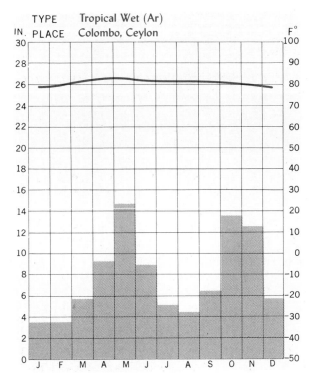

Figure 6.4 A representative station with tropical wet climate: average monthly temperatures (shown by the green line and read from the scale at right) and average monthly precipitation (shown by the green bars and read from the scale at left). Monthly temperatures are much more uniform than monthly amounts of precipitation. Note that Colombo has no dry month.

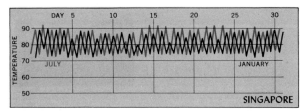

Figure 6.5 Daily maximum and minimum temperatures for the extreme months at a representative station with tropical wet climate (Ar). Diurnal solar control is almost complete, as shown by the regular daily rise and fall of temperature.

Precipitation

Annual Amount and Origin. Tropical wet climate coincides fairly well with the earth's belt of heaviest annual precipitation (compare Plates 1 and 2).[2] Annual rainfall usually varies from 70 to well over 100 in. In most equatorial regions conditions are relatively ideal for the rainmaking processes. The air is warm, humid, and unstable. The surface circulation is convergent, so that general ascent is prevalent. Rain-generating weak atmospheric disturbances are numerous. The result is an abundance of cumulus cloud and heavy showery rainfall, commonly accompanied by thunder and lightning. More rain usually comes during the warm afternoon and early evening hours, when solar heating makes the humid air increasingly unstable and buoyant; but night rains are frequent too.

Days with rain are numerous, but certainly not all days are rain-days. The showery weather comes in spells of several days' duration, separated by brief periods of clearer skies. Thus rainfall does not have the daily regularity characteristic of the temperature element. Weak atmospheric disturbances probably account for the spells of wet weather. Therefore the shower activity is predominantly organized, being concentrated in the disturbance and moving with it. Ordinarily it is not random or haphazard in its disturbance. Thus while irregular, nonperiodic weather changes are much weaker here

be expected where there are such excessive humidity and abundant cloudiness. The cooling is usually sufficient, however, to cause surface condensation in the near-saturated air, so that radiation fogs and heavy dew are common.

Figure 6.5 shows the daily march of temperature for the extreme months at a representative station within tropical wet climate. It is a temperature regime in which sun is almost completely in control. Temperature changes show a marked diurnal regularity and periodicity, rising to about the same height each day and falling to about the same level each night, so that one 24-hr period almost duplicates every other. Irregular invasions of cool air, a feature common in the middle latitudes, are rare.

[2] An unusual and puzzling feature of the eastern equatorial Pacific is the narrow belt of greatly reduced rainfall along the equatorial pressure trough, flanked by zones of much heavier rainfall to the north and south.

CLIMATIC DATA FOR REPRESENTATIVE STATIONS
WITH TROPICAL WET CLIMATE

Belém, Amazon Valley, 1°18'S

	J	F	M	A	M	J	J	A	S	O	N	D	Yr	Range
Temp., °F	77.4	77.0	77.2	77.9	78.4	78.4	78.4	78.6	78.4	79.0	79.3	78.6	78.3	2.3
Precip., in.	13.4	16.0	17.2	13.5	11.3	6.9	5.7	5.0	4.7	3.6	·3.4	6.9	108	

Stanleyville, Congo Basin, 32'N

	J	F	M	A	M	J	J	A	S	O	N	D	Yr	Range
Temp., °F	77.2	77.0	77.4	77.5	76.6	75.7	74.3	74.3	75.2	75.6	75.7	75.7	76.0	3.1
Precip., in.	3.3	4.1	6.9	5.6	6.1	3.5	4.4	8.9	7.5	9.8	6.7	2.8	69.4	

Singapore, 1°18'N, 153°52'E

	J	F	M	A	M	J	J	A	S	O	N	D	Yr	Range
Temp., °F	79.5	80.5	81.5	81.5	82.0	81.5	81.5	81.0	81.0	80.5	80.5	80.5	80.5	2.5
Precip., in.	9.9	6.8	7.6	7.4	6.8	6.8	6.7	7.7	7.0	8.2	10.0	10.1	95.0	

Belize, British Honduras, 17°31'N

	J	F	M	A	M	J	J	A	S	O	N	D	Yr	Range
Temp., °F.	74.8	76.8	79.2	79.2	81.9	82.4	82.6	82.6	82.0	79.3	76.1	73.6	79.3	9
Precip., in.	5.1	2.6	1.6	1.5	4.1	9.1	9.6	8.5	9.4	11.0	10.2	6.3	79.0	

Manaus, Amazon Valley, 3°1'S

	J	F	M	A	M	J	J	A	S	O	N	D	Yr	Range
Temp., °F.	79.2	79.2	79.5	79.2	79.3	79.9	80.2	81.5	82.2	82.0	81.7	80.2	80.4	3
Precip., in.	10.5	9.7	10.6	10.5	7.6	4.0	2.5	1.5	2.3	4.9	6.0	8.5	78.6	

than in the middle latitudes, they still occur, at least as far as rainfall is concerned.

Seasonal Distribution. Perhaps two subtypes, based on seasonality of precipitation, may be recognized in the tropical wet climate. What has usually been considered the archetype of equatorial climates is the one whose abundant rainfall is distributed throughout the year, without even a single dry month (see data for Singapore; also Fig. 6.4). But probably the more common and widespread is the subtype which, though it has equally as much annual rainfall, also has one, or at most two, dry months in which rainfall is less than about 2.3 in. (see data for Manaus). Usually dense rainforest prevails in both subtypes. And in both, the amount of rainfall during the wet months may vary widely, so that the annual rainfall curve of a tropical wet station is likely to be much more irregular with a much greater range than its temperature curve.

Resource Potentialities of the Tropical Wet Realm

Although approximately 10 percent of the earth's land surface has a tropical wet climate, this realm contains much less than 10 percent of the earth's population. The tropical wet areas show wide variations in population densities: the New World tropics are far emptier than those of the Old World.

Tropical wet regions have the most lavish and prolific vegetation of all climates. There is no dormant season for plant growth imposed by either a season of cold or a long season of drought. Since plants grow more continuously and rapidly here than in any other climate, these regions would seem to offer the highest potential for food production. (An offsetting factor, however, is the handicap this climate imposes upon the comfort, and perhaps health and general well-being, of the people who live in it.)

But while the climate provides a bountiful atmospheric environment for growing crops, this asset is seriously counterbalanced by the infertile residual soils (those derived from the underlying rock) from which the abundant rains have leached out mineral plant foods and organic material. The topsoil of tropical wet areas is exhausted by a few years of cropping, so the native farmer is obliged to give each cultivated plot a long period of fallowing in which to recuperate. On the other hand, many of the soils have a coarse granular structure, which makes them friable and easy to till.

Wild vegetation in these parts of the world is lush and evergreen. No other climate produces such a dense forest. For a native farmer who must clear the land, this forest is a serious handicap. But at the same time it provides a great potential resource of wood and lumber, although logging this timber and transporting it involves many problems.

Unoccupied, or meagerly occupied, land is still abundant in some tropical wet regions. The value of these areas for future settlement is a controversial topic. At present there appears to be more optimism about their future than ever before. Of the earth's three extensive types of land with meager population, there seems to be more hope for expansion of settlement in the wet tropics than in either the cold or the dry lands.

Tropical Wet-and-Dry Climate (Aw)

This climate differs from the tropical wet type in two principal ways: first, it usually has less total annual precipitation; second, the rainfall is more seasonal in character, for typically there is a dry season of over two months. These climatic differences result in replacement of the dense evergreen rainforest typical of *Ar* climate by lighter deciduous forest (i.e., composed of trees that shed their leaves during the dormant season). There are also many areas of intermingled woodland and grass, so that wet-and-dry type is sometimes called *savanna* (grassland with scattered trees) climate.

Location

On the hypothetical continent (Fig. 6.2), tropical wet-and-dry regions are located on the poleward and interior sides of the tropical wet climate, lying between it and the dry climates. Toward the rainier eastern part of the continent, the poleward side of wet-and-dry climate is adjacent to the subtropical humid regions of the middle latitudes.

Tropical wet-and-dry climate is typically located from about latitudes 5°–10° to 15°–20°. It may extend still farther poleward on the eastern side of a continent. This places wet-and-dry in an intermediate position between the ITC and its unstable air masses on the equatorial side, and the subtropical anticyclones with their stable subsiding and diverging air masses on the poleward side (Fig. 6.3). With the north-south shifting of solar energy belts during the course of a year, and hence a similar migration of pressure and wind belts, latitudes about 5 to 15° are alternately encroached upon by the wet ITC and its rainbringing disturbances at the

CLIMATIC DATA FOR REPRESENTATIVE STATIONS WITH TROPICAL WET-AND-DRY CLIMATE

Navrongo, Ghana, 10°53′N

	J	F	M	A	M	J	J	A	S	O	N	D	Yr	Range
Temp., °F	81	85	89	90	87	82	80	79	79	82	82	80	83	10
Precip., in.	0.0	0.2	0.6	1.9	4.4	5.7	7.9	10.4	9.0	2.7	0.2	0.1	43.1	

Timbo, Guinea, 10°40′N

	J	F	M	A	M	J	J	A	S	O	N	D	Yr	Range
Temp., °F	72	76	81	80	77	73	72	72	72	73	72	71	74	9.7
Precip., in.	0.0	0.0	1.0	2.4	6.4	9.0	12.4	14.7	10.2	6.7	1.3	0.0	64.1	

Calcutta, India, 22°32′N

	J	F	M	A	M	J	J	A	S	O	N	D	Yr	Range
Temp., °F	65	70	79	85	86	85	83	82	83	80	72	65	78	21
Precip., in.	0.4	1.1	1.4	2.0	5.0	11.2	12.1	11.5	9.0	4.3	0.5	0.2	58.8	

Cuiabá, Brazil, 15°30′S

	J	F	M	A	M	J	J	A	S	O	N	D	Yr	Range
Temp., °F	81	81	81	80	78	75	76	78	82	82	82	81	80	6.6
Precip., in.	9.8	8.3	8.3	4.0	2.1	0.3	0.2	1.1	2.0	4.5	5.9	8.1	54.6	

Normanton, Australia, 17°39′S

	J	F	M	A	M	J	J	A	S	O	N	D	Yr	Range
Temp., °F	86	85	85	82	78	73	72	75	80	85	88	87	81	15
Precip., in.	10.9	10.0	6.1	1.5	0.3	0.4	0.2	0.1	0.1	0.4	1.8	5.6	37.5	

time of high sun, and by the drier parts of the trades and the subtropical anticyclones at the time of low sun. The result is a rainy summer and a dry winter.

Comparison of Plate 2 and Fig. 6.2 shows that most of the extensive regions with tropical wet-and-dry climates actually are located on the world's continents in approximately the positions indicated on the hypothetical continent. This is the case with South America and Africa, both north and south of the equator; southern Asia; and northern Australia. Other smaller regions of *Aw* climate can also be found on Plate 2.

Temperature

Temperature conditions which were described for tropical wet climate largely apply to the wet-and-dry type as well. The differences are modest. In tropical wet-and-dry the annual range of temperature, though still small, is somewhat greater: usually over 5°, but seldom over 15 or 20° (see the preceding table). The diurnal range, which continues to exceed the annual, is usually highest in the dry season, when the sky is clearer and humidity low. Diurnal temperature regularity is still strong (Figs. 6.6, 6.7).

Often the hottest period precedes the time of highest sun, rather than coinciding with it or following close upon it, as is normal (Fig. 6.6). This is because high sun is the time of rain and cloud, which somewhat reduce air temperatures (see the preceding table). Thus March, April, and May are usually warmer than June and July, which are the rainier months for the Northern Hemisphere wet-and-dry climate.

Precipitation

Annual Amount. Since the two tropical climates do not differ much in temperature, rainfall becomes the critical element in distinguishing between them. Characteristically the wet-and-dry type has 40 to 60 in. of annual precipitation, which is somewhat less rain than in tropical wet. This reduction in rainfall reflects the transitional nature of the wet-and-dry climate, located as it is between very wet ITC

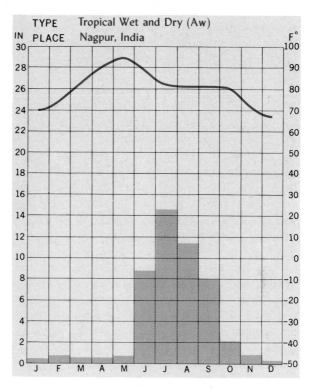

Figure 6.6 Average monthly temperatures and precipitation amounts for a representative station with tropical wet-and-dry climate (Aw) in India. Note that the highest temperatures are in May preceding the rains.

climates equatorward and dry climates of the subtropical anticyclones poleward. Within tropical wet-and-dry climates, therefore, rainfall usually decreases in a poleward direction (Fig. 6.6).

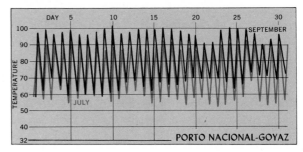

Figure 6.7 Daily maximum and minimum temperatures for the extreme months at a station with tropical wet-and-dry climate (Aw) in Brazil. Note the dominance of the periodic or solar control; also the large diurnal range of temperature at this interior station. September is hotter than January because it is less cloudy.

Seasonal Distribution. But it is the seasonality of precipitation, more than the smaller annual total, that mainly differentiates the two climates of the humid tropics. *Aw* climate has a marked dry season of more than two months' duration, characteristically at the time of low sun. In that season desert weather prevails, for usually the drought is intense. The trees lose their leaves, the rivers shrink, the soil cracks, and the landscape is parched and brown. All nature appears dormant. Dust, as well as smoke from grass fires set by native farmers, fill the air, so that visibility is usually low. But during high sun, or summer, convective showers are numerous and the daily weather is like that of tropical wet regions (Fig. 6.6).

This marked seasonal rhythm of alternating drought and rains again shows the intermediate position of *Aw* between subtropical anticyclones poleward (*cT* air) and ITC and equatorial westerlies equatorward (*mT* air). A poleward migration of pressure and wind belts with the sun brings ITC rains to the wet-and-dry climate in summer and anticyclonic drought in winter. Most emphatically, rainfall follows the sun. It should be obvious, however, that when *Aw* climate in the Northern Hemisphere is having its wet season, its counterpart in the Southern Hemisphere will be in the grip of drought. The relative lengths of the wet and dry seasons vary; the farther from the equator and the ITC, the shorter the wet season and the longer the dry.

Variability of Rainfall. Not only is rainfall in tropical wet-and-dry climate less in total amount, and more seasonal in its distribution, than in tropical wet; it also fluctuates more from year to year and hence is less reliable. One year may bring property damage and crop losses due to excessive rains; in the following one there may be even more severe losses from drought.

Upland Tropical Climate

In tropical latitudes on several continents, especially Africa and South America, there are extensive upland areas with only moderate elevation. These

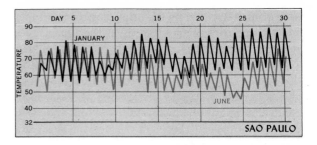

Figure 6.8 Daily maximum and minimum temperatures for a station with tropical wet-and-dry climate on the Brazilian upland at nearly 24°S. Note the lower temperatures imposed by altitude and also by the latitude. Although solar control is dominant, some nonperiodic air-mass control is also evident here on the margins of the tropics.

have many of the usual features of tropical humid climates but differ chiefly in their somewhat lower temperatures, which of course are a result of higher altitude (Fig. 6.8). Parts are even sufficiently high that temperatures for one or more months may be below the minimum set for tropical climates. In the climate groupings used here, these extensive uplands of tropical Africa and South America are still classed as tropical humid, usually of the wet-and-dry type; but on Plate 2 they are set apart from the more standard lowland variety by a light stippling. (Climatic modifications imposed by altitude are discussed in Chap. 9.)

Resource Potentialities of the Tropical Wet-and-Dry Realm

Close to 15 percent of the earth's land area has tropical wet-and-dry climate. On a population map of the earth, many wet-and-dry regions, especially those in the New World and Australia, are conspicuous for their scarcity of people. Peninsular India is the most striking exception, for there human life is abundant. The wet-and-dry parts of Africa are intermediate in population density.

Although temperatures are constantly high in tropical wet-and-dry climate, the dormant season imposed by drought makes the productiveness of this realm considerably less than that of tropical wet climate. The smaller total amount of precipitation, and its variability as well, increase this disadvantage.

Because of the reduced climatic energy, the vegetation cover is a less luxuriant forest, composed of smaller trees, more widely spaced, and usually deciduous. Over large areas, grasslands made up of tall coarse grasses are intermingled with woodland. Much of the woodland is of little value commercially, and the mature natural grasses are too tall, coarse, and unnutritious to support an important commercial grazing industry.

Not much is known about the mature soils of the wet-and-dry climate, but generally they appear to be leached and infertile like those that develop under the rainforest. As in most regions of infertile or difficult soils, the most attractive sites for cultivation are the fresh, young, unleached new alluvial surfaces (i.e., surfaces deposited by running water fairly recently in geologic time).

Selected References for Chaps. 6–10

Atlas of American Agriculture. Part 2, Climate. 3 sections: "Frost and the Growing Season"; "Temperature, Sunshine and Wind"; "Precipitation and Humidity." U.S. Government Printing Office, Washington, D.C. Contains excellent and detailed maps of the climatic elements.

Blair, Thomas A. *Climatology, General and Regional.* Prentice-Hall, Inc., Englewood Cliffs, N.J., 1942.

Brooks, C. F., A. J. Connor, et al. *Climatic Maps of North America.* Harvard University Press, Cambridge, Mass., 1936.

Climate and Man. Yearbook of Agriculture, 1941. U.S. Department of Agriculture, Washington, D.C. Contains an abundance of climatic data on foreign countries as well as on the United States.

Critchfield, Howard J. *General Climatology.* 2d ed. Pp. 145–221. Prentice-Hall, Inc., Englewood Cliffs, N.J., 1966.

Hare, F. K. *The Restless Atmosphere.* Pp. 116–182. Harper & Row, Publishers, Incorporated, New York, 1963.

Haurwitz, Bernard, and James M. Austin. *Climatology.* McGraw-Hill Book Company, New York, 1944.

Kendrew, W. G. *Climatology.* 2d ed. Oxford University Press, Fair Lawn, N.J., 1957.

———. *Climates of the Continents.* 4th ed. Oxford University Press, Fair Lawn, N.J., 1953.

Miller, A. Austin. *Climatology.* 3d ed. E. P. Dutton & Co., Inc., New York, 1953.

Trewartha, Glenn T. *The Earth's Problem Climates.* The University of Wisconsin Press, Madison, Wis., 1961.

———. *An Introduction to Climate.* 4th ed. McGraw-Hill Book Company, New York, 1968.

Ward, Robert De C. *Climates of the United States.* Ginn and Company, Boston, 1925.

Sources of World Climatic Data

Monthly Climatic Data for the World. U.S. Weather Bureau.

Tables of Temperature, Relative Humidity, and Precipitation for the World, Parts I, II, III, IV, V, and VI, 1958. Great Britain Meteorological Office.

World Weather Records. Issued 1921–1930 and 1931–1940 as Smithsonian Institution Miscellaneous Collections; 1941–1950 by the U.S. Weather Bureau, 1959.

7

The Subtropical Climates (C)

Middle-latitude climates, of which the subtropical is one group, lack the constant heat of the tropics and the constant cold of the polar regions. They have a very definite seasonal rhythm in temperature conditions. Thus temperature is as important as rainfall, or even more so, in differentiating the various types of middle-latitude climates. In the tropics, seasons are designated as wet and dry; in the middle latitudes, they are called winter and summer, and the dormant season for plant growth usually is one of low temperature rather than of drought.

Subtropical climates have the warmest summers and mildest winters within the humid middle latitudes. They are positioned along the equatorward margins of these latitudes, forming a kind of transition group between tropical climates farther equatorward and the more severe middle-latitude climates farther poleward. Most parts of the continental subtropics are subject to occasional killing frosts in winter. In some marine locations, however, frosts may be rare or even absent.

Within the subtropical belt, two types of humid climate are recognized: subtropical dry summer on the west side of a continent, and subtropical humid on the east.

Subtropical Dry-summer Climate (Cs) (Mediterranean)

In its simplest form this climate is characterized by three striking features: (1) a concentration of the year's modest amount of precipitation in the winter season, while summers are usually nearly or completely dry; (2) warm-to-hot summers and notably mild winters; and (3) abundant sunshine and meager cloudiness, especially in summer. Quite deservedly this climate with its bright, sunny weather, blue skies, few rainy days, and mild winters—and its usually abundant fruit, flowers, and winter vegetables—has acquired a glamorous reputation. It is unique in being the only one of the earth's humid climates with drought in summer and a strong rainfall maximum in winter.

The subtropical dry-summer type has strongly marked climatic characteristics which are fairly well duplicated in the five regions where it occurs: the borderlands of the Mediterranean Sea, central and coastal southern California, central Chile, the southern tip of South Africa, and parts of southern Australia.

Location

Subtropical dry-summer areas typically are found on the tropical margins of the middle latitudes (30°–40°) along the western sides of continents (Fig. 6.2, Plate 2). Situated thus on the poleward slopes of a subtropical high, this type lies between the subsiding air of an oceanic anticyclone's stable eastern end, on the one hand, and the rainbringing cyclones and fronts of the westerlies, on the other. With the north-south shifting of wind belts during the course of a year, these west-side subtropical latitudes are joined to the dry tropics at the time of high sun and to the humid middle latitudes at low sun. Tropical constancy therefore characterizes them in summer, middle-latitude changeability in winter. In other words, this subtropical dry-summer, or Mediterranean, type is a transitional climate situated between low-latitude dry climates equatorward and cool, temperate marine climates farther poleward.

In both central Chile and California, mountains terminate this type abruptly on the land side. As for southern Africa and southwestern Australia, their poleward tips barely reach into the middle latitudes, so that on these continents the subtropical dry-summer climate occupies the southern and southwestern extremities rather than having a west-coast location. Only in the region of the Mediterranean Sea Basin, which is a major route of winter cyclones, does this type of climate extend far inland, penetrating for 2,000 miles or more and affecting extensive areas. It is for this reason that the subtropical dry-summer type is often called Mediterranean climate.

The subtropical interior and eastern margin of a continent, where the summer anticyclone is relatively weak and where there is a tendency toward a monsoon wind system, is a type location that does not favor a dry summer.

Temperature

Because of its subtropical location, dry-summer climate has little cold weather. The annual temperature range is small for middle latitudes.

Two subdivisions of this type may be recognized, based mainly on the degree of summer heat, which in turn is largely a function of location. First and much more extensive, a warm-summer subtype (Csa) is situated either inland from the coast or on a coast bordered by warm water. Second, cool-summer subtype (Csb) occupies limited areas where coasts are washed by cool ocean currents—mainly in coastal California and Chile.

Except along cool-water coasts, average summer-month temperatures are hot, 75 to 80° +

being common (Fig. 7.1). The heat is dry, like that of the semi-arid climates. Afternoon July temperatures in the Great Valley of California are likely to reach 90° or above, and 100° is not uncommon.

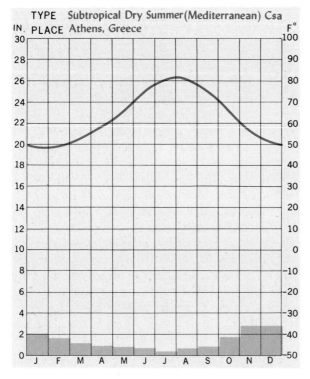

Figure 7.1 A subtropical dry-summer station, hot-summer subtype (*Csa*).

The land blazes under a pitiless sky. Because the air is dry and there are few or no clouds, night cooling is rapid and daily ranges are large, resembling those of dry climates (Fig. 7.2).

But temperature conditions along the cool-water coasts of subtropical Chile and California are significantly different from this. Santa Monica on the California coast has an average warmest-month temperature of only 66°. So does Valparaiso, Chile, in sharp contrast to the hot interior (Fig. 7.3). In such locations summer fog and low stratus cloud are frequent. Winter temperatures too are somewhat milder than those inland, with the total effect that the annual temperature range is abnormally small—only 9° at San Francisco, and 11° at Valparaiso. Diurnal ranges also are small (Fig. 7.4).

It is for the mild, bright *winters* with their pleasant temperatures that dry-summer climate is justly famed. People of the colder, higher latitudes seek it out for comfortable winter living. To residents in the upper Mississippi Valley, the word "winter" has a congealing sound, but to Californians it signifies gentle weather and a green landscape. The absence of severe winter cold is due both to the subtropical location and to the dry-summer region's proximity to the sea on the windward western sides of continents. Usually the winter months have average temperatures between 45 and 55°, with coastal locations being somewhat milder than those inland (Figs. 7.1, 7.3). At midday the temperature com-

CLIMATIC DATA FOR REPRESENTATIVE SUBTROPICAL DRY-SUMMER STATIONS

Red Bluff, California (Interior)

	J	F	M	A	M	J	J	A	S	O	N	D	Yr	Range
Temp., °F	45	50	54	59	67	75	82	80	73	64	54	46	62.3	36.3
Precip., in.	4.6	3.9	3.2	1.7	1.1	0.5	0.0	0.1	0.8	1.3	2.9	4.3	24.3	

Santa Monica, California (Coast with cool water)

	J	F	M	A	M	J	J	A	S	O	N	D	Yr	Range
Temp., °F	53	53	55	58	60	63	66	66	65	62	58	55	59.5	13.6
Precip., in.	3.5	3.0	2.9	0.5	0.5	0.0	0.0	0.0	0.1	0.6	1.4	2.3	14.78	

Perth, Australia (Coast)

	J	F	M	A	M	J	J	A	S	O	N	D	Yr	Range
Temp., °F	74	74	71	67	61	57	55	56	58	61	66	71	64	19
Precip., in.	0.3	0.5	0.7	1.6	4.9	6.9	6.5	5.7	3.3	2.1	0.8	0.6	33.9	

Naples, Italy (Coast with warm water)

	J	F	M	A	M	J	J	A	S	O	N	D	Yr	Range
Temp., °F	48	49	53	59	65	72	77	77	72	64	56	51	62	29
Precip., in.	4.8	3.5	1.7	1.8	2.2	0.7	0.6	1.3	4.3	4.6	4.1	4.7	34.3	

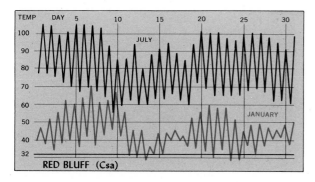

Figure 7.2   An interior subtropical dry-summer station in California (Csa). Note the hot summer and the large diurnal range of temperature. Solar control is dominant in summer, but irregular, nonperiodic air-mass control is conspicuous in winter.

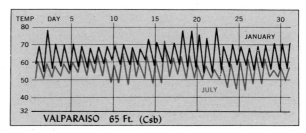

Figure 7.4   The same cool-summer subtype (Csb) as in Fig. 7.3. Note the small diurnal range of temperature and the low summer (i.e., January) temperatures.

monly rises to 55°–65°; at night it may drop to 40 or 45° and on occasion even to freezing (Figs. 7.2, 7.4).

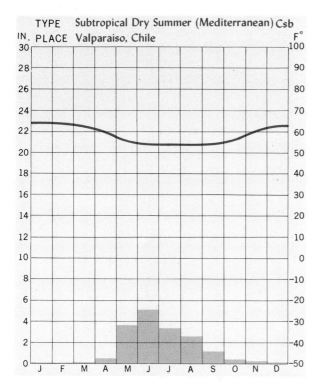

Figure 7.3   A Southern Hemisphere subtropical dry-summer station, coastal cool-summer subtype (Csb).

It is not because of their frequency and severity that frosts are so much dreaded in these regions of sensitive fruit and vegetable crops. Rather, it is their infrequency that tempts farmers to take a chance on the frost hazard, with the result that losses are sometimes appalling. Ordinarily the growing season does not quite extend over the whole year, for frosts do occasionally come during the three winter months. They usually occur on only a few nights, however, and only rarely are they severe. Never does the thermometer remain below freezing during the midday hours.

During a period of 41 years at Los Angeles, California, near the Pacific Coast, there were 28 in which no killing frost occurred, so that the growing season was 12 months long. However, at Sacramento, inland from the coast, the temperature usually drops below 32° on several winter nights each year.

Frosts in subtropical dry-summer regions are mainly the result of radiation cooling following an advection of polar air by winds in a cold anticyclone. Subfreezing temperatures are usually confined to a shallow layer of surface air, especially in topographic depressions (low spots) where air drainage concentrates the chilled air. For this reason such sensitive crops as citrus are customarily located on slopes.

Precipitation

Annual Amount. As a general rule dry-summer climate has too little rather than too much annual rainfall. A great many dry-summer areas just escape being semiarid. Normal precipitation is 15 to 25 in., which means that this climate type is classified as subhumid rather than humid. It is usually bordered by steppe climate along its equatorward margin, so that it is driest along this frontier and rainfall amounts increase poleward. Thus San Diego in southernmost California receives only 10 in. of rain; Los Angeles, less than 100 miles farther north, 15 in.; and San Francisco, about 250 miles still farther north, 20 in. In other words, rainfall mounts with increasing distance from the influence of the subtropical anticyclone. The general deficit of water and the variation in rainfall amounts from year to year are reflected in the large-scale use of irrigation water. Most of the modest rainfall on lowlands originates in cyclonic storms or along fronts—disturbances which are characteristic features of the middle-latitude westerly winds.

Seasonal Distribution. To an unusual degree the year's rainfall is concentrated in the cooler half of the year. Winter in the dry-summer climate is usually the rainiest of the four seasons, while summer often is desertlike (Figs. 7.1, 7.3). At Los Angeles, over three-quarters of the year's rain comes during the 4 months from December to March, and only 2 percent from June to September. The rainfall regime, therefore, is that of the deserts in summer and that of the cyclonic westerlies in winter.

    This seasonal alternation of drought and rain is, as previously indicated, a consequence of the north-south migration of wind and rainfall belts following the course of the sun. A poleward shifting of the sun in summer brings these subtropical latitudes along west coasts under the influence of the stable eastern margin of a subtropical anticyclone. Subsiding and diverging air, temperature inversions, a near absence of atmospheric disturbances, and in some locations, cool ocean water along the coast, all join to produce aridity (Fig. 7.5). But in winter, when the sun, and therefore the wind and rainfall belts, move to their southernmost limits, these same latitudes largely escape the effects of the anticyclone. Instead they come under

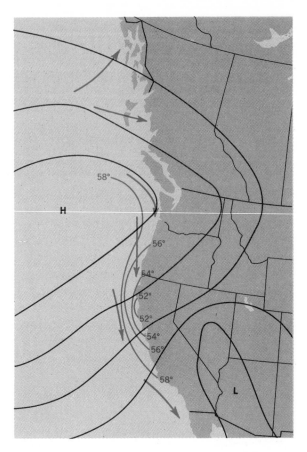

Figure 7.5 Pressure, winds, and temperatures of the ocean water along the Pacific Coast of the United States in midsummer. Cool-summer coastal climates and drought are a consequence of these controls. *(After Patton.)*

the influence of the westerlies with their cyclonic storms and frontal systems (Fig. 4.12). Although winter is distinctly less sunny than summer, it is by no means a season of prevailing overcast.

    Lowlands in dry-summer climates do not have a snow cover, and even snowfall is rare. In central and southern California, annual snowfall averages less than 1 in., and there is none at all along the coast south of San Francisco. But highlands adjacent to dry-summer climates may have a moderate to heavy snowfall and a snow cover, whose meltwater is an invaluable source of irrigation for the drier lowlands.

Seasonal Weather

Daily weather is less fickle in the subtropical climates than it is farther poleward, where traveling cyclones and anticyclones are more numerous and better developed. A typical *summer* day in non-coastal California resembles one in a low-latitude desert. Moreover, one day is much like another, with drought, brilliant sunshine, low relative humidity, high daytime temperatures, and marked nocturnal cooling. Along seacoasts there is often a daily sea breeze, which greatly moderates the desert heat.

In *autumn,* as the cyclonic belt creeps equatorward following the course of the sun, an occasional cyclone arrives, accompanied by its cloud cover and rain. The dry and dusty land begins to assume new life under the greening effect of the precipitation. *Winter* brings an increase in the frequency and strength of cyclones, and it is then that irregular, nonperiodic weather changes are most marked. Rainy days are sandwiched between sunny ones when the daytime hours are comfortably mild, even though the nights may be chilly, with occasional frosts. *Spring* is a delightful season in the Mediterranean year: fresh and yet warm. This is the harvesting period for many grains. Passing cyclones gradually become fewer as summer approaches.

Resource Potentialities of the Dry-summer Realm

Although this is the most restricted of all the climatic realms, embracing less than 2 percent of the earth's land surface, it is one of the most unusual and attractive. The near absence of snow and cold, the plentiful fair weather and sunshine, the abundance of fruit and flowers—all have given this dry-summer realm a reputation far out of proportion to its size. Certainly, in contributing to pleasant living, climate is one of the realm's major resources.

The subtropics approach the bountiful temperature regime of the tropics more nearly than any other part of the middle latitudes. Their almost tropical temperature conditions, combined with their proximity to the great markets of the middle latitudes, give the two subtropical realms a unique commercial advantage. In them farmers can grow certain warmth-loving or frost-sensitive crops, some of a luxury type—citrus, figs, viniferous grapes, rice, sugar cane, cotton—which thrive in few other parts of the middle latitudes. The subtropical climates likewise enable farmers to produce out-of-season vegetables and flowers for the markets of regions farther poleward, where a season of severe cold imposes a long dormant period.

On the other hand, the dry-summer realm's relatively meager total precipitation and long summer drought place definite climatic limitations upon agricultural production. These factors also tend to limit the kinds of crops grown, causing emphasis on drought-resistant perennials, such as the olive and the vine, and on annuals which mature quickly, such as barley and wheat. The large-scale development of irrigation within this realm represents man's attempt to overcome the handicap of summer drought.

It is fortunate that the usual 15 to 25 in. of rain is concentrated in the cooler months of the year, when evaporation is at a minimum. If the same modest amount fell mainly during the hot summer, when evaporation is excessive, much less of it would be effective for plant growth and the climate would be semiarid.

Modest precipitation and summer drought produce a vegetation cover of woody shrubs and widely spaced, stunted trees; some dry-summer regions also have scattered patches of desert bunchgrass. This plant cover is of some value for grazing, particularly of sheep and goats. Only on the wetter mountain slopes do dry-summer forests have genuine commercial value; the stunted trees and the bushes of the valleys and lower slopes are useful chiefly as checks to erosion.

On mountain and hill slopes, the soils of dry-summer regions are inclined to be thin and stony, and a large part of them remains uncultivated. It is the young alluvial soils of the valleys which are the attractive sites for farming.

Subtropical Humid Climate (Cf)

Subtropical humid areas differ from subtropical dry-summer ones in three main ways: (1) Characteristically they are located on the eastern rather than the western side of a continent, (2) ordinarily they have more annual precipitation, and (3) this precipitation may be distributed throughout the year or else may be concentrated in the warmer months; either way, summer is a humid season.

Location

In latitudinal positions the two subtropical climates are similar, both being on the equatorward margins of the intermediate zones from about 25 or 30° to 35 or 40° (Fig. 6.2 and Plate 2). But since the humid subtropical type is characteristically situated on the eastern side of a land mass, it is affected by a different pattern of weather controls. It comes under the influence of the weaker subsidence and less stable air in the western limb of an oceanic subtropical anticyclone. In this location there is also some tendency for a monsoon system of winds, which in turn favors summer precipitation. In addition, warm ocean currents parallel these east coasts.

Although both subtropical types of climate lie on the tropical margins of the middle latitudes, they are usually flanked by quite unlike climates to north and south. While the subtropical dry-summer type characteristically changes into dry climate on its equatorward side, subtropical humid is bounded by tropical humid climates there. Similarly, the dry-summer climate usually merges into a mild, rainy marine climate on its poleward side, while (in Asia and North America, at least) subtropical humid adjoins severe continental climates. Because of these differences in the neighboring climates, north and south winds advect air masses with markedly different temperatures and humidities into the two subtropical climate types.

Temperature

Logically, in view of their similar latitudinal positions, the two subtropical climates are fairly similar in temperature (Fig. 7.6). Of course, since there are no cool ocean currents along subtropical east coasts, the humid type has no cool-summer subtype. *Summer* is normally hot, with monthly averages around 75 to 80°. In contrast to the dry heat of California, high humidity in conjunction with high temperature produces sultry, oppressive weather resembling that of the humid tropics. Not only are the days hot and sultry; nights are oppressive as well. The slow night cooling in the humid air results in only average diurnal ranges of temperature (Fig. 7.7). July daily maxima in the United States Gulf Coast region usually reach 90 to 100°. Summer temperatures are slightly less high in the Southern Hemisphere.

Winters are of course relatively mild in these subtropical latitudes, average cool-month temperatures usually varying between 40 and 50°.

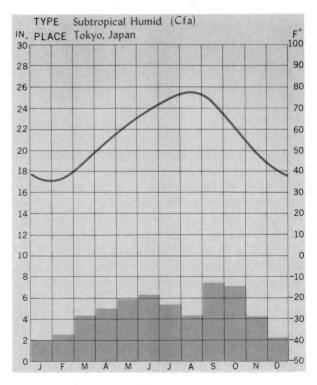

Figure 7.6 Compare with Figs. 7.1 and 7.3. Seasonal rainfall distribution here is quite different from that in the dry-summer climate.

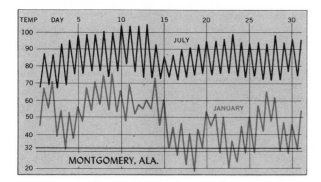

Figure 7.7 Daily maximum and minimum temperatures for the extreme months at a subtropical humid station in the United States. Note the strong periodic, or solar, control in summer. By contrast, winter shows strong nonperiodic or air-mass control.

Still, there are important regional variations depending on the size of the continent. In January, Shanghai, China, averages 38°; Buenos Aires, Argentina, 50°; Dallas, Texas, 45°. Midday winter temperatures are pleasantly mild, around 50 or 60°, and on winter nights minimum temperatures of 35 to 45° are usual. However, passing cyclones and anticyclones result in irregular spells of warmer and colder weather (Fig. 7.7).

Nighttime freezing temperatures may be expected occasionally during the winter months, but the number of freezes is not large. The growing season is long—from 7 or 8 months up to almost, if not quite, the entire year. Daytime temperatures normally rise above freezing. In the humid subtropics of both Asia and North America, freezes are more frequent and more severe than in their Southern Hemisphere counterparts. The United States Gulf states, which are completely open to invasions of polar air, are especially prone to severe freezes.

Precipitation

Since the western limb of an oceanic subtropical anticyclone usually provides an environment favoring rain, precipitation is relatively abundant in the humid subtropics. Rainfall varies considerably be-

tween regions, however. Chiefly it is the interior western margins that are driest.

As a rule there is no marked dry season. More often than not, summer is the wettest, and winter has the least rain. But in parts of East Asia, where the winter monsoon is strong, winter may be genuinely dry.

In the summer, sunshine is relatively abundant, although less so than in the dry-summer subtropical climates. Much of the summer precipitation is of the showery, convective type developing in warm, humid *mT* air which has been made unstable by a heated land surface. Most of the showers usually occur in conjunction with the passage of weak disturbances, in which convergence acts to lift the unstable air (Fig. 7.8). Clouds are mainly of the

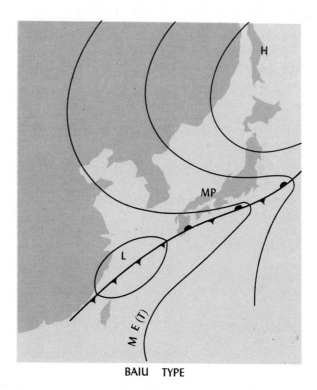

BAIU   TYPE

Figure 7.8 A weak low of the early summer period in subtropical eastern Asia. It is disturbances of this type which produce a large part of the rainfall in the Asiatic humid subtropics. *(From Trewartha, Japan: A Geography. The University of Wisconsin Press, Madison, Wis.)*

CLIMATIC DATA FOR REPRESENTATIVE SUBTROPICAL HUMID STATIONS

Charleston, South Carolina

	J	F	M	A	M	J	J	A	S	O	N	D	Yr	Range
Temp., °F	50	52	58	65	73	79	82	81	77	68	58	51	66.1	31.4
Precip., in.	3.0	3.1	3.3	2.4	3.3	5.1	6.2	6.5	5.2	3.7	2.5	3.2	47.3	

Shanghai, China

	J	F	M	A	M	J	J	A	S	O	N	D	Yr	Range
Temp., °F	38	39	46	56	66	73	80	80	73	63	52	42	49	42.8
Precip., in.	2.8	2.0	3.9	4.4	3.3	6.6	7.4	4.7	3.9	3.7	1.7	1.3	45.8	

Sydney, Australia

	J	F	M	A	M	J	J	A	S	O	N	D	Yr	Range
Temp., °F	72	71	69	65	59	54	52	55	59	62	67	70	63	20
Precip., in.	3.6	4.4	4.9	5.4	5.1	4.8	5.0	3.0	2.9	2.9	2.8	2.8	47.7	

Dallas, Texas

	J	F	M	A	M	J	J	A	S	O	N	D	Yr	Range
Temp., °F	45	47	56	65	73	81	84	83	77	66	55	47	65	35
Precip., in.	2.2	2.0	2.7	3.9	4.4	3.1	2.5	2.1	2.9	2.8	2.5	2.4	33.6	

cumulus type. The North American humid subtropics have the highest frequency of thunderstorms in the United States. Hurricane rainfall, which is confined to the North American and Asiatic sectors, accounts for a portion of the summer-fall precipitation there.

Winter precipitation is chiefly cyclonic in origin. Gray, overcast days with rain are unpleasantly chilly. Snow falls occasionally when a vigorous winter cyclone swings well equatorward, but it infrequently stays on the ground for more than a few days. Even on the northern margins of the United States Gulf Coast region, snow falls on only 5 to 15 days a year.

Seasonal Weather

Irregular, nonperiodic weather changes are usually less noticeable in the humid subtropics than they are farther poleward, where the conflict between air masses is more marked and cyclonic storms are more numerous.

In *summer,* when the storm belt is farthest poleward, irregular weather changes are at a minimum (Fig. 7.7). Because the sun largely controls the weather, diurnal regularity of temperature is a characteristic feature; humid, sultry days are the rule. Frequent spells of showery weather accompanying weak disturbances alternate with periods

of several days in which no rain falls. To an unusual degree the weather resembles that of the wet tropics.

In North America and Asia, late summer and fall are the dreaded hurricane season. Although these storms are not numerous, their severity more than makes up for their infrequency. Sunny autumn days furnish delightful balmy weather. With the approach of winter the equatorward-advancing cyclonic belt produces a gradually increasing number of gray, cloudy days and begins to import unseasonable temperatures.

In *winter* the belt of cyclonic storms is farthest equatorward, so that irregular weather changes are more frequent and extreme. Tropical air masses may arrive and push daytime temperatures to well above 60 or even 70°, only to be followed by northerly winds of polar origin which reduce temperatures as much as 30° within 24 hr, resulting occasionally in severe freezes. Certainly there are many bright, sunny winter days, distinctly pleasant and exhilarating out of doors. As spring comes, the cyclonic belt retreats and regular diurnal sun control is gradually reestablished.

Resource Potentialities of the Humid Subtropics

Without doubt, subtropical humid is the most productive climate of the middle latitudes. Temperature and rainfall combine to create the closest approach to humid tropical conditions outside the low latitudes. The more abundant precipitation of the humid subtropics, together with the lack of a genuinely dry season, make this realm potentially more productive than its west-coast counterpart. To be sure, its sultry tropical summers are not ideal for human comfort, but they are nonetheless excellent for luxuriant plant growth.

The abundant climatic energy, expressed in rainfall as well as temperature, results in equally abundant wild vegetation. This usually consists of forests, although grasses may replace trees in regions of more modest precipitation. The character of the forests varies so much among humid subtropical regions that generalizations are difficult to make.

Trees grow more rapidly in the humid subtropics than they do in other climates of the middle latitudes, so that natural or artificial reforestation is a quicker process than it is farther poleward.

Usually the mature forest soils of the humid subtropics are low in fertility, a factor which provides a serious offset to the effects of the bountiful climate. This inferiority of the soil is not surprising, however, considering the high leaching power of the many rains and the low humus-producing character of forest vegetation. Where grasses replace forests, as they do in the subhumid portions of the subtropics, the soils are darker in color and much more productive. The lower rainfall results in less leaching, and the grasses provide a greater abundance of organic matter.

8

The Temperate Climates (D)

This group of climates occupies a medial latitudinal position within the intermediate zones, since it is located between the subtropical climates equatorward and the boreal climates poleward. Admittedly the name "temperate," defined as moderate, is not well suited to the continental climate, one of the types within this group. But for want of a better title, temperate is used here to designate the climates with temperatures that are intermediate between boreal cold and subtropical heat.

Two main types comprise the temperate group: a mild one designated as oceanic or marine (*Do*), and a more severe one called continental (*Dc*) (Fig. 6.2). The boundary delimiting the oceanic type is the coldest-month isotherm of 32° (to 36°, usually farther inland). An annual temperature range of 36° has also been suggested.

Temperate Oceanic Climate (Do)

Location

This mild marine climate typically lies on the western or windward side of middle-latitude continents, poleward from about 40°, where onshore westerly winds advect sea climates to the land (Fig. 6.2, Plate 2). In its general atmospheric characteristics, therefore, it is like the ocean from which the air is imported. Warm ocean currents add their effects to those of the ocean proper. Of course, this oceanic type of climate cannot develop over any extensive area on the eastern, or leeward, side of a large continent in middle latitudes.

On its equatorward side, temperate oceanic climate normally adjoins the subtropical dry-summer type. It extends far into the higher middle latitudes, where it is eventually terminated by the boreal or tundra type. The depth to which the oceanic climate penetrates inland from the west coast depends largely on the presence (as in North America and Chile) or absence (as in Europe) of mountain barriers (compare Fig. 6.2 with Plate 2).

Temperature

Since this is an ocean-controlled climate, it does not have large seasonal extremes of temperature. The annual temperature curve is relatively flat, for summers are on the cool side, and winters are

mild for the latitude. Thus the annual range is small (Fig. 8.1).

Certainly "temperate" is a most suitable

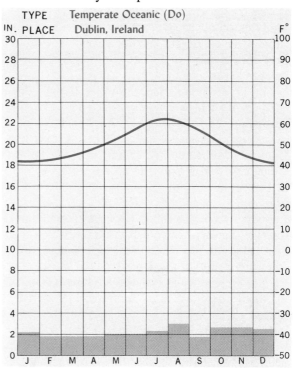

Figure 8.1   Monthly temperature and rainfall for a temperate oceanic station in western Europe. Note the small annual range of temperature and the modest amount of precipitation well distributed throughout the year.

CLIMATIC DATA FOR REPRESENTATIVE TEMPERATE OCEANIC STATIONS

Valentia, Ireland

	J	F	M	A	M	J	J	A	S	O	N	D	Yr	Range
Temp., °F	44	44	45	48	52	57	59	59	57	52	48	45	50.8	15
Precip., in.	5.5	5.2	4.5	3.7	3.2	3.2	3.8	4.8	4.1	5.6	5.5	6.6	55.6	

Paris, France

	J	F	M	A	M	J	J	A	S	O	N	D	Yr	Range
Temp., °F	37	39	43	51	56	62	66	64	59	51	43	37	50.5	29
Precip., in.	1.5	1.2	1.6	1.7	2.1	2.3	2.2	2.2	2.0	2.3	1.8	1.7	22.6	

Hokitika, New Zealand

	J	F	M	A	M	J	J	A	S	O	N	D	Yr	Range
Temp., °F	60	61	59	55	50	47	45	46	50	53	55	58	53	16
Precip., in.	9.8	7.3	9.7	9.2	9.8	9.7	9.0	9.4	9.2	11.8	10.6	10.6	116.1	

Portland, Oregon

	J	F	M	A	M	J	J	A	S	O	N	D	Yr	Range
Temp., °F	39	42	46	51	57	61	67	66	61	54	46	41	53	28
Precip., in.	6.7	5.5	4.8	3.1	2.3	1.6	0.6	0.6	1.9	3.3	6.5	6.9	43.8	

name for this oceanic climate. The pleasantly cool *summers* are excellent for human comfort and efficiency, though they are too cool for the best growth of some cereal crops. Average summer-month temperatures of 60 or 65° are 5 to 10° lower than those of the continental interior in similar latitudes. Only occasionally are midday temperatures uncomfortably warm.

Winters are milder for the latitude than summers are cool. Thus the coastal lands of western Europe are 20 to 30° too warm for their latitudes in January. And while Seattle is only 5° cooler than Montreal (in the interior) in July, it is 27° milder in January. Winter isotherms tend to roughly parallel the coastline, with the temperatures decreasing more rapidly inland than poleward. This is evidence that land-water control is stronger than latitude. Average January temperatures range from somewhat below 40° to slightly over 45°. Annual ranges vary from about 15 to 25 or 30° (Fig. 8.1).

Freezing temperatures are more frequent and more severe than in the subtropical dry-summer climate to the south. Still, the growing season is long considering the latitude. In the American North Pacific Coast region, 6 to 8 months are characteristic. At Paris, France, frost normally occurs only on about half the nights during the three winter months. However, winter usually is severe enough to produce a dormant season for plant life. During occasional cold spells, temperatures may remain constantly below freezing for several days in succession (Fig. 8.2). Such cold spells occur when

there is a westward and southward thrust of anticyclonic polar air from the interior of the continent (Fig. 8.3).

While the magnitude of the irregular temperature fluctuations is not as striking in these marine climates as it is in the continental interiors, still the passage of cyclones and anticyclones, with the resulting changes in wind direction, is bound to cause some degree of weather variability (Figs. 8.2, 8.4).

Precipitation

Annual Amount. Temperate oceanic climates are humid, and they usually have adequate precipitation in all seasons (Fig. 8.1). The total varies greatly from region to region, however, depending upon the amount of surface relief. Where lowlands prevail, as they do in western Europe, rainfall is only moderate (usually 20 to 35 in. per year), but the

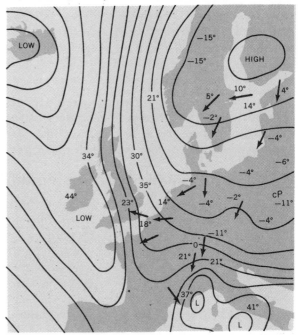

Figure 8.3 Weather controls favoring unseasonably low winter temperatures in western Europe. A cold anticyclone to the north and east is delivering cold *cP* air to the regions west and south of its center. Temperatures shown are the night minima. *(After Kendrew.)*

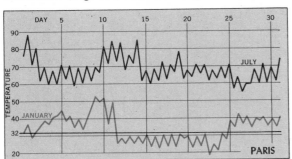

Figure 8.2 A marine-climate station in western Europe inland from the coast. Nonperiodic air-mass control of temperature is conspicuous.

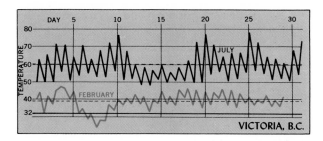

Figure 8.4 A marine station on the Pacific coast of Canada. Note the small diurnal range, especially in winter, when cloudy skies prevail. Dotted lines represent the two monthly averages.

humid marine climate extends well inland. Where there are highland barriers, as in Chile and western North America, precipitation is excessive on the windward slopes, but dry climates prevail to the east of the mountains. The evaporation rate is relatively low, so that small totals of precipitation are highly effective.

Snow is more common than in the subtropical climates, but in lowlands it ordinarily lies on the ground for only 10 to 15 days during the year. In highlands, however, snowfall is heavy, and a deep snow cover persists for several months. In the past, mountain snowfields have created numerous valley glaciers, whose erosive action has formed the irregular fiorded coasts of Norway, southern Chile, and British Columbia.

Seasonal Distribution. Sufficient precipitation at all seasons and no marked period of drought are typical of temperate oceanic climate (Fig. 8.1). Thus normally there is no dormant season imposed upon vegetation because of a rainfall deficiency; the winter period of dormancy is due entirely to low temperature. Both in the locations closest to the ocean and in the areas lying nearest to the dry-summer type, winters commonly are somewhat rainier than summers, even though there are only a few places—parts of Washington and Oregon, for example—that have one or more summer months which are really dry.

Origin. Over lowlands, where orographic effects are

absent, the precipitation is chiefly frontal, or cyclonic, in origin. While much of it falls as long-continued steady but light rain from a gray overcast (Fig. 8.5), some is in the form of showers which originate in fresh *mP* air made unstable by turbulence over the land. Because of the general lack of high temperatures, temperate oceanic regions have few thunderstorms.

Although the total amount of precipitation on lowlands is modest, the number of rain-days is unusually high. Thus the frequent rains are light to moderate ones. For example, while Paris receives only about 23 in. of precipitation a year, this amount is spread over 188 days.

This oceanic climate is one of the earth's most cloudy types. Dark, gloomy, overcast weather

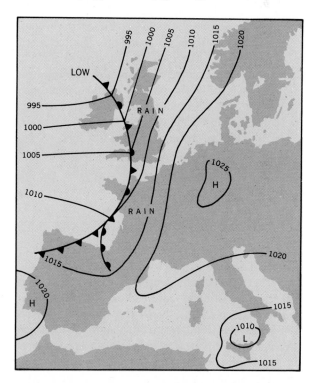

Figure 8.5 A strongly occluded storm in western Europe, producing light but steady and widespread rainfall, a low cloud ceiling, and low visibility. Most of the cyclones that affect western Europe are in an advanced stage of occlusion. Over lowlands, such storms tend to produce much cloud but only a modest amount of precipitation.

is very common. Over extensive areas in western Europe, average cloudiness is greater than 70 percent, the sun sometimes remaining hidden for several weeks in succession, especially in winter and fall.

Seasonal Weather

Cyclonic storms are numerous, so that the non-periodic weather element dominates temperate oceanic climate (Fig. 8.2). *Fall* and *winter,* in spite of mild temperatures, are stormy seasons with frequent periods of gloomy, dripping cyclonic weather (Fig. 8.5). Spells of bright, crisp anticyclonic weather associated with *cP* air masses are the exception, but when they do occur this climate is likely to have its most severe freezes.

As *spring* advances, cyclones become fewer and sunshine more abundant. The air is still cool, but the sun is strong; thus in western Europe, late spring is acclaimed the most delightful season. *Summer* temperatures bring a sense of physical well-being, and where sunny days are numerous, as in the American Pacific Northwest, a more pleasant summer climate would be hard to find. When cloudy, rainy days do occur in summer, however, they may be unpleasantly chilly.

Resource Potentialities of the Temperate Oceanic Realm

Two of the most significant climatic elements affecting the potential productivity of the marine realm are (1) its unusually long frost-free season, considering its latitude, and (2) its relatively mild winters. To be sure, there is a marked dormant season imposed by frost, so that most of the sensitive and of out-of-season crops which are grown in parts of the subtropics are largely excluded from this realm. Still, the frost-free period of 6 to 8 months and the relatively mild winters permit fall sowing of many cereal crops, and animals can graze out-of-doors nearly 12 months, if not the entire year. Storage of animal feed for winter use is therefore not a large-scale operation, as it is in the more severe continental climates.

Somewhat offsetting the advantages of the mild winters and the long frost-free season in this oceanic climate is the deficiency of summer heat. While warm-month temperatures of 60 to 65° are ideal for human comfort, and may represent the optimum conditions for physical activity as well, they are not the best conditions for a crop such as corn. On the other hand, the climate is almost perfect for grass, so that pastures are usually excellent and hay and forage crops thrive.

The adequate amount of annual rainfall and the fact that there is usually no season of marked drought are climatic assets of the first magnitude for crop growth generally. Another asset is the dependability of the precipitation year in and year out, a feature which is reflected in uniformly high crop yields.

In these mild west-coast regions the original vegetation cover was chiefly forest, both broad-leaf deciduous and needle-leaf types. These forests have largely been removed from the lowlands, but they still cover extensive areas in some highlands. The earth's finest coniferous forest is located in the North American sector. While the podzolic soils of this humid climate are leached and only moderately fertile, they are suitable for a wide variety of crops. However, under constant cultivation they deteriorate rapidly unless given proper care.

This is the first of the climatic realms discussed here where surface and drainage features resulting from glaciation are at all prominent. Except on the European lowlands, the glacial features affecting temperate oceanic regions were produced chiefly by mountain or valley glaciers. Where highlands closely approach the sea (as they do in the higher latitudes of Pacific North America, Norway, Scotland, southern Chile, and the southern island of New Zealand) the heavy snowfall has been conducive to the development of valley glaciers. These have created fiorded coast lines, ragged in outline, with many long, narrow, and steep-walled arms of the sea as well as innumerable islands.

In western Europe, extensive continental glaciers once covered most of the area south to about the Elbe River in Germany and all but the southernmost parts of England and Ireland. On the highlands, commonly of resistant crystalline rock, ice scouring removed the weathered rock and soil, grooved and polished the bedrock, and gouged out many lake basins. On the lowlands, composed of less resistant rocks, features associated with ice deposition are conspicuous. Among these are numerous lakes and swamps.

Temperate Continental Climate (Dc)

Location

Scarcely "temperate" in the sense of lacking extreme seasonal temperatures, this fairly severe climate is nevertheless found in some of the earth's most prosperous and well-developed regions in both Anglo-America and Eurasia. In this respect it is unlike the other continental climate, the much more severe boreal type located farther poleward, in which population is very sparse. Since the temperate continental type is a land-controlled climate and consequently a product of broad continents in middle latitudes, it does not occur in the Southern Hemisphere. This thermally severe climate type is generated only in Eurasia and North America.

Temperate continental climate, as might be expected, has an interior and lee (east) location in both North America and Eurasia. Its latitudinal spread is some 10 to 20°, extending from about 35 or 40° on the south to 50 or 60° on the north (Fig. 6.2, Plate 2). But there are differences in location on the two continents. In Eurasia, where lack of mountain barriers on the west side allows oceanic air to enter the continent freely, this climate is positioned both to the west and to the east of the dry interior. In North America, however, it lies only to the east of the dry climates (Plate 2). In both eastern Asia and eastern North America, temperate continental climate is bordered by boreal climates on the north and subtropical humid ones on the south. But in Europe and western Asia, it meets Mediterranean and dry climates on its southern margins.

It may seem somewhat surprising that this land-controlled climate should extend eastward to the ocean margins in both Asia and North America.

But remember that the prevailing west-to-east atmospheric circulation in these latitudes makes deep and persistent entrance of maritime air on the lee, or east, side unlikely.

Temperature

Seasonal temperatures are relatively severe; winters are cold and summers warm to hot (Figs. 8.6 to 8.9). Depending largely on latitudinal location, the average July temperature may vary from 75° or even more (in the south) to 65° (in the north). The January average shows a much greater variation: from zero or below in the north to 25° or above in the south. As a consequence, the annual range of temperature is large everywhere, and it increases both from south to north and from the coast toward the interior. At Peoria, Illinois (41°N), for example, the January and July averages are 24 and

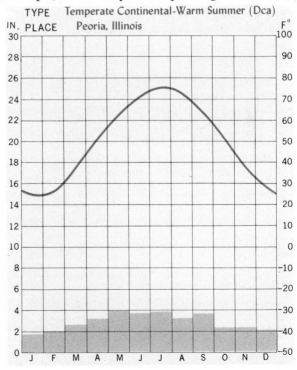

Figure 8.6   A station representing the warm-summer subtype of temperate continental climate. The large annual range of temperature and the rainfall maximum in the warm season are characteristic.

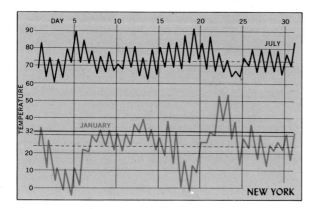

Figure 8.7   Daily maximum and minimum temperatures for the extreme months at a station with temperate continental climate, warm-summer. Nonperiodic air-mass control is conspicuous, especially in winter.

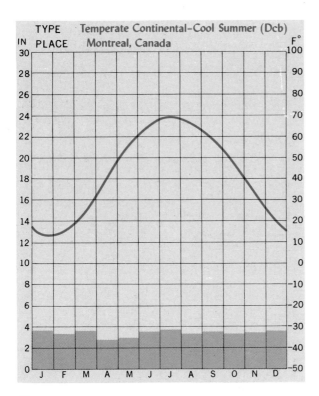

Figure 8.8   Temperature and rainfall conditions at a station with temperate continental climate, cool-summer. Note the large annual range of temperature. At this station there is no seasonal concentration of precipitation, a feature characteristic of the northeastern United States and adjacent parts of Canada, where winter cyclones are numerous.

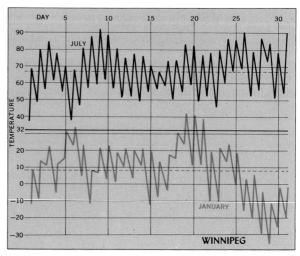

Figure 8.9   Temperate continental climate, cool-summer. Note the very large and irregular temperature changes, evidence of strong air-mass control associated with cyclones and anticyclones.

75°, giving an annual range of about 50°. But at Winnipeg, Canada (about 50°N), the comparable figures are −4° and 66° and the range is 70°. Similarly, New York City on the Atlantic Coast has a range of 42°, while Omaha, Nebraska, at a comparable latitude but inland, records 55°.

The length of the frost-free season likewise changes from south to north, approaching 200 days on the southern margins and declining to about 100 days on the subarctic side. This feature creates large latitudinal contrasts in agricultural land use.

Average temperatures in winter and summer are not only extreme but also variable from one year to another. In marine climates one winter is apt to be much like another, but continental climates show wide departures from their normal seasonal temperatures. Average winter temperatures are distinctly lowered by the snow cover in the continental, boreal, polar, and highland climates; indeed, only in these climates does the snow cover last long enough to have a marked influence upon winter temperature.

Seasonal Gradients.   In continental climates there are great differences between summer and winter in the rate of change in temperature in a north-south direction (Fig. 8.10). This reflects the similar seasonal gradients in solar radiation (Fig. 2.4c, d). In winter the isotherms are much more closely spaced than in summer; in the central and eastern United States, for instance, the temperature gradient is two to three times as steep in January as in July. Thus sudden and marked temperature changes associated with shifts in wind direction are much more likely in winter than in summer (Fig. 8.7).

Temperature Subtypes of Continental Climate

Temperate continental climates may be divided into two subtypes: a more moderate one with warm-to-hot summers and cool winters (*Dca*), and a more severe one (*Dcb*) located poleward, which has less hot summers and more rigorous winters (Figs. 8.6, 8.7, and 8.8, 8.9). A suggested boundary separating the two is the isotherm of 72° for the warmest month. In the warmer subdivision the frost-free, or growing, season is about 5 or 6 months, and in the colder one only 3 to 5 months. The snow cover is deeper and lasts longer in the more northerly subtype. (See climatic data for stations representing each subtype.)

Precipitation

Annual Amount. Moderate amounts of annual rainfall (20 or 25 in. to 40+ in.) concentrated in summer are the rule. Although this is a humid climate, there are larger areas where annual precipitation is too little than where it is too much. This is to be expected of land-controlled climates whose winters are cold, because of both the distance from the ocean and the lower humidity content of the cold winter air.

 Rainfall decreases from the seaward margins toward the interiors, and usually toward higher latitudes as well. The interior parts are definitely subhumid.

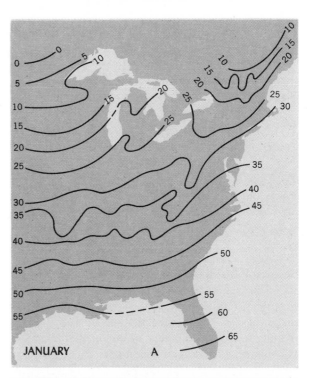

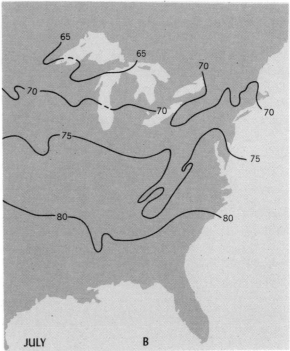

Figure 8.10 Isotherms for the extreme months. Surface-temperature gradients in the temperate continental climates of the central and eastern United States are much steeper in winter than in summer.

CLIMATIC DATA FOR REPRESENTATIVE STATIONS IN THE TEMPERATE CONTINENTAL WARM-SUMMER SUBTYPE *(Dca)*

Peoria, Illinois

	J	F	M	A	M	J	J	A	S	O	N	D	Yr	Range
Temp., °F	24	28	40	51	62	71	75	73	65	53	39	28	51	52
Precip., in.	1.8	2.0	2.7	3.3	3.9	3.8	3.8	3.2	3.8	2.4	2.4	2.0	34.9	

New York City

	J	F	M	A	M	J	J	A	S	O	N	D	Yr	Range
Temp., °F	31	31	39	49	60	69	74	72	67	56	44	34	52	43
Precip., in.	3.3	3.3	3.4	3.3	3.4	3.4	4.1	4.3	3.4	3.4	3.4	3.3	42.0	

Bucharest, Rumania

	J	F	M	A	M	J	J	A	S	O	N	D	Yr	Range
Temp., °F	26	29	40	52	61	68	73	71	64	54	41	30	51	48
Precip., in.	1.2	1.1	1.7	2.0	2.5	3.3	2.8	1.9	1.5	1.5	1.9	1.7	23.0	

Mukden, China

	J	F	M	A	M	J	J	A	S	O	N	D	Yr	Range
Temp., °F	8	14	30	47	60	71	77	75	61	48	29	14	44	69
Precip., in.	0.2	0.3	0.8	1.1	2.2	3.4	6.3	6.1	3.3	1.6	1.0	0.2	26.5	

Seasonal Distribution. Although there is precipitation in winter, summer is normally the season of maximum rainfall (Fig. 8.6). This concentration of much of the year's precipitation in the warmer months is another hallmark of continental climates. It is the result of several conditions: (1) Low temperatures make the specific humidity, or reservoir of water vapor in the atmosphere, much lower during the winter than it is in the warm-to-hot summers. (2) During winter the settling air in the continental seasonal anticyclone is also conducive to low specific humidity. This same settling and divergence make for temperature inversions and increased stability of the atmosphere. (3) Convection is at a minimum during the winter months, for at that season the cold snow surface tends to increase the stability of air masses. In summer, on the other hand, the warm land surface has a tendency to make the air masses moving over it unstable. (4) Because of the seasonal extremes of temperatures and hence of pressure, a tendency toward a monsoon system of winds develops. This leads to an outflow of dry, cold *cP* air in winter, and to an inflow of tropical maritime (*mT*) air with high rainfall potentialities in summer.

Typically the summer maximum is greatest in two locations: within the deep continental interiors, and in regions where a monsoon circulation is strong, as in eastern Asia. In the subhumid interior locations the time of maximum rainfall is often

CLIMATIC DATA FOR REPRESENTATIVE STATIONS IN THE TEMPERATE CONTINENTAL COOL-SUMMER SUBTYPE *(Dcb)*

Madison, Wisconsin (Marginal in location)

	J	F	M	A	M	J	J	A	S	O	N	D	Yr	Range
Temp., °F	17	20	31	46	58	67	72	70	62	50	35	23	46	55
Precip., in.	1.2	1.3	1.9	2.6	2.7	3.4	3.5	3.3	4.1	2.3	2.0	1.4	30.6	

Montreal, Canada

	J	F	M	A	M	J	J	A	S	O	N	D	Yr	Range
Temp., °F	13	15	25	41	55	65	69	67	59	47	33	19	42	56
Precip., in.	3.7	3.2	3.7	2.4	3.1	3.5	3.8	3.4	3.5	3.3	3.4	3.7	41	

Moscow, U.S.S.R.

	J	F	M	A	M	J	J	A	S	O	N	D	Yr	Range
Temp., °F	12	15	23	38	53	62	66	63	52	40	28	17	39	54
Precip., in.	1.1	1.0	1.2	1.5	1.9	2.0	2.8	2.9	2.2	1.4	1.6	1.5	21.1	

Harbin, China (Marginal in location)

	J	F	M	A	M	J	J	A	S	O	N	D	Yr	Range
Temp., °F	−2	5	24	42	56	66	72	69	58	40	21	3	38	74
Precip., in.	0.1	0.2	0.4	0.9	1.7	3.8	4.5	4.1	1.8	1.3	0.3	0.2	19.3	

shifted to early summer, so that June becomes the wettest month. The summer maximum makes these severe climates with their short frost-free season much more productive than they would be otherwise, because in their case it is essential for crops that rainfall be concentrated in the warm growing season.

But in spite of a prevalent summer rainfall maximum, over extensive areas evaporation exceeds precipitation during the warmest months. As a result, a deficiency of water commonly occurs at the peak of the growing season. This may be reflected in seared pastures and lawns, and occasionally in stunted crops.

Winter precipitation is largely frontal or cyclonic in origin. In North America, *mT* Gulf air masses move poleward up the Mississippi River Valley with no mountains to interfere. These air masses are drawn into frequent passing cyclonic storms, so that they come into conflict with cold polar air masses and are forced to ascend over them. Widespread frontal precipitation results. Thus the North American continental climate has a moderate amount of winter precipitation. This amount increases eastward, until along the Atlantic seaboard winter is equally as wet as summer (Fig. 8.8). In northeastern Asia, where the outward-flowing winter monsoon is stronger, *mT* air is unable to advance far poleward, so that winter precipitation in northern China and Manchuria is very meager. For example, Peking, which receives 25 in. a year, has 9.4 in. in July and only 0.1 in. in January (see climatic data for Mukden).

A portion of this climate's winter precipitation is in the form of snow, and a permanent snow cover, varying from a few weeks to several months in duration, is typical (Fig. 8.11). In those parts of the northeastern United States and southeastern Canada where winter cyclones are particularly numerous and well developed—the Great Lakes region, the St. Lawrence River Valley, northern New England, and the Canadian Maritime Provinces—snow becomes very deep. Northern New England and northern New York have more than 7 ft of snowfall during an average winter, and snow remains on the ground for more than 4 months.

More of the *summer* rainfall is in the form

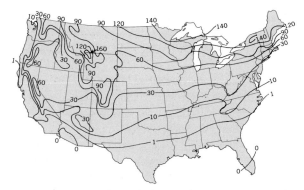

Figure 8.11   Number of days with snow cover in the United States.

of convective showers and thunderstorms. This is because the warm, humid summer air has been made buoyant and unstable by heating from below as it travels over a warm land surface. Of the summer rainfall at Madison, Wisconsin, 75 to 90 percent occurs in thunderstorms. Preponderantly these showers are connected with some form of extensive atmospheric disturbance and so are organized in their distribution. Such showery rainfall is local in character and fickle in occurrence.

Seasonal Weather

Nonperiodic Weather Changes. In no other type of climate are rapid nonperiodic weather changes so pronounced as in the temperate continental, for it is in these regions that the conflict between polar and tropical air masses reaches a maximum. The cold season, when the sun, and with it the storm belt, has retreated farthest south, is the time when the continental climates have the strongest nonperiodic control of weather. At that season diurnal sun control is usually subordinate. Weather conditions are dominated by moving cyclones and anticyclones associated with rapidly shifting polar and tropical air masses, as well as by the fronts that develop along their boundaries. Many times the daily rise and fall of temperature with the sun is obscured by the larger nonperiodic oscillations caused by invasions of polar and tropical air masses (Figs. 8.7, 8.9). The central and eastern United States, since it is freely open to the movements of air masses from both north and south, is a region of unusual storminess. Storm control is less marked in eastern Asia. In summer, air masses are more stagnant, fronts are fewer, and the weather is more regular and sun-controlled.

Special Seasonal Weather Types. The normal cycle of weather changes which take place with the passage of a well-developed cyclone, followed by an anticyclone, was described in Chap. 5. In reality, however, there is an almost infinite variety of possible weather changes, depending upon the season, the size and intensity of the atmospheric disturbance, the nature of the air masses involved in the storm, the track it follows, and the patterns of the above-surface atmospheric circulation. As a consequence, no satisfactory classification of weather types has ever been developed. Nevertheless, everyone is familiar with some weather types which are sufficiently distinctive, and so frequently repeated, that they have been given names: warm wave, cold wave, Indian summer, blizzard, and January thaw are illustrations. But the less distinctive unnamed ones are much more numerous. No real comprehension of temperate continental climates is possible without an appreciation of this variety of weather types which in combination produce the seasons. It requires a study of the daily weather map, or synoptic chart, together with a firsthand observation of weather conditions. A few weather types characteristic of continental climates are illustrated in Figs. 8.12 to 8.15. These are worth careful study.

Winter, the season of maximum temperature gradients and strongest air-mass contrasts, is the period of greatest weather variety. A well-developed anticyclone arriving from arctic Canada as a mass of fresh *cP* air may produce bitterly cold weather with subzero temperatures (Fig. 5.11). This sharp drop in temperature brought by the northwest wind is the well-known *cold wave.* If the cold anticyclone has unusually steep pressure gradients, blizzard-like conditions with violent winds may usher it in. But if it is composed of modified *mP* air from west of the Rocky Mountains, skies will be clear and temperatures only moderately low. This kind of anticyclone produces some of the finest winter weather. A deep cyclonic storm,

especially if it originates in the Texas area and takes a route northeastward across the country, will probably bring widespread heavy snowfall to the humid continental climates of the Mississippi Valley and the East (Fig. 8.12). If a vigorous cyclone travels a more northerly route, the weather is milder and the rain area is more extensive. Or a weak low following a route to the north of the Great Lakes may give generally gray overcast weather, but only modest amounts of rain or snow (Fig. 8.13). These are only a few of the huge number of weather types which combine to produce the winters of humid continental climates.

In *summer,* temperature gradients are weaker, air-mass contrasts are less striking, and altogether the weather element as controlled by passing atmospheric disturbances is less well developed. But while sun control and diurnal regularity are relatively stronger than at other seasons, nonperiodic weather irregularities do occur. A somewhat stagnant warm anticyclone to the south and east may envelop the temperate continental area of the United States in a prolonged *heat wave,* bringing

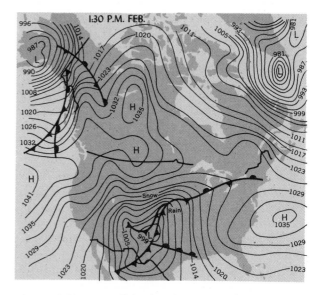

Figure 8.12 A well-developed winter (February) storm originating in the Texas area and moving northeastward across the United States. Such storms are likely to bring heavy precipitation, much of it in the form of snow on the northern side of the storm.

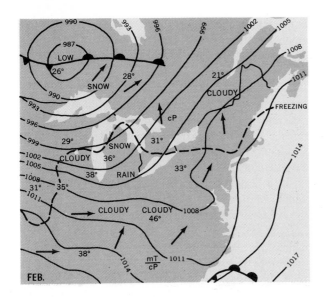

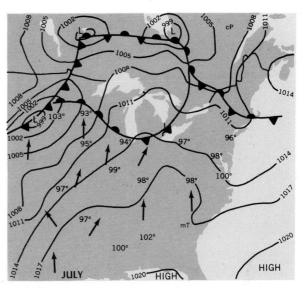

Figures 8.13   A common winter weather type: A February cyclone traveling on a northern track is producing cloudy, mild weather and light precipitation over extensive areas of the northern central United States. Temperatures shown are for 1:30 A.M.

Figure 8.14   A summer weather type in the form of a July heat wave over the central and eastern parts of the country. Temperatures shown are the maxima for the 12 hr preceding. Tropical air from the warm anticyclone over the Gulf of Mexico and western Caribbean controls the weather.

a succession of days when the daily maximum temperature is between 90 and 100° (Fig. 8.14). Such a heat wave may be suddenly ended by the arrival of a V-shaped cyclonic storm with a well-developed cold front and severe thunderstorms (Fig. 5.8*b*). Following the passage of the cold front with its strong convectional activity, there may be several days of delightfully cool weather because an anticyclone with polar air dominates the weather.

In *spring and fall,* the transition seasons, there is a more even struggle between storm and sun control. One and then the other takes over, so that summer and winter conditions tend to alternate. Mild, warm days in April and early May, with a regular diurnal rise and fall of the thermometer resembling summer, may be followed by winter conditions as a passing cyclone lays down a snow cover and the following *cP* invasion drops the temperatures to an unseasonable freeze (Fig. 8.15).

Autumn brings some of the loveliest days of the year, but likewise some of the rawest and gloomiest. Bright, clear weather, with warm midday temperatures and crisp, frosty nights, comes with

anticyclonic control. In October and November, after a severe frost and perhaps even a snowfall, a hot-wave type of gradient (Fig. 5.12) may be reestablished, leading to a temporary return of near summer conditions. The result is those much-cherished spells of warm weather with hazy, smoky atmosphere, known as Indian summer. But at this season well-developed cyclonic storms may also bring raw, gray days with chilly rain, and occasionally a temporary snowy winter landscape may be seen as early as October.

Resource Potentialities of the Temperate Continental Realm

Since this is one of the greatest producing realms of the earth, natural assets of a high order must be present. Climatically, however, it is less bountiful than the humid subtropics, chiefly because of the shorter growing season, but also because of a greater overall deficiency of heat. This tends to exclude many of the more sensitive crops, as well as those requiring a long period between frosts. As a result,

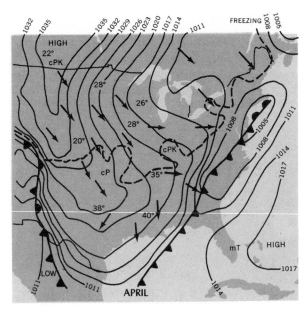

Figure 8.15 A spring weather type. Here a cold anticyclone advancing southward as a mass of cold *cP* air with northwest winds carries low temperatures deep into the subtropics and results in a severe spring (April) freeze in the north central states. Temperatures shown are for 1:30 A.M.

farmers in this climate place greater dependence upon quick-maturing annuals. Compared with the subtropics, there is also a shorter period during which livestock can forage for their food, and a much longer one during which they must be protected against cold and given feeds that have been stored in barns and granaries.

A further climatic handicap is that extensive areas have rainfall which is only modest in amount and which tends to be undependable. Relatively wide fluctuations in crop yields from year to year reflect these disadvantages. A factor which somewhat compensates for the modest and variable precipitation is that it is concentrated in the warm growing season.

Forests in the more humid portions and tall-grass prairie in the subhumid interiors—this is the pattern of native vegetation within temperate continental climates. In their virgin state, the prairies provided some of the finest natural grazing land on earth. Almost all the prairie has long since

come under cultivation, however, for it constitutes some of the world's best agricultural land. The original forests of the more humid regions were of different types: a representative north-south cross section would show conifers predominating toward the northern margins of the realm, with mixed forests and purer stands of deciduous broadleaf trees farther south. The virgin forests of the temperate continental realm were among the finest and most extensive of the earth.

Soils in the humid continental realm vary widely, depending upon the nature of the climate, the original vegetation, and the recency of glaciation. Moderately fertile soils (*podzolic* types) which are characteristic of areas with mixed or deciduous forests, represent the best of the forest soils. On the cooler poleward margins of the humid continental realm, where needle trees tend to replace the broadleaf varieties, the soils are inferior, for here they are more strongly leached of mineral plant foods and have a much lower humus content. On the other hand, some of the earth's superior soils are found in the subhumid sections of the realm where prairie grasses used to predominate. The lower rainfall results in less leaching, and the grasses provide an abundance of organic matter, so that the soils are high in soluble minerals and dark in color. Such excellent soils partly compensate for the less abundant and less reliable rainfall.

Considerable areas in both the North American and European sectors of the temperate continental realm have been subjected to recent glaciation by continental ice sheets. Where the irregularities of the land surface are relatively great or the bedrock is resistant—as, for example, in New England, northern New York State, and parts of Sweden and Finland—ice erosion has been dominant, so that soils are often thin and stony and lakes are numerous. In other regions where ice deposition prevailed, the drainage lines have been disrupted, creating many lakes and swamps and a rolling and somewhat patternless terrain of rounded hills and associated depressions. There the soils are usually deep, but they vary greatly in composition and quality.

9

The Boreal (*E*), Polar (*F*), and Highland Climates

Boreal (Subarctic) Climate (*E*)

Location

This group of climates has much in common with the temperate continental, except that it is located farther poleward and is distinctly more severe. In fact, it is so severe that over most of the very large area which has a boreal climate, general cereal agriculture is impossible, and population is sparse or even absent.

Boreal, or subarctic, climate is to be found only in the higher middle latitudes (50 to 55 or 65°) of the great Northern Hemisphere continents (Fig. 6.2, Plate 2). On its poleward side it usually borders on tundra, one of the polar climates. This northern boundary is approximately the northern limit of forests. On its southern margin, boreal climate usually adjoins continental climates or, in some locations, dry climates.

Temperature

Long and bitterly cold winters, very short summers, brief falls and springs, and unusually large annual ranges—these are the main temperature characteristics of boreal climate (Fig. 9.1). Thus the boreal group represents land-controlled climate at its maximum development (Fig. 9.2).

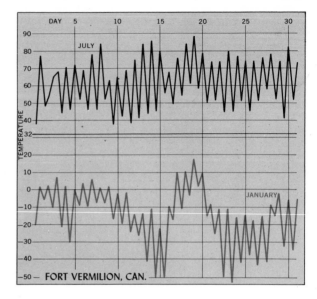

Figure 9.2 A boreal station in Canada. Note the unusually strong nonperiodic air-mass control of temperature changes in winter. Summer shows greater diurnal regularity.

By reason of both its length and its severity, *winter* dominates the climatic calendar. Frosts may arrive in late August, and ice begins to form on ponds in September. At Yakutsk, Siberia, the average monthly temperature drops 37° (from 16 to −21°) between October and November. Within an extensive area in northeastern Siberia, near the center of the great thermal winter anticyclone, the average January temperature is below −50°, and January temperatures of −76° and lower have been recorded. At Oimyakon, Siberia, the cold pole or region of lowest minimum temperatures, the thermometer has fallen as low as 95° below zero. However, these are the extremes in subarctic winters; over most of the North American and European sectors, average January temperatures of zero to −15° are the rule. It is common, however, for the average temperatures of 6 or 7 months to be below freezing and for averages of 2 to 3 months to be below zero. The low temperatures, combined with the long daily period of darkness (which is obviously partly responsible for them), make the winter weather depressing and hard to bear. Because of the excessive and long-continued cold,

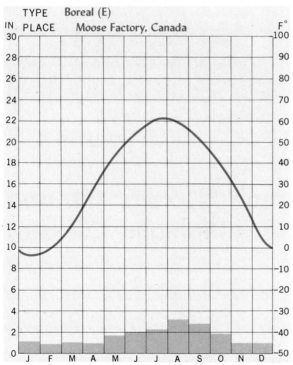

Figure 9.1 Cool summers, severe winters, large annual ranges of temperature, and modest precipitation, usually concentrated in summer, are characteristic of boreal (subarctic) climate.

large areas of the boreal realm are permanently frozen down to great depths (Fig. 9.3).

Spring, like autumn, is very short indeed. At Yakutsk the mean temperature rises 25° between April and May, and 18° between May and June.

The most striking characteristic of *summer* in the subarctic is not so much coolness but brevity.

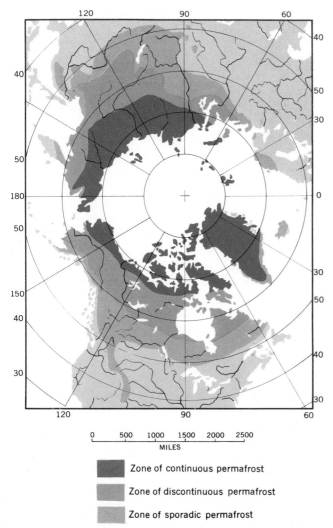

120   90   60

40

40   50

30

50

180   0

50

30

150   50

40   40

30

30

120   90   60

0   500   1000   1500   2000   2500
MILES

Zone of continuous permafrost

Zone of discontinuous permafrost

Zone of sporadic permafrost

Figure 9.3 Distribution of permafrost in the Northern Hemisphere. *(After Black.)*

Typically the warmest month, July, has an average temperature in the 60s, which is no lower than that of many stations in temperate oceanic climates farther south. Moreover, it is not uncommon for midday temperatures to reach 80° and above (Fig. 9.2). But July's modest warmth is fleeting, for June and August averages are between 50 and 60°, and May and September are in the 40s. As a rule the average period between killing frosts is only 50 to 80 days, and many stations occasionally have freezing temperatures even in July and August. Average temperatures of 50° or above occur only during a period ranging from 1 to 3 months.

Somewhat compensating for the briefness and coolness of summer is the unusually long period of daylight in these higher latitudes. Thus at 60°N, June days have an average 18.8 hr of possible sunshine.

Precipitation

Precipitation in the boreal realm is meager—most of it under 20 in., and large parts under 15 in. These low figures are related to low temperatures and associated low specific humidity, the well-developed winter anticyclone with its settling air and diverging wind systems, and the great breadth of the land masses in the subarctic latitudes. In lower latitudes, areas with less than 20 in. of precipitation would be classed as semiarid. But where there are such low temperatures, and therefore low evaporation rates, and where the ground is frozen so much of the year, this amount of precipitation is sufficient for a humid climate and for forest growth.

The year's precipitation is concentrated in the warmer months, when the specific humidity of the air is highest and atmospheric stability is least (Fig. 9.1). The especially low winter temperatures and the strong winter anticyclone mentioned above both operate to inhibit the processes making for precipitation in that season. Winters are especially dry over east-central Siberia: the three midwinter months have less than 10 percent of the annual precipitation, while the three summer months account for about 60 percent. The meager winter

CLIMATIC DATA FOR REPRESENTATIVE BOREAL STATIONS

Fort Vermilion, Alberta, Canada (58°27′N)

	J	F	M	A	M	J	J	A	S	O	N	D	Yr	Range
Temp., °F	−14	−6	8	30	47	55	60	57	46	32	10	−4	27	74
Precip., in.	0.6	0.3	0.5	0.7	1.0	1.9	2.1	2.1	1.4	0.7	0.5	0.4	12.3	

Moose Factory, Canada (51°16′N)

	J	F	M	A	M	J	J	A	S	O	N	D	Yr	Range
Temp., °F	−4	−2	10	28	42	54	61	59	51	39	22	5	30	66
Precip., in.	1.3	0.9	1.1	1.0	1.8	2.2	2.4	3.3	2.9	1.8	1.1	1.1	21.0	

Yakutsk, Siberia, U.S.S.R. (62°13′N)

	J	F	M	A	M	J	J	A	S	O	N	D	Yr	Range
Temp., °F	−46	−35	−10	16	41	59	66	60	42	16	−21	−41	12	112
Precip., in.	0.9	0.2	0.4	0.6	1.1	2.1	1.7	2.6	1.2	1.4	0.6	0.9	13.7	

precipitation in boreal regions is in the form of dry, hard snow, which produces a snow cover of variable depth that persists for as many as 7 months.

Almost all boreal precipitation on lowlands originates in cyclonic storms. Thunderstorms are rare. There are enough disturbances at all seasons to cause marked nonperiodic weather changes, even though winter has much settled anticyclonic weather (Fig. 9.2).

Resource Potentialities of the Boreal Realm

This is one of the most extensive of the earth's geographic realms, but it is also one of the least productive and populated. In subarctic regions the extractive industries—those based on extracting natural resources, such as hunting, fishing, mining, and logging—are unusually important, but these are capable of supporting only a meager population. The landscape therefore is composed predominantly of natural features: man has left only a faint imprint.

The boreal realm is fundamentally handicapped by a niggardly climate, whose brief cool summers set very definite and very low limits upon agriculture. At present commercially successful farming is not likely in regions where the frost-free season is less than 80 or 90 days, as it is in all except the most southerly portions of the subarctic.

Subarctic Eurasia and North America are covered by what is largely a virgin coniferous forest. Conifers usually occupy about 75 percent of the forest area; such deciduous trees as birch, poplar, willow, and alder take up most of the rest. The forest is not impressive, either in the size of the trees or in the density of the stand, so that it does not represent nearly so great a potential supply of forest products as its area might seem to indicate. Most subarctic timber is probably more valuable for pulpwood and firewood than for good lumber. Moreover, the inaccessibility of these northern forests and their great distance away from world markets considerably reduce their resource value.

In addition to the rigorous climate, the soils of boreal regions are impoverished—a combination which presents almost insurmountable difficulties to the farmer. The needles from the coniferous forest provide little organic material for the soil, while the groundwater, which is high in organic acids derived from the carpet of half-decayed needles, causes an excessive leaching of soil minerals.

After climate and soils, the third handicap to agricultural settlement within the subarctic realm is deficient drainage. This prevalence of poorly drained land is partly the result of permanently frozen subsoil and rock, a condition called *permafrost,* which exists in continuous or discontinuous form throughout much of the boreal and tundra area in North America and northern and eastern Siberia (Fig. 9.3). Summer thaw penetrates only 2 to 14 ft. Most of subarctic North America, and Scandinavia, Finland, and western Soviet Russia, have an abundance of lakes and swamps, which is a consequence of continental glaciation.

Polar Climates (F)

Just as the tropics lack a cool season, so the polar regions lack a period of warmth. It is the prevalence of monotonous heat that typifies the low latitudes. In the high latitudes, monotonous cold is the distinctive feature, and the greatest handicap.

Location

Polar climates are confined to the high latitudes of the earth, largely poleward of latitude 60°. The poleward limit of forest growth is commonly accepted as the equatorward boundary of polar climates. Over the great continents, this vegetation boundary coincides approximately with the 50° isotherm for the warmest month. Here during much of the winter the sun is constantly below the horizon, so that darkness prevails and cold is intense. Moreover, while in summer the sun may never set, it is never far above the horizon, and its oblique rays deliver little energy at the earth's surface.

In the Southern Hemisphere, the only extensive nonoceanic area with polar climates is the Antarctic Continent, the approximate center of which is at the South Pole. Since the Arctic is almost a landlocked sea, except for the frozen ocean, the polar climates there are confined to the northern borders of Eurasia and North America and to the island continent of Greenland.

Polar climates may be subdivided into two types, with the *warmest-month* isotherm of 32° serving as the boundary between them. (1) Where the average temperatures of all months are below freezing, the growth of vegetation is impossible, and a permanent snow-and-ice cover prevails. These are the *ice cap* climates. (2) Where one or more of the warm-season months has an average temperature above 32° (but not over 50°), so that the ground is free from snow for a short period and a meager and primitive vegetation cover is possible, the climate is designated as *tundra*.

Tundra Climate (Ft)

Tundra climate on land areas is almost exclusively limited to the Northern Hemisphere; in the Southern Hemisphere, oceans prevail in latitudes where this climate normally would develop. The most extensive tundra areas include most of North America's Arctic Archipelago, the coastal borders of Greenland, and the parts of both Eurasia and North America which rim the Arctic Ocean. (Fig. 6.2, Plate 2).

Temperature

A long cold winter and a very short cool summer are the rule in tundra climate (Fig. 9.4). Since the average temperature of the warmest month by definition is between 32 and 50°, even midsummer is raw and chilly, like March and April in southern Wisconsin, or January in the Gulf states. Usually only 2 to 4 months have average temperatures above freezing. At Pond's Inlet, a tundra station at

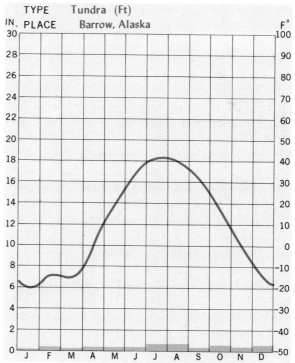

Figure 9.4 A tundra station on the north coast of Alaska. Note the large annual range of temperature, the cool summer, and the meager precipitation.

CLIMATIC DATA FOR REPRESENTATIVE TUNDRA STATIONS

Sagastyr, Siberia, U.S.S.R. (73°N, 124°E)

	J	F	M	A	M	J	J	A	S	O	N	D	Yr	Range
Temp., °F	−34	−36	−30	−7	15	32	41	38	33	6	−16	−28	1	77
Precip., in.	0.1	0.1	0.0	0.0	0.2	0.4	0.3	1.4	0.4	0.1	0.1	0.2	3.3	

Upernivik, western Greenland (73°N, 56°W)

	J	F	M	A	M	J	J	A	S	O	N	D	Yr	Range
Temp., °F	−7	−10	−6	6	25	35	41	41	33	25	14	1	16	61
Precip., in.	0.4	0.4	0.6	0.6	0.6	0.6	1.0	1.1	1.0	1.1	1.1	0.5	9.2	

about 73°N in Canada, the average July temperature is 42°, with the thermometer rising to about 50° at midday and sinking to about 35° at night. Daily ranges in tundra areas are small in both summer and winter. Killing frosts may occur at any time, although it does not freeze on most July nights (Fig. 9.5). The continuous but weak summer sun frees the land of its snow cover for a few months, but the subsoil remains frozen, so that the surface is wet and poorly drained. Tundra vegetation consists of lichens, mosses, sedges, and bushes.

Precipitation

Given the low temperatures of these high latitudes, the modest annual precipitation, usually less than 10 or 12 in., is not surprising. In continental locations the year's precipitation, nearly all of it cyclonic in origin, is concentrated in the warmer

months of the year when the specific humidity of the air is highest (Fig. 9.4). This is less the rule in marine-controlled areas. The meager winter snowfall is dry and powdery, so that the strong winds sweep the level surfaces bare. It has been estimated that 75 to 90 percent of the surface of Arctic tundra lands is nearly free of snow at all seasons.

Ice-cap Climate (Fi)

This least well known among the world's climatic types extends over the great permanent continental ice sheets of Antarctica and Greenland and over the perpetually frozen ocean in the vicinity of the North Pole. Only fragmentary weather data have been obtained from these deserts of snow and ice where no month's average temperature rises above freezing.

Temperature

Since both Antarctica and Greenland are ice plateaus whose higher interior parts have average elevations of over 9,000 ft, any recorded surface-air temperatures for the interiors presumably would be some 30°± higher if reduced to sea level. From the higher parts of both ice plateaus, weak downslope gravity winds drain toward the lower margins. Very strong surface temperature inversions prevail on 80 to 90 percent of the days.

At Eismitte in high interior Greenland, the average coldest-month temperature is about −53° and that of July +12°, providing a range of 65°.

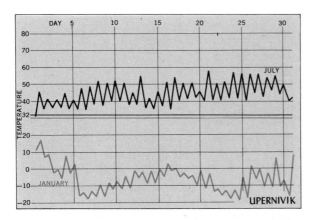

Figure 9.5　Daily maximum and minimum temperatures for the extreme months at a tundra station in Greenland.

CLIMATIC DATA FOR REPRESENTATIVE ICE-CAP STATIONS

Little America, coastal Antarctica (79°S, 164°W)

	J	F	M	A	M	J	J	A	S	O	N	D	Yr	Range
Temp., °F	22	(9)*	(−7)*	−24	−27	−29	−34	−34	−29	−14	9	24	−11.3	58
Precip., in.	No data													

Eismitte, interior Greenland (70°54′N, 40°42′W, 9,941 ft)

	J	F	M	A	M	J	J	A	S	O	N	D	Yr	Range
Temp., °F	−42	−53	−40	−24	−4	4	12	1	−8	−32	−46	−37	−22	65
Precip., in.	No data													

* Estimated.

At the South Pole station in interior Antarctica, average monthly temperatures in 1958 remained below −70° for the 6-month period April to September. The warmest month averaged −10° and the coldest −75° (Fig. 9.6). Certainly these are the lowest summer temperatures on the earth, and the winter temperatures match—or probably are somewhat lower than—those of northeastern Siberia. To be sure, these data for both Greenland and Antarctica reflect conditions in the higher interiors; weather in the lower marginal areas is not so severe (see the data given in the table for Little America). In ice-cap climates, short-time temperature fluctuations do occur. These variations, which reach a maximum in winter, are associated with invasions of low-pressure systems whose clouds reduce the rate of heat loss.

Precipitation

If little is known about the temperatures of ice-cap climates, still less is understood concerning their precipitation. There is no doubt that it is meager, and probably all of it falls in solid form. It is likely

that most of the inland snow originates in the cyclonic storms that move along the margins or penetrate the interior regions of the ice plateaus.

At Eismitte in interior Greenland, 12 in. of snow, or 3 to 4 in. of water, fell in 204 days in one year. At the South Pole station on the ice plateau of Antarctica, a recent year had only 17 days with measurable precipitation, but there were 248 days with some precipitation, even though the amounts were usually too small to measure. The annual fall totaled only 0.48 in. of water equivalent. There were 100 overcast days and 165 that were clear. It is believed that on the average, the whole Antarctic Continent receives less than 4 in. of water equivalent annually. The intensely cold atmosphere and consequent low specific humidity, the extreme stability of the air, and the rarity of upslope winds all act to inhibit precipitation.

Highland Climates

There is no such thing as a highland *type* of climate. Mountain country has an almost endless variety of climates, depending on altitude and on exposure to sun and winds. Thus different altitudes have different climates; valley weather contrasts with that of the exposed peak; windward slopes differ from leeward slopes; and southern exposures are unlike those facing north. And these many kinds of highland climates are multiplied again by differences in latitude and continental location. For in many ways, highland climates are low-temperature

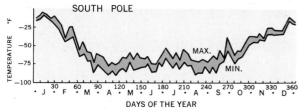

Figure 9.6 Five-day means of maximum and minimum air temperatures at the surface, 1958, South Pole, Antarctica. (*After Sabbagh.*)

variants of climates at low elevations in similar latitudes.

Because this great complexity of climates within highlands would be impossible to illustrate on a small-scale map, they have been grouped together under a single designation on Plate 2. Generally, regions with an elevation below 4,000 or 5,000 ft are not included.

Atmospheric Pressure in Mountains

At low elevations the minor changes in air pressure from day to day, or from season to season, cannot be directly perceived by the human body. But the very rapid decrease in the atmosphere's weight with increasing elevation, and the consequently very low atmospheric pressure that prevails on high mountains and plateaus, cause the pressure element to be genuinely important in highland climates. Physiological effects (faintness, headache, nosebleed, nausea, weakness) of decreased pressure aloft are experienced by most people at altitudes above 12,000 or 15,000 ft. Sleeplessness is common and exertion is difficult.

Solar Energy

Intensity of sunlight increases with elevation in the cleaner, drier, thinner air of mountains. Dust, clouds, and water vapor, the principal scattering, reflecting, and absorbing elements of solar radiation in the atmosphere, are concentrated at lower elevations. On a clear day, probably three-fourths of the solar energy penetrates to 6,000 ft, but only one-half to sea level. This greater intensity of sunlight at high altitudes has an important effect upon soil temperature and, both directly and indirectly, upon plant growth.

Temperature

The most important climatic change resulting from increased elevation is the decrease in air temperature (on the average, about 3.6° per 1,000-ft rise, as stated in Chap. 2), which occurs in spite of the increased intensity of solar energy. Quito, Ecuador, situated on the equator at an elevation of 9,350 ft (see the following table), has an average annual temperature of only 55°, which is about 25° lower than that of the adjacent Amazon lowlands. Because the dry and more dust-free air at Quito is incapable of absorbing much solar or earth radiation, the air remains chilly. Yet for the same reason the sunlight itself is strong, so that the climate is one of cool shade and hot sun. One is never warm except in the sun.

Importance of Vertical Change. The vertical rate of temperature change along mountain slopes is several hundred times greater than the north-south horizontal gradient over continental lowlands. Consequently in the tropics, where lowlands are continuously and oppressively hot, the cooler highlands may become the centers of population concentration. Such is the case in much of tropical Latin America. There is a striking vertical zonation, not only of contrasting climates but also of agricultural and vegetation belts, in tropical highlands (Fig. 9.7). Thus in tropical valleys where there is a luxuriant rainforest, such heat-requiring crops as rubber, bananas, and cacao thrive. Somewhat higher they may give way to an economy based on coffee, tea, maize, and a variety of food crops. On the still higher and cooler slopes, middle-latitude cereals and potatoes become more important, as does animal grazing, the natural pastures for which

CLIMATIC DATA FOR A HIGHLAND STATION IN THE TROPICS

Quito, Ecuador (9,350 ft)

	J	F	M	A	M	J	J	A	S	O	N	D	Yr	Range
Temp., °F	54.5	55.0	54.5	54.5	54.7	55.0	54.9	54.9	55.0	54.7	54.3	54.7	54.7	0.7
Precip., in.	3.2	3.9	4.8	7.0	4.6	1.5	1.1	2.2	2.6	3.9	4.0	3.6	42.2	

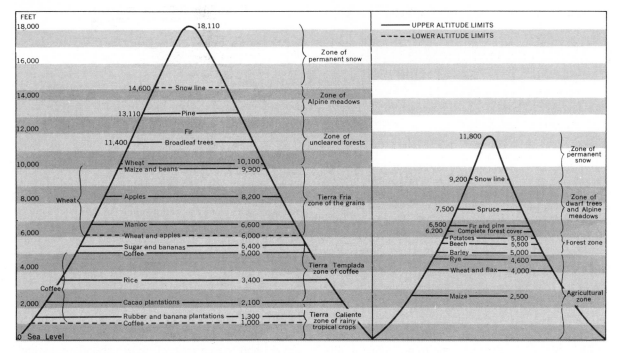

Figure 9.7 Vertical temperature zones and altitudinal limits of selected crops and vegetation types on a tropical mountain (left) and a middle-latitude mountain (right). *(After Sapper.)*

are terminated along their upper margins by the permanent snowfields.

By contrast, highlands in middle latitudes are less attractive climatically and have fewer vertical zones of contrasting vegetation and agriculture (Fig. 9.7). Here even the lowlands are none too warm, so that any reduction in temperature with altitude, resulting in a cooler summer and a shorter growing season, materially reduces the opportunities for agricultural production.

Diurnal and Seasonal Temperatures. The thin, dry air of mountains and high plateaus permits not only the entry of strong solar radiation by day but also the rapid loss of earth radiation at night. This results in rapid daytime heating and rapid night cooling. Thus large diurnal ranges of temperature are characteristics of highland climates (Fig. 9.8).

At high altitudes in tropical highlands, this results in many days with night freezing and daytime thawing. Such frequent and rapid oscillation between the two has marked effects upon vegetation and soil. The great temperature difference between day and night in tropical highlands stands in contrast to the very small difference between the average temperatures of the warmest and coldest months, or the annual range. This combination of a large daily and a small annual range of temperature is one of the distinctive features of high plateau and mountain climates in the tropics.

Although the temperature is lower on a tropical mountain than on an adjacent lowland, the two locations have similar temperature patterns. Monotonous repetition of seasonal and daily weather belongs alike to tropical highlands and plains (Figs. 9.8, 9.9). For instance, at Quito the temperature difference of less than 1° between the warmest and coolest months is very similar to that in the Ama-

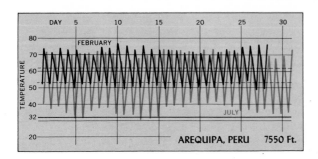

Figure 9.8 Daily maximum and minimum temperatures of the extreme months at a tropical mountain station located at moderate altitudes. Note the diurnal regularity of temperature change, indicating sun control. Diurnal range is greater in July, the drier season, when there is the least cloud.

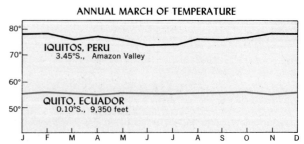

Figure 9.9 A comparison of the annual march of temperature at Iquitos, a lowland station, and Quito, a highland station, both in equatorial latitudes. Note the generally lower temperature at Quito. On the other hand, a small annual range of temperature is characteristic of both stations.

zon lowland in the same latitude. Mexico City at 7,474 ft has an average annual temperature 17° below that of Veracruz, in the same latitude but on the coast; yet their annual ranges are almost identical—11.5 and 11°, respectively. In other words, the pitch changes; the tune remains the same. High-altitude climates in the tropics provide the unique feature of a cold climate with a small annual range of temperature.

Precipitation

For the reasons given in Chap. 4's discussion of orographic precipitation, highlands have heavier precipitation than the surrounding lowlands. This is a fact of great importance, especially in dry climates. There, no matter what the latitude, the heavier highland precipitation (including snowfall) is critical. Not only are settlements attracted to the humid slopes and to the well-watered mountain valleys, but streams descending from the rainier highlands carry the influence of highland climate

far out on the dry lowlands. There the mountain waters (including meltwater from snowfields) are put to multiple uses—irrigation, power development, and in some places, transportation.

In addition, because mountains in regions of drought are "islands" of heavier precipitation, they are likewise islands of heavier vegetation cover, and sometimes of more abundant agricultural production. In dry lands, highlands are likely to bear a cover of forest, in contrast to the meager grass and shrub vegetation of the surrounding lowlands.

Winds and Weather

On exposed mountain slopes and summits, where the effects of ground friction are reduced, winds are strong and persistent. By contrast, protected mountain valleys may be relatively quiet areas. Highland regions are particularly subject to numerous local winds and their accompanying weather, occasioned by the great variety of relief and exposure present. It is common in valleys and along heated slopes to have an upslope wind by day,

CLIMATIC DATA FOR A REPRESENTATIVE HIGHLAND STATION IN MIDDLE LATITUDES

Longs Peak, Colorado (8,956 ft)

	J	F	M	A	M	J	J	A	S	O	N	D	Yr	Range
Temp., °F	23	22	26	33	41	51	55	55	48	39	31	24	37	33
Precip., in.	.07	1.2	2.0	2.7	2.4	1.6	3.6	2.2	1.7	1.7	0.9	0.9	21.6	

when convection is at a maximum, and a down-slope wind at night. Where well-developed cyclonic storms are present, as in the middle latitudes, the passing low-pressure system may induce a down-slope wind, nondiurnal in character, known as the foehn or chinook. Such winds are characterized by great dryness and unseasonable warmth.

In highlands the weather shifts within a 24-hr period are likely to be greater than on adjacent lowlands. Violent changes from hot sun to cool shade, from chill wind to calm, from gusts of rain or possibly snow to intense sunlight—these give the daily weather an erratic quality. Even in the tropics, the complex sequence of weather within a day is in marked contrast to the uniformity of the average daily and monthly temperatures.

10

The Dry Climates (B)

Since the dry-climate group is the only one which is not defined in terms of temperature criteria, and the only one which cuts across the latitudinal temperature zones (Fig. 6.1), its discussion has been postponed until last. A dry climate may be defined as one in which the annual water loss by evaporation exceeds the annual water gain by precipitation. A water deficiency prevails.

Since the amount of water lost through evaporation increases with temperature, this loss is greater in warm climates than in cold ones. Thus the amount of annual rainfall which distinguishes between dry and humid climates varies: warm dry climates can have more annual rainfall and still be dry than cool dry ones can.

Based on annual rainfall amounts, two subdivisions of dry climate are commonly recognized: (1) the *arid,* or *desert,* type and

(2) the *semiarid,* or *steppe,* type. In general the steppe is a transitional belt surrounding the desert and separating it from the humid climates beyond (Fig. 6.2). The boundary between arid and semi-arid climates is an arbitrary one, but commonly it is defined as one-half the amount of annual rainfall separating steppe from humid climates.

Location. Of all the climatic groups, dry climates are the most extensively developed over the continents, occupying more than one-quarter of the earth's land surface. As Fig. 6.1 and Plate 2 show, they are a feature of tropical, subtropical, temperate, and boreal temperature zones.

In the tropics and subtropics, dry climates are concentrated between about latitudes 15 or 20° and 30 or 35°—zones which are influenced by the subtropical anticyclones. Here the dry climates characteristically are shifted away from the windward eastern side of a continent toward its western and central parts.

In the middle latitudes, drought conditions are most fully developed in the deep interiors of the great land masses. These regions are farthest removed from oceanic sources of moisture, and they are dominated by a cold anticyclone in winter.

Temperature. Since dry climates exist in a wide range of latitudes from tropical to boreal, it is impossible to make valid generalizations about their average annual temperatures. Some are hot, some are cold, some are intermediate.

As a class, however, continental dry climates have relatively severe seasonal temperatures compared with the average for any particular latitude. In other words, summers in dry climates on continents are likely to be abnormally warm or hot, and winters abnormally cool or cold, relative to the seasonal temperatures of humid land climates in the same latitude. Thus large annual ranges of temperature are also typical. These seasonal extremes and large annual ranges are results of the leeward and interior locations of most dry climates, as well as of the prevailing clear skies and dry atmosphere.

Even more striking, however, are the large

daily extremes and daily ranges of temperature. Clear, cloudless skies and relatively low humidity permit an abundance of solar energy to reach the earth by day, but likewise allow a rapid loss of earth energy at night. The meagerness of the vegetation cover in deserts also contributes to the large diurnal ranges, for it is too sparse to prevent the surface from becoming intensely heated by day and rapidly chilled at night.

Precipitation and Humidity. Rainfall in the dry climates is always scanty. In addition, it is so variable from year to year that even the low average cannot be depended upon (Fig. 10.1). Significantly also, there are more years when rainfall is below the average than above, for it is the occasional humid year which tends to lift the average. A useful general rule is that dependability of precipitation commonly decreases with decreasing amount. Therefore two handicaps—meagerness and unreliability of rainfall—seem to go together.

With a few exceptions, relative humidity is low in the dry climates, 12 to 30 percent being usual for midday hours. Conversely, potential evaporation is characteristically high. Thus there is little cloudiness and much sunshine: direct sunlight, as well as that reflected from the earth, is blinding in intensity.

Absolute humidity, on the other hand, is not always low. Desert air in warm and hot climates usually contains a considerable quantity of water vapor, even when the air is far from saturated.

Winds. Dry regions are often windy places, since the sparse, stunted vegetation exerts very little frictional drag upon air movement. In this respect dry lands are like the oceans. Moreover, the rapid daytime heating of the lower air over deserts leads to strong convectional overturning. This interchange of lower and upper air tends to accelerate the horizontal surface currents during warm hours when convection is at a maximum. "In the desert the wind is almost the only element of life and movement in the domain of death and immobility. A journey in the desert is a continuous strife against

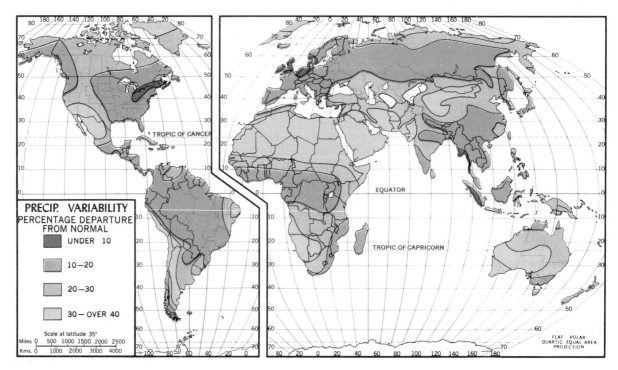

Figure 10.1 Variability or undependability of annual rainfall is at a maximum in dry and subhumid climates. *(After Biel, Van Royen, and others.)*

the wind charged with sand and, in moments of crisis, a painful physical struggle" (Gautier). Nights are usually much quieter.

Because of the strong and persistent winds, desert air is often murky with fine dust which fills the eyes, nose, and throat, causing serious discomfort. Much of this dust is carried beyond the desert margins to form the loess (deposit by wind) of bordering regions. Heavier, wind-driven rock particles, traveling close to the surface, are the principal tool of the wind in sculpturing desert landforms.

In the classification of climates employed here, dry climates, including both steppe and desert, are divided into two great subgroups based upon temperature contrasts. One is the dry climates of the tropics-subtropics, or hot steppes and deserts. The other is the dry climates of middle latitudes, or the cold (in winter) steppes and deserts associated with the temperate and boreal groups.

Tropical-Subtropical Dry Climates (BWh and BSh)

Location

As noted previously, hot steppes and deserts coincide fairly well with the subtropical anticyclones and their dry trades. But because subsidence is weaker in the western part of an oceanic cell, dry climates do not ordinarily extend to the adjacent eastern side of a continent, which is also the windward side. The drought-making effect of strong subsidence along the eastern flanks of an oceanic anticyclone (west side of continent) may be strengthened by the stabilizing influence of the cool ocean water which is found along several of the western coasts. Both controls probably act to intensify the aridity and extend it farther equatorward along the western sides of continents (see especially Peru and southwestern Africa in Plate 2).

CLIMATIC DATA FOR REPRESENTATIVE STATIONS IN TROPICAL-SUBTROPICAL DESERTS

Jacobabad, West Pakistan

	J	F	M	A	M	J	J	A	S	O	N	D	Yr	Range
Temp., °F	57	62	75	86	92	98	95	92	89	79	68	59	79	41
Precip., in.	0.2	0.3	0.2	0.2	0.1	0.3	0.9	0.9	0.2	0.1	0.1	0.2	3.5	

William Creek, Australia

	J	F	M	A	M	J	J	A	S	O	N	D	Yr	Range
Temp., °F	83	83	76	67	59	54	52	56	62	70	77	81	68	30.5
Precip., in.	0.5	0.4	0.8	0.4	0.4	0.7	0.3	0.3	0.4	0.3	0.4	0.3	5.4	

Precipitation

In their driest parts, tropical-subtropical deserts are the most rainless regions of the earth. The majority of these areas receives less than 10 in., and large parts less than 5 in. Cairo, Egypt, averages only 1 in., and in sections of the Chilean desert no rain may fall for several years in succession. Actually, average figures are not particularly useful in describing the scanty rainfall of deserts, since it is so erratic, undependable, and inconsistent in its seasonal concentration. What little rain does fall is largely of the shower type; what few clouds form are mainly cumulus.

The steppes, while somewhat less arid than the deserts, have the same highly variable and undependable rainfall. Steppe areas lie less at the heart, and more on the margins, of the subtropical highs, so that during the course of a year they are encroached upon briefly by rainbearing winds and their atmospheric disturbances. Thus total annual rainfall may amount to 15 to 25 in.

Those tropical steppes which are located on the equatorward margins of the deserts, and therefore lie between them and the tropical wet-and-dry regions, are likely to have a brief period of relatively heavy rains at the time of high sun, for then the ITC and its unstable air and numerous disturbances are farthest poleward. Rainfall periodicity in these steppes is like that of the adjacent tropical wet-and-dry climate except that the dry season is longer and the total precipitation less (see the data for Kayes in the following table).

Belts of steppe which lie on the poleward side of tropical deserts, and usually in fairly close proximity to the subtropical dry-summer type, have nearly all their rainfall in the cool season. Like the nearby Mediterranean climates, they receive rain from fronts associated with middle-latitude cyclones, which usually travel more equatorward routes in winter than in summer because of sun migration (see the data for Benghazi).

As mentioned earlier, cloudiness is meager and sunshine abundant in dry climates. In the

CLIMATIC DATA FOR A REPRESENTATIVE STATION IN TROPICAL-SUBTROPICAL STEPPE WITH HIGH-SUN RAINFALL

Kayes, Mali, 14°20'N

	J	F	M	A	M	J	J	A	S	O	N	D	Yr	Range
Temp., °F	77	81	89	94	96	91	84	82	82	85	83	77	85	19.2
Precip., in.	0.0	0.0	0.0	0.0	0.6	3.9	8.3	8.3	5.6	1.9	0.3	0.2	29.1	

CLIMATIC DATA FOR A REPRESENTATIVE STATION IN TROPICAL-SUBTROPICAL STEPPE WITH LOW-SUN RAINFALL

Benghazi, Libya, 32°8'N (Marginal in location)

	J	F	M	A	M	J	J	A	S	O	N	D	Yr	Range
Temp., °F	55	57	63	66	72	75	78	79	78	75	66	59	69	24
Precip., in.	3.7	1.8	0.7	0.1	0.1	0.0	0.0	0.0	0.1	0.3	2.1	3.1	11.9	

Sonora Desert of northwestern Mexico and adjacent parts of the United States, about 75 percent of the possible sunshine is received in winter, and 90 percent in the other seasons. The blinding glare of direct and reflected sunlight is a characteristic feature.

Temperature

Seasonal Temperatures. It has been pointed out earlier that dry climates are characterized by relatively large seasonal and diurnal extremes of temperature for the latitude. In the low-latitude dry climates specifically, scorching, dessicating heat prevails during the period of high sun. Average hot-month temperatures are usually between 85 and 95°, and those of the winter season between 50 and 60° (Fig. 10.2). Thus annual ranges are 25 to 30° or even more. Such relatively large seasonal differences are not found in any other tropical cli-

mates. They reflect the greater seasonal extremes of solar energy here, as well as the clear skies, low humidity, and sparseness of vegetation.

Daily Temperatures. The temperature difference between day and night may equal or even exceed that between winter and summer. Midday readings of 100 to 110° are common in summer (Fig. 10.3), and over 130° has been recorded. At a station in Death Valley, California, the daily maxima in 1960 reached or exceeded 100° for 136 consecutive days. On summer nights the temperature may drop to 75 or 80°, which is a welcome relief after the parching daytime heat, but is still relatively warm.

During winter, midday temperatures are pleasantly warm, averaging 65 to 75°, while nights are distinctly chilly, with minimum temperatures dropping to 45 to 55°. Thus diurnal ranges of 25 to 35° are characteristic.

Daily Weather

Solar control dominates daily weather in the tropical dry climates (Fig. 10.3). One day is like another, with temperature rising to about the same level during the period of afternoon heat and falling to nearly the same minimum at night. Some non-

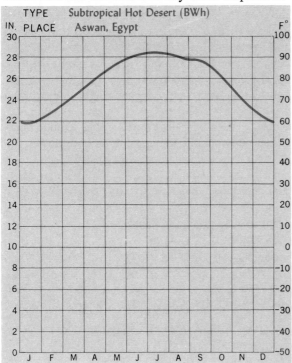

Figure 10.2 A hot-desert station in subtropical latitudes. Note the relatively large annual range for the latitude. Precipitation amounts are too low to plot on the graph.

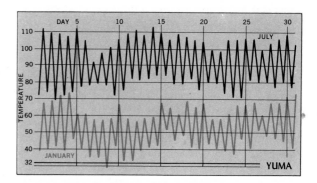

Figure 10.3 Daily maximum and minimum temperatures for a hot-desert station, located on the northern margins of the subtropics in Arizona. Although solar control is dominant, nonperiodic air-mass effects associated with passing cyclones and anticyclones are fairly conspicuous at this latitude, especially in winter.

periodic variety in weather is found in the more marginal parts, where disturbances bring spells of showery or rainy weather on the low-latitude frontier in summer and the poleward frontier in winter. On the poleward margins, some nondiurnal temperature variations are likewise derived from passing middle-latitude fronts accompanied by invasions of polar air (Fig. 10.3).

Cool Marine Dry Climates (Bn)

The normal features of tropical-subtropical dry climates—hot summers, large annual and diurnal temperature ranges, low humidity, and little cloudiness—are considerably modified along the littorals of several deserts, where cool ocean currents fed by upwelling parallel the coast (Fig. 10.4). Cool currents have a marked influence on weather along the desert coasts of Peru and northern Chile, and the Kalahari in southwestern Africa. They also affect the Atlantic coasts of the Moroccan Sahara, northwestern Mexico, and Somaliland in eastern Africa. Note that most of these regions are found along tropical west coasts, and that they center in latitudes 20°–30°, although in some instances they may extend equatorward to nearly 10°. The Somali coast in eastern Africa is the principal exception to west-coast location.

In most such coastal dry climates, three features of temperature contrast strikingly with those of the usual tropical dry climates: (1) Summer temperatures are markedly lower, (2) the annual range of temperature is greatly reduced, and (3) the daily range of temperature is likewise abnormally small (compare Figs. 10.5 and 10.6 with Figs. 10.2 and 10.3; also see climatic data for Lima).

Rainfall along these cool tropical desert coasts is exceedingly low—even lower than in much of the interior desert—because they are most directly under the influence of the stable eastern end of an oceanic subtropical anticyclone and perhaps also the stabilizing effects of the cool coastal water. For a distance of nearly 2,000 miles along the desert coasts of Peru and northern Chile, annual rainfall is only about 1 in.

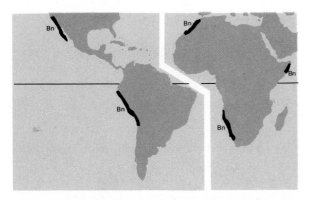

Figure 10.4 Distribution of cool coastal dry climates (Bn) in tropical and subtropical latitudes. Characteristically this subtype of tropical-subtropical dry climate is located along coasts paralleled by cool ocean currents fed by upwelling. Temperature inversions are common, and fog is frequent.

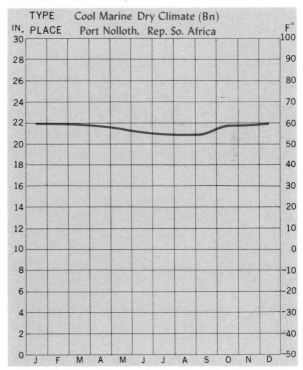

Figure 10.5 A marine desert station located on a coast paralleled by a cool ocean current. Temperatures are abnormally low, and the annual range is very small. Compare with Fig. 10.2. Precipitation is too low to plot on the graph.

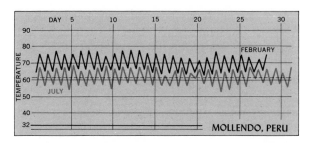

Figure 10.6 Daily maximum and minimum temperatures for a low-latitude desert station located on a coast paralleled by a cool ocean current. Note the abnormally low average temperatures and the small daily ranges. Compare with Fig. 10.3.

But although precipitation is meager, fog and low stratus clouds are abundant, so that the bright sunshine common to most deserts is greatly reduced, especially in winter. Much of the fog and stratus cloud owe their origin to the cool water and the prevalent temperature inversion.

Middle-latitude (Temperate and Boreal) Dry Climates (BWk and BSk)

Location

As mentioned earlier, dry climates in middle latitudes usually are found in the deep interiors of the great continents, far from the oceans, which are the principal sources of the atmosphere's water vapor (Fig. 6.1, Plate 2). Further intensifying the aridity of these deep interiors is the fact that parts are largely surrounded by mountain or plateau barriers which block the entrance of humid maritime air masses. Where high mountains closely parallel a coast, as in western North America, dry climates approach relatively close to the sea. Many of the very driest parts are low in altitude and have basin-like configurations.

Owing to an unusual combination of circumstances, dry climates actually reach the east coast in Patagonia (Argentina). There the land mass is so narrow that all of it lies in the rain shadow of the Andes, where descending currents create drought conditions. These same mountains disrupt the cyclonic storms that cross the continent from the west.

Temperature

Dry climates of middle latitudes differ from their counterparts in the tropics mainly in that they undergo a season of severe cold. Otherwise they have many features in common with the tropical-subtropical dry climates. Because of their interior locations on large continents, seasonal temperatures are relatively severe, and annual ranges are consequently large. Their wide latitudinal spread of 15 or 20°, however, makes it impossible to give representative overall temperature figures (see Figs. 10.7, 10.8, and the following tables). Diurnal ranges are also large (Fig. 10.8).

Patagonia in Argentina is again somewhat the exception. There the narrow land mass and the cool waters offshore result in temperatures that are more marine than continental, so that summers are unusually cool and winters relatively mild.

Precipitation

Probably no middle-latitude deserts are so rainless as the most arid tropical deserts. In all likelihood, some precipitation falls every year. Unlike the dry climates of the low latitudes, those of middle latitudes receive a part of their total precipitation in the form of snow, although the amount is small. The snow cover varies in depth and duration depending chiefly on latitude.

CLIMATIC DATA FOR A REPRESENTATIVE DESERT STATION ON A COOL-WATER COAST

	J	F	M	A	M	J	J	A	S	O	N	D	Yr	Range
Lima, Peru														
Temp., °F	71	73	73	70	66	62	61	61	61	62	66	70	66	12.8
Precip., in.	0.0	0.0	0.0	0.0	0.0	0.2	0.3	0.5	0.5	0.1	0.0	0.0	1.8	

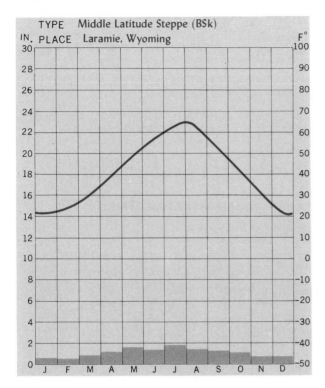

Figure 10.7 A middle-latitude steppe station. Winters are characteristically cold. Annual range of temperature is relatively large. The modest precipitation is concentrated in the summer.

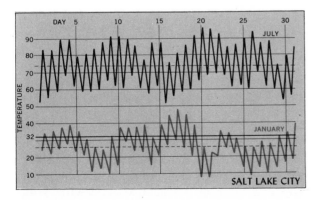

Figure 10.8 Daily maximum and minimum temperatures for a middle-latitude steppe station (BS). Note the strong nonperiodic air-mass control, especially in winter. A large diurnal temperature range is typical of summer.

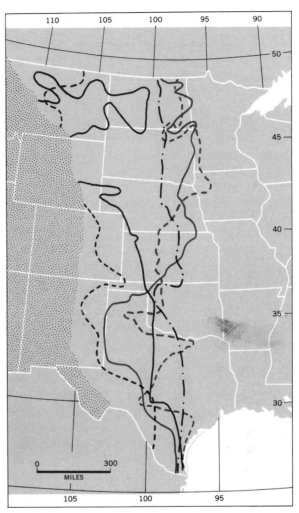

Figure 10.9 Wide fluctuations in the location of the annual boundary separating dry from humid climates over a period of 5 successive years in the semiarid-subhumid region east of the Rocky Mountains. Black dots indicate the mountain-plateau area. *(After Kendall.)*

Most middle-latitude dry climates receive the greater part of their precipitation in the warmer months. As previous chapters have shown, this is a characteristic of continental climates in general, humid as well as dry. Chiefly it is the parts which lie closest to subtropical latitudes, and therefore to the subtropical dry-summer type, that may have more precipitation in winter than in summer.

CLIMATIC DATA FOR REPRESENTATIVE STATIONS IN MIDDLE-LATITUDE DESERTS

Santa Cruz, Argentina

	J	F	M	A	M	J	J	A	S	O	N	D	Yr	Range
Temp., °F	59	58	55	48	41	35	35	38	44	49	53	56	47.5	24
Precip., in.	0.6	0.4	0.3	0.6	0.6	0.5	0.7	0.4	0.2	0.4	0.5	0.9	6.1	

Kuche, Sinkiang, China (3,182 ft)

	J	F	M	A	M	J	J	A	S	O	N	D	Yr	Range
Temp., °F	10	26	45	56	65	71	76	73	65	54	35	19	49	66
Precip., in.	0.1	0.1	0.2	0.1	0.1	1.3	0.7	0.3	0.2	0.0	0.1	0.3	3.4	

Fallon, Nevada. (3,965 ft)

	J	F	M	A	M	J	J	A	S	O	N	D	Yr	Range
Temp., °F	31	36	41	50	56	65	74	72	61	51	40	32	50.6	42.7
Precip., in.	0.6	0.5	0.5	0.4	0.6	0.3	0.1	0.2	0.3	0.4	0.3	0.6	4.7	

CLIMATIC DATA FOR REPRESENTATIVE STATIONS IN MIDDLE-LATITUDE STEPPES

Williston, North Dakota (Marginal in location)

	J	F	M	A	M	J	J	A	S	O	N	D	Yr	Range
Temp., °F	6	8	22	43	53	63	69	67	56	44	27	14	39.2	62.7
Precip., in.	0.5	0.4	0.9	1.1	2.1	3.2	1.7	1.7	1.0	0.7	0.6	0.5	14.4	

Ulan Bator (Urga), Mongolia (3,800 ft)

	J	F	M	A	M	J	J	A	S	O	N	D	Yr	Range
Temp., °F	−16	−4	13	34	48	58	63	59	48	30	8	−17	28	79
Precip., in.	0.0	0.1	0.0	0.0	0.3	1.7	2.6	2.1	0.5	0.1	0.1	0.1	7.6	

Saratov, U.S.S.R.

	J	F	M	A	M	J	J	A	S	O	N	D	Yr	Range
Temp., °F	11	13	21	43	60	69	74	69	56	42	28	17	43	63
Precip., in.	1.1	1.0	0.8	1.0	1.3	1.8	1.2	1.3	1.1	1.4	1.4	1.2	14.5	

Middle-latitude steppes, like their counterparts in the tropics, occupy transitional, or intermediate, positions between deserts and the humid climates (Fig. 6.2 and Plate 2). Since they have more precipitation than deserts, the steppes are somewhat better utilized and populated. But just because of this, and because the rainfall is unreliable, they are also regions of greater economic catastrophe (Figs. 10.1 and 10.9). A succession of humid years may tempt settlers to push the agricultural frontier toward the desert. Then drought years come, crops fail, and disaster follows.

Resource Potentialities of the Dry Realm

As previously stated, dry climates cover over one-quarter of the earth's land surface. It seems unfortunate that such an unproductive climate should be so extensive. For the most part, dry lands coincide with great blank spaces on the world popula-tion map, as do parts of the wet tropics and nearly all of the cold polar and subarctic lands. Indeed, these three climates—the dry, the cold, and the constantly hot—offer the greatest obstacles to a large-scale redistribution of population on the earth.

Owing to the shortage and extreme year-to-year variability of rainfall, it appears that the earth's dry climates are doomed to remain relatively unproductive. Neither artificial rainmaking by cloud seeding nor methods for converting sea water into freshwater seem likely to create any large increase in dry-land agriculture in the near future. Possibly agriculture can be expanded by an increased use of irrigation and of drought-resistant plants cultivated by dry-farming methods. But again, it is hard to be optimistic about the promise of either of these techniques for opening up extensive new areas of dry land to agricultural settlement.

The niggardly desert climate is responsible for a sparse vegetation cover which has relatively low resource value. Some deserts are almost completely barren wastes; in others there is a thin mantle of widely spaced woody shrubs with some short desert bunchgrass, but even the grazing value of this vegetation is very low. Semiarid regions have short, shallow-rooted, widely spaced grasses with a considerably higher grazing value than that of the desert shrub; i.e., they are capable of supporting more livestock per unit area. This grass is a great natural asset of the steppes, but grazing is an industry which can support only a small population.

Soils are not important in deserts, largely because the rainfall deficiency makes it impossible to farm them. In the middle-latitude steppes the very modest amount of leaching and the organic material derived from the root mat of the grasses make for excellent dark, fertile soils. Unfortunately this admirable soil resource of middle-latitude semiarid lands cannot be exploited to anything like its capacity because of the precipitation handicap. It is the old story: fruitful soils and prolific climates ordinarily do not go together.

11

Water

The surface zone of the earth includes a surprising amount of water. More than two-thirds of the solid earth is covered by it (Fig. 1.1); it is present in large quantities beneath the solid surface; and it is a normal constituent of the atmosphere. Unlike any other common substance near the earth's surface, water occurs as a solid, a liquid, or a gas within the range of temperatures that are normal there. Certainly no other material is more ubiquitous than water, or more changeable under ordinary conditions.

Water is important in physical geography for a variety of reasons: It is one of the three major elements of weather and climate; it is the prime agent in the sculpturing of the land; and it is indispensable for the existence of life. Its vital place in the organic complex has been well summarized as follows:

"Where there is life there must be water. There is no organism today, plant or animal, which is not highly dependent on it. . . . A seed will not sprout without water. Indeed the cells which make up a seedling . . . are largely water. Water has a basic role in the formation of the protein molecule, the fundamental material for all living matter, plant and animal. No less than light it is essential to photosynthesis, the biochemical process by which . . . plants obtain the principal raw materials for their growth. . . . Apart from fat, the tissues of all animal bodies are 70 to 90 per cent water."[1]

Man, of course, needs water to keep himself alive and to produce the plant and animal organisms he uses for food. But in addition, a modern industrial and commercial society must have a huge continuous supply of it—far beyond that needed for drinking and raising food. No other economic resource is so important in modern life.

Besides the water being held in chemical bond in the materials of the deep interior of the earth, there is an enormous amount of water near the surface. The outermost 3 miles of the solid-liquid earth contain three times as much water as all other substances put together, and six times as much as the next most abundant compound, feldspar. The following table provides an estimate of the distribution of this vast supply.

As the table shows, most of the water near

APPROXIMATE DISTRIBUTION OF THE WATERS OF THE EARTH
(In Cubic Miles of Liquid Equivalent)

In the solid earth

Above sea level	1,085,000
Below sea level to a depth of 2½ miles	1,255,000
In the subcrustal zone	19,400,000

On the solid earth

In soil, plants, and animals	3,400
In lakes and streams	53,000
In icecaps and glaciers	7,200,000
In the ocean basins	315,000,000

In the atmosphere

In solid, liquid, and vapor	3,600
TOTAL	344,000,000

[1] Edward A. Ackerman. *Water Resources in the United States.* Reprint 6. Resources for the Future, Inc., Washington, D.C., 1958. P. 2.

the surface is ocean water—a topic which will be treated in the next chapter dealing with the seas. Only a small proportion of the surface supply of water exists outside the ocean basins: some is in the atmosphere as vapor, as cloud-forming droplets, or as ice particles; some is in the tissues of plants and animals; the remainder occurs as liquid or ice on or very close to the land surface.

Properties of Water. Water has many characteristics that make it unique among the common inorganic materials. Two of these qualities which are important in producing major environmental contrasts are its dissolving power and its occurrence in solid, liquid, and vapor forms.

Pure water is scarcely ever found in nature, for as soon as liquid water forms in the atmosphere, it dissolves carbon dioxide and becomes weak carbonic acid (H_2CO_3). When this acid reaches the solid earth, it instantly begins to dissolve other compounds. Water, with carbonic acid and other "tools," is able to dissolve almost every constituent of the earth's crust. As a consequence, it is the great carrier of food for the organic life which subsists on the minerals of the crust. Because of this unique high solvent power, billions of tons of dissolved materials are constantly in transit on the land. They ultimately find their way to the oceans, to be added to that complex chemical solution, sea water, which itself supports an abundant and vast array of life forms.

As previously observed, water is the only natural substance that can occur in the solid, liquid, and vapor states within the temperature range at the surface of the earth. As temperatures vary from place to place and time to time, large amounts of water (1) are more or less locked in storage as ice, (2) are evaporated from the ocean and transported as vapor, only to be condensed again as precipitation, and (3) exist as varying volumes of liquid in rivers, lakes, and oceans.

Other properties of water play important roles in helping to create differences in the environment, such as water's expansion upon freezing, its capacity for absorbing and transmitting heat, and its surface tension—the highest of any fluid. Because of this surface tension, water can be held within the soil by capillary force,[2] so that soil solutions are available to the feeding roots of plants.

The Hydrologic Cycle

Practically all the water (liquid and vapor) near the surface of the earth is in constant circulation in some way. This occurs by means of a vast distilling process which is in continuous operation: the hydrologic cycle. As Chap. 4 mentioned, whenever liquid water and the requisite energy meet, some of the water evaporates and becomes a part of the atmosphere. In turn, all this condenses and falls back to the earth's surface.

[2] When a liquid, through surface tension, moves or is retained in fine interstices or "tubes" such as occur in the soil, it is said to be held there by capillary force or capillary action.

Functioning of the Cycle. Water may be evaporated from a variety of places, such as the transpiring surfaces of plants and animals, the soil, snow, lakes and streams, and especially the ocean surface. Solar radiation is the ultimate source of energy for these processes, which together are called *evapotranspiration.*

As a constituent of air masses, water vapor moves with the advectional and convectional currents of the atmosphere. Chiefly, it condenses aloft as clouds composed of water droplets or ice particles, and some of these coalesce and fall as precipitation. Of this precipitation, a portion returns to vapor again before it reaches the earth's surface; the rest falls directly back into the ocean reservoir or onto the land surface. The hydrologic cycle in its entirety is very complex. The brief description which follows is illustrated diagrammatically in Fig. 11.1.

Over land areas, precipitation generally ex-

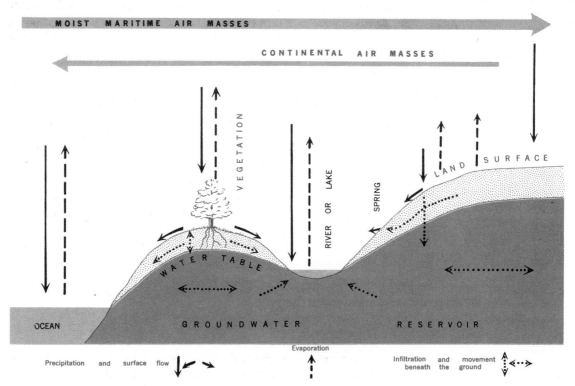

Figure 11.1 Some of the major relationships between the hydrologic cycle and waters on the land. The vertical and horizontal circulations within the ocean are not diagrammed. For these, see Chap. 12.

ceeds evaporation; consequently much of the water that falls on the land is ultimately destined to return, as liquid, to the ocean reservoir. Its movement in that direction is not likely to be very direct, however. Although some falls upon lake or stream surfaces and thus starts back immediately, most is shed on the ground and must find its way to a stream. Once in a stream, this *surface water,* responding to the pull of gravity, may flow either directly into the ocean or toward some enclosed basin on the land. In such a basin it may evaporate or sink beneath the land surface. Where there is no such topographic interruption to its return to the ocean, the stream of surface water continues on its course, sometimes being delayed in a freshwater lake or swamp, but always moving downward. On the way, some of it may leave the stream by sinking into the stream bed.

A large proportion of the water that falls on the land returns seaward in the form of vapor rather than of liquid flow. Continental air masses absorb vast amounts of water through evaporation as they move out of the continental interiors.

A portion of the water that falls on the land neither evaporates again nor enters a stream, but instead sinks downward into the loose soil. Some of this is taken up by plant roots, which pass it upward through the stems to the leaves, where it is again evaporated through the leaf pores. A fraction of the water in the soil may move upward by capillary force, but some continues downward to become part of the *groundwater.* This is water that infiltrates the cracks and pore spaces of the rocks in the outer zone of the solid earth, as well as the looser material that commonly covers the rocks. Within the groundwater reservoir the water may move laterally as well as vertically. Some of it discharges directly into the ocean, below sea level. But by far the larger part drains by seepage and springs into streams and rivers, thus becoming surface water.

If we try to follow the history of a specific mass of water during a long period, we find many interruptions and complications which are not evident from a general summary of the hydrologic cycle. For example, some water may become locked up in ice masses in polar or high-altitude regions, or may be held in mineral crystals in rock formations, or may even be trapped in the pore spaces of sediments accumulating at the bottom of the sea, there to remain for uncounted years or perhaps even whole geologic eras. However, these kinds of complications do not greatly affect the geographically significant fact about the hydrologic cycle, i.e., that water flows from the sea to the land and back via evaporation and precipitation.

Variations over the Earth. There are great differences over land areas in the operation of the hydrologic cycle. This results from the variations in all the conditions that cause weather and climate to differ, plus the complications caused by differences in vegetation cover, soil and rock character, and many other factors.

Regions that have a great deal of surface water, a damp soil, and a denser vegetation cover will probably furnish a proportionately large amount of water to the atmosphere. Likewise, the clearer, windier, and warmer an area, the greater will be the possibility of transferring water from the land to the air. Thus the climatically or seasonally dry lands, generally being clear, windy, and warm, have a high *potential* rate of evapotranspiration. But because there is little surface or soil water and meager vegetation in these areas, the *actual* rate is relatively low.

The timing of the hydrologic cycle is also a complex matter. It is known that at particular times, there are significant variations in the total amount of water involved in the cycle and the proportions existing in each part of it. There is also a definite pattern to the annual regime, i.e., the timing of the functioning of the cycle during a year. And just as the spatial variations of the climatic elements result in significant geographical patterns, so there are general spatial patterns in the functioning of the cycle. Our knowledge of these is much scantier than our knowledge of the variations in climatic elements; nevertheless, the patterns of the hydrologic cycle constitute a fundamental part of the earth's physical geography.

Waters on the Land

The water that falls on the land is fresh, and land-based life has largely evolved to depend upon this kind of water in various ways. Besides the fact that the very existence of life requires it, water is a mineral which, while only one of a long list of minerals used by man, exceeds all others in the urgency of its need and in the quantity required.

Water as a Resource. Until recently a relatively small amount of water was required to supply the needs of man. Beginning with the Industrial Revolution, however, water steadily increased in significance, until today it is certainly the most used material in our complex modern life. Quite apart from its uses in place—that is, for such things as outdoor recreation and surface transportation—it is required for a large variety of home, industrial, and agricultural purposes. It is our major industrial and home solvent, coolant, and waste carrier; virtually all manufactured electricity requires water; and almost all industrial production requires amazing amounts of it. For example, a steel mill uses perhaps 65,000 gal of water for each ton of steel it produces; 1 gal of gasoline requires some 10 gal of water for its preparation; and vast amounts are used for irrigation.

As the population of the earth increases, and as more and more of that population congregates in cities to earn its living in industry, the supply of water per capita increases. The per capita average total consumption of water for all uses in 100 cities of more than 100,000 population in the United States is the equivalent of about 150 gal per day. At the extreme, the great industrial city of Chicago supplies its homes and factories with about 255 gal per day for each of its residents—the highest per capita rate of consumption in the United States.[3]

[3] N. Durfor and E. Becker. *Public Water Supplies of the 100 Largest Cities in the United States,* 1962. P. 6. U.S. Geol. Survey Water Supply Paper 1812, Washington, D.C., 1964.

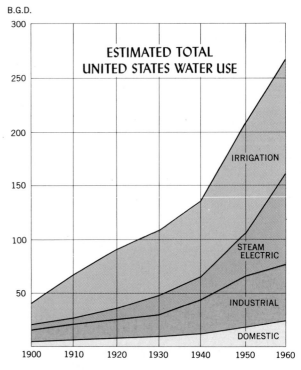

Figure 11.2 From 1900 to 1960, it is estimated that water used in the United States rose from less than 50 billion gal per day (BGD) to more than 250 BGD. *(Based upon various estimates, including 1955 Annual Report of Resources for the Future, and Mackichan and Kammerer.)*

In general the use of water is increasing at a considerably faster rate than population is. Figure 11.2 shows that water consumption in the United States has risen more than five times since 1900, although the population has little more than doubled in that period.

Withdrawal and Nonwithdrawal Uses. Water may be obtained either by using surface supplies—that is, the water in lakes, streams, and rivers—or by tapping groundwater supplies by means of springs or wells. However obtained, its uses may be classified as withdrawal and nonwithdrawal. When water is diverted for use from its source, whether the source is a well or stream, this is called a withdrawal use. When it is used in place (e.g., for navigation or recreation) it is called a nonwithdrawal use.

Water for withdrawal use must meet stringent purity requirements; for most purposes it must be fresh, and only the water precipitated from the atmosphere is generally of that quality. Thus regions of abundant precipitation usually, although not always, have ample sources of fresh water close at hand, and inhabitants may use it lavishly. In dry regions, on the other hand, sources are not ample, and it may be used only sparingly. These differences are of critical significance in human geography.

Since the amount of water for withdrawal uses varies from place to place, the total amount consumed in the world is a meaningless figure. Some ideas of the magnitude may be gained from knowing that the average domestic use of water in the United States is nearly 75 gal per person per day, and that even under the most primitive living conditions anywhere on earth, a person requires at least 5 gal per day. Although domestic use has the highest priority, it accounts for only a minor portion of the total amount consumed. The quantities withdrawn for irrigation, industry, and steam power production are incomparably larger.

Withdrawal supplies are obtained both from the surface water in streams and lakes and from the groundwater reservoir. Surface water is by far the more important, since it is usually easier to obtain. The proportion of the United States supply which comes from each source is illustrated in Fig. 11.3.

Surface Water

Not only is surface water the major source for withdrawal uses, but the most important nonwithdrawal uses—such as navigation, waste disposal, recreation, and the sustaining of wild life—depend almost entirely upon surface water supplies. Surface water can be divided into two major parts: the water held in more or less temporary storage, and the water known as surface runoff, which is in the process of draining off the land.

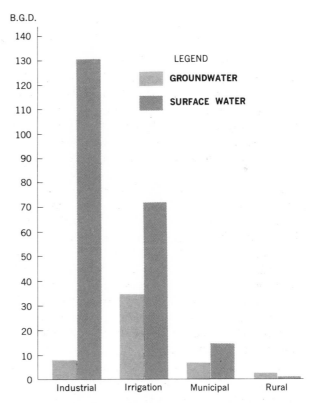

Figure 11.3 Estimated withdrawal use of surface and groundwater in the United States in 1960, in billions of gallons per day (BGD). *(From Mackichan and Kammerer.)*

Water Storage

Surface water temporarily held in storage on and in the upper portion of the land includes the water in the loose materials and rock above the saturated groundwater reservoir, the water in ice and snow on the surface, and the water in the tissues of plants and animals. For shorter or longer periods and in larger or smaller amounts, some portion of the total supply of surface water is always in storage.

Figure 11.4 gives a generalized picture of the average distribution of storage water by latitudinal zones. This graph might be said to show the latitudinal variation of "average wetness." The general symmetry of the two hemispheres is, of course, to be expected. In addition, the latitudinal variations within a hemisphere clearly reflect the

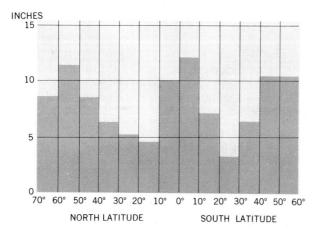

Figure 11.4 General distribution of the water detained in temporary storage on and near the surface of the land at various latitudes, expressed as a depth per unit area. Values are the averages of computed monthly totals. Since the storage water of one month may be carried over to the next, the graph does not reveal the total amount of water involved. *(Data from van Hylckama.)*

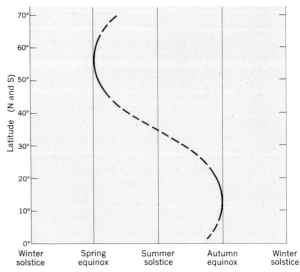

Figure 11.5 Highly schematic diagram showing the season of maximum water detention on the land at the various latitudes in both hemispheres. Where the relationship is less clear, the curve is shown as a broken line.

heavy precipitation in the tropics and the lower precipitation and higher evaporation in the sub-tropics. The large values shown for the cooler regions in the higher middle latitudes are results of the winter storage of snow and ice, as well as the lessened evaporation at all seasons.

The annual variations in the amount of water in storage at the various latitudes also exhibit some symmetry; i.e., similar latitudes have similar regimes. Figure 11.5 shows schematically for each latitude the season of the year when the most water is likely to be detained. In the higher latitudes, late winter and spring are usually the seasons of maximum storage. This is because low winter temperatures have allowed very little winter evaporation and have locked up a large volume of water in snow and ice. In the lower latitudes, the maximum storage occurs during and shortly after the wet season.

Surface Runoff

The drainage in streams, called surface runoff, comes from three immediate sources: (1) the rain-water that remains after losses due to soil infiltration and evapotranspiration (evaporation and transpiration by plants), (2) the water released from storage, and (3) the water that emerges from the underground (groundwater) reservoir.

Measurement of Runoff. The annual runoff of a watershed (a landform drainage region) is determined from the amount of water its streams discharge expressed as a volume per unit of time. The total annual volume is divided by the area of the drainage region to obtain a quotient of a depth of water, and averages of these values for a number of years are mapped. Although this is the same method by which precipitation is expressed, maps of average annual runoff provide a somewhat more generalized picture of variations from place to place.[4]

[4] This is because the volume of runoff for a region can only be obtained from one point—a stream-gauging station—and the total runoff is then equally apportioned to all parts of the watershed. Consequently, a map of runoff shows only the general pattern of variation, not the actual amount that drains at every point.

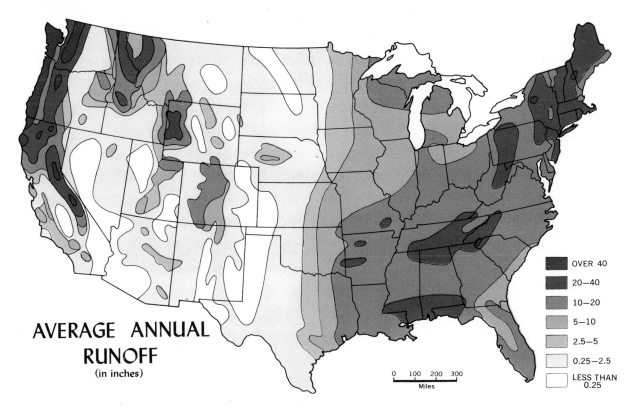

AVERAGE ANNUAL
RUNOFF
(in inches)

OVER 40
20—40
10—20
5—10
2.5—5
0.25—2.5
LESS THAN 0.25

0   100   200   300
Miles

Figure 11.6   The average annual runoff in the United States. *(Generalized from a map by the U.S. Geological Survey.)*

Figure 11.6 is a map of the average annual runoff of the United States. If it is compared with the map of average annual precipitation in Plate 1, a general correlation between the two can be seen.

Stream Flow. Much of the time, surface runoff is largely fed by emerging groundwater. However, when water accumulates on the land surface, as it often does during a shower, for example, most of it quickly collects in channels. One recognized listing of stream channels distinguishes between those that contain flowing water only a part of the time and those that do so all the time. The first kind, if they contain water with some regularity, are called intermittent streams; the second are termed permanent streams.

Unchannelized movement of water in a thin layer over the land surface (sheetflow) occurs when the accumulation of water on a sloping sur-face exceeds the channeling and water-infiltering capacity of the surface forms and materials. Heavy rains and snowmelt, relatively gentle slopes, and a surface material with a slow infiltration capacity (such as a "tight" clay or frozen soil) all tend to produce sheetflow.

Where there is not enough slope to draw off the water, it simply collects as temporary "standing water" in swamps, marshes, and shallow lakes.

Yearly Variations in Runoff. Marked variation from place to place and from time to time is a characteristic of both total amounts of runoff and the proportions supplied from various sources. Short-term minor variations result from differences in individual storms, while seasonal variations result from differences in the amounts of annual precipitation and in the release of storage water.

The proportion of runoff supplied from the groundwater reservoir is subject to the least fluctuation.

Figure 11.7 shows the *areal* variation of the annual runoff in the United States for the water year 1960, which was a fairly ordinary year. Figure 11.8 shows the *temporal* variations in the annual runoffs for 30 years averaged for a number of stations in the middle western United States. From the two figures it will be seen that both types of variability are relatively high.

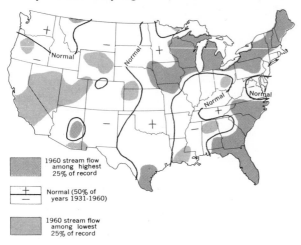

Figure 11.7   The geographical distribution of departures from normal (1931–1960 average for the United States) of annual runoff for the water year 1960. The 1960 water year is from October, 1959, to September, 1960. *(Generalized from Busby.)*

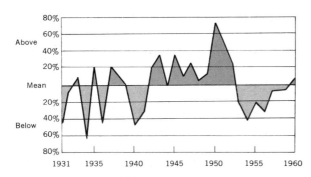

Figure 11.8   The temporal distribution of variations in runoff shown as percentage departures from the mean for 1931–1960 in the middle western region of the United States. *(After Busby.)*

Regimes of Runoff. Since one may observe that direct surface runoff increases after a rainy period, while drainage from the underground reservoir fluctuates relatively little, one might expect that the annual runoff regime would also reflect seasonal variations in precipitation amounts. In many large areas of the world, however, the annual variation in runoff is much more closely regulated by the release of storage water, and in those regions peak runoff generally is associated with the period of peak storage. In the tropics the peak runoff does come after the high-sun period of peak precipitation, but in a large part of the middle and higher latitudes in the Northern Hemisphere the maximum runoff occurs after the spring equinox.

The graph in Fig. 11.9 illustrates the aver-

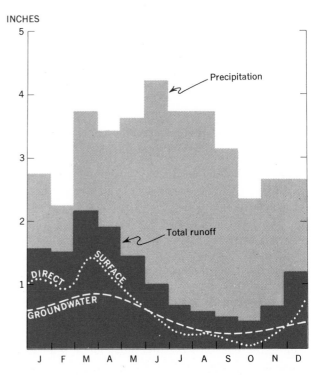

Figure 11.9   Twenty-five-year (1921–1945) combined averages of precipitation and total runoff as measured at the Hocking and Mad Rivers, near Athens and Springfield, Ohio. The dotted and dashed white lines show the proportions of the total runoff supplied from direct surface runoff and from groundwater. *(From U.S. Geological Survey.)*

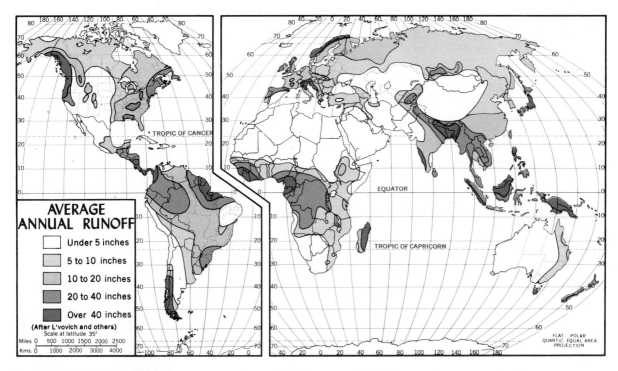

Figure 11.10   World map of average annual runoff, highly generalized. For some large areas few data are available.

age regime of runoff for an area in Ohio. As winter wanes, temperatures (and consequently evaporation) are still relatively low, and the top layer of soil is likely to be frozen. Both rainfall and melting snow and ice contribute considerable direct surface runoff. But as temperatures rise and plants begin to grow, an increasing proportion of the precipitation and storage water is subtracted through evapotranspiration. Thus even though precipitation reaches a maximum in the summer, surface runoff has by that time decreased, and groundwater, an equalizing influence, provides a larger proportion of runoff water. In the autumn the decreases in both plant growth and air temperatures again allow an increase in direct surface runoff as well as a steady replenishment of the groundwater reservoir.

Concentration of surface runoff in the early part of the warm season tends to increase poleward. Soggy ground and flooding are common springtime phenomena in areas with humid climates in the middle and higher latitudes. The large

surface runoff at this time of year often covers man's encroachments on natural drainage channels, flooding farmlands and roads on the low areas adjacent to streams and large rivers.

Distribution of Surface Water

World Map of Annual Runoff. The world map of average annual runoff (Fig. 11.10) suggests some general correlations with world climate and precipitation patterns. For example, the areas of copious precipitation generally have the greatest runoff. There are two such major areas: the regions of abundant tropical rainfall, where runoff is high despite the extremely high evapotranspiration; and the areas with oceanic climates, where relatively large amounts of precipitation are combined with cool temperatures and consequent low evaporation rates. But Fig. 11.10 also shows that low runoff zones can extend into humid climatic areas well beyond the dry-land boundaries, for in many of these humid regions a great part of the precipitation comes in the high-sun season and is quickly lost to evapotranspiration.

Factors Affecting the Amount of Annual Runoff. The distribution of surface runoff illustrated in Fig. 11.10 is a result of many variables. By far the most important are the climatic factors, which tend to operate over extensive areas in contrast to the more local effect of factors associated with the land surface.

Climatic Factors. As already observed, runoff tends to vary directly with precipitation; but differences in the nature of the precipitation are also important. Where heavy or very frequent showers occur, a greater proportion of the fall will immediately become runoff because other factors come into play. For example, the rate of ground infiltration will decrease as a consequence of saturation or compaction of the soil.

Figure 11.11 shows that actual runoff is heavy in the tropics in spite of the high evapotranspiration there, because rainfall is proportionately even heavier.[5] The subtropical areas, owing to their generally high temperatures and low precipitation, are the zones of lowest annual runoff. The middle and higher latitudes, where evaporation rates are relatively low, have the highest ratios of annual runoff to annual precipitation.

Land-surface Factors. Primarily as a result of variations in permeability, the land surface adds complexity to the general distribution of annual runoff that is basically determined by the climatic pattern. Large areas are covered with surface materials that permit rainfall to percolate quickly to considerable depths, where the water is beyond the reach of plant roots and the evaporation process.

---

[5] Water held in storage near the surface, as well as that which percolates down to the groundwater reservoir, is merely delayed, not lost as a potential source of runoff. On the other hand, any water that is evaporated is lost. Consequently, the total runoff is the amount of precipitation minus the loss due to evapotranspiration.

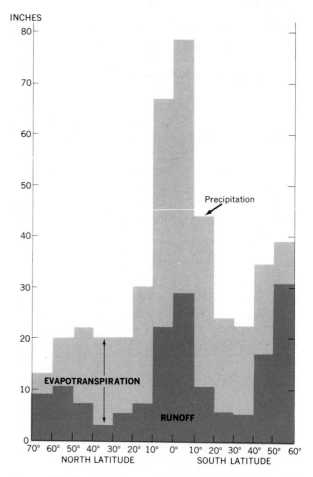

Figure 11.11 Comparison of the average annual total runoff with average annual total precipitation on the land per unit area according to latitude. The vertical difference between the two green areas represents the loss through evapotranspiration. *(From L'vovich and Drozdov.)*

Thus surfaces underlain by pervious lavas and limestones are capable of absorbing vast quantities of water rapidly. Commonly these areas are notoriously low in direct surface-runoff amounts. Also, sandy and gravelly areas are likely to have porous surface materials and thus low direct runoff. Such areas, both small and large, fringe many mountainous regions, particularly in dry-climate lands. On the other hand, in areas with very low permeability in marginal sections of dry climates, rainfall collects in surface depressions, so that a large proportion of it evaporates. In general, there is likely to be more variability in annual runoff from place to place in the dry areas of the earth than elsewhere.

Lakes, Swamps, and Marshes. As has been mentioned throughout this chapter, surface runoff sometimes accumulates in lakes or ponds. If a water area is shallow enough to allow vegetation to grow through the thin covering of water, it is called a swamp, marsh, muskeg, or bogland. By definition, all such bodies of water, as distinguished from streams, must lie in basinlike depressions of the land surface.

The existence of basins in a surface runoff system markedly affects the character of both the water and the runoff process. Water leaving a lake tends to be clear and to have a relatively uniform temperature, and it has been considerably modified by the biological processes at work in the lake. But the most significant effect of a lake on the runoff process is its regulation of the rate of flow.

A lake acts as a reservoir, detaining water during times of heavy surface runoff and releasing it later at a more uniform rate. This has great utility to man in at least two ways: It reduces both the incidence and severity of downstream flooding; and at the time of minimum flow, it raises the volume of the stream above what it would otherwise be. The maintenance of a higher minimum volume is advantageous in many ways. For example, two nonwithdrawal uses, navigation and the production of hydroelectric power, are generally limited by the minimum flow—the former by its depth, the latter by its volume.

Basins containing lakes, swamps, or marshes occur for many reasons. In some parts of northern North America and Europe, there are literally tens of thousands of major and minor basins resulting from glaciation. Lakes and swampy areas are also common on the flat lowlands adjacent to many stream channels and near their mouths, as well as on coastal areas of unusually gentle pitch. In all these types of areas, the drainage of the land is poor; that is to say, the rate of

precipitation is high enough and the rates of runoff and evaporation are low enough so that the balance among them results in "standing" water.

In dry regions, most basins are not filled to overflowing by the meager surface runoff; hence they are not quickly integrated into stream drainage. These basins of interior drainage may contain temporary lakes, most of which have salt water. This is because the surface streams feeding into them are charged with minerals in solution, which gradually become concentrated by evaporation.

Great structural deformations of the earth's crust have created numerous lake basins, including some of the world's most outstanding lakes. Lakes Tanganyika and Nyasa in Africa, as well as the Dead Sea, are examples of lakes that have developed in huge down-dropped trenches.

Where natural lake basins are absent, man may form artificial basins (Fig. 11.12). More and more of these reservoirs are being constructed in areas where the regime of surface runoff has a large range between maximum and minimum flow (Fig. 11.13).[6]

Man-made lake basins are subject to the same forces as natural basins. Thus, although man can easily prevent the outlets from eroding deeper and draining the reservoir, it is very difficult to control the silt content of the inflow in order to keep the basin from filling with sediment. This requires careful planning and regulation of the land use in an entire drainage basin, and such a complex long-range program is not easy to carry out.

Withdrawal Surface Water as a Resource

As a resource, withdrawal surface water differs from groundwater in a number of important respects. Because surface waters are partly derived from the immediate runoff of rain water, they usually have a greater range of temperature, are more colored and turbid, and are softer (less mineral-

[6] N. O. Thomas and G. E. Harbeck, Jr. *Reservoirs in the United States.* U.S. Geol. Survey Water Supply Paper 1360-A, Washington, D.C., 1956.

Figure 11.12   The Hiwassee Dam of the TVA impounds a lake 22 miles long with a shoreline of 180 miles. Note the contour that extends up the "drowned" tributary valleys. *(Tennessee Valley Authority.)*

ized) than the groundwaters of the same region. Surface waters generally contain significant quantities of sediment and organic matter, including bacteria. Consequently, users of withdrawal surface water must as a rule treat it in several ways: (1) for the destruction of bacteria by chlorination or other means of disinfection, (2) for the coagulation of very fine sediment and colloidal matter, and (3) for the removal of sediment by filtration. Water used for irrigation must not have too high a mineral content, and water for many industrial uses, ranging from boilers to canning, must have various mineral specifications.

The large industrial and municipal withdrawal uses of water also commonly are associated with serious problems of pollution when the effluent (the used water) is returned to surface drainage. Pollution profoundly affects recreation and wild-

life, as well as the municipal supplies of communities downstream who may also use the surface water.

In many areas of the world, cities have grown up without an adequate, easily obtainable supply of surface (or ground) water, and water must be transported great distances by aqueduct. For example, Los Angeles brings water from the Owens River–Mono County area on the eastern side of the Sierra Nevada, nearly 300 miles away, and from the Colorado River on the California-Arizona border. Denver and Colorado Springs now bring water, by way of tunnels, from the western slope of the Rocky Mountains as far as 100 miles away.

The provision of water for the rapidly increasing urban areas in industrial societies is an exceedingly difficult problem. As an extreme ex-

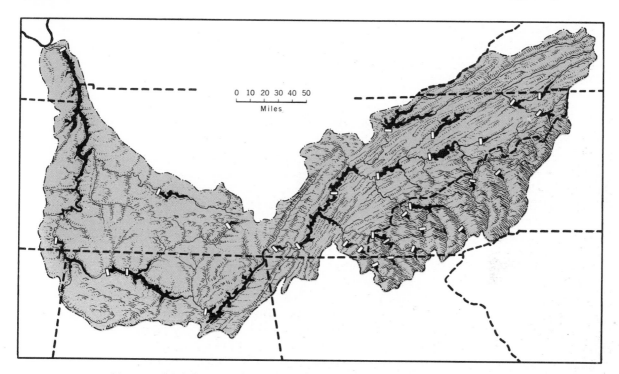

Figure 11.13 Highly generalized diagram of the Tennessee River drainage basin, showing the numerous reservoirs which have been integrated into the scheme of natural surface runoff. Dotted lines represent state boundaries; and the little, white rectangles, dams. Many projects of this nature, large and small, are being carried out in parts of the world where surface runoff is subject to great fluctuation. *(Drawn by Norman J. W. Thrower.)*

ample, New York City uses more than 1.2 billion gal of water per day. Because the city is not located near a large lake, it obtains this tremendous supply from a variety of areas. Quite apart from the Hudson River, New York City depends on seven different watersheds that gather water from a combined area half again as large as Rhode Island. Water is taken from more than 1,000 streams, small and large; it is stored in 27 artificial and natural reservoirs, some of which are as far as 120 miles away; and it is brought to the city by means of more than 350 miles of aqueducts and tunnels.[7]

As the cost of providing fresh water steadily increases, man is turning to the great sources of saline water, primarily the oceans. The basic prob-

lem is simply the cost of converting saline to fresh water. However, with the price of fresh water rising and the cost of converting saline water decreasing as a result of power and engineering economies and developments, the two will no doubt soon be equal for significant areas of the earth. The effects of such a development will be profound indeed.

Groundwater

Some of the precipitation that falls on the land sinks into the porous soil and the bedrock beneath. Ultimately some of it will penetrate far enough to become part of the saturated reservoir of fresh water that underlies all the continental areas of the earth at a greater or lesser depth.

Generally, water beneath the surface is called groundwater, as distinguished from surface water. Yet, as indicated in the preceding discussion

[7] A. Van Burkalow. "The Geography of New York City's Water Supply: A Study of Interactions." *Geog. Rev.*, Vol. 49, pp. 369–386, 1959.

of surface water, a portion of the water that seeps downward does not go far, but is stored temporarily in the upper section. Much of this water never penetrates deeper. It may shortly be lost by evapotranspiration or may emerge to become surface runoff. In the preceding section, this water was treated as a part of surface water; in the discussion below, its groundwater aspects will be considered. More accurately, this water near the surface, at least in humid areas, is in a transition state between surface water, groundwater, and atmospheric water.

Groundwater Zones

Basically, liquid water responds to two great forces: that of gravity and that of molecular attraction. The force of gravity pulls water directly downward. On the other hand, molecular attraction, through surface tension and capillarity, tends to cause water to adhere to surfaces in a thin film or to creep into crevices and tiny channels, and to remain suspended there in spite of the pull of gravity. As a volume of water moves downward from the surface of the ground, a portion is left behind as a consequence of molecular attraction. The upper portion of the ground is therefore commonly damp, although by no means saturated.

Several zones or layers of groundwater are recognized (Fig. 11.14). Water derived from immediate precipitation, from melting snow, or from the surface runoff of some other area first passes into the *zone of soil water*. This upper section of the soil, usually consisting of fine materials with a large admixture of organic substances, can absorb and retain a considerable quantity of water until some of it passes into another stage of the hydrologic cycle by evapotranspiration, leaving the soil either by direct evaporation, or through the roots and transpiring surfaces of plants. When the zone of soil water is holding all the water it can retain, it is said to be at *field capacity*.

Some of the water that enters the zone of soil water in excess of field capacity will be quickly lost through evapotranspiration. The remainder of

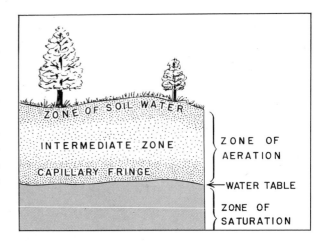

Figure 11.14 Zones of subsurface water. In many places not all the zones occur.

the excess will gravitate into an *intermediate zone* below the reach of most plant roots. There it will adhere to the surfaces of rock particles, the sides of cracks, and other openings. Although these voids may be temporarily filled during a time of copious groundwater, usually they are not. Air also circulates among these spaces.

The intermediate zone and the zone of soil water above it are collectively called the *zone of aeration*. The amount of water in this zone fluctuates as a consequence of losses from evapotranspiration.

The downward-moving water that does not pause in the zone of aeration ultimately enters the *zone of saturation*, where all the pore spaces, cracks, and other openings among the earth particles and the bedrock itself are filled with water.

Immediately above the zone of saturation, and thus at the bottom of the zone of aeration, is a region called the *capillary fringe*. Here surface tension holds the water which is above the saturated zone in interconnected voids or "tubes" so small that water cannot drain out of them. These extend some distance into the zone of aeration. Water may creep upward a short way from the saturated zone into the capillary fringe, but the fringe is primarily supplied from above. The thickness of the capillary fringe depends upon the sizes of the voids; the smaller they are, the thicker it will be. Thus in sandy areas, the thickness may be 1 ft or less, while in clay areas, where the soil particles are much smaller, it may be 3 ft or more. The capillary fringe is important because in areas where the availability of groundwater is critical to plant growth, the capillary fringe may provide a source of water for deep-growing plant roots.

The Water Table

The top of the saturated zone, or the contact surface (interface) between the zones of aeration and saturation, is called the *water,* or *groundwater, table.* By definition it is a continuous surface, and it has much the same sort of configuration that the land surface does, except that its ups and downs are somewhat more subdued. The water table coincides with, or even intersects, the land surface in some low places; and although it rises beneath hills, it is proportionately farther below the land surface at their summits.

There is no need here to go into the complex physical laws governing the horizontal and vertical movements of groundwater, but one factor that basically accounts for much of the configuration of the water table should be understood. A slope is required for water to flow, and the rate of flow varies directly with the slope. The slope of the water table is called the hydraulic gradient, and it is expressed as the ratio of the head (vertical height or "fall" of the water) to the horizontal distance between the intake and discharge points, i.e., the places where water enters and leaves the table (Fig. 11.15). Therefore, if one postulates a constant rate of flow, the greater the distance between the places where the water enters the saturated zone and where it discharges, the higher the head must be. Water in the saturated zone near a discharge point can escape with little head, while that farther away will pile up higher until the rate of addition to the saturated zone balances the rate of flow.

Since the additions to the saturated zone change from time to time, the elevation of the

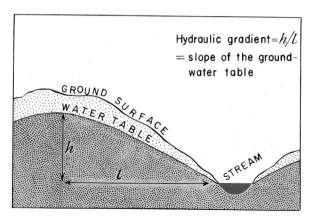

Figure 11.15 The hydraulic gradient.

groundwater table will change, rising higher during periods of net groundwater recharge and falling during periods of net discharge. This will have significant effects on vegetation and stream levels (Fig. 11.16). Similarly, the level of water in ordinary wells, being at the elevation of the water table, will tend to fluctuate with precipitation both seasonally and over the long term (Fig. 11.17).

Groundwater Discharge

Water added to the groundwater reservoir must ultimately leave it either by emergence into the surface water supply (outflow to streams), or by evapotranspiration. Streams may be classed as effluent or influent in their relationship to groundwater. Effluent streams are those which are fed where the stream channel intersects the water table, so that water drains into the stream from the groundwater reservoir. Influent streams are those from which water feeds into the ground; here the water table lies beneath the bottom of the stream channel (Fig. 11.18).

The streams of humid climatic regions tend to be effluent streams, and because of the progressive addition of outflowing groundwater, they generally increase in volume downstream. Dry-land streams tend to have the opposite characteristics. A stream that is situated where its valley is in a variable relationship with the fluctuating water table

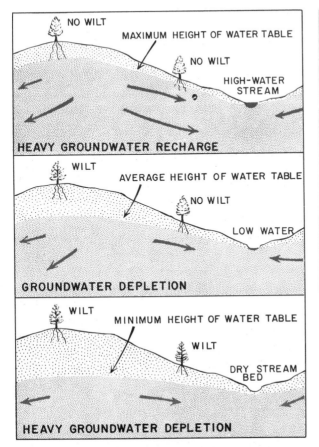

Figure 11.16 Fluctuations in the level of the groundwater table have important effects upon streams and vegetation.

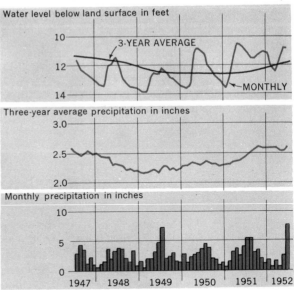

Figure 11.17 Monthly and 3-year averages of the levels of the water in a well at Antigo, Wisconsin, in relation to monthly and 3-year averages of precipitation for a period of 5 years. A 3-year average for any month is the average of it and the preceding 35 months. *(After Geological Survey, Water Supply Paper 1234.)*

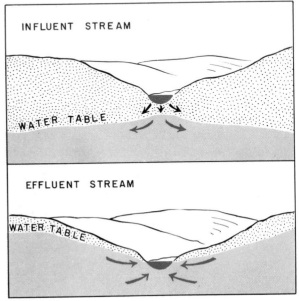

Figure 11.18 Cross sections of an influent and an effluent stream.

will change from time to time, being effluent when the water table is high and becoming influent or even drying up entirely when the water table is low.

Where groundwater discharges onto the land surface instead of at or below the level of a flowing stream, a spring exists. Springs result from a variety of conditions involving the position of the water table, the configuration of the land surface, and the nature and arrangement of the bedrock and its covering. Figure 11.19*A* shows where springs would develop on the sides of a valley which has eroded below the usual level of the water table. Springs of this type are common; often they are the main water sources for small brooks at the headwaters of rivers. The spring site in Fig. 11.19*B*,

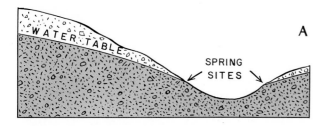

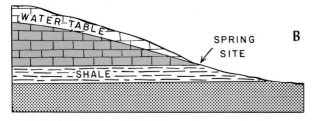

Figure 11.19 Two of the many possible conditions of surface, material, and structure that are related to the occurrence of springs.

on the other hand, resulted from the movement of water downward through the green-shaded porous formations and then horizontally along the top of an impervious layer of shale. Such subsurface conditions tend to produce many such springs, so that water may issue at about the same elevation throughout a region.

Occurrence of Groundwater

The depths and thicknesses of the groundwater zones have great influence on the characteristics of other elements in physical geography, such as soils and vegetation. The number of variables involved is large, but the most important factors that affect the character of the groundwater reservoir in any place are first, the precipitation and evaporation of the area, and second, the porosity and permeability of the water-bearing materials.

Precipitation and Evaporation. The greater the precipitation and the less the evaporation, the more water is available to percolate downward to the saturated zone, and consequently the higher the groundwater table is likely to be. In some areas

the balance of these two factors maintains a level of the groundwater table that commonly intersects the undulations of the land surface, giving rise to numerous lakes, swamps, and streams. By contrast, in dry climates and in areas where meager precipitation occurs at the time of high temperatures, the water table is likely to be deeply buried everywhere except in the lowest valleys.

Porosity and Permeability. *Porosity* is the ratio (percentage) of the volume of the interstices in a mass of material to the total volume. This ratio depends upon many factors, but primarily upon the shape, arrangement, and assortment of the particles in the material. Unconsolidated or loosely cemented sands and gravels, some kinds of rocks such as sandstone, and greatly fractured bedrock are porous because the sum of the spaces is large.

Permeability refers to the ease with which water can move within a porous material. Permeability—or conversely, impermeability—depends primarily on molecular attraction, which tends to retard the movement of water.

The average size of the particles in a mass is inversely related to the amount of surface area. That is, the smaller the particles, the larger the total surface area. The larger the surface area, the greater the volume that can be retained by molecular attraction (surface tension). Hence fine-textured (finely divided) materials tend to be relatively impermeable.[8] The permeability of the soil is strongly affected by its organic material. In general, the more organic material there is, the more water the zone of soil water can absorb and transmit—i.e., the more permeable it is.

Infiltration. The movement of water into the soil is known as infiltration. The rate at which infiltration takes place varies with porosity and permeability, and with time as well. In general, assuming that

[8] For example, the total surface area of all the particles in a given volume of clay may be five thousand times that of the same volume of gravel, making the permeability of the gravel much greater, while the porosity of the two materials could well be the same.

the zone of soil water is only normally damp at the beginning of a rainfall, the rate of infiltration will be high. It will rapidly decline in most kinds of soil, for the soil spaces become clogged because of the movement of soil particles and the swelling of the components from being moistened.

Aquifers. Beneath the ground surface, some rock formations and accumulations of certain materials hold large supplies of water and allow it to move easily. Called *aquifers,* these formations are relatively widespread, since they are normal products of the gradational processes. The rocks with the name of sandstone and some limestones (i.e., consolidated rocks), as well as beds of gravel and

sand (unconsolidated materials), are well-known aquifers.

The pattern of aquifers in any place is likely to be very complex, for few areas are underlain by undisturbed materials. The pattern in the United States is shown in Fig. 11.20. National and state agencies are continuously making detailed studies of the occurrence of aquifers, since their depth, their extent, and the quality of their waters are matters of great concern in most areas.

The Water Balance

The amount of moisture in the soil, the additions by precipitation, the downward losses by gravity,

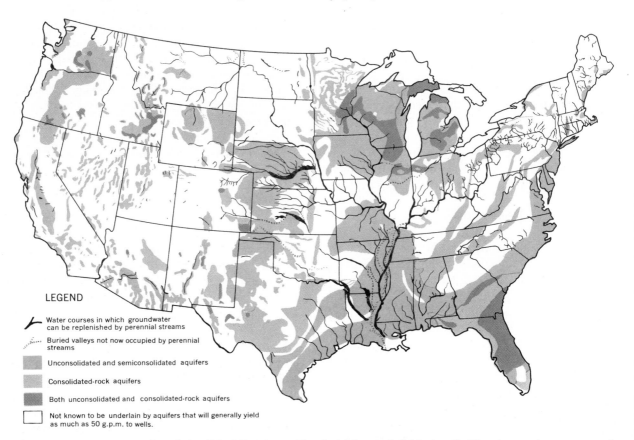

LEGEND

Water courses in which groundwater can be replenished by perennial streams

Buried valleys not now occupied by perennial streams

Unconsolidated and semiconsolidated aquifers

Consolidated-rock aquifers

Both unconsolidated and consolidated-rock aquifers

Not known to be underlain by aquifers that will generally yield as much as 50 g.p.m. to wells.

Figure 11.20 Major aquifers of the United States capable of yielding to individual wells 50 gal per min or more and containing not more than 2,000 parts per million of dissolved solids. *(Based upon a map by H. E. Thomas, U.S. Geological Survey.)*

and the upward losses by evapotranspiration change in their relationship with one another from time to time and, of course, from place to place. The annual pattern of the changes at a place is known as the water balance. This functioning of the hydrologic cycle as it affects the variations in groundwater is an important topic in the study of physical geography. It involves the interaction of many variables, such as temperature, precipitation, and winds, as well as the pattern of vegetation growth, which is both a consequence and a contributing factor.

The manner in which water is made available to the soil and used from the soil by plants during the course of a year (often called the water budget) can be represented graphically as in Fig. 11.21.[9] This shows the water balance at Rockford, Illinois, a station representative of the middle western United States. During the winter months, there is a surplus of water (as a consequence of low temperatures) which is above the amount necessary to bring the upper sections of the soil to field capacity. In spring as temperatures rise, plants begin to utilize the soil moisture. But even though the withdrawal by evapotranspiration now exceeds the amount added by precipitation, soil moisture is still available, because the soil had previously reached field capacity.

Early in summer, the combination of high evaporation and the great withdrawal because of the transpiration of rapidly growing plants depletes the soil moisture to the point where even the increased warm-season rainfall cannot maintain the supply. A period of water deficiency follows, lasting until September. As autumn progresses, plant requirements decrease rapidly, lower temperatures reduce evaporation rates, and precipitation is again

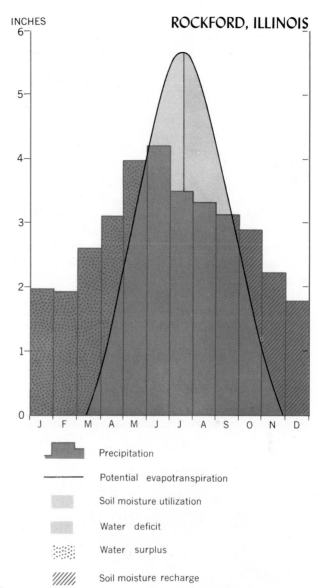

Figure 11.21   The average water balance at Rockford, Illinois, based on mean monthly values. (Data from Thornthwaite, Mather, and Carter.)

[9] The measurement of evapotranspiration is difficult, and so far it has been more practicable to compute a close estimate by means of an empirical equation devised by C. W. Thornthwaite. Since there is no net loss of water in the hydrologic cycle, the sum of actual evapotranspiration and runoff must equal precipitation. But since neither evapotranspiration nor runoff is as simple to measure as precipitation, maps of these two factors are at present not nearly so reliable as maps of precipitation.

available for the recharge of the soil. By midwinter the soil has been recharged, and the cycle begins to repeat.

Notice particularly that in the humid climate with high-sun precipitation represented by

Fig. 11.21, recharge does not take place at the time of maximum precipitation. Maximum recharge ordinarily occurs during the period of maximum precipitation only in the humid tropics, where potential evapotranspiration rates are relatively constant, and in those subtropical areas having a maximum of precipitation during low sun.

Groundwater as a Resource

Throughout the world, groundwaters are not as important a source of water supply as surface waters. Nevertheless, the groundwater reservoir is extensively utilized, especially in places where surface supplies are limited or have undesirable qualities, and in smaller cities and villages, in suburban areas, and on farms.

Mineralization. Almost no water is free from dissolved or suspended material. Since groundwater ordinarily has been filtered through the earth, sometimes for many years, before it again comes or is brought to the surface, it is relatively free from suspended materials. On the other hand, it commonly contains dissolved minerals. Some of these, such as sulphur or iron, may give it a dis-

agreeable taste or make it unfit for certain industrial processes; while some minerals may have tonic, laxative, or other medicinal qualities.

Among the most abundant of the dissolved minerals or salts often found in groundwater are compounds of calcium, sodium, and magnesium. In humid regions, most of the readily soluble sodium compounds have long since been removed from the upper portion of the ground. However, limestones and other limey rocks furnish calcium and magnesium carbonates (CO_3) and bicarbonates (HCO_3) which, although they do not much affect the taste of water, give it a quality called "hardness," which does have an influence on its domestic and industrial utility.

Hardness usually is stated as the number of parts of dissolved mineral (expressed as $CaCO_3$ equivalent) per million parts of water (ppm). Groundwater is usually harder than surface water (Fig. 11.22). Some very soft water may contain as little as 5 to 10 ppm, and water containing as much as 60 ppm still is considered soft; but if it contains more than 120 to 180 ppm, it is considered hard water. In regions of lime-containing sedimentary rocks, well waters in common use contain 300 to 500 ppm and, in a few places, as much as 700 to

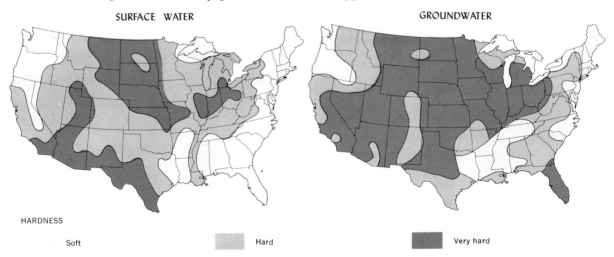

SURFACE WATER   GROUNDWATER

HARDNESS

Soft   Hard   Very hard

Figure 11.22 Approximate hardness of surface and groundwaters in the United States. Note that only limited sections of the northeast, northwest, and south central regions have both soft groundwater and soft surface water, and that hard groundwater occurs more widely than hard surface water. *(Generalized from various sources.)*

800 ppm. Generally, the groundwaters that supply some 10 percent of the urban population in the United States are twice as hard as the surface waters used for that purpose (160 ppm compared with 80 ppm, approximately). Hard waters, if not "softened" by chemical treatment, may cause serious problems in the home and in certain industrial processes. This is because of their chemical reactions, especially reactions which produce precipitates that coat utensils and tanks and reduce the effective diameters of pipes.

Springs and Wells. In the United States thousands of farmhouses and many villages are located upon sites originally chosen because spring water was available there. Large numbers of these springs, most of them on valley slopes, still are flowing and provide a water supply for rural families. There are many springs that are noted for the purity or the medicinal quality of their waters, and in some localities the bottling and shipping of these waters is a considerable industry. Sometimes thermal and medicinal springs with special properties have served as reasons for population concentration; around them health and recreational resorts of considerable size have grown up.

Wells are simply holes that extend below the water table so that groundwater may be brought to the surface through them. Formerly, many wells were dug by hand, and they were seldom deep. Millions of such wells still are in daily use in nearly all parts of the world, although their shallow and open construction makes them particularly subject to surface pollution.

A *driven* well is obtained by forcing a point (a pointed length of pipe with screened holes in it) into the ground, and by adding successive sections of pipe as the point goes down. If the point enters an aquifer, such as a bed of gravel, the water will run into the holes and may be pumped out. Since the pipe forms a casing from the surface all the way to the aquifer, there is less likelihood of pollution than with a dug well. Driven wells are usually shallow and can only be put down in unconsolidated materials.

A *drilled* well results from boring a hole into the solid bedrock until a rock aquifer is pierced. The hole is then cased (lined with metal) at least in its upper portion. The hole may be deepened until the rate of flow into it provides the water supply desired. Of all wells, it is ordinarily only drilled ones that extend very far beneath the surface, tap large supplies of water, and merit the term deep wells.

Artesian Wells. Any well in which water rises of its own accord above the level of the tapped aquifer is an artesian well. Artesian wells are possible with several types of underground structure, two of which are illustrated in Fig. 11.23. The favorable situation must include the following conditions: The aquifer must be exposed in a region of sufficient precipitation to fill it with water; it must dip beneath a capping layer of some impermeable material; it must extend into a region where the land surface is lower than it is at the exposed end; and there must be enough partial constriction (or total blockage) of the aquifer so that the water which collects in its lower portion comes under pressure. Groundwater will then rise in a well, or even flow from the opening, as long as the rate of

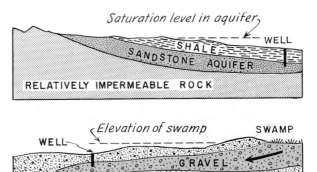

Figure 11.23 *Above:* A structural artesian condition like that which occurs in the northern Great Plains of the United States. The shale forms an impervious cap to the aquifer. *Below:* A local artesian condition that might be found in an area of glacial deposition. In this case the impervious material is finely divided glacial material (clayey till).

recharge exceeds the rate of loss through natural seepage and through withdrawal from the well.

Notable artesian structures underlie some truly large areas—for example, the northern Great Plains region of the United States. There porous rocks, especially sandstones, occur at considerable elevation near the Rocky Mountains and incline eastward, under suitable capping layers, toward the lower plains. They yield artesian waters for farms and ranches as far away as the eastern Dakotas. Likewise, parts of the east central dry lands of interior Australia are blessed with artesian structures which supply water for farming and sheep raising. Artesian structures also occur over large areas in northern Africa and central Argentina.

Effects of Withdrawal on the Groundwater Reservoir. It is important to understand that the total amount of water in the hydrologic cycle does not appreciably change, and that the groundwater reservoir at any place is in cyclic equilibrium with respect to its discharge and recharge. The reservoir rises and falls in response to the fluctuations (short-term and long-term) of the climatic components of the cycle, but nevertheless it is in overall balance between inflow and outflow. This can be termed the hydrologic equation. It follows that any tapping of the reservoir by wells must result in a lessening of the available water in the reservoir, simply because this tapping causes an increase in outflow. Groundwater, then, is *not renewable* in the same sense that surface water is; serious problems of depletion have already occurred in many areas because of "overuse."[10]

When water is withdrawn from a well at a rate greater than lateral movement of groundwater can supply it, a cone of depression forms around the well. As long as the withdrawal exceeds the rate that water can be supplied, the cone steadily deepens and widens (Fig. 11.24). Obviously, if withdrawal continues to exceed the water's rate of lateral movement, the cone will continue to deepen

[10] H. E. Thomas and L. B. Leopold. "Ground Water in North America." *Science,* Vol. 143, pp. 1001–1006, March, 1964.

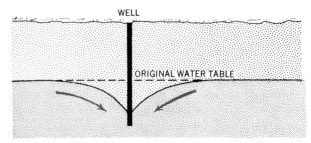

Figure 11.24 The development of a cone of depression around a well. If withdrawal continues to exceed the rate of lateral movement, the cone will ultimately reach the bottom of the well.

until it reaches the bottom of the well. The cone may even intercept the cones of other wells, thereby reducing their yields; but in any case the natural discharge will be decreased somewhere. The gradual lowering of the water table which is involved will, of course, increase the costs of pumpage and perhaps necessitate further drilling.

In numerous places where wells are located near the sea, the depletion of the fresh groundwater supply has caused salt water to move toward the well (Fig. 11.25). This is, of course, a form

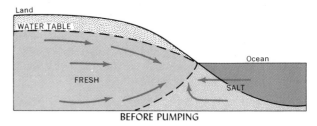

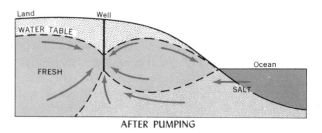

Figure 11.25 Pumping from the groundwater reservoir near the ocean may result in salt water mixing with the fresh water in the well.

of contamination, and the remedies are expensive. One method is to force fresh water into the aquifer at strategic places, both in order to "hold back" the salt water mechanically and in order to reduce the net outflow from the reservoir by recharge.

Selected References for Chap. 11

Ackerman, E. A., and G. O. G. Löf. *Technology in American Water Development*. Resources for the Future, Inc., and The Johns Hopkins Press, Baltimore, 1959.

Bue, D. *Principal Lakes of the United States*. U.S. Geol. Survey Circ. 476, Washington, D.C., 1963.

Carroll, D. *Rainwater as a Chemical Agent of Geologic Processes: A Review*. U.S. Geol. Survey Water Supply Paper 1535G, Washington, D.C., 1962.

Durfor, N., and E. Becker. *Public Water Supplies of the 100 Largest Cities in the United States, 1962*. U.S. Geol. Survey Water Supply Paper 1812, Washington, D.C., 1964.

Highsmith, R.M. "Irrigated Lands of the World." *Geog. Rev.,* Vol. 55, pp. 382–389, 1965.

Hoyt, W. G., and W. B. Langbein. *Floods*. Princeton University Press, Princeton, N.J., 1955.

Kuenen, P. H. *Realms of Water*. John Wiley & Sons, Inc. (Science Editions), New York, 1963.

Langbein, W. B., et al. *Annual Runoff in the United States*. U.S. Geol. Survey Circ. 52, Washington, D.C., 1949.

Mackichan, K. A., and J. C. Kammerer. *Estimated Use of Water in the United States, 1960*. U.S. Geol. Survey Circ. 456, Washington, D.C., 1961.

McGuinness, C. L. *The Role of Ground Water in the National Water Situation*. U.S. Geol. Survey Water Supply Paper 1800, Washington, D.C., 1963. (Contains a very large bibliography.)

Miller, D., J. Geraghty, and R. S. Collins. *Water Atlas of the United States*. Water Information Center, Port Washington, N.Y., 1962.

Perrin, N. "New York Drowns Another Valley." *Harper's Magazine,* Vol. 227, pp. 76–83, 1963.

Thomas, H. E. *The Conservation of Ground Water*. McGraw-Hill Book Company, New York, 1951.

———— and L. B. Leopold. "Ground Water in North America." *Science,* Vol. 143, pp. 1001–1006, March, 1964.

Thornthwaite, C. W., J. R. Mather, and D. B. Carter. Three water-balance maps of eastern North America. Resources for the Future, Inc., Washington, D.C., 1958.

Water. Yearbook of Agriculture, 1955. U.S. Government Printing Office, Washington, D.C.

12

The Seas

The land surfaces upon which man lives and from which he derives most of his sustenance occupy what may seem a surprisingly small fraction of the whole surface of the globe. Nearly 71 percent of the earth is covered by the oceans, and all the land masses are completely surrounded by water, forming huge islands in the continuous sea. Moreover, the sea is also deep, its volume being many times as great as that of the portions of the continents which lie above sea level. The sea, not the land, is the prevalent environment on earth, foreign though it is from the human point of view.

Though man does not live in the sea, he has much to do with it, for it serves him as a route of transport; a source of food and, increasingly, of minerals; a modifier of his climate; and a partitioner of his lands.

Movements of Ocean Waters

As Chap. 11 described, the earth's waters move continually through the great distilling process of the hydrologic cycle. At any given time more than 90 percent of the total volume of water is contained in the immense reservoir of the oceans. For the oceans, taken as a whole, evaporation exceeds precipitation; for the lands, the reverse is true. Consequently, much of the water that falls on the land must move back to the sea through the various direct and indirect forms of runoff.

But once this water reaches the sea, it by no means comes to rest. The waters of the oceans, like those of the lands, are constantly moving. Their movements, which are of several distinct kinds, have important effects upon the patterns of many other marine phenomena, including temperatures, sea life, coastal erosion, and navigation.

Waves

Waves are the smallest and most localized of the movements of ocean waters. They are an important factor in the operation of oceangoing ships, and an even more important one in shaping the coastline by erosion and redistribution of the eroded material.

Most waves are generated by the wind, though they may continue far beyond the area stirred by the wind and long after it has ceased to blow. Where waters are deep and wind velocities are low or moderate, wave movements are smoothly progressive, with each water molecule describing essentially a circle as the wave impulse passes. The water rises on the front of the wave, moves forward as the crest passes, drops down the rear slope, and moves backward in the succeeding trough (Fig. 12.1). With high wind velocities, the crest of the wave is tipped forward and breaks, forming a whitecap.

Near the shore, where the depth of water decreases, an approaching wave is slowed by friction from below. The crest rises, steepens, and finally crashes forward in the form of a breaker. It is here that the erosional effect of the waves is greatest.

The height of waves in the open sea and the length between their crests depend upon the velocity of the wind, the length of time it has blown, and the distance it has driven the waves across the surface (called the fetch). Up to a certain point, wave height and length become greater with increasing values of wind velocity, duration, and fetch.

There are significant variations among the oceans in the frequency of occurrence and direction of movement of high waves. In latitudes equatorward of 30°, winds of gale force are relatively rare except in hurricanes and local squalls. High waves are correspondingly rare, a fact that is recognized in the heavier loading permitted to ships operating in tropical waters.

On the other hand, the North Atlantic and North Pacific Oceans, along with the corresponding latitudes in the southern seas, the "roaring 40s"

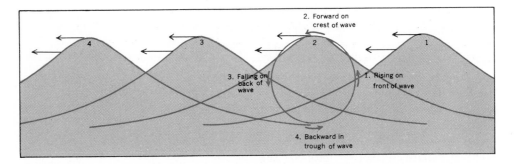

Figure 12.1   How a water particle moves in a circle during the passage of a wave in the open sea.

and 50s, are notorious for the long, high waves that may be encountered during winter blows. Wind velocities of 45 to 80 mph with long duration and long fetch generate waves as great as those in the smaller but more intense hurricanes of lower latitudes. Such storm waves have on occasion caused minor damage to even the largest ocean liners and have forced them to reduce speed and change course to prevent further battering and to lessen the violence of their rolling.

Currents and Drifts

Even if wave movements are ignored, the waters of the oceans are not stationary. They take part in a broad system of continuous circulation that involves practically the entire water mass. The pattern of movement is three-dimensional, but the deeper parts of the system will not be considered here. Of the surface movement, much the larger part is a slow, relatively inconspicuous transfer, at an average rate of about 2 miles per hour, that affects only shallow depths. These slow movements are more correctly spoken of as *drifts*, in contrast to the deeper and more rapidly flowing *currents*, which are usually confined to localities where discharge takes place through narrow channels. An example is the Florida Current, which achieves velocities of 4 to 6 miles per hour in making its exit from the Gulf of Mexico through the narrow strait between Florida and Cuba.

The main lines of the circulation system are determined by the winds, though the flow patterns of wind and sea are not identical. Owing to the Coriolis deflection caused by earth rotation, surface currents are driven to the right of the direction of air movement in the Northern Hemisphere and to the left in the Southern Hemisphere. Complications in this pattern arise from the shape and depth of the ocean basins and from density contrasts associated with differences in the water's temperature and salinity.

General Pattern. Except for the polar seas, all the great oceans exhibit broadly similar patterns of surface currents and drifts. This is a natural outcome of the general similarity of the prevailing wind patterns described in Chap. 3.

The most conspicuous elements of the circulation are great elliptical whirls about the subtropical oceanic high-pressure cells (Fig. 12.2). On the equatorward sides of the anticyclones in both hemispheres, the surface waters are driven steadily westward in the trade-wind zones. These are the Equatorial Currents. In the Pacific and Indian Oceans, and much less markedly and consistently in the Atlantic Ocean, the Equatorial Currents are separated by an eastward-moving Equatorial Countercurrent, which coincides approximately with the position of the intertropical convergence zone (ITC). Upon reaching the western sides of the ocean basins, the Equatorial Currents swing poleward around the ends of the high-pressure cells, bathing the eastern shores of the continents with waters warmed by their long journey through the tropics.

At about latitude 40°, westerly winds and

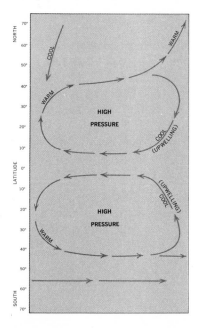

Figure 12.2 Generalized scheme of ocean currents.

deflection cause the waters to turn slowly eastward across the ocean in the form of a west-wind drift. In the eastern part of the sea the drift divides, a part of it being driven by the winds equatorward along the coast as a relatively cool current until it again joins the Equatorial Current and thus completes the low-latitude circuit. In the Northern Hemisphere, however, a considerable portion of the west-wind drift is carried poleward by the stormy southwesterlies, its relatively warm waters washing the west coasts of the continents and eventually entering the Arctic Ocean. The Arctic, compensating for this receipt of warm water, produces an outward flow of cold water that passes down the western side of the ocean into the middle latitudes. In the Southern Hemisphere much of the west-wind drift continues clear around the earth in the unbroken belt of ocean that occupies the southern middle latitudes.

If this idealized pattern is compared with a somewhat generalized map of actual currents (Fig. 12.3), it will be seen that the concept is basically valid. In the Atlantic and Pacific Oceans the subtropical whirls, west-wind drifts, and arctic currents are clearly distinguishable. In the Indian Ocean only the Southern Hemisphere pattern is well developed.

Convergence, Divergence, and Vertical Motions. Examination of the map of surface currents in Fig. 12.3 discloses several areas in which currents characteristically diverge or converge. Divergence occurs at the western ends of the Equatorial Currents and in the eastern parts of the middle-latitude west-wind drifts. Convergence takes place at the eastern ends of the Equatorial Currents and in western parts of the middle-latitude oceans, where the poleward-moving warm currents meet the equatorward-flowing cold currents from the polar seas. Slow convergence also occurs in the middle of the subtropical anticyclonic whirls.

Where surface convergence occurs, surface waters must sink. If there are no significant density differences involved, the sinking takes place throughout the area of convergence. But if the converging currents differ in density, the denser waters sink beneath the less dense, in a manner comparable to the behavior of converging air masses at

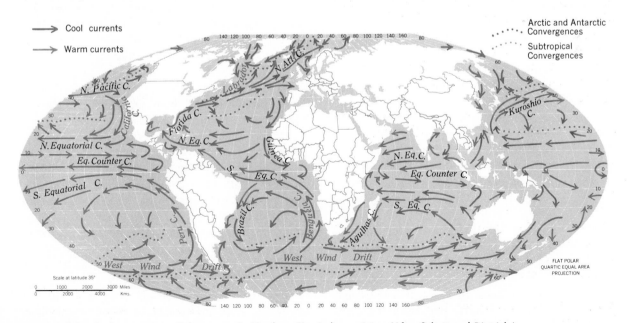

Figure 12.3   Surface currents of the oceans in Northern Hemisphere winter. *(After Schott and Dietrich.)*

a front. At the important zones of convergence in the middle latitudes, the cold polar waters plunge deeply below the warm waters that have come from the tropics. The polar waters then continue their direction of flow for thousands of miles at great depth. The convergence zone is relatively turbulent, but there is remarkably little mixing of the contrasting waters.

Surface divergence is accompanied by the rising of water from below. In most of the areas of divergence the movement is sluggish and diffuse. Along the subtropical west coasts of the continents, however, equatorward-moving winds drive the surface waters away from the coasts, and large volumes of cold water rise to the surface near the shore from depths of several hundred feet. This vigorous upwelling reinforces the low temperatures of the equatorward-moving currents. For example, during the summer the water temperature along the coast of central California, where the upwelling is strongest, is actually lower than that much farther north along the coast of Oregon and Washington. Upwelling in these areas has profound effects upon the climate of the coastal strip and upon sea life in the coastal waters.

Tides

Nearly all shores of the open seas experience the distinct periodic rises and falls of sea level known as the tides. Like most familiar natural phenomena, they have been known and studied from very early times, and along the way they have become a symbol of the certainty and inflexibility of natural processes. But an understanding of how and why the tides vary from place to place has been slow in coming, and even now it is not securely grasped. The basic factors that produce the tides are not especially obscure, but the actual mechanism of tidal activity on the earth is exceedingly complex and can be no more than briefly summarized here.

Forces Causing the Tides. In a system such as that of the earth and the moon, one body does not revolve about the other; instead, both bodies revolve about the center of gravity in the pair. Since the earth is much heavier than the moon, the center of gravity of the earth-moon pair lies just within the earth on the side nearest the moon. Around that point the center of the moon moves in a large circle, while the center of the earth travels in a small circle. It should be noted that this movement of the earth is a *revolution* about the center of gravity, not a *rotation*.

Of the forces involved in such a system, two are important to the tides: (1) the gravitational pull of the moon upon the earth, and (2) the centrifugal reaction to that pull which necessarily accompanies the small revolution of the earth. The gravitational pull decreases rapidly with increasing distance from the moon, and hence is significantly greater on the side of the earth nearest the moon than on the side opposite. The centrifugal reaction, on the other hand, is the same everywhere on the earth, for as the center of the earth travels around the center of gravity of the pair, all other points on the earth follow circular paths of the same size and move at the same speed.

At the center of the earth, the gravitational pull and centrifugal reaction must be equal in strength. This means, however, that on the side toward the moon the greater gravitational strength will cause a net moonward pull, and on the opposite side the lesser gravitational strength will result in a net pull away from the moon (Fig. 12.4). The effect upon the fluid oceans will be to draw a flow of water toward both the point nearest the moon and the point farthest from the moon, raising the water levels at those two places and consequently depressing them elsewhere. As the earth makes a complete rotation, each point in the ocean, therefore, will receive two outward pulls, one reaching a maximum when the point is on the side toward the moon and the other when the point is on the side away from the moon. Because the moon rises about 50 min later each day, the successive maxima at a given point come at intervals of about 12 hr, 25 min.

The moon, like the sun, changes its latitude seasonally, reaching maxima of slightly more than 28½° N and S. Hence, except when the moon is overhead at the equator, one of the two points of

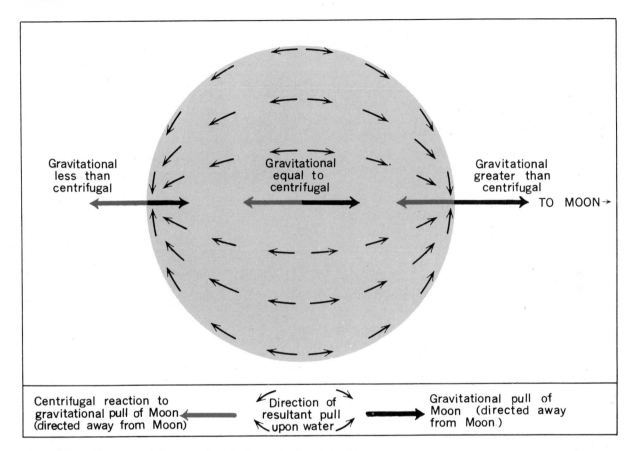

Figure 12.4   The principal forces involved in the production of the tides.

maximum tidal force will be located north of the equator and the other will be precisely opposite, at the same distance south of the equator. Therefore any place not on the equator will experience one stronger and one weaker tidal pull during the course of a single rotation.

The sun also generates tidal forces, in precisely the same manner as the moon. However, the distance between the sun and earth is so many times greater than that between the earth and moon that the tide-producing forces are much smaller. In fact, the effects of the sun do not appear as separate tides, but simply as modifications of the lunar tides.

At times of new moon and of full moon, the earth, moon, and sun are nearly in line, so that the lunar tides and the solar tides occur in the same places, and the height of the solar tides is added to that of the lunar tides. This causes the high tides of those periods to be unusually high and the intervening low tides to be unusually low. These are the periods of *spring tide,* which occur every two weeks. When the moon is at its first and third quarters, the earth-sun line is nearly at right angles to the earth-moon line. The solar tides then fall between, and detract from, the lunar tides, causing the difference between low and high tide to be less pronounced than usual. These are the periods of *neap tide,* which also recur every two weeks.

Variations over the Earth. The seas are not continuous, but form a series of interconnected basins of many shapes and sizes. Therefore the tides do not actually behave as simple progressive bulges moving westward about the earth. Instead, each major ocean basin and bordering sea tends to respond separately to the rhythmic pulls of the tidal forces. In each basin the water develops an oscillatory or swashing movement of the sort that may be produced by tilting or swinging a basin of water. Because of the deflection caused by earth rotation, most of the oscillatory movements become circular. The wave of high tide swings about a central pivot, counterclockwise in the Northern Hemisphere, clockwise in the Southern.

Most basins respond most actively to the twice-daily pull of successive maxima of tidal forces, so that they have two high and two low tides per day. A few, however, because of their particular size and depth, respond more actively to the once-daily pull exerted by the stronger of the two tidal maxima, and thus yield only one high and one low tide per day. Most of the Gulf of Mexico, parts of the eastern Caribbean, and several basins around the margin of the western Pacific have only one daily tide. Elsewhere two is the rule, although often one is higher than the other. In Fig. 12.5 the graph for New York shows the common pattern, while that for Honolulu shows a pronounced alternation of tidal heights.

The average difference in water level between low and high tide at any place is called its mean tidal range. The range is determined by several factors. In the open seas, ranges are least at the points or areas around which the tidal movements swing and increase outward from those centers. Common tidal ranges on exposed coasts are between 3 and 10 ft. In nearly enclosed bodies of water, such as the Mediterranean and Baltic Seas and the Gulf of Mexico, ranges are commonly less than 1 ft. However, if the connection with the open ocean is broader and the range in the adjacent ocean is large, even a semienclosed sea may experience substantial tides. For example, ranges exceeding 6 ft occur in the North Sea, the Persian Gulf, and the Sea of Okhotsk. Even inland lakes and ponds have their tides, but the ranges are so small as to be negligible.

Most places of great tidal range are situ-

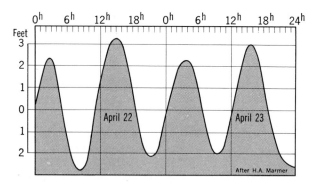

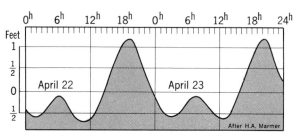

Figure 12.5   The intervals and amounts of tidal rise and fall during a 48-hr period at New York (top) and Honolulu (bottom). *(Adapted from Marmer, The Sea. Appleton-Century-Crofts, Inc., New York, 1930.)*

ated on funnel-shaped bays or estuaries, where the range increases from the bay mouth toward its head. Thus Liverpool has a range of 29 ft, while the head of the Bay of Fundy, Nova Scotia, has 42 ft and, at time of spring tide, sometimes as much as 50 ft of extreme tidal range.

Some important harbors, notably those of the British Isles and the adjacent coasts of Europe, are seriously inconvenienced by their large tidal ranges. In the ports of London, Rotterdam, Hamburg, and Bremen, among others, it has been necessary to construct docking basins with lock gates to maintain water levels high enough to keep moored vessels afloat at low tide and to decrease the inconvenience of change of level while loading and unloading.

Tidal Currents.   In order to raise or lower the water level in a semienclosed bay, sound, or lagoon, water must flow in or out through the opening. If the tidal range is large and the bay is large, the volume of water pouring through a narrow entrance will also be great. The resulting velocities of the current through the opening may become high enough (not infrequently 5 to 10 miles per hour) to carry out erosion that deepens the channel and maintains the opening against bar development.

Such strong tidal currents may also make it difficult to handle ships in the entrance channels and to dock large vessels. In the days of sail, ships were often compelled to await a favorable direction of tidal current before they could enter or leave a harbor.

Properties of Sea Waters

Surface Temperatures. Surface temperatures of the seas range from about 28.4°F, which is the approximate freezing point of sea water, to about 86°F—a much smaller range than temperatures have on the land. Seasonal changes in surface temperature at a given place are also remarkably small, amounting to no more than 2 to 7° in tropical waters and 9 to 15° in the upper middle latitudes. Between day and night, sea surface temperatures vary no more than a fraction of a degree. This extreme conservatism of ocean temperatures is highly important to the earth's climates, as has been noted.

Although the seasonal changes of surface temperatures are small, they are not so slight as to be unimportant, particularly in the middle and high latitudes. Many thousands of square miles of the ocean surface in the Arctic and Antarctic freeze during the winter and thaw again during the summer, and additional areas are invaded seasonally by icebergs. In middle-latitude waters, where winter cooling of the surface is especially great, an "overturning" commonly occurs during the winter. The chilled surface waters become cold enough and therefore dense enough to sink, while slightly warmer waters from below come to the top.

The sea is heated chiefly by absorption of radiation from the sun and from the atmosphere. It is cooled largely by outward radiation and by the evaporation of water from the surface. Since solar radiation is relatively evenly distributed through the low latitudes and decreases significantly from tropics to poles, it is not surprising to find that ocean temperatures follow essentially a latitudinal pattern (Fig. 12.6). The tropical seas are warm, and variations from place to place are small. Poleward of the tropics, temperatures fall off rapidly with increasing latitude.

However, the fact that sea surface isotherms do not strictly follow the parallels of latitude indicates that solar radiation is not the only control. Air temperatures also have an effect, particularly in lowering sea temperatures near the eastern coasts of continents in the middle latitudes during the winter. Much more important, however, is the circulation of ocean water in the great surface current systems. These bring warm water into the middle latitudes on the western sides of the oceans and move it across to the eastern sides, while they bring cool water equatorward on the eastern sides of the subtropical oceans and on the western sides in the high latitudes (Fig. 12.3).

The effects of these movements of the ocean waters may be seen in Fig. 12.6. The average sea temperature on the coast of southern Japan, washed by a warm current, is nearly 10° warmer than that in southern California, in the same latitude but washed by a cool current reinforced by upwelling. Between Labrador, flanked by a cold Arctic current, and northern Ireland, in the path of the warm west-wind drift, the difference is more than 15° in August, and during the winter it is nearly twice that.

The importance of sea surface temperatures in affecting air-mass characteristics, moderating the air temperatures of coastal areas dominated by sea air, causing coastal fogs, etc., has already been emphasized in preceding chapters.

Salinity. Sea water is a complex substance. To be sure, only 3.5 percent of it, by weight, is anything but pure water, and most of this small amount of impurity is common salt (sodium chloride). The remainder is largely dissolved salts of magnesium, calcium, and potassium. But there are also minute

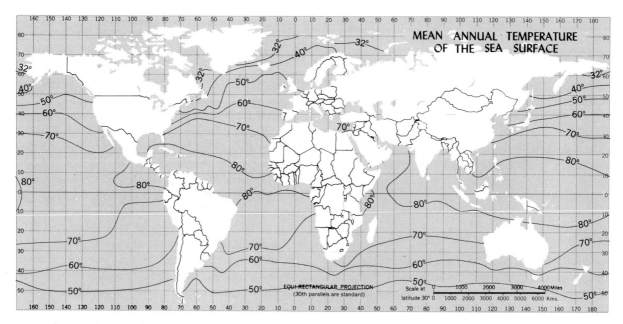

Figure 12.6   Surface temperatures of the oceans show a basic latitudinal pattern. The variations in this pattern are caused mainly by the great surface current systems. (*Modified from Schott, Geographie des Indischen und Stillen Ozeans, and Geographie des Atlantischen Ozeans. C. Boysen, Hamburg, 1935, 1941.*)

quantities of an immense number of other substances—so many that a complete listing here is impossible. Most of these impurities were probably formed by chemical decomposition of rock materials on the lands and were then dissolved by groundwater or surface water and carried into the seas by streams. Some may have been derived from volcanic gases and dust in the atmosphere. In either case, evaporation of water from the sea surface leaves the salts behind and thus tends to concentrate them in the ocean waters.

The degree of concentration of dissolved salts, called the *salinity* of the water, varies somewhat from place to place, being affected principally by the relative rates of precipitation and evaporation. Heavy rainfall lowers the surface salinity by dilution; strong evaporation raises the salinity by removal of water and concentration of salts. Average surface salinity is about 35 parts per thousand, and values greater than 38 or less than 32 are rare in the open seas (Fig. 12.7).

The highest salinities in the open sea are found in the dry, hot subtropics, where evaporation is great. Nearer the equator salinities decrease because of heavier rainfall. In the cooler middle latitudes salinities are relatively low because of the decrease in evaporation and the considerable rainfall. Surface salinities are also generally low in Arctic and Antarctic waters, chiefly because of the effect of melting ice, which releases quantities of fresh water.

In coastal waters and nearly enclosed seas, on the other hand, the salinity often departs greatly from the mean. In hot, dry, nearly isolated seas, such as the Red Sea and the Persian Gulf, the salinities reach 38 to 40 parts per thousand, because the water is subject to strong evaporation but cannot mix freely with less saline waters from the depths of the open sea. On the other hand, near the mouths of large rivers, or in almost enclosed seas into which large rivers flow, such as the Black Sea and the Baltic Sea, dilution by fresh water reduces the salinity below 20 parts per thousand.

The mean density of sea water becomes

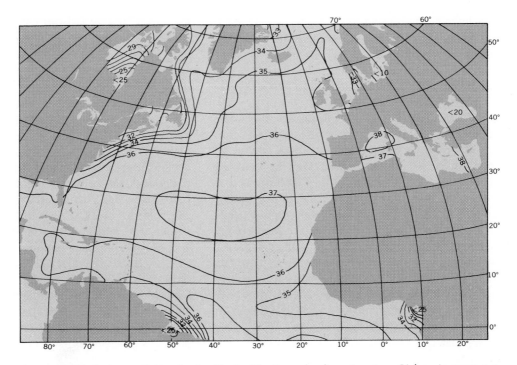

Figure 12.7 Surface salinities in the North Atlantic and adjacent waters. (Values in parts per thousand.) *(Modified from Dietrich, General Oceanography: An Introduction. Interscience Publishers, Inc., New York, 1963.)*

greater with increasing salinity. Thus where evaporation is rapid, the surface water becomes excessively saline and dense and tends to sink, being replaced by water from beneath.

Sea Life

Major Classes of Marine Organisms. The myriad forms of life that exist in the sea may be divided into three groups according to their mobility. The most familiar are the free-swimming forms, which include the larger fish, Crustacea, and sea mammals that are able to move about over a considerable distance in search of food. A second group is made up of the sessile forms—those plants, shellfish, corals, etc., that are more or less permanently attached to the bottom. The third and perhaps least familiar group is the *plankton*. These are small, sometimes microscopic organisms, both plants and animals, that are incapable of much self-determined movement either because they have no means of locomotion or because they are so very small. Instead, they drift with the water in which they live.

The plant plankton (phytoplankton) are the most fundamental source of food for sea life in general. The animal plankton (zooplankton) and all other forms of sea creatures either feed directly upon these tiny plants or eat other animals that do. If the phytoplankton were removed from the sea, all sea life would soon perish. Thus life in the seas, like that on the lands, is ultimately dependent upon plants, which can synthesize living material from carbon dioxide in the presence of light.

Nutrients in the Sea. Like other plants, the phytoplankton need not only carbon dioxide and light, but also a large number of nutrient elements (chiefly phosphorus, nitrogen, and silicon) which enter into their structures and regulate their life functions. Abundant life in the sea can be expected only near the surface where solar radiation is sufficient, and only where abundant nutrients are present in the surface waters.

In general, nutrient substances tend to be depleted in surface waters because they are consumed by the plant life that exists there, and to be ample in deeper waters because they are released there by the decomposition of dead organisms that have sunk down from the surface layers. Maintenance of life in the surface waters thus depends on mechanisms that replenish the depleted supply of nutrients, both by bringing nutrient-rich deeper waters to the surface and by carrying in nutrients from the organically rich continents. Coastal waters generally, and areas near the mouths of major rivers in particular, tend to be relatively high in nutrients brought from the land. As for the processes that carry deeper waters to the surface, several have been discussed previously: winter overturning in the upper middle latitudes, upwelling along the subtropical west coasts, rising of water with the divergence of surface currents, and various forms of turbulence, either along the margins of well-defined currents and boundaries between water masses of contrasting density, or associated with storm wave action in shallow waters.

The greatest concentrations of nutrients in the surface seas are found (1) in the upper middle latitudes, especially toward the eastern sides of the oceans where divergence occurs; (2) along the subtropical west coasts of continents; (3) in diverging western equatorial waters; (4) along the margins of such well-defined currents as the Gulf Stream and the Kuroshio; and (5) in shallow coastal waters. Perhaps the poorest surface waters in terms of nutrient supply are in the interiors of the great subtropical anticyclonic whirls, where continuous slow convergence and sinking of saline waters occur without a compensating rise of water from below in the same area. As a consequence these regions are notably poor in sea life; they have been called the "deserts of the sea."

Fish and Sea Mammals. Fish can be grouped according to their very different habits of swimming, spawning, and feeding. Some fish, including such important commercial varieties as cod, haddock, hake, halibut, flounder, and sole, live and feed far below the surface, commonly at depths of 200 ft or more. As a class these are referred to as *demersal* fish. The first three named are highly mobile and, as adults, feed chiefly upon other fish and invertebrates. Halibut, flounder, and sole, on the other hand, belong to the flatfish group and are remarkably well adapted to living directly upon the sea bottom, where they feed chiefly on mollusks, worms, and other bottom-dwelling organisms. The young of both groups feed on plankton.

A second major class are the *pelagic* fish—those that spend most of their time near the surface. Many of these, including herring, mackerel, and sardines, characteristically travel in large groups or shoals. Others, such as tuna, eels, and sharks, do not congregate to the same degree. Most pelagic fish are strong swimmers and move about over long distances. Many are plankton feeders.

A few saltwater fish, notably salmon, spawn in freshwater streams rather than in the bordering seas. This characteristic leads to large concentrations of the fish near the mouths of major rivers during the spawning season—a factor which, like the shoaling habits of herring, has affected the techniques of fishing.

In addition to fish and shellfish, the living resources of the sea include numerous sea mammals, some of which are valuable for their skins, oil, bone, or flesh. Seals and sea lions spend much time on shore, where they breed and bear their young. Whales and porpoises, also great travelers, are strictly water dwellers. Many of the largest whales subsist chiefly on plankton, while most of the smaller whales, as well as porpoises, seals, and walruses, are largely fish eaters.

Since they gather in places which are rich in plankton, fish and sea mammals are concentrated on the continental shelves, in areas of upwelling or turbulence, and in the seasonally overturning waters of the higher latitudes. The bottom-dwelling forms of sea life—including oysters and other shellfish, crabs, lobsters, and sponges, many of which are valuable to man—are most abundant in the shallow waters of the same areas.

The waters of the North Atlantic and the North Pacific, especially the continental shelf areas poleward of about latitude 30°, are noteworthy for their immense populations of fish. The corresponding waters of the Southern Hemisphere also appear to be rich in sea life, though they are less well known. Certain of the most abundant fish of the Northern Hemisphere, including herring, do not occur naturally in southern waters.

It is commonly believed that the warm tropical seas are generally less densely populated by fish than the cooler waters of the globe. Yet while this may be true, fish are abundant enough in the warm oceans to permit many peoples of the tropical coasts to derive a large part of their food from the sea. It seems clear that in the warm waters of the low latitudes there is a greater variety of species than in the higher latitudes, but that the number of individuals in any single species is likely to be much smaller. For example, there are no known tropical counterparts of the tremendous

shoals of herring and sardines that are found in cooler waters.

Fisheries. The great commercial fisheries line the margins of the North Atlantic and North Pacific Oceans, where fish exist in unparalleled abundance and where the adjacent lands have populous markets (Fig. 12.8). The shallow waters off China, Japan, and eastern Siberia are the world's most productive fishing ground. Japan has been for many years the leading nation in total catch, her annual production in recent years amounting to nearly one-sixth of the world total. China and the Soviet Union also now rank among the leading producers. Leading products of the cold waters in this area are herring and the great king crabs; sardines, tuna, and mackerel come from the warm waters.

The stormy waters of the eastern North Atlantic and the North Sea rank second to the western North Pacific in their yield of fish, though they produce scarcely half as much. All the countries fronting on these rich waters, from Iceland to Portugal, are important fishing nations and have a long tradition of maritime activity. Cod, haddock,

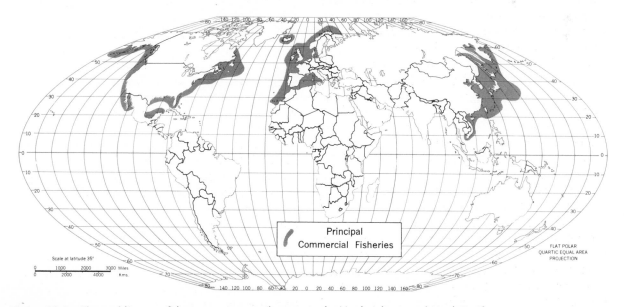

Figure 12.8 The world's great fisheries are in coastal waters in the North Atlantic and North Pacific.

mackerel, and especially herring are the chief products of the commercial fishery here. Northwestern Europe and Iceland are the leading region of the world in export of fish.

The coastal waters and, more significantly, the offshore banks of New England, Newfoundland, and Maritime Canada rank third in annual productivity. The North Atlantic Banks, extending as broad, shallow submarine platforms from Nantucket to the eastern coast of Newfoundland, are among the world's great producing regions for cod, herring, mackerel, haddock, and halibut.

The fishery of the Pacific Coast of North America has tended generally to decline and to shift its centers of activity. The salmon fishery was once important in northern California, Oregon, and Washington, but now it is confined largely to Alaskan waters—where Soviet and Japanese vessels, as well as American, compete for the available supply. Overfishing, together with unknown biological factors, have also reduced the California sardine fishery. Tuna fishing is important in the upwelling waters from southern California down the coast of northern Mexico.

Because of their value, many of the large sea mammals have been ruthlessly hunted and their numbers greatly reduced, especially in the Northern Hemisphere. The whale fishery is now largely in Antarctic waters. Even there, several of the most valuable species are in danger of extinction, as are the fur seals of the Bering Sea.

In fishing, as in whaling and sealing, improved methods and a growing rate of consumption are threatening the future of the industry by depleting the resource. At present the problem is localized, although several major areas have already declined significantly in output. It can only be hoped that a realization of the gravity of the problem, together with increasing scientific knowledge of the numbers, habits, and reproductive capabilities of the various species, will serve to adjust the harvest to fit the production rates before disastrous depletion occurs.

Selected References for Chap. 12

Carson, Rachel. *The Sea around Us*. Oxford University Press, Fair Lawn, N.J., 1951.

Dietrich, Günter. *General Oceanography: An Introduction*. English translation by Feodor Ostapoff. Interscience Publishers, Inc., New York, 1963.

King, C. A. M. *Introduction to Oceanography*. McGraw-Hill Book Company, New York, 1963.

Lake, Philip. *Physical Geography*. 3d ed. Cambridge University Press, New York, 1955.

Sverdrup, H. U., M. W. Johnson, and R. H. Fleming. *The Oceans: Their Physics, Chemistry and General Biology*. Prentice-Hall, Inc., Englewood Cliffs, N.J., 1942.

Von Arx, W. S. *An Introduction to Physical Oceanography*. Addison-Wesley Publishing Company, Reading, Mass., 1962.

13

Land-surface Form;
Changes in the Earth's Crust

Land-surface Form. The continents upon which man lives display a great and often pleasing variety of surface forms. High lands and low, level expanses and steep slopes, crests and valleys are arranged in endless combinations. In fact the diversity of forms is so great and the pattern so complex and so vast that the task of assembling a coherent picture of the continental surfaces has proved to be surprisingly slow and difficult. Many large areas are still poorly mapped, and few sections of the surface have been systematically and analytically described.

Yet in spite of the difficulty, man has learned much about the geography of land-surface form. He has learned to recognize distinctive combinations of features or characteristics that recur in different parts of the earth, and he has even discovered a certain crude order in the arrangement of the major features of the continents. He has also made a good beginning toward understanding how the more distinctive types of surfaces have been produced by natural processes operating in different strengths, combinations, and sequences over immensely long periods of time.

Nevertheless, the systematic study of land-surface form and its development is still young. Like the other earth sciences, it is undergoing a startlingly rapid transformation as new data are collected and new methods of investigation are brought to bear. Some of the changes, conflicts, and gaps in theory are so basic that they cannot reasonably be omitted from even an introductory treatment.

Time and Process in Surface-form Development. The shortness of man's life span led ancient peoples to develop a false idea of the permanence of the natural features of the earth's surface. Since they could see little change in surface forms, even over several generations, it was natural for them to think of the landscape as essentially unchanging. Only along certain rivers and seacoasts and near unusually active volcanoes could significant changes be noticed, and these could be regarded as exceptions—perhaps as willful acts of the gods.

But now that something is known of both the vast reaches of geologic time and the extreme changeability of land surfaces, we realize that man's short life is a poor yardstick with which to measure and understand the rates of earth-shaping events. It is like trying to conceive the distance from the earth to the moon in inches: the numbers are so large that they are meaningless. It is difficult to realize how much can be accomplished over millions of years by the almost imperceptibly slow processes which can be seen at work today. Yet a stream that is eroding its bed at the modest rate of just over 1 in. per century can cut a canyon 1,000 ft deep in a million years, which is not a long period of geologic time. In the history of the earth's surface development, there has been ample time

for slow processes to change the surface drastically and repeatedly. The lands in their present form are in no way permanent but represent only a momentary stage in a long and complex history of change.

The natural processes responsible for these changes may conveniently be grouped into two major sets: (1) those that deform the rocky crust of the earth or locally alter its composition (*tectonic processes*), and (2) those that move earth materials about from place to place over the surface, picking up here and depositing there (*gradational processes*). These two sets of processes are active at the same time; and as will be seen, they commonly work in opposition to one another. At any moment in earth history the land surface reflects the existing state in the never-ending war between tectonics and gradation.

Changes in the Crust—
The Tectonic Processes

The Crust and the Earth's Interior. Man knows nothing of the deep interior of the earth by direct observation. His deepest mines are but a few thousand feet deep, and even his deepest borings have rarely penetrated more than 4 or 5 miles—scarcely more than $\frac{1}{1,000}$ of the way to the center. But geophysicists, by computing the speed of earthquake waves passing through the interior, mapping the pattern of terrestrial magnetism, measuring differences from place to place in the acceleration of gravity, and calculating the mean density of the earth, have been able to piece together a crude but revealing picture of what the internal structure of the globe must be. A simplified version of that picture is shown in Fig. 13.1.

Although it has extremely high temperatures (possibly 1000 to 3000°C), the interior of the earth appears to be mostly solid. This is because the melting point of its substances is raised by the great pressure from the overlying materials. The exceedingly dense core, thought to be largely nickel and iron, is solid toward the center, but may be molten in its outer part. The thick surrounding mantle, less dense than the core, is evidently wholly

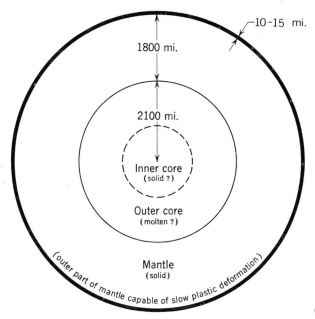

Figure 13.1 Diagram of the internal structure of the earth. The heavy outer line represents the crust, too thin to be shown at correct scale.

solid. It is believed to be composed of some of the denser substances found in common surface rocks. Near its outer limit the mantle changes abruptly, so that its thin surface shell, which is low in average density, consists of the familiar types of rocks well known to geologists. This shell, averaging 10 to 15 miles thick, is called the crust, a term which reflects the earlier belief that everything beneath it was molten.

Although it seems very rigid, the crust is actually not so in terms of the tremendous forces (including the force of gravity) that act upon it. Furthermore, the dense outer layers of the mantle just beneath it, although they are solid, are believed to be capable of exceedingly slow flowage or other deformation such as might be expected of an almost inconceivably viscous fluid. This combination of relatively weak crust and somewhat unstable underpinning sets the stage for deformation of the crust itself, provided only that there are forces strong enough to bring it about. Since there is abundant evidence that the crust has in fact

been extensively warped, folded, and broken, it is clear that such forces do exist, though as yet they are little understood.

Continents and Ocean Basins. The continents are not simply upraised sections of a uniform crust, but are fundamentally different from the low-lying ocean basins. The crust forming the continents has an average thickness of perhaps 25 miles, compared with about 4 miles for that beneath the deep-sea floors. Also, the predominant rocks of the continental masses are much less dense than those of the ocean basins. The continents appear to be formed primarily of granites and closely related rocks, often overlain by a thin skin of sedimentary strata and underlain by a layer of denser materials (Fig. 13.2). But beneath the ocean basins only the thin, dense lower layer is present, probably composed largely of basalt, a fine-grained dark rock that is common in lavas.

The surfaces of the continental masses stand higher than the ocean floors, but their bases lie deeper in the mantle underneath. The situation is comparable to that which would occur if a thick block of pine were floated in a tub of water next to a thin block of heavier oak. The upper surface of the pine block would stand higher than that of the oak block, and its base would lie deeper in the water. All evidence suggests that this analogy is a reasonable one. The crust does behave as if it were buoyed up by a denser mantle that is capable of plastic adjustment to the varying weights above it.

Little is known about the origin of the ex-

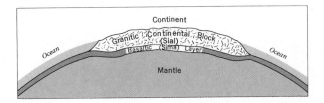

Figure 13.2 The structure of continents and ocean basins is fundamentally different. The terms *sial* and *sima* are sometimes used to refer to the granitic layer (rich in silicon and aluminum) and the basaltic layer (rich in silicon and magnesium), respectively.

tensive "rafts" of granitic rocks that form the continents. Much of their rock material appears to be very ancient, and there seems little doubt that the continents have been in continuous existence since a very early period in earth history. However, the nature and distribution of the thin sedimentary rock cover makes it clear that from time to time parts of the continental platforms have been submerged beneath shallow seas. There is also complex evidence suggesting that at least some of the continents have grown in extent during their lifetime.

Evidence of Crustal Change. Most of our knowledge of what has happened to the crust in past times comes from observations of the rock layers and masses that are exposed at the surface or have been reached by deep borings or excavations. Rock strata that were originally laid down horizontally are now often found gently or steeply inclined. Some layers of well-consolidated rock have been bent into sharp folds (Fig. 13.3) or shattered. Rocks containing fossils of sea animals are found in mountain ranges thousands of feet above sea level. Great fractures sometimes cut through thick series of massive rock strata, and often there is clear evidence of slippage along the breaks, with

Figure 13.3 Portion of a small folded rock structure exposed in a stream valley. *(Stose, U.S. Geological Survey.)*

displacements occasionally amounting to many feet or even many miles. Such observations indicate clearly that the crust has been subjected to almost every conceivable form of bending, breaking, uplift, and depression. This crustal deformation is sometimes referred to as *diastrophism*.

Although rock structures provide most of the evidence for diastrophism, some of our knowledge comes from movements that have been observed in historical time. Slow vertical movements of the crust have been recorded at many places, usually along seacoasts, where the sea surface provides a ready reference level. Here such occurrences as the gradual submergence of ancient buildings, emergence of old harbor works, and progressive disappearance of low-lying coastal plains can be used to indicate the direction and rate of deformation. From this kind of evidence it has been determined, for example, that parts of the Baltic Coast of northern Europe are rising at about 3 ft per century, while the outer part of the Mississippi River Delta in Louisiana is apparently sinking at a similar rate. More rapid movements have also been measured. Changes of level of several feet occurred along much of the south coast of Alaska during the great earthquake of 1964.

Displacements of rocks along fractures have been frequently observed, usually as rapid movements during earthquakes. The individual displacements are ordinarily quite small, but there have been conspicuous exceptions. In the violent San Francisco earthquake of 1906, a section of a road was offset laterally 21 ft. In northeastern India a sudden vertical displacement of 35 ft occurred during a great earthquake in 1897.

Other evidence indicates crustal changes of quite a different sort. Rock materials of types known to develop by crystallizing from a molten state are found in sheets and masses within and upon the crust, lying in close association with rocks of wholly different kinds. The relationships make it clear that the molten materials have been forced or have melted their way into the other rocks from below, and that in some instances they have emerged upon the surface before solidifying. All the diverse phenomena involved in the formation, movement, and emplacement of these molten materials in and upon the crust are referred to collectively as *vulcanism*. The actual examples of surface vulcanism that have been observed by man are especially dramatic. Graphic accounts of ancient volcanic eruptions are among the earliest recorded observations of events that have significantly changed the surface of the earth.

Diastrophism—Warping and Folding. In many places deforming stresses have been applied to the crust so slowly that the rock strata, confined by the great weight of overlying materials, have bent or buckled rather than broken. The resulting deformation can range from the gentlest warping to remarkably tight and complex folding.

Few sections of the crust have escaped some warping. Even in such tectonically stable areas as the North American Middle West, southern England and northern France, or the central and western Sahara, the rock strata are gently warped into broad structural domes and basins, though inclinations are rarely more than a few degrees from the horizontal. Some parts of the continental platforms have been shallowly depressed below sea level, as in Hudson Bay; elsewhere, sections of the shallow sea floor have been upwarped,

bringing fossil-bearing marine sediments well above the sea surface.

Some broad belts of the crust have been thrown into systems of folds that range from small wrinkles to great wavelike structures measuring many miles from crest to crest and thousands of feet from base to top. The arch or crest of a simple fold is called an anticline; the trough is a syncline. A one-sided simple fold is a monocline or flexure (Fig. 13.4). In many mountainous areas, such as the Alps, the Himalaya, and the Northern Rockies, deformation has been so vigorous that folds have been tightly jammed together, overturned, broken, and greatly displaced, producing structures of astonishing complexity. Such intense deformation can be explained only by extreme lateral compression of those sections of the crust, involving horizontal movements of many miles.

Diastrophism—Fracturing and Faulting. Like warping, fracturing of the crust is worldwide. Systems of cracks, often in roughly parallel sets, can be seen in almost all exposed rocks. Ordinarily there has been no appreciable displacement along these small fractures, which are known as joints (Fig. 13.5).

Where stresses have been more severe, however, there have been repeated vertical or horizontal slippages along the fracture planes, with

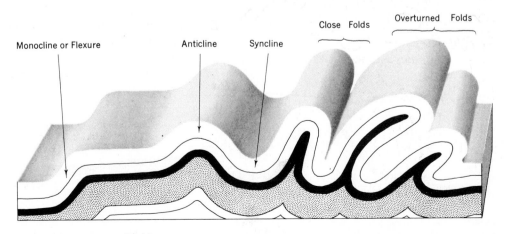

Figure 13.4   Types of folds.

Figure 13.5 Jointing in granite. Three sets of joint planes are visible, roughly perpendicular to each other. *(Cross, U.S. Geological Survey.)*

are called faults. Stresses producing the displacements may be compressional, tensional (stretching), or shearing (roughly parallel to the fault plane). The resulting movements may be vertical, horizontal, or both. Some simple types of faults are shown in Fig. 13.6. If the displacement is vertical and extends to the surface, a cliff, called a fault scarp, is produced. If the displacement is largely horizontal, linear features such as roads, fence lines, and streams are offset along the fault.

Blocks of the crust bounded on either side by faults are sometimes raised, lowered, or tilted. Raised blocks are called horsts; depressed blocks are grabens. Death Valley in California, the great "rift valleys" of East Africa (Fig. 13.7), and the trough occupied by the Red Sea are examples of grabens. Some of the small ranges of Nevada and western Utah are horsts and tilted fault blocks. The Sierra Nevada of California is a huge tilted block with an immense fault scarp on its eastern side (Fig. 13.8).

cumulative displacements of hundreds or thousands of feet. Fractures along which displacements occur

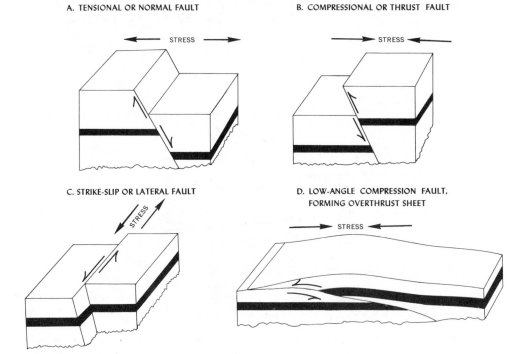

Figure 13.6 Types of faults.

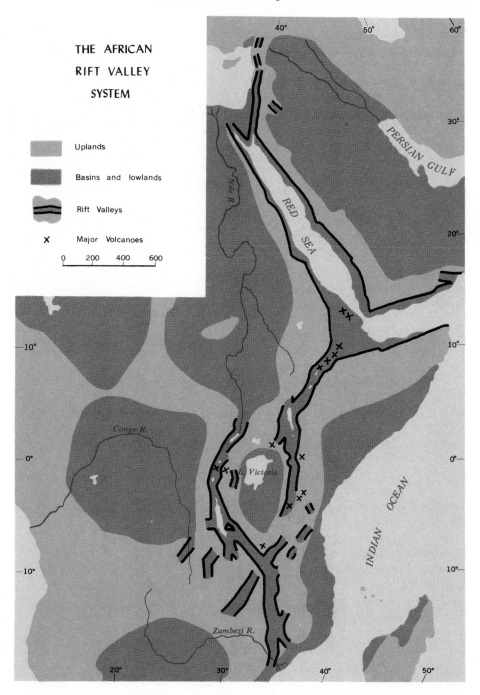

Figure 13.7   An immense system of grabens or "rift valleys" extends through much of East Africa and neighboring areas. (Compiled from various sources, chiefly Machatschek, Das Relief der Erde, vol. 2, Gebrüder Borntraeger, Berlin, 1955.)

Figure 13.8 The rugged eastern face of the Sierra Nevada of California is an eroded fault scarp that rises nearly 8,000 ft above its base in the section shown. The peak at the far right is Mount Whitney (14,495 ft), highest summit in the United States outside of Alaska. *(Spence Air Photos.)*

Of course, large-scale folding or faulting does not occur in single swift cataclysms. By human standards the time scale is slow. A great fault scarp like that of the Sierra Nevada was probably produced by a long series of small displacements occurring over a period of many hundreds of thousands of years. Extensive systems of folds like those of the Appalachians or the Alps may have required millions of years for their development.

Vulcanism. Normally both the crust and the layers of material beneath it are in the solid state, in spite of the high temperatures that prevail below the surface. Yet repeatedly during geologic history, large masses of material immediately beneath the crust or in the deeper crust have become molten and forced their way toward the surface. The development of these molten masses is not well understood, but they appear to form most frequently in areas of active crustal deformation.

The molten rock makes its way upward partly by melting the rocks above it and partly by forcing its way into fractures. As it does so, hot gases are given off and groundwater is boiled into steam, generating high pressures. The various rising materials sometimes burst out upon the surface, causing the usually spectacular events known as volcanic activity or extrusive vulcanism. Most of the molten material, however, cools and hardens into solid rock before reaching the surface. This subsurface part of the activity is called intrusive vulcanism.

Intrusive Vulcanism. Rock masses formed by intrusive vulcanism occur in a vast range of forms and sizes (Fig. 13.9). The largest, known as batholiths, are immense bodies of granite or similar rocks measuring tens or even hundreds of miles across and thousands of feet in thickness. Much of the unbroken expanse of mountains in the Rockies of central Idaho, for example, is carved out of a batholith measuring about 100 by 250 miles. Much of the Sierra Nevada of California is underlain by an even larger batholithic mass. Deep intrusive

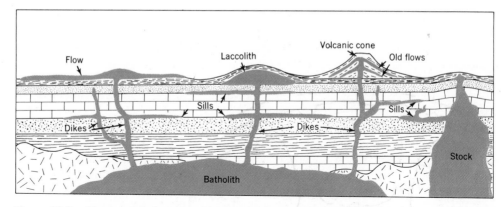

Figure 13.9   Characteristic features of intrusive and extrusive vulcanism.

masses similar in character to batholiths but much smaller in size are called stocks.

When molten material under great pressure enters the rocks near the surface, it often makes its way into joints and other fractures, where it solidifies into vertical sheets known as dikes; or it works in between the layers of stratified rocks to form horizontal sheets called sills. Sometimes in this situation, the overlying rock is bulged upward by the intrusive material, forming a great blister. The hardened filling of such a blister is called a laccolith. The filling of a volcanic vent forms a volcanic plug or neck.

Extrusive Vulcanism. In extrusive vulcanism, much rock material, along with quantities of gases and steam, is forced out onto the surface of the earth. This material may be emitted rather quietly as molten rock or lava, or may be vigorously blown out as solid rock in particles ranging from fine dust to large boulders.

Some volcanoes characteristically erupt in a series of explosions, often of tremendous force. This is especially likely to happen when the vent of the volcano has been sealed over by quick-hardening lavas, allowing extreme pressures to build up underneath. Vesuvius is a familiar example of an explosive volcano. Krakatau, in Indonesia, and Katmai, in Alaska, have produced two of the greatest explosions of human record. Each mountain nearly destroyed itself by blasts of almost incredible violence. In the products ejected by explosive volcanoes, the percentage of solid material (ash) is naturally great (Fig. 13.10).

Figure 13.10   The volcano Parícutin, Mexico, in violent eruption. Typical steep-sided cinder cone. *(American Museum of Natural History.)*

By way of contrast, many volcanoes emit slow-cooling lavas that have little tendency to plug the vents. Eruptions of these volcanoes are quieter and normally produce a much lower percentage of ash. The volcanoes of Hawaii are of this type.

Lava flows and ash deposits are the most extensive products of extrusive vulcanism. Near a vent these products may pile up to great thickness, forming a volcanic cone. Most lava accumulations cover no more than a few square miles of the earth's surface. In a few places, however, layer after layer of highly fluid, slow-cooling lava, usually basaltic, has emerged through extensive systems of vents and has spread out over hundreds or thousands of square miles. In the Columbia Plateau region of the northwestern United States, successive flows over a long period covered an area of more than 100,000 square miles to an average depth of ½ mile. Similar accumulations cover large parts of peninsular India, Ethiopia, and southern Brazil.

World Pattern of Crustal Disturbance. Crustal disturbance has not been evenly distributed over the world in any given period of geologic history—nor, indeed, for the whole span of geologic history. The majority of the deformed rock structures that exist today were produced long ago. Thus, for example, the folds of the Rocky Mountains developed about 70 million years ago, while those of the Appalachians are more than 200 million years old. Many of the complex structures of central and eastern Canada date far back into early geologic time, some probably more than a billion years ago. These records of ancient events exist now only because later diastrophism or erosion has not destroyed them. Some areas of the crust do not appear to have been subjected to anything more than mild warping for hundreds of millions of years. Others seem to have undergone strong and repeated disturbances over a long span of geologic time and are still being actively changed today.

Since earthquakes commonly accompany the fracturing and displacement of rocks, their pattern of occurrence should indicate where the greatest diastrophic activity is centered at the present time. Figure 13.11 shows that the principal earthquake regions lie in a belt which circles the basin of the Pacific Ocean and extends westward across southern Eurasia. Comparison with Plate 3 will reveal a close correlation with the high-mountain

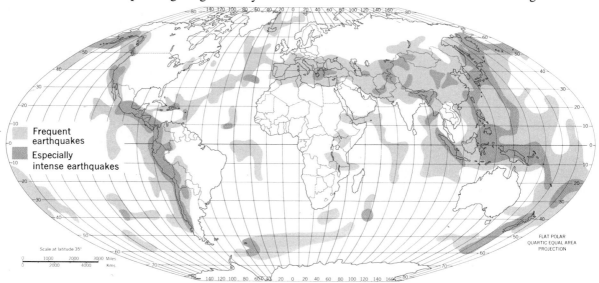

Frequent earthquakes

Especially intense earthquakes

Scale at latitude 35°

FLAT POLAR QUARTIC EQUAL AREA PROJECTION

Figure 13.11   The principal earthquake regions of the world. (*Adapted from Leet, Causes of Catastrophe. McGraw-Hill Book Company, New York, 1948.*)

regions of the world, which is not surprising, since high mountains are themselves indicative of strong tectonic activity in late geologic time.

Volcanic activity is much more localized than diastrophism, but it occurs chiefly in areas that are also diastrophically active (Fig. 13.12). Deep-seated masses of molten rock seem to develop most frequently in places where the crust has been profoundly deformed. Moreover, the fracturing associated with diastrophism provides zones of weakness through which the molten rock can most readily move toward the surface.

Causes of the Deformation. Not surprisingly, geologists and geophysicists have put much effort into the attempt to determine the origin and pattern of the forces that have so clearly, repeatedly, and powerfully deformed the crust. Many interesting and ingenious hypotheses have been devised, but so far none has proved wholly satisfactory as a comprehensive explanation of the observed facts of deformation.

The most widely respected hypotheses at the present time are probably those that ascribe major crustal movements to slow convectional cur-rents in the solid but plastic mantle underneath. Perhaps because of differences in radioactivity or in the rate of heat loss through the crust, temperature differences may occur deep in the mantle. Over "hot spots" rising currents might then develop, spreading out at the base of the crust, while over cooler areas currents would converge and sink. The horizontally moving currents at the base of the crust would drag the crust along with them. Crustal jamming would then occur in the zones of convergence, while stretching would result in the zones of divergence (Fig. 13.13). Some theorists believe that the continental blocks themselves have been strongly displaced relative to one another over long periods of geologic time.

Unfortunately space does not permit comprehensive treatment of this intriguing body of speculative research. Much of it rests upon assumptions concerning the nature and environment of the mantle that are themselves not yet securely based. It remains true that neither the existence nor the pattern of the largest of all geographic features—the continents, ocean basins, and great mountain belts—can at present be accounted for with any certainty.

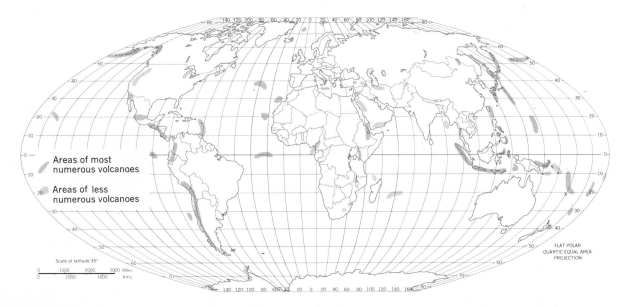

Figure 13.12   The principal volcanic regions of the world. *(Adapted from Sapper, Vulkankunde.)*

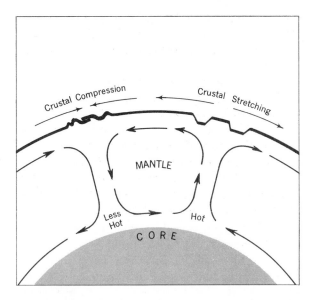

Figure 13.13 The theory of convectional currents in the earth's mantle.

Importance of Tectonic Activity. From the point of view of the development of land-surface form, the tectonic processes, whether they involve crustal deformation or vulcanism, produce two significant kinds of results: surface irregularities and rock structures. Surface irregularities caused by tectonic activity are many and varied. Fault scarps, broad domes and basins, high-standing horsts and depressed grabens, anticlinal ridges and synclinal troughs—all are examples of diastrophic surface forms. Vulcanism produces cones and craters, laccolithic bulges, and tongues or plains of lava.

We rarely find these tectonic landforms in a "pure" state; usually they have been modified by gradation, sometimes sufficiently to make the original feature scarcely recognizable. The local differences in elevation produced by tectonics provide the energy required for the movement of streams, glaciers, and gravity-powered slides and flows of earth. But as soon as these agents begin to act, they begin to destroy the very irregularities that brought them to life. By the geologic time scale, such destruction proceeds swiftly, erasing even great mountain systems in a few tens of millions of years and smaller features in much less time. Thus the surface irregularities produced by tectonics, though important, are not particularly long-lived.

On the other hand, warped, folded, and faulted rock structures, which reach deep into the crust, can persist for eons. Erosion may quickly strip off their upper parts, but the lower parts remain untouched unless later tectonic activity reworks them. And as long as these structures remain, their distinctive arrangements of diverse rock materials affect the form and arrangement of the surface features that the gradational agents produce (Fig. 13.14).

Rock Materials and Rock Breakdown

Rock types are important to the study of land-surface form both because they differ greatly in their resistance to the agents that disintegrate and decompose them and because they yield very different products when they are chemically decomposed. These contrasts in behavior stem from differences in (1) the chemical composition of the materials that form the rocks, (2) the size, arrangement, and cohesiveness of the grains or particles, and (3) the detailed structure of the rock— that is, whether it is thin-bedded, platy, or massive.

Figure 13.14 Differential erosion has left resistant volcanic dikes standing like walls above the surrounding surface. Near Spanish Peaks, southern Colorado. *(Stose, U.S. Geological Survey.)*

Minerals. Rocks are made up of particles of substances called minerals, each of which has its own well-defined chemical composition and physical properties. Some minerals are soluble or otherwise chemically unstable under conditions that are common near the earth's surface. Others are highly stable under normal surface conditions and thus resist decomposition. Some minerals are physically hard and difficult to break; others are easily crushed or split. Although there are hundreds of known minerals, a relatively small number make up the great bulk of the crust. Some of the commonest of these are listed in the table below. Several of the entries in the table refer to groups of closely related minerals (for example, the feldspars or the clay minerals) rather than single members of the group.

Some of these common minerals are formed during the cooling and crystallization of molten materials. Others are usually products of the decomposition of more complex minerals. In the table, for example, the feldspars, micas, pyroxenes, amphiboles, and magnetite fall into the first class, while the clays, calcite, dolomite, hematite, and limonite belong to the second. Silica can develop in either way.

The great differences among minerals in hardness and chemical stability are transmitted to the rocks which they compose, and because of their varied mineral composition, the rocks themselves vary in physical and chemical resistance. Although it is not within the scope of this book to discuss the hundreds of recognized types of rocks, the student of land-surface form should know something about the nature and origin of rocks, and should become generally familiar with the characteristics and relative resistance of some of the commonest varieties.

Rocks. Geologists usually classify rocks primarily by their mode of origin. The three principal classes are (1) *igneous* rocks, which have crystallized from a molten state; (2) *sedimentary* rocks, which have developed through the consolidation of loose sediments deposited by the various agents of gradation

COMMON ROCK-FORMING MINERALS

Name	Composition	Hardness	Chemical stability	Distinctive characteristics
Silica (quartz and related minerals)	Silicon dioxide	Very hard	Very stable	Transparent or various light colors
Feldspars	Aluminum silicates with potassium, calcium, or sodium	Hard	Moderately stable to moderately unstable	Pink or grey; smooth faces common
Micas	Aluminum silicates with potassium, iron, or magnesium	Soft	Moderately stable	Transparent or black; thin flakes and sheets
Pyroxenes and amphiboles	Silicates of calcium, magnesium, iron, and sometimes aluminum	Hard	Moderately unstable	Dark green or black
Clay minerals	Hydrous aluminum silicates	Soft	Stable	Earthy; light colors
Calcite	Calcium carbonate	Soft	Very unstable	Usually transparent, white, or light colors
Dolomite	Calcium-magnesium carbonate	Rather soft	Unstable	Usually transparent, white, or light colors
Hematite, magnetite, limonite	Iron oxides	Variable	Stable	Black, red, or yellow; often earthy

or through chemical precipitation of substances carried in solution; and (3) *metamorphic* rocks, which have been formed through the alteration of other rocks, chiefly by great pressure and heat or by the work of mineralized groundwaters or hot gases.

By definition, igneous rocks are associated with vulcanism and form the various intrusive bodies, lava flows, and ash deposits. Most are composed of interlocking particles or grains of the commoner igneous minerals, such as quartz, feldspars, micas, and amphiboles or pyroxenes. In general, those of the larger and deeper intrusions, which have cooled slowly, are coarse-grained, while those of the more quickly cooled surface flows and narrow dikes and sills tend to be fine-particled. Among the abundant coarse-grained igneous rocks are granite (made up chiefly of quartz and feldspar), diorite (mostly feldspars), and gabbro (pyroxenes, amphiboles, and feldspars). The fine-grained counterparts of these three are, respectively, rhyolite, andesite, and basalt. Except for lavas, ash deposits, and thin sills, the igneous rocks are massive rather than layered.

In contrast, sedimentary rocks are characteristically stratified, with layers or beds of varying thickness (Fig. 13.15). One group of common sedimentary rocks, called clastic rocks, are simply deposits of loose gravels, sands, silts, or clays that have been cemented together by some substance— most commonly silica or calcium carbonate, but sometimes iron oxides or clay. Conglomerate (cemented gravel), sandstone (sand), and shale (clay) are examples of this group. Limestones, dolomites, rocksalt, and gypsum are examples of rocks formed by the precipitation or removal of the particular mineral substance from solution, usually in lakes or shallow seas.

Metamorphic rocks, since they may be produced by various processes and from any kind of rock, are an extremely complex and diverse group. Some are distinctly foliated (divided into well-defined bands, sheets, or plates), while others are more massive. Some, especially those formed from sedimentary rocks, may be stratified. Among

Figure 13.15 Stratified sedimentary rocks cut by a normal fault. Separations between individual strata are bedding planes. *(Winchester, U.S. Geological Survey.)*

the foliated types are gneiss (a coarse-banded rock commonly derived from granite, diorite, or conglomerate), schist (a more finely foliated rock that may develop from gabbro, basalt, shale, etc.; shown in Fig. 13.16), and slate (a firm-plated material usually derived from shale). More massive metamorphic rocks include fine-particled hornfels (from shale), coarsely crystalline marble (from limestone), and granular or nearly structureless quartzite (from sandstone).

Processes of Rock Breakdown. None of the agents of gradation is able to work very effectively against solid, massive bedrock. Therefore the processes of decomposition and disintegration are highly important preliminaries to the work of surface erosion.

Figure 13.16 Foliated schist. Lighter-colored band cutting across foliation is a granitic dike intruded after the schist was formed.

Together these processes are commonly referred to as *weathering,* though the term is hardly appropriate if applied to the diastrophic shattering of rock far below the surface. Two interrelated groups of processes contribute to rock breakdown. One is simply mechanical breaking of the rock, or *disintegration.* The other is chemical alteration of the rock minerals, or *decomposition.* The two go on at the same time and actually aid one another, for the cracking of rock makes it easier for chemical agents (chiefly water) to penetrate, and conversely, decomposition weakens rock masses so that they can be broken more easily.

In spite of the basic simplicity of the disintegration process, the various ways by which it is accomplished in nature are imperfectly known. Probably the most important methods of rock breaking are (1) the formation of joints during

crustal deformation or in response to stresses developed during the cooling or compaction of rocks, (2) the expansion of water as it freezes in rock crevices, and (3) the wedging effect of the growth of plant roots in rock crevices. In addition, all scraping, grinding, scouring, and striking of the rock surface by hard, heavy, or fast-moving objects may dislodge fragments from the larger mass. The extreme temperature changes that accompany forest fires or lightning strikes cause enough uneven expansion and contraction to strain rocks to the breaking point. Rock disintegration may thus be expected everywhere; but it is probably farthest advanced where crustal deformation has occurred, where plant roots are especially abundant, and where alternate freezes and thaws are frequent.

The principal agent of rock decomposition is water—especially water which contains certain dissolved substances, such as carbon dioxide, that make it more aggressive chemically. Most water in the ground does contain these impurities, which are washed down from the atmosphere, given off by plant roots, or released during organic decay. High temperatures also contribute to decomposition, not only by keeping water unfrozen, but by increasing the rate of chemical reaction. The rotting of rock is therefore most rapid and complete in moist areas, especially the humid tropics, and most retarded in arid or very cold regions. Some decomposition occurs, however, even where the climate is arid or cold.

The chemical processes involved in decomposition attack firm rock in several ways. Some minerals are actively removed in solution. The rest, as a rule, soften and swell and are eventually altered to yield substances that are softer, more soluble, or finer-particled than the original minerals, so that the rock is weakened or even destroyed. As an example, the hard mineral hornblende, one of the amphiboles, decomposes into calcium and magnesium carbonates (which are soluble), iron oxides and clays (which are fine-particled), and silica in such fine-particled form (colloidal) that it is easily removed by water.

The end products of disintegration are

simply rock fragments—usually rather angular ones. Decomposition, on the other hand, characteristically produces a mass of fine soil particles and more or less rounded fragments of somewhat rotten rock. If erosion does not remove these products, they accumulate to form a surface layer of debris called the *regolith* (Fig. 13.17). In humid areas the regolith is composed predominantly of fine debris from decomposition. In dry and cold areas, however, the angular products of disintegration are more evident, not because they are more abundant there than elsewhere, but simply because they are not hidden by finer debris (Fig. 13.18).

Rock Resistance. It has already been emphasized that different types of rocks, because of their mineral composition and detailed structure, differ greatly in their response to the weathering processes. Some are very resistant in almost any environment; others are universally weak. Still others may yield readily to decomposition in humid climates but prove surprisingly resistant in a desert environment.

In humid climates the most important factor in resistance is the chemical stability of the minerals which compose the rock. Thus rocks made up largely of silica are likely to be especially resistant; those composed chiefly of feldspars, pyroxenes, and amphiboles will be intermediate in resistance; and those composed of or cemented by

Figure 13.18 Angular rock debris at elevation of 14,000 ft on Torreys Peak near Georgetown, Colorado. Repeated freeze and thaw at this high altitude favors rapid shattering of rock. Larger fragments measure 1 to 3 ft across.

the soluble salts and carbonates decompose readily. Other things being equal, massive, impermeable rocks resist decomposition better than jointed, thin-bedded, or foliated rocks containing the same minerals. The most resistant of all common rocks is quartzite, which is tightly structured and composed wholly of silica. Among the rocks that are fairly resistant in humid climates are granite, rhyolite, gneiss, silica-cemented sandstones and conglomerates, and some dolomites that contain much silica. Lower on the scale but still moderately resistant are gabbro, diorite, andesite, basalt, slates, the thicker-banded schists, most conglomerates, and some silica-rich limestones. Moderately weak rocks include dolomites, thin-plated schists, thick-bedded shales, and lime-cemented sandstones. Weakest of all are pure limestones, marbles, rocksalt, and thin-bedded shales. However, all the types listed are subject to significant variations.

In dry regions, where chemical weathering is feeble, the physical structure of the rock appears to be very important. Massive, fine-grained rocks—such as rhyolites, basalts, quartzites, and even thick-bedded, fine-particled limestones—seem to endure better than coarse-grained granites, porous sandstones, all thin-bedded sedimentary rocks, and highly foliated metamorphic rocks. Weathering as

Figure 13.17 Bedrock grading upward into regolith of rock fragments and soil.

a whole, however, proceeds much more slowly in arid regions than in humid ones.

Selected References for Chaps. 13 to 17

Dury, George. *The Face of the Earth*. Penguin Books, Inc., Baltimore, 1959.

Fenneman, Nevin M. *Physiography of Western United States*. McGraw-Hill Book Company, New York, 1931.

————. *Physiography of Eastern United States*. McGraw-Hill Book Company, New York, 1938.

Flint, R. F. *Glacial and Pleistocene Geology*. 2d ed. John Wiley & Sons, Inc., New York, 1961.

Gilluly, J., A. C. Waters, and A. O. Woodford. *Principles of Geology*. 2d ed. W. H. Freeman and Company, San Francisco, 1958.

Hammond, E. H. Map and text: Classes of Land-surface Form in the United States. 2 sheets. U.S. Geol. Survey, Washington, D.C., 1966.

Hunt, C. B. *Physiography of the United States*. W. H. Freeman and Company, San Francisco, 1967.

King, Lester C. *The Morphology of the Earth: A Study and Synthesis of World Scenery*. Hafner Publishing Company, Inc., New York, 1962.

Leet, L. D., and S. Judson. *Physical Geology*. 2d ed. Prentice-Hall, Inc., Englewood Cliffs, N.J., 1958.

Leopold, L. B., M. G. Wolman, and J. P. Miller. *Fluvial Processes in Geomorphology*. W. H. Freeman and Company, San Francisco, 1964.

Raisz, Erwin. Map: Landforms of the United States. 6th ed. Ginn and Company, Boston, 1957.

Sharpe, C. F. S. *Landslides and Related Phenomena*. Columbia University Press, New York, 1934.

Shelton, John S. *Geology Illustrated*. W. H. Freeman and Company, San Francisco, 1966.

Strahler, A. N. *Physical Geography*. 2d ed. John Wiley & Sons, Inc., New York, 1960.

Thornbury, W. D. *Principles of Geomorphology*. John Wiley & Sons, Inc., New York, 1954.

————. *Regional Geomorphology of the United States*. John Wiley & Sons, Inc., New York, 1965.

Trewartha, G. T., A. H. Robinson, and E. H. Hammond. *Physical Elements of Geography*. 5th ed. McGraw-Hill Book Company, New York, 1967.

14

Sculpturing the Land Surface

The Sculpturing Agents and Their Work. Whenever soil or rock material is moved from one place to another across the earth's surface, the surface form is changed. The agents that are the most active movers of earth materials—running water, glacier ice, wind, waves, and gravity—are therefore the principal sculptors of the land's surface form. Gravity, an important earth mover in its own right, is also the direct or indirect source of power for the other agents. Hence when material is picked up and moved by any agent, it is most likely to come to rest at a point lower than where it began. The long-run effect is for the higher parts of the surface to be lowered by removal of material and for the low sections to be raised by deposition, thus reducing the overall irregularity. It is for this reason that the agents working at the surface are often called the gradational agents.

It is convenient to divide the work of any sculpturing agent into three parts: erosion, transportation, and deposition. This division is somewhat artificial, especially that between erosion, which is the detaching of material from its initial position, and transportation, the carrying of the material away from the point of erosion. However, the laws governing the processes do differ, and they can be understood best when they are examined individually. It is also necessary to consider the work of the different sculpturing agents separately, for each agent has its own peculiarities and produces its own distinctive results.

Before the 1930s, surprisingly little was actually known about the mechanics of erosion, transportation, and deposition by the different sculpturing agents. Most earlier students had based their concepts of the gradational processes largely upon inference drawn from observing the landforms themselves. Unavoidably, the inferences were not all correct. During the past few decades careful field observation, simulation of natural conditions in laboratory experiments, and the application of physical theory have greatly advanced our understanding of the agents, especially water and wind. Much still remains to be learned, however.

Running Water

For the world as a whole, running water is the most important long-distance transporter of earth material. In company with the short-haul activities of gravity-induced movements of regolith on slopes (which are called *mass movements*), it has been at work almost everywhere. Although some landscapes show the effects of some other agent more clearly, running water has left its marks on all but a few.

Origin and Mechanical Effects of Surface Flow

Direct and Indirect Runoff. As already described in Chap. 11, the water that falls to the land surface as precipitation follows two different downward paths (Fig. 14.1). Some of it flows down the sur-

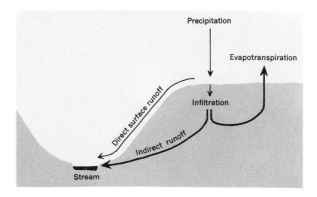

Figure 14.1 Relationships among precipitation, infiltration, runoff, and evapotranspiration.

face of the slope as *direct surface runoff*. The rest soaks into the regolith as infiltration water. If precipitation is slow and gentle, if the regolith is highly permeable, or if surface runoff is slowed by the levelness of the land or by a dense cover of vegetation, a relatively high percentage of the precipitation will soak in. On the other hand, heavy downpours, fine-particled regolith, steep slopes, and an absence of vegetation all favor direct surface runoff.

Direct surface runoff begins to move as a thin sheet of water on the upper slopes. Because it seeks the lowest place and the easiest line of movement, it soon becomes concentrated into well-defined threads of flow. These join other threads in progressive fashion, thus forming larger and larger streams and rivers. The smaller streams are referred to as tributaries of the larger streams that they join. A major stream together with all its tributaries is called a stream system, and the entire area of land drained by a given stream system is the drainage basin of that system. The line separating one drainage basin from the next is a divide.

Of the water that infiltrates the ground, much is taken up by plant roots and returned to the atmosphere by evaporation from the leaves. Most of the remainder, however, moves both downward and laterally through the regolith and bedrock, eventually reappearing at the surface through seepages and springs on the lower slopes and in the valley bottoms. Since this water eventually enters the streams, it may be referred to as *indirect runoff*. Direct and indirect runoff together constitute the total runoff of the drainage basin.

Water Erosion. Water dislodges particles from the land surface by five principal means: (1) the impact of raindrops striking against a bare soil surface; (2) the direct frictional drag of a flowing sheet or stream of water upon the underlying bed; (3) the work of eddy currents in the flowing water, which help to loosen particles from the bed and flip them up into the moving mass; (4) the impact or friction against the bed created by particles already in motion; and (5) the dissolving of soluble minerals with which the water comes in contact.

Frictional drag, eddy current activity (turbulence), and the strength of particle impact all increase rapidly as the speed of the flowing water increases. Also, frictional drag increases as the depth of the water becomes greater. Speed of flow depends chiefly upon the steepness of the gradient, the depth of the water, and the roughness of the bed. Thus running water has the greatest erosional force in deep, steep-gradient channels and is least effective in thin sheets and upon gentle slopes.

Erosion is also affected by the particle size and cohesiveness of the material over which the water flows. Up to a certain point, the smaller the particles, the easier they are to erode, with the maximum ease of erosion in the very fine sand or coarse silt range (about 0.2 to 0.5 mm diameter). But the finer silts and still finer clays are surprisingly difficult to erode, probably because the particles fit tightly together and tend to cling to each other. Of course, if particles are actually cemented together, resistance to erosion is greatly increased.

Most of the land surface lies outside of well-defined stream channels. In these areas erosion depends strongly upon the vegetation cover, which not only protects the soil against raindrop impact, but also greatly slows the rate of runoff and increases the percentage of infiltration. A well-vegetated slope on which almost no measurable erosion has been occurring may be disastrously stripped and gullied in a single rainstorm if the vegetation is removed (Fig. 14.2).

Figure 14.2 Erosion by sheetflow and gullying on a slope whose grass cover had been thinned by overgrazing. *(W. H. Lathrop, Soil Conservation Service.)*

Erosion by solution, though it occurs almost everywhere, is especially rapid in places where such soluble rocks as limestone and dolomite are exposed to the moving water. The work of solution by groundwater is more frequently emphasized in the literature, but solution by surface runoff is also very important as a gradational process.

Transportation by Running Water. Particles that have been dislodged from a slope or a stream bed are transported in several ways (Fig. 14.3). Materials too heavy to be raised from the bottom are simply rolled or shoved along by the force of the current and the impact of other particles. Somewhat smaller grains are thrown up into the current by eddies and then carried downstream until they settle, strike the bottom, and bounce up again, thus proceeding by a series of leaps. This process is called saltation. Still smaller particles are so light that they can be kept off the bottom by the churning eddy currents. These particles are said to be in suspension. The load of particles which are moved along the bottom, together with the heavier part of the load moving by saltation, is referred to as the bed load. The lighter part of the load in saltation is usually grouped with the load in suspension under the name of the suspended load. Still other material is carried invisibly in solution.

Clay and silt particles are almost always carried in suspension, and even fine sands will move in suspension at modest stream velocities. Gravels, on the other hand, are nearly always moved as bed load. Usually coarse sands are too, except in the swiftest streams. A heavy bed load tends to "get in its own way": friction among its particles becomes excessive, and the particles underneath are masked by those above. For this reason, it seems probable that there are stringent limits to the amount of coarse debris that a stream of given depth, width, and velocity can keep in motion at a given time. On the other hand, the concentration of suspended load can reach remarkably high values. Occasionally, samples taken from muddy streams in flood have contained several pounds of suspended matter per cubic foot of water.

The concentration of load carried in solution depends chiefly upon the climate and the presence of exposed soluble rocks. Streams in the moister sections of the United States commonly carry as much as one-fourth to one-half of their total load in solution—a surprisingly high figure that indicates the importance of this often-neglected process.

Deposition by Water. Deposition occurs whenever (1) the velocity of flow drops below the value necessary to keep in motion all the material being transported, (2) the volume of water decreases below the amount needed to carry all the load, or (3) tributary streams, sheetflow erosion, or other agents dump more load into the stream than it can handle. Under any of these conditions the heavier

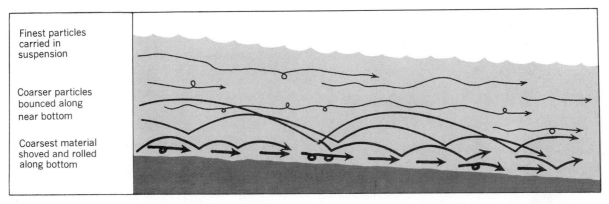

Finest particles carried in suspension

Coarser particles bounced along near bottom

Coarsest material shoved and rolled along bottom

Figure 14.3   Ways in which solid materials are transported by running water.

and coarser elements of the bed load are most readily dropped, while the suspended load is most easily kept in motion. All stream-deposited materials are referred to as *alluvium*.

A particularly common location for deposition induced by decreased velocity of flow is in the slack water on the inner sides of stream bends, where accumulations known as point bars develop. More extensive deposition occurs where the velocity is checked as the stream enters a lake, a reservoir, or the sea, or as it emerges from a steep mountain canyon onto a gently sloping plain.

A downstream decrease in volume of water occurs chiefly in the dry lands. Rivers such as the Nile, the Colorado, and the Indus enter deserts from moister regions and receive no important contributions of runoff during their desert passage. Because of evaporation and infiltration, the volume of water in the river shrinks and deposition occurs all along the course.

Sometimes glaciers, gravity-induced earth movements, or unusually heavy slope erosion will feed more coarse load into a given section of a stream than the stream can transport. Under these circumstances deposition will occur along the channel for some distance below the point where the material enters.

Stream Channels and Discharge

Well-defined streams of runoff carve elongated grooves or *channels* large enough to accommodate their waters. The volume of water that passes through a given cross section of the channel in a unit of time is called the *discharge* of the stream. The discharge of any stream fluctuates continually, chiefly in response to the occurrence and intensity of precipitation or, in some cases, of snowmelt. A stream at high water often discharges five to fifteen times as much as at low water, and in the drier climates many streams dry up completely between rains.

The discharge of a stream is measured by the product of the cross-section area of the stream and the velocity of flow. The same discharge could be carried by a wide, shallow channel or a narrow, deep one. However, frictional drag in a shallow channel is greater than in a deep one, so that a steeper gradient is needed in the shallow stream to maintain a given velocity of flow.

During high-water periods a stream deepens and increases its velocity, thereby gaining increased erosional power, which it expends in scouring its bed and undermining its banks. By repeated erosion of this kind, the channel eventually achieves dimensions and a gradient that are adjusted to handle the more frequently occurring high-water discharges. Observations indicate that most streams have channels large enough to be filled bankfull once every year or two. The less frequent discharges of even greater amounts cause the stream to overflow its banks, producing floods.

As discharge recedes following high water, the stream simply shrinks within its channel and becomes relatively inactive. If it is transporting bed load, it may deposit much of this as discharge decreases, only to set the load in motion again at the next period of high water. Undoubtedly most channel erosion other than solution occurs at high water, and most deposition during periods of receding discharge.

The typical stream channel is considerably wider than it is deep and has a more or less flat floor with inclined sides. The steepness of the sides and the ratio of width to depth appear to depend principally upon the materials that form the banks and bed. Loose, easily caving sands yield wide, shallow channels with gently inclined sides (Fig. 14.4B). More cohesive sediments give steeper sides and greater depth (Fig. 14.4A). Channels cut in well-consolidated bedrock are the deepest, narrowest, and steepest-walled of all.

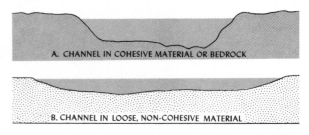

Figure 14.4   Characteristic cross sections of stream channels.

Meandering and Braided Channels. Nearly all streams of fluid that are not narrowly confined show a clear tendency to develop rhythmic swings from side to side. Such sinuosities can be seen even in the atmospheric jet streams, as well as in clearly defined ocean currents like the Gulf Stream and in river channels.

Where these winding patterns are best developed in rivers, it has been discovered that successive bends are quite regularly spaced along the stream at intervals of about six or seven times the width of the channel. Similarly, it has been found that many channels develop alternate deep spots

(pools) and shallow sections (riffles) at essentially the same spacings (i.e., from one pool to the next). In winding channels the pools regularly fall at the outsides of the bends, the riffles in the straighter sections between. It is evident that the sinuosity and the depth changes are closely related in their development, but the relevant theory is beyond the scope of this book.

The smoothest and most regular winding, called meandering, is most often found in streams that are flowing on broad surfaces of predominantly silty alluvium, though some sand is commonly present as bed load (Fig. 14.5A). Point bars form in

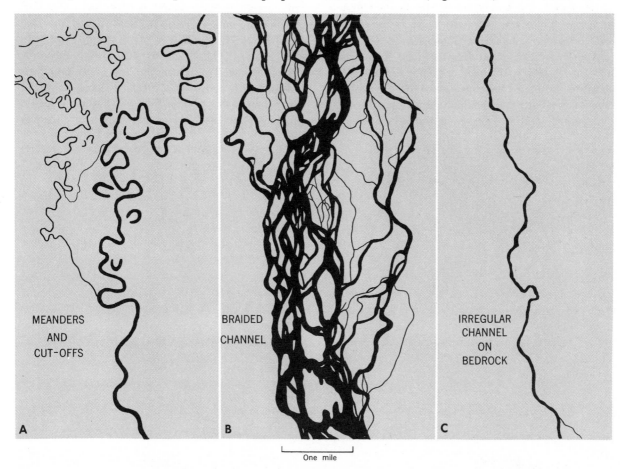

MEANDERS
AND
CUT-OFFS

BRAIDED
CHANNEL

IRREGULAR
CHANNEL
ON
BEDROCK

A

B

C

One mile

Figure 14.5   Characteristic stream channel patterns. A: A stream flowing on fine-textured alluvium commonly displays a pattern of shifting meanders. B: A stream moving sandy or gravelly bed load often develops a braided pattern. C: Streams cutting in bedrock characteristically have relatively narrow, irregular channels. *(From U.S. Geological Survey topographic sheets: Fairbanks D-1, Fairbanks C-1, and Fairbanks A-4, Alaska.)*

the slack waters on the inside of each bend just downstream from the sharpest curve, while the opposite bank is undercut and caves in (Fig. 14.6). As a result, each meander loop tends to enlarge and migrate slowly downstream. Often one loop will break through to join the next loop downstream, thus cutting off the intervening segment of the channel, which then slowly fills with sediment.

Channels cut in bedrock usually develop narrow and irregular bends rather than true meanders (Fig. 14.5C), though there are conspicuous exceptions. The generally high but variable resistance of the bank materials inhibits and irregularizes the lateral movement of the channel that is necessary if meanders are to form.

Streams flowing in loose sands and transporting quantities of sand as bed load form channels of a highly distinctive type (Fig. 14.5B). Because the banks cave so easily, the channel becomes very wide and shallow. Sand bars form in midchannel, and the narrowed threads of flow to

either side erode their outside banks. In time these channels also develop bars, become subdivided, and widen by bank caving. The ultimate result, called a braided channel, is a wide band composed of many narrow subchannels separated by bars. Because the frictional drag in the narrow, shallow ribbons of flow is so great, braided channels can keep their sandy bed load in motion only by maintaining relatively steep gradients.

Downstream Changes in Channels. Streams in humid lands normally increase in discharge from head to mouth because of the water supplied by tributaries. To accommodate this increased flow, the channel must increase in width, depth, or velocity of flow. Examination of many channels indicates that as a rule all three increase, width most and velocity least. Until recently it was generally believed that because most streams decrease in gradient toward the mouth (Fig. 14.7), their velocities must also decrease, but measurements disclose that

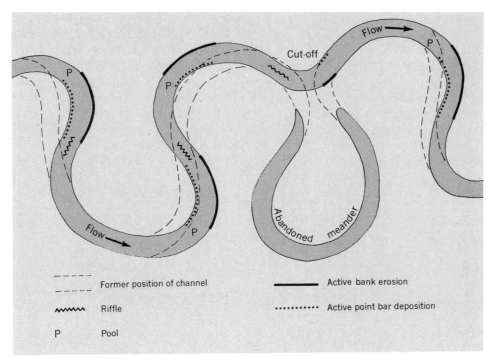

Figure 14.6 Characteristic features of a meandering channel.

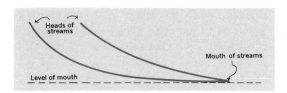

Figure 14.7 Characteristic lengthwise profiles of stream channels.

the greater depth and width actually reduce the frictional drag enough to permit the speed to rise slightly. Recent investigations have suggested that stream channels tend to develop toward a condition in which the downstream changes in width, depth, and velocity (and therefore gradient) are neatly adjusted to provide a constant rate of energy loss along the stream.

The reason for the characteristic downstream decrease in gradient is not wholly clear, though some contributing factors can be suggested. For example, a stream cannot cut below the level of its mouth (baselevel). From the beginning of development, the lower reaches of a stream are close to baselevel and thus have little vertical distance through which they can cut. Therefore one would expect those sections to achieve gentle and limiting gradients early, while the upper reaches of the stream are still far above baselevel and still steep. The particle size of the material in the stream bed also plays a part. Other things being equal, fine material can be eroded and transported on gentler gradients than coarse material. A stream segment on coarse bed material cannot cut down to the gentle gradients that a stream segment on fine materials can. Because of continued wear and tear, the average size of particles in the stream bed tends to diminish downstream, a circumstance which favors a concave profile.

There may be significant irregularities in gradient in an actively eroding stream flowing over contrasting materials. As a result of differing rates of erosion, falls and rapids may develop on the resistant rocks, while gentler stretches occur where water flows over weak materials (Fig. 14.8). Some other irregularities in gradient may result from diastrophic disturbance of the channel, or from blocking by lava flows or landslides. In time, however, these various irregularities are gradually smoothed out, and the profile assumes the characteristic form.

Changes in Channels through Time. Geomorphologists have long believed that stream channels undergo relatively rapid change until they reach some kind of balance or equilibrium, beyond which change is very slow or negligible. In classical geomorphology it was usually thought that the stream cut down actively until it reached a very gentle gradient near baselevel. At that time it ceased to cut down, but began to meander and to cut laterally, thereby widening its valley.

In modern geomorphology a stream is be-

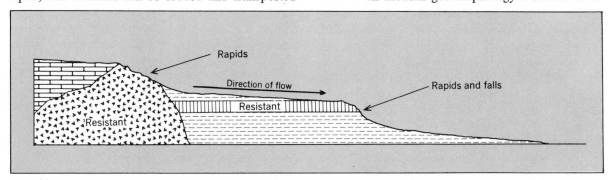

Figure 14.8 Rock resistance may affect stream profiles. Weaker rocks erode more rapidly and allow the stream to achieve gentler gradients, while resistant outcrops, because they yield more slowly and are undercut from below, develop steep gradients, rapids, and falls.

lieved to alter its channel rapidly by widening, deepening, and changing its gradient until each segment of the channel is nicely adjusted to carry the more frequent high-water discharges, together with the sediment load fed to it from above. This condition of equilibrium does not necessarily involve a gentle gradient, nor need the stream be near baselevel. If the stream is flowing on coarse bed materials or is carrying a coarse bed load, the gradient will have to be substantial. Furthermore, the stream may adjust its channel by widening with little or no deepening, especially where bank materials are loose. Valley widening, with or without meandering, may occur at any stage and is not dependent upon lateral erosion by the stream itself. The rather small number of careful investigations of stream channels that have been made suggest that many channel segments are well adjusted to the discharges and loads they carry, and thus appear to be in a near-equilibrium state.

However, the very fact that quantities of sediment are being passed through stream channels to their mouths makes it clear that progressive erosion is going on in some places in the drainage basins while deposition is occurring in others. Probably erosion in the small, steep headwater channels, together with unchanneled sheetflow and mass movements of regolith on the slopes, is responsible for most of the sediment load in major channels.

Causes of Channel Modification. Any major change in a stream channel, whether in width, depth, or gradient, is brought about by some significant change in the environment of the stream. For example, diastrophic uplift of a drainage basin would raise its streams farther above baselevel and thus give them room and energy for further downcutting. At first, the only parts of the system that would be affected would be those where the stream gradients were actually increased, perhaps around the margins of the uplifted area. In time, however, the downcutting would work its way progressively upstream into the remainder of the basin.

Increased erosion could also be caused by increased high-water discharges. These might result from a climatic change, especially an increase in the intensity of downpours, or from a thinning of the vegetation that would allow more surface runoff. In some instances discharge might be increased by the natural diversion of a sizable stream into the drainage basin, or by invasion of the basin by an extensive glacier. Other things being equal, an increase in discharge will cause an erosional deepening or widening of the channel—commonly both.

Finally, a channel could be forced to change by an increase or decrease in the supply of bed load. Increased direct surface runoff in the headwater area, especially if the vegetation cover were not dense, would stimulate erosion on the slopes and hence would increase the amount of sediment being dumped into the streams. Unless the increase in discharge was exceptionally great, the increase of bed load would cause extensive deposition in the channels. Deposition can also be induced in a given stream by damming (either natural or artificial) or by raising the water level at the mouth. In either instance, deposition will occur only in the section where the flow has been checked.

Valleys and Valley Systems

The fact that nearly all streams occupy valleys much deeper than the channels themselves indicates that most streams pass through a period of progressive downcutting. Not all the excavation of a valley is done by the stream itself, however. As soon as valley walls are exposed above the stream surface, other agencies such as slope wash, gullying, and gravity-induced movements of regolith will attack them, driving them back, sometimes reducing their steepness, and thereby widening the valley. In general, narrow or steep-walled valleys result from resistant materials, small runoff down the valley sides, and rapid downcutting. On the other hand, loose or thin-bedded materials, slow downcutting, and much local surface runoff tend to produce wider valleys and more gently sloping walls.

As the branches of a given stream system

cut down progressively, they carve a corresponding valley system and create an erosional landscape in which the principal elements are the valleys themselves and the higher-standing lands (interfluves) between them. As the valleys deepen, widen, and increase in number, the erosional landscape passes through a developmental sequence.

In traditional geomorphology, the sequence has commonly been presented as a simple, idealized series of steps, based upon certain assumptions (Fig. 14.9). In this scheme, the larger streams are considered to form their valleys first. Then tributary valleys form at the margins of the main valleys and gradually extend themselves by headward erosion into the previously uncut upland. As long as there are few valleys and much uncut upland, the

landscape is said to be "youthful." When the tributary net is complete, so that no uncut upland remains, and the major streams have cut down almost to baselevel, "maturity" has been reached. From there on, slow valley widening continues at the expense of the interfluves, which are eventually reduced to low, narrow remnants, at which time the landscape has arrived at "old age." The whole area has then been reduced near baselevel, and no significant further development is possible unless the area is uplifted again. The "cycle of erosion" has been completed.

In the light of more recent findings, however, it seems apparent that this sequence is far from universal. It has long been realized that the cycle may be interrupted at any stage, especially by diastrophic events, so that old age is rarely achieved. It now also seems probable that stream cutting can become stabilized far above baselevel, and it is clear that valley form and development depend heavily upon the mode and amount of runoff and the nature of the materials of the surface, stream bed, and valley side—not upon time alone. While progressive headward growth of valleys does often occur (Fig. 14.10), it cannot be assumed. Conditions that favor a high percentage of infiltration may virtually preclude tributary growth because they result in a lack of surface runoff, thus making the achievement of maturity almost impossible. Conversely, ample precipitation combined with impermeable but erodable materials may per-

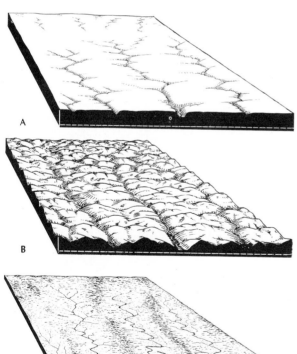

Figure 14.9 Ideal stages in the progressive development of a stream-eroded landscape. A. Youth—few tributaries, broad, undissected interfluves. B. Maturity—complete tributary net; valley sides everywhere. C. Old age—broad lowlands; low, narrow divides. (V. C. Finch.)

Figure 14.10 Gullies developing through headward extension. (F. W. Lehmann, C. B. & Q. Railroad Co.)

mit almost immediate development of the tributary net, and hence the development may bypass youth. Several questions concerning the late stages of erosional development will be discussed in Chaps. 16 and 17.

The Work of Groundwater Solution

Groundwater moving along joints and bedding planes of some rocks may remove so much material in solution that the rock becomes honeycombed with cavities, large and small. This occurs especially in limestones, and to a lesser degree in dolomites and lime-cemented sandstones. Under particularly favorable circumstances huge caverns may be formed. With a few exceptions, it is only in such large solution cavities that freely flowing streams occur beneath the surface.

Some of the cavities formed by solution, especially those developed along vertical joints, are open to the surface as steep-walled fissures or pits, sometimes remarkably deep. In other instances surface depressions are formed by the collapse of the roofs of caverns. Most solution depressions are small and shallow; but in some areas of thick, pure limestones, progressive solution, aided by collapse, has led to the development of enclosed valleys and basins hundreds of yards across. Though there are many specific terms used for features of various sizes and shapes, the general name for solution-produced depressions is *sinks*.

The Work of Gravity

Gravity as an Earth-moving Agent. The force of gravity is well known as a contributing factor in the operations of all other gradational agents. But the work of gravity as an essentially independent gradational agent is much less familiar, and in the past its importance was grossly underestimated. Now, however, geomorphologists realize that the downslope movement of regolith under the largely unaided urging of gravity is one of the most widespread and effective of all the means of gradation, perhaps scarcely less important than running water

itself. Such gradational activity is called *mass movement* or *mass wasting*.

Some kinds of mass wasting can occur on gentle slopes and in dry regolith; but as a general rule, mass movements, particularly the more rapid forms, are more common where slopes are steep and where there is much water in the ground. Saturation of the regolith is especially likely as a result of long-continued rains or the seasonal melting of large quantities of snow. It is not surprising that actual flowing of the surface mantle occurs rather frequently in areas which have a pronounced rainy season or a rapid seasonal thaw, but only infrequently elsewhere.

Kinds of Mass Movements. On steep slopes, masses of regolith and fractured bedrock sometimes break loose and fall, slide, or tumble at high speed into the valley below. Such landslides and rockfalls are usually small, often involving only a single block. Some, however, are huge, sending thousands of tons of soil and rock thundering down the mountainsides, overwhelming whatever lies below. One of the larger recorded slides occurred in the Gros Ventre Mountains of western Wyoming in 1925 (Fig. 14.11). A mass of 50 million cu yd of material moved about 2,000 ft downslope and a short distance up the opposite side of the valley. The debris dammed a stream, forming a large lake which eventually overtopped its dam, washed out a part of it, and swept down the valley, causing damage and loss of life.

Landslides are often triggered by erosional or excavational undermining of the steep slope, by slight earthquake shocks, or simply by heavy rains that have loaded the soil with water. Steeply inclined joints or bedding planes often provide breakaway points and slippage surfaces, especially when they have been lubricated by infiltrating water.

In areas with heavy clay subsoils, long-continued rains or melting snow can saturate the subsoil, causing it to become plastic and to flow downslope, carrying the overlying material with it. Such movements, called earthflows, are much slower than landslides, though still perceptible, and

Figure 14.11   The Gros Ventre landslide of 1925, near Jackson, Wyoming, produced an immense scar on the mountainside and temporarily dammed the creek in the valley below. *(U.S. Forest Service.)*

may occur even on relatively gentle slopes. Like landslides, however, they usually involve a clearly defined mass of material and are sharply bounded (Fig. 14.12).

In high-latitude and high-altitude areas, the deeper ground may remain frozen for some time after the surface layers have thawed. Since the water from melting snow and ice cannot escape downward by infiltration, the surface layers become so wet as to be jellylike. The soil may then ooze slowly downhill over an entire broad slope. This process, known as solifluction, is common now in subpolar and high-altitude areas, and appears to have been active around the margins of the great ice caps during the Ice Ages.

Oddly enough, the most widespread, most continuous, and hence most important of all forms of mass movement is the slowest and least evident of all. This form, called creep, is not a single pro-

cess, but rather the sum total of all processes by which individual soil particles can be moved a fraction of an inch downhill. Cracks, burrows, and root cavities are slowly filled by particles which tumble into them, mostly from the uphill side. Frost crystals lift particles, which then settle farther downhill with the next thaw. Soil expands or swells when it is wetted, heated, or frozen, and contracts again when it dries, cools, or thaws—and such expansion and contraction is greatest in the downhill direction because of gravity. Soil is forced downhill by the prying action of wind-blown trees and shrubs, or by the weight of walking animals. In these and other ways the soil on all slopes is slowly and steadily moved downward, grain by grain. Though the movement itself is imperceptible because of its slowness, its results are visible in various forms (Fig. 14.13).

Aided only by unchanneled sheetflow,

Figure 14.12 Earthflow resulting from rain saturation of the ground on a shaly slope in eastern Ohio. The upper margin of the scar shows tension cracks; the lower section shows bulges from flowage under the sod. *(Soil Conservation Service.)*

Figure 14.13 Common evidences of creep: *A.* Moved joint blocks. *B.* Trees with curved trunks. *C.* Downslope bending and drag of fractured and weathered rock. *D.* Displaced posts, poles, etc. *E.* Broken or displaced retaining walls. *F.* Roads and railroads moved out of alignment. *G.* Turf rolls downslope from creeping boulders. *H.* Stone line near base of creeping soil. *(From C. F. S. Sharpe, Landslides and Related Phenomena. Columbia University Press, New York, 1934. Reproduced by permission of author and publisher.)*

mass movement accomplishes all the gradational activity there is on the slopes and uplands that lie between stream beds. And since these sections of the surface have a total area many times as large as that of the stream beds themselves, the accomplishment is great.

The swifter and more localized forms of mass movement, such as landslides and earthflows, leave obvious marks on the surface. Normally there is a sunken scar on the upper slope where the material has broken loose, and at the lower end of the scar a jumbled, humpy accumulation of the debris that has come down. Blocks on prominent cliffs often break loose singly, falling and rolling to the base, where they may form accumulations known as talus slopes (Fig. 14.14).

These rapid and concentrated forms of mass movement are important chiefly in mountainous and hilly areas where steep slopes prevail. In many of those areas they undoubtedly account for a large part of the transfer of debris from the slopes to the valley bottoms, where it may be carried away by streams or ice tongues. Because of their concentrated occurrence, they are probably

Figure 14.14   An extensive talus slope at the foot of a cliff. Beartooth Range, Montana.

less important in total result than the unobtrusive but more widespread creep.

Creep, however, does not produce well-defined landforms. Instead of forming scars and localized accumulations, it moves all the regolith downward and thus drives back the entire expanse of a slope. The material that has crept down may be carried away by streams or other transporting agents, or it may accumulate in a thickening sheet, gentling the lower part of the slope and masking it against further weathering and erosion. In humid areas that have a thick mantle of weathered material and a well-established cover of vegetation, creep may proceed at a significant rate even though surface erosion outside of stream channels may be negligible. On the other hand, where the vegetation cover is sparse or open, surface erosion by rainwash is the more important process, though creep will still occur.

The Development of Slopes. The majority of slopes, especially the steeper ones, have no doubt originated as stream valley sides. Others may have begun as tectonic forms (fault scarps, flanks of folds, volcanic slopes, etc.) or as erosional or depositional features produced by waves, glaciers, or the wind. Once formed, slopes are modified by the combined action of weathering, mass wasting, and channeled or unchanneled surface runoff. Weathering produces regolith, runoff and mass wasting move it downward, and streams or other gradational agents remove it from the foot of the slope. We have surprisingly little conclusive knowledge about the actual course followed by slope modification. Although the processes involved are familiar, their relative importance and rates of action under different circumstances are as yet poorly defined.

Slope steepness appears to depend chiefly upon (1) the physical strength of the underlying material, (2) the coarseness of the regolith, and (3) the rate of downcutting or undercutting, if any, at the slope base. The strength and cohesiveness of the material sets an upper limit to steepness, beyond which the slope will collapse and slump back to or below the limiting angle. The coarseness of the regolith tends to define the lower limit of possible steepness, for the finer the material, the gentler the slope on which it can be moved. Rapid downcutting or undercutting by a stream, a glacial tongue, or wave erosion at the slope base will tend to keep the slope steep, while the absence of this kind of attack may permit the slope to become gentler. Thus very steep slopes are usually associated with rapid deepening of valleys or with undercutting of slopes formed in strong, massive bedrock or highly cohesive sediments. Gentle slopes commonly indicate weak or loose materials and an absence of active erosion at the base of the slope.

For convenience, the many existing theories of slope development can be gathered into two groups (Fig. 14.15). According to the first group, slopes become progressively more gentle. Throughout the course of development the characteristic slope form is convex in its upper part and concave below. According to the second group, slopes tend to be driven back without significant gentling. However, as the steeper slopes retreat they leave behind gentler footslopes, usually concave.

Recent scientific thought suggests that these contrasting versions of the developmental sequence may in fact represent two special cases near the ends of a broad range of actual occurrences. Progressive gentling is probably characteristic where regolith removal is slow and debris can accumulate on the lower part of the slope, masking it against further attack while the upper part continues to be eroded. On the other hand, if regolith is stripped from the slope about as soon as it is formed, no masking occurs, and the slope maintains steepness while retreating. Convexity of the upper slope

seems to be especially common where rocks are weak or weathering is rapid, for regolith then forms quickly. Active creep in the thick regolith then rounds off the slope near the crest above the level at which channeled slope erosion occurs.

The Work of Moving Ice

Development of Glaciers. Glaciers are not simply inert masses of ice and snow but rather tongues or sheets of ice so thick that they can actually be deformed by the force of gravity. The deformation is much like the flow of very viscous liquids—say, the traditional "molasses in January." Glaciers rarely move more than a few inches per day, though exceptional rates of more than a hundred feet per day have been recorded.

Since ice must become 150 to 200 ft thick before it will begin to flow, glaciers can form only where ice accumulates over a period of years. If more snow falls during a cold season than can be melted during the following summer, the unmelted residue is added to the snow of the next year, and so on. The old, buried snow changes gradually into solid ice under the effects of compression combined with partial melting and refreezing. In this way a great thickness of ice can be built up in a relatively short time.

Circumstances favorable to glacier growth are most often encountered in areas having unusually heavy winter snowfall but short, cool summers. At present most of the ice-covered area of the earth is in Antarctica and Greenland. Elsewhere glaciers are confined to the moister and colder mountain regions. Dryness and summer heat are enemies of glacier development, and many high mountain ranges and even some large areas within the polar circles have no glaciers at all because their snowfall is insufficient to last out the summer.

The ice in a glacier follows the paths of least resistance, moving generally downslope and away from the center of thickest accumulation (Fig. 14.16). As it spreads beyond the region of accumulation into neighboring areas where elevation is lower, summers are warmer and longer, or

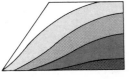
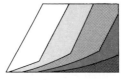

A. PROGRESSIVE GENTLING   B. PARALLEL RETREAT

Figure 14.15 Two theories of slope development.

Figure 14.16 Nysne Glacier, Peary Land, northern Greenland. Note the collecting basins from which the glacier flows and the surface markings that indicate the flowing movement. Ridges of ice-deposited debris (moraines) border the ice tongue, and a braided stream of meltwater flows across the sand and gravel it has washed out from the ice margin. *(Geodetic Institute, Copenhagen, copyright.)*

annual snowfall is less, its outer margins are attacked by melting. The ice continues to spread, however, until its edge reaches the point of balance between the rate of supply and the rate of melting. Thereafter, as long as conditions do not change, the edge of the glacier remains in the same place, though the ice is in continuous movement from the source to the edge. If climatic conditions change so that the supply of ice is lessened or the rate of melting is increased, the glacier begins to shrink. On the other hand, if melting is decreased or the ice supply is increased, the edge of the glacier advances until it reaches a new point of equilibrium.

Former Continental Glaciers. If glaciers had never been more extensive than they are now, they would not be familiar as sculptors of the land, for the surfaces beneath existing glaciers are effectively hidden. However, it is well known that at several times during the last million years glaciers of tremendous size spread over large parts of the Northern Hemisphere continents (Fig. 14.17). In North

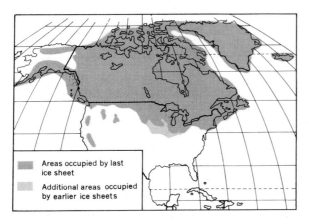 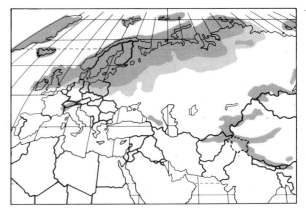

Areas occupied by last ice sheet

Additional areas occupied by earlier ice sheets

Figure 14.17 Extent of former continental glaciers in North America and Eurasia. *(Adapted from Flint, Glacial and Pleistocene Geology. 2d ed. John Wiley & Sons, Inc., New York, 1961.)*

America they originated to the east and west of Hudson Bay and, at one time or another, invaded all of Canada and the northeastern and north central United States. In Eurasia they developed in the Scandinavian highlands and spread over most of northern Europe and northwestern Siberia. Most of eastern Siberia and much of Alaska were not glaciated in spite of their coldness, probably because of insufficient snowfall. There were no continental glaciers in the Southern Hemisphere except on Antarctica, because there are no large land masses in the upper middle latitudes where they could have grown.

At the same time that these continental ice sheets developed, there was a general expansion of glaciers in high mountain valleys all over the world. For example, in the western United States, the Rocky Mountains, which now are almost bare of glaciers, were heavily glaciated—much as the Alps and high Himalaya are now.

Why such immense glaciers developed during this great ice age, or *Pleistocene period,* is not at all clear. Unquestionably there were climatic changes in the direction of cooler summers and greater snowfall in the source regions, but the reason for these changes lies in the realm of theory. The many possible factors that have been suggested include fluctuations in the output of energy from the sun, outpourings of volcanic dust into the atmosphere, and changes in the shapes and elevations of the continents and in the connections between the oceans.

Even the course of glacial history is most imperfectly known. It is generally believed that ice sheets formed, spread, fluctuated, and finally melted away several times (probably four) during the Pleistocene period. The last major expansion (called *Wisconsinan* in North America) reached its maximum close to 20,000 years ago and did not finally disappear from the northern edge of the United States until perhaps 8,000 years ago. Glaciation reached approximately its present state in the world only about 5,000 years ago. The most recent major expansion fell well within the period when man had become widely established over the earth and must have had profound effects upon his existence. By the time the last ice sheet had vanished, history had reached the early stages of the sedentary civilizations of Babylon and Egypt.

The effects of glaciation were widespread and complex. The surfaces actually covered by the ice were modified by erosion and deposition. They were also evidently considerably depressed by the weight of the ice, rising again when the ice melted away. Valleys and plains adjacent to the ice were strewn with debris carried from the glacial edge by meltwater. Throughout the world sea levels dropped several hundred feet as more and more water was transferred to the ice sheets, then rose again as the glaciers wasted away. Accompanying the whole glacial sequence was a complex series of climatic changes, which affected not only the glaciated areas but much of the rest of the world as well.

Erosion by Glaciers. The investigation of how glaciers erode and deposit is greatly complicated by the fact that it is impossible to see just what is happening underneath glaciers now in existence. Many of our notions of how glaciers rework the surface are inferred from the forms left behind in areas where the ice has lately melted away. Hence knowledge has grown slowly, and strong differences of opinion remain.

Apparently glaciers can erode in three ways. First, and probably the most important by far, is the process known as plucking or quarrying. In this the plastic ice molds itself about particles of the regolith or blocks of bedrock and then drags them out of place as the ice mass moves forward (Fig. 14.18). Quarrying is most effective where the surface materials are loose, thin-bedded, or jointed. A second erosional technique is that of grinding or abrasion. Quarried rocks which are partly embedded in the lower surface of the ice are dragged across bedrock outcrops like grains on a giant sheet of sandpaper, scraping and gouging as they go. Grooved and polished rock surfaces show the work of this process. Third, and probably least important, is a bulldozerlike shoving effect, which may occur where the ice edge readvances over loose heaped-up debris dropped earlier.

Undoubtedly the chief accomplishment of glacial erosion is the stripping of the regolith from the surface over much of the area covered. However, the ice also quarries actively in strongly jointed or conspicuously weak bedrock. Projecting crags are removed or reduced in size. Bottleneck valleys lying in the direction of ice movement seem especially liable to strong erosion. But generally speaking, the extensive and thick continental ice sheets were not strongly channeled, so that their erosional work was inclined to be patchy, producing irregular depressions rather than integrated valleys. Erosion by glacial tongues in mountain valleys, on the other hand, is narrowly confined.

Transportation by Glaciers. Glaciers are highly competent and indiscriminate transporting agents, able to carry material of all sizes, including immense boulders. The debris eroded by the glacier itself is carried near the base of the ice. But mountain valley glaciers may also transport quantities of material that has been dumped onto them by

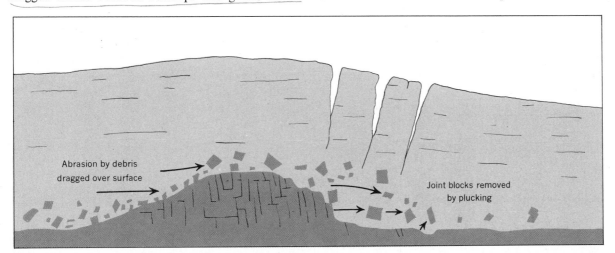

Figure 14.18   A glacier erodes mainly by plucking and abrasion.

mass movement or surface erosion on the steep valley sides. This material is concentrated near the surface of the ice, though some may eventually become covered by so much snow that it reaches considerable depth.

Deposition by Glaciers. A glacier deposits its load by melting away from it. Melting occurs toward the outer margins of the ice, and works both upward from the ground and downward from the upper surface (Fig. 14.19).

As a result of melting on the lower surface, the debris carried in the lower part of the ice is lodged beneath the glacier. Melting downward from above exposes more and more debris on the surface of the ice, so that the lower ends of some mountain valley glaciers are almost completely obscured by a thick cover of rock and sand. This surface debris is deposited at the edges of the glacier as the ice melts.

There is no mechanism for selectivity in either the transporting or depositing process. Therefore glacial deposits are commonly jumbled mixtures of material varying in size from clay to huge boulders (Fig. 14.20). By this characteristic they can usually be easily distinguished from water-laid deposits, which almost always show some degree of sorting and layering. The unsorted debris deposited directly by the ice is called *till*. The specific deposits themselves are called *moraines*. The sheet of till believed to have been laid down

Figure 14.20 Exposure of glacial till, showing the unassorted clay, pebbles, and boulders of which it is composed. *(Ernest Muller.)*

by lodgment beneath the ice is the ground moraine; the thicker accumulations deposited along the ice edge are marginal moraines.

Moraines can be found throughout the glaciated area, for at some time or other every place overrun by the ice will have been in the

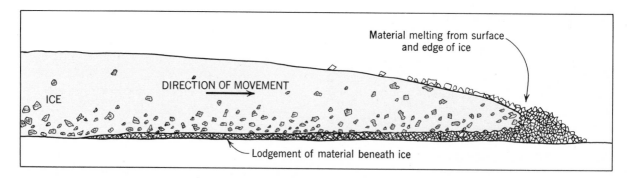

Figure 14.19 Near its edge, an ice sheet melts on both upper and lower surfaces. Thus some of the debris it contains is lodged beneath the ice, while the rest is dropped at the outer margin.

vicinity of the glacial margin. Within the depositional area, however, the till is unevenly distributed in patches, heaps, ridges, and blankets of unequal thickness. The deposits are normally thickest in valleys, in areas "downstream" from sources of easily eroded material that furnish quantities of till, and in the outer parts of the glaciated area where the melting zone may have remained longest. Deposits are often thin or absent altogether on hilltops, in areas of especially resistant rock, and in the source regions from which the ice was continually moving outward.

Meltwater flowing from the ice margin may carry out quantities of debris, which are deposited as alluvium across plains or in valley bottoms (Fig. 14.21). Such deposits, called outwash, are not strictly glacial, but outwash and till deposits are both commonly included under the general term of *glacial drift*.

In varying degrees, till deposition modifies the landscapes over which it is laid down. The resulting surface features depend upon the thickness and stoniness of the till and upon the form of the underlying surface. The tendency of moraine deposition to be irregularly heaped and to be con-

centrated in valleys has the effect of obscuring old drainage lines and of leaving behind an irregular surface of rises and depressions without well-organized valley systems. It was noted above that glacial erosion has somewhat similar effects.

Because there is a significant difference in age between early and late Pleistocene glacial deposits, the surface features that the ice produced also show a considerable difference in their freshness and degree of preservation. Those formed by the late Wisconsinan ice sheets are generally clearly defined and little altered. Those formed during the middle and early Pleistocene, and even some early Wisconsinan surfaces, are commonly so changed by stream erosion and mass movement as to be unrecognizable. Only the distinctive character of the materials themselves reveals the glacial history of these "old drift" areas.

The Work of the Wind

Where and How Wind Works. The wind is a much less important sculptor of surface forms than are water, gravity, and ice, chiefly because wind can erode only under certain limited conditions. Wind erosion is active only if the surface is nearly bare of vegetation, and then only if the surface material is fine and dry. For this reason the work of the wind is largely confined to deserts or semideserts and to those few areas in humid regions—such as beaches, river beds at low water, and, nowadays, plowed fields—which have little plant cover.

Where it is able to work, the wind erodes, transports, and deposits in much the same manner as running water, except that it does little channeling. It erodes by frictional drag, eddy currents near the surface, and the impact of particles already being carried (sandblasting effect). It moves material by rolling or bouncing particles along the ground or by carrying them in suspension. It deposits where surface irregularities, including vegetation, check its speed near the ground, or where its velocity decreases simply because of the atmospheric pressure pattern. Rain falling through the

Figure 14.21 A cut through a deposit of glacial outwash. Rudely sorted and stratified sand and gravel washed free of clay. *(Wisconsin Geological Survey.)*

dust-laden air will often carry most of the suspended material down with it.

The wind can rarely move material larger than coarse sand. Sand is carried as "bed load" of the airstream—that is, by rolling or low bouncing —and seldom rises more than a few feet above the ground even in high winds. Silt and clay can be carried in suspension and thus may reach great heights and travel long distances. For example, fine red soil traceable to the plains of western Oklahoma has fallen on the deck of steamers in the Atlantic.

Wind Erosion (Deflation). Erosion by the wind, like that by ice, tends to be widespread or patchy rather than channeled. Thus it may lower the surface rather uniformly over a broad area without producing any pronounced surface forms. On occasion, however, deflation scours out shallow depressions in places where the vegetation has been destroyed, where the material is especially loose and fine, or where the wind velocity is increased by a natural bottleneck. It is common for the wind to winnow out the finer particles from mixed surface material, leaving behind a coarse-textured gravelly or stony cover sometimes called desert pavement (Fig. 14.22).

Wind Deposition. The deposition of fine suspended material is so extensive and unconcentrated that it modifies the surface significantly only if it continues for a long time and leaves a very thick

Figure 14.22 Sandblasted rock fragments and pebbles left behind by selective wind erosion on the floor of Death Valley, California. *(Eliot Blackwelder.)*

layer. Most of the widespread deposits of silty, unlayered, buff-colored, calcium-rich material called *loess,* common in the middle western United States, eastern Europe, and north China, are believed to have originated as wind-blown silt.

By contrast, sand tends to accumulate in heaps rather than smooth sheets, and thus sand deposition does produce distinct landforms. These features, known as sand dunes, are common in some desert regions and along many coasts.

Man's Effects upon Gradation

Man has had and will no doubt continue to have a profound modifying influence upon the activities of the gradational agents. He has not produced any known effects upon glaciers and their work, but he has (sometimes intentionally, sometimes unintentionally) wrought major changes in the operations of running water, mass movement, and the wind.

The most widespread of his modifying activities has been the thinning or complete clearing of the vegetation cover from immense areas, especially in the humid and moister semiarid parts of the earth. Obvious gullying and less obvious but often measurable sheetwash on lands once protected by a natural vegetation cover demonstrate the tremendously enhanced rates of erosion that clearing and cultivation have brought. The soil swept from the slopes is dumped into streams, increasing their loads and contributing to their rates of deposition. The same loss of vegetation cover also permits much more direct surface runoff and decreases infiltration, thereby causing greater fluctuation in stream discharges, including higher and more frequent floods. Especially on the semiarid fringes of agricultural areas, clearing has enabled the wind to strip untold quantities of topsoil from plowed fields in dry weather and to spread it broadcast over the lands to leeward of the source.

By building dams, man creates lakes that trap the streams' sediment load (which will eventually fill the lakes). Below the dams the clearer streams are then enabled to erode more actively. Especially in the great metropolitan districts, huge areas of watershed are now largely roofed or paved, greatly increasing the direct runoff and affecting stream discharges. Improperly designed bridges, culverts, and embankments sometimes so confine stream channels that during high waters the scouring of swift currents in the narrowed sections undermines and washes out these structures. The excavation of quarries, road cuts, and building foundations often undercuts unstable slopes, triggering landslides that overwhelm the works below.

Even so brief and incomplete a catalogue conveys something of the magnitude of man's role in changing the natural processes at work on the surface. Not all his activities result in disaster; many have been at least temporarily beneficial. But in view of his far-reaching power to alter the natural scheme of things, it is critically important that he improve his understanding of natural processes to the point where he can predict the long-term and indirect effects of his projects as well as the immediate and the obvious.

15

Characteristics and Classes
of Land-surface Form

Characteristics of Land Surfaces

Because there are so many types of land surfaces distributed over the earth without apparent order, it may seem that an understanding of their nature and arrangement, or even a systematic description of them, is beyond the ability of a beginning student. Actually, however, it is quite possible to describe the land surface objectively, specifically, and, if desired, quantitatively.

If one carefully compares many small areas in order to determine precisely how the land-surface form of each is unlike that of the others, one soon accumulates a long list of specific differences. And if this list is analyzed, it becomes apparent that the many differences can be grouped under the four headings of slope (or inclination), surface material, arrangements, and dimensions. That is, the differences between any two sections of the land surface can be expressed in terms of these four major sets of properties.

Slope. Slope refers simply to the inclination of the land surface at a particular spot. Normally any section of the surface measuring a few miles across is made up of many small bits of sloping land, each one differing from its neighbors in steepness. Steep slopes, gentle slopes, and slopes of intermediate steepness may all be present in a single area. However, one area may differ greatly from another in the predominance of each of these major slope classes. For example, a section of the Texas coastal plain near Corpus Christi is 95 percent occupied by very gentle slopes (Fig. 15.1*B*), while in a section of hilly southwestern Wisconsin only 30 percent of the area is gently sloping, with intermediate and steep slopes occupying the greater part of the area (Fig. 15.1*A*). It is doubtful that any other single bit of information could tell as much about the fundamental contrast between these two regions.

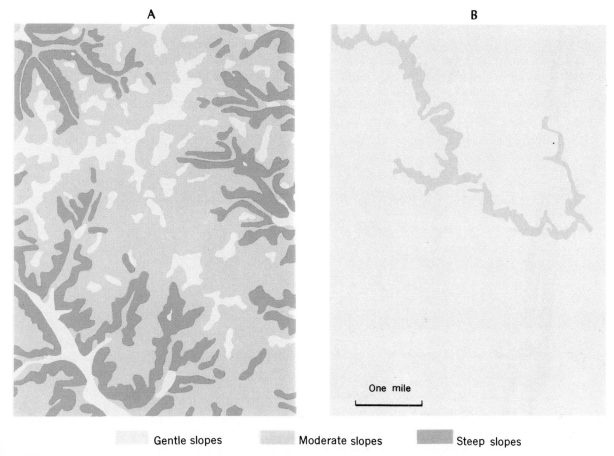

A   B

One mile

Gentle slopes   Moderate slopes   Steep slopes

Figure 15.1   An example of contrast in slope. A is from the hill land of southwestern Wisconsin; B from the coastal plain near Corpus Christi, Texas. *(From U.S. Geological Survey topographic sheets: Boaz, Wisconsin, and Petronilla, Texas.)*

The figures not only suggest the contrasting appearance of the areas but also hint at important differences in the usefulness of the land.

Surface Material. Most of the earth's land surface is covered with relatively fine-particled mineral matter with some partially decomposed organic debris mixed in (Fig. 15.2A). Wherever such soil (using the term in a very broad sense) does not make up the surface layer, that fact is worth knowing. Surfaces of bare bedrock, loose sand, cobbles and boulders, permanent ice, and standing water are fundamentally different from soil surfaces, in appearance and feel as well as in origin and function (Fig. 15.2B and C).

The character of the bedrock many feet below the surface and the chemical and detailed physical properties of even the surface layers do not as a rule belong in a list of terrain elements. But clearly the gross physical nature of the surficial materials cannot be omitted from a terrain description without running the risk of serious misrepresentation. It would, for example, be futile to attempt a characterization of Finland or of much of northern and eastern Canada without mentioning that standing water and exposed bedrock together probably occupy as much or more of the area than soil does. The ice cap of Antarctica, the sand-dune seas of the Libyan Sahara, and the great coastal marshes of South Carolina and Georgia all owe much of their distinctive character to their unusual surface materials.

Arrangements. Arrangements are the relative positions of features within an area. Streams, ridge crests, peaks, areas of gentle slope, steep bluffs, and exposures of bare rock are all set upon the land surface in distinctive horizontal arrangements or patterns that are best seen from an airplane or on a map. In some regions pattern is one of the most striking of all characteristics, especially where it departs from the usual treelike arrangement of valleys or streams and of the ridges between them that is illustrated in Fig. 15.3A. The remarkably parallel arrangement of ridges in the middle belt of the Appalachians between central Pennsylvania and northern Alabama (Fig. 15.3B), the random dotting of small isolated volcanic hills on the plains of

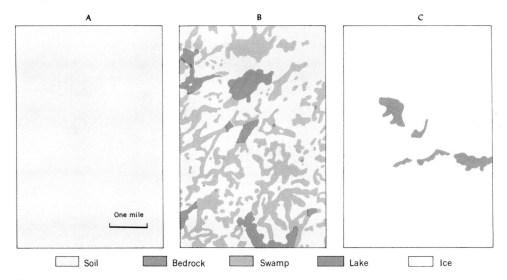

Soil   Bedrock   Swamp   Lake   Ice

Figure 15.2 An example of contrast in the nature of surface material. A is from rolling prairies of northwestern Missouri, B from morainic plains of northern Minnesota, C from mountains of southern Alaska. *(From U.S. Geological Survey topographic sheets: Bethany, Missouri, Ely, Minnesota, and Seward A-8, Alaska.)*

south central Oregon (Fig. 15.3*C*), and the aimless maze of lakes, swamps, and streams in northeastern Minnesota (Fig. 15.2*B*) are indispensable ingredients of any meaningful description of these regions. The patterns establish the character of the terrain; they are highly significant clues to the geological history of the region; and they are clearly reflected in the patterns of other phenomena such as soils, native vegetation, and agricultural utilization of the land.

     Vertical arrangements are also significant, especially profiles, a profile in this sense being the change of slope or gradient along a given line. Profiles can illustrate such characteristics as the cross-section forms of valleys; the evenness, jaggedness, or presence of deep clefts in major mountain crests; and the various changes in gradient of streams from their headwaters down to their mouths. Regional contrasts in these are sometimes striking and important (Figs. 15.4, 15.5). The student of earth history finds cross-section profiles of valleys and divides and the lengthwise profiles of streams espe-

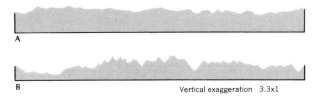

Vertical exaggeration 3.3x1

Figure 15.4 The continuously high crest line of the Sierra Nevada of California (A) contrasts with the deeply serrated crest of the Cascade Range in Washington (B). *(From Army Map Service series 1:250,000: Fresno and Wenatchee sheets.)*

cially valuable, for they may sometimes be used to determine previous uplifts of the earth's crust, earlier variations in stream discharge, and the effects of rock character upon the processes of erosion. These examples will suggest that profiles of the terrain may relate also to other aspects of geography, including utilization of the land by man.

Dimensions. Dimensions give scale to the characterization. Without a knowledge of such numerical values as the height of ridges, the width and depth

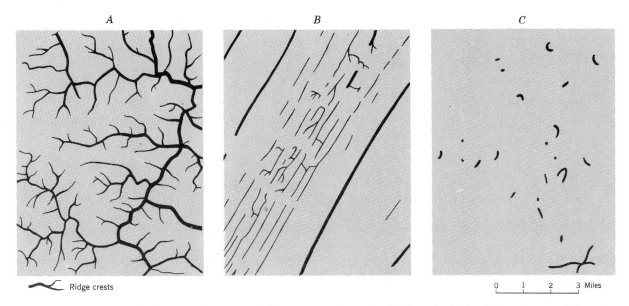

Ridge crests   0   1   2   3 Miles

Figure 15.3 An example of contrast in pattern of ridge crests and summits. A is from the hill land of southwestern Wisconsin, B from the Appalachian Ridge and Valley region of central Pennsylvania, and C from an area of volcanic cones in south central Oregon. *(From U.S. Geological Survey topographic sheets: La Farge, Wisconsin, Orbisonia, Pennsylvania, and Newberry Crater, Oregon.)*

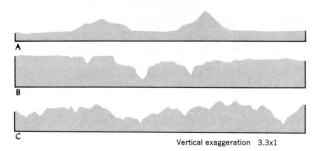

Vertical exaggeration 3.3x1

Figure 15.5 Contrasting transverse profiles in areas of high relief. A is from the Basin and Range province in Nevada, B from the Colorado Plateaus in northern Arizona, and C from the Northern Rocky Mountains in Idaho. *(From U.S. Geological Survey topographic sheets: Sonoma Range, Nevada, Diamond Creek, Arizona, and Lolo, Idaho.)*

of valleys, the spacing of streams, and the size of patches of gently sloping land, it is impossible to visualize a landscape that is being described.

Important dimensions in the horizontal plane are the spacings of valleys, ridges, and streams, the widths of patches of gentle slope, steep

slope, or distinctive surface material, and the sizes of lakes or swamps. Areas similar in other characteristics are sometimes strikingly different in horizontal dimensions (Fig. 15.6). Areas in which widths and spacings of features are relatively large are spoken of as coarse-textured; those in which horizontal dimensions are small are fine-textured.

In the vertical direction, dimensions are given by various expressions of local relief, or difference in elevation within a limited area. For a general expression of local relief, the difference in elevation between the highest and lowest points in the area is sometimes used. Or a figure may be used that indicates the average or prevalent height of crests above the adjacent valley bottoms. The relief along crest lines, on local uplands, and along valley floors or streams may also be of interest.

Local relief is a characteristic of considerable descriptive value, suggesting at once something of the scale of features and the degree of irregularity within the area being considered (Fig.

A

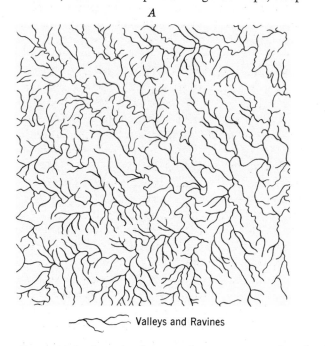

Valleys and Ravines

B

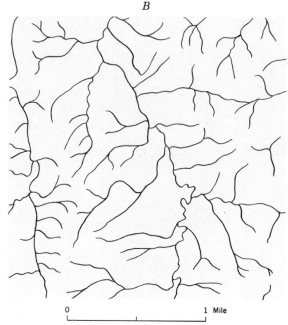

0   1 Mile

Figure 15.6 Example of contrast in texture, or spacing of valleys and ravines. The patterns are similar, but the textures are strikingly different. A is from the White River Badlands of southwestern South Dakota, B from central Missouri. *(From U.S. Geological Survey topographic sheets: Cuny Table East, South Dakota, and Nelson, Missouri.)*

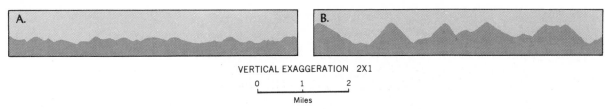

VERTICAL EXAGGERATION 2X1

0   1   2

Miles

Figure 15.7 Contrasting local relief in two areas of rough lands. *A is from the Missouri Ozarks, B from the Appalachian Highlands in central West Virginia. (From U.S. Geological Survey topographic sheets: Round Spring, Missouri, and Bald Knob, West Virginia.)*

15.7). If the local relief in an area a few miles wide is only 50 ft, it is evident that the surface must be either nearly flat or marked by only small roughnesses. But a local relief of 5,000 ft immediately suggests a landscape of considerable grandeur, though without specifying what form its great features may take. When combined with data on slope and profiles, local relief is one of the most revealing of all generalized expressions of terrain character.

Classes of Land Surfaces

The preceding section suggested how a land surface, even a complex one, might be effectively analyzed by considering it in terms of specific characteristics. Many characteristics can be described in quantitative terms, others with reasonable precision by words or diagrams. A complete and systematic description of the land-surface form of an area employs all available techniques—verbal, numerical, cartographic, and pictorial—in order to be objective, precise, and clear. With such specific and systematic information, it becomes possible to compare, characteristic by characteristic, any one bit of the earth's surface with any other bit.

When large numbers of terrain samples from all over the world are compared, certain combinations of major characteristics occur again and again in widely separated places. Given these similarities, it becomes possible to define a number of general classes of terrain that may be recognized whenever they occur, and that together make up the entire surface of the continents. These are anal-

ogous to the climatic types defined in earlier chapters.

Major Classes of Land-surface Form. The scheme of classification used here is based upon three major characteristics: relative amount of gently sloping land, local relief, and generalized profile. On the basis of the first two characteristics alone we may distinguish among (1) *plains,* having a predominance of gently sloping land, coupled with low relief, (2) *plains with some features of considerable relief,* also dominated by gently sloping land but having moderate to high local relief, (3) *hills,* with little gently sloping land and with low to moderate relief, and (4) *mountains,* which have little gently sloping land and high local relief.

The second group, plains with some features of considerable relief, may be further subdivided on the basis of whether their gently sloping land occurs in the lower part of the profile or in the upper part. If most of the gentle slopes lie at relatively low levels, with steep slopes rising above them, the surfaces may be designated *plains with hills or mountains.* If, on the other hand, most of the nearly level land lies relatively high, with canyon walls or long lines of bluffs (escarpments) dropping down from it, the surfaces may be called *tablelands.* If the relief is slight or if the amount of gently sloping land is not large, this profile distinction is less significant, so it is not used here as a basis for subdividing plains, hills, and mountains.

Figures 15.8 and 15.9 give examples of the principal classes of land-surface form. The accompanying table shows schematically how the classes are defined.

Figure 15.8 Examples of the three smoother classes of land-surface form. A is the rolling plain of the Appalachian Piedmont near Durham, North Carolina; B is Canyon de Chelly and vicinity in northeastern Arizona, a well-defined tableland; and C shows the Hopi Buttes, near Winslow, Arizona, a plain with hills and mountains. (A, courtesy of North Carolina State Highway Commission; B and C, Spence Air Photos.)

A

B

Figure 15.9   Examples of the two rougher classes of land-surface form. A is hill land from the Allegheny-Cumberland section of the Appalachian Highlands in western West Virginia; B is high-mountain country in the Alaska Range, central Alaska. (A, J. L. Rich. Courtesy of the Geographical Review, American Geographical Society, New York; B, Bradford Washburn.)

MAJOR CLASSES OF LAND SURFACES

Slope	Local relief	Profile	Class
More than 90% gentle slope	0–300 ft	Any	**Plains** (Flat plains if more than 80% gentle slope and 0–100 ft local relief)
	More than 300 ft	More than 50% of gentle slope is in upper half of elevation range	**Tablelands**
		More than 50% of gentle slope is in lower half of elevation range	**Plains with hills or mountains**
Less than 50% gentle slope	0–1,000 ft	Any	**Hills**
	1,000–3,000 ft	Any	**Low mountains**
	More than 3,000 ft	Any	**High mountains**

It must be fully understood that within each of these major classes of land surfaces, which are defined here in terms of only two or three characteristics that seem particularly important to visualization or to utility, there exists a vast variety, based upon differences in other characteristics. Some plains, for instance, are conspicuously flat and swampy, others are rolling and well drained, and still others are simply broad expanses of smooth ice. Similarly, some mountains are low, smooth-sloped, and arranged in parallel ridges, while others are exceedingly high, with rugged, rocky slopes and great glaciers and snowfields. The classification outlined in the accompanying table is intended to bring out only the most striking contrasts and to provide a basis for systematic discussion of land surfaces, their origins, and the general surface character of the various continents.

Terminology and the Problem of Scale. In discussing land surfaces it is important to distinguish clearly among the concepts of (1) surface characteristics or properties, (2) classes or types of surfaces, and (3) individual surface features. Suppose, for example, that an arbitrarily chosen area of the land surface in the Texas Panhandle, measuring a few miles each way, is examined carefully. Taken as a unit it is found to possess the *characteristics* of predominant gentleness of inclination, small overall range of elevation, wide spacing of valleys, tree-like valley pattern, almost universal soil cover, and a large majority of the surface area lying in the upper half of the elevation range. Following the scheme of classification just described, the area is designated as belonging to the *class* of surfaces called "plains." Examined in a different way, the same area is made up of many *features,* including valleys of various sizes, smooth uplands, stream channels (mostly dry), individual slopes, terraces, sand bars in the stream channels, and several small and shallow depressions in the uplands. Such characteristics, classes, and features all have a place in land-surface description, and all will be used in the succeeding discussions.

Many of the common terms that characterize land surfaces are used in more than one way. Some have, in addition to their technical meaning, a rather loosely defined usage in common speech. Some refer to features as well as classes of surface form. Many serve to designate features of vastly different orders of magnitude. In the preceding paragraph, for example, an area of several square miles in the Texas Panhandle was classified as "plain," because it displays the necessary characteristics of predominantly gentle slopes and low relief. However, this same area of the surface is also part of a much larger region called the High Plains, which is the southern part of a still larger region known as the Great Plains, which in turn is the western part of the huge Interior Plains of North America, which reach from the Rocky Mountains to the Appalachians. Not every small section of the High Plains, Great Plains, or Interior Plains would classify as "plain" according to the definition given in the preceding section. But taken as a whole, each of these regions would contain more plain surface than any other kind.

"Plain" also appears as a part of various terms that refer to specific kinds of features, such as "floodplain," "delta plain," "till plain," or "pediplain." Here again differences of scale enter in. A delta plain, for example, may be the patch of smooth ground a few yards wide formed by a small creek flowing into a tiny mountain lake, or it may be the delta plain of the Hwang Ho, measuring more than 300 miles across and occupying a large part of northeastern China. Similar differences in usage and in scale of reference are encountered with "mountains," "hills," and "tablelands," as well as with such designations as "valley," "terrace," "slope," or "ridge."

These variations of usage need not cause confusion, provided the distinctions among characteristics, classes of surfaces, and kinds of surface features are clearly understood, and provided one is aware of the varying scales at which given kinds of features or surfaces may occur.

World Pattern of Land-Surface Form

Broad Aspects of the Pattern

Plate 3 shows the distribution over the earth of the major classes of land-surface form. In addition to the seven classes defined above (flat plains are mapped as a separate class), the few broad ice caps of the world have also been shown.

The following table, which was derived directly from Plate 3, shows that the major types of land surfaces are neither equal in total extent nor evenly distributed among the continents. The more irregular types of plains are especially widespread, suggesting that conditions favoring the development of such surfaces have been common in late geologic time. On the other hand, the formation of tablelands and flat plains requires sets of circumstances that have not occurred so widely. It will be seen later that each of these kinds of surfaces demands rather specific and limited circumstances in order to develop at all.

The world's pattern of land-surface form is undeniably complex. However, a study of Plate 3 and other maps of surface form reveals broadly systematic arrangements and general similarities and variations among the continents that help to reduce the apparent chaos.

A useful starting point in considering the world pattern is the cordilleran belts, the great bands that contain most of the world's major mountain systems together with various basins and lands

PERCENTAGE OF CONTINENTAL AND WORLD LAND AREAS OCCUPIED BY MAJOR LAND-SURFACE TYPES

	North America	South America	Eurasia	Africa	Australia; New Zealand	Antarctica	World
Flat plains	8	15	2	1	4	0	4
Rolling and irregular plains	23	30	30	44	51	0	30
Tablelands	9	10	3	5	1	0	5
Plains with hills or mountains	18	18	11	22	19	0	15
Hills	8	5	10	11	12	0	8
Low mountains	10	11	21	13	12	1	14
High mountains	16	11	23	4	1	1	13
Ice caps	8	0	0	0	0	98	11
Percentage of world area	16	12	36	20	6	10	100

of lesser roughness. The principal cordilleran systems form a nearly continuous ring about the Pacific Ocean Basin and thrust a long-arm westward through southern Eurasia to the Atlantic. Sometimes they are described as a group of three arms radiating from a "knot" in the Pamir region of the Afghanistan-U.S.S.R. frontier (Fig. 15.10). Thus both of the Americas and Eurasia have long cordilleran segments running along one side of the continent, forming for each an immense "backbone" to which the less rugged remainder of the continent is attached. Africa and Australia lack such well-marked cordilleran bands, though in each of them there is a relatively rough zone running from north to south through the eastern part of the land mass.

Near the Atlantic margins of both the Americas and Eurasia there is secondary rough land, less rugged than the cordilleran belt opposite it. Between the two rough belts lie the most extensive plains of these three continents. In Africa and

Australia the pattern is more patchy, with large areas of plains intermingled with areas of moderate roughness comparable to the secondary rough lands of the cordilleran continents. The Antarctic Continent is so largely covered by ice that little is known of the form of its bedrock surface, except that it is in part ruggedly mountainous. The "continent" beneath the ice may actually involve more than one land mass.

Patterns of Individual Continents

North America. North America is a roughly average continent in the proportional occurrence of the various types of land-surface form. Along its western side is a broad and complex cordilleran belt that occupies most of Alaska, more than a quarter of Canada and the United States, and all but an interrupted east-coastal strip in Mexico and Central America. In the United States and northern Mexico, where it achieves a width of about 1,000

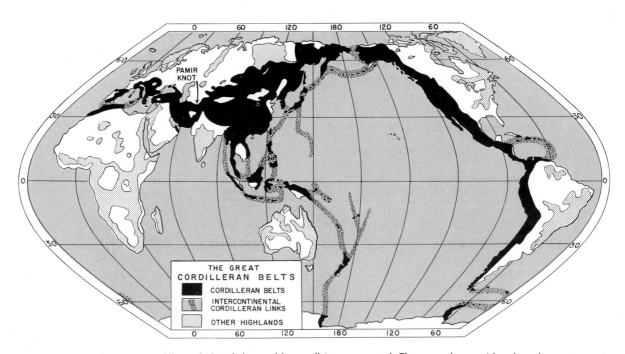

Figure 15.10 The great cordilleran belts of the world are all interconnected. They may be considered as three great arms radiating from the Pamir knot, two of them embracing the basin of the Pacific Ocean, the third reaching westward across southern Europe.

miles, the cordillera is made up of loosely linked mountain strands separated by extensive basins and tablelands, considerable parts of which do not drain to the sea. North and south of this section it becomes narrower and more continuously rough.

The extensive secondary rough land of North America includes the Ozark-Ouachita and Appalachian–New England areas, irregular margins of the great Canadian Shield (the area of ancient resistant rocks in central and eastern Canada), and the major portion of the Arctic Islands. Most of this area is made up of hills and low mountains, but in the eastern Arctic the ruggedness becomes extreme and ice caps become prominent. Greenland accounts for nearly one-tenth of the world's area of ice cap.

The North American plains lie between these two bands of rougher land, with a further extension along the Atlantic Coast in the southeastern United States. The interior plains, with significant exceptions, are irregular and rise gradually toward the west, reaching elevations of 3,000 to 6,000 ft at the base of the Rocky Mountains. The northern sections are notable for their abundant lakes and swamps. The southeastern plains are low and frequently marshy near the coast, rising and becoming better drained and more irregular inland.

South America. South America is similar to North America in having a western cordillera, secondary rough lands to the east, and extensive plains between. However, the nature of the three parts is strikingly different.

The South America cordillera, the Andes, is higher, more continuous, and much narrower than that of the northern continent, its greatest width being no more than 500 miles. Except in the extreme north and south there are no real breaks in the mountain wall, and in the central section the elevation of the divide continuously exceeds 10,000 ft for a distance of 2,000 miles. In the widest central section are broad basins at great elevation, strongly resembling those of the high uplands of Tibet.

The secondary rough land is in two sec-

tions, separated by the lower Amazon plains. The northern and smaller section, known as the Guiana Highlands, is largely a loose array of groups and ranges of low mountains rising from the plains. The much larger Brazilian Highlands are a great platform that rises gradually from the Amazon lowlands toward the southeastern margin, where it drops abruptly to the sea. Most of the rough part of this section is along the high southeastern edge; the interior parts are upland plains and tablelands.

The plains of South America occupy nearly half the continent and form the major part of the drainage basins of its three greatest river systems, the Orinoco, the Amazon, and the Paraguay-Paraná. They lie at low elevations and, especially in the southern basin, contain larger areas of flat land than are found in North America. The plains reach broadly to the Atlantic near the river mouths, and on the west they abut directly, at low elevation, against the foot of the Andes. Only in the extreme south is there a more elevated section, the Plateau of Patagonia, a counterpart of the High Plains of North America.

Eurasia. Eurasia is by far the largest, the roughest, and the most complex of the continents. Less than one-third of its area is plain, and that is split into numerous pieces. Like the Americas, it may be regarded as having a cordillera, a secondary rough land, and intervening plains; but these are vastly different in form, position, and proportion from those in the New World continents.

The Eurasian cordillera covers nearly half of its land mass. In the west, from Spain to western Iran, it is of moderate width, and is composed of loosely linked mountain systems separated by broad, low basins, some drowned by the sea, and broken by numerous low gaps such as the valley of the Rhone River and the straits of the Bosporus and Dardanelles. Two strands of mountains, completely separated from the rest by the narrow straits of the Mediterranean, form the Atlas Mountains of northwest Africa. In the Middle East the basin levels become higher and the low breaks disappear. In and just beyond the Pamir knot the mountains surge to extreme heights and begin the fanwise spreading that carries the cordillera into all parts of eastern Asia. This section of the continent, with its tangled ranges and huge intermontane basins, is the most complex and extensive cordilleran area in the world. The belt even continues into the sea along the rugged island chains of Indonesia and Japan and hurdles the Bering Sea to join with the backbone of the Americas. Along the northern margin of the cordillera are a number of areas of hills, low mountains, and tablelands, the largest being the extensive upland of central Siberia.

The principal plain of Eurasia occupies much of the northwestern quarter of the continent. Like the plains of South America, this great wedge of smooth land lies at low elevations, even to the very foot of the cordilleran ranges. As in North America, the northern part of the plain contains many lakes and swamps. The flat lowland of northwestern Siberia is the most extensive swampland in the world. The dry southeastern part of the plain does not drain to the open ocean but to the immense salt lakes called the Caspian and Aral Seas. In addition to this most extensive plain, Eurasia possesses several others of considerable size, most notably those of Iraq, of north India and Pakistan, and of north China and Manchuria.

The secondary rough land of Eurasia is small and divided, occupying the Scandinavian Peninsula and much of the British Isles. It is largely open hill-and-low-mountain country, though in Norway it achieves considerable elevation. The Ural Mountains form a curious and unique isolated north-south band of rough country in interior Russia.

The Arabian and Indian Peninsulas are an element in Eurasian geography that has no counterpart, for location, in the Americas. These peninsulas, lying beyond the cordillera, are both tilted platforms, highest on the west, that bear some resemblance to the Brazilian Highlands and are even more closely related to sections of Africa. The Arabian Peninsula may in all respects be considered a detached fragment of Saharan Africa, just as the African Atlas is a detached strip of Europe. There is little to distinguish its surface from that of

northeastern Africa, which faces it across the Red Sea. Peninsular India is higher and more irregular, much like southeastern Brazil and parts of west central Africa.

Africa. Africa differs from the three continents already discussed in that it has no true cordilleran backbone. High mountains are scarce. Surfaces smoother than hill lands make up nearly three-quarters of the total area. From the southern Sahara southward, Africa may be regarded as a series of broad, shallow basins separated by somewhat higher swells or thresholds. Generally speaking, the basin surfaces are largely plains, while the swells are commonly hill-studded plains or are carved into hills or low mountains. The long line of swells that traverses eastern Africa from north to south is especially high, and in many places is rugged and broken. The detached block of Madagascar is somewhat similar to the rougher sections of this swell. This central and southern part of Africa is moderately elevated (principally to the south and east), and the outer swells drop with varying degrees of abruptness to the sea or to relatively narrow coastal plains.

Saharan Africa is generally lower than the southern part of the continent. It is largely plain and low tableland, with several areas of hilly or mountainous terrain. The trough of the Red Sea and the rugged swell adjacent to it separate the Sahara from the similar Arabian Peninsula.

Australia. Australia somewhat resembles northern Africa, being largely low-lying and smooth-surfaced. Along the eastern margin of the continent runs a swell of moderate elevation and roughness—the closest approach to an Australian cordillera. As in northern Africa, most of the interior is dry, and considerable areas of it do not have through drainage to the sea.

By way of contrast, New Zealand is distinctly cordilleran, with predominantly rough terrain that also characterizes the Indonesian and other islands north and northeast of Australia along the same general structural line.

16

Plains

Origin of Plains. The only facts true of all plains, as they are defined here, are that most of their slopes are gentle and their local relief is small. Within these broad limits they can vary significantly. Plains can be strongly rolling or nearly flat; they can be marshy or dry, low-lying or elevated, boulder-strewn or silt-covered. But the two characteristics by which they are defined are important enough to justify setting plains apart, for their smoothness not only makes them visually distinctive but also renders them more useful to man, on the average, than any other class of land-surface form.

Most plains owe their existence to a dominance of gradation over tectonics. High relief can occur only if some crustal disturbance has raised parts of the surface well above their surroundings in relatively recent time. If tectonic activity has been slight and gradation has long had the upper hand, relief is ordinarily small. Where relief is small and valleys are shallow, gentle slopes usually predominate. The short valley side slopes, which have the steepest inclination in the landscape, often take up less space than the more gently inclined uplands and valley floors. And because stream downcutting is commonly slow, even the valley sides themselves may be gentle, especially if the materials are weak or there is much surface runoff. Areas of low relief are often depositional surfaces, and except for some sand dunes and stony moraines, deposition rarely creates steeply sloping landforms.

Many of the world's most extensive plains, such as those in the middle western United States, and those east of the Andes in South America, lie in areas where the crust has been particularly stable during late geologic time. However, plains can also occur in areas of active crustal disturbance. Much of the upland of central and southern Africa, for instance, appears to be a broad erosional surface which has been uplifted recently enough that valley cutting has not yet had time to penetrate far inland from the coastal escarpments. Some large structural depressions in the great cordilleran belts have served as receptacles for the deposition of debris from the surrounding highlands, and their floors are broad alluvial plains. The Central Valley of California, the Ganges Plain of northern India, and the Tigris-Euphrates Valley of the Middle East are examples.

The detailed forms of individual plains are the product of recent work by the various sculpturing agents. Plains commonly bear the marks of more than one agent or process, but as a rule the effects of one—most often running water or glaciation—predominate. Because each agent tends to produce associations of features that are peculiarly its own, plains are grouped in the following sections according to the agents primarily responsible for their characteristic landforms.

Plains Eroded by Running Water

Running water and mass wasting are the most universally active of the earth-sculpturing agents. To-

Figure 16.1 Elements of a stream-eroded plain.

gether they have produced the integrated valley systems that are the distinctive features of the most widespread class of plains. The surfaces of these stream-eroded plains are made up of three characteristic elements: (1) the slopes that form the valley sides, (2) the relatively smooth uplands or interfluve crests, and (3) the lowlands or valley floors (Fig. 16.1). The uplands are usually more or less modified remnants of whatever erosional or depositional surface existed in the area before the cutting of the present valleys began. The valley sides have been formed by stream downcutting and reworked by surface runoff and mass wasting. The valley floors have developed either as gentle footslopes left behind as the valley walls have been eroded back or as alluvial features produced by stream aggradation.

Because many variable factors are involved in the formation of each of these elements, it is predictable that plains eroded by running water will show much variety. The chief differences are expressible in terms of completeness of the valley systems, patterns of the valley systems, and cross-section forms of the valleys and interfluves.

Youthful and Mature Plains. Some stream-sculptured plains are distinctive because of the incompleteness of their valley systems. Their major valleys are widely spaced and tributaries are short, so that large parts of the plain have no valleys at all (Fig. 14.9A). Many other plains of this class, by contrast, have completely developed valley systems, with tributaries reaching into every part of the surface (Fig. 14.9B). In the first group interfluve uplands are the dominant element of the landscape; in the second the plains may be made up almost wholly of valley sides. In Chap. 14 these contrasting landscapes were identified with the "youthful" and "mature" stages of the idealized erosion cycle. At the same time it was suggested that the ideal sequence is not always followed, and that some surfaces are persistently youthful while others are mature almost from the outset.

The most important factors controlling tributary development are the amount and velocity of direct surface runoff and the vulnerability of the surface material to erosion. Therefore the conditions favorable to abundant and effective runoff—namely, frequent and intense rainfall, impermeable surface materials, relatively steep slopes, and sparse vegetation—all favor quick development of a dense network of tributaries and hence quickly maturing landscapes. Conversely, gentle and infrequent precipitation, flat surfaces, permeable materials, and a dense plant cover inhibit tributary development and thus prolong youth or, in extreme cases, prevent the attaining of true maturity.

An excellent example of a maturely dissected plain is the Appalachian Piedmont, which extends along the eastern foot of the Appalachian Highlands from New York City to Atlanta, Georgia. The Piedmont is an erosional plain developed primarily on granites and gneisses under a rainy climate. The sandy clay regolith is low in permeability but is readily gullied. In spite of a forest cover, the abundant surface runoff has carved a complete and fine-textured network of valleys, so that the plain is rolling, in places almost hilly, with broadly rounded interfluves and narrow-bottomed valleys (Fig. 15.8A).

A very different landscape is found in the High Plains, the vast smooth upland that stretches from the Platte River of western Nebraska southward into western Texas and eastern New Mexico, broken only at wide intervals by valleys crossing from west to east (Fig. 16.2). Most of the larger streams rise in the neighboring Rockies; relatively little surface runoff is generated within the area itself. The semiarid climate, the permeable materials (originally alluvium from the mountains), the protective cover of grassland sod, and the initial flatness of the depositional surface have all helped to inhibit tributary growth. Although the plain has apparently been exposed to erosion throughout Pleistocene time, at least, and although some valleys have achieved widths of several miles, the area remains obstinately youthful. Short tributaries form narrow fringes of dissected "river breaks" along each major valley, but headward extension into the broad uncut uplands seems to be proceeding no more rapidly than widening of the valleys themselves (Fig. 16.3). Achievement of true maturity appears unlikely. It should be carefully noted that erosional youth and maturity are distinguished from one another on the basis of degree of dissection of the upland, not the width of valleys.

Figure 16.2 The remarkably smooth surface of the High Plains in southwestern Kansas, an old depositional plain upon which stream erosion has made little headway. (U.S. Soil Conservation Service.)

In the plains of older glacial drift and loess in the middle western United States, tributary development appears to be progressive but to proceed at widely varying rates. In eastern Nebraska, southern Iowa, and northern Missouri, dissection is mature (Fig. 16.4), while in eastern Missouri and central Illinois much uncut upland remains. The causes of this variation have received little study, but it seems probable that the more persistently youthful sections were initially flatter than those upon which tributary development has advanced rapidly.

In youthfully dissected plains, the broad, smooth interfluves are most likely to be the principal sites of farmlands, towns, and transportation routes. Some uplands of such plains are so flat as to be poorly drained, especially if their soils are fine-textured. Valley sides, on the other hand, are well drained, but they are sometimes too steep, gullied; or thin-soiled to be useful. The bottoms of major valleys in youthful plains may contain much usable land, though it may be subject to flooding. Minor valleys are usually narrow. In plains of early maturity, roads and towns are most likely to be

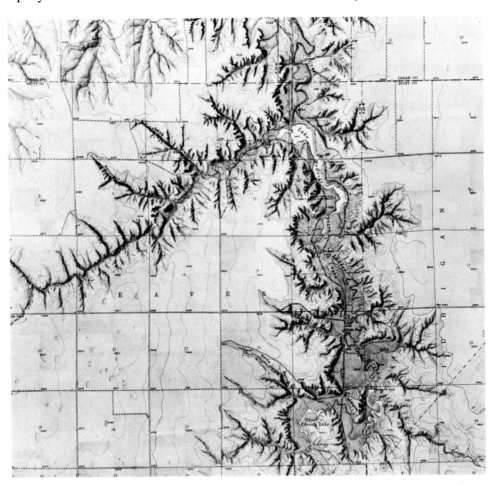

Figure 16.3 A youthful plain, showing smooth interfluve uplands and narrow fringes of river breaks along major valleys. The large squares are 1 mile each. (*Reproduced from U.S. Geological Survey topographic sheet: Lake McBride, Kansas.*)

Figure 16.4   The rolling surface of a mature plain in northwestern Missouri.

found on the broad-crested interfluves. But once the interfluves have been narrowed, the wider valleys may provide the preferred sites for transport and settlement. The localization of farmlands often depends upon how steep and dissected the valley sides are.

Valley Widening—Old-age Surfaces. Even when a stream channel has achieved stability, the walls of its valley continue to be attacked by weathering, surface runoff, and mass wasting. Under this attack they are driven back or worn down so that the valley is widened or opened out. In the advanced stages of erosional development the valley floors widen into broad lowlands and thus become the dominant elements of the surface. Interfluves gradually become narrower and lower until only small remnants (called *monadnocks* after Mount Monadnock in New Hampshire) are left. The stage of old age has been achieved.

Two different schools of thought, intimately related to the contrasting theories of slope development discussed in Chap. 14, have arisen regarding the nature and formation of old-age erosional surfaces. According to one hypothesis, valley widening is accomplished by flattening and rounding of slopes, aided in the late stages by lateral erosion by meandering streams. The end product, a smooth, alluvially veneered plain with low,

rounded monadnocks, is called a *peneplain* (Fig. 16.5*A*). According to the other hypothesis, valley widening proceeds by parallel slope retreat and the evolvement of a gently inclined floor, called a *pedi-*

A. PENEPLAIN

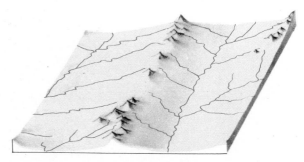

B. PEDIPLAIN

Figure 16.5   Differences between old-age erosion surfaces as conceived according to the peneplain concept (*A*) and the pediplain concept (*B*).

ment, at the foot of the retreating slope. The end product, consisting of greatly expanded, gently concave pediments surrounding relatively steep-sided interfluve remnants, is called a *pediplain* (Fig. 16.5*B*).

It has already been suggested that both forms of slope development probably occur, along with numerous variations in between. However, it is becoming increasingly doubtful that lateral erosion by meandering streams is an important means of producing broad lowlands. It seems likely that the lowlands formed under the first hypothesis of slope development should be gently concave slopes, possibly shallowly dissected and mantled with fine regolith moved downward largely by creep, rather than flat, alluviated floodplains of great width. Surfaces of the peneplain form do occur, as do extensive surfaces of the pediplain type. Narrower alluviated valley bottoms may occur with either.

Many pediments and pediplains are remarkably smooth, while others are corrugated by numerous shallow valleys or rills (Fig. 16.6). Some scholars prefer to restrict the term pediplain to the smoother type, which they consider to be a product of relatively dry environments. It may be more meaningful, however, to extend the term to both varieties and to suggest that the differences stem from the kind of load carried by the streams which form them. Thus the smoother varieties, usually sloping bedrock surfaces thinly veneered

with alluvium, may be formed when the streams are heavily charged with bed load and so tend to form broadly spreading, shifting channels of the braided type. On the other hand, if the streams carry little or no bed load, regardless of the climatic regime, the channels may remain narrow and may therefore tend to cut well-defined rills rather than to smooth the surface more broadly.

It must be emphasized that many of these ideas regarding the evolution of erosional landscapes are highly conjectural. Changing understandings of stream channel behavior and the mechanisms of slope development have cast strong doubts upon simple classical concepts, but it is too early to formulate a wholly coherent theory well backed by evidence.

Valley Patterns. Ordinarily stream patterns develop as a consequence of the arrangement of slopes upon which the runoff is established. The usual result is a pattern in which the principal streams flow in somewhat irregular courses down the regional slope of the land, with tributaries following the same general trend and joining the main streams at acute angles. The pattern is thus treelike or *dendritic*. If the regional slope is slight, the branching is wide like that of an oak (Fig. 16.7*A*); if the slope is steeper, the tributaries are more nearly parallel and the pattern resembles the branches of a poplar (Fig. 16.7*B*).

Figure 16.6 Small erosionally reduced mountain ranges surrounded by extensive pediments, near Oro Grande, Mojave Desert, California. These pediments show both smooth and corrugated sections. *(John S. Shelton.)*

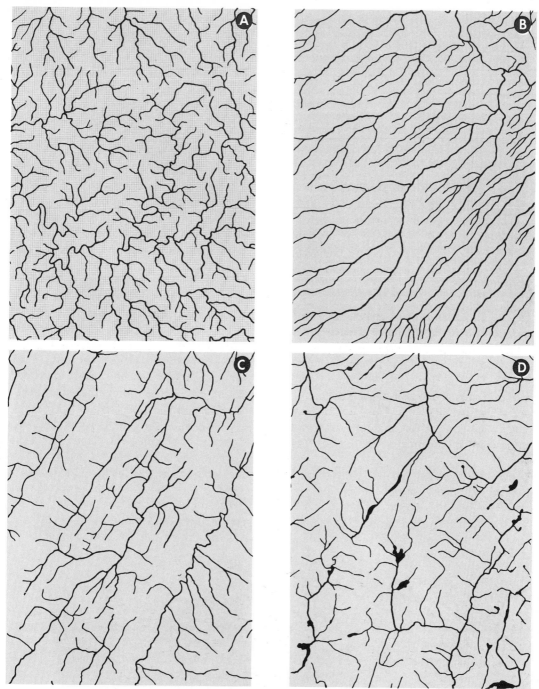

Figure 16.7 A: Random dendritic stream patterns develop where there are no strong local contrasts in rock resistance. B: If the original surface has a pronounced inclination, the dendritic pattern is drawn out in a downslope direction. C: Erosion on parallel bands of rock of contrasting resistance results in parallelism of many stream segments. D: Erosion on strongly fractured or jointed rocks sometimes produces angular stream patterns. (*From Army Map Service series 1:250,000: Charleston, Moab, Charlottesville, and Lake Champlain sheets.*)

A channel pattern which is not dendritic usually means either that the slope on which the streams formed was rather steep and had some peculiarity of shape, or that there are strong local differences in rock resistance. An example of the first case would be an array of relatively straight channels radiating from a center, as they might on the slopes of a new volcanic cone. The effect of the second condition is simply to favor the development of channels where the rock materials are most easily weathered and eroded. The zones of weakness may be joint planes (often occurring in parallel sets), fault lines, or bands of outcrop of relatively weak rock. The resulting stream systems commonly display peculiarly parallel or angular patterns (Fig. 16.7C and D).

Effects of Rock Resistance—Cuestaform Plains. More important than the details of stream pattern are the larger features produced by broad-scale differential erosion. Lands underlain by relatively resistant rocks tend, in the course of time, to retain more youthful forms and higher elevations than the weak-rock zones around them. Some monadnocks and isolated hill groups, for example, owe their preservation to the superior resistance of their rocks.

One very common type of structure consists of stratified rocks, usually sedimentary, in which there are sharp contrasts in resistance between one stratum, or group of strata, and the next. If the strata are horizontal, a particularly resistant layer may become widely exposed at the surface through the erosional stripping of weaker materials from above it. Such a surface is called a stripped plain. On the other hand, if the strata are gently inclined, so that they outcrop at the surface in wide parallel bands of alternating resistance, differential erosion will produce a landscape consisting of parallel strips of highland and lowland. The higher strips, called *cuestas,* are usually asymmetrical in cross section, with a gradual rise along the surface of the resistant stratum on one side (called the dip slope), and an abrupt drop or escarpment on the other (Fig. 16.8). In some cuestas the escarpment is steep and regular and the dip slope smooth and well defined. More commonly, however, especially if there is much surface runoff and the sustaining rock layer is thin, the cuesta is merely a belt of rougher country between lower and smoother lands to either side. Dip slopes always follow the inclination of the strata, while escarpments face in the opposite direction. Hence around a structural basin, cuesta escarpments face outward, while around a structural dome they face toward the center (Fig. 16.9).

Much of the middle western United States is occupied by cuestaform plains. Throughout this area the strata are gently warped into a series of domes and basins that have suffered long erosion. Extensive formations of silica-bearing limestones and dolomites and thick sandstones are the chief cuesta makers, and many of the escarpments can be traced for scores or even hundreds of miles.

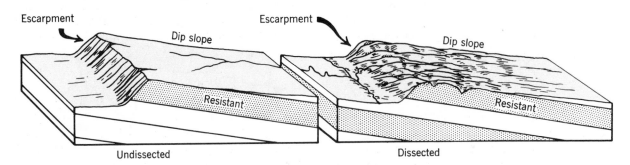

Figure 16.8 Form and structure of cuestas. Example at left is sharp and regular. Dissected form at right is more typical, especially in humid regions.

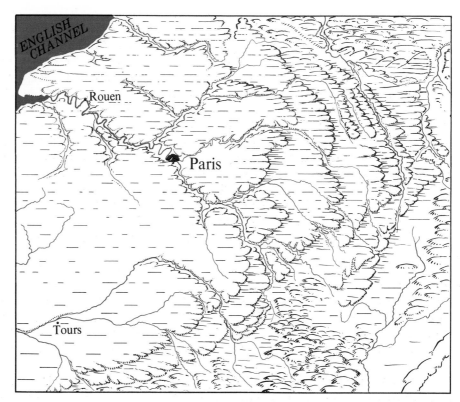

Figure 16.9 Paris lies near the middle of a broad structural basin, surrounded by cuestas with prominent out-facing escarpments. *(V. C. Finch.)*

Other strikingly cuestaform surfaces are found in the Gulf Coastal Plain from Alabama to Texas, and in northeastern France and southern Great Britain.

Effects of Solution. Although solution is an important means by which running water erodes, little is yet known about the specific effects of solution upon the forms of stream-eroded valleys. Steep valley walls and smoothly meandering valleys appear to be unusually common in areas of soluble rocks, but they are not confined to such rocks, nor do all valleys in soluble rocks have them.

Features produced by groundwater solution have been much more intensively studied. It has already been mentioned that the most characteristic are subsurface cavities of various sizes and the similarly varied surface depressions called sinks (Fig. 16.10). Sinks are rather common sub-

sidiary landforms on stream-eroded plains in limestones and dolomites, where they most often appear on the wider interfluves. But in some plains integrated stream valleys are rare, and solution depressions, usually arranged in no systematic pattern, occupy much of the surface. Runoff does not go far before disappearing into a sink or enlarged joint crack. Some of the sinks are narrow-mouthed open pits; some are broad, steep-walled, and flat-floored, with clayey soil; and some are plugged with clay so that lakes or swamps form in them. If the depressions are numerous and small, the landscape often bears a close similarity to morainic terrain (Fig. 16.11). The regolith is commonly thin and patchy, however, for pure limestones and dolomites yield little debris when they are weathered.

Subsurface cavities are not often large, though they may thoroughly honeycomb the soluble

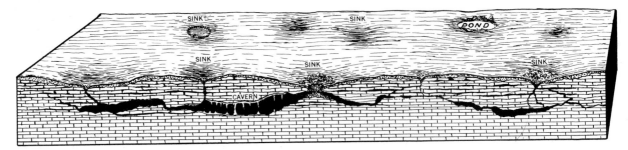

Figure 16.10 Sinks and their relation to solution cavities beneath the surface. *(V. C. Finch.)*

strata in which they occur. Great caverns such as Mammoth Cave, in Kentucky, and Carlsbad Cavern, in New Mexico, can develop only in unusually thick and pure limestone formations. Some of these larger caves are many miles in length, with passages on several levels, and immense rooms that may reach lengths of several hundred feet and heights of more than a hundred. The most spectacular caves are those with many pendants and pinnacles (stalactites and stalagmites), which are deposited by dripping water containing calcium carbonate in solution.

Sinks are common in many parts of the United States, but only two large areas of almost exclusively solution terrain exist, one in central and northern Florida and the other in south central Kentucky. The Florida region is low and gently rolling, with hundreds of shallow depressions, many of them filled with water. It has many large springs, as well as some areas of steep-walled solution valleys. Part of the Kentucky area is somewhat similar, but the section near Mammoth Cave is much rougher, with sinks of unusual size and depth.

Probably the most noteworthy area of solution topography in the world is in western Yugoslavia, where a truly mountainous surface of great ruggedness has been sculptured almost wholly by solution in thick limestones. The region is called the Karst (meaning barren land), and from this example the term "karst topography" has often been extended to cover all solution landscapes, however unlike the original they may be.

Figure 16.11 Limestone plain with numerous small sinks, some containing ponds. Near Park City, Kentucky, south of Mammoth Cave. *(W. Ray Scott, National Park Concessions, Inc. Courtesy Kentucky Geological Survey.)*

Plains Deposited by Water

The surfaces of alluvial deposits are almost invariably plains—usually conspicuously smooth plains. However, they are not featureless. Stream channels are present in various forms and patterns, and because streams shift their channels readily in loose alluvial materials, scars of abandoned channels are almost as characteristic as active streams. Usually there are also various slight swells and depressions resulting from unequal deposition. The depressions often contain swamps or shallow lakes.

Floodplains. When stream aggradation occurs on the floor of a well-defined valley, a floodplain is formed. It was formerly though that floodplains were essentially erosional features, planed off by laterally swinging streams and only thinly veneered with alluvium. However, numerous borings indicate that in the majority of examples, the alluvial fill is relatively deep and has been laid down in a characteristic erosional valley bottom. Thus most floodplains appear to be truly depositional features, resulting from the adjustment of a stream to an increase in sediment load relative to discharge. The surface features of the floodplain, like the form of the stream channel itself, depend chiefly upon the particle size of the alluvium and the width of the alluvial strip relative to that of the channel.

Silty Floodplains with Sinuous Channels. Streams flowing on predominantly silty materials and carrying little coarse bed load usually develop undivided sinuous channels. If the alluvial plain is wide enough (commonly more than twelve to fifteen times the channel width), the stream can develop complex sequences of smooth meanders which will shift and migrate as described earlier (Fig. 16.12C). If, on the other hand, the alluvial strip is relatively narrow, meandering is distorted by contact with the bedrock valley walls. The channel will cross the floodplain, follow the base of the valley wall for a distance, then swing back again to the other side, and so proceed (Fig. 16.12B). In these circumstances the crossover sections migrate rapidly,

eroding their banks on the down-valley side and constructing bars on the up-valley side. On the wide floodplains, cutoff meanders in various stages of sedimentary filling are common features (Fig. 16.13). On the narrower varieties, old channel scars are abundant, but they do not have the same horseshoe pattern.

On floodplains with sinuous channels, most deposition is probably in the form of point bars. During floods, however, some suspended load is spread over the entire surface. The greater part of the suspended material is dropped where the velocity is abruptly checked as the overflow leaves the deeper channel itself. For this reason, the

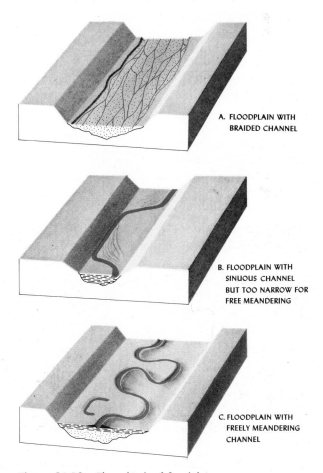

A. FLOODPLAIN WITH BRAIDED CHANNEL

B. FLOODPLAIN WITH SINUOUS CHANNEL BUT TOO NARROW FOR FREE MEANDERING

C. FLOODPLAIN WITH FREELY MEANDERING CHANNEL

Figure 16.12   Three kinds of floodplain.

Figure 16.13 Broad, silty floodplain, showing meandering natural channel with cut-off meanders and meander scars (top). Straightened artificial channel (center) shows formation of point bars and beginnings of meander development. *(Production and Marketing Administration.)*

accumulation is thickest in strips on either side of the channel, but thins down farther from the stream. The thicker sections, called natural levees, are slightly higher and therefore better drained than the rest of the floodplain, which is sometimes called the backswamp (Fig. 16.14). Narrower floodplains rarely have natural levees, presumably because the channel shifts too rapidly to allow them to form. The Missouri River Valley in central Missouri illustrates the narrower version of the silty

floodplain, while the lower Mississippi is the classical example of the freely meandering stream with natural levees and backswamps.

Sandy Floodplains with Braided Channels. The broad band of bars and channels characteristic of streams flowing in loose sand often occupies the entire width of a floodplain (Fig. 16.12A). If the plain is unusually broad, the active channel may not cover all of it at any one time (Fig. 16.15),

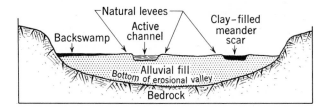

Figure 16.14 Features characteristic of broad silty flood-plains, shown in cross section. The highest ground is along the natural levees.

but the easy lateral shifting of such a channel may cause all parts of the plain to be reworked over a period of several decades.

Braided channels are especially typical of the heavily loaded streams that drain glacial margins, or that emerge from steep mountain valleys where erosion is active onto plains where the coarse debris is dropped. Most of the streams of the Great Plains (such as the Platte and the Arkansas), and many Alaskan rivers (for example, the Copper and upper tributaries of the Yukon), furnish excellent examples of braided channels and their related floodplain forms.

The Use of Floodplains. Floodplains are often eagerly sought as agricultural lands because of their flatness, their loose and relatively fine material, and their easy access to water. Sometimes, though by no means always, their soils are more fertile than the older soils on the neighboring uplands. However, floodplain agriculture is always beset by the problem of floods, with their destructiveness to crops, buildings, and livestock. Even apart from floods, much of the land is likely to be permanently swampy or subject to waterlogging by heavy rains. While these problems can be attacked by various

Figure 16.15 The braided channel of the Rio Grande in northern New Mexico. During flood the entire belt of channels and sand bars will be covered with water. *(Spence Air Photos.)*

Figure 16.16   Alluvial terraces are created by renewed downcutting in an older alluvial deposit.

flood-control and drainage programs, such measures are expensive and not always worth the cost and effort they involve.

Alluvial Terraces.   After a floodplain has been formed, the stream may start eroding again as a result of an increase in discharge or gradient, or a decrease in the amount of sediment load being fed into it. It will then cut down into its earlier deposit, leaving only shelflike remnants along the valley sides (Fig. 16.16). In some valleys several such alluvial terrace levels may be seen, indicating that the stream has repeatedly alternated between deposition and erosion. Because of the lack of flood danger, alluvial terraces are sometimes preferred sites for settlements, roads, and farmlands.

Deltas.   Where a stream flows out of its confined channel into a lake or the sea, its velocity quickly diminishes, and therefore so does its ability to carry its sediment load. The sediment is deposited about the stream mouth, forming in time a low, spreading alluvial surface known as a delta.

The alluvium is usually dropped on either side of the main entering current and in a bar opposite the end of the channel. The channel then divides around the bar, and both branches extend seaward, eventually subdividing again. In this way the stream acquires numerous branching outlets known as distributaries, and the delta grows outward and laterally from the original mouth (Fig. 16.17).

Except for the distinctive distributary channels, the surface features of deltas are usually much

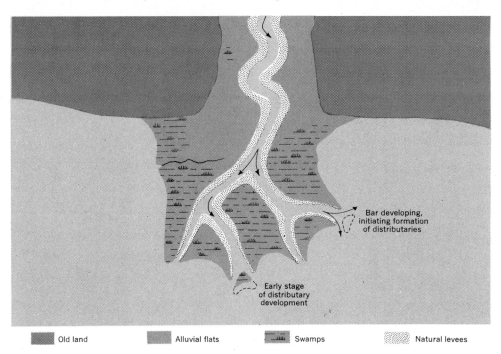

Bar developing, initiating formation of distributaries

Early stage of distributary development

Old land   Alluvial flats   Swamps   Natural levees

Figure 16.17   Characteristic features of a silty delta plain: alluvial flats with large swampy areas, natural levees, and branching distributaries of the stream channel.

like those of floodplains developed in similar materials. Silty deltas—for example, the Mississippi's—are characteristically flat, with sinuous channels bordered by well-developed natural levees, which may provide the only well-drained land. Between them are extensive backswamps, often permanently wet and usually grading into tidal marshes along the outer margin of the delta (Fig. 16.18). In contrast, channels on sandy deltas are characteristically braided, gradients are steeper, and there are no natural levees and relatively little bordering marshland.

Some deltas reach great size. Those of the Mississippi, the Nile, the Volga, and the Ganges, for example, all exceed 100 miles in width, and that of the Hwang is a plain more than 300 miles wide. Many large deltas are not conspicuous on the map because they are built in the inner ends of arms of the sea. The Colorado, Sacramento–San Joaquin, and Tigris-Euphrates are examples.

Not every stream has a delta. Some carry little sediment to their mouths, either because the stream system is erosionally inactive throughout or, more commonly, because most of the load has been deposited in lakes or other spots along the stream course. For example, most of the sediment from the headwaters of the St. Lawrence River is trapped by the Great Lakes, while that of the Congo is dropped in the shallow structural basin through which the river passes before plunging down the coastal escarpment to reach its mouth. Neither of these rivers has a delta. In some other streams the relatively small amount of sediment brought to the mouth is dropped into deep water or is spread across the sea floor or along the coast by wave and current action, so that no delta is formed.

As a group, deltas offer major problems to human utilization, chiefly because of their pervasive swampiness. Nevertheless, the pressure of population upon available agricultural land is so great in some parts of the world that marshy delta lands have been diked off and drained, and are now able

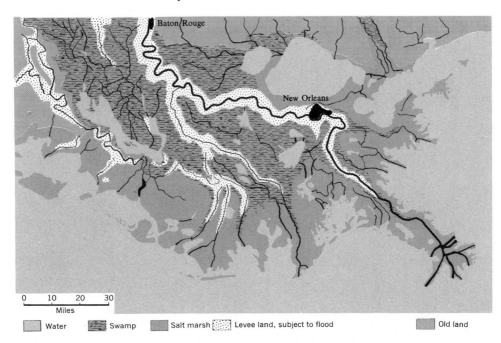

| | Water | | Swamp | | Salt marsh | | Levee land, subject to flood | | Old land |

Figure 16.18 The Mississippi River Delta has fringing areas of salt marsh, areas of wooded swamp, and narrow strips of natural levee. Note that the levee lands grow narrow downstream and disappear. *(Adapted from V. C. Finch.)*

to support great numbers of people. This is true, for example, of large areas in the Yangtse and Ganges deltas. Perhaps the most remarkable instance of delta reclamation is in the Netherlands. All but a small part of that nation is made up of formerly marshy land or even shallowly submerged sea floor in and adjacent to the great combined delta of the Rhine, Maas, and Scheldt Rivers (Fig. 16.19). Over a period of many centuries small tracts have one after another been diked, ditched, and pumped dry, adding a total of several thousand square miles of agricultural land to this densely populated and intensively cultivated country. All such reclaimed land is called polder land.

Alluvial Fans and Piedmont Alluvial Plains. The bases of abrupt mountain fronts, especially in dry and subhumid climates, are characteristic sites for

Figure 16.20 Alluvial fans at the foot of a mountain range in the Mojave Desert, southeastern California. (J. L. Balsley, U.S. Geological Survey.)

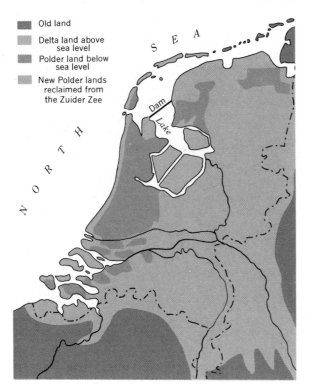

Old land

Delta land above sea level

Polder land below sea level

New Polder lands reclaimed from the Zuider Zee

Figure 16.19 Nearly all the Netherlands occupies low-lying alluvial land or reclaimed shallow sea floor on and adjacent to the delta of the Rhine, Maas, and Scheldt Rivers.

another type of alluvial feature. The steep, swift streams of the mountain canyons become heavily charged with coarse bed load, especially at high-water periods, and emerge upon the plains below as actively aggrading braided streams. As each channel shifts from side to side, pivoting about the canyon mouth, it constructs a smoothly semicircular *alluvial fan,* shaped like a flat half cone (Fig. 16.20). Often several channels, diverging from the canyon mouth, are active at the same time. As a rule the coarsest material and steepest slopes are found at the apex of the fan.

At the foot of an elongated mountain range, many fans may form side by side, eventually growing together to produce an extensive, gently sloping *piedmont alluvial plain* ("piedmont" simply means "foot of the mountain"). Often the outlines of the individual fans can still be discerned in the generally smooth surface (Fig. 16.21). Some plains of this type reach great size, extending out several tens of miles from the mountain front, with very gentle gradients on their lower slopes.

Piedmont alluvial plains often develop in association with pediments, which they sometimes resemble closely in surface form. In one common arrangement, a pediment extends out some distance from the mountain front, but the lower slopes of the plain still farther out are thickly covered with alluvium. However, if the rate of alluvial deposition is sufficiently rapid, alluvium accumulates in fans right at the mountain foot, and no bedrock pediment appears.

In dry climates, water flows on the surface of the fans and piedmont alluvial plains only during rainy spells or periods of snow melt. Low-water flow soaks into the alluvium near the head of the fans, but it is often brought to the surface again by shallow wells and conveyed through ditches to the lower slopes of the plain, where it is used for irrigation. Sometimes the streams are dammed in the narrow canyons and their waters payed out from the reservoirs onto the fan surfaces as needed.

Piedmont alluvial plains are common features in the North American West, notably around the small but steep ranges of Nevada, eastern California, and western Utah and in the southeastern part of the Central Valley of California. Much of Los Angeles stands on a plain of this type that has

Figure 16.21   General view of Death Valley, California, from the south. The smooth slope below the mountains to the left of the valley is a piedmont alluvial plain, formed by the merging of many large alluvial fans. The portion of the valley shown is more than 50 miles long and 15 miles wide. *(John S. Shelton.)*

been built out into the sea from the high mountains north of the city. Extensive piedmont alluvial plains also occur east of the central Andes, south of the western Himalaya in Pakistan and northwestern India, and about the bases of many of the high ranges in Russian Turkistan and central Asia.

Lake Plains and Coastal Plains. On lake bottoms and coastal sea bottoms, sediments are likely to be spread broadly and evenly by waves and currents, forming surfaces that are unusually smooth, with only a very gentle slope away from the shore. Many of the world's flattest and most featureless plains represent surfaces of this kind that have become exposed through the disappearance of the lake or a change in the relative level of land and sea.

Newly emerged coastal plains are especially widespread and extensive. Typically they are low, smooth, and poorly drained, with broad coastal marshes where the nearly level surface merges with the sea (Fig. 16.22), and other swamps in shallow depressions in the depositional surface. Beachlines and low wave-eroded scarps mark the position of former shorelines. Stream gradients are extremely gentle, and erosion often makes little headway even in the loose sandy, silty, or clayey materials. Extensive coastal plains occur along the northern margin of the U.S.S.R., around

Figure 16.22 The flat, marshy surface of the Florida Everglades, part of a relatively new plain not yet dissected by streams. (The water in the foreground is a drainage ditch.) (V. C. Finch.)

the shores of Hudson Bay and the Arctic fringe of Alaska, and on the east coast of Central America. The outer zone of the Atlantic and Gulf Coastal Plain between New Jersey and the Mexican border is an excellent example of the type. Local relief in this plain is generally less than 50 ft, and stream erosion is shallow and incomplete. Extensive coastal marshes, together with swamps both in the valley floors and on the uplands, give the region nearly two-thirds of all the ill-drained lands of the conterminous United States (that is, the United States exclusive of Alaska and Hawaii). This factor, together with the sandiness of much of the regolith, greatly restricts agricultural usefulness.

The exposed floors of former lakes are in most respects similar to newly emerged coastal plains. Abandoned shorelines, flatness, patches of swamp, and shallow remnant lakes smaller than the original one are typical. Lakes are short-lived by the scale of geologic time, for they are inevitably subject to filling with sediment or to draining by downcutting of the outlet. Some lakes have disappeared through evaporation, because the climate has become drier. Other dry-land lake beds fill during periods of major runoff but become partially or completely exposed during dry periods.

Lake plains are especially abundant in glaciated country, for both deposition and erosion by the ice produce numerous shallow depressions in which lakes can accumulate. These will be discussed in the following section on glaciated plains.

In North America most of the prominent lake plains outside the glaciated area occupy structural basis in the dry West. The lakes existed during times when the basins were receiving more runoff than they do now—probably at various moist periods during the Pleistocene, or in some instances even more recently. The two largest lakes, named Bonneville and Lahontan, covered huge areas in western Utah and western Nevada, respectively (Fig. 16.23). Great Salt Lake is a shrunken remnant of Lake Bonneville, and the Bonneville Salt Flats, famous for automobile speed trials, are part of the former lake floor.

Among the larger lake plains elsewhere in

the world are one which occupies part of the smooth elevated basin of the Congo River and another in the Chad Depression along the southern margin of the Sahara.

Complex Alluvial Plains. Several of the world's most extensive alluvial plains cannot be adequately discussed under any single heading. They combine floodplains, deltas, piedmont alluvial plains, and in some cases coastal or lake plains in a single smooth surface. Most of them have formed either in great structural depressions or immediately adjacent to high mountain systems, or both.

One of the finest North American examples is the alluvial plain of the lower Mississippi, which extends some 600 miles southward from southern Illinois to the Gulf Coast, with a width varying from 30 to nearly 150 miles. This great plain includes not only the floodplain and delta of the Mississippi, but also the floodplains of several large tributaries, broad areas of older and slightly higher alluvial surfaces built by the Mississippi and its western tributaries at a time when their bed loads were heavy and their channels braided, and a number of still higher and older alluvial terraces (Fig. 16.24). The plain has developed in a shallow crustal sag that has long received sediment from the north, west, and east. The present alluvial fill, which ranges in thickness from about 100 ft at the north to 400 ft in places near the coast, appears to have been laid down during and since the major rise of sea level that accompanied the melting of the last Pleistocene ice sheet. Beneath the alluvium is a typical erosional plain formed when the sea level was low.

Other somewhat similar complex alluvial plains are found in the Central Valley of California, the Po Valley of northern Italy, the Tigris-Euphrates Valley of the Middle East, and the lower basins of the Indus and Ganges river systems in Pakistan and northern India. A combined piedmont alluvial plain, delta, and multiple floodplain complex, widely mantled with loess, extends broadly eastward from the central Andes to the Paraguay River and the Atlantic.

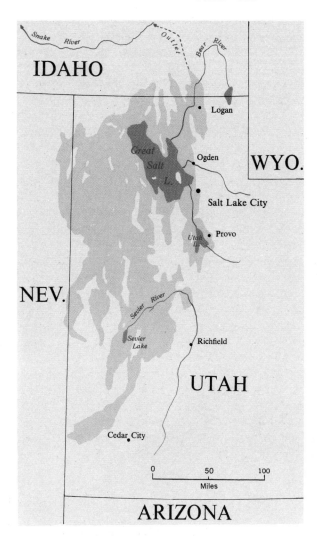

Figure 16.23   Great Salt Lake, Utah Lake, and Sevier Lake occupy small portions of the area once covered by Pleistocene Lake Bonneville.

Climate and Plains of Stream Gradation. Gradational plains in different climates differ from one another not so much in the specific features they possess as in the relative frequency with which certain kinds of features occur. Probably the most distinctive climatic environments for land-surface-form development are the humid and well-vegetated, the very dry, and the very cold.

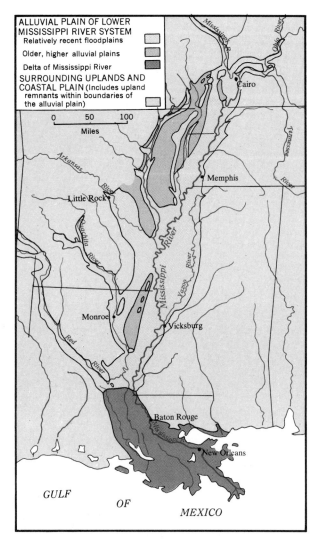

Figure 16.24 The complex alluvial plain of the lower Mississippi River system. *(After Fisk, Geological Investigation of the Alluvial Valley of the Lower Mississippi River. U.S. Army Corps of Engineers, 1944.)*

In humid areas, the significant conditions are, as a rule, a thick protective cover of vegetation, considerable runoff, permanent major streams, and rapid weathering. The rapid weathering tends to favor the accumulation of a fine-textured regolith. This regolith, aided by the vegetation cover, tends to favor infiltration and creep rather than surface

erosion on the slopes. However, the infiltrated water reappears via springs to feed a reasonably close network of permanent streams. Thus the erosional topography is often moderately dissected but smooth-sloped. The large runoff and the perennial flow of streams through to the sea discourage thick inland alluvial accumulations, especially fans. Where highly resistant rocks reduce the effectiveness of weathering or where high relief permits unusually rapid valley deepening, terrain more rugged than the norm may develop.

In dry areas, the significant factors for terrain development are slow weathering, sparse vegetation, impermanent streams, and occasional locally abundant runoff. Under these conditions regolith accumulates slowly and may be quickly swept away during the rare downpours of rain. Hence uplands and slopes tend to be closely gullied and to show much exposed bedrock or coarse regolith. Desert lowlands, however, are often thickly and smoothly covered with alluvium, for stream discharge usually dwindles rapidly when a shower ceases or the stream leaves the area of rainfall, and the heavy load stripped from the uplands is soon dropped. Dry areas that have weak surface materials often display features smoother and more rounded than the average. In areas where surface materials are unusually permeable or in which rains are gentle as well as rare, the landscape may be unusually subdued and very nearly unchanging.

Structural basins in dry lands may not receive enough water to overflow the depression rim and cut an outlet channel. Thus they persist as areas having no drainage outlet to the sea. The Great Basin of Nevada and western Utah, the Chad Depression near the southern margin of the Sahara, and the Aral-Caspian Depression in the southern U.S.S.R., which receives the waters of the mighty Volga as well as several other large rivers, are all regions of interior drainage.

Very cold regions are somewhat similar to dry regions in that vegetation is sometimes rather sparse and weathering is slow. They are also as a rule weak generators of runoff. The slow accumulation of regolith may leave many outcrops of bedrock, but surface erosion and gullying are generally less significant than in dry regions. On the other hand, mass movement, especially solifluction, is very active, as are various small-scale processes of soil movement produced by the frequent growth of ice crystals in the soil. In many areas subsoils remain frozen through much or all of the year, thereby inhibiting subsurface drainage so that the flatter surfaces are usually swampy and strewn with shallow lakes.

Plains Modified by Glaciation

Glacial Modification of the Surface. The great continental ice sheets of the Pleistocene period covered about 30 percent of the land area of the earth (Fig. 14.17), as compared with the 10 percent, chiefly in Antarctica and Greenland, now occupied by glaciers and ice caps. Within the area of Pleistocene glaciation, however, distinctively glacial landforms are well preserved only in those section occupied by the last, or Wisconsinan, ice sheet. Not all these areas are plains, but their surface features effectively illustrate the patchy, irregular, unchanneled erosional and depositional activity of the great ice sheets. That activity virtually obliterated the old stream courses and produced a surface in which there were many shallow enclosed depressions and few continuous valleys. For this reason lakes, swamps, and aimlessly wandering streams are found almost everywhere in the lately glaciated country, though they are uncommon in stream-eroded landscapes.

Most of the glaciated area is dominated by depositional features. Only in scattered sections where there is no drift or where the drift is very patchy are scoured bedrock surfaces broadly exposed. By chance, both the Scandinavian and Canadian areas in which the glaciers originated are underlain largely by ancient "shields" of resistant rocks. Conversely, the broad outer zones of the glaciated plains in both continents are areas of weaker sedimentary strata. Since the weaker rocks yield more readily to weathering and erosion, it is not surprising that the areas which they underlie

are in general more thickly covered with drift than the hard-rock areas. However, the smoother sections of even the shields are also primarily drift plains, although the drift is relatively thin and bedrock outcrop is frequent.

In general, drift deposition tended to make the surface smoother than it had been. Drift was deposited more thickly in valleys than on hilltops, while glacial erosion was somewhat more active on the crests than in the valleys. If the relief of the original surface was slight, the drift might completely obscure the older forms, producing an entirely new surface. If, on the other hand, the original terrain was hilly or the drift rather thin, the old hilltops may still protrude.

Because some glacial drift is put down underneath the body of the ice itself, while some is deposited at the ice margin and some is laid down by the streams of meltwater flowing from the ice, a drift plain is a highly complex surface (Fig. 16.25). The most extensive and fundamental element in this complex is the till plain or ground moraine, which covers most of the glaciated area. Marginal moraines are arranged about the margins of the till plain and also upon its surface, often in broad festoons, one behind the other (Fig. 16.26). Bordering them, either beyond the till plain or upon its surface, are sheets of sandy and gravelly outwash or beds of fine sediments that accumulated in temporary lakes.

Till Plains. The till sheet or ground moraine is a widespread mantle of debris, in part lodged beneath the glacier and in part let down onto the ground when the ice edge melted back or the glacier wasted away. The till plain is characteristically a gently undulating surface produced by uneven deposition (Fig. 16.27). Broad, low swells and wide, shallow depressions are arranged according to no systematic pattern. Lakes and swamps accumulate in the depressions, and streams wander aimlessly from one depression to another (Fig. 16.28). Even the larger lakes are usually quite shallow. In the till plains of North America, thousands of the smaller lake-filled basins left at the retreat of the last gla-

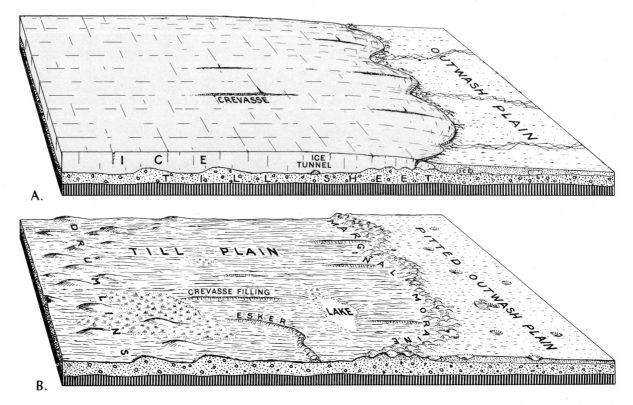

Figure 16.25 Relationships of several kinds of drift deposits to the parts of the glacier by which they were formed. A shows a plain partly covered by the margin of an ice sheet. B shows the same plain after the ice has disappeared. Since till extends beneath the outwash at right, the marginal moraine is recessional. *(Adapted from V. C. Finch.)*

cier have already been filled with sediment or drained by natural processes and converted into marshes.

Rising above the undulating surface in a few localities are sizable groups of low, smooth, half-egg-shaped hills composed of till. Each hill is usually a considerable fraction of a mile in length and is elongated in the direction of glacier flow, with its steeper end facing the direction from which the ice came (Fig. 16.29). These features, known as drumlins, were deposited beneath the marginal sections of the ice sheets and were streamlined by ice movement, but the exact manner of their formation is not known. Extensive fields of drumlins occur in eastern Wisconsin, western New York, and several parts of central Canada.

While many areas of till plain, such as those in northern Iowa, Illinois, Indiana, and Ohio, are excellent agricultural lands, some others are not. Many sections are excessively sandy or stony, and nearly all are plagued with problems of poor drainage. Even in the productive plains of the middle western Corn Belt, thousands of square miles of land have arrived at their high value only through the installation of untold thousands of miles of drainage tile. Elsewhere great numbers of marshes and swamps have been ditched and drained. Unfortunately, very extensive areas of till plain, largely in the Soviet Union and Canada, lie poleward of the climatic limits of profitable agriculture and are further burdened with infertile soils.

Marginal Moraines. Pleistocene marginal moraines

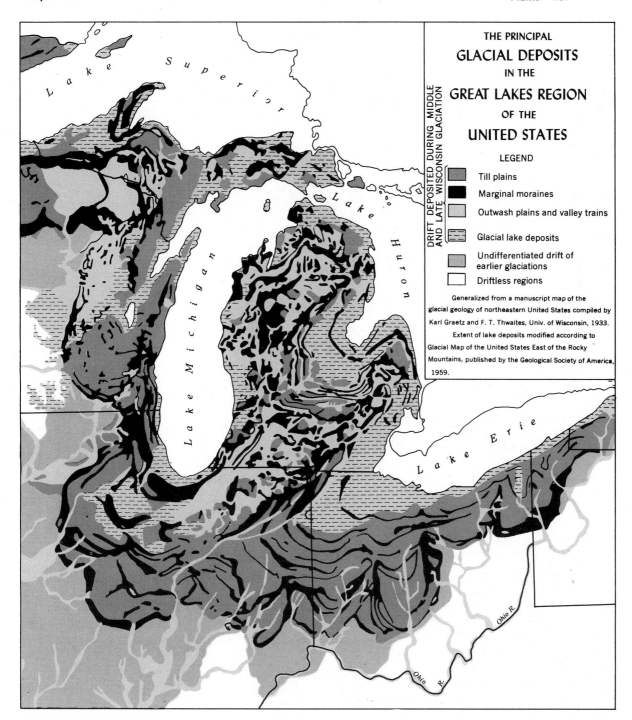

DRIFT DEPOSITED DURING MIDDLE AND LATE WISCONSIN GLACIATION

THE PRINCIPAL
GLACIAL DEPOSITS
IN THE
GREAT LAKES REGION
OF THE
UNITED STATES

LEGEND

Till plains

Marginal moraines

Outwash plains and valley trains

Glacial lake deposits

Undifferentiated drift of earlier glaciations

Driftless regions

Generalized from a manuscript map of the glacial geology of northeastern United States compiled by Karl Graetz and F. T. Thwaites, Univ. of Wisconsin, 1933.

Extent of lake deposits modified according to Glacial Map of the United States East of the Rocky Mountains, published by the Geological Society of America, 1959.

Figure 16.26   Glacial deposits of the Great Lakes region. *(Modified from F. T. Thwaites.)*

Figure 16.27 The undulating surface of a till plain. *(Wisconsin Geological Survey.)*

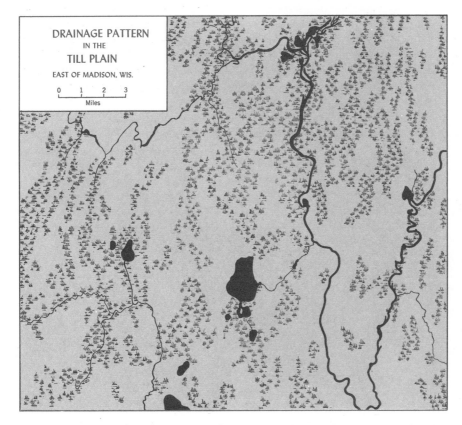

Figure 16.28 Typical aimless drainage pattern on a portion of a till plain in eastern Wisconsin.

Figure 16.29 Two drumlins in tandem on a till plain near Weedsport, central New York. Ice moved in direction from right background toward left foreground.

are relatively thick heapings of drift that accumulated around the edge of a glacier during periods when the ice margin remained nearly stationary for a considerable time. The location of marginal moraines reveals the position and pattern of the ice edge at various times during glacial wastage. Moraines put down where the ice was at its most advanced position are called terminal moraines. Recessional moraines are those built upon the till plain behind the terminal moraine during the general period of glacial wastage.

The surface of a well-developed marginal moraine is usually higher, stonier, and more irregular than that of the neighboring till plain (Fig. 16.30). The depositional processes involved in the construction of a moraine are complex. Some material is dropped in heaps and ridges by melting; some is laid down in alluvial cones against the ice front by meltwater running off the glacier surface; and some is bulldozed up by brief local readvances of the ice edge. The gravel cones and piles of till form many small, rounded knobs or ridges, and between these are small hollows or depressions, some of which contain ponds or swamps. Generally speaking, moraines in stony and gravelly drift are more upstanding and have rougher, more broken surfaces than moraines in clay drift. For example, the clay moraines of northeastern Illinois, though large in volume, form low, gentle swells that would hardly be recognized by a person familiar only with the hilly, stony moraines of eastern Wisconsin or western Minnesota.

The highest and broadest marginal moraines represent situations in which either the ice

Figure 16.30 Small kettle ponds surrounded by boulder-strewn knobs in a marginal moraine near Whitewater, Wisconsin. (V. C. Finch.)

edge oscillated over a limited zone for an unusually long time or a vast mass of drift accumulated in the narrow zone between two slightly separated lobes of the ice sheet. Oscillation of the ice edge accounts for the unusually broad belts of hummocky moraine in west central North Dakota and western Minnesota, as well as those across northern Europe south of the Baltic Coast. An example of an interlobate moraine is the remarkably high and rough Kettle Moraine of eastern Wisconsin.

Glaciated Surfaces with Little Drift. In the rougher parts of the crystalline shields of Canada, Scandinavia, and Finland, the thin preglacial cover of regolith was stripped from large areas, and the resistant bedrock underneath, though it was vigorously scoured by the ice, yielded little new drift. As a result, naked bedrock is broadly exposed in rounded knobs and hills, steep, quarried bluffs, and more level expanses scarred by elongated grooves and innumerable shallow depressions (Fig. 16.31). Joints, fault lines, and other zones of weakness show unusually clearly because they have been etched out by selective erosion. Sparse accumulations of stony drift fill the bottoms of many of the valleys and basins. Drainage is in complete dis-

order. Lakes are even more abundant than in the areas of deeper drift (Fig. 16.32). Streams wander from one overflowing basin to the next in seemingly aimless pattern. Falls and rapids are numerous and, in these areas of hard rock, are highly persistent.

Ice-scoured surfaces of this kind offer little of value to man. Their thin, stony, and patchy soils, irregular surfaces, and large amounts of standing water virtually exclude agriculture. Rapids and falls provide some water-power sites, and valuable mineral deposits have been discovered in some areas, but for the most part they remain among the more thinly settled parts of the earth.

Outwash Surfaces. Meltwater draining from the edge of the ice sheets usually carried a heavy load of sediment, much of it coarse, and therefore the meltwater channels were normally braided and actively aggrading. The finer suspended load was transported far beyond the ice edge, but the sands and gravels of the bed load were deposited in great quantity in the marginal zone.

Some glacial streams flowed in definite valleys and for this reason laid down deposits, referred to as valley trains, that are in all respects like other floodplains formed by braided streams. Many chan-

Figure 16.31 The scoured, bare uplands and rock basins of a glaciated surface with little drift. This site is near Great Bear Lake in northern Canada.

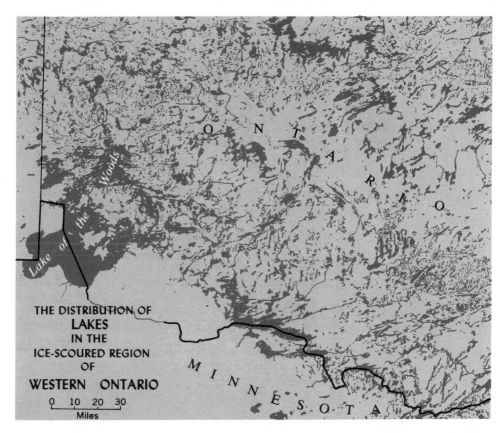

Figure 16.32 Sprawling lakes, mainly in rock basins, occupy much of the thinly drift-strewn plain of western Ontario. *(After Map 24A, Province of Ontario, Department of Surveys.)*

nels, however, were not confined by valley walls, but were able to shift freely back and forth, spreading their debris fanwise to form smooth outwash plains similar to piedmont alluvial surfaces with particularly gentle gradients (Fig. 16.33). This situation was no doubt especially common during the period of ice wastage, for then the meltwaters were released upon the surface of the till plains deposited shortly before.

During the wastage of the ice sheets, large blocks or masses of stagnant ice were left in front of the retreating glacial margin by uneven melting. Outwash from the main ice front continued to be deposited around them and in some instances buried them. When each block or mass eventually melted away, often long after outwash deposition in that area had ceased, its disappearance left a

steep-walled depression in the otherwise smooth surface. Many of the small lakes of northern Wisconsin and southern Michigan are associated with pitted outwash plains of this kind.

Some streams of meltwater built narrow deposits of outwash at the bottoms of deep crevasses or in ice tunnels through which they flowed beneath the outer part of the ice sheets. If the ice melted away without destroying the fragile feature, it remained as a sinuous ridge of gravel somewhat like an abandoned railroad embankment. Such ridges are called eskers (Fig. 16.34).

Because of the sandy and gravelly materials of which outwash plains are composed, they commonly have rather low agricultural value compared with the less stony varieties of till plain. They do, however, afford valuable and abundant re-

Figure 16.33　The nearly flat surface of an outwash plain. *(Wisconsin Geological Survey.)*

sources of sands and gravels for constructional use. The large commercial gravel pits of the Great Lakes region are located mainly in outwash plains.

Glacial Lakes and Lake Plains. Most of the numerous lake plains in the areas of Pleistocene glaciation are no more than the sediment-filled relics of small postglacial lakes that formed on the irregular drift surface. However, others, some of them very large, represent the beds of lakes that existed briefly in places where northward-flowing streams were dammed by the edge of the ice itself during the maximal and wasting stages of glaciation.

The largest of all these marginal lakes oc-

Figure 16.34　The narrow, sinuous ridge of an esker, made up of stratified drift. *(John R. Randall.)*

cupied much of the basin of the Red and Nelson Rivers in Manitoba and surrounding sections during the last major period of glacier recession. At its greatest extent this lake, known as Lake Agassiz, covered an area larger than that of all the present Great Lakes combined, and drained southward via the Minnesota and Mississippi Rivers (Fig. 16.35). It finally disappeared when melting uncovered the outlets into Hudson Bay. Much of its bed is now the flat and fertile Red River Plain, though other sections are occupied by large swamps and lakes. The former outlines of Lake Agassiz are marked by beach ridges and other shoreline features.

The Great Lakes had a complex history during late glacial times. For a considerable period the ice blocked the St. Lawrence outlet and even covered the northern parts of the lake basins themselves. The lakes in the exposed parts of the basins rose and overflowed through various southern outlets, most of which led to the Mississippi River system. At their highest levels the lakes spread well beyond their present bounds. Chicago, Detroit, and Buffalo are among the many cities now located on the smooth plains that mark former extensions of the lake floors (Fig. 16.26).

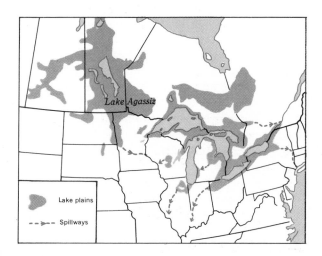

Figure 16.35 Glacial lake plains in the United States and Canada.

Where marginal lakes found new outlets across low divides into other drainage basins, the outflow carved large spillways that still exist though they are no longer traversed by streams. Some rivers blocked by the ice developed new courses that paralleled the ice front for long distances. Some of these new valleys were cut down to levels lower than those of the former channels, so that the rivers continued to flow in them even after the glaciers disappeared. The present courses of the Missouri and Ohio Rivers are probably largely of glacial-margin origin, as are sections of the Mississippi Valley north of St. Louis. Similar marginal valleys, most of them not now followed by streams, run from east to west across the plains of Poland and northern Germany.

The Great Ice Caps. It has been estimated that if the great ice caps that still cover most of Greenland and Antarctica were to be completely melted, they would release enough water to raise the level of the seas nearly 250 ft. The Antarctic ice sheet alone covers an area about $1\frac{2}{3}$ times as large as the conterminous United States. Both ice sheets reach extreme thicknesses of more than two miles.

The surface of each ice cap rises rapidly from the coast to a high plateaulike interior. In Antarctica the average elevation is about 6,000 ft, and the maximum is more than 14,000 ft. The highest elevation in Greenland is above 10,000 ft. Over large areas the bottom of each ice cap is below sea level, a fact which suggests that the land surface has been significantly depressed by the weight of the overlying ice.

For the most part, the surfaces of the ice caps are relatively smooth upland plains. Only near their margins and about the scattered mountain masses that project through them do they become rough and crevassed. At their margins both ice caps descend toward the sea through gaps in mountain ranges, breaking into tongues and lobes as they do so. Where the ice reaches the sea, great masses split off from the edges to form icebergs, some of which drift hundreds of miles from their source before melting away.

Plains Modified by the Wind

Wind-eroded Surfaces. Wind-sculptured plains are largely confined to the dry parts of the world, and even there the effects of wind action are usually less important than the work of water. Except for the few great "seas" of sand dunes, wind-produced features are mostly minor details on surfaces shaped primarily by other agents.

The most important effects of deflation occur where the wind picks up quantities of fine material from the bare floors of alluviated desert basins, thereby lowering the surface over a broad area (Fig. 16.36). Only occasionally do clearly excavated depressions appear, usually on bare patches within areas otherwise covered by vegetation. Local destruction of the vegetation by animals, excessive alkalinity, or any other cause opens up a bare spot where deflation may go to work, producing a shallow "blowout." Generally, however, the wind erodes so broadly and so gradually that its importance can scarcely be estimated.

As a by-product of its selectivity, deflation is largely responsible for the widespread occurrence of gravel-clad surfaces in the deserts. Only the finer silts and clays are picked up; pebbles and coarse sand may not even be moved along the ground. In this way the coarser materials become concentrated at the surface (Fig. 14.22). Where there is no coarse material in the regolith, however, the finer dust may be stripped off to considerable depth.

Sand-dune Areas. The popular conception of the desert plain as a sea of wind-blown sand is not well

Figure 16.36 Bare surface lowered by deflation. Note mounds protected by shrubs and tufts of grass. (*A. M. Piper, U.S. Geological Survey.*)

founded. Not many large desert areas are so much as one-fourth sand-covered. However, there are many regions of sandy desert, the largest being in the central and eastern Sahara and in southern Arabia, which derive their abundant sands chiefly from the disintegration of sandstone or granitic rocks or from accumulations of sandy alluvium in dry basins (Fig. 16.37).

Unlike fine silt and clay, sand is rolled or bounced along the ground like the bed load in a stream, and tends to accumulate in heaps, ridges, or sheets that assume an astonishing variety of shapes. Where sand is thick and abundant, dunes commonly form as a series of great waves transverse to the dominant wind direction, similar in form to wind-driven waves in the sea (Fig. 16.38). However, where strong winds may come from several directions, the waves are distorted into arrays of pyramids and other complex forms (Fig. 16.39). Where the sand is less plentiful, the dunes are usually separated from one another. Some take the form of almost perfect crescents (*barchans*) with the horns pointing downwind; others are long, peaked ridges (*seifs*), oriented parallel to the direction of strong winds (Fig. 16.38).

Most dunes that are barren of vegetation, and especially those occurring in areas of fairly constant wind direction, are actively moving. High winds drift sand up their gentle windward slopes and over their crests, where the grains drop in the shelter of the steep leeward slopes. By this process the dune form is maintained while the whole feature slowly migrates. Rates of movement vary from imperceptibly slow to as much as 100 ft per year.

There are many regions of the world in which sand dunes have become fixed by the growth of a grass cover on them, in some instances undoubtedly indicating a long-term increase in rainfall. One such region forms a broad belt across Africa along the southern margin of the Sahara. In north central Nebraska a large area of once-active dunes, probably Pleistocene in origin, is now anchored by a thick cover of grass.

Loess Plains. The deposition of wind-blown loess may cover the land with an extensive blanket of

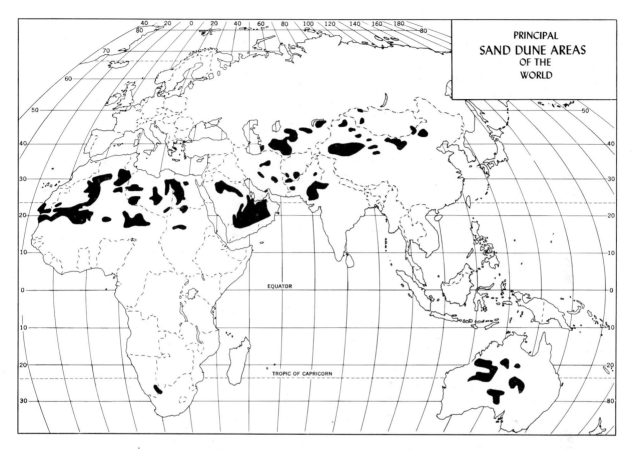

PRINCIPAL
SAND DUNE AREAS
OF THE
WORLD

Figure 16.37 Extensive areas of sand dunes are largely confined to the deserts of the Eastern Hemisphere continents.

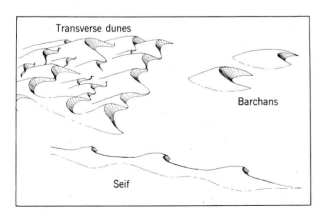

Transverse dunes

Barchans

Seif

Figure 16.38 Common types of sand dunes. In all the examples, the prevalent direction of strong winds is from left to right.

silt several inches or even many feet thick. The thinner accumulations do not greatly change the form of the preexisting terrain. But thick loess deposits may reduce the unevenness of a plain somewhat, and may display low, inconspicuous dunelike features on their surfaces.

Loess has certain physical peculiarities that permit the development of distinctive features by stream erosion and mass wasting. Owing perhaps in part to the angularity of its particles, it has the property of standing in near-vertical faces when cut through by streams or artificial excavations. If the vegetation is thin, gullying is very likely to occur, leading to rapid and intricate dissection. Erosional slopes are steep and often much scarred by slumping, so that eroded loessial landscapes have an unusually broken appearance (Fig. 16.40).

Figure 16.39 The complex, wind-rippled forms of one of the small patches of sand dunes in the American desert. Death Valley National Monument, California. (G. A. Grant, National Park Service.)

Figure 16.40 An eroded and slumped hillside in deep loess in central Nebraska.

Particularly extensive loess deposits occur in the interior of the United States (Fig. 16.41), the southern parts of the great plain of northwestern Eurasia from France into the U.S.S.R., the northern interior of China, and parts of the Pampa of Argentina. Some of these deposits appear to have been blown out from alluvial plains in neighboring dry regions; others are thought to have been obtained from broad valley trains and outwash plains around the glacial margins during Pleistocene time.

Loessial soils are friable and often highly fertile. As a consequence the loess plains of the world are in most instances productive agricultural regions, though soil erosion is a perennial problem.

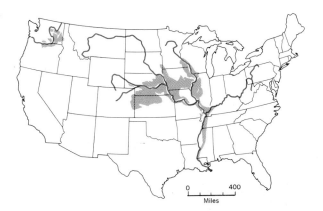

Figure 16.41 Areas of deep loess (more than 8 ft) in the United States. (From map: *Pleistocene Aeolian Deposits of the United States, Alaska, and Parts of Canada.* Published by Geological Society of America, 1952.)

Selected Lists of United States Topographic Quadrangles

The topographic quadrangles listed at the ends of Chaps. 16 through 18 have been selected from those published by the U.S. Geological Survey because they illustrate certain land-surface types and features described in the text.

Because of the great progress made during the last three decades in accuracy of representation, recently published sheets have been chosen wherever possible. To provide uniformity as well as adequate-sized samples of the terrain, the selection has been largely confined to sheets on the scales of 1:62,500 or 1:63,360. Where maps with other scales have been chosen, the scale has been noted.

In recent years the Geological Survey has issued a number of sheets in shaded relief with contours, as well as in the regular contour editions. Because of the unusually graphic quality of these maps, they are especially useful for classroom teaching.

Attention should also be called to the series of contour maps at the scale of 1:250,000, published by the Geological Survey and now available for the entire United States (though some of the sheets for Alaska are as yet issued only in reconnaissance editions). This set of maps is especially useful for regional study of land-surface form, because larger features and regional contrasts are often shown much more effectively than on the larger-scale topographic sheets. Most sheets of this set cover areas measuring 1° of latitude by 2° of longitude. Because of the diversity of features shown on each sheet, no attempt has been made to include maps of this series in the lists.

Copies of all topographic maps listed may be obtained from the U.S. Geological Survey, Denver 25, Colorado, or Washington 25, D.C. Also obtainable are index sheets showing the topographic maps published for each state, an index for the sheets of the 1:250,000 series, and a folder giving instructions for the use of topographic maps and a key to the symbols employed.

Maps Showing Plains

Plains Eroded by Running Water

Youthfully Dissected Plains

Carlinville, Ill. (Smooth old-drift upland; sharply incised dendritic valleys suggestive of progressive headward erosion)

† Rose Hill, N.C. (Smooth newly emerged coastal plain; shallow dissection; early youth)

† Sandon, Kans. (Smooth upland of High Plains; margin of river breaks at north edge)

† Sheets listed under more than one heading
* Shaded relief editions available

Maturely Dissected Plains

Chula, Mo. (Gently rolling; widening main valleys with meandering streams; carved in loess-covered old drift)

Cowpens, N.C. (Strongly rolling section of Appalachian Piedmont; fine texture of dissection; monadnock hill)

† Sherman, Miss. (Cuestaform plain on weak strata of Gulf Coastal Plain; western section rough mature; eastern section very late mature)

Cuestaform Plains

Fredonia, Kans. (Two well-marked escarpments on indurated sedimentary rocks)

† Sherman, Miss. (Much-dissected cuesta and lowland; weak sedimentary rocks)

†* Mammoth Cave, Ky. (Irregular sandstone escarpment overlooking limestone lowland; solution features)

Plains Showing the Effects of Solution

†* Mammoth Cave, Ky. (Small and large sinks on limestone plain and in hills of sandstone underlain by limestone)

Interlachen, Fla. (Broad, shallow sinks, some with lakes; sand-covered limestone)

Holt, Fla. Smooth limestone upland cut by angular, steep-walled solution valleys fed by springs)

Plains Deposited by Water

Wide Floodplains; Meandering Streams

Caspiana, La. (Meanders; cutoffs; shifts of channel marked by county boundary)

† Mellwood, Ark.–Miss. (Meanders of Mississippi River; artificial cutoffs; natural levees; meander scars; swamps)

† Belle Plaine, Minn. (Meanders and cutoffs)

Narrow Floodplains; Sinuous Streams

Columbia, Mo. (Sinuous Missouri River confined by narrowness of floodplain; steep limestone bluffs; smaller meandering and sinuous streams; entrenched meanders in limestone)

Hermann, Mo. (Missouri River floodplain among hills; bluffs; old channel scars)

Floodplains with Braided Channels

†* Ennis, Mont. (Wide, braided channel; artificial lake; alluvial terraces; alluvial fans)

† Tyonek (A-8), Alaska (Braided channel below mountain glaciers)

Fairbanks (C-1), Alaska (Wide, braided channel of major stream)

Alluvial Terraces

†* Ennis, Mont. (High gravel terraces at several levels; braided channel; alluvial fans)

† Manito, Ill. (Broad outwash terrace above modern floodplain; sand dunes)

Delta Plains

† East Delta, La. (Outer margin of Mississippi Delta: distributaries; narrow natural levees; backswamps; irregular shoreline)

† Donaldsonville, La. (Inner part of Mississippi Delta; wide natural levees; backswamps)

Rio Vista, Calif. (Agriculturally developed delta; diked and drained peat lands among distributaries)

Alluvial Fans and Piedmont Alluvial Plains

†* Ennis, Mont. (Large, well-defined fan; alluvial terraces)

† Wheeler Peak, Nev. (Several fans merging into piedmont alluvial plain; basin of interior drainage; alkali flat)

Visalia, Calif. (Broad piedmont alluvial plain; fanwise channels and irrigation ditches)

†* Sequoia and Kings Canyon National Parks, Calif. (1:125,000) (Piedmont alluvial plain at foot of high fault scarp)

Lake Plains and Newly Emerged Coastal Plains

Meldrim, Ga. (Swampy coastal plain; low terrace; beginnings of dissection)

† Rose Hill, N.C. (Smooth coastal plain; low terrace; shallow valley system)

Emerado, N.D. (Margin of former glacial Lake Agassiz; very smooth; several former beachlines)

† Buckley, Ill. (Small, flat lake plain behind low marginal moraine)

Complex Alluvial Plains (Lower Mississippi)

† Clarksdale, Miss. (Recent floodplain, now abandoned; many meander scars)

Wynne, Ark. (Old higher alluvial plain originally formed by braided channels; strip of isolated bedrock upland)

See also Mellwood, Ark.–Miss.; Donaldsonville, La.; and East Delta, La., listed above.

Plains Modified by Glaciation

Till Plains

† Belle Plaine, Minn. (Undulating till plain; small lakes; cut by one broad valley)

Madison, Wis. (Till over irregular bedrock surface; large lakes in partially drift-filled preglacial valley; marshes)

Horicon, Wis. (Drumlins; lakes; huge marsh occupying sediment-filled lake basin; stream course affected by drumlins)

Marginal Moraines

†* Kingston, R.I. (1:24,000) (Rolling glaciated surface over irregular bedrock; hummocky moraine; shore features)

† Jackson, Mich. (Broad belt of hummocky moraine; pitted outwash on east side; lakes and swamps)

† Buckley, Ill. (Broad, low, smooth clay moraine; lake plain to northeast; beginning dissection)

Vergas, Minn. (Unusually broad and rough moraine; kames; kettles; no stream dissection)

Outwash Features

† Jackson, Mich. (Pitted outwash area in broad morainic zone)

† Manito, Ill. (Broad outwash terrace or valley train; sand dunes; modern floodplain)

† Saponac, Me. (Prominent esker; bedrock control of drift surface)

Plains Modified by Wind

Sand Dunes

* Ashby, Neb. (Large clumped sand hills, now grass-covered)

† South Bird Island, Tex. (Coastal dunes on mainland and on broad offshore bar)

† Manito, Ill. (Irregular small dunes on outwash terrace)

† Provincetown, Mass. (1:24,000) (Irregular coastal dunes associated with beaches and spits)

Loess Surfaces

Utica, Neb. (Smooth surface with shallow wind-formed irregularities; sharply dissected at edges)

Broken Bow SW, Neb. (1:24,000) (Sharply dissected loess hills; small remnants of depositional surface)

17

Surfaces Rougher than Plains

Hill and Mountain Lands

In common speech, the words "hill" and "mountain" are used indiscriminately for any land surfaces of predominantly steep slopes and considerable vertical development. In this text, however, the terms are used more restrictively, following the definitions given in Chap. 15. Hill and mountain lands are distinguished from all other classes of surfaces by the fact that the majority of their slopes are not gentle. Mountains have greater local relief than hills: the class boundary is set at 1,000 ft of relief.

Steep slopes are characteristic of hills and mountains, but they are rarely as steep as is popularly supposed. Slope angles of 10 to 25° are common; those greater than 50 or 60° are found only on limited

Figure 17.1 The Sulphur Spring Range, northwest of Eureka, Nevada, a linear mountain range rising more than 2,000 ft above its base. At the lower left are several well-defined shorelines of a lake that covered the basin floor in Pleistocene time. *(John S. Shelton.)*

steeper faces. Local relief reaches extremes of 10,000 to 15,000 ft, but values between 500 and 5,000 ft are more characteristic.

In Chap. 15 the term *cordilleran belt* was applied to the major mountainous zones of the continents. These belts, in turn, are commonly made up of more or less well defined *mountain* *systems,* such as the Rocky Mountains, the Alps, or the Himalaya. *Mountain ranges* are elongated chains of ridges and peaks that possess an overall unity of form and structure (Fig. 17.1). *Mountain groups* are similar, but more compact in outline (Fig. 17.2). Ranges and groups may be isolated or they may form parts of the larger systems.

Figure 17.2 Abajo Mountains, a mountain group in eastern Utah. This dissected laccolith is about 6 miles in diameter and rises nearly 4,000 ft above the upland of the Colorado Plateaus. *(W. Cross, U.S. Geological Survey.)*

Origin and Development

The two distinguishing characteristics of mountains —high relief and steep slopes—both result, directly or indirectly, from strong uplift in relatively recent geologic time. The importance of uplift to the development of high relief was noted in Chap. 16, and in Chap. 13 attention was called to the broad correspondence between the patterns of current tectonic activity and the great cordilleran belts.

Steep slopes naturally accompany high relief. Streams that have far to go to reach stable gradients usually cut down rapidly, thereby producing steep-sided, often canyonlike valleys. Hill lands with low relief, though much less common, do occur where conditions are especially favorable to the development of steep slopes. Perhaps the most frequent circumstance under which they form is the combination of copious surface runoff and materials that are easily gullied but cohesive enough to support steep valley walls.

Tectonic Background. Mountain and hill lands are all carved from uplifted or upbuilt sections of the crust. Some hill lands—the Ozarks, for example— are developed on parts of the crust that have been simply upwarped but are otherwise undistinguished. Most of the major mountain systems, on the other hand, are underlain by an unusually great thickness of sedimentary or metamorphosed sedimentary rocks. This fact is interpreted to mean that for long periods in the past these areas were huge elongated depressions in the crust (*geosynclines*) into which quantities of sediments were carried from the higher adjacent lands. The complex folded, faulted, and intruded structures existing in the areas today indicate that after sedimentation the geosynclines were subjected to strong lateral compression, commonly accompanied by vulcanism. The reasons for the formation and later compression of the geosynclines are not well understood (p. 193).

In most of the mountainous areas, deformation appears to have occurred several times, with long quiet periods between. As a rule the most violent deformation has taken place rather early, during the period of strong lateral compression of the geosyncline, and the principal complex structures have formed then. Later diastrophism tends to take the form of progressively simpler and smaller uplifts of the already deformed structure.

This sequence of events produces successive generations of mountains in the same area of crustal disturbance. Each generation is reduced or even destroyed by gradation before the next major uplift occurs. The mountains that exist now are simply the most recent generations, brought into being by uplifts within the last few million years. But the complex structures from which they have been carved commonly date back to much earlier and much more intense deformations. Thus, for example, the Appalachians are developed on structures more than 200 million years old, and the Rockies on structures 70 million years old. Yet the existing mountains in both areas are the result of uplift and erosion that has occurred, in all probability, well within the last 5 million years. Some rough lands are known to have been uplifted just before or during the Pleistocene period, and in some uplift is going on actively today.

Structure. The rock structure of the upraised portions of the crust from which mountains or hills are carved may be of almost any sort. In the Appalachian Highlands, for example, the western part is developed on nearly horizontal sedimentary strata, the central part on parallel open folds in sedimentary strata, and the eastern part on a highly complex structure of intrusive and metamorphic rocks (Fig. 17.3). The massive ranges of the Middle and Southern Rocky Mountains are carved from relatively simple broad anticlines (Fig. 17.4). The Sierra Nevada of California and most of the smaller ranges in Nevada and western Utah are raised and tilted fault blocks. The Cascade Range in Oregon is an upraised belt of folded igneous and metamorphic rocks capped by thick deposits of relatively recent lava and ash. The Alps are sculptured from an intensely folded and thrust-faulted structure of unbelievable complexity which involves nearly all classes of rocks.

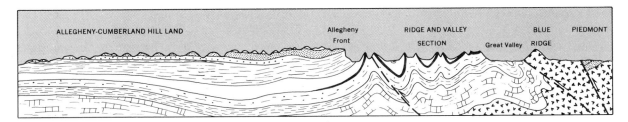

Figure 17.3 Schematic cross section of the northern Appalachian Highlands, showing general relationships of surface form to structure.

These structures, even though they may be ancient, affect the landforms of the present generations of mountains and hills because of local differences in resistance of their rocks. In some mountainous areas, the recent tectonic events have themselves controlled the overall form and the drainage pattern of the rough land, especially where the disturbance has involved large-scale faulting or extrusive vulcanism. More commonly, however, the patterns, features, and outlines of hill and mountain lands are the result of differential erosion upon an inherited structure of much greater age.

Sculpture. Most hill and mountain forms are erosional; the occasional uneroded fault scarps, volcanic cones, lava flows, and alluvial features are exceptions. Undoubtedly the principal sculpturing agents are stream erosion and mass wasting, including the more rapid forms of the latter. However, glaciation, either local or continental, has been important in many regions, and in some mountainous areas valley glaciers are still prominent features of the landscape.

The characteristic sequences of repeated

uplift and reduction have left their mark on the surface forms of most rough lands. Each new generation of hills or mountains begins with the upraising, with more or less distortion, of a gradational surface formed during the reduction of the preceding generation. If the earlier mountains were largely destroyed, this inherited surface is usually a pediplain or peneplain, sometimes combined with extensive alluvial plains. These surfaces may be remarkably smooth, cutting across the diverse structures and burying some irregularities beneath the alluvium. More commonly, however, the earlier generation of mountains was not completely destroyed, and the surface, when uplifted, was still highly irregular and imperfect, with numerous peaks and ridges, or even sizable groups or ranges, remaining along the principal divides or on areas of more resistant rocks. Since the new uplift, valley cutting and related processes have attacked the inherited surface, in some instances virtually destroying it. But on many rough lands much of the old surface remains, forming a broad upland between the newer valleys. Many of the highest peaks of existing mountains are actually

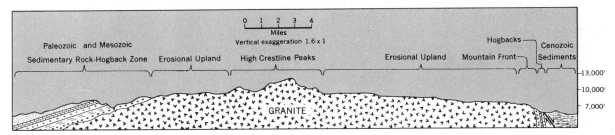

Figure 17.4 Cross section of the Big Horn Range, Wyoming, showing the anticlinal structure and the erosional forms that are characteristic of the ranges of the region. *(From U.S. Geological Survey topographic sheets: Cloud Peak and Fort McKinney.)*

the larger monadnocks left over from the preceding generation (Fig. 17.5).

Extensive hill lands are rarely, if ever, simply worn-down mountains. Areas like the Ozarks and the hill lands of eastern Kentucky and West Virginia have moderate relief because they have been carved from broad sections of the crust that were only moderately uplifted. Where mountains have been greatly lowered by erosion, their valleys have usually widened so much that only separated clumps or lines of high-standing remnants are left.

Surface Features

Valleys. Because the latest uplift and associated environmental changes have disturbed their equilibrium, most streams in rough lands are actively cutting down. Their gradients are characteristically steep and irregular, with many rapids and falls. Valley widening is so slow relative to deepening, especially in resistant rocks, that valley cross sec-

tions are commonly V-shaped or even slitlike (Fig. 17.6). Where rocks are weaker, valley sides may be much more widely flaring. If the principal streams have been able to achieve stable gradients, their valleys may have widened significantly and developed open floors. In this way the Alps, the Cascade Range in Washington, and the mountains of northern New England, all of which have open main valleys with gentle gradients, contrast with the Rockies, the Sierra Nevada, the Himalaya, and much of the Andes, where even the major streams flow through narrow gorges.

In the majority of rough lands most major streams assume their courses in accordance with the pattern of slopes on the uplifted surface. They are then referred to as *consequent* streams. If the uplift has involved little distortion of the inherited surface, the consequent drainage may have virtually the same pattern as that before uplift occurred. But if the inherited surface has been tilted, arched, or warped during uplift, the new stream pattern may be quite different, with the streams flowing down the flanks of the uplifted mass, what-

Figure 17.5   Deeply dissected rolling erosional surface of the pediplain type at elevations of 9,000 to 10,000 ft atop the Colorado Front Range near Boulder, Colorado. In the background the peaks along the Continental Divide, which are remnants of the previous generation of mountains, reach elevations above 13,000 ft. *(T. S. Lovering, U.S. Geological Survey.)*

ever its form. As erosion proceeds, differential resistance may affect the pattern, with tributaries tending to develop more readily on the weaker materials. Tributaries growing along weak-rock belts are called *subsequent* streams.

Sometimes a consequent stream crosses a belt of resistant rock with weaker materials on either side, or flows on a cover of alluvium or other sediments over the top of a buried ridge. As erosion proceeds, the resistant belt may be left standing as a ridge between weak-rock valleys, or the sedimentary cover may be removed from the buried ridge. In either event, the consequent stream is then found cutting directly across the resulting ridge in a discordant canyon called a water gap if it is short (Fig. 17.7), or a *dioric valley* if it is longer. A stream that has been thus let down onto the structure from a smooth erosion surface or a sedimentary cover is called a *superimposed* stream. If the stream has maintained an earlier course while a fault block or anticlinal ridge has been slowly raised across it during uplift, the stream is referred to as *antecedent*. In the Middle and Southern Rockies, few major streams leave the mountain area without passing through dioric valleys, most of them produced by superimposition of the streams from an earlier alluvial cover that buried lesser ranges.

Slopes, Uplands, and Crests. The steep slopes characteristic of rough lands are liable to especially rapid erosion and active mass wasting. Hillside soils are typically thin and stony because of the continual stripping of the surface. Outcrops and cliffs of bedrock are common, especially on resistant materials, and blocks detached from such cliffs often roll down and form talus accumulations at the bottom of the slope.

Particularly high mountains are subject to various processes associated with repeated freeze and thaw, frozen subsoils, and the presence of snow and ice on the surface. Mechanical weathering is especially rapid on exposed rock faces, and solifluction is more active than stream gullying on the high-altitude slopes where permeable regolith

Figure 17.6 Narrow gorge of Wind River in Owl Creek Mountains, Wyoming. Note highway at left and railway tunnels at right. *(William C. Warner.)*

can accumulate. The results of local valley glaciation on such mountains will be discussed in a subsequent section.

Where there is little local contrast in rock resistance, and especially if humid climate and abundant vegetation permit regolith to accumulate, slopes may be quite smooth (Fig. 17.8). On the other hand, contrasts in resistance of horizontal strata, or even strongly developed joint systems in resistant rocks, can produce striking steplike or architectural forms like those that give such spectacular quality to the northern Swiss Alps or the mountains of Glacier National Park (Fig. 17.9).

In general, slopes that are poorly protected by vegetation tend to become closely gullied, particularly so if the materials are cohesive but easily eroded. The famed Badlands of the western Dakotas, carved out of weakly cemented sandy silts, are a striking example (Fig. 17.10).

Most rough-land crests and uplands are

Figure 17.7   Winter aerial view along one of the parallel ridges of the Appalachian Ridge and Valley region in Pennsylvania. The ridge is maintained by a resistant stratum that dips steeply to the left. The Susquehanna River cuts through the ridge, forming a water gap. *(Litton Industries—Aero Service Division.)*

simply what has been left by the cutting of adjacent valleys. Some, however, owe their preservation to unusual resistance of their rocks. Crest lines and divides are most likely to be continuous, high, and broad during the early stages of erosional develop-

ment. In time, however, the uplands become narrowed to sharp crests, and these, in turn, become deeply notched and irregularly lowered. Most often the principal divide lies somewhere near the center line of a mountain range or system, but some up-

Figure 17.8   Smooth mountain slopes developed in relatively homogeneous rocks, northeastern Washington. *(U.S.D.A. photograph.)*

lifts are conspicuously asymmetrical. The tilted fault block of the Sierra Nevada of California is a noteworthy example (Fig. 17.11).

It has already been noted that some uplands represent remnants of an uplifted gradational surface, and that some prominent peaks are mo-

Figure 17.9   Steplike mountain slopes developed on horizontal strata of varying resistance, Glacier National Park, Montana. *(National Park Service.)*

Figure 17.10   Rugged, closely gullied terrain in Badlands National Monument, South Dakota.

nadnocks which remained on that surface. Uplands and peaks with these origins are widespread in the Rocky Mountains (Fig. 17.5) and the Sierra Nevada. In other mountain systems, such as the Cascade Range and the Andes of Ecuador and Bolivia, some of the highest peaks are recent volcanic cones.

Effects of Differential Erosion. Some of the effects of differential erosion upon patterns of crests and valleys and upon the detailed forms of slopes have been briefly mentioned above. In general these effects are not unlike those encountered in lands of lesser roughness. However, because complex rock structures are almost the rule in mountainous areas,

and because relief is great, the results of differential erosion are both more common and more strongly developed than in plains lands.

The most striking effects of differences in resistance are found in the patterns of crests and valleys. Prominent joint systems or patterns of metamorphic foliation may produce some degree of parallelism or rectangularity (Fig. 16.7C and D). Most remarkable, however, are the arrays of parallel ridges and valleys that have developed through deep erosion of parallel folds in sedimentary strata of contrasting resistance. The steeply dipping resistant strata on the flanks of the folds form long, sharp-crested ridges, similar in development to cuestas, but with escarpment and dip

Figure 17.11   Cross section of the Sierra Nevada of California in its highest section. Position of eastern faults is approximate. Compare with Fig. 13.8. *(From U.S. Geological Survey topographic sheet: Sequoia and Kings Canyon National Parks.)*

Figure 17.12   View southeastward across the Ridge and Valley section of the Appalachian Highlands toward Harrisburg, Pennsylvania. Ridge in the foreground, rising 1,500 ft above its base, is supported by a quartizite stratum in the crest of a sharp anticline. All other ridges shown are monoclinal. Note multiple water gaps of Susquehanna River to left of center in background. *(John S. Shelton.)*

slopes of about equal steepness. Monoclinal ridges of this kind are often called hogbacks. The majority of the even-crested parallel ridges of the middle, or Ridge-and-Valley, section of the Appalachians are hogbacks, though the term is rarely applied in that area (Fig. 17.12). Hogbacks are also common features on the upturned strata along the flanks of the great eroded anticlines that form the ranges of the Middle and Southern Rockies (Figs. 17.4, 17.13). In areas of open folding such as the middle Appalachians or the Jura of France and Switzerland, the uncovering of resistant strata in the floors of synclines or the crests of anticlines has created other distinctive forms of ridges (Fig. 17.14).

Figure 17.13 View northward along eastern margin of Colorado Front Range near Denver. Massive crystalline rock at extreme left; outcrops and hogbacks on steeply inclined sedimentary strata in center. Mesa in right background is capped by resistant lava flow. *(T. S. Lovering, U.S. Geological Survey.)*

Valley Glaciers. Snows fall on almost all high mountains, but valley glaciers are found only in mountains that receive unusually heavy winter snowfall or have a short or cool melting period. Glacial tongues 5 to 10 miles long are common in the Canadian Rockies and the Alps, while in southern Alaska and in the Himalaya and adjacent mountains, some glaciers reach lengths of 10 to 50 miles (Fig. 15.9*B*). In the Rocky Mountains and the Sierra Nevada of the western United States, on

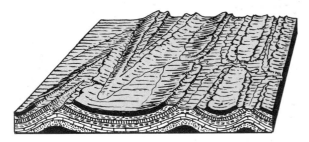

Figure 17.14 Erosional mountains carved from folded structures. *(V. C. Finch.)*

the other hand, long, warm summers restrict glacier development to a few tiny patches, generally less than a mile in length. However, during the glacial periods of the Pleistocene, glaciers were much more extensive in these and other mountains over most of the world.

The snow that feeds mountain glaciers accumulates in high valley heads, into which it is swept by winds and by avalanches from the slopes above. From these collecting basins ice flows in great tongues down the valleys into the zone of melting (Fig. 14.16). The upper parts of the glaciers are often concave, with snow-covered, sometimes smooth surfaces. Toward the lower ends, however, the snow cover disappears in the summer, exposing rough surfaces deeply slashed in places by open cracks or crevasses, especially at sharp turns and unusually steep gradients in the valley (Fig. 15.9*B*). Wastage of ice by melting and evaporation uncovers masses of rock debris that has been carried on and in the ice, so that the lower ends of many glaciers are almost obscured by a cover of rubble.

Effects of Valley Glaciation. Valley glaciers tend to increase the roughness of mountainous areas, for like streams, they tend to erode and enlarge the valleys in which they flow. They work vigorously, clearing weathered rock and talus from the valley bottoms and sides, plucking in jointed bedrock, scouring and quarrying on rock projections and spurs, and dumping their transported load farther down the valleys and along the edges of the ice tongues.

Because of this activity the walls of glaciated valleys are often steeper and freer of regolith than those of typical stream-eroded valleys. Frost shattering attacks these bare walls, driving them back and dropping the debris onto the ice below. Such steepened, smoothed, and straightened walls give many glaciated valleys a troughlike form with a crudely U-shaped cross section. This form appears to be best developed in resistant rocks that have strong vertical jointing.

Glaciated valley floors commonly descend in a series of irregular steps and are marked by lakes strung like beads along a cord. Some of the lakes occupy shallow depressions in the bedrock; others are dammed by moraines. Between the lakes the streams may plunge over waterfalls or rapids (Fig. 17.15). These typically irregular profiles are probably due largely to differential erosion, in which the ice plucks most actively in weaker and more closely jointed rocks and on the steeper gradients of the preglacial valley floor. Tributary valleys often enter the main valley in discordant fashion, their mouths appearing as notches far up the valley side. The streams issuing from these "hanging" valleys must drop in waterfalls or steep cascades to reach the main valley floors.

Valley heads, like valley walls, are abrupt and steep, sometimes looking as though they had been scooped out of the mountainside by a gigantic power shovel. These features, called *cirques,* appear to be the result of glacial plucking, frost shattering, and talus removal at the headwall of the valley. Rapid retreat of the cliffed valley sides and cirque walls eventually leads to the formation of knife-edge ridges and sharp peaks of great ruggedness (Fig. 17.16).

Because of the quantities of debris that are carried onto the moving ice from the valley walls, mountain glaciers are often heavily laden with

Figure 17.15   Head of a glaciated mountain valley. A large cirque in background, with precipitous rock walls and a small remnant glacier. Characteristic stepped-down valley profile with lakes and waterfalls. *(Hileman, from Glacier National Park.)*

Figure 17.16 Valley-glaciated mountains of the alpine type, showing a large cirque, a small glacier, and the characteristic steep rock walls and sharp peaks and ridges. The large lateral moraines in the middleground indicate that the glacier was once larger than it is now. Mount Athabasca, Alberta, Canada. *(Canadian Pacific Railway Co.)*

rubble, and consequently they build moraines that sometimes reach startling size. Lateral moraines are strung along the slopes at the sides of the ice tongues, and end moraines curve across the valleys like dams. Eskers, outwash deltas, and valley trains are also found, in all respects similar to those associated with continental glaciers.

This combination of abrupt slopes, sharp peaks and ridges, much exposed bedrock, numerous lakes, and prominent moraines gives glaciated mountains a spectacular quality that is further enhanced if glaciers are still present. Except for moraines, these characteristics can also occur in mountains that have never been glaciated, but the recurrent presence of several of them together is the special mark of mountain glaciation. Ranges in which the glacial features are notably rugged and in which glacial tongues still exist are called alpine mountains.

Effects of Continental Glaciation. Many mountain and hill areas in the northern continents were completely overrun by the great Pleistocene ice sheets, with results generally similar to those on glaciated plains. The ice tended, in general, to smooth the surface by eroding away crags and small spurs and by depositing drift in the valleys and ravines (Fig. 17.17). Where valleys in weak rocks were oriented in the direction of glacial flow, glacial erosion was unusually vigorous, sometimes excavating basins such as those occupied by the Finger Lakes of western New York. Lakes are common in all glaciated hill lands, especially in the drift-clogged valleys. The northern Appalachians and Adirondacks in New York State, the uplands and mountains of New England, most of the Laurentian highlands of eastern Canada, and most of northern Scandinavia are rough lands that have been modified by overriding continental glaciation.

Figure 17.17 Smooth, drift-covered slopes in glaciated section of Appalachian Highlands near Syracuse, New York.

Volcanic Mountains. While many of the world's rough lands are carved out of volcanic rocks, relatively few mountain chains have been constructed primarily by volcanic activity. The most truly volcanic mountains are the cones that have been built up by the accumulation of lava and ash about eruptive vents. Cones form as essentially isolated features, ranging from insignificant hillocks to magnificent peaks thousands of feet high and several miles in diameter. As a rule, cones formed by explosive eruption of ash and cinders are steep-sided, while those formed by the outpouring of slowly hardening lavas are broad and gentle. Parícutin (Fig. 13.10) and Vesuvius are examples of the steep-sided class, the Hawaiian volcanoes of the broad and gentle type. The majority of cones, however, are made up of both lava and ash and are intermediate between the two extremes. Fujiyama, the beautiful dormant volcano of central Japan, is such a composite cone (Fig. 17.18).

Fresh volcanic cones are usually smooth and symmetrical in form, with one or more well-defined craters. After eruptive activity ceases, however, erosion soon breaches the crater and rough-

ens the slopes. Eventually extinct cones become so reduced that they can scarcely be recognized for what they are. Mount Rainier, Mount Hood, and the other great peaks of the Cascade Range of Washington and Oregon are cones eroded by both streams and glaciers (Fig. 17.19). Agathla Peak in northeastern Arizona (Fig. 17.20) and Shiprock in northwestern New Mexico are the last resistant remnants (plugs and dikes) of once-great cones. Occasionally destruction of a cone is hastened by explosion or collapse, which forms an immense

Figure 17.18 The symmetrical cone of Fujiyama rises more than 12,000 ft above Suruga Bay and its bordering alluvial plains. *(H. Suito.)*

Figure 17.19 Mount Hood is an extinct composite volcanic cone, deeply eroded by water and ice. *(U.S. Forest Service.)*

Figure 17.20 Agathla Peak, a great volcanic neck in northeastern Arizona. This resistant core alone has survived the erosional destruction of a large volcanic cone. *(American Museum of Natural History.)*

depression (caldera) larger than any normal crater (Fig. 17.21).

In a few places—for example, the island of Java—clusters or lines of cones form mountain groups or ranges by themselves. More often, however, the cones are incidental features built upon mountains of diastrophic and erosional origin, as in the Cascade Range and the northern and central Andes. Some other mountains—for example, the San Juan Mountains of southwestern Colorado and the Absaroka Range of northwestern Wyoming—are made up largely of thick masses of extrusive rocks, but are wholly erosional in their present form. Some large laccoliths have been eroded into isolated mountains or mountain groups (Fig. 17.2).

Resource Value of Rough Lands. As a group, hill and mountain lands are the least habitable of the five major classes of land surfaces. Steep slopes, narrow crests and valley floors, thin and stony soils, and abundant rock outcrops make much of the land unfit for productive use. The small areas that are cultivable are often poor in quality, and many are subject to destructive erosion if tilled. As a rule, the great majority of the land that is not hopelessly barren is best kept in forest or grass cover which both utilizes and helps to preserve the soil. Not surprisingly, lumbering and grazing are important activities in many rough lands.

The intense tectonic activity that produces the complex structures common to many mountainous areas is often responsible as well for the formation of certain mineral deposits, especially metallic ores. These have been important attractions to settlement in some regions, but they are commonly spotty in occurrence and short-lived as bases for habitation.

The attractive scenery, clear air, and conditions favorable for camping, hiking, and fishing have come to be an economic resource of great value to some hill and mountain lands, especially those readily accessible to large centers of population. New England, the Catskills, the Colorado Rockies, and the Sierra Nevada are among the many notable mountain tourist centers. No doubt

Figure 17.21 Crater Lake, Oregon, occupies a deep caldera formed by the collapse and destruction of the upper part of a great volcanic cone. Wizard Island (center) was formed by later eruptions. *(Oregon State Highway Department.)*

the most famous of all mountains are the Alps, a magnificent and intensively developed tourist attraction easily reached from anywhere in Europe.

Steep gradients, narrow and tortuous valleys, and high divides are among the numerous factors that tend to make hill and mountain belts barriers to travel and transport. However, there is much variation from region to region. Some mountains are easily traversed by way of valleys that cut completely through them. The Columbia River gorge through the Cascade Range and the Hudson Valley through the New England–Appalachian Highlands are examples of such passageways that have become important routes of trade. Other mountain divides have relatively low gaps that may be approached by gentle-gradient routes from either side, thus presenting less difficulty than the general ruggedness or summit elevations might suggest. The Alps and the Northern Rocky Mountains offer several such pass routes. Some ranges, however, have such continuously high crests and such steep and difficult approaches that they are unusually difficult to cross. The southern Sierra Nevada in California, the central Andes, and the tremendous wall of the Himalaya are excellent examples.

Tablelands, and Plains with Hills or Mountains

Large areas of the continents are occupied by surfaces in which much gentle slope and relatively high relief are combined. These surfaces would, indeed, be plains, if they did not have certain widely spaced features with steep slopes and considerable height or depth. The distinction has already been drawn between those surfaces in which relief is provided chiefly by canyons or cliffs falling away below a smooth upland (tablelands) and those in which spaced hills or mountains rise above an extensive plain (plains with hills or mountains).

Since smooth surfaces usually imply a dominance of gradational processes, and since high relief cannot occur without significant uplift of a part of the crust, it is clear that these rough-and-smooth surfaces are combinations in origin as well as in configuration. Commonly the smooth plain and the interrupting irregularities must be accounted for by quite separate series of events.

Tablelands

Origin. Most tablelands are surfaces that began as plains but have been unusually deeply incised by streams. The distinguishing profile of the tableland, with its broad upland and widely spaced valleys, is simply a high-relief version of the familiar profile of erosional youth. In most tablelands the deep downcutting has been made possible by a general uplift of the plain, amounting to hundreds or even a few thousands of feet, during relatively recent geologic time.

Preservation of the uplifted plain surface against mature dissection during such deep cutting requires that tributary development be unusually slow. Hence the conditions that retard tributary growth—flatness, permeable surface materials, a continuous vegetation cover, light rains, and resistant surface strata—are even more important to the existence of tablelands than to the maintenance of youthful plains. It is not surprising that many table-

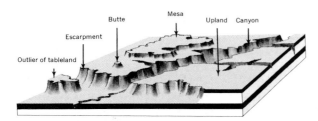

Figure 17.22   Characteristic features of tablelands.

lands are capped by unusually resistant rock strata or by sheets of permeable sand or gravel. Nor is it mere coincidence that most tablelands are found in rather dry areas. In many dry regions local runoff is slight, and canyon cutting can be accomplished only by a few permanent or seasonally active streams that enter the region from more humid areas nearby. Between these few canyons the upland may be only shallowly etched by small rills and gullies.

Canyons and Escarpments. The detailed features of tablelands are chiefly products of recent gradational activity, and are not fundamentally different from those already discussed in connection with plains and rough lands. However, canyons and escarpments, and the various smaller features that are associated with erosion of horizontal rock strata in dry climates, are particularly common and deserve special attention (Fig. 17.22).

The existence of canyons is favored by the very factors responsible for tablelands in general. Late, strong uplift permits rapid downcutting. Limited surface runoff, slow weathering, and resistant caprocks inhibit valley widening. Although canyons are narrow and deep, the eye tends to exaggerate their proportions. The Grand Canyon of the Colorado is nearly ten times as wide from rim to rim as it is deep, and even the seemingly slitlike gorge of its tributary, the Little Colorado, is twice as wide as deep (Fig. 17.23).

The lines of cliffs, or escarpments, that form the margins of tablelands or separate one upland level from another originate either as fault scarps, canyon walls, or bluffs produced by differential erosion. They are continually driven back by weathering and erosion but retain their steepness. As they retreat, the tableland surface above them becomes smaller and smaller and eventually disappears. Because of small-scale differential weathering and gullying, most escarpments are highly irregular, with many spectacular buttresses and towers separated by niches and ravines (Fig. 17.24). Often fragments of the tableland are detached from the main mass by erosion, forming flat-topped, steep-walled hills or columns in front

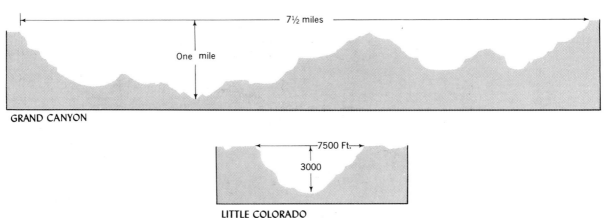

GRAND CANYON

LITTLE COLORADO

Figure 17.23   Cross-section profiles of the Grand Canyon of the Colorado at Powell Memorial and of the canyon of the Little Colorado about 2 miles above its mouth. Vertical and horizontal scales are the same. *(From U.S. Geological Survey topographic sheet: Grand Canyon National Park, East Half.)*

Figure 17.24   The ragged edge of an escarpment that is being driven back by erosion. Painted Desert, northeastern Arizona. *(Spence Air Photos.)*

of the escarpment. As a class such features are called outliers. In the American West the more extensive ones are called mesas, the smaller ones buttes (Fig. 17.25).

Upland Features. The upland surfaces of tablelands may exhibit any type of configuration. Some are typical stream-eroded or alluvial plains. Others are covered by glacial drift or broad sheets of lava.

Figure 17.25   Mesa (left background) and buttes (center), Monument Valley, Arizona. *(I. J. Witkind, U.S. Geological Survey.)*

Figure 17.26 The Grand Canyon of the Colorado River, Arizona, is cut in nearly horizontal strata of varying resistance. View from North Rim. *(U.S. Department of the Interior, National Park Service.)*

Still others are roughened by fault scarps or small volcanic cones.

The features of uplands developed on roughly horizontal strata in dry climates are often simply small-scale editions of the larger elements that make up the tablelands themselves. Narrow, steep-sided ravines, low escarpments and ledges maintained by individual resistant strata, and small mesas and buttes are characteristic.

The surfaces of tablelands are in many places smooth enough to be easily crossed and even to be used agriculturally. However, they are often rather dry and may be so far above the streams that they cannot be irrigated. Some uplands are rough, rocky, or gravelly. The canyons and escarpments may provide major obstacles to transportation and may even make access to the uplands locally difficult.

Occurrence of Tablelands. Considering the world as a whole, extensive tablelands are not especially numerous compared with other types of terrain. In North America, the broadest areas of the type are all in the relatively dry western part of the continent (Plate 3).

The huge expanse of the Colorado Plateaus in northern Arizona, northwestern New Mexico, eastern Utah, and western Colorado is developed on gently warped sedimentary strata of considerable but varying resistance. The area was uplifted as a great block, with marginal faulting, and has since been deeply cut by the Colorado River and several large tributaries, all of which originate in the more humid mountains and higher plateau margins surrounding the tableland itself. The upland surface is a complex of cuestaform and stripped plains, with many rugged escarpments, rock terraces, mesas, and buttes. The larger canyons, notably the Grand Canyon of the Colorado, are among the most spectacular features of their kind (Fig. 17.26).

Much of eastern Washington, Oregon, and southern Idaho is covered with thick sheets of basalt lava. In some sections the lava plain is practically undissected, and in other areas it has been upfolded and carved into mountains. However, in southwestern Idaho, north central Oregon, and parts of eastern Washington, the plain has been converted into a tableland by deep incision of the Snake and Columbia Rivers and their numerous tributaries that emerge from the neighboring mountains. One of the noteworthy features of the area is the Grand Coulee, a now-abandoned channel cut by the Columbia River at a time when its present course around the western side of the basalt area in central Washington was blocked by late Pleistocene ice (Fig. 17.27).

Other extensive tablelands occur just east

Figure 17.27 The Columbia River at Grand Coulee Dam, Washington. The broad, steep-walled Grand Coulee, a great valley cut by the Columbia River when it was temporarily diverted by a continental glacier in late Pleistocene time, stretches southward into the distance. *(F. B. Pomeroy, Bureau of Reclamation, Department of the Interior.)*

of the Rocky Mountain front, especially in eastern Montana, Saskatchewan, and Alberta. These have only modest relief and represent erosional plains, mostly on weak sedimentary rocks, that have been incised by streams emerging from the mountains to the west.

In South America the principal tablelands are the sandstone and lava-capped uplands of interior Brazil and the dissected piedmont plain of the Patagonian Plateau east of the Andes in southern Argentina. Broad areas of southern Russia, somewhat similar to the aforementioned low tablelands east of the North American Rockies, are among the chief areas of the class in Eurasia. The African continent is sometimes referred to as a plateau because its margins are abrupt and much of its interior is a relatively smoother upland. However, only a few sections actually have a tableland configuration, chiefly the cuestaform *hammadas* of the northern Sahara.

Plains with Hills or Mountains

Nature and Origin. Like tablelands, plains with hills or mountains are two-part surfaces. Unlike tablelands, however, the plain in this type of surface forms a floor, while the relief is provided by widely spaced hills and mountains that rise above it. As with tablelands, the plain is ordinarily the product of widespread gradation, while the mountains or hills testify to tectonic activity that has at some time carried all or part of the area well above baselevel or above its surroundings.

At least two fundamentally different sequences of events combine gradation and tectonics in such a way as to generate surfaces of this class. In the first sequence, a high-standing surface is reduced by long-continued erosion to early old age, in which only a few remnants of the highland are left standing upon an erosional plain. In the second sequence some kind of tectonic activity raises widely spaced irregularities upon an already existing plain. Examples of surfaces formed by each of these sequences are numerous, as are areas in which the two appear to have been combined.

Erosional Types. In earlier sections it was stressed that erosion of a mountainous area or other highland does not produce lower but still continuous mountains or hills. Instead, the valleys widen at the expense of the mountains between them, eventually becoming very broad and merging with one another to form a low-level plain of irregular outline. For a long time, however, numerous steep-sided ridges, isolated peaks, and small groups of hills or mountains may remain standing upon such a plain.

The most extensive development of mountain-studded plains of erosional origin has occurred in Africa and South America. Large parts of the hard-rock uplands of central and western Africa are smoothly rolling erosional plains surmounted by remnant ranges or groups, and in some areas by peaks so isolated as to resemble islands rising from the sea. Similar terrain, though generally less advanced in reduction, occupies the eastern parts of the Guiana and Brazilian Highlands of South America (Fig. 17.28).

In North America a narrow strip of the Appalachian Piedmont just east of the mountain front displays a similar granite erosional surface dotted with monadnocks (Fig. 17.29). Erosional plains surmounted by buttes, mesas, and hogbacks occur in parts of Wyoming, eastern Montana, and the western Dakotas. Many parts of New England and of central and eastern Canada are hard-rock erosional plains with monadnocks, but have been much modified by glaciation. Essentially similar terrain occupies much of eastern Sweden and northern Finland.

Figure 17.28 Remnant hills left standing upon an erosional plain developed on ancient resistant rocks in British Guiana. *(D. Holdridge. Courtesy of the Geographical Review, American Geographical Society, New York.)*

Figure 17.29 Near the western edge of the Appalachian Piedmont, numerous monadnocks remain standing upon an erosional plain developed on igneous and metamorphic rocks. Big Cobbler Mountain in northern Virginia. (J. L. Rich. Courtesy of the Geographical Review, American Geographical Society, New York.)

Tectonically Roughened Types. In the second sequence of development, the tectonically produced roughnesses may be volcanic cones, domes, anticlines, or, most commonly, horsts or tilted fault blocks. In some areas of the type, the plains between the mountains appear to have been little disturbed by diastrophism; in others they have been actively downwarped or downfaulted so as to form enclosed depressions.

The upraised features are attacked by erosion as soon as they begin to appear, and are therefore usually found in more or less dissected form. It is not uncommon for the mountains to have been much reduced by erosion, and the plain thereby expanded through pediment formation. In this event the surface as it now exists represents a combination of the two sequences of development.

One of the largest continuous areas of plains with hills and mountains is the North American Basin and Range province, which occupies much of the southwestern United States and nearly all northern Mexico (Plate 3). From southern Oregon to Mexico City, this landscape of dry plains and generally small but rugged mountain ranges extends without a break and with only moderate internal variation. Most of the ranges are believed

to have originated as raised and tilted fault blocks, though there are some volcanic cones, chiefly at the extreme northwest and near the southern end of the province in central Mexico.

Except for the volcanic areas, the principal internal differences in the Basin and Range province are in the degree of erosional reduction of the mountains and in the amount of alluviation and drainage integration on the plains. Thus in most of Nevada and western Utah, and in parts of eastern California, the mountains are bold, relatively steep-sided ranges and the plains are deeply alluviated basins with interior drainage (Fig. 16.21). In southern Arizona and southeastern California, on the other hand, the mountains are small, irregular remnants of once larger ranges, surrounded by extensive pediments (Fig. 16.6). Alluviation is much thinner, and drainage is largely integrated, with few basins of interior drainage remaining. Evidence is strong that the Nevada-Utah area has undergone a relatively late renewal of tectonic disturbance which did not involve the long-eroded landscape farther south.

Plains with hills and mountains of tectonic origin are widespread, especially in the cordillera of Eurasia. From Turkey to the Pamir knot the terrain is similar to the Basin and Range province of North America. In central Asia the basins and ranges are on a truly grand scale, and Tibet is noteworthy for the fact that even its basin floors are at elevations of 10,000 to 16,000 ft. The central Andes of southern Peru, Bolivia, and northern Chile are remarkably similar to Tibet, though some of the prominent peaks are volcanic.

Because of the discontinuity and wide spacing of their peaks and ranges, plains with hills or mountains rarely offer serious hindrance to through transportation. Where soil, water, and climate are favorable, the plains also furnish valuable agricultural land. Unfortunately, large areas of this class, such as the North American Basin and Range province, the central Andes, and the Middle East and central Asia, are excessively dry, and many of their basins are floored with coarse alluvium and saline deposits. However, some alluvial plains have usable soils that can be irrigated by water from the adjacent mountains.

Maps Showing Surfaces Rougher than Plains

Hills and Mountains

Stream-eroded

Structural Effects Minor or Not Evident

* Dutchman Butte, Ore. (Low mountains; V-shaped valleys and sharp crests; steep slopes; dendritic pattern)

Iaeger, W. Va. (Low mountains; V-shaped valleys and sharp crests; steep slopes; fine texture of dendritic valleys)

Drynob, Mo. (Ozark Hills; steep slopes; rounded crests; ingrown meanders; a few sinks)

Structural Effects Evident

* Orbisonia, Pa. (Sharp-crested parallel monoclinal ridges; water gaps) (Near Fig. 17.12)
* Maverick Spring, Wyo. (1:24,000) (Eroded structural dome; concentric hogbacks)

Loveland, Colo. (Hogbacks at Rocky Mountain front; dendritic dissection on granite rocks) (Near Fig. 17.13)

Glaciated

Mountain Valley Glaciers

† Tyonek (A-8), Alaska (Numerous large glaciers; glacial tongue damming lake; medial and terminal moraines; braided meltwater stream)

† Blying Sound (D-8), Alaska (Large ice field with glacial tongues descending to sea level; fiord)

† Mount Rainier, Wash. (1:125,000) (High, eroded volcanic cone among erosional mountains; radial glacier system)

Mountains Modified by Valley Glaciation

* Rocky Mountain National Park, Colo. (Many cirques; troughs; cirque and valley lakes; stepped valley profiles; hanging valleys; huge lateral moraines)

†* Sequoia and Kings Canyon National Parks, Calif. (1:125,000) (Cirques; deep troughs; sharpened crests; lakes; stepped valley profiles; huge moraines; eroded fault scarp; complete cross section of Sierra Nevada) (Figs. 13.8, 17.11)

Mount Bonneville, Wyo. (Many cirques; troughs; sharpened peaks and ridges; stepped valley profiles; hanging valleys; morainic terrain on upland to west)

Hills and Mountains Modified by Continental Glaciation

Tully, N.Y. (Smooth, rounded slopes; open, trough-like valleys; large marginal moraines; small lakes; bedrock channels cut by meltwater; ice-contact outwash terraces) (Near Fig. 17.17)

* Monadnock, N.H. (Smoothed knobs; ponds; swamps; Mount Monadnock, a large remnant of preglacial erosion)

Tectonic Features

Volcanic Cones

Lassen Volcanic National Park, Calif. (Cones, various sizes and degrees of erosion; lava flows; most recently active volcano in conterminous United States)

†* Bray, Calif. (Several cones, variously eroded; craters; lava flows)

† Mount Rainier, Wash. (1:125,000) (Large, glaciated, inactive cone among erosional mountains)

Crater Lake National Park and Vicinity, Ore. (Lake-filled caldera; recent cone in lake; smaller cones; large dissected cones; photos and text) (Fig. 17.21)

Fault Scarps

Hurricane, Utah (Little-eroded fault scarp of Hurricane Cliffs; erosional scarps; hogbacks; sand dunes)

†* Sequoia and Kings Canyon National Parks, Calif.

(1:125,000) (High, rugged, dissected scarp of Sierra Nevada; glaciated mountain forms) (Figs. 13.8, 17.11)

† Wheeler Peak, Nev. (High, rugged, dissected scarp of tilted fault block; alluvial fans)

Tablelands

Uplands and Canyons

* Portage, Mont. (Low tableland of northern Great Plains; smooth upland with low escarpment and outlier; narrow canyons)

Canyon del Muerto, Ariz. (Broad, smooth upland in Colorado Plateaus; deep, steep-walled canyons) (Fig. 15.8B)

Bright Angel, Ariz. (1:48,000) (Deepest part of Grand Canyon of Colorado River; cliffs and benches; text) (Figs. 17.23, 17.26)

* Grand Coulee Dam, Wash. (Lava upland of Columbia Plateaus; wide canyon of Columbia River; abandoned channel of Columbia; great dam and lake) (Fig. 17.27)

Escarpments

Johnston, Utah (Two high escarpments in Colorado Plateaus; outliers)

Agathla Peak, Ariz. (Ragged escarpment and outliers

in Monument Valley area; volcanic neck) (Figs. 17.20, 17.25)

Plains with Hills and Mountains

Erosional Types

* Warm Springs, Ga. (Irregular remnant ridges rising above Appalachian Piedmont; water gaps)

* Antelope Peak, Ariz. (Southern Basin and Range province; fault-block ranges much reduced by erosion; extensive pediments and piedmont alluvial plains)

† Saponac, Me. (Residual mountains on rolling erosional surface; continental glaciation; esker)

Tectonically Roughened Types

† Wheeler Peak, Nev. (High, rugged, tilted fault-block range in northern Basin and Range province; alluvial fans; piedmont alluvial plains; interior drainage; alkali flat)

Sonoma Range, Nev. (1:250,000) (Large area of Basin and Range province; numerous fault-block ranges, variously eroded; basins of interior drainage)

†* Bray, Calif. (Plain surmounted by several volcanic cones; northwest corner of Basin and Range province)

18

The Margins of the Lands

Factors of Coastal Development

Positioning the Shoreline

Erosion and deposition by waves and currents, deposition by streams and glaciers from the adjacent lands, organic accumulations, and various tectonic happenings have all left their mark on the landforms of the world's coastal zones. More fundamentally important than any of these, however, have been large changes in the relative levels of land and sea, for these changes have actively moved the shorelines about and are responsible for their present location and many aspects of their detailed pattern.

The Continental Shelf. That the continents end and the oceans begin at the shoreline seems obvious. But if this statement is changed to say that the continental platforms end and the ocean basins begin at the shoreline, it is neither obvious nor true. Along most continental margins the sea bottom does not drop off abruptly to great depths just outside the shoreline. Instead it usually falls away very gradually to depths of 400 to 600 ft, and then plunges steeply for thousands of feet to a more gently sloping apron or to the relatively smooth floor of the deep sea. The gently sloping shallow zone is called the continental shelf; its steeper outer margin is the continental slope (Fig. 18.1). It is entirely reasonable to regard the shelf and slope as parts of the continents, for they are regularly underlain by sediments of continental origin and other rocks of relatively low density that differ sharply from the dense materials beneath the adjacent deep-sea floor.

Widths of the continental shelf vary from less than a mile to as much as 400 miles. The widest shelves are commonly found adjacent to low-lying plains on the continents. Mountainous coasts, on the other hand, are often bordered by narrow shelves or by none at all (Fig. 18.2).

Changes of Sea Level. A change in the relative levels of land and sea can be produced in two quite different ways. First, the land itself can be raised or lowered by crustal movement. Second, the sea surface can be raised or lowered, either by a change in the amount of water in the oceans or by a tectonic alteration of the total volume of the basins in which the oceans rest. These things have all happened frequently and on a large scale in relatively recent time, producing two kinds of changes in the position of the shoreline: (1) If the land rose or the sea level sank, the shoreline migrated seaward across the continental shelf. (2) If the land sank or the sea level rose, the shoreline moved landward.

The changes in sea level that accompanied the formation and disappearance of the great Pleistocene ice sheets were especially significant for the earth as a whole. Since the water that formed the glaciers originally came from the sea and was returned to the sea when the ice melted, the sea level sank as each ice sheet grew, and rose again as the ice melted. When the last glaciation was at its maximum, the sea level is believed to have been nearly 400 ft lower than it is now, thus exposing as dry land vast areas of what is now continental

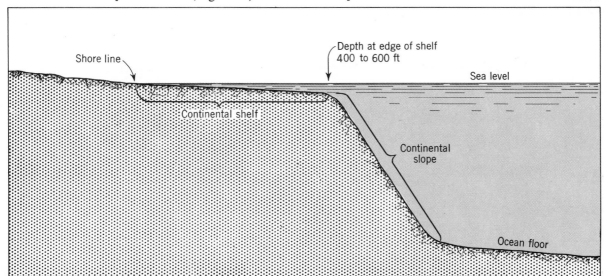

Figure 18.1   Relation of continental shelf and continental slope to shoreline and ocean floor.

shelf. Thereafter the water surface rose irregularly, probably reaching its present level no more than five or six thousand years ago. Tectonic raising and lowering of some coastal lands, especially in the far north and around the Pacific rim, have occurred even more recently.

As a result of these events, the shorelines have only lately attained their present positions; indeed, in some places the shore is still shifting because of changes in the level of the land. The effects of these movements of the shoreline may be clearly seen in the present outlines of certain coasts and in various features repeatedly encountered in the coastal zones.

Modification of the Shoreline

The Work of Waves and Currents. Along the thousands of miles of the world's coasts and lake shores, the work of waves and currents is a prime factor in shaping the surface forms. Though waves and currents also occur in the open seas, they can erode only along the shore and in shallow water, where their activity can reach to the bottom. Waves themselves probably accomplish little erosion at depths greater than 30 or 40 ft, though wave-generated currents can carry material along the bottom in much deeper water.

In waves of the open sea, the motion of individual water particles is a simple oscillation, with little net forward motion (Fig. 12.1). The wave form moves forward without transporting the material itself, just as waves may be seen to move across a field of standing grain or along a shaken rope. But when a wave enters shallow water, the lower part of the oscillation is retarded by frictional drag against the bottom. As a result, the wave form steepens, becomes higher, leans forward, and finally topples or breaks, throwing a great mass of water violently forward and downward (Fig. 18.3).

Waves break when they reach water which is only slightly deeper than the wave height. On coasts where the water deepens gradually offshore, the larger, more powerful waves break far out, and the plunging water scours upon the shallow bottom. Inside the breaker line, smaller waves continue landward, finally rolling or breaking against the shore and sending a swash of sand-laden water up the beach. Where the water maintains a depth of 10 to 20 ft close to the shore, waves break only

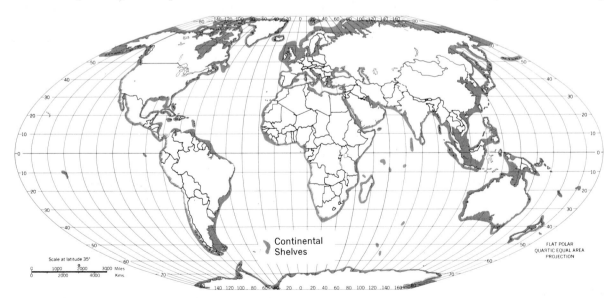

Figure 18.2 World map of continental shelves.

Figure 18.3   A wave breaking. *(F. P. Shepard.)*

when they have almost reached the land, and expend their energy directly against the shore itself. In either case, the water thrown onto the shore by waves or swash is drawn seaward again by gravity, flowing beneath oncoming waves as an undertow current which is sometimes strong enough to move debris along the bottom.

Large storm waves fling tons of water (and sometimes sand and rock as well) against the shore or the shallow bottom, probably generating as great an erosional force as any found in nature. Even relatively small waves can accomplish significant erosion. A few exposed coasts in weak materials are being driven back at rates of several tens of feet per century.

Material dislodged by erosion is transported and redeposited by the waves themselves or by undertow or other wave-generated currents. Much is cast up on neighboring beaches. Flat, gentle waves usually produce a net deposit of sand upon the beach, while the undertow accompanying wind-driven storm waves usually accomplishes net removal. Some debris may be transported long distances along the shore by currents. Considerable material may be spread over the zone between the breaker line and the shore, but as a rule only fine suspended material is carried out beyond the breakers. Coarse gravel and cobbles (shingle) as well as sand may be thrown up into a bar just inside the breaker line.

Where the direction of the wind is oblique to the shoreline, the diagonal shoreward motion of the waves and the direct offshore motion of the undertow combine to move both water and debris along the shore by zigzag in-and-out paths (Fig. 18.4). If the prevailing winds come from one direction, there may be a large and continual longshore transport of material in the direction of the wind movement.

Other Agents of Shoreline Modification. Several other agents besides waves and shore currents contribute to coastal modification. Streams carry huge quantities of sand and mud to their mouths, where this debris may be either added to deltas that build the shore seaward or distributed along the coast on beaches and bars by wave-generated currents. Stream-borne materials are responsible for filling many shallow bays and lagoons.

Pleistocene ice sheets, moving beyond the shorelines as we know them today onto the then-exposed continental shelves, deposited large amounts of debris that now form shoreline features. Long Island, for example, is composed largely of moraine and outwash, while most of the numerous islands in Boston Bay are drumlins. In Antarctica and parts of Greenland and Alaska, glacial ice itself forms parts of the shorelines.

In volcanic areas, lava flows and unusually thick accumulations of ash sometimes encroach upon the sea. Some islands, such as Hawaii, are wholly volcanic.

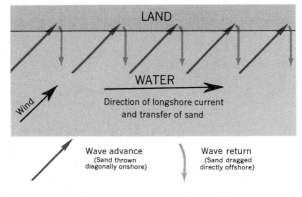

Figure 18.4   Longshore transport of sand by waves and currents.

Several types of floating or rooted plants thrive in sheltered waters and help to fill shallow inlets and lagoons with their own debris. But by far the most important organic modifiers of the shorelines are the corals, small colonies of tiny animals that secrete about themselves structures of calcium carbonate taken from the sea. Both living corals and the broken structures of earlier generations contribute to the growth of limestone reefs that may become very extensive.

Nearly all coasts have been formed by the combined action of several of the agencies thus far discussed. A single shoreline, for example, might bear the marks of wave erosion and deposition, stream deposition, and both a fall and a rise of sea level. For this reason, classifications of shorelines by origin are rarely satisfactory, and none will be attempted here.

Shoreline Features

Bays and Gulfs. Some deep gulfs, including the Red Sea, the Persian Gulf, and the Gulf of California, occupy great structural depressions formed by sharp downfolding or downfaulting (Fig. 18.5). A number of broader and shallower bordering seas, such as Hudson Bay and part of the Gulf of Mexico, appear to be the result of gentler downwarping of sections of the continental margin. But except for these and for some inlets or coves caused by differential wave erosion, most bays and gulfs have been formed through the drowning of erosional topography by a rising sea level. It is not surprising to find such coastal indentations so widely distributed, since the sea level rose perhaps 400 ft all over the world during the melting of the last continental glacier.

When the sea level rises, a new shoreline is established on the former land surface. At first this shoreline will follow all the wanderings of a contour line upon that surface. If the submerged surface was a smooth alluvial slope, its contours were regular and the new shoreline will be similarly regular. But if the surface was an erosional surface, as is more often true, its contours were

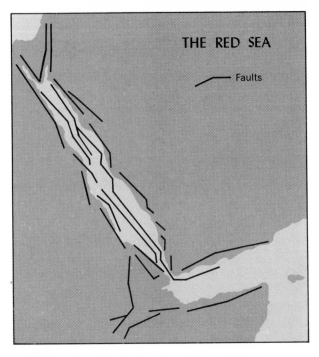

Figure 18.5 Map of the Red Sea and its surroundings, showing the relation of its outline to major fault lines. *(Adapted from Machatschek, Das Relief der Erde, Vol. 2. Gebrüder Borntraeger, Berlin, 1955.)*

probably highly irregular, and the shoreline resulting from its drowning will also be irregular. The sea penetrates the valleys, forming bays, while the higher divides remain above water as peninsulas or headlands. Individual embayments resulting from submergence are called drowned valleys. Those at the mouths of rivers are called estuaries.

Drowned Valleys; Estuaries. If the gradients of the valleys drowned are gentle, the resulting embayments reach far into the land. On the other hand, the drowning of steeply pitching valleys produces short indentations. Since the form and pattern of the bays follow the form and pattern of the valleys that have been drowned. some estuaries are dendritic, others are simple and parallel, and still others are highly irregular.

An especially fine example of an estuarine shoreline is the Atlantic Coast of the United States in Delaware, Maryland, Virginia, and North Carolina (Fig. 18.6). There the drowning of a dendritic system of broad river valleys having particularly gentle gradients produced estuaries of unusual size and length. Other strikingly estuarine coasts occur in northwestern Spain, Greece and western Turkey, western Ireland and Scotland, southern China, and southern Japan. The coasts of New England, Nova Scotia, and Newfoundland have an unusually complex outline as a result of the drowning of an irregular glaciated surface (Fig. 18.7).

The extensive stretches of the world's coastlines that are not impressively estuarine are rarely, if ever, completely free of existing or former estuaries. Most of these coasts have steep-gradient valleys that yielded only small estuaries, and in many instances even these have been filled by the deposits of swift-flowing streams. Thus, for ex-

Figure 18.7 The drowned glaciated shoreline of Casco Bay, Maine, has many rocky islands, peninsulas, and narrow inlets.

ample, the Pacific Coast of the United States, though it has few large estuaries, has many sediment-filled valley mouths that were once small bays.

Fiords. Several mountainous coasts of the world are distinguished by large numbers of narrow, deep, and spectacularly steep-walled bays, some of which penetrate unusually far into the land. These magnificent estuaries, known by their Norwegian name *fiord,* are drowned ice-scoured mountain valleys (Fig. 18.8). The principal regions of fiords are the coasts of (1) Norway, (2) Greenland, northern Labrador, and the eastern Arctic Islands, (3) British Columbia and southern Alaska, (4) southern Chile, and (5) western South Island, New Zealand (Fig. 18.9).

Some of the largest fiords are nearly 100 miles long, 2 to 4 miles wide, and have depths in places exceeding 1,000 ft. Such extreme depths, together with the basinlike form of many fiord bottoms, suggest that glacial tongues of unusual thickness may have been able to erode even below the lower sea levels of Pleistocene time. However, the problem is complicated by the fact that all the fiorded coasts were greatly depressed by the weight of the ice, and have not yet fully recovered their preglacial level.

Figure 18.6 The middle Atlantic coast of the United States exhibits a remarkably fine development of estuaries.

Figure 18.8   Geiranger Fiord, a spectacular drowned glacial valley on the coast of Norway. *(C. d'Emery, Manugian Studio, Courtesy of Norwegian America Line.)*

Cliffs and Benches. Coastal cliffs and benches are produced chiefly by wave erosion. On exposed steep coasts, storm waves breaking directly against the land undercut the coastal slopes, forming sea cliffs. If the materials are weak, the cliffs are usually fairly regular. In resistant rocks, however, joints and other local inequalities favor differential erosion, and the resulting cliffs are often spectacular, with many niches and caves, projecting buttresses, rock arches, and detached pinnacles and rocky islets (Fig. 18.10).

As the sea cliff retreats landward, it leaves behind an eroded bench which inclines gently seaward a little below sea level. The material eroded from the cliff may be carried along the shore or dragged seaward into deep water. Accumulation of some of this debris at the outer margin of the bench may extend it a short distance to seaward (Fig. 18.11). Wave-cut benches sometimes reach widths of a considerable fraction of a mile, but as they widen, the wave attack on the cliff is likely to become weaker and eventually cease.

In many places sea cliffs and marine benches have been either submerged or left high and dry by changes of relative levels of land and sea. Submerged benches are usually hard to identify because they have been obscured by later deposition. Cliffs and benches that are now exposed

Figure 18.9 The intricate coastlines of British Columbia–southern Alaska and Norway are typical of fiorded coasts.

Figure 18.11 Development of sea cliff and wave-cut terrace.

above sea level, on the other hand, are common and often prominent coastal features. Some coasts display a whole series of such terraces, rising like steps from the present shore (Fig. 18.12).

Along tectonically active coastlines, raised shorelines are often warped and sometimes occur hundreds of feet above the present sea level. However, elevated shorelines also occur along stable coasts, though usually at elevations well below 300 ft. Many of these terraces have been attributed to the high stands of sea level that occurred during the interglacial periods of the Pleistocene. Because the successively lower shorelines appear to be successively younger, it has been suggested that the Pleistocene oscillations of sea level were superimposed upon a general lowering of the sea surface, which may have resulted from a diastrophic lowering of parts of the ocean floors.

It should be emphasized that elevated shorelines occur along coasts that also display estuaries which indicate a late rise of sea level.

Figure 18.10 A wave-cut cliff and rocky islets on the exposed coast of Anacapa Island, Channel Islands National Monument, California. (*Roger Toll, National Park Service.*)

Figure 18.12 Well-defined marine terraces on coastal hillside, Palos Verdes Hills, southern California. Three terraces are visible. (*W. P. Woodring, U.S. Geological Survey.*)

This is true even on such a remarkably estuarine coast as that of Virginia and North Carolina. Most coasts show evidence which is entirely compatible with the idea of an oscillating sea level during glacial times.

Beaches, Bars, and Spits. On protected sections of the coast, or even on exposed coasts that are not too frequently swept by destructive storm waves, relatively gentle wave action tends to move sand or gravel onto the shore, creating beaches. Along a smooth coast, the beaches may form a continuous strip many miles in length. On irregular coasts, however, the sediment is usually concentrated in the indentations, the headlands often being swept clear and subjected to active erosion. Through the erosion of headlands and the accumulation of beaches in the indentations, an irregular shoreline is gradually straightened by wave action. (Fig. 18.13).

Debris that is moved parallel to the shore by obliquely striking waves and longshore currents continues to shift until it comes to an angle in the shoreline, to the sheltered or deeper waters of a bay, or to a protected position between a close-in island and the shore, where it is dropped. Gentle waves that come more directly from seaward may then carry the material onto beaches or build it up into bars across the mouths of bays or between island and shore. Sometimes the line of a coast is extended beyond a major angle through the growth of a long, often curved bar or *spit* (Fig. 18.14).

Some flat, relatively storm-free coasts that are abundantly supplied with alluvial sands have been built seaward for considerable distances by the successive formation of beaches or bars, one in front of the other. Conversely, some other coasts show evidence of a reduced supply of sediment, accompanied by gradual wastage of beaches and bars.

Figure 18.13 A sandy beach has accumulated in this sheltered bay, while the headland beyond has been swept clear by wave action. Cape Sebastian, Oregon. *(Oregon State Highway Commission.)*

Offshore Bars. Along coasts where shallow water causes the waves to break far from shore, long strips of sand, called offshore bars, form just inside the line of breakers. Such bars may touch the land at projecting points, but elsewhere they are separated from it by shallow lagoons a few yards to several miles in width. Most are broken at intervals by openings through which tidal currents pass.

Many offshore bars appear to be simply elongated spits, built by longshore currents combined with constructive wave action. On the other hand, some bars are not in contact with the land and appear to be out of reach of land-derived sediments. These, at least, may have been formed wholly by constructive wave action just inside the erosional site of the breaker line. It is, however, difficult to understand how incipient sand bars could have survived their formative periods in such storm-swept waters as those at Cape Hatteras.

Offshore bars are unusually well developed along the south Atlantic and Gulf Coasts of the United States, where they are almost continuous. Many of the famous beach resorts, such as Atlantic City, Palm Beach, Miami Beach, and Galveston, are built on them and are reached from the mainland by bridges or causeways. In North Carolina broad estuarine lagoons (sounds) are enclosed by an especially far-flung cordon of offshore bars, the outermost point of which is Cape Hatteras, famous for the number of ships that have been driven aground on its sandy shoals (Fig. 18.15).

All beaches and bars composed of sand are subject to significant changes with time. They normally widen or lengthen during periods of gentle wave action, and they may be greatly altered, reduced, or even destroyed during violent storms. Shingle features are considerably more durable, and may grow even during storms.

In hurricanes the unusually high water levels and huge waves cause beaches and bars to be literally overwhelmed. The greatest loss of life in any natural disaster in the United States occurred in a hurricane at Galveston, Texas, in 1900. Wind-driven water completely covered the city to a depth of several feet, and nearly 5,000 people died. The

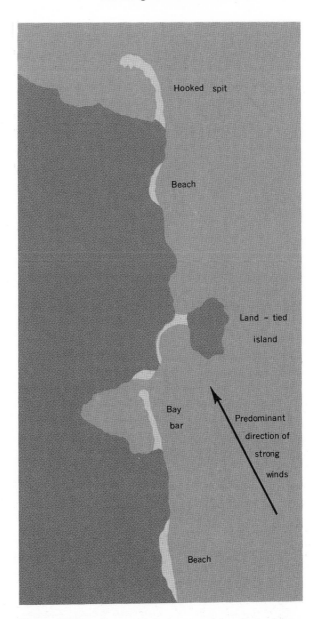

Figure 18.14 Characteristic types and locations of bars, spits, and beaches.

construction of a high sea wall has effectively forestalled a repetition of the catastrophe.

Coral Reefs and Atolls. Reefs of limestone comprised principally of the crumbled skeletal struc-

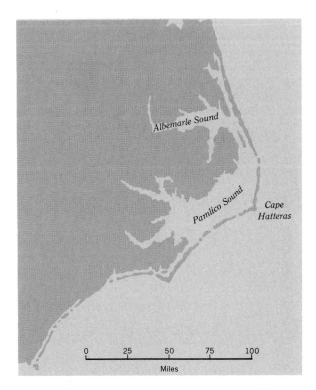

Figure 18.15 Offshore bars and sounds along the coast of North Carolina.

tures of colonies of corals are common features along tropical coasts. Most coral reefs form narrow coastal fringes in shallow water. Fringing reefs grow with such rapidity in clear, shallow, warm waters that they build a shoreline seaward in spite of wave and current erosion. Corals can also grow abundantly in shallow waters at a considerable distance from shore and thereby form a barrier reef separated from the mainland by a broad lagoon. The great reef that parallels the northeast coast of Australia for 1,000 miles is the largest example.

Some small reef-encircled islands, mostly volcanic, seem to have undergone slow submergence while the coral fringe about them has continued to grow. The encircling reefs now appear at the surface as low, more or less complete coral rings, called atolls, which enclose shallow lagoons. Midway, Wake, Bikini, Kwajalein, and Eniwetok are all of this general type (Fig. 18.16). Borings

and seismic investigations made in several Pacific atolls have revealed accumulations of coral rock several thousand feet thick atop the volcanic bases. This thickness represents the amount of subsidence that has occurred since the volcanic island was originally formed (Fig. 18.17).

Islands

The existence of isolated masses and bits of land surrounded by the seas, occurring sometimes in groups or strings and sometimes quite alone in midocean, has never failed to stir man's interest and curiosity. It is hard to avoid feeling that such peculiar features, strangely rising from the open sea, must have some unique and startling mode of origin. Yet this is a false notion, for the processes that produce islands are not different from those that produce high-standing features on the continental masses themselves.

Some islands, for example the British Isles, the islands of eastern Denmark, the Arctic Islands of Canada, Vancouver Island, and Prince Edward, Cape Breton, and Long Islands, appear to be no more than detached portions of the continental masses. The channels that separate them from the mainland may well have been cut during low stands of sea level in glacial times and then drowned during the postglacial rise of sea level.

Other islands, however, have been formed by tectonic disturbance. Some are raised or tilted fault blocks. Santa Catalina and neighboring islands off southern California, the several islands of the Gulf of California, and in a more complex manner, the islands of Tasmania and Madagascar, all originated in this way. But by far the greatest number of islands are either volcanic cones built up from the sea floor or complex folded, faulted, and eroded masses similar to the continental mountain systems—or else combinations of the two.

Isolated volcanic islands are very common, especially in the western Pacific. There the ocean floor is dotted with dozens of great cones (Fig. 18.18). These include not only the currently active cones, such as those of the Hawaiian Islands, but

Figure 18.16 Coral reefs and sandy islets enclose a quiet lagoon at Wake Island, a small atoll in the central Pacific. Shallow reefs show as light-colored submerged areas ringed with white strip of heavy surf, best seen in right foreground. *(Official U.S. Navy photograph.)*

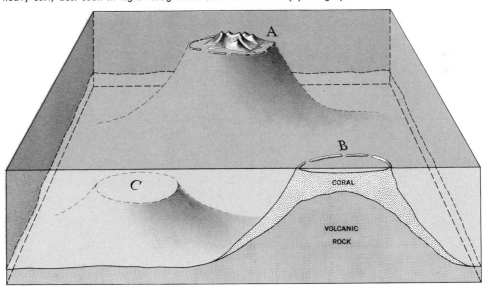

Figure 18.17 Volcanic islands and coral reefs. *A* is a modern volcanic island surrounded by a barrier reef, suggesting the beginnings of submergence. *B* is an atoll, formed by continued growth of coral above a volcanic island that has slowly submerged. *C* is a former volcanic island, its top planed off by wave erosion, which submerged too rapidly to permit the maintenance of coral growth.

also the many more inactive, eroded cones, such as those of Tahiti, Samoa, Ponape, and Truk. As previously mentioned, many cones have slowly become submerged, leaving on the surface only the atolls maintained by the continuing growth of a cap of coral on the sinking peaks. Some cones sank too rapidly to permit the maintenance of coral growth and are now completely submerged, flat-topped features (Fig. 18.17).

Other isolated volcanic islands occur in the Indian and Atlantic Oceans. In the Atlantic several of these, including the Azores, Ascension and Tristan da Cunha, are cones built along the great Mid-Atlantic Ridge, a complex faulted, structural swell, somewhat similar to a continental cordilleran belt, that runs almost squarely down the middle of the Atlantic Ocean Basin from north to south.

Complex folded and faulted islands most commonly occur off the coasts of similarly struc-tured mountainous parts of the continents. Among these are most of the islands of the Mediterranean (including Corsica, Sardinia, Sicily, and Crete) and many others, such as Borneo, Newfoundland, and Kodiak.

Many curving strings of islands, known as island arcs, festoon the borders of the continents, especially in the western Pacific. They include the lesser West Indies, the Aleutians, the Kurils, the Ryukyus, the Marianas, and such larger masses as Japan, the southern islands of Indonesia, and the eastern Philippines. These island chains are in part volcanic and in part complex folded structures. In most instances, they are bordered on their seaward side by ocean-bottom trenches of tremendous depth (Fig. 18.19). The island arcs and trenches are known to be among the most active tectonic zones on earth. They appear to represent sites where deformation is proceeding actively because

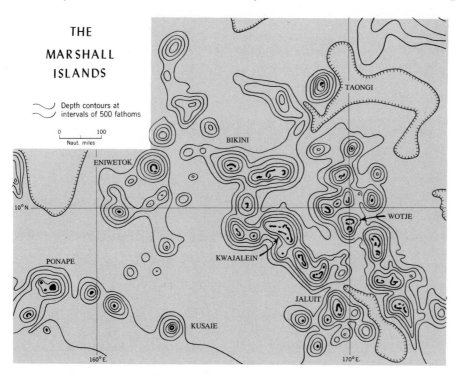

THE
MARSHALL
ISLANDS

Depth contours at
intervals of 500 fathoms

0   100
Naut. miles

TAONGI

BIKINI

ENIWETOK

10° N.

WOTJE

PONAPE

KWAJALEIN

JALUIT

KUSAIE

160° E.   170° E.

Figure 18.18 The Marshall Islands are coral atolls which have formed about the sum-mits of thickly clustered volcanic cones that rise more than 15,000 ft from the ocean floor in the west central Pacific. *(Modified from Depth Curve Chart of the Adjacent Seas of Japan, Maritime Safety Agency, Tokyo, 1952.)*

Figure 18.19   The Kuril Islands, stretching northeastward from Japan, are a typical island arc, with an associated trough, or deep. *(Modified from Depth Curve Chart of the adjacent Seas of Japan, Maritime Safety Agency, Tokyo, 1952.)*

of lateral compression of the crust. Vulcanism is common in the islands, usually toward the concave side of the arc. In many respects the arcs correspond closely to certain of the great curving continental mountain systems, such as the Himalaya, the Alps-Carpathians, and the northern Andes.

Coasts and Harbors

There are many significant relationships between coastal characteristics and human activities, chiefly those involving navigation and the development of harbors. Clearly the configuration of the shoreline

and of the bottom close to shore are factors that must be taken into account in locating or improving ports or channels.

It must be kept in mind, however, that a port is a result of human needs and work, rather than a feature of physical geography. The value of a harbor depends upon its own physical characteristics, but even more upon whether it is located where a harbor is needed.

A deep and well-protected bay well connected with a productive or populous hinterland is a resource of incalculable value. It is only natural that many significant ports have developed on estuaries and fiords or in waters sheltered by reefs, bars, or offshore islands. But even such "natural" harbors as those of New York, San Francisco, Rio de Janeiro, and Sydney have required much dredging and reshaping to provide enough deepwater docking space to handle their immense traffic.

Some of the most commodious and sheltered bays are of almost no value as harbors because the land behind them is unproductive, sparsely populated, or inaccessible. The magnificent fiords of southern Chile, for example, are almost unused because they are backed by a wild, storm-swept, mountainous, and nearly uninhabited land.

On the other hand, some of the world's busiest ports have been developed where no natural harbor existed, because the hinterland required a shipping and receiving facility for its products and imports. The harbor of Los Angeles—and to an even greater degree that of Callao, the port of Lima, Peru—are largely man-made. At both places long breakwaters have been built to protect an otherwise exposed section of coast. At London, Rotterdam, Bremen, and Hamburg, shallow estuaries have been heavily dredged to provide sufficient entrance depth, and basins that can be closed off by lock gates have been excavated to provide docking space unaffected by the excessive rise and fall of the tides.

Maps Showing Shoreline Features

Bays and Gulfs

Estuaries

† Kilmarnock, Va. (Branching estuaries of dendritic valleys; low terrace; small spits; bottom contours)
† Point Reyes, Calif. (Branching estuary; drowned erosional valley along fault zone; spits; cliffs; small delta)
Boothbay, Maine (Highly irregular coast of drowned rock-controlled glaciated surface; many drowned valleys; islands)

Fiords (All sheets have bottom contours)

Sumdum (D-5), Alaska (Long, twisting, narrow fiord; deep basin and shallow mouth; small mountain glaciers; stagnant ice tongue; cirques, troughs)
† Blying Sound (D-8), Alaska (Large fiord with deep basin and shallow sill; smaller fiords; large ice field and glacial tongues) (Blying Sound (C-8) extends coverage southward, showing mouth of fiord; smaller fiords; islands)

Features of Marine Erosion and Deposition

Sea Cliffs

† Point Reyes, Calif. (High sea cliffs; offshore rocks and islets; estuaries; spits)
Point Sur, Calif. (Mountainous coast with sea cliffs; offshore rocks; islet tied to land by bar)

Beaches, Bars, and Spits

† Provincetown, Mass. (1:24,000) (Large hooked spit; bay bar; smaller spits; beaches; dunes; bottom contours)
†* Kingston, R.I. (1:24,000) (Several spits and bay bars; beaches; drowned glacial coast; moraine)
† Point Reyes, Calif. (Spits and bay bars; sea cliffs; estuaries)
† South Bird Island, Tex. (Broad offshore bar with dunes; lagoon; large estuaries; dunes on mainland; bottom contours)

Elevated Shorelines

Redondo Beach, Calif. (1:24,000) (At least six marine terraces discernible on coastal hillsides)
† Kilmarnock, Va. (Low terrace; smooth plain below and dissected plain above; estuaries)
† Rose Hill, N.C. (Low terrace; youthful dissection)

Selected References for Chap. 18

King, C. A. M. *Beaches and Coasts.* Edward Arnold (Publishers) Ltd., London, 1959.

Kuenen, Ph. H. *Marine Geology*. John Wiley & Sons, Inc., New York, 1950.

Shepard, Francis P. *Submarine Geology*. Harper & Row, Publishers, Incorporated, New York, 1948.

Steers, J. A. *The Coastline of England and Wales*. 2d ed. Cambridge University Press, New York, 1964.

Thornbury, W. D. *Regional Geomorphology of the United States*. John Wiley & Sons, Inc., New York, 1965.

Williams, W. W. *Coastal Changes*. Routledge & Kegan Paul, Ltd., London, 1960.

Wooldridge, S. W., and R. S. Morgan. *An Outline of Geomorphology: The Physical Basis of Geography*. 2d ed. Longmans, Green & Co., Ltd., London, 1959.

19

Wild Vegetation

The extraordinary diversity of the wild vegetation (i.e., vegetation which is not cultivated or domesticated) that still mantles large parts of the continents is one of the earth's most striking embellishments. It has been said that vegetation is the apparel of scenery, for the way a rural region looks is to an important degree determined by its plant cover. Forested areas stand in marked contrast to wild grasslands, and both of these to the desert's sparse mantle of shrub. The green woodland in leaf gives a totally different scenic effect from the somber leafless grove in winter. In some places the esthetic aspect of wild vegetation has considerable resource value as an attraction for travelers and tourists.

But besides being decorative, wild vegetation has additional practical utility for man. In the preagricultural stage of his development, wild vegetation and the animal life which subsisted on it provided the

the essentials for his food, shelter, fuel, and clothing. As civilization advanced and population multiplied, spreading more widely over the earth, the original vegetation cover on much of the land surface was consumed, destroyed, changed, or obliterated. The result is a greatly altered landscape consisting of modified wild vegetation, tilled fields, and planted pastures—as well as areas which, being occupied by cities, towns, highways, and railways, have little or no vegetation. But even in this twentieth century, wild grasslands for animal grazing, and forest products in the form of lumber, fuel, pulp, and food, make a significant contribution to man's economic well-being.

Moreover, since the wild vegetation of an area is an expression of the total physical environment, past as well as present, it can serve as an indicator of the overall environmental potential, especially as a guide to judging the suitability of land for reforestation or for specific crops. Long after the original vegetation has disappeared and agriculture is well established, the soil continues to bear the imprint of the type of plant cover under which it developed. Significantly, many classifications of climate (see Chaps. 6 to 10) and soils (see Chap. 20) continue to make use of wild vegetation as an indicator, as shown by some of the type names used and the boundaries chosen.

The Grouping and Arrangement of Plants. Although there is an almost infinite variety of wild plant forms mantling the earth's land surface, it can be observed that these plants exist in distinct groupings. Such a grouping is not a haphazard collection of plants, but rather an organized colony composed of different sizes and species, whose highly interdependent members have evolved in, and share, the same environment. Called *plant communities,* they vary in extent from subcontinental size down to small local units. The broadest classes of plant communities are forest, grassland, desert shrub, and tundra.

These communities may be subdivided into *formation types.* For example, the forest community may be separated into tropical rainforest,

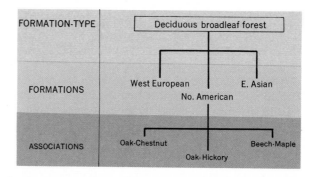

Figure 19.1 The rankings of one formation type among plant communities. For simplicity, only North American associations are shown in the diagram; Europe and East Asia have other DBF associations.

coniferous forest, deciduous broadleaf forest, and several others. Each of the formation types may be further subdivided into large regional *formations* (North American deciduous broadleaf forest, European DBF, East Asian DBF, etc.), and each of these again into *associations* (oak-hickory forest, beech-maple, and chestnut-oak) (Fig. 19.1). It is with the extensive plant communities, formation types, formations, and associations that this chapter will deal.

Causes of Regional Variations

The remarkable diversity of the earth's mantle of wild vegetation is a result of the interaction of heredity or evolution, natural environment, and the effects of human interference.

Evolution

The first land plants were simple primitive forms such as algae and fungi. From these the present complex vegetation forms have evolved over eons of time. It is a general rule that vegetation, left to itself, will evolve from relatively simple communities of small plants, to much more complex ones dominated by large plants. Such a developmental series of plant communities is called a *plant succession.*

The prime cause of the development of

higher and more complex plant species from lower forms, and of the differentiation of these species over the earth, is believed to be a natural selection of inheritable characteristics that are beneficial in the struggle for existence with other plants. In the competitive struggle of any and all life forms, including plants, it is those individuals having slight physical advantages in structure or function over their fellows that come to prevail. Among the characteristics most important in the evolutionary process are migrational abilities, potential for adjusting to climatic change, and habitat preferences.

Environment

The present broad patterns of distribution of great plant associations or vegetation types appear to be closely related to environmental factors. And while the natural environment varies widely over the earth, it is nevertheless made up of the same basic components: solar energy, climate, underlying bedrock, soils, water, terrain, and the wild fauna and flora. Together these elements compose a complex of mutually interacting phenomena called the *biotic complex* (Fig. 19.2). Unlike animals, plants do not have the power of locomotion, cannot construct shelters, and do not generate heat, so they are unable to escape the effects of the surrounding environment to the same degree.

Climate. Climate is the master element in the broad-scale patterns of plant communities, for the distribution of wild vegetation over the earth reflects climatic conditions more than any other single factor. Not only does climate operate directly through its components of light, temperature, precipitation, and wind, but indirectly it affects plants through the weathering of rocks, the soil-making and leaching processes, and organic decay. Still, climate is only a permissive factor, for many plants which could otherwise flourish are eliminated by competition. For example, grass is quite at home in the climatic conditions which exist in most forest regions; it has been excluded not by the climate but by competition, for grasses cannot tolerate the shade beneath the tree cover.

If the climate of an extensive region remains unchanged over a long period of time, its plant life gradually evolves through a succession of stages until at last it becomes stabilized. Because of common physical needs and tolerances, certain plants, although unrelated to one another, are repeatedly found growing together in similar environments. The most complex type of plant formation—the last in the plant succession—that can develop under a particular climate, and is in equilibrium with that climate, is known as a *climatic climax vegetation*. It is likely to persist relatively unchanged for an indefinite period. Accordingly the climax vegetation associations are the extensive plant formations which correspond with the major types of climate. Examples of widespread climatic climaxes are the tundra of the poleward margins of North America and Eurasia, the subarctic coniferous forest of the boreal climates of the same continents, and the tropical rainforest of those equatorial latitudes which have abundant rainfall and little or no dry season. But although a climax plant-formation type, such as tropical rainforest, is similar in general appearance throughout the world because its dominant species are very alike in form, actually

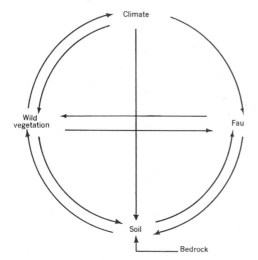

Figure 19.2 The complex of interacting and interdependent natural phenomena is often referred to as the biotic complex. *(After Eyre.)*

its different continental subdivisions may contain quite unlike species. Climax plant communities are not sharply delimited; rather, they merge imperceptibly through zones of transition called *ecotones,* where the species of one community are intermingled with those of another.

It should not be assumed that a homogeneous climatic climax vegetation is bound to prevail everywhere within a general climatic type, even though the climate remains unchanged over a long period of time. In some parts of a climatic region, a variety of factors (such as terrain slope, exposure, soil and drainage) may operate to arrest progress toward the climatic climax, so that there will be intermediate stages known as *subclimax* plant communities. Thus, in a region of varied relief there may be a complex patchwork of climax and subclimax vegetations, for very steep hillsides and extremely flat lowlands both are arresting factors which hinder progress toward the climatic climax. On steep slopes the soil cannot accumulate to the necessary depth, while the flat plain may be so poorly drained and marshy as to inhibit the development of larger trees. Subclimax vegetation resulting from relief variety is likely to persist indefinitely. Human intrusion in the form of set fires, logging operations, tillage and the grazing of domesticated animals are other varieties of interference with development of climatic climax vegetation.

Among the more important climatic elements acting on plants are sunlight, temperature, and precipitation. Each of these influences vegetation directly and indirectly in a great many ways, through processes too complex for elaboration here.

Temperature is critically important, since it affects the speed of the chemical activity that goes on within the plant and so conditions the life processes. For example, temperature is closely connected with photosynthesis, the process by which plants break down carbon dioxide into carbon and oxygen, retaining the carbon to build tissues. To a significant degree temperature determines the growing, reproductive, and dormant periods of plants. As a consequence the great world vegetation zones appear to be closely aligned with temperature belts. Temperature also indirectly affects the water requirement of plants, because it is a major factor determining the rate of evaporation.

Different species resist cold in a variety of ways. Some make the adjustment by retarding growth and arresting certain functions, such as assimilation and respiration, during the period of low temperatures. This may result in a marked external change, such as leaf fall in middle-latitude deciduous trees. Certain other plants, such as coniferous trees, lapse into dormancy during a cold season without showing any outward change. In some species the plant completes its entire life cycle during the warm period. The vegetative portions perish completely during the season of cold, and it is only by means of a seed, which is capable of greater and more prolonged resistance to low temperatures, that the plant survives. These are the *annuals,* such as the cereals, for instance. They stand in contrast to *perennials,* whose vegetative parts live on year after year.

Sunlight, quite independently of temperature, influences plants through its variations in intensity and duration. For example, light is essential for photosynthesis, and in most plants the rate at which the process occurs is closely related to the intensity of light.

Precipitation supplies the necessary soil water for plants. Water, taken in mainly at the roots, is the principal ingredient of sap, in which soil nutrients must be dissolved before they can be assimilated by plants. Loss of water by transpiration, which occurs chiefly through the leaves, aids in the circulation of sap inside the plant and is also associated with certain chemical changes furthering assimilation of nutrients.

Drought-resistant plants, known as *xerophytes,* have a variety of structures which provide a defense against their arid environments. Roots commonly are long or spreading. To reduce evaporation, leaves may be small and thick, may have a covering of wax or hairs, or may even be replaced by thorns or scales. By contrast, *hygrophytes,* which are adapted to humid environments, have scarcely any defense against evaporation and water deficiency. Many plants—deciduous trees, for example—become xerophytes in the dormant cold or dry season and hygrophytes during the warm or wet season of active growth.

Soil. The soil environment affects plant life chiefly through its temperature, chemical composition, and water retentiveness. Porous, coarse, and stony soils may induce a xerophytic vegetation even in regions of moderate rainfall. Soils with excessive amounts of salt or lime support only meager or special communities of plants, and the same is true of soils covered with raw and highly acid humus.

Biotic Factor. Organisms modify vegetation in a variety of ways; a few examples are the injurious effects of overgrazing by wild herbivorous animals, some plants' needs for pollinating insects, and the relationships that exist between hosts and parasites. Man himself, as herdsman, cultivator, fire carrier, and constructor of cities and transportation systems, has been the most widespread and drastic modifier of the earth's vegetation mantle. By his activities much of the earth's original plant cover has been replaced by tilled crops or has been exploited and depleted in varying degrees, so that over extensive areas only vestiges of the former wild vegetation remain.

World Map of Vegetation

How to generalize the complexities of the plant cover and present any meaningful simplification of the distribution of world vegetation types on a small-scale map is a baffling problem. On Plate 5 no attempt has been made to show either cultivated vegetation, such as crops, or human settlements. Instead the entire land surface is represented as having some kind of cover of wild or natural vegetation. Where the climatic climax vegetation is known with some assurance, even though it may have disappeared long ago, it is this which is shown. But still, this is only what would be found over much of a region if all its slopes had gentle gra-

dients, all its land were well drained, and none of its environment had been disturbed by man. In those extensive areas where the climax of past times is in doubt, Plate 5 shows the commonest type of wild vegetation which exists there now. Keep in mind that what appear to be homogeneous vegetation regions on this small map are actually an intricate patchwork of plant communities, for the limitations of scale are obvious. Actual patterns of vegetation are extremely complex, even within existing climatic climax formations.

Principal Types of Wild Vegetation

In a classification based largely on appearance or physiognomic character, the earth's main communities of land vegetation are forest, grass, desert shrub, and tundra, the latter composed chiefly of herbaceous plants other than grass. The distribution of these classes over the earth is mostly, though not entirely, controlled by environment—chiefly by climate. The meagerest and lowliest vegetation is characteristic of the deserts, either cold or dry. Tundra is largely confined to climates where the summers are so cool and short as to exclude forest and, to some extent, grass. Desert shrub is a product of climates that are extremely deficient in rainfall. On the other hand, some arid regions have a sparse plant cover which is more grass than shrub, so it is not always true that shrub indicates greater aridity than grass.

Just how to assess the relative environments of forest and grassland is controversial. At one time it was believed that they occupy mutually exclusive types of climate, but the weight of evidence appears to be against such a hypothesis. As mentioned earlier, it now seems that grasses are meager or absent in forested regions less because the climate and soil are unfavorable than because they cannot tolerate the shade beneath a continuous forest cover. Consequently they are crowded out in environments where the more complex and exacting tree thrives. Trees, on the other hand, have certain characteristics that make them less tolerant of certain unfavorable environments than grass. The very height of a tree makes it more susceptible to drying winds than the lowly grass. This same height requires large amounts of water to transport mineral nutrients from roots to crown. In addition, the soft green shoots annually produced by trees require a sufficiently long growing season free from cold or drought so that they can mature. It is correct to say, therefore, that grasses tend to dominate in environments which permit vegetation but are hostile to trees. The worst conditions for trees are water-saturated soils, dry subsoils, desiccating winds, and periodic burning of the vegetation cover by man.

Main Types of Wild Vegetation

1. Forest associations
   a. Low-latitude forests
      a^1 Tropical rainforest
      a^2 Lighter tropical forest (including semideciduous, deciduous, and shrub-thorn forest)
   b. Middle-latitude forests
      b^1 Mediterranean schlerophyll woodland and shrub
      b^2 Broadleaf forest
         (1) Deciduous
         (2) Evergreen
      b^3 Needle-leaf or coniferous forest
2. Grassland associations
   a. Tropical grasslands (savanna)
   b. Middle-latitude grassland (prairie and steppe)
3. Desert shrub
4. Tundra

Forests and Their Distribution[1]

Low-latitude Forests

Tropical Rainforest. This most luxuriant type of woodland community is the climax vegetation of tropical lowlands and slopes where rainfall is both abundant and well distributed throughout the year. No long dry season can be tolerated.

---

[1] Trees are classified as either (*a*) broadleaf or (*b*) needle-leaf (conifers); (*a*) deciduous or (*b*) evergreen. Evergreens are those which retain some foliage throughout the year, while deciduous trees periodically lose their leaves and are therefore bare for a portion of the year. Broadleaf trees are both evergreen and deciduous; conifers are, with a very few exceptions, evergreen.

There are three distinct regional formations of tropical rainforest: American, African, and Indo-Malaysian. The American sector is the largest, with its most extensive development occurring in the Amazon Basin (see Plate 5 for other regions).

This forest type has three principal characteristics: (1) There is a great variety of different species of trees—far greater than in middle-latitude forests. But although species are numerous, rainforest trees are remarkably similar in general appearance and structure. (2) Vertical stratification in the forest is developed to an unusual degree. This feature arises from the fact that the various species have different height limits and arrange themselves in several layers (Fig. 19.3). The result is a forest with a number of tree tiers, each lower one reflecting an increasing tolerance for the shade imposed by the canopy above. (3) The number of climbers, lianas, and epiphytes is unusually large. The giant lianas have the appearance of great cables interlacing the branches of the forest crown and binding the individual trees together. Even when a large tree breaks off near the base, it may be prevented from falling by the lianas that entwine it.

Luxuriant, complex, exuberant—such is the character of tropical rainforest. In external appearance it presents a richly varied mosaic of

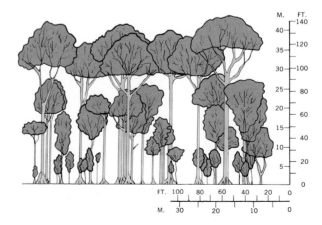

Figure 19.3 Profile diagram of tropical rainforest in Trinidad, West Indies. Note the several stories of trees. *(After Beard.)*

many shades. Leaves are monotonously alike, however, in size, shape, and leathery texture, the latter being a response to the intense midday sun and high temperature. Tropical rainforest is evergreen broadleaf. There is no dormant period when the forest as a whole is bare and without foliage: leaf shedding is a sporadic event rather than a seasonal one for all species. Individual trees without leaves may be observed at any time.

From the inside the tropical rainforest is dense, with trees which vary greatly in height and diameter growing close together. The tallest ones may rise to 150 ft but rarely exceed this height. Trunks are relatively slender and do not branch until near the top. Their bark is thin and smooth. Such a multistoried forest produces a dense canopy of shade, and the forest floor is deep in gloom. As a result, the forest undergrowth of low shrubs and herbaceous plants is poorly developed. In contrast, what is called *jungle* has a thick and impenetrable undergrowth. Jungle conditions are characteristic chiefly of sections where more light reaches the forest floor—for example, along rivers and coasts, on precipitous wet slopes, and in abandoned agricultural clearings.

There is reason to believe that the tropical rainforest has persisted relatively unchanged from very remote times. Recently these forests have been rudely disturbed by the spread of Western civilization to the tropics, with associated clearing of the trees for plantations and an expanding native agriculture. It is estimated that tropical rainforest may still comprise as much as half of the earth's forest area, but at the accelerated rate at which it is being destroyed, much of it may disappear within a few generations.

Lighter Tropical Forest. This term covers a considerable variety of woodland types—semievergreen, deciduous, and thorn shrub—whose characteristics and precise distributions are not sufficiently well known to permit showing them individually on a world vegetation map such as Plate 5. As a rule, where soils and drainage do not interfere, evergreen tropical rainforest gives way at its climatic limits

to semievergreen forest. With declining rainfall, this in turn passes over to deciduous woodland, and finally to thorn woodland and desert shrub.

Within the *semievergreen forest* some of the dominant trees are evergreen and others deciduous. This is commonly referred to as "monsoon forest," since it occurs in humid regions with a distinct dry season. Ordinarily, the trees are not so tall as in the rainforest, and the vertical structure of the forest is simpler.

Because of its seasonal leaf fall, the *deciduous forest* is better adapted to withstand a longer season for drought than is the semievergreen type. Trees are somewhat shorter, their trunks are more gnarled and crooked, and they branch closer to the ground (Fig. 19.4). Crowns are commonly umbrella-shaped, lianas are few, and there may be some development of grass under the forest.

In the still more drought-resistant *thorn forest,* trees are even lower in stature. Trunks are more gnarled, crowns are more spreading, and species are fewer. The forest is dominated by low bushy trees and tall shrubs, many of which carry long spikes or thorns.

Doubtless some of the woodland types included under the general heading of lighter tropical forest are true climatic climaxes; others are actually

Figure 19.4 Lighter tropical forest (semideciduous) in the Congo. The shade is not dense, so that coarse grass mantles the forest floor. *(From Shantz and Marbut, 1923; courtesy of the American Geographical Society.)*

transition associations of mixed forests and forest-and-grass; while the ecological status of some is unknown. Their type location is the transition belts between tropical rainforest with its abundant, well-distributed rainfall on one side, and the deserts on the other. Not only is there less rainfall in lighter tropical forests than in tropical rainforests, but it is also more variable and seasonal. These forests usually have a distinct and fairly long dry season. As shown in Plate 5, the lighter tropical forest occupies the same general type location as wooded savanna and savanna.

Resource Value of Tropical Forests. While relatively few native peoples depend on the tropical forests for their main food supply, many do earn their livelihood by gathering such wild forest products as tagua nuts (vegetable ivory), Brazil nuts, vegetable gum, and rattan (used for wickerwork). Until fairly recently, wild rubber was also important. While reserves of timber in the tropical forest are enormous, there are serious handicaps to the exploitation of this resource. Chief of these is the great number of tree species. If only one, or even a few, particular kinds of trees are desired, they are so widely scattered that the selective logging required is very expensive. And if clean cutting of the forest (i.e., cutting down all timber in a given area) is resorted to, then there is the problem of marketing the great variety of woods obtained. Currently the main commercial kinds of timber logged from tropical forests are hard, durable cabinet woods such as mahogany, teak, and rosewood, whose high value justifies the expense of selective logging.

Middle-latitude Forests

Mediterranean Sclerophyll Woodland and Shrub. This formation type is closely identified with the subtropical dry-summer, or Mediterranean, climate (compare Plates 2 and 5). It is an unusual woodland in that while it is predominantly both evergreen and broadleaf like the tropical rainforest, it is

Figure 19.5   Sclerophyllous evergreen woodland and shrub in California. *(U.S. Department of Agriculture.)*

able to tolerate summer drought and heat. This is accomplished through a variety of structural adaptations which aid in conserving water—dwarf forms, thick bark, small, leathery, often shiny leaves,[2] and extensive or deep root systems.

It is a formation predominantly composed of woody shrubs and widely spaced dwarf trees (Fig. 19.5). Tall trees are rare. This bush thicket is called *maquis* in the Mediterranean lands and *chaparral* in California. Probably a part of the present maquis was once a mixed evergreen forest, which subsequently has deteriorated as a consequence of human intrusion in the form of cutting, burning, grazing, or cultivation. In other areas, especially in the harsher Mediterranean environments, maquis very likely represents climax communities. Its chief economic importance is the watershed protection it provides.

Needle-leaf or Coniferous Forests. Within the more humid parts of the middle latitudes are two great forest groups: needle leaf (conifer) and broadleaf. Over extensive transition belts they exist as a mixed conifer-broadleaf forest.

Of the two types, conifers are more primitive and ancient. They are predominantly evergreen in character; larch is the important exception. The growth and fall of needles are continuous processes and not confined to a single period or season; hence this forest never appears bare. Unlike broadleaves, most of which permit large water losses through transpiration, the hard, narrow needles of conifers are xerophytic in character. Thus leaf shedding is not necessary to protect the conifer against a season of drought or of severe cold with frozen ground. On the whole, conifers are less demanding as regards both climate and soil than broadleaf trees, and consequently they tolerate a wider range of environmental conditions.

Subarctic Coniferous Forest. Coniferous forests

reach their maximum extent in the severe boreal climates of subarctic northern North America and Eurasia, where they exist in wide and continuous east-west belts stretching from Atlantic to Pacific. On its northern frontier along a sinuous boundary, the subarctic coniferous forest gradually grades into tundra where, chiefly because of the cool and short summer, the cimate is hostile to all trees.

Within the harsh subarctic environment, the more tolerant conifers greatly predominate over broadleaves, although varieties of the latter, such as birch, aspen, alder, and willow, are scattered throughout in groves and thickets. Among the most common needle trees are spruce, fir, pine, and larch or tamarack, with the combinations of species varying from region to region and locality to locality.

Figure 19.6 Side view of subarctic coniferous forest in Canada. Note the small size of trees. *(U.S. Forest Service.)*

[2] It is this leaf characteristic which has given the entire type the name *sclerophyll*—meaning an exceptional development of protective tissue that produces foliage resistant to water loss.

In these boreal climates growth is slow, so that trees are relatively small in both girth and height (Fig. 19.6). Over extensive areas where strong ice scour prevails and bedrock is widely exposed, the forest cover is usually thin, and in places even absent (Fig. 16.31).

On the shaded floor of the subarctic forest, undergrowth is scanty or nonexistent, in part stifled by the thick blanket of slowly decomposing needles. Little organic matter is made available to the soil, for needle leaves are a poor source of humus to begin with, while the low temperatures and deep shade act to retard decomposition and discourage the activity of soil fauna.

Since enormous areas of the subarctic forest in North America and the U.S.S.R. remain almost unpopulated, the tree resource is largely unused. But along parts of this forest's southern margins which border on regions of denser settlement, there has been large-scale logging for pulpwood during the last half century, so that extensive cutover and burned-over areas exist.

Conifers in Temperate and Subtropical Middle Latitudes. South of the great belts of subarctic conifers, and therefore in climates which are less severe except at high altitudes, there are other less extensive areas of needle trees which represent a more valuable forest resource. Not only are they composed of larger trees and superior timber species, but they lie closer to important markets. Coniferous forests in the lower middle latitudes are situated in both highlands and lowlands. Highland conifers are widely distributed in North America, Europe, and Asia; lowland nonboreal conifers are found chiefly in North America.

In dry western North America, broken belts of conifers extend southward from the subarctic following the rainier highlands and, continuously, the moist coastal lowlands (Fig. 19.7). In the highlands the harsh subarctic climate is duplicated in modified form. Vertical zonation of forest types is a prominent feature. In general the highland forests, with their thinner stands of usually smaller trees, are not ,as valuable for timber as the rich

coast forest, which forms a continuous belt extending from southern Alaska southward along the coastal lowlands and lower slopes as far as California. In this rainier and milder climatic environment, large trees, dense stands, and good-quality timber combine to make the forest of the American Pacific Coast states, British Columbia, and Alaska the most extensive area of high-grade conifers anywhere in the world (Fig. 19.8).

Dominant climax varieties in this coastal forest are western hemlock, western red cedar, Sitka spruce, and in California, the gigantic redwood. Douglas fir, though widespread, is considered a subclimax resulting from depredations by man and fire. In such a mild and humid climate it may be wondered why there is not a broadleaf deciduous forest instead of conifers. Summer dryness in the southern half of this forest area may be a partial answer. Another possibility is that the broadleaf species were largely exterminated by the rigors of the Pleistocene climate, while the conifers were able to survive.

East of the Rockies, lowland conifers extend southward from the subarctic into humid southeastern Canada and adjoining parts of the northeastern United States—Minnesota, Wisconsin, Michigan, New York, and northern New England (Fig. 19.7). Because of its fine-quality timber this lake forest of white pine, red pine, and hemlock suffered such rapid and complete cutting in the late nineteenth century that little of the original stand has survived. Regeneration has been minor. Today much of the lake forest region remains as unattractive cutover land whose second growth of poplar and shrub has only modest commercial value. In Eurasia before logging reduced them, valuable coniferous forests south of the subarctic usually occupied highlands, although they were occasionally found in some sandy lowlands as well.

Another conifer-dominant forest in the subtropical southeastern United States is separated from the lake conifers by a wide belt of broadleaf and mixed forest (Fig. 19.7). In general it coincides with the Atlantic-Gulf Coastal Plain, where sterile, sandy soils, which are low in mineral nutrients and

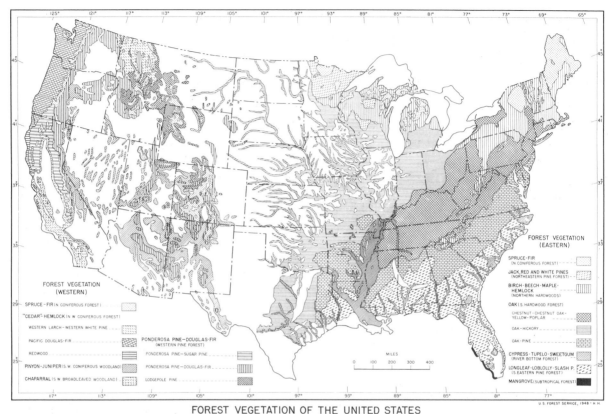

FOREST VEGETATION OF THE UNITED STATES

Adapted from Shantz and Zon's "Natural Vegetation" map of the United States in the "Atlas of American Agriculture"

Figure 19.7 Forest types and regions. *(U.S. Forest Service.)*

do not retain water, are widespread. Conifers are at less of a disadvantage on these soils than broadleaf trees. The prevailing species are pines—loblolly, shortleaf, pitch, longleaf, and slash. Still, many broadleaf trees (oak, hickory, and poplar) do grow in this forest—apparently most thickly on the sites with better soils. The southern pine-dominant forest does not represent a climatic climax type, for the subtropical humid climate is highly suitable for broadleaf varieties. Probably within the soil-terrain environment of the Coastal Plain, fires, both natural and man-set, have been the decisive factor maintaining the pine dominance, for such trees suffer less injury from fire than do most broadleaf varieties. If protected from fire, much of the southern pine forest would no doubt

be replaced by an oak-hickory association. The Coastal Plain conifers are one of the nation's main sources of lumber and pulpwood.

Broadleaf and Mixed Forests

Broadleaf forests in middle latitudes may be either deciduous or evergreen. Deciduous forms dominate in the climatically more severe Northern Hemisphere, evergreen species in the milder Southern Hemisphere. The changeover from needle-leaf to broadleaf forest characteristically takes place in a transition zone of mixed forest where the two types intermingle.

Since the climatic environments of both broadleaf and mixed forests are eminently suited for agriculture, most of these forests have been

Figure 19.8   Interior view of the Douglas fir forest in the United States Pacific Northwest. The stand is dense and trees are large. *(U.S. Forest Service.)*

swept away in the process of agricultural settlement. Extensive remnants exist mainly in highlands or rough lands.

Broadleaf deciduous forest evolved in the humid subtropical and temperate climates of the middle latitudes. In the summer period of active growth this forest is characterized by a lush foliage of thin leaves, which it sheds upon entering the dormant winter period. In North America the main block of broadleaf deciduous forest is situated in the eastern humid half of the United States (see Fig. 19.7). Oak, hickory, maple, basswood, and chestnut are the common trees. Several forest associations are recognized. A somewhat similar forest is to be found in the middle latitudes of Europe and northeastern Asia (Plate 5).

In central eastern North America, transitional belts of mixed forest flank the broadleaf deciduous forest on both its north and south sides and separate it from the coniferous forests (Figs. 19.7, 19.9). A somewhat similar pattern is observable in Europe and in eastern Asia.

As indicated earlier, broadleaf evergreen forest belongs chiefly to the Southern Hemisphere. It is represented also in subtropical eastern Asia and along the oceanic margins of the Gulf Coastal Plain in the United States.

Grasslands

Grasses are able to tolerate a wide range of environmental conditions—from tropical to polar temperatures, and from desert lands to swamplands. Compared with the more complex tree, grasses suffer less from the vicissitudes of climate, fires, and the depradations of animals. Their wide range is also fostered by the smallness and lightness of their seeds.

At one time, the fact that many of the earth's extensive grasslands are typically located between humid climates and deserts led plant geographers to the conclusion that they represented a climatic climax of semiarid and subhumid regions. Many authorities now doubt that such is universally the case.

Figure 19.9   A dominantly broadleaf deciduous forest (oak-hickory) in northern Indiana. Much of this type of forest occupied good agricultural land and as a consequence was destroyed in the process of settlement. *(U.S. Department of Agriculture.)*

Figure 19.10   Tall coarse grass with low trees in the wooded savanna of Africa north of the equator. Height of the grasses is about 8 ft, so that they reach into the lower branches of the short trees. *(From Shantz and Marbut, 1923; courtesy of American Geographical Society.)*

Tropical Grasslands or Savanna

Savannas may be either treeless or wooded. They differ from middle-latitude grasslands in certain respects: They more frequently contain trees; they do not have a continuous sod cover—the grasses occur in discontinuous tufts; and the grasses are markedly coarser (Fig. 19.10). Tropical grasses vary greatly in height, reaching 10 to 12 ft in the more luxuriant stands found in parts of Africa. The blades of mature savanna grasses are harsh and leathery; mainly it is the fresh young shoots which are palatable to grazing animals. Although grazing is often the principal economy of savanna areas, no important commercial livestock industry has developed there. Among native peoples it is common practice to burn off the old grass toward the end of the dry season in order to make room for new growth at the beginning of the rains.

Most of the world's extensive savannas coincide with tropical wet-and-dry climates. But that climate type may not necessarily be the cause of the savanna. It is debatable whether there is such a thing as a "savanna climate" in which savanna grasses represent the true climatic climax. Increasingly, plant geographers have tended to conclude that many, if not most, savannas are a consequence of human intervention in the form of set fires and livestock grazing. In some areas, however, savanna vegetation seems to be the result of waterlogging of the soil in the wet season, followed by extreme soil dryness in the dry season. Thus the origin of the earth's savannas continues to be something of an enigma.

Middle-latitude Grasslands

Grasslands in middle latitudes typically are located in semiarid and subhumid climates (Plate 5); and many ecologists view them as the climatic climax vegetation of such environments. In this feature of origin they may differ from savannas. They also differ in that they generally have no trees, except along stream courses and along their contact zones with forest.

In the midcontinent grasslands of interior North America east of the Rockies, two, or sometimes three, subdivisions are recognized (Fig. 19.11). The tall-grass prairie, or true prairie (which has mostly been replaced by farmland), used to occupy the more humid eastern parts, and

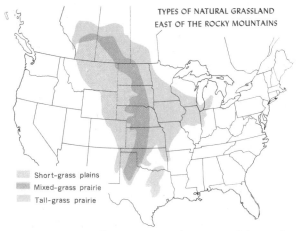

TYPES OF NATURAL GRASSLAND
EAST OF THE ROCKY MOUNTAINS

Short-grass plains
Mixed-grass prairie
Tall-grass prairie

Figure 19.11   Tall-grass prairie, short-grass plains, and a two-story mixed-grass transition zone are found in the mid-continent grasslands. *(After J. Richard Carpenter.)*

Figure 19.12   Midgrasses on the Great Plains in Colorado at the end of a season of exceptional rainfall. Ordinarily, only shortgrasses grow this far west. *(U.S. Forest Service.)*

the short-grass steppe, or plains, still exists in many of the drier western parts. Between them is a transition zone called the mixed-grass prairie, which consists both of midgrasses 2 to 4 ft tall and of shorter grasses, which together form an upper and a lower story (Fig. 19.12). It is possible that the two-story mixed-grass prairie originally also prevailed on the plains area farther west, and that the midgrass species were largely killed out by overgrazing. West of the Rockies extensive vegetation areas of the original short bunchgrass still exist, mainly in Washington, Oregon, Idaho, and California.

The tall-grass prairie was dominated by tall, luxuriant, deep-rooted grasses which reached heights of 5 to 8 ft in the more humid eastern parts. Usually there were many showy flowering plants intermingled with the grasses. A notable feature of the American prairie, and one difficult to explain, is the far eastward thrust of grassland. It extends in the form of a wedge even into central Illinois and western Indiana (Fig. 19.11), where the climate is humid and therefore seems favorable to forest development. Some authorities maintain that this humid prairie has a higher concentration of summer rainfall variability and regional drought than the forested regions both to the north and to the south. Others believe that the humid prairie region was climatically capable of supporting forest, but was prevented from doing so by grass fires (set both by lightning and by man) which killed the woody plants but not the grass, and by the injurious effects of grazing animals.

Outside Anglo-America, important middle-latitude grasslands used to exist north of the equator in the southern U.S.S.R. and in northeastern China. In the Southern Hemisphere, they were mainly in Argentina–Uruguay–southeastern Brazil, the veld of southern Africa, and the southern island of New Zealand. In all of them, large parts have been converted to tilled land.

Desert Vegetation

Some soilless, windswept, rocky deserts, and some areas of moving sand dunes, may be devoid of all vegetation, but these are the exception. Most desert regions have some plant life, although almost invariably it is sparse. Desert plants are of several types, and each has a different way of surmounting the handicaps of its arid environment.

Desert shrub is the most widespread form of arid-land vegetation. The deciduous species make use of leaf shedding in order to withstand drought. The evergreen varieties have protective structures such as small, thick, and leathery leaves with shiny, waxy surfaces. In both types of shrub, root systems are unusually well developed—some in depth and others in breadth. In the United States the two most widespread desert shrubs are sagebrush and creosote bush, the second of which grows chiefly in the hotter and more arid Southwest.

Arid-land vegetation also includes leafless, thorny succulents such as the cacti, certain salt-tolerant plants, and a variety of short-lived transients (Fig. 19.13). The shallow-rooted cactus is distinguished by its large water storage capacity, which permits it to survive between infrequent rains. In addition, its outer surface is hard and waxy, which reduces losses of water by transpiration, while its spines protect it against animals attracted by its interior water supply. Fleshy, succulent, salt-tolerated plants are characteristic of areas which have highly alkaline soils as a consequence of poor drainage. Like the cacti, they are able to store water in leaves and stem. The so-called transients, usually small in size, include many flowering annuals, but also grasses and tuberous plants. They are able to tolerate the aridity chiefly because growth is rapid and their life cycles can be completed in a brief period of time. In the form of seeds, tubers, or corms, they are able to remain

Figure 19.13   Desert shrub and cacti in the vicinity of the Superstition Mountains in Arizona. *(U.S. Forest Service.)*

dormant during periods of drought. Subsequently they are stimulated to germination and growth by a period of showers.

Tundra Vegetation

The lowly dwarf vegetation comprising the Arctic tundra of northernmost North America and Eurasia is a reflection of the harsh environment. This includes strong drying winds, a short growing season of only a month or two with occasional summer frosts, and shallow, infertile, poorly drained soils underlain by permanently frozen ground.

In the climatically more favorable parts, the climax vegetation usually is one in which grasses and sedges dominate, with an understory of lichens and mosses. Where the environment is harsher, grasses and sedges decline, while lichens, and to a lesser extent mosses, become dominant. Dwarf shrubs are scattered throughout both communities and may become the dominants in some local areas. Tundra vegetation also includes a great variety of ephemeral plants with bright flowers. Yet even at the height of the short growing season when many species are in flower, the general color of the tundra is drab or yellowish. On its southern boundary, the tundra makes contact with the subarctic forest along a very sinuous zone, with tundra communities dominating the exposed interfluves, and forest growing in the protected valleys and lower slopes. Throughout the tundra, the pattern of vegetation distribution is likely to be very patchy; plant groupings change with minute variations in slope, exposure, and drainage. Tundra vegetation has little economic significance except in connection with the grazing of reindeer.

Mountain Vegetation

Mountain areas are characterized by an unusual variety of local environments existing in close juxtaposition. The vegetation responses to these variations are so complex that it is impossible to describe them in detail or to represent them on a small-scale map such as Plate 5. Only a few broad generalizations about mountain vegetation are given here.

On the lower slopes of highlands, the vegetation cover may resemble that of the surrounding lowlands. But with increasing altitude, temperature decreases rapidly, while solar energy, rainfall, and wind speeds increase. Changes of vegetation fall into a rough vertical zonation of plant life, but with many interrupting local variations.

Conifers, with their strong tolerance for the vicissitudes of mountain climates and soils, comprise the largest element of mountain forests in middle latitudes, and they are also found at high elevations even in the tropics. Within the coniferous zone, pines usually predominate at lower elevations, but fir and spruce take over near the upper climatic limits of forest. Above these limits, which vary in altitude, trees will not grow because of low temperatures, a short growing season, diurnal freeze and thaw, strong winds, and thin soils that alternate between saturation and aridity. Alpine pastures and meadows predominate in this zone and furnish summer grazing for flocks and herds brought up from farms or ranches at lower elevations. Above the alpine pastures, the meager, lowly mountain vegetation bears considerable resemblance to that of the Arctic tundra. But it is by no means uniform, since there are important variations in the plant associations on south (sunny) and north (shady) slopes, on wet and dry flanks, and in windy and protected locations.

Selected References for Chap. 19

Atlas of American Agriculture. Sec. E., "Natural Vegetation," U.S. Government Printing Office, Washington, D.C., 1924.

Cain, Stanley A. *Foundations of Plant Geography.* Harper & Row, Publishers, Incorporated, New York, 1944.

Climate and Man. Yearbook of Agriculture, 1941. U.S. Department of Agriculture, Washington, D.C.

Eyre, S. R. *Vegetation and Soils: A World Picture.* Aldine Publishing Company, Chicago, 1963.

Gleason, Henry A., and Arthur Cronquist. *The Nat-*

ural Geography of Plants. Columbia University Press, New York, 1964.

Grass. Yearbook of Agriculture, 1948. U.S. Department of Agriculture, Washington, D.C.

Haden-Guest, Stephen, John K. Wright, and Eileen M. Teclaff (eds.). *A World Geography of Forest Resources.* The Ronald Press Company, New York, 1956.

Kuchler, A. W. Potential Natural Vegetation of the United States. Map (65 × 40) and accompanying manual (156 pp., comprising text, bibliography, and legend descriptions, and 118 illustrations of vegetation types). Special Publication No. 36., American Geographical Society, New York, 1964.

————. World Natural Vegetation. Colored Map in *Goode's World Atlas.* Pp. 16–17. Rand McNally & Company, Chicago, 1964.

Polunin, Nicholas. *Introduction to Plant Geography.* McGraw-Hill Book Company, New York, 1960.

Richards, P. W. *The Tropical Rainforest: An Ecological Study.* Cambridge University Press, New York, 1952.

Trees. Yearbook of Agriculture, 1949. U.S. Department of Agriculture, Washington, D.C.

Weaver, J. E. *The North American Prairie.* Johnsen Publishing Company, Lincoln, Neb., 1954.

20

Soils

Most of the land area of the earth is covered by a layer of disintegrated rock material—the normal result of weathering processes. Only in limited localities does bare bedrock protrude or ice cover the surface. Much of this disintegrated-rock veneer is residual, that is, it has accumulated on top of the bedrock from which it formed. Some of it, however, has been moved—either locally by mass movement, or for some distance by gradational agents such as glaciers or running water. Except when frozen, this mantle is somewhat porous, so that both air and water circulate among the particles. The top of the layer, being exposed to sunlight, is regularly bathed with vital energy.

Normally, this loose covering becomes a dynamic complex of inorganic substances teeming with life—a complex called soil. The processes which form it include many that go on only under the influence of organisms, both living and dead, ranging from higher animals, earthworms, and abundant forms of microscopic life such as bacteria, to vegetation, which is particularly important. For this reason the soil extends downward only so far as life and its contributions do, which is usually no more than a few feet.

It would be difficult to overemphasize the significance of soil. The many chemical elements on which human life depends are primarily needed in the form of organic compounds, such as proteins, fats, carbohydrates, and vitamins; and these come from the soil either by way of plants that man consumes directly, or as animal products derived from plants. The soils of some areas can support a large and healthy human population, but in even larger areas the reverse seems to be true.

The Elements of Soil

In order to study the essential characteristics of soils as they vary from place to place, one must appreciate that their physical, chemical, organic, and inorganic qualities bear the same relation to the geography of soil that the climatic elements do to the geography of climate. The most important elements of soil character are (1) fertility—that is, the chemical constituents affecting its nutritional quality; (2) texture—the sizes of the inorganic particles; (3) structure—the arrangement of these particles; (4) organic components; (5) water and air relationships within the soil; and (6) the profile —the distinctive arrangement of horizontal layers that commonly develops as a soil matures.

These elements of soil character differ systematically from place to place according to the operation of the controls of soil development— just as the elements of climate vary according to the action of the climatic controls. But soils have a larger number of significant elements, and the contrasts between soils of adjoining localities tend to be more abrupt.

Fertility. The existence of all life on land is ultimately dependent upon the ability of plants to obtain from the soil many of the chemical elements required for their photosynthetic construction of carbohydrates and their biosynthetic production of protein and other essential foods.[1] The available supply of these critical chemical elements is referred to as the soil's fertility. A high fertility does not necessarily mean a productive soil, however; for example, a dry-land soil may be very fertile even though it is too dry to be productive.

Plants need some chemical elements in relatively large amounts: these include oxygen, carbon, hydrogen, nitrogen, sodium, calcium, potassium, phosphorus, sulphur, magnesium, and iron. Others are required only in very small amounts: manganese, copper, zinc, iodine, and boron. Although some of these are available directly from the gases of the atmosphere, others are derived from the water in the soil, the organic material in the soil (e.g., nitrogen), and the soil's inorganic matter (e.g., the metallic elements calcium, potash, and phosphorus).

Plants obtain the mineral nutrients they need by means of an ion exchange between the plant roots and the nutrients available in the soil solution.[2] Many factors affect this complicated process, but the basic requirement is that the essential minerals be present in the soil: if a sufficient supply is not there to begin with, the soil cannot be fertile unless the minerals are added artificially.

Supply and Removal of Fertility Elements. The supply of essential minerals in a soil may be reduced in several ways: by erosion; by excessive use, or overcropping; and especially, by leaching, the removal of elements in solution by soil water per-

---

[1] W. A. Albrecht. "Soil Fertility and Biotic Geography." *Geog. Rev.,* Vol. 47, pp. 87–105, 1957.

[2] The processes by which a plant obtains its nourishment are very complex and as yet not completely understood. A root takes in water from the soil by capillary pressures and the osmotic pressures of the solution. Nutrients are obtained by the exchange of the plant's ions (electrically charged particles in solution) for the nutrient ions available in the solutions on the surfaces of the soil particles that are in contact with the root.

colating downward. A deficiency may be partially remedied in several ways: by appropriate mineral fertilizing; by fallowing, that is, letting the land lie idle so that natural decomposition provides an additional supply of minerals; and by manuring, that is, returning a major proportion of the plant growth to the land in the form of animal excreta and plant refuse.

Certainly, the most universal factor affecting the fertility of soils is leaching. Though to some extent, temperature, vegetation, and other factors contribute to leaching, it is caused mostly by the water from precipitation. Thus humid regions tend to have less fertile soils than dry regions.

Acidity and Alkalinity. Some of the water molecules in a solution are broken into hydrogen ions and hydroxyl ions. If there is a preponderance of hydrogen ions, the solution is said to be acid. The degree of acidity or alkalinity of a solution is expressed by the pH scale, which extends from 0.0 to 14.0, with the midpoint, 7.0, indicating neutrality. pH values below 7.0 indicate acidity, which increases as the pH numbers become smaller.[3]

The solubility of many elements is affected by the pH of the soil solution. For example, if the pH of an acid soil is raised (made less acid), some elements, such as iron, manganese, or copper, may become less soluble and hence less available to plants. At higher pH values the lack of availability of these elements may actually result in a deficiency. On the other hand, if such elements are abundantly available (as in a very acid soil), they may be toxic to plants.[4] The microorganisms in the soil function best when the pH of the soil is near neutral, and each kind of plant has its individual pH preference and range.

[3] A pH value is the reciprocal of the logarithm of the concentration of hydrogen ions. Therefore, a pH value of 5.0 indicates ten times the concentration of hydrogen ions of a pH value of 6.0, and a pH value of 4.0 indicates ten times the concentration of a pH value of 5.0—and accordingly, one hundred times the concentration of a pH value of 6.0.

[4] W. H. Allaway. "pH, Soil Acidity, and Plant Growth." *Soil.* Yearbook of Agriculture, 1957. Pp. 67–71. U.S. Government Printing Office, Washington, D.C.

The most important factor determining the pH of a soil is the amount of leaching to which it is subjected. Humid lands usually have acid soils, which favor the production in plants of bulk carbohydrates such as starches, sugars, fats, and cellulose, as opposed to the proteins that are nutritionally more significant to animals.

Texture. The potential productivity of a soil depends upon several physical characteristics in addition to its chemical fertility. One of the more important is its texture—the relative proportions of the various sizes of particles that constitute the inorganic part of the soil complex. These weathered rock fragments, which commonly occupy nearly one-half the volume of the upper portion of the soil, are grouped in size classes ranging from sands (the largest) to clays. The accompanying table shows the class limits assigned by soil scientists. The various combinations of percentages of the textural classes that occur in a soil are given specific names. *Loam* is the general term assigned to

TEXTURE CLASSES

Name	Diameter, mm
Sand:	
Very coarse sand (fine gravel)	2.00–1.00
Coarse to medium sand	1.00–0.25
Fine to very fine sand	0.25–0.05
Silt	0.05–0.002
Clay	less than 0.002

combinations that include moderate amounts of all three. Figure 20.1 shows the relative proportions of sand, silt, and clay in the various textural classes.

Some of the fragments in a soil have diameters that are considerably less than a micron (.001 mm). These particles, often clay crystals, are negatively charged, and they adsorb—that is, attract and hold on their flat surfaces—ions which enter into the exchange involved in plant feeding. These and other finely divided materials are called *colloids*. Since the chemical reactions within a soil which make nutrients available to plants take place largely on

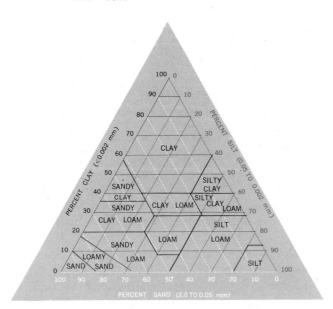

Figure 20.1 The textural triangle used by the soil scientists of the U.S. Department of Agriculture. In order to find the textural class, they enter the percentages of sand, silt, and clay on the appropriate scales and follow the hatch lines to the intersection of the three lines.

the surfaces of the particles, the average size of the fragments is important. The smaller the average size, the more specific surface, or total surface per unit mass, there will be. Consequently, the potential reactivity of a soil, which is its physical ability to provide an ionic food supply, varies directly with the specific surface.

The texture also markedly affects the retention and movement of water within a soil. For example, a soil's field capacity (the maximum amount of water it can hold after any excess has drained away) varies inversely with the average size of the particles. Hence sandy soils have relatively poor water retention, so that they dry out quickly after rains.

Usually the texture of a soil is different at different depths. Water which is pulled downward by gravity may carry down the smaller soil particles, mostly the clay and colloidal fractions, and thus reduce their proportion in the upper part. This mechanical removal of solid material is called

eluviation. The load removed by eluviation may be deposited lower in the soil; such charging of a layer with fine material from above is called illuviation. Because this shifting of particles is accomplished by water, the upper portions of the soils of humid lands commonly tend to be eluviated as well as leached.

Structure. The term "structure" refers to the character and arrangement of the small clumps or groups of individual soil particles that develop in most soils. These units, called peds, are very significant to the productivity of a soil because peds permit pore space to develop between them, allowing air, water, and root penetration. A favorable structure greatly eases problems of management—that is, the treatment of the soil in order to develop its maximum productivity.

There is a variety of ways in which the fragments may become aggregated in peds and in which they may cleave when broken apart. The principal distinct forms of peds are spheroidal (granular or crumb), blocky, prismatic, and platy (Fig. 20.2). In some poorly structured soils the amount of pore space may be less than 20 percent of the soil volume, whereas in highly structured clays it may exceed 60 per cent. Most soils suitable for agriculture include amounts of pore space comprising 35 to 50 percent of the soil volume.

Good structure, which includes a high percentage of pore space, commonly is found in soils of fine texture that have considerable organic content. In contrast, sandy soils are essentially without structure; each sand particle acts as an individual unit. A favorable structure is promoted by the presence of lime, colloids, and organic material that form gluey films which help the soil particles to stick together. However, a good soil structure may be destroyed by improper treatment.

Organic Components. It is the presence of living organisms and dead organic matter that makes soil different from mere disintegrated rock. The role played by this organic content in a functioning soil is critical. It includes the following actions: (1)

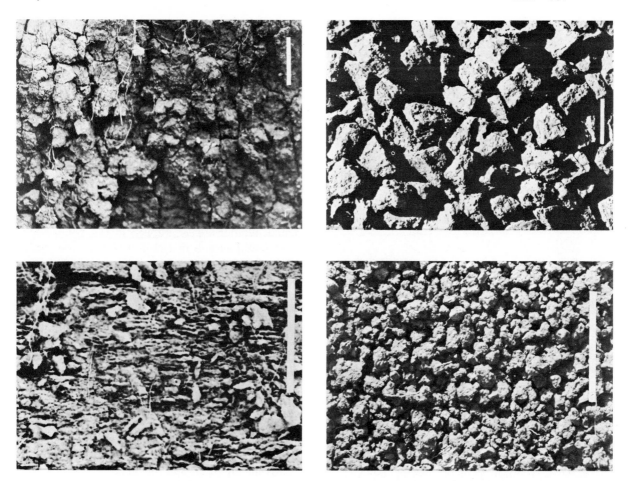

Figure 20.2   The principal forms of soil structure: upper left, prismatic; upper right, blocky; lower left, platy; lower right, spheroidal (granular). In each photogaph the white line represents 1 in. The peds in the photographs at upper and lower left are in place in the soil; those at upper and lower right have been removed from the soil and spread on a flat surface. (Photographs by Roy W. Simonson.)

The decomposed organic material directly supplies plant food—especially nitrogen[5] and some of the essential mineral elements, such as calcium, mag-

[5] Plants must have nitrogen in rather large amounts. They get it in the soluble form of nitrates. These can be added artificially in chemical fertilizers; in nature, nitrates are produced largely through the work of microorganisms which are able to take nitrogen gas and transform it. Legumes and some other plants play an important role in this connection, since their roots act as hosts to these nitrogen-transforming bacteria (Rhizobia). Other soil organisms make nitrogen available through their ability to decompose the remains of plants and animals, which are then incorporated in the soil.

nesium, and phosphorus. (2) The dead organic tissues provide the major food source for the living microorganisms of the soil, which in turn affect the health and quality of the higher forms of organic life supported by the soil. (3) Organic decomposition yields complex acids which contribute to further weathering of mineral matter. (4) The dead tissues have a high water-holding capacity, which helps the soil retain a supply of water for the soil solution and at the same time retards the leaching of dissolved minerals. (5) Organic matter promotes the development of a favorable soil structure.

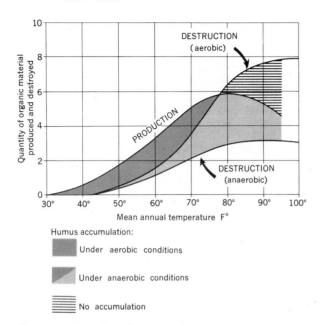

Humus accumulation:

Under aerobic conditions

Under anaerobic conditions

No accumulation

Figure 20.3   In humid climates, these are the relative rates of production of vegetative matter and its destruction by aerobic and anaerobic microorganisms (decomposition) as generally related to average temperatures. Thus in regions with average temperatures above about 77°, no humus is likely to be produced. *(After Senstius.)*

The soil microorganisms (bacteria, fungi, and protozoa), which may total as much as 1,000 lb per acre, perform many functions in addition to helping make nitrogen available. For example, they rot organic matter, and they produce antibiotics which promote the quality and health of plants. Higher forms of life, such as earthworms and many kinds of insects, are also active in the soil. Insects help in the disintegration of plant remains. Insects and earthworms together affect the porosity of soil with their burrows and galleries, as well as carrying out extensive transporting and overturning of the soil. The many thousand earthworms which may inhabit an acre of soil can bring as much as 20 tons of material to the surface in a year. This is an important aid in the vertical mixing of the soil materials.

The decomposed plant and animal remains of the soil are called *humus.* They break down to a jellylike consistency, which ultimately reaches the colloidal state and which has highly complex physical and chemical properties.

Regional Variations in Humus Accumulation. Some soils have very small amounts of humus; some are richly supplied with it. Generally, other things being equal, the production of humus is closely associated with moisture and temperature relationships.[6] For the earth as a whole the creation of vegetative matter (plant growth) takes place only above freezing, and the amount of volume produced tends to increase with temperature up to the range of 75 to 85°F. At higher temperatures it decreases. This general relationship is graphed in Fig. 20.3, which also shows that in a moist and aerated environment the organic material which has been produced tends to be destroyed by microorganisms during the process of decomposition. These aerobic microorganisms (i.e., microorganisms which thrive only in the presence of free oxygen) begin to function around 40°F, and their destructive ability increases with temperature well beyond the range of 75 to 85°F. Until such temperatures are reached, however, the relative rate of destruction remains below that of production. When translated into latitudinal terms, this means that humus can accumulate in all nonpolar humid climates, except in those low-latitude regions where average temperatures are approximately 77°F and higher.

The curve in Fig. 20.3 representing the destruction of organic matter in environments without air, such as swamps, shows that anaerobic microorganisms (i.e., microorganisms which can live without free oxygen) are much less active as agents of decomposition. Hence there can be a continuous accumulation of humus in such environments at any latitude. This accounts for the relatively large accumulation of peat in swamps, both now and in former ages.

In a subhumid climate the volume of vegetative production by the characteristic grasses and shrubs is, of course, below that of a humid climate, but the activity of the microorganisms is propor-

[6] M. W. Senstius. "Climax Forms of Rock-weathering." *Amer. Scientist,* Vol. 46, pp. 355–367, 1958.

tionately even less as a result of the lack of moisture (Fig. 20.4). Consequently, humus can accumulate in subhumid climates at any latitude.

Water and Air. Perhaps only 50 percent of the volume of an average, good-quality surface soil consists of inorganic particles, dead organic material, and living organisms. Water and air circulating within the pore spaces make up the other 50 percent. Water and the gases of the air are an integral part of the inorganic and organic chemical reactions that occur in the soil, and hence are just as much constituents of soil as the solids are. Although plants derive their food from the soil solutions, relatively few types of plants are able to thrive in soils in which the pore space is always filled with water; most of them require soils which contain air as well.

Immediately following a rain, the pore spaces of a soil may be filled with water which displaces the air. In this condition the water is in excess of field capacity, and the surplus will move downward. This surplus is called free or gravitational water (Fig. 20.5). The water which remains, capillary water, is held to the surfaces of the soil

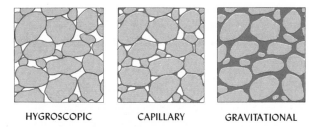

HYGROSCOPIC   CAPILLARY   GRAVITATIONAL

Figure 20.5 Forms of soil water. Grey areas represent individual soil particles greatly magnified; green margins, water; white areas, air spaces.

particles and in the voids between them by surface tension. When the amount of capillary water is diminished by plant use or direct evaporation, capillarity may cause some water to move horizontally, or even creep upward a short distance, from zones where it is more abundant. In fine-textured soil, water may move in this fashion with relative ease. In coarse-textured soils, both the field capacity is low and the movement of capillary water is limited. After a drought when the supply of capillary water has been depleted, there is still a molecular film called hygroscopic water on the surfaces of the soil particles (Fig. 20.5). It adheres firmly, does not move from one place to another, and is resistant to both evaporation and absorption by plant roots.

The supply of soil water varies from region to region and depends upon the ratio of precipitation to evapotranspiration and the amount of free drainage there is. Where precipitation is relatively high in proportion to evapotranspiration, there will be more gravitational water and hence more leaching, and the soils will tend toward an acid reaction (pH below 7.0). In sites where the groundwater table coincides with the land surface, or in localities where an impervious layer exists in the subsoil, there may be a more or less permanent supply of gravitational water near the surface. This creates a waterlogged as well as an acid soil. On the other hand, in arid regions the occasional gravitational water may move downward only a short distance, carrying with it dissolved salts, and then move upward again through capillarity and be lost by evapotranspiration. In this way lime and other salts may

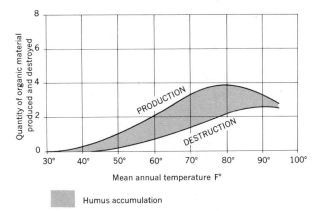

Humus accumulation

Figure 20.4 In semiarid climates, these are the relative rates of production of organic material and its destruction by aerobic microorganisms. Less organic material is produced than in a humid climate, but the soil microorganisms are even less active owing to the decreased moisture. The result is that humus production continues at higher temperatures. *(After Senstius.)*

accumulate in definite layers or even at the surface in dry-land soils. Consequently, the soils of sub-humid areas tend to have an alkaline reaction (pH above 7.0).

Profile. In the development of soil, one set of processes—such as the accumulation of organic matter, illuviation, or eluviation—tend to produce more or less distinct layers called horizons, which have different chemical and physical properties. These are designated as A, B, and C horizons, reading from the top down. The thicknesses of the horizons vary greatly; in some types of soil they are thin, in others so thick and irregular that for purposes of better description, each horizon is further subdivided as A_1, A_2, A_3, etc. (Fig. 20.6).

The horizons within a profile are distinguished from one another in texture, structure, chemical characteristics, and many other qualities. Organic life and debris are most abundant in the A horizon. In humid regions the A horizon is usually subjected to leaching and eluviation and is left poorer in soluble substances and coarser in texture as a result. The B horizon, in contrast, may be one of illuviation as well as a zone of nutrient enrichment, since some of the materials carried in solution from the layer above may be deposited in it. The C horizon is the little-changed parent material from which the solid fraction of the soil was derived.

Another set of developmental processes tend to churn or mix the soil materials, so that distinct and contrasting horizon development is inhibited.[7] These processes include the mixing of soils by animals; tree fall; expansion and contraction, which occurs in freezing and thawing, and which also occurs when certain clay-rich soils are alternately dried and moistened; mass movements; and the like. Some tropical black-clay soils, for example, are known as "self-plowing" and hence have simple profiles; yet they may have been in existence ten times as long as the Michigan podzol diagrammed in Fig. 20.6 with its clearly defined horizons.

[7] F. D. Hole. "A Classification of Pedoturbations and Some Other Factors of Soil Formation. . . ." *Soil Sci.,* Vol. 91, pp. 375–377, 1961.

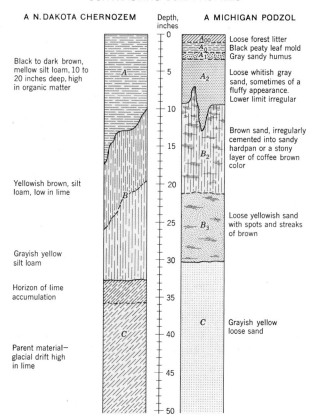

Figure 20.6 Some characteristic profile elements within the profiles of two different soils.

Color. Among the more striking characteristics of the surfaces and horizons of different soils are their distinctive colors. Since color is generally significant as an indicator of the soil's physical or chemical condition, it is usually included in the descriptions of horizons, and even large soil classes may have colors as parts of their names.

Among the commonest soil colors are shades of red, brown, or yellow, which are caused primarily by various forms, degrees of hydration, and concentrations of the oxides of iron. Blue and gray-blue tints are common in the structureless clay concentrations of waterlogged soils. In some humid regions a gray or whitish color often indicates a lack of iron oxides, which have been lost because of strong leaching. In arid regions, on the other hand, the same color may denote a concentration of soluble salts. Black and dark-brown soil colors usually (but not always) indicate a considerable content of organic matter. In many soils two or more color-forming elements are present, giving rise to intermediate colors, such as yellowish-brown or grayish-brown.

Pan Layers. Some soils develop a dense or compact horizon known as a pan layer. This layer can markedly affect soil productivity because of its interference with root penetration and, in some instances, water penetration. Pan layers are caused by a variety of factors, the two most common being large amounts of gravitational water in humid regions, and precipitation of carbonates in dry regions. Both of these conditions result in a strongly illuviated or cemented horizon.

There are many kinds of pan layers, which have been grouped into several general types.[8] The name claypan is applied to a compact layer of uncemented clay, which may be created either by a high concentration of clay in the original subsoil or by illuviation. Claypans are relatively widespread in the very smooth or flat lands of both the humid middle latitudes and the subhumid and arid regions.

Another group of pan layers, hardpans, are the results of chemical cementation. Hardpans occur widely in all latitudes. In humid regions, where the cementing agent is commonly iron, hardpans are most widespread in the tropics, commonly developing into an ironstone called laterite. Hardpans in dry regions are typically cemented by calcium carbonate and are called caliche, which is restricted mostly to the warmer dry areas.

The Controls of Soil

The individual characteristics of a soil, its distinctive elements, result from the interaction of a number of controls, the most important of which are (1) the initial or parent material, (2) climate, (3)

8 Eric Winters and Roy W. Simonson. "The Subsoil." *Advances in Agron.,* Vol. 3, pp. 31–45, 1951.

organisms in the soil, (4) land-surface form, (5) time, and (6) changes made by man.

Each control varies in its effect and relative importance from place to place on the earth. Some of these variations are systematically arranged, such as those deriving from climatic factors, while others are not, such as those which primarily depend upon the character of the bedrock or the form of the land surface. Generally, world patterns of soils are more subject to internal variation than world patterns of climate.

Initial Material. The loose, thin, inorganic covering of the earth's surface, however it may have come into existence, contains a combination of rock particles of particular chemical composition which have weathered to a particular array of fragment sizes. Whatever the processes of development in a soil, they are not likely to erase completely the fundamental qualities deriving from this initial or parent material.

The textural characteristics of the initial material are significant because they affect the degree to which water and air can circulate. The mineral, or chemical, content is extremely important in that under natural conditions (i.e., without changes made by man), it is largely the source of the soil's fertility. An inadequate supply of a critical chemical element in the parent material can be counteracted only by artificial fertilization or by some catastrophic event, such as a flood, volcanic eruption, or dust storm. Thus the initial material may be thought of as a limiting factor with respect to some of the soil's textural and most of its initial fertility characteristics.

Climate. Climate directly affects the rate and depth of weathering of rocks and the amount of water percolating through or evaporating from the soil. Prevailing high temperatures promote deep weathering and other rapid chemical activity in the soil, while cold temperatures slow them down. Alternating wet and dry seasons develop soil characteristics which differ from those of continuously rainy regions, and the total amount of precipitation is directly related to the leaching of the important bases—that is, the salts of calcium, phosphorous, potassium, etc.—from the soil.

Climate also acts as an indirect control through its influence upon the organic life of a soil and on the plants (and animals) which subsist upon it. (Note that the soil and the vegetation growing "in" it are all parts of a single system.) Since most vegetation can flourish only within certain temperature and moisture ranges, these establish definite climatically based zones of plant life on the earth. Through the character of their vegetative products—for example, their needle leaves, broad leaves, thick or sparse root systems, etc.—plants markedly affect the character of the soil in which they grow. Furthermore, as observed earlier, the temperatures which occur in a region have an important effect on the rate of accumulation of humus (Figs. 20.3, 20.4).

Organisms in the Soil. Plant and animal organisms are a control as well as an element, since organisms and their tissues affect the soil in many ways. For example, when plants and animals die, much of their remains are incorporated in the soil complex, and the microorganisms (bacteria, protozoa, fungi, etc.) in the soil are primary agents in the decomposition of these remains. Some microorganisms also are able to change atmospheric nitrogen into a form that can be utilized by plants.

Burrowing organisms and plant roots add to the porosity of the soil by their penetration of it. Moreover, deep-rooted plants bring minerals up from the subsoil and hold them in their tissues. When the plants die and decay, these minerals are then returned to the upper soil layers.

Land-surface Form. Differences in slope can have a great effect on moisture and air conditions within the soil. Even more important, they influence the rate of surface erosion. Maximum development of soil profiles such as those shown in Fig. 20.6 will ordinarily take place on undulating but well-drained uplands with free underdrainage and only slight surface erosion. The slow rate of erosion on such

sites allows the soil-forming processes to penetrate relatively deeply below the surface. Soils which have been formed under such circumstances and which have reached a balance possess well-defined profiles and are termed mature. The soils of steep slopes generally fail to develop these characteristics, because accelerated surface erosion restricts the profile development, by thinning the horizons and limiting the vegetative cover so that the organic content is reduced. Soils of poorly drained or marshy areas develop quite different profiles from other soils, primarily because they remain waterlogged and air cannot penetrate them.

Time and Man. Because the soil-forming processes do not advance at the same rates in the various earth environments, time is not a constant control. There is no specific period in which a soil develops its particular characteristics. Some may reach a condition of relative balance comparatively quickly, possibly in less than a hundred years; others may require thousands.

Man has greatly modified vast areas of soil by making changes that fall in all the classes of controls. He may have altered the parent material by adding mineral fertilizers, removing salts, taking out more nutrients by cropping than are replaced naturally, or even adding toxic materials. He may have changed the land-surface form relationships by checking or accelerating erosion, or he may have caused subsidence by draining or mining. He may have affected the climate in many ways, such as by adding carbon dioxide to the atmosphere, creating smog and toxic gases, or clearing and burning vegetative cover, which in turn affects wind velocities and humidities. He may have added organic matter by manuring, or he may have removed it by overcropping, burning, or plowing.[9] All soils are, of course, always undergoing change; that is an ever-present characteristic of the environment. But because man has been so active in his tilling of the soil, it is likely that nearly mature soils are largely

[9] O. W. Bidwell and F. D. Hole. "Man as a Factor of Soil Formation." *Soil Sci.,* Vol. 99, pp. 65–72, 1965.

restricted to those which have never been cultivated. On the other hand, it is important to keep
in mind that the immature or man-modified soils of
an area usually have qualities closely related to
those of the actual or hypothetical mature soil of
the region.

Soil Classes and Regions

In many ways a soil is similar to a living organism:
for one thing, some of its characteristics are heredi-
tary, such as those derived from its inorganic an-
cestry, while others are due to environmental

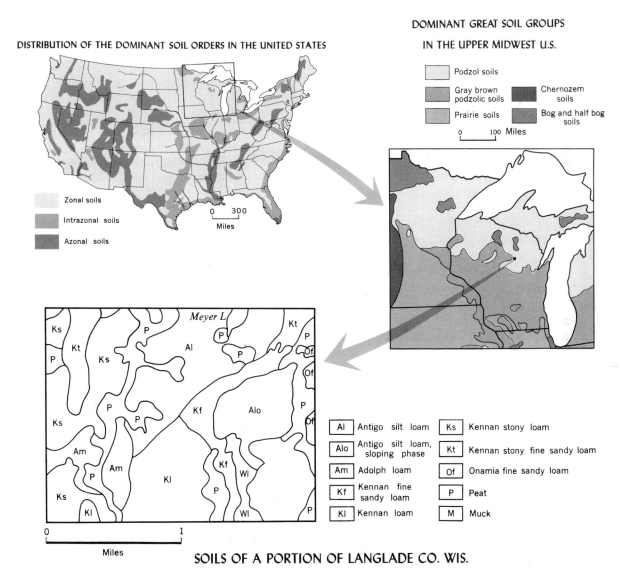

DISTRIBUTION OF THE DOMINANT SOIL ORDERS IN THE UNITED STATES

Zonal soils

Intrazonal soils

Azonal soils

DOMINANT GREAT SOIL GROUPS

IN THE UPPER MIDWEST U.S.

Podzol soils

Gray brown
podzolic soils

Chernozem
soils

Prairie soils

Bog and half bog
soils

0   100   Miles

Al	Antigo silt loam	Ks	Kennan stony loam
Alo	Antigo silt loam, sloping phase	Kt	Kennan stony fine sandy loam
Am	Adolph loam	Of	Onamia fine sandy loam
Kf	Kennan fine sandy loam	P	Peat
Kl	Kennan loam	M	Muck

SOILS OF A PORTION OF LANGLADE CO. WIS.

Figure 20.7 Soils maps of different scales show different degrees of detail in the classification of soils. Note the area
covered on one map in relation to the scale of the adjacent map. *(Generalized from maps of the Soil Surveys of the United
States and Wisconsin.)*

influences. Generally, the environmental controls, especially climate and living organisms, tend to be dominant in the development of a soil. But the number of combinations of important soil qualities is very large, and the systematizing help of a classification is needed to study their occurrence over the earth.

Soil Classification. The most comprehensive genetic grouping is that of the three soil orders: zonal soils, intrazonal soils, and azonal soils. Their distribution in the United States is shown on the small map in Fig. 20.7. Zonal soils have well-developed characteristics based largely upon the dominance of climate and vegetation among the soil-forming processes. Intrazonal soils have more or less well-developed characteristics, but their development was dominated by factors other than climate and vegetation—for instance, excessive or poor drainage, unusual parent material, or excessive evaporation. Azonal soils do not have well-developed soil profiles; wind-blown sand areas or recent aluvium are examples of the azonal order.

This system of classification then proceeds through suborders to divisions called great soil groups, of which there are approximately forty in the United States. Each great soil group is composed of families, which are in turn composed of series, which are divided into types. The soil type is the fundamental element in the classification system.[10]

The Soil Conservation Service of the U.S. Department of Agriculture has developed a new system of classifying soils based more on their distinctive properties and less on their genesis. Called the 7th Approximation, its proposals are now under study and seem likely to be generally accepted.[11]

[10] There are thousands of soil types. A type is distinguished by a textural description added to a series name which is a geographical name: for example, a Miami silt loam. Soil types can be further described as divided into phases: for example, stony phase or steep phase.
[11] Soil Survey Staff. *Soil Classification, A Comprehensive System: 7th Approximation. Soil Conservation Service, USDA.* U.S. Government Printing Office, Washington, D.C., 1960.

Instead of three orders, there are ten in the new proposal, followed by numerous suborders, great groups, subgroups, families, and series. The names of the ten new orders from the 7th Approximation are given in the table of major world soil categories opposite.

A World View of Soils. In order to provide the reader with a worldwide view of soil as a component of the geographical environment and to aid the study of how the soil relates to the other elements of physical geography, the following table was formed by grouping the numerous kinds of soils into ten broad descriptive categories. To select these ten, the dominant great soil groups of the earth, primarily from the zonal order, were first sorted into eight general categories: those which are listed under no. 1 and no. 2 in the first column of the table. Two other categories were then added and grouped under no. 3: alluvial soils (azonal), because alluvial areas are significant regions of human use; and the soils of areas with high local relief, because such areas have tremendous internal variety in soils, just as they do in climate. The second column of the table shows how the major great soil groups fit into these ten basic categories. The names of the corresponding orders of the 7th Approximation are given in the third column. The distribution of the ten broad soil categories over the earth is shown in Plate 6.

Soil Regions and Soil Genesis

Figure 20.8 illustrates schematically the distribution of the first eight broad soil categories shown in the table and their spatial associations with world climates and vegetation. The diagram of these elements, plotted on a kind of hypothetical continent, demonstrates in simplified form the correspondence one would observe by careful study of the maps in Plates 2, 5, and 6. Among the generalizations that could be made from such a study, the most important is that there are fundamental differences between the soils of humid lands and those of dry lands.

BROAD DESCRIPTIVE SOIL CATEGORIES BASED UPON DOMINANT GREAT SOIL GROUPS

Descriptive soil categories	Great soil groups	7th Approximation orders
1. SOILS OF THE HUMID REGIONS a. **Tundra soils**	Tundra Humic-Gley	Entisols, Inceptisols, and associated Histosols
b. **Podzolic soils of the high latitudes**	Brown Podzolic Podzol	Spodosols and associated Histosols
c. **Podzolic soils of the middle latitudes**	Gray-wooded Gray Podzolic Noncalcic Brown Degraded Chernozem Gray-brown Podzolic	Alfisols
d. **Podzolic soils of subtropical latitudes**	Red-yellow Podzolic Reddish-brown Lateritic	Ultisols
e. **Latosolic soils**	Reddish latosols and a variety of imperfectly known latosolic, lateritic, latosolic-podzolic, latosolic-chernozemic, and other soil groups	Oxisols
2. SOILS OF THE SUBHUMID AND DRY REGIONS a. **Chernozemic soils**	Prairie Chernozem Reddish Prairie Rendzina Brown Chestnut Terra Rossa	Mollisols (middle latitudes)
b. **Grumusolic soils**	Regur Black Clay Reddish Brown Reddish Chestnut	Vertisols
c. **Desertic soils**	Desert Reddish Desert Sierozem Solonchak Solonetz	Aridisols
3. OTHER SOILS a. **Alluvial soils**	Alluvial	Entisols
b. **Soils of areas with high local relief with complex soil associations**		Entisols, Inceptisols, and Lithic intergrades of other orders

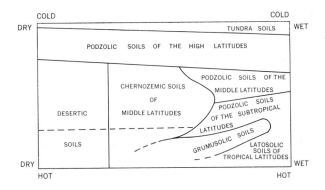

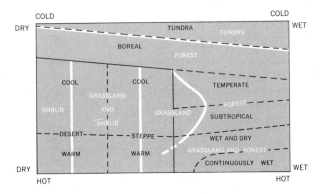

Figure 20.8 Diagrams showing the generalized spatial correspondence on the earth between (top) the broad categories of soils and (bottom) the major climatic zones. Also in the bottom diagram, the white lines and lettering indicate the dominant vegetation characteristics. On each diagram, average annual temperature increases from the top toward the bottom, and moisture conditions increase from left to right.

Soil Formation in Humid Areas.

Most soils of humid regions have developed under natural vegetations of forest or woodland. Except in areas with very high temperatures, the production of organic matter exceeds its destruction; consequently humus accumulates. Humus is formed primarily on the surface, however, and is therefore incorporated into the soil rather slowly. Also, there is a net downward movement of soil water in humid regions; accordingly the soils as a whole are much leached, usually light-colored, and acid. The net result is that they are comparatively low in both organic matter and mineral plant foods.

The chemical soil-forming processes, and the soil profiles, are notably different between warm and cool humid regions. In general, solution and eluviation dominate in the humid tropics, producing a latosolic soil. In latosols there is relatively little humus accumulation because of the activity of microorganisms (Fig. 20.3). Weathering is deep, and the basic minerals and much of the silica have been leached out of latosols, leaving a concentration of reddish iron and aluminum oxides in the upper sections. Horizon differentiation is poor.

By contrast, in the cool humid regions of the higher latitudes, the soil-forming process creates a podzolic soil. Abundant decaying organic material produces compounds which combine with iron and aluminum and thereby permit the removal of these metals from the A horizon and their deposition in a strongly illuviated B horizon. Horizon differentiation is marked, and silica which remains in the lower section of the A horizon forms an ash-gray horizon between the black layer of humus and the dark-brown B horizon.

The soils of humid areas are sometimes called pedalfers (from *ped,* soil; *al,* aluminum; *fer,* iron) because their iron and aluminum content is high in comparison with the soils of dry regions.

Soil Formation in Dry Areas.

Because of the relative lack of water, leaching is not a major factor in the development of dry-land soils. Consequently they have a considerable, and in some places excessive, content of soluble alkaline compounds. Calcium and magnesium may be plentiful in these areas, and because of the low rainfall and high evaporation, the soils usually have neutral or basic reactions (pH values of 7.0 or more). The general process by which the calcium content of the soil is kept high in drier regions is known as calcification. Because there is a delicate relationship between the downward moving water heavily charged with lime and its precipitation as a result of loss by evapotranspiration, an actual horizon of lime concentration often develops.

Although there are some significant differences between the soils of the warm dry regions and those of the cool, the most important differences are those between the soils of the very arid or desert regions and the soils on the subhumid margins of the dry regions. The typical desertic soil is light-colored, high in saline or alkaline minerals, and low in organic matter. On the other hand, the chernozemic soil of the barely subhumid region is black or dark brown, neutral or only moderately alkaline, and high in organic content. In some of the subhumid sections, the alternation of wet and dry seasons and the particular vegetation cover have combined to produce a clay-rich soil, called a grumusol, with unusual cracking characteristics. Because of the abundance of calcium in the soils of the dry areas of the earth, they are sometimes called *pedocals*.

Soils of the Humid Regions

It was noted above that the mature soils of the humid areas include two extreme categories, and of course there are several which are intermediate. They will be considered here in the same order given in the table of soil categories: that is, the tundra soils of the treeless high latitudes; the podzolic soils which are found principally in the regions of coniferous boreal forests and the higher middle-latitude mixed forests; the podzolic soils of the middle-latitude areas; the podzolic soils of subtropical areas; and the latosolic soils of the tropical rainforest and other areas of tropical climate and vegetation.

Tundra Soils (Entisols, Inceptisols, and Associated Histosols).[12] The extensive treeless regions of the Arctic fringe in both North America and Eurasia contain a complex of soils that are markedly affected by the long cold periods and the characteristically poor drainage. Because of the intense frost action and slow weathering, many of the soils are young, and not much horizon development has taken place (Entisols). The low temperatures, combined with clay layers and especially with permafrost (permanently frozen ground), cause poor drainage and waterlogging, and therefore result in little eluviation or illuviation (Inceptisols). The intense, long-continued cold keeps vegetative decomposition at a minimum, and as a consequence many of the soils contain raw humus or peat (Histosols).

A large part of the tundra is poorly drained and consists of bog and hummocky marshland. The soils are similar to the glacial marsh and bog soils found in middle latitudes, many of which have been drained and made into farmland. This could not be done in the tundra, however, even if the climate were to allow agriculture. Large areas in the Arctic cannot be drained, are unsuited to tillage, and support a natural vegetation useful only as pasture.

Podzolic Soils of the High Latitudes (Spodosols). The mature Podzol is the great soil group characteristic of regions having a humid boreal climate. It and similar podzolic soils usually develop under a natural vegetation of conifers or mixed broadleaf–needle-leaf forest. Conifers do not require abundant alkaline soil elements for their growth, and since they are mainly shallow-rooted trees, they draw only small supplies of the soil bases to the surface, even where these are available in the parent material. Thus there is little chemical reaction to oppose the tendency toward soil acidity, and pH values are generally in the vicinity of 5.0.

The effects of the long, cold boreal winter and moderate summer temperatures, as well as the forest litter of resinous pine needles, are to retard bacterial action and to prevent the formation of a surface layer of half-decomposed humus several inches thick. This spongy material, which represents the accumulation of many years, retains water, becomes highly acid, and makes any downward-moving soil water acid. The effect of the strongly acid solutions upon the soil minerals is to dissolve the available iron and aluminum and remove them from the surface soil. Consequently, beneath the layer of humus the A horizon of these soils is strongly leached. In addition, it has lost most of its clay and colloidal constituents by eluvia-

---

[12] Where applicable, the corresponding 7th Approximation names are given in parentheses.

tion, it is poor in the mineral elements of soil fertility, and it is nearly structureless. Because of the removal of the iron, the upper layer becomes grayish white (the name Podzol is derived from a Russian word meaning ashes), as shown in Fig. 20.9. Beneath the gray-white A horizon, and sharply different from it, there is typically a dense, brown, acid B horizon, strongly illuviated, containing iron

Figure 20.9 Profile of a Podzol soil in Ontario. Note the typical heavy leaching of the light-colored lower A horizon and the strongly illuviated dark-colored upper part of the B horizon. *(Photograph by G. A. Hills, Ontario Department of Lands and Forests.)*

and aluminum sesquioxides (Fe_2O_3, Al_2O_3) and appreciable amounts of organic carbon. These materials often cause the cementation of pellets which can become dense enough to constitute a pan layer.

Without improvement, the podzolic soils of high latitudes are poor soils for most farm crops. Under cultivation, the surface layer of organic matter is soon lost, and the grayish surface soil requires lime, fertilizer, and good management to keep it productive and to prevent its poor structure from becoming a hindrance to tillage.

Podzolic Soils of the Middle Latitudes (Alfisols). These soils develop in temperate continental climates under broadleaf deciduous or mixed conifer and broadleaf forests (compare Plates 2, 5, and 6). They also tend to have a dark surface layer of organic material, but it is not so thick, so poorly decomposed, or so acid as that associated with the podzolic soils of colder climates (Fig. 20.10). pH values are usually between 5.0 and 6.0. Moreover, the organic material derived from broadleaf forests contains more lime, potash, and other bases than that from coniferous forests, and it can be easily mixed with other parts of the soil by earthworms. The A horizon is leached, but it is neither so impoverished nor so bleached as the A horizon of the true Podzol. Generally it is stained with a brown hydroxide of iron, and the admixture of organic matter gives it a grayish-brown color. The illuviated B horizon is commonly yellowish-brown and heavier in texture than the A horizon. The C horizon is the little-changed parent material of the soil.

On the whole, the podzolic soils of middle latitudes have better structures than other forest-land soils, maintain them better under cultivation, and respond more readily to the application of lime and organic fertilizers. However, they lose their quality under continuous cropping unless they are managed carefully, limed, and well fertilized.

Associated Soils. In the Northern Hemisphere, where most of the podzolic soils occur, a surprising variety of other kinds of soils are associated with the podzolic soils of the high and middle latitudes.

Among these are alluvial soils (Entisols), either fertile river deposits or the infertile sands and gravels associated with glacial outwash. Alluvial soils lack any marked horizon development and tend to be low in humus, and those that are sandy dry out quickly.

Also common are types of soils that have been affected by poor drainage, such as the dark-colored soils formed in marshy or boggy places where peat and muck have accumulated (Histosols). In them the surface layers are composed largely of organic matter derived from the remains of grasses, sedges, and other marsh plants. They commonly are underlain by sticky compact clays that are light shades of gray tinged with blue. These plastic clays are termed gley, and they occur where a high groundwater table allows the formation of ferrous iron compounds, which cause the blue tints. The process of gleization can occur anywhere if the soil is periodically waterlogged. Such soils are common in the numerous depressions and high-water-table areas of glaciated plains. If drained, many can be productive.

In the glaciated regions of North America and northern Europe there are also considerable areas of rocky ground providing what is called a lithosol—a stony soil with few soil characteristics.

Podzolic Soils of the Subtropical Latitudes (Ultisols). As shown on Plate 6, these soils are dominant in only a few areas, but they occur in regions of considerable agricultural importance, such as southern China and the Cotton Belt of the United States. Their upper horizons generally are brown clays and loams. Their B horizons usually are deep, with colors varying from red to yellow and often showing mottles of laterite (i.e., iron concentrations; see the subsection on laterite below). The generally lighter colors of these soils result from less complete oxidation of the iron content. They have also been more or less affected by podzolization, so that in them a thin top layer of darker organic material is commonly underlain by a lighter A horizon and an illuviated acid B horizon of clay-enriched material.

Figure 20.10 Profile of a podzolic forest soil (Gray-brown Podzolic) in the middle latitudes. Compare this with Fig. 20.9 and note that in the Gray-brown Podzolic soil the organic matter is better mixed and the effect of bleaching in the A horizon is not so marked. *(Photograph by G. A. Hills, Ontario Department of Lands and Forests.)*

The inherent agricultural capacity of these soils is not high, but with careful management they are productive. They are generally low in calcium and other alkaline substances, and the supply of organic matter is seldom abundant. Under cultivation, the red and yellow colors of the B horizon usually predominate, becoming distinctive elements of the landscape.

Latosolic Soils (Oxisols). Vegetation variations are much more complex in the humid regions of the tropics, and the soils also show great variety. Where grasses predominate, soils tend to be dark; where forest prevails, soils are lighter. Even the podzoli-

Figure 20.11 Profile of a yellowish-red latosol formed from gneiss northwest of Rio de Janeiro, Brazil. Latosol profiles are typically deep and commonly do not have as much horizon differentiation as podzols. There is some darkening of the upper portion by organic matter. Plant roots extend to depths below 5 ft in this soil. Numbers on ruler show feet. (Photograph by Roy W. Simonson, Soil Conservation Service, U.S. Department of Agriculture.)

zation process is known to occur. Because our knowledge of tropical soils is insufficient at present to differentiate them clearly or generalize properly about them, these areas are shown on Plate 6 with less detail than most of the other soil regions.

In tropical humid localities the high temperatures and abundant precipitation combine to promote deep and intense weathering. This results in the removal of the iron and aluminum compounds of silica, as well as the bases, from the surface soil, while quartz and the reddish sesquioxides of iron and aluminum remain. The texture is commonly clay size, but surprisingly porous, with a tendency toward granular structure. The high temperatures and moist conditions are favorable to microorganisms as well as to plant life, and there is little humus accumulation where temperatures are continuously high (Fig. 20.3). Because of the heavy leaching, the soils are predominantly acid, commonly with pH values around 5.0. The profiles are unusually deep, sometimes extending more than 10 ft, and the horizon differentiation is gradual or diffuse (Fig. 20.11).

Many latosolic soils are very permeable; consequently, they are capable of being tilled immediately after heavy rains, and since they dry out quickly they are subject to drought. Being intensively leached, the upper horizons are generally low in plant foods, both mineral and organic, and are not usually capable of sustained cropping without fertilization. Since they are porous, some require irrigation in dry seasons. Tropical soils are obviously adapted to the growth of deep-rooted crops, such as oil palms, which utilize the deeper supply of nutrients, the intense tropical sunlight, and the abundant rains for the production and storage of fats, starches, sugars, and other carbohydrates instead of proteins.

Laterite. In horizons of tropical soils that are occasionally saturated with water, the sesquioxide of iron together with some quartz and clay commonly forms soft nodules, called laterite. This segregation of iron occurs as a layer within the profile. With alternate wetting and drying it tends to solidify and form a hardpan with coarse tubular-like pores filled with clayey material. Thus it becomes a sort of ironstone, which is sometimes even used for building material (Fig. 20.12).

Soils of the Subhumid and Dry Regions

In the more humid sections of the dry regions, the luxuriant grasses, combined with the slower activity of microorganisms, produce a large and deep supply of humus. Since there is relatively little leaching, sufficient lime is available to combine with the large amount of organic colloids and clays in these dark soils, thus promoting excellent structural conditions in all the soil horizons.

As one moves from the subhumid to the semiarid and finally to the arid sections, a change occurs in the character of the soils (Fig. 20.8). Less moisture means less leaching, more calcification, less vegetative cover, and therefore less humus and a lighter soil color. In some areas the evaporation of surface waters may even lead to salinization, the process of widespread and complex salt accumulation.

Although there are no abrupt changes along which boundaries can be readily drawn, the soils of the subhumid and the arid extremes are different enough so that at least three groups can be recognized: (1) the chernozemic soils of the relatively humid portions of the subhumid areas, (2) the grumusolic soils of some tropical and subtropical areas with wet and dry seasons, and (3) the desertic soils of the shrub-covered arid regions.

Chernozemic Soils (Mollisols). The majority of these soils have developed under a grass vegetation in which the plants are closely enough spaced to form a sod providing an abundance of humus. Since chernozemic soils are located on the more humid margins of the dry regions, there is some leaching, but not enough to remove all the calcium carbonate and other bases which are generally available for exchange to plant roots. The process of calcification takes place in most soils of this category, except for those in the most humid sections. Also, a horizon of lime accumulation usually occurs at

Figure 20.12 A stack of laterite bricks cut from a layer about 6 ft thick near Colombo, Ceylon. The handle of the small pick is about 18 in. long. *(Photograph by Roy W. Simonson, Soil Conservation Service, U.S. Department of Agriculture.)*

some depth—nearer the surface in regions of abundant lime and low rainfall, and farther down in soils that are better supplied with moisture or are derived from parent materials poor in line.

Plate 6 shows the world distribution of these excellent, highly fertile soils. Their use in farming reaches its peak in the middle latitudes, especially on the gently undulating uplands along the prairie-steppe margin in such areas as the United States and southern Russia. The chernozemic category includes several well-recognized soils such as the Prairie, the Chernozem itself, the Chestnut, the Brown, and variants of these.

Prairie Soils. Adjacent to some of the forest-soil regions are very dark brown soils known as Prairie or Brunizem soils. Found widely in the United States, Russia, and South America, they appear to have formed under a natural vegetation of tall grasses. Because they develop in climates which generally have sufficient moisture to be classed as humid, leaching has lowered the available calcium to the point where they have pH values less than 7.0, therefore being neutral to slightly acid. They have fine granular textures, and because they are in relatively humid areas they have no horizon of lime accumulation.

Chernozem Soils. The name for the entire category

Figure 20.13 Profile of a Chernozem formed from glacial till in South Dakota. The A horizon extends to a depth of a little over 1 ft, while the B horizon extends to nearly 2½ ft. The white spots in the bottom of the B and in the C horizon are carbonate accumulations. *(Photograph by Roy W. Simonson, Soil Conservation Service, U.S. Department of Agriculture.)*

encompassing the soils of the middle-latitude sub-humid regions is taken from the specific name of a soil, Chernozem, from Russian words for black and earth. Normally this soil is one of the most fertile of the chernozemic category. It is formed under a dense vegetation of somewhat shorter prairie and steppe grasses. Average annual precipitation in Chernozem areas is sufficiently low (about 20 in. in the United States) so that this soil contains an abundance of lime and the less soluble alkaline minerals. The deep A horizon of the Chernozem is high in humus and is colored black or very dark brown (Fig. 20.13). The B horizon is lighter brown or yellow. Horizon differentiation tends to be gradual. The soil structure is granular and porous; when tilled, it crumbles into a fine seedbed; and it has a large capacity for holding water. pH values usually range from 7.0 to just below 7.0. In a Chernozem soil the horizon of lime accumulation generally lies 3 to 5 ft beneath the surface—still within reach of the grass roots, which have in it an inexhaustible source of calcium.

Other Chernozemic Soils. On the drier margins of Chernozemic areas, the sod is not so luxuriant and the precipitation is less. These conditions give rise to Chestnut and Brown Soils, the darker Chestnut commonly lying adjacent to the Chernozem while Brown is nearer to arid regions. Owing to smaller amounts of humus, the A horizon is brown or grayish-brown, and the B horizon is considerably lighter. In the more tropical areas the soils are reddish-brown—signifying less humus, more leaching, and greater concentration of iron and aluminum sesquioxides. These soils usually have pH values in the vicinity of 8.0 and commonly include a zone of lime accumulation, which is relatively near the surface (1 to 4 ft) because of the slight precipitation. In some localities the lime is so abundant that it forms a tough hardpan layer. In general, however, these soils are easily tilled.

In several humid regions, areas of dark-colored soil high in humus are found in association with podzolic and latosolic forest soils. This soil type, called Rendzina, is similar to Prairie soil, but it developed from soft clayey limestones, with lime in such abundance that the supply which is made available by weathering exceeds the rate of loss through leaching. Since calcium is necessary for tall grasses, the original vegetation apparently was prairie rather than forest. This, in turn, produced a dark soil of the chernozemic type. Because Rendzinas exist only as small patches (being intrazonal, they can occur anywhere), they are not shown on Plate 6 except where they lie adjacent to other chernozemic soils. Examples of Rendzinas are found in the soils of the Black Prairies of Alabama and Texas.

Within the Mediterranean region there is a related class of dark reddish soils called Terra Rossa. These have commonly formed on the harder limestones, but sometimes they have even developed on basic igneous rocks. They contain an exceptional amount of clay in the upper horizons.

Grumusolic Soils (Vertisols). These are soils of the dry lands of tropical and subtropical areas with wet and dry seasons. They have a variety of origins: some of them weathered from basic igneous rocks with an unusual mineral content, such as the Regur soils of central India; many others developed from limestones. They were usually formed under grass with scattered woody vegetation, and they have a dark-colored A horizon which resembles chernozemic soils. But in many instances, this darkness may be caused by a complex of factors only indirectly related to organic accumulation, for the grumusolic soils are no more than moderately rich in organic material. On the drier margins their color tends to be reddish brown, because they have less humus and the tints of the iron oxides are more noticeable.

A widespread characteristic of these soils is a high content of clays that swell when wetted and then crack open when dried out (Fig. 20.14). Rainfall tends to drain into these cracks rather than moistening the entire soil, thus wetting a lower layer, which may then expand. As a consequence grumusolic soils are unstable and cause severe problems of management.

Figure 20.14   Cracks in a clay soil in Arizona as a result of drying. The average size of the blocks is about 1 sq ft. *(Photograph by Soil Conservation Service, U.S. Department of Agriculture.)*

Desertic Soils (Aridisols). Where aridity prevents any vegetation but widely spaced desert shrubs, the soil contains little organic matter, lighter colors predominate, and the reds, browns, yellows, and grays of weathered rock particles are widely exposed. Their light colors are accentuated by the accumulation of salt, lime, and other whitish substances near the soil surface, or even upon it (Fig. 20.15).

Several classes of soil fall into this general category. They are distinguished primarily by the kinds and concentrations of alkaline materials they contain. The common desertic soil of the middle latitudes (called Sierozem) has a brownish-gray A the soils become redder. Poor drainage and rapid evaporation lead to salinization, and where high concentrations of a variety of soluble salts occur, the soil is called Solonchak. If the salts contain an unusually large proportion of sodium resulting in a darker-colored, hard B horizon, the soil is called Solonetz. In the western part of the United States these are termed alkali soils.

No doubt, the larger parts of the great deserts are not covered with mature soils. Instead there are patches of bare rock, expanses of desert gravels, tracts of dune sands, and other areas of immature soil. There is generally an abundance of elements conducive to fertility, so that if water can be made available, many such areas are capable of becoming productive.

Alluvial Soils (Entisols)

Alluvial soils probably support a larger proportion of the world's population than any other great soil category. Where they are extensive enough, they have been shown as a separate group on Plate 6, even though there is great variety among these soils because their character is largely derived from the source materials of the specific alluvial products. Their textures may range from sands through silts to clays; their color may range from the light-colored gray, buff, or reddish alluvium derived from desertic soils to the dark-colored alluvium derived from chernozemic soils; and they may be more or less rich in plant nutrients. They are usually free from stones and easily cultivated, but in many areas they are poorly drained. In general there is little horizon development, except where surface cultivation has provided it. As a consequence alluvial soils are considered immature azonal soils.

Not all alluvial soils are productive. In many areas they are too wet or too dry; or they occur where the growing season is too short; or they may be too subject to flooding. In Far Eastern areas, where rice is commonly grown in alluvial paddy lands, the alluvial soils are probably more generally utilized than elsewhere in the world.

Figure 20.15 A desertic soil in California that has a high concentration of whitish salts at the surface. Note the cracking. *(Photograph by Soil Conservation Service, U.S. Department of Agriculture.)*

horizon above an even lighter-colored B horizon. Calcium carbonate accumulation is prominent near the surface and may even have become somewhat cemented into caliche. In the more tropical regions,

Selected References
for Chap. 20

Albrecht, W. A. "Physical, Chemical and Biochemical Changes in the Soil Community." In William L. Thomas, Jr. (ed.). *Man's Role in Changing the Face of the Earth*. The University of Chicago Press, Chicago, 1955. Pp. 648–673.

———. "Soil Fertility and Biotic Geography." *Geog. Rev.,* Vol. 47, pp. 87–105, 1957.

Bidwell, O. W., and F. D. Hole. "Man as a Factor of Soil Formation." *Soil Sci.,* Vol. 99, pp. 65–72, 1965.

Bunting, B. T. *The Geography of Soil*. Aldine Publishing Company, Chicago, 1965.

Eyre, S. R. *Vegetation and Soils: A World Picture*. Aldine Publishing Company, Chicago, 1963.

Hole, F. D. "A Classification of Pedoturbations and Some Other Processes and Factors of Soil Formation. . . ." *Soil Sci.,* Vol. 91, pp. 375–377, 1961.

Jenny, H. *Factors of Soil Formation*. McGraw-Hill Book Company, New York, 1941.

Lowdermilk, W. C. *Conquest of the Land through Seven Thousand Years*. Ag. Inform. Bull. No. 99, Soil Conservation Service, USDA., 1953.

Orvedal, A. C., J. Kubota, and Howard M. Smith. "Major Soil Profiles and Their Relationship with Climate." *Frost Action in Soils*. Highway Research Board (National Research Council) Rept. 2, pp. 1–10, Washington, D.C., 1952.

Robinson, G. W. *Soils: Their Origin, Constitution, and Classification*. 3d ed. John Wiley & Sons, Inc., New York, 1959.

Senstius, M. W. "Climax Forms of Rock-weathering." *Amer. Scientist,* Vol. 46, pp. 355–367, 1958.

Simonson, Roy W. "Changing Place of Soils in Agricultural Production." *Sci. Monthly,* Vol. 81, pp. 173–182, 1955.

Soil. Yearbook of Agriculture, 1957. U.S. Government Printing Office, Washington, D.C.

Soil Survey Staff. *Soil Classification, A Comprehensive System: 7th Approximation*. Soil Conservation Service, USDA. U.S. Government Printing Office, Washington, D.C., 1960.

Thorp, James, and Guy D. Smith. "Higher Categories of Soil Classification Order, Suborder and Great Soil Groups." *Soil Sci.,* Vol. 67, pp. 117–126, 1949.

Winters, E., and R. W. Simonson. "The Subsoil." *Advances in Agron.,* Vol. 3, pp. 31–45, 1951.

21

Mineral Resources

In the portion of the solid (and liquid) earth within man's reach, there are many substances that he has learned to use to his material advantage. These are the various elements and their inorganic or organic compounds, which are loosely classed as mineral resources. Minerals are employed in a great many ways: as materials for tools and other useful objects, as sources of energy, as substances for road building, as mineral fertilizers, and so on, almost without end. The list of mineral resources is long, and it continues to grow each year as man learns at an ever-increasing rate to use the substances he finds in the earth.

Although many minerals, such is iron and aluminum, are comparatively abundant and widely dispersed in the earth's surface layer, they occur in relatively small quantities in any one locality. Because it is costly to collect any mineral in this dispersed state, man is most interested in those places where the mineral content has somehow become sufficiently concentrated to form what is called a deposit. The geography of mineral deposits—that is, their comparative distribution and the distribution of related phenomena—is a subject of considerable importance to human societies.

The dependence of civilization upon mineral resources has grown rapidly in recent decades. Since the beginning of the twentieth century more minerals have been extracted from the earth than in all previous history. As man's scientific understanding and technological skill grow, it is to be expected that his dependence upon minerals will also increase.

To classify the mineral resources according to the use to which each is put would not be completely satisfactory, for many of them serve a variety of needs. Instead, the long list of minerals may be separated into three major categories which are only partly based on use: (1) the mineral sources of energy, (2) the metallic minerals, and (3) the nonmetallic minerals.

Mineral Sources of Energy

With man's ability to draw upon mineral sources for fuel and power, he can accomplish tasks which are far beyond his own meager muscular potential and that of domestic animals. His major sources for such power are what are called the mineral fuels. To be sure, there are other sources of power, such as falling water, wood, the tides, or the winds, but man depends primarily on three organically derived fuels: coal, petroleum, and natural gas. A fourth inorganic source provides nuclear energy which, although its use is steadily increasing, is not likely to supplant the others for some time yet. To recognize the potentialities which regions or countries have for human use, and to appreciate their industrial development and their economic problems, one must know their relation to these basic physical earth resources.

Some of the sun's energy is built into the tissues of all living plants and animals. In the normal course of events, this energy will be released after death during the process of decay—as, for example, in the liberation of heat when oxygen combines chemically with a decomposing substance. But if the complete decomposition of an organic material is prevented, it becomes a potential source of usable quantities of heat that can be obtained by inducing combustion later.

Firewood is an example of this kind of energy sources which has been a relatively short time in the making. Coal, petroleum, and natural gas are sources of energy that have been stored a long time. At certain times in the geologic past, conditions of physical geography occurred which caused the retardation of the decomposition of vast amounts of organic material and allowed them to be transformed into these three fuels. The formation of considerable deposits of these materials, called "fossil" fuels, required the interaction of a large number of physical phenomena.

In marked contrast to the fossil energy sources, man has very recently learned to unlock and control the energy available in the nuclei of the atoms of fissionable material such as uranium 235 or 233, and the atoms of fusionable material such as deuterium. When an atom of a fissionable material is broken into atoms of other substances, or when the fusion of atoms occurs, an enormous amount of energy is released which can provide the heat needed to drive a steam power plant. In power equivalents, the supplies of these materials are enormously greater than the fossil fuels, and they are widely distributed.

In recent years there has been a very rapid increase in the use of energy from mineral sources, and world production in all classes continues to rise. But coal, which until recently had always supplied the lion's share, has slipped (though only relatively) to second or third place in many areas. By far the greatest increases have been in the use of natural gas, and the total energy produced from oil and gas now rivals that from coal. This trend is even more marked in the United States than in the rest of the world (Fig. 21.1).

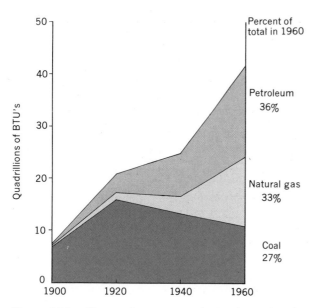

Figure 21.1 Changes in energy production from mineral sources in the United States, 1900–1960, and the percentage of total energy production supplied from these sources in 1960. The 4 percent unaccounted for was supplied largely by hydroelectric power. *(From various sources.)*

Petroleum and Natural Gas

Besides the fact that petroleum and natural gas are important energy sources in themselves, a large variety of special fuels, to say nothing of lubricants, can easily be prepared from these minerals. Their versatility has enabled man to reduce the significance of distance dramatically since the first oil well was drilled a little more than a century ago. Both can be transported easily, in or out of pipes, and their energy equivalent is greater than that of coal. For these and many other reasons, petroleum and natural gas have become critical items in the inventories of modern nations.

Structural Associations of Petroleum. Petroleum hydrocarbons, which probably originated from small marine organisms whose remains were prevented from complete decay, are found only in sedimentary rocks. They saturate the pore spaces of permeable rocks, especially sandstones and limestones, just as the surrounding rocks are saturated

by groundwater. Structures containing petroleum are commonly overlain by others filled with water (Fig. 21.2). This places the oil under pressure and concentrates it in limited deposits, called pools, in some form of structural pocket or trap from which the oil and gas cannot escape upward.

Oil and gas are obtained by drilling wells. If the petroleum is under considerable pressure from associated gas, it may be forced upward when the drill reaches it. But even in such a well, the oil must eventually be raised by pumping. Moreover, since the oil is contained in the small pore spaces in the pervious rock, much of it exists as a film clinging to the rock particles, and not all of this can be recovered. Even with the most improved methods, a considerable portion of the oil remains in the ground when the expenditure for pumping becomes unprofitable.

Petroleum and Gas Regions. Petroleum and gas deposits are restricted to those areas of the world containing considerable thicknesses of sedimentary rocks—areas which are commonly called sedimentary basins because of the manner in which they were formed. In addition, the continental-shelf areas less than 200 meters in depth which fringe

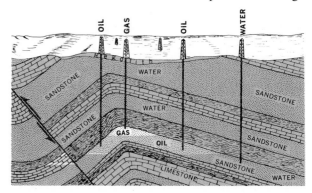

Figure 21.2 Two types of subsurface structures (fold and fault) in which petroleum and gas may be entrapped. Note the relation between the locations of several wells and the nature of their products. As can be seen, the existence of the structure entrapping the major oil and gas pool would not be evident from the surface relief. More than three-fourths of the world's oil is obtained from these kinds of structures.

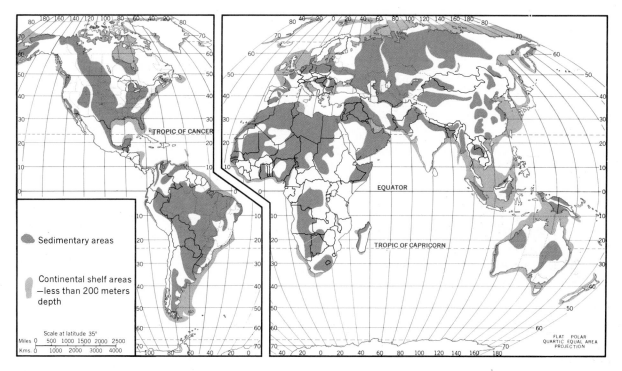

Figure 21.3 Generalized map of the sedimentary basins and continental-shelf areas indicating where the occurrence of petroleum and gas is not unlikely. *(From various sources.)*

many of the continents are largely covered with sediments. These also can contain oil (Fig. 21.3). Moreover, there are vast amounts of petroleum-impregnated shale, as well as lesser amounts of tar sand, from which the oil can be extracted, but neither source is now much utilized.

Natural gas sometimes occurs in physical association with petroleum deposits, but more often it does not. On the other hand, it is commonly found in connection with exploration for petroleum, so it is logical that gas has been developed as a resource by the oil industry.

Current estimates place the world reserve of petroleum at about 1,250 billion barrels, natural gas at somewhat more in energy equivalent, and recoverable oil from tar sands and oil shales at somewhat more than the reserves of gas. Almost all the known deposits of liquid petroleum and natural gas are concentrated in the Northern Hemisphere. And two circles with radii of a little

less than 2,000 miles would outline areas that probably contain some three-quarters of these reserves. The centers of these circles are approximately at 20°N Lat and 85°W Long in the Western Hemisphere, and 35°N Lat and 35°E Long in the Eastern (Figs. 21.4 and 21.7). The two areas include the central and southern United States and the land adjacent to the Caribbean Sea on the one hand, and the Middle East, North Africa, Europe, and neighboring areas of the U.S.S.R. on the other.

Western Hemisphere. There are several regions in the United States where petroleum and gas occur in great volume, and both the production and consumption of these fuels in the United States far exceed those of any other country. In recent times productive deposits have been discovered in Canada, and the regions bordering the Caribbean are also important producers of petroleum, especially for export. The several regions are shown in their overall relationship in Fig. 21.4. Each of these regions includes a number of subdivisions. Some of them contain both oil and gas, some yield oil but not much gas, and other yield gas alone.

In the United States the Midcontinent oil and gas region contains several widely scattered deposits, including hundreds of pools in Kansas, Oklahoma, southeastern New Mexico, southern Arkansas, northwestern Louisiana, and central, western, and eastern Texas (Figs. 21.5 and 21.6). Pipelines now carry both gas and oil to industrial consumers far to the north and east.

The Gulf Coast region includes pools found in many locations, primarily in eastern Texas and Louisiana. The deposits also extend out into the continental shelf, and considerable offshore development is taking place.

In the Rocky Mountain region, numerous fields are distributed over a large area which is mainly in Wyoming, although it extends northward into Montana, southward into Colorado, and eastward into North Dakota. The California fields are more productive, but both areas are far behind the

Figure 21.5 The principal oil-producing areas of the United States.

Midcontinent and Gulf Coast regions. The Eastern Interior region includes several fields of minor importance in Ohio, Indiana, Illinois, and Michigan. Among these the greatest producer is the field located in southeastern Illinois and adjacent Indiana.

Until recently, oil production in Canada was restricted to small amounts produced in scattered areas. But with discoveries in the vicinity of Edmonton in central Alberta, Canadian production and reserves have greatly increased, and Canadian status in the world oil market will doubtless continue to rise. Most of the production is in Alberta, with some in British Columbia to the northwest and in Saskatchewan and Manitoba to the southeast (Fig. 21.4).

Included in the Caribbean region are sev-

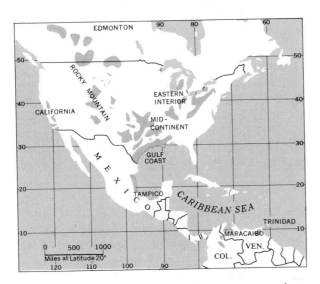

Figure 21.4 The principal oil- and gas-producing regions of the Western Hemisphere. Note the area that would be included by a circle with a 2,000-mile radius centered at 20°N Lat and 85°W Long (just east of the Yucatan peninsula).

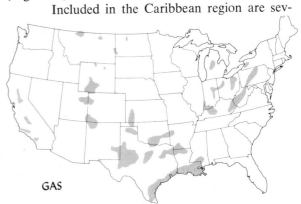

Figure 21.6 The principal natural-gas-producing areas of the United States.

eral areas of considerable importance. The chief among them is located in northern South America, mainly in the Maracaibo and Orinoco River Basins of Venezuela, but including smaller areas in Colombia and the island of Trinidad (Fig. 21.4). Venezuela has perhaps 8 to 10 percent of the world's known reserves. A second productive area in eastern Mexico near Tampico and Tuxpan is fourth in production in the Western Hemisphere. There is some evidence of widespread unexploited petroleum deposits in South America beyond the Caribbean borders, but only Argentina has any significant production.

Eastern Hemisphere. The oil-producing areas in the Eastern Hemisphere are so extremely fragmented by national boundaries that the casual observer may not realize at first that its major producing deposits are as localized as those of the Western Hemisphere. Although deposits of oil and gas have been found in many localities in Europe, Asia, Africa, and Australia, the region of greatest present output and largest proved resources is confined to an area more or less centered in the Middle East and extending west into North Africa and Europe and north into the U.S.S.R. (Fig. 21.7). The only other area that produces a significant amount is Indonesia, and its output is less than 4 percent of the hemisphere's total.

The petroleum deposits of the Middle East are located in several countries near the Persian Gulf, mainly in Kuwait, Saudi Arabia, Iran, and Iraq (Fig. 21.7). These areas, taken together, produce more than three-fourths as much oil as the United States, most of which is exported to the great consuming area of Europe. Finally, the proved reserves of the region are perhaps just over half the world's known supply. The greatest producer is Kuwait, a tiny sheikdom of less than 6,000 square miles at the head of the Persian Gulf.

The major producing areas in the U.S.S.R. are in several sections west and south of the Ural Mountains. By far the largest share is contributed by fields between the Volga River Valley and the Urals. Other important producing areas lie south,

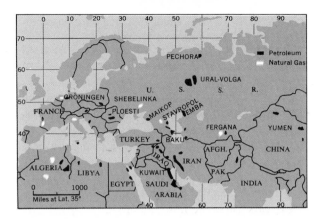

Figure 21.7 The principal oil- and gas-producing regions of the Eastern Hemisphere. The only significant producing area not shown is Indonesia. Note the area that would be included by a circle with a 2,000-mile radius centered at 35°N Lat and 35°E Long (between Cyprus and Syria at the eastern end of the Mediterranean Sea).

near Saratov, Volgograd (Stalingrad), on the north flank of the Caucasus Mountains, and across the Caspian Sea in Turkestan. The U.S.S.R. is the second major producer of petroleum in the world.

Europe, outside the U.S.S.R., is one of the great petroleum-consuming areas, but it produces less than 3 per cent of the world's total. The leading production is in the Ploesti area of Romania in southeastern Europe. Natural gas is rapidly assuming importance as a fuel in Europe, as it is elsewhere. There are extensive deposits of it in northern Italy and southeast France, and only recently one of the world's largest single deposits of natural gas was discovered in the province of Groningen in the Netherlands.

Production of petroleum and natural gas in Africa is mostly confined to the northern part, where northern Algeria and Libya are the major areas of production. These countries are becoming significant suppliers in the world market; already, liquified natural gas from North Africa is being transported by sea to Europe.

Eastern and southeastern Asia, so far as is now known, contain only small deposits, widely scattered, from Sakhalin southward. The most important are in the Indonesia region, especially Sumatra, Borneo, and New Guinea.

Coal

Coal is sedimentary rock derived largely from the unoxidized remains of plant tissues. The carbon-bearing tissues were preserved from ordinary decay by their submergence in swamp waters and subsequent burial and compaction by layers of clays, sands, and limes. The burial ultimately made these beds of organic material members of a series of horizontal sedimentary rocks. Some eight hundred years ago in the Western World, it was found that these "black rocks" would burn. By the eighteenth century millions of tons were being mined each year.

Except for occasional off years, the world production of coal has steadily increased. Although in the United States petroleum and natural gas together have supplanted coal as the major source of inanimate energy, coal still leads in the world as a whole. It is used for many purposes: space heating, the generation of electricity, the smelting of metals, and a host of other industrial, metallurgical, and chemical operations.

There are four classes of coals, but broadly speaking, all coal was initially similar to the first class, peat. Peat is the partially preserved, crumbled, and blackened organic remains that may be seen in present-day swamps and bogs. The other three forms represent successive changes in peat when it underwent compression and the loss of water and gases (Fig. 21.8). Thus a second class, somewhat

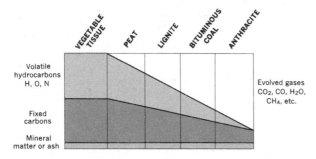

Figure 21.8 Stages in the metamorphosis of vegetable material into coal of various types. *(After Newberry.)*

more compact than peat, is the crumbly brown coal or lignite. Further transformation—additional losses of volatile constituents and corresponding increases in the relative content of fixed carbon—produces a "soft" black class of coal called bituminous. There is an almost endless list of slightly different grades of bituminous coal, the most widely used class. Further compression still, often associated with warping and faulting and sometimes with heating, produces the class of "hard" coal called anthracite, which is mostly carbon. → p118.

One of the most significant distinctions among the various bituminous coals is based upon suitability for the manufacture of coke, which is used in the blast-furnace extraction of iron from its ore. Coke is mainly the hard carbon that remains after sulphur and the injurious volatile constituents have been driven off by roasting bituminous coal in special ovens. The metallurgical requirements of coke are so stringent that only a small proportion of the world's bituminous deposits can be used to produce it. Consequently, the areas where iron can be smelted economically are seriously restricted.

Structural Associations of Coal. Since the original position of swamp deposits is nearly horizontal, the coal beds of many coal deposits still have an essentially horizontal position, a condition that markedly simplifies the problems of mining. Mining is also affected by the fact that individual swamps seldom are very large for individual beds, or seams of coal, are not usually extensive. However, this is not necessarily true of coalfields, which are areas containing many associated coal beds. In these regions conditions favorable to coal formation existed widely and for long periods. Numerous swamps flourished and then dried up, and their organic accumulations were buried by earthy sediments at the same time that other swamps were coming into existence nearby. If subsidence of an entire area took place, newer swamps may have formed above the remains of the older, but separated from them by layers of inorganic sediments. Accordingly, in some coalfields the beds are widely distributed both in area and in vertical sequence.

The various structural and situational relationships in which coal occurs markedly affect its accessibility (Fig. 21.9). In some localities of nearly horizontal structure, beds are found so close to the surface that they may be strip-mined by power shovels after the removal of only a few feet of covering earth or rock (Fig. 21.10). In areas with somewhat greater relief, the horizontal seams are mined with giant augers (Fig. 21.11). In most coal-mining regions, however, the beds are far enough underground that it is necessary to sink shafts to reach them.

Shafts sunk into the ground for any mining purpose are in effect dug wells, and they commonly extend below the water table. As a consequence,

one of the great technical problems of mining is to remove the water that flows out of the saturated rocks into the shafts and drifts (horizontal passages).

Coal Regions. There is a vast amount of still-unmined coal in the world. Present estimates of the total minable reserve, which are probably about right, total several trillion tons—enough for many hundreds of years at the present rate of use. But the reserve is very unevenly distributed over the earth.

Three general features of its geographical distribution are significant: First, almost all the known minable reserve lies in the Northern Hemi-

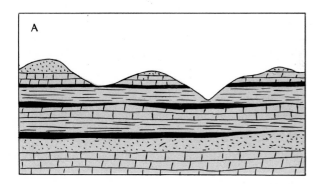
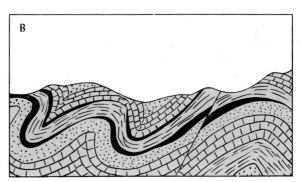
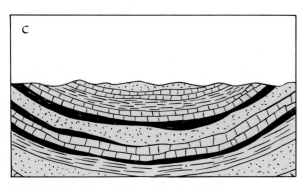

Figure 21.9 Several surficial and structural relationships of coal: (A) a stream-dissected hill-land area, such as in the western Pennsylvania coalfields; (B) a highly folded and faulted area, such as in the Pennsylvania anthracite region; (C) an area underlain by a gentle synclinal or basin structure, such as in southern Illinois; and (D) an area where erosion has removed some of the coal beds, while the rest occur on the flanks of the upland, such as on either side of the Pennine Upland in England.

Figure 21.10 Giant furrows turned by power shovels in the process of strip mining in southern Illinois. The 4-ft-thick bed of coal exposed in the bottom of the trench is mined out before the next furrow is turned.

sphere. Second, about 50 percent of this reserve is in deposits in Asia—the vast majority of them located in the U.S.S.R. and China. The rest of the reserve consists of 34 percent in North America, 13 percent in Europe, and the remaining 3 percent among all of Africa, South America, and Australia.[1] Third, it is estimated that about four-fifths of the total lies within the boundaries of only three nations: the United States, the U.S.S.R., and China, in that order (Fig. 21.12). Of the rest of the Northern Hemisphere reserve, a considerable proportion (approximately one-eighth of the total) occurs in the countries of western and central Europe. It should be noted that if the continent of Europe, not including the U.S.S.R., is taken as a whole, it ranks first in coal production—ahead of the United States, the U.S.S.R., and China.

[1] M. King Hubbert. *Energy Resources.* National Academy of Science–National Research Council, Washington, D.C., 1962. Pp. 36–37.

Thus the known coal reserves are concentrated within a relatively few national areas. Quite the opposite is true of usable deposits, however. Many small deposits scattered over the earth contain amounts which are very important to the economies of the places where they occur. For example, Japan, with only about 0.2 percent of the world's reserve, extracts about 50 million metric tons annually to support its highly developed complex of heavy industry. At least 35 countries each produce a million or more tons of coal per year.

North America. The Appalachian region is much the most important coalfield of North America. It contains numerous workable beds of good-quality coal, some of which have the characteristics required for the manufacture of blast-furnace coke (Fig. 21.13). The deposits occur mostly within the dissected Appalachian hill country, and they are noted for the ease with which they are mined, since the coal beds, which are traversed by innumerable deeply incised stream valleys, often are exposed along the valley walls (Fig. 21.9A). Three-fourths of the coal output of the continent is obtained from the Appalachian field, including most of the American export coal and most of the coal used in the eastern and northeastern industrial districts of the United States. The northern section of the field is the most productive.

The Interior region of the United States is also abundantly provided with coal deposits (Fig. 21.13). Again the coal generally is bituminous, although not of coking quality. Among the several sections of this region, the eastern part located in Illinois and Indiana is by far the greatest producer. In it the rocks have a broad synclinal (saucerlike) structure (Fig. 21.9C), while the coal beds in the central portion are so deeply buried that mining operations are concentrated mainly on the margins of the field.

The remaining producing areas in North America, ranging from the Rocky Mountain fields to the small deposits in Nova Scotia, are locally important but do not approach the productivity of the Appalachian and Interior fields.

Figure 21.11 A giant mechanized auger removing more coal from a "bench" previously stripped with power shovels. *(Photography by Courier-Journal and Louisville Times.)*

Europe. A relatively narrow belt containing numerous coalfields extends from the British Isles eastward across western and central Europe (Fig. 21.14). The leading nations of western and central Europe, in order of production as well as in availability of proved reserves of good-quality coal, are the United Kingdom, West Germany, and Poland. An indication of the wide availability of coal in western Europe is the fact that coal is produced in more than 20 countries. Only the United Kingdom and Germany, however, have large deposits of coking-quality coal.

British coalfields contain coal of bituminous quality or better, and only two parts of the island are far from a deposit: the ancient crystalline rock region of the Scottish Highlands, and the plain of southeastern England. Most of the readily accessible coal in Britain has been mined, and the remaining seams are increasingly costly to utilize.

The numerous coalfields of continental Europe include coal of many types, among them the lower grades of coal and even peat, all of which are used much more in continental Europe than in Great Britain or the United States. The most productive portion of the western section lies in the Ruhr River Valley, the center of the heavy iron and steel industries of Germany (Fig. 21.14). The Ruhr Valley contains a reserve of coking coal reputed to be larger than any other in continental Europe. The eastern end of the central European coal belt is also highly productive. The major deposits lie in East Germany and in the Silesian deposits of Poland and adjacent portions of Czechoslovakia.

The coalfields of the European U.S.S.R. are limited to some locally useful deposits of lignite south of Moscow and in the central Ukraine, and to the productive Donets field in the eastern

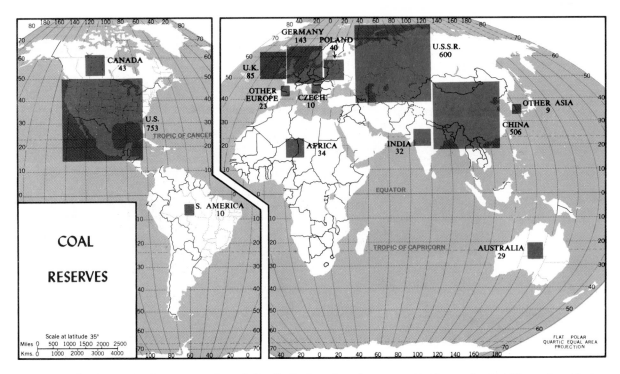

Figure 21.12 Diagrammatic representation of the distribution of coal reserves. Numbers refer to billions of metric tons. *(After Hubbert.)*

Ukraine. This great deposit contains coal of all qualities, including coking coals, and supplies the large industrial areas of this region (Fig. 21.14).

Asia. Nearly 50 percent of the world's coal reserves lie in deposits in Asia. They are about evenly divided between the U.S.S.R. and China (Fig. 21.12). Most of the large reserve of good-quality coal in the U.S.S.R. is in Siberia, where the Kuznetsk field is the major producer (Fig. 21.15). This field is estimated to be tremendously rich in high-quality reserves; indeed, it is considered second only to the Appalachian coalfield in the United States. The Karaganda field (located midway between the Kuznetsk and Ural areas) and the Abakan field to the east are also significant producing areas.

    Smaller coalfields lie on both flanks of the Ural Mountains, in the region west of Lake Baikal, in the Tunguska region north of Lake Baikal, and

far to the east in Siberia. In the isolated forest areas of northern and eastern Siberia are extensive coal deposits whose boundaries and reserves are imperfectly known.

    Of the widely distributed deposits of coal in eastern and southern Asia, Communist China has by far the greatest amount (Fig. 21.16). Coal is found in many parts of China, but the greatest deposits are in North China and Manchuria. The provinces of Shansi and Shensi have the largest reserves of good-quality coal. The coalfields of Manchuria, which support a considerable industrial community, are especially valuable because they contain good coking coal. China is already the third-largest national producer after the United States and the U.S.S.R., and as the country continues to grow industrially, coal production will also rise.

    Other Asian countries that have important coal supplies are India and Japan. Those of India

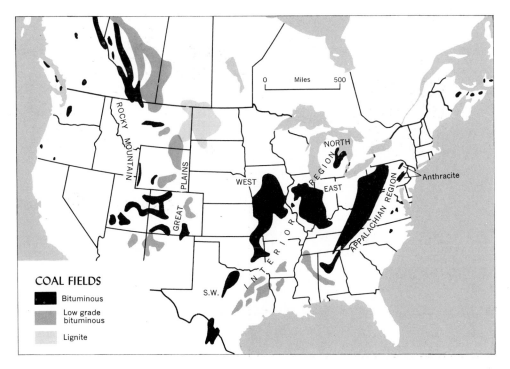

Figure 21.13   Principal coal deposits of North America, showing the distribution of major classes of coals.

are located in the Damodar Valley in the northeastern part of the Deccan Plateau, about 150 miles inland west of Calcutta. They are now being intensively used in the iron and steel industries of the same region. India's reserve of coal is large, but the supply of coking coal is limited. In Japan, unfortunately for its industrial establishment, the reserve of coal is relatively small and scattered, and many

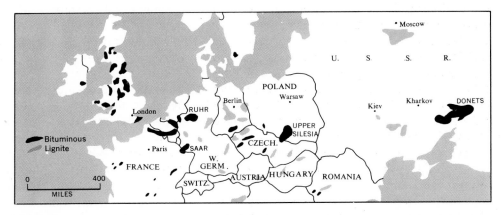

Figure 21.14   Principal coal deposits of west central and eastern Europe, including the western U.S.S.R.

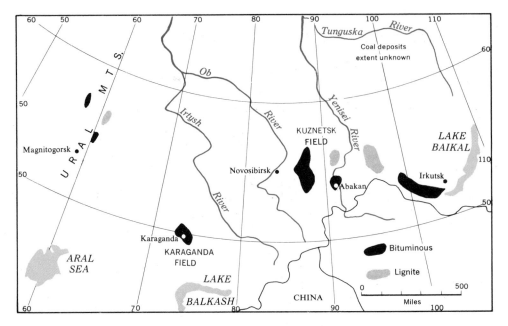

Figure 21.15   Principal coal deposits of western Siberia.

of the beds are badly faulted. The most productive field is that in northern Kyushu, followed by those of central Hokkaido.

South America, Africa, and Australia. Hardly 3 percent of the world's coal reserves are contained in South America, Africa, and Australia together. This small amount is unevenly distributed, with southern Africa and Australia having the most and being about equally endowed (Fig. 21.17). In each case the production meets the needs of the region. Of all the continents South America has the least coal; it contains only a few small, scattered deposits.

Sources of Nuclear Energy

The only alternatives now known to coal, oil, and gas as sources of energy are solar radiation, water power, and nuclear energy. Solar radiation is difficult to concentrate, and the amount of energy potentially available from water power is relatively limited. Within the present generation, however, man has learned to control the release of some of the energy in the nucleus of the atom by fission and fusion. Both operations liberate astounding amounts of energy, and since there is a relative abundance of the materials used in these processes, man can look forward to a practically unlimited supply of energy from mineral sources.[2] To date only fissioning has had any practical development, and many such atomic power stations are already in operation in several countries. But it will be some time yet before atomic energy contributes more than a token to the total peaceful energy production of the world.

Minerals for Fission. The production of power by fission utilizes U-235, one of the isotopes of uranium, with or without the other fissionable materials: U-233, another isotope of uranium, or Pu-239, plutonium. U-235 is relatively scarce, and U-233 and Pu-239 are produced by "breeding"— that is, by processing in an atomic furnace, or pile, two other minerals which occur much more abun-

[2] *Ibid.* Pp. 106–141.

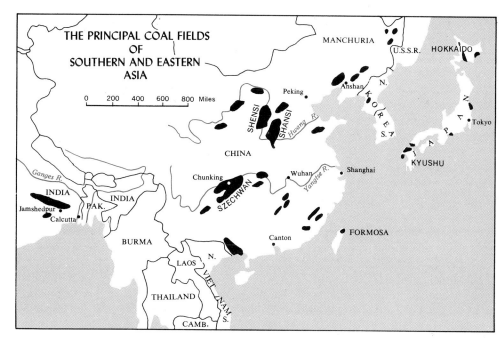

Figure 21.16   Principal coal deposits of southern and eastern Asia.

dantly than U-235: namely, uranium 238 (from which the small amount of U-235 is obtained) and thorium 232 (several times as abundant as U-238). Accordingly, the locations throughout the world of deposits of uranium 238 and thorium 232 will ultimately assume a significance comparable to that of petroleum distribution.

Nuclear fuel deposits of uranium and thorium are scattered throughout the world in all continents. Full information on their extent and accessibility is not yet available. So far as is known, these deposits tend to be concentrated in areas of crystalline rocks—for example, granite and the sedimentary rocks derived from it. The most productive uranium areas have probably been the Katanga region of the Congo in Africa, north central Canada near Great Bear Lake, southeastern Canada in southern Ontario, and the Colorado Plateau area in the southwestern United States. Thorium, which is more abundant, is found in eastern Brazil, the coastal area of southern India and Ceylon, stream deposits of Malaya and Indo-

nesia, and central Florida and the western Carolinas in the United States.

Uranium and thorium occur as normal constituents of granite, but usually in small percentages. Nevertheless, because of the vast amount of granite in the world, there is no possibility of the depletion of this source within the foreseeable future, even if the richer concentrations become scarce.

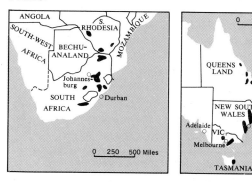

Figure 21.17   Principal coalfields of southern Africa and Australia.

The potential supply of mineral atomic energy, although almost unlimited, cannot be tapped without creating some troublesome problems. Probably the most difficult and disquieting is how to dispose safely of the waste products of the fission process, which remain radioactive and biologically dangerous for long periods. This problem has not yet been solved.

Minerals for Fusion. Energy can be obtained from fusion by combining isotopes of hydrogen to form helium. Although the process is not yet developed to the practicable stage, the supply of raw material is essentially unlimited, since the needed isotopes, principally deuterium, are relatively abundant in sea water. It is estimated that potentially the energy obtainable by fusion from only 8 cu km of sea water is equivalent to the total world supply of the fossil fuels.[3] Furthermore, the product of the process, helium, is not radioactive, as are the products of fission.

Metallic Minerals

Some of the elements of the earth's crust, such as iron or copper, are called metallic. Man learned early to use these, and the development of civilization and the course of human events have been strongly influenced by their geographical occurrence.

Early in history, metals were largely valued for making weapons, utensils, tools, and sewers; but beginning with the Industrial Revolution their utilization (combined with the use of inanimate energy from fossil fuels) has increased a thousandfold. Within the past century, the power-driven machines that are mostly composed of metals have made it possible for man to become a mobile being, and they have increased his productivity and efficiency beyond his greatest expectations.

Metals are sometimes used in the pure state, as, for example, copper or gold; but commonly they are mixed to produce a more desirable

3 *Ibid.* P. 121.

alloy. Bronze (copper and tin) and brass (copper and zinc) are examples of long-known alloys. The most important alloys today, however, are the steels, made by mixing other metals with iron. Without steel our modern high-speed metalworking machines and efficient technologic processes would be impossible.

A few metals, such as copper, aluminum, and especially iron, may be thought of as fundamental resources. For example, huge amounts of iron are required in an industrial society, and iron is of such comparatively low specific value, i.e., low value per ton, that the ready availability of iron ore is considered a matter of major importance by the great nations. Although other metals, such as chromium or tungsten, are critical for some processes, they are used in relatively small quantities and can hardly be called basic mineral resources. Because of their high specific value, this category of metals can move freely in international trade—unless, of course, restrictive trade regulations are imposed to prevent it. In a sense, the whole world draws upon the same sources of supply of these metals.

Structural Associations of Metallic Minerals

An ore is a deposit of metallic mineral (or one of its chemical compounds) which has somehow become sufficiently concentrated to be used practicably. Some metals, such as copper, occasionally occur in the native state. But more often the metallic elements are found in chemical combination with other elements (in such forms as sulphides, sulphates, oxides, or carbonates), from which they must be set free by smelting. Usually the desirable mineral is also intermingled with some quantity of unwanted rock material, called gangue, from which it must be separated by mechanical means. The natural concentration of metallic minerals into ore deposits takes place by a variety of processes that can be grouped in three general categories: (1) igneous activity, (2) weathering, and (3) sedimentation.

Compounds of chromium, nickel, copper,

lead, and zinc are examples of metals commonly found in association with crystalline rock masses as a result of igneous activity. Either these compounds may become concentrated within the igneous mass itself during its cooling and crystallization, or they may intrude or be chemically precipitated from circulating groundwater in the rock zone adjacent to the cooling mass.

Weathering processes, the second category, produce concentrations of metallic ores in several ways. The decomposition of rock masses in warm climates may involve a chemical change, such as the transformation of the unusable silicate of aluminum to the usable ore of aluminum, which is a hydrous oxide called bauxite. Or undesirable components may simply be removed by leaching, thereby effectively concentrating the remainder; as, for example, when the removal of a large portion of the silica from an iron formation concentrates the iron oxide. Finally, a mineral may be leached from one zone and precipitated in a more usable form at a lower level, an example of which is the transformation of the sulphide of copper into the readily soluble sulphate.

The third category, which is the normal sedimentary alluvial process, includes the many minerals that are transported along with other materials by running water and, because of the relative weight of the minerals, become concentrated as placer deposits in the beds of present or former streams. For example, a majority of the world's tin supply comes from placer deposits.

Regions of Concentration of Metallic Minerals

In general, no matter how the ultimate concentration of a usable ore came about, it very often began with the segregation of elements that occurs as a result of heat and pressure in rock masses. It is not surprising, therefore, that ores containing metallic minerals are commonly associated with regions primarily composed of igneous or crystalline rocks. Although there are some notable exceptions, it is generally true that the great areas of tectonically undisturbed sedimentary rocks are relatively poor

in the ores of many metals. Within these very broad generalizations, a few of the better-known regions of mineral production can be identified.

The Canadian Shield is highly productive of metallic minerals and has large possibilities for future discoveries. Its ancient crystalline rocks contain not only rich iron ores but a wealth of other metals. These include most of the world's supply of nickel and large amounts of gold, silver, cobalt, copper, uranium, and others.

The American cordilleran region, from Alaska to Cape Horn, is also noted for the abundance and variety of its mineral products. At least half the world's copper is found here, in deposits as far separated as Chile, Peru, Arizona, Montana, and Alaska. Gold, silver, lead, and zinc are sufficiently abundant that Mexico, the United States, and Canada rank high in the production of each of them. The Andean countries of South America are important producers of platinum, tin, and tungsten, and have an appreciable output of other metals. It was the gold of this region that prompted its conquest by Spain.

In central and southern Africa the crystalline rocks include several highly productive mineral regions. Within that vast area are the Rand, the world's leading gold-producing district, and such important centers in the production of copper as the Katanga region in Zambia and the adjacent Congo. There are also districts producing chromium, manganese, and uranium, and important localities from which most of the world's diamonds are mined.

Among other mineral regions of world renown are the following: (1) Areas of igneous and crystalline metamorphic rocks in southern and western Australia have yielded gold, silver, lead, zinc, and minor quantities of other metals. (2) The crystalline rocks of the highlands of eastern South America, in Brazil and the Guianas, contain deposits of iron ore and bauxite. In addition, these highlands yield important quantities of manganese, thorium, gold, and precious stones, and are known to contain deposits of several other metals which are as yet little developed. (3) A large region of crystalline rocks in eastern Asia extends from Korea on the south to the shores of the Sea of Okhotsk on the north, and thence westward in southern Siberia. From it comes a great part of the gold that makes the U.S.S.R. one of the leading producers of that metal. The region contains vast areas which are relatively unexplored geologically. (4) The highlands of southeastern Asia yield the largest part of the world's tin, tungsten, and several other metals. (5) The cordilleran region of southern Europe, the Mediterranean borderlands, and the Middle East have important deposits of iron, chromium, zinc, and bauxite. (6) The Ural region of the U.S.S.R. is an area of great variety in its metallic treasures: iron, ferroalloys, aluminum, copper, and the precious metals.

As was observed earlier, there are a few metals, such as iron, aluminum, and copper, whose ores are needed in large quantities in order to satisfy fundamental demands of modern civilization. To these must be added a class of metals needed for alloying with iron to make steel—the ferroalloys, which are not needed in large amounts but which are indispensable to the modern uses of iron. Iron, aluminum, copper, and the ferroalloys are found in a variety of places and in many kinds of deposits.

Iron. Iron usually occurs in chemical combinations, the more important ones being the oxides named hematite (Fe_2O_3), magnetite (Fe_3O_4), and limonite (hydrous oxides), and the carbonate named siderite ($FeCO_3$). The oxides particularly are scattered widely though thinly over the earth, but to be usable as an ore a concentration must contain at least 25 to 35 percent of the metal. Iron-bearing minerals sometimes contain as much as 70 percent iron, but ore deposits seldom consist solely of these minerals; instead the iron content of a mass is reduced by associated gangue minerals, especially silica.

There are many places which have substantial deposits, but since at present iron must be separated from the ore by the use of coke, it is important that these two ingredients be readily

accessible to each other. The world's populated plains are tributary to the basin of the North Atlantic Ocean and include the only three areas in which abundant deposits of both iron and coking coal are closely associated. These are eastern North America and the Caribbean, northwestern Europe, and the U.S.S.R. They are the present world centers of heavy iron and steel manufacture, as well as of the many other industries that depend on abundant iron and steel. Some of the world's greatest reserves of iron ore are in Brazil and India, but Brazil has almost no coking coal, and India has only a limited supply. China has large reserves of coal but no known comparable supply of ore.

Western Hemisphere Deposits. In the Western Hemisphere there are several regions of unusual present and potential future iron-ore production. The outstanding ones are those associated with the crystalline rocks of the Canadian Shield, in both the United States and Canada.

The United States has the most renowned iron deposits—those of the Lake Superior district (Fig. 21.18). These ores are mostly hematite of high quality, the average iron content being 50 percent or over. Some of the deposits are easily mined by power shovel, though these are rapidly being depleted (Fig. 21.19). The proximity of the Lake Superior ores to regions of manufacture and market is fortunate. The Great Lakes, with the canals connecting Lakes Superior and Huron, provide a deep waterway almost from the mine to the very margin of the Appalachian coalfield and the heart of the American industrial region.

The remaining reserves of easily mined, high-quality ore in the Lake Superior district are not large, and an alternative ore, taconite, is now being used. Because its iron content is only about 25 percent, taconite is first "beneficiated"—that is, artificially concentrated and pelletized so that the product contains some 60 per cent iron.

Iron deposits are found elsewhere in the United States besides the Lake Superior district, but the reserves are limited. The most-used deposit is in Alabama, where iron is mined in the same

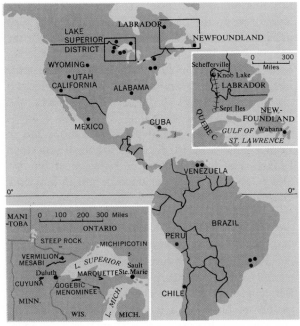

Figure 21.18 The major Western Hemisphere iron deposits. The insets show the Lake Superior and Labrador districts in greater detail.

district with the coal and limestone required for its smelting (Fig. 21.20).

Canadian deposits in the Canadian Shield occur particularly in the western Ontario region northwest and northeast of Lake Superior. Another

outstanding concentration is in the Knob Lake–Schefferville district in the eastern part of the shield (Fig. 21.18). Much of the ore in this district is hematite with an iron content exceeding 60 percent, and open-pit mining is practiced.

Deposits in Venezuela supply a large share of the iron-ore imports of the United States. High-grade ores are located near the lower Orinoco River, so that the ore is easily moved by water to the smelting centers of the eastern United States. Other Latin American deposits are in Brazil, Chile, Peru, Mexico, and Cuba. The extremely large reserve of Brazilian ore lies some 200 miles north of Rio de Janeiro in the crystalline rocks of the Brazilian Plateau. Mining operations in this vast deposit are just beginning.

Eastern Hemisphere Deposits. Throughout the Eastern Hemisphere there are many iron deposits (Fig. 21.21), some of which now produce abundantly for local consumption. However, only a few appear to rank among the major world reserves. The largest, which contains perhaps a quarter of the world's supply, is in India in the Bihar-Orissa region about 150 miles west of Calcutta. This vast deposit of excellent quality is utilized in connection with the coals of the same general area.

The great iron deposits of the U.S.S.R. rival those of the United States. The major pro-

Figure 21.19 Mining ore in an open pit in northern Minnesota. Open-pit ore of high quality is no longer abundant in the Lake Superior district. *(Oliver Iron Mining Company.)*

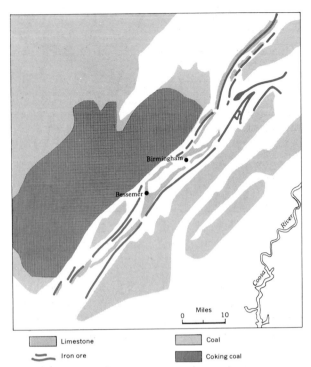

Figure 21.20 The distribution of minerals essential for iron smelting in the Birmingham, Alabama, industrial region.

ducing areas are at Krivoi Rog in the Ukraine, and near Magnitogorsk and several other areas in the Ural section. A smaller concentration occurs in the Kerch region, and there are several other places,

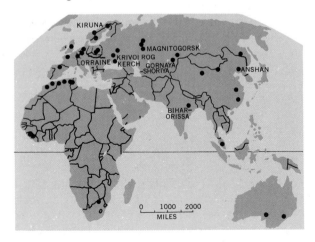

Figure 21.21 The major Eastern Hemisphere iron deposits.

not now utilized, of lesser significance. The Krivoi Rog deposit, the richest and normally the most productive, is located about 300 miles west of the Donets coal basin. The ores at Magnitogorsk are used in association with coal from several small fields farther north in the Ural region, and especially with the coal of the distant Kuznetsk and Karaganda fields in Siberia.

The large iron deposits of Europe are in France and Sweden. Sweden has less iron than France, but Swedish iron is superior in quality. Other less important ore deposits are in England, Germany, and Spain.

The Lorraine iron ores of France include the largest single iron reserve in western Europe and one of the large deposits of the world. They occur in the northeastern part of the country and extend into Luxembourg and a short distance into Belgium (Fig. 21.22). The Lorraine ores consist mainly of limonite, a hydrous oxide of iron, and are relatively low in quality, averaging only about 25 to 35 percent iron. The iron ores of Sweden, which are noted for their high quality, are mainly magnetite and average 55 to 65 percent iron. The largest deposits are situated in the crystalline rocks of the far northern part of the country in the Kiruna district. Since there is almost no coal and relatively little iron manufacture in Sweden, most of this ore is exported.

Throughout Africa, Asia, and Australia, iron-ore deposits occur in many places. Some of them now produce in sufficient quantity to fill the needs of local industry—as, for example, those of southern Australia and southern Africa. Deposits are found at many places in China, and production seems to be spreading from the major area, Anshan in Manchuria. Algeria, Morocco, and Tunis are largely exporters.

Ferroalloys. For the manufacture of finished products, the modern industrial world does not use much iron in the state in which it comes from the blast furnace. Instead, iron is alloyed with various other metals and nonmetals to make steels which have special qualities—steels that are stainless,

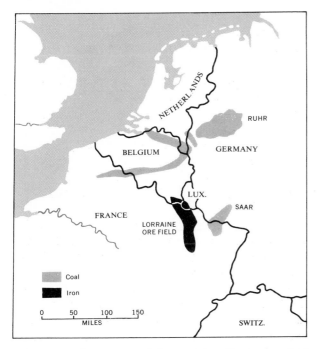

Figure 21.22 Location of the great Lorraine iron-ore field of France in relation to nearby coalfields.

tough, able to hold an edge, capable of withstanding high temperatures, etc. The main ferroalloying metals are manganese, chromium, nickel, tungsten, molybdenum, vanadium, and cobalt; the nonmetals are carbon and silicon. The three most-used metals are manganese, chromium, and nickel.

The major alloying metals are in great demand, although they are not needed in large quantities; comparatively, their combined annual production would probably not be the equivalent of 1/25 of the iron ore mined. In terms of quantity, the one most used is manganese, which is an ingredient in the manufacture of all steel. About 13 lb of manganese is used in making each ton of steel in the United States.

In general the ferroalloys are associated with crystalline and igneous rocks (Fig. 21.23). The world's major known deposits of manganese are in the U.S.S.R., mainly in the southern Ukraine and Georgia. Other major producers are India, the Union of South Africa, Ghana, Brazil, and Mo-

rocco. The largest reserves of chromium are found in southern Africa, Turkey, the U.S.S.R., and the Philippines. Canada is the world's greatest nickel producer.

Although the United States actually produces more alloying elements than any other nation, and leads in the production of several, virtually all its supplies of the most-used three—manganese, chromium, and nickel—must be imported.

Copper. If the importance of metals were to be evaluated on the basis of the tonnage produced, all would pale alongside iron and the ferroalloys. At least ten times as much iron is produced as all other metals combined, and perhaps a third of all these other metals consists of the ferroalloys. Nevertheless, other metals are equally vital to industrial societies. Copper, tin, aluminum, lead, and zinc, to name only a few, have uses for which they are superior to anything else. For example, copper has become the basis of the modern electrical world.

Unlike iron, copper is not widely distributed. And whereas a deposit of iron must contain a high percentage of the metal in order to be usable, a deposit of copper that yields as little as 1 percent is considered an ore. The occurrence of copper ore conforms to the generalization stated earlier: it is found in regions of crystalline rock or in areas of recent tectonic activity.

Western North America, western South America, and south-central Africa, in that order, account for some three-quarters of the known copper resource (Fig. 21.24). None of the great industrial nations, except perhaps the U.S.S.R., is self-sufficient in copper production.

In North America, which produces approximately a third of the world's copper, the copper reserves are located in both the United States and Canadian sections of the western cordillera, and in the Canadian Shield. South American copper ores, also located in the cordilleran region of that continent, are concentrated in Chile and southern Peru. Chile has perhaps the greatest single known deposit. In Africa, copper ores are located in the

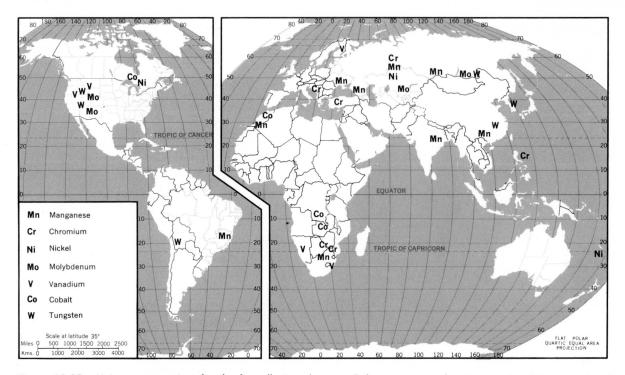

Figure 21.23 Major source regions for the ferroalloying elements. Only manganese, chromium, and nickel are produced in large quantities.

Katanga region of the southern Congo and in adjacent Zambia. Copper reserves outside these regions are small, and so is production; the largest producer elsewhere is the U.S.S.R.

Aluminum. Like iron, aluminum is an abundant element in the earth's crust and is widely distributed; but the only usable concentration known at present is bauxite, an ore which is composed of hydrous oxides of aluminum associated with silica and iron oxide. For the most part, bauxite resulted from weathering and leaching in a warm moist climate, and most deposits are near the surface.

Australia and West Africa have huge reserves of bauxite: those of Australia are on the Cape York Peninsula, and those of Africa are in Ghana and Guinea. Most production, however, presently takes place on other continents: in the Caribbean region, especially Jamaica and Surinam; in British Guiana; in the northern Mediterranean

borderland in Europe (France, Greece, Hungary, Yugoslavia); and in the U.S.S.R. The only known deposits of consequence in North America are in the Ouachita Mountain region of Arkansas.

Nonmetallic Minerals

Man has used the nonmetallic minerals of the earth's crust much longer than he has used either the metallic minerals or the mineral fuels. Very early, he learned to fashion implements and utensils from stones and clay, and he employed rock in the construction of many things. Modern civilization has expanded its use of these materials, demanding ever-increasing amounts for both traditional and new purposes. Road building, architectural construction, and such industries as chemicals, glassware, and fertilizers use volumes of nonmetallic mineral substances that perhaps exceed and certainly rival all the fuel and metallic minerals combined.

Some nonmetallic minerals are employed in their natural states, while others pass through processes of industrial manufacture and appear as components in goods having hundreds of uses. Rocks, sands, clays, salts, abrasives, fertilizers, gems, and many others make up the long list. Most of them are found in a variety of grades. Nonmetallic minerals are essential qualities of the natural equipment of regions, and no limited portion of the earth contains all of them.

As a class the nonmetallic minerals do not have the similarities and regularities in geographical distribution that, to some extent, the fuels and metallic minerals do. It is impossible to make an overall statement regarding their places of origin, although the general locations of some of the individual substances can be named. This brief section will treat only those nonmetallic minerals that are

relatively essential and are required in great quantity.

Salt. Sodium chloride (NaCl), one of the common rock minerals (halite), is used in large volume as a food, a food preservative, and a basic raw material from which industry derives a number of the useful compounds of sodium and chlorine. Owing to its solubility in water, salt is not abundant in the zone of free groundwater circulation in humid climates, but inexhaustible supplies are available for human use from several sources.

The sea, for example, contains $2\frac{2}{3}$ lb of salt for every 100 lb of water. Natural brines, which are the waters of ancient seas, can be found saturating deeply buried sedimentary rocks cut off from general groundwater circulation. Deposits of rock salt, called evaporites, probably resulted from the evaporation of water in the arms of ancient seas or in former arid interior drainage basins. These rock

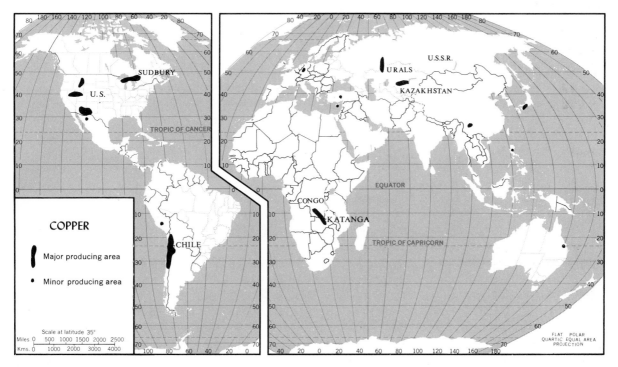

Figure 21.24 Copper-producing areas. The United States, Chile, and the Katanga region in Africa lead in production, followed by the U.S.S.R. and Canada.

salt deposits now are sedimentary rocks deep underground, and because of their fine-grained, nonclastic texture they are practically impervious to groundwater. In addition to all these sources of salt, there are limited surface incrustations of it in interior drainage basins in dry climates. Salt is found in so many places that few parts of the world are without some local supply. For industrial uses, salt is obtained largely by mining rock salt or by pumping brines, either natural brines or those produced by pumping water down to bodies of rock salt.

The industrial regions of North America are supplied with salt from abundant reserves. Thick beds of rock salt underlie large areas in central and western New York, northeastern Ohio, southeastern Michigan, and peninsular Ontario. Other large reserves are found in the buried salt domes of the Louisiana and Texas Gulf Coast, in deposits in central Kansas, and at various places in the southwestern states. The industrial centers elsewhere in the world likewise are well provided with salt. There are large deposits in western England, central Germany, Austria, and the southern U.S.S.R.

Sulphur. Great amounts of sulphur, primarily in the form of sulphuric acid, are used in a variety of industrial processes. These include the manufacture of fertilizer, chemicals, and paper, as well as the refining of oil. The demand continues to increase.

Deposits of sulphur are of two types: native sulphur (that is, not combined with other elements); and sulphur from pyrites (various sulphides, especially iron sulphide, FeS_2). The two sources supply about equal amounts of sulphur. Some sulphur is also obtained as a by-product of smelting and refining operations. In the Western Hemisphere, most of the sulphur is taken from areas adjacent to the Gulf of Mexico, where native sulphur is associated with salt domes that have thrust upward into overlying sedimentary rock. It is "mined" by the Frasch method: Superheated water is forced into the deposit to melt the sulphur, and the mixture is brought to the surface by compressed air, all in a continuous process. Elsewhere it is obtained by mining pyrite, or as a by-product. There are large world reserves of pyrites. In addition to the United States, Italy, Japan, and the U.S.S.R. are leaders among the many countries which produce sulphur.

Mineral Fertilizers. In farming areas, continuous cropping and accelerated erosion usually remove the elements of soil fertility faster than they can be resupplied by natural processes. The most-needed nutrients—nitrogen, calcium, potash, and phosphorus—are, moreover, among those especially susceptible to depletion. The volume of agricultural production can be increased markedly in areas of initial or induced low soil fertility by adding these elements. For each of the four, there are known mineral deposits which can be drawn upon for the manufacture of fertilizers.

Nitrogen, although largely unavailable to plants in the gaseous form, is now provided by combining it with nonmetallic minerals after obtaining it from the atmosphere or as a by-product of the coking of coal. Its production from mineral deposits in arid lands has practically ceased.

Calcium, in the form of calcium carbonate, is readily available in the limestones of many regions. The other two soil nutrients are much less abundant, and notable deposits of them are considered to be resources of great importance. Potash,[4] for example, is obtained in small quantities from the ashes of wood, seaweed, and other substances; but the principal commercial sources are deposits of complex minerals. There is a large reserve of potash, and it is widely produced. The United States has great supplies in deposits in southeastern New Mexico. In Eurasia the major production is in Alsace in France, in West and East Germany, and in the U.S.S.R.

Mineral sources of phosphorus, which is an indispensable constituent of all living cells, occur

---

[4] Potash is a term generally used to refer to simple potassium-bearing compounds, such as potassium carbonate (K_2CO_3—lye), potassium hydroxide (KOH), or potassium oxide (K_2O).

principally in rock form as various calcium phosphates. This rock is believed to have been formed from the alteration of limestone by the chemical action of groundwater which had first passed through accumulations of bird and fish remains.

The world reserve of phosphate is very large. Valuable beds of phosphate rock usually occur as local pockets in limestone strata. The principal sources in Europe are located near the Mediterranean coast of Africa in Tunis, Algeria, and especially Morocco, which contains a tremendous reserve. The United States is supplied mostly from extensive beds in western Florida, with small amounts from central Tennessee and the Northern Rocky Mountain region. In the U.S.S.R., phosphate is obtained mostly from the Kola Peninsula.

Building and Crushed Stone. A great variety of rocks is used in tremendous quantities for many types of construction work. Since many parts of the earth contain stone or gravels of stream or glacial origin, it may seem that rock, in this broad sense, is one of the universal items of regional equipment, like the air; but that is not true. Some regions are endowed with large quantities of rock, or with rock of unusual quality; others have almost none.

Indeed, a few regions of considerable size are practically devoid of any kind of rock. Among these are the great deltas of the world, where silt covers hundreds of square miles and rock is buried to great depths. Larger still are certain plains of older alluvium, or regions of deep accumulation of wind-blown dusts. Among these are the Pampa of Argentina and similar areas in the American Corn Belt, where such materials cover the rock strata deeply. In these regions there are areas that do not even have any crude rock or gravel with which to surface roads.

By far the greatest demand for rock is in the crushed form for general construction purposes; only a small fraction is needed as dimension stone for building (exterior walls, etc.). Limestone accounts for three-quarters of the total consumption, being heavily used for such purposes as road construction, fluxing, cement, and fertilizing. Where rock is available, it is seldom transported far from its place of origin unless it has some particular quality to recommend it to a wider market, because stone is very heavy and has a low specific value.

An abundant supply of rocks with some special quality is a valuable resource, especially if the region where they occur is also located near a large market. In New England's region of igneous intrusion and metamorphosed sediments, for example, beautiful and massive granites, slates of parallel cleavage, and excellent marbles all are produced near a good market. The even-textured and easily worked gray and buff-colored Bedford limestones of southern Indiana, as well as the Lannon stone of Wisconsin, also have a national market. Some stone of unique quality, such as the statuary marble of Italy, has practically worldwide markets.

Sand, Lime, Gypsum, and Clay. Sand, mostly forms of quartz (SiO_2), is needed in vast quantities in construction as an ingredient of concrete, mortar, and plaster. It is widely used in foundries and for abrasives, and it is the chief raw material in the manufacture of glass. It shares with clay and calcium compounds a place of great importance as a raw material of industry generally. Lime (calcium carbonate, $CaCO_3$, that has been calcined—that is, heated to drive off the carbon dioxide) and clay are required in the manufacture of cement. Clay, of which there are many kinds, is basic to the brick, tile, and pottery industries. Gypsum (hydrous calcium sulphate, $CaSO_4 \cdot 2H_2O$) is widely used in plaster materials.

These substances are common almost everywhere. There are, for example, river sands, beach sands, wind-blown sands, sands in glacial deposits, and pure sandstones. There are unconsolidated marls, soft chalks, and other limestones from which lime may be obtained. Deposits of gypsum and anhydrite (anhydrous calcium sulphate) are relatively widespread. There are river clays, marine clays, residual clays, and shale rocks.

Indeed, most regions have more than one of these minerals.

Qualities differ, however, and needs for particular grades often cannot be supplied locally or even regionally. For example, common clays are good enough for the manufacture of ordinary brick and tile, but not for special purposes. Kaolin, which is used for fillers and pottery and which must be particularly pure, is valuable enough to be traded internationally. It is usually found in residual deposits, where it has weathered from coarsely crystalline feldspars. Good grades of glass sand, free from iron and clay, may be transported hundreds of miles to major centers of glass manufacture. Thus some regions have economic advantages from particular natural endowments even in these common substances. Indeed, some have achieved international fame through their products, such as the regions of pottery clays in southern England, northern France, and Bavaria.

Selected References for Chap. 21

Alexander, J. W. *Economic Geography*. Prentice-Hall, Inc., Englewood Cliffs, N.J., 1963.

Frasché, D. F. *Mineral Resources*. Publication 1000-C, National Academy of Science–National Research Council, Washington, D.C., 1962.

Fryer, D. W. *World Economic Development*. McGraw-Hill Book Company, New York, 1965.

Hubbert, M. K. *Energy Resources*. Publication 1000-D, National Academy of Science–National Research Council, Washington, D.C., 1962.

Jones, C. F., and G. G. Darkenwald. *Economic Geography*. The Macmillan Company, New York, 1965.

Leet, L. D., and S. Judson. *Physical Geology*. Prentice-Hall, Inc., Englewood Cliffs, N.J., 1958.

Lydolph, P. E., and S. Shabad. "The Oil and Gas Industries of the U.S.S.R." *Ann. Assoc. Amer. Geographers,* Vol. 50, pp. 461–486, 1960.

Miller, E. W. "World Patterns and Trends in Energy Consumption." *J. Geog.,* Vol. 58, pp. 269–279, 1959.

———. "Mineral Regionalization of the Canadian Shield." *Canadian Geographer,* No. 13, pp. 17–30, 1959.

Pounds, N. J. G. *The Geography of Iron and Steel*. Hutchinson & Co. (Publishers), Ltd., London, 1959.

Pratt, E., and D. Good. *World Geography of Petroleum*. The American Geographical Society and Princeton University Press, New York, 1950.

Rodgers, A. "Coking Coal Supply: Its Role in the Expansion of the Soviet Steel Industry." *Econ. Geog.,* Vol. 40, pp. 113–150, 1964.

Steel, R. W. "The Copper Belt of Northern Rhodesia." *Geography,* Vol. 42, pp. 83–92, 1957.

Thoman, R. S., E. C. Conkling, and M. H. Yeates. *The Geography of Economic Activity*. 2d ed. McGraw-Hill Book Company, New York, 1968.

Van Royen, W., and Oliver Bowles. "The Mineral Resources of the World." *Atlas of the World's Resources*. Vol. II. Prentice-Hall, Inc., Englewood Cliffs, N.J., 1952.

Voskuil, W. H. *Minerals in World Industry*. McGraw-Hill Book Company, New York, 1955.

Zimmerman, E. C. *World Resources and Industries*. Rev. ed. Harper & Row, Publishers, Incorporated, New York, 1951.

INDEX

Map Section

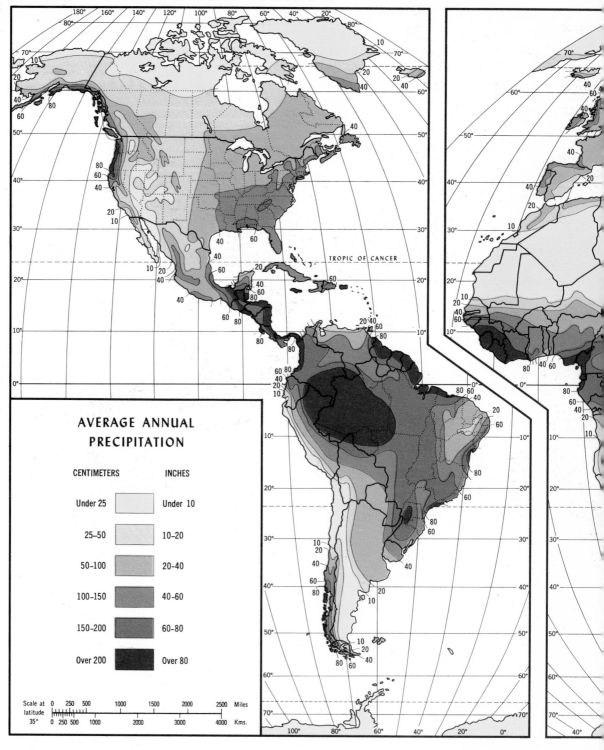

AVERAGE ANNUAL PRECIPITATION

CENTIMETERS		INCHES
Under 25		Under 10
25–50		10–20
50–100		20–40
100–150		40–60
150–200		60–80
Over 200		Over 80

Scale at latitude 35°

Miles: 0 250 500 1000 1500 2000 2500
Kms.: 0 250 500 1000 2000 3000 4000

TROPIC OF CANCER

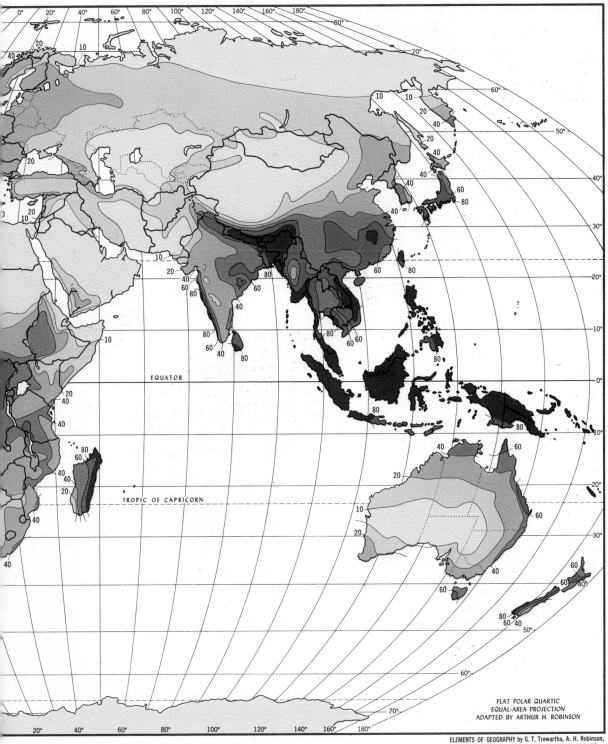

FLAT POLAR QUARTIC
EQUAL-AREA PROJECTION
ADAPTED BY ARTHUR H. ROBINSON

ELEMENTS OF GEOGRAPHY by G. T. Trewartha, A. H. Robinson,
and E. H. Hammond. © McGraw-Hill Book Co., N.Y., 1967.

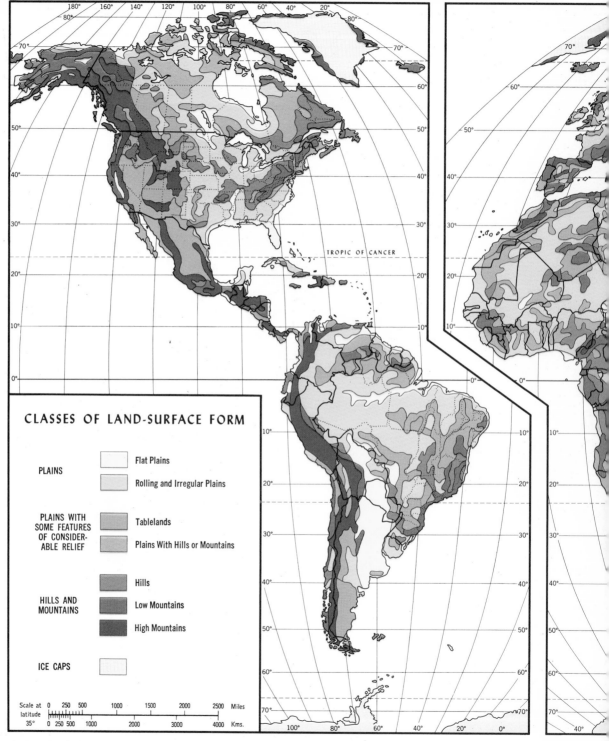

CLASSES OF LAND-SURFACE FORM

PLAINS

- Flat Plains
- Rolling and Irregular Plains

PLAINS WITH SOME FEATURES OF CONSIDERABLE RELIEF

- Tablelands
- Plains With Hills or Mountains

HILLS AND MOUNTAINS

- Hills
- Low Mountains
- High Mountains

ICE CAPS

Scale at latitude 35°

| Miles | 0 | 250 | 500 | 1000 | 1500 | 2000 | 2500 |
| Kms. | 0 | 250 500 | 1000 | 2000 | 3000 | 4000 |

TROPIC OF CANCER

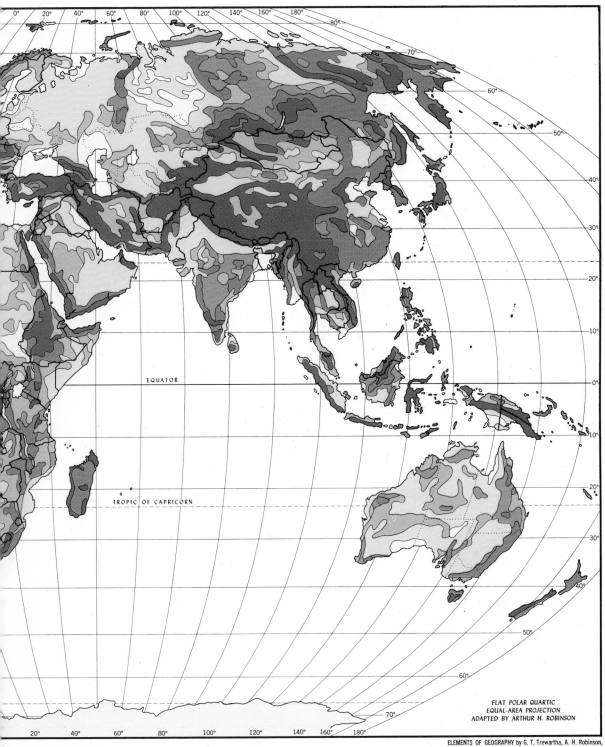

EQUATOR

TROPIC OF CAPRICORN

FLAT POLAR QUARTIC
EQUAL-AREA PROJECTION
ADAPTED BY ARTHUR H. ROBINSON

ELEMENTS OF GEOGRAPHY by G. T. Trewartha, A. H. Robinson,
and E. H. Hammond. © McGraw-Hill Book Co., N.Y., 1967.

4 LITHIC REGIONS

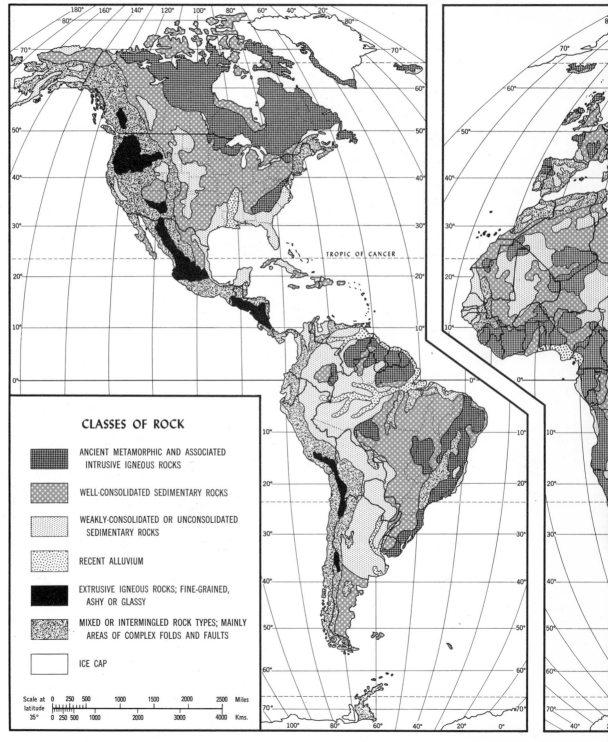

CLASSES OF ROCK

- ANCIENT METAMORPHIC AND ASSOCIATED INTRUSIVE IGNEOUS ROCKS
- WELL-CONSOLIDATED SEDIMENTARY ROCKS
- WEAKLY-CONSOLIDATED OR UNCONSOLIDATED SEDIMENTARY ROCKS
- RECENT ALLUVIUM
- EXTRUSIVE IGNEOUS ROCKS; FINE-GRAINED, ASHY OR GLASSY
- MIXED OR INTERMINGLED ROCK TYPES; MAINLY AREAS OF COMPLEX FOLDS AND FAULTS
- ICE CAP

Scale at latitude 35°
0   250   500   1000   1500   2000   2500   Miles
0   250 500   1000   2000   3000   4000   Kms.

TROPIC OF CANCER

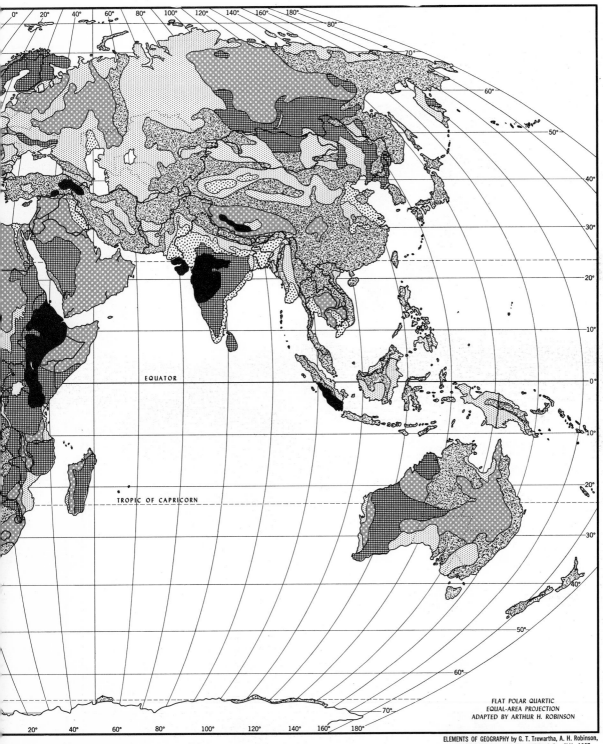

EQUATOR

TROPIC OF CAPRICORN

FLAT POLAR QUARTIC
EQUAL-AREA PROJECTION
ADAPTED BY ARTHUR H. ROBINSON

ELEMENTS OF GEOGRAPHY by G. T. Trewartha, A. H. Robinson, and E. H. Hammond. © McGraw-Hill Book Co., N.Y., 1967.

5 WILD VEGETATION

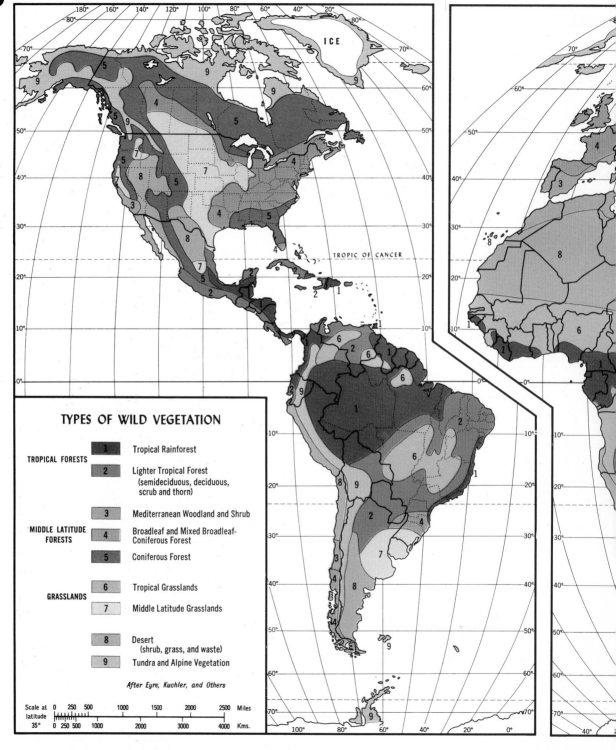

ICE

TROPIC OF CANCER

TYPES OF WILD VEGETATION

TROPICAL FORESTS

1	Tropical Rainforest
2	Lighter Tropical Forest (semideciduous, deciduous, scrub and thorn)

MIDDLE LATITUDE FORESTS

3	Mediterranean Woodland and Shrub
4	Broadleaf and Mixed Broadleaf-Coniferous Forest
5	Coniferous Forest

GRASSLANDS

6	Tropical Grasslands
7	Middle Latitude Grasslands
8	Desert (shrub, grass, and waste)
9	Tundra and Alpine Vegetation

After Eyre, Kuchler, and Others

Scale at latitude 35°

0   250   500   1000   1500   2000   2500   Miles

0   250   500   1000   2000   3000   4000   Kms.

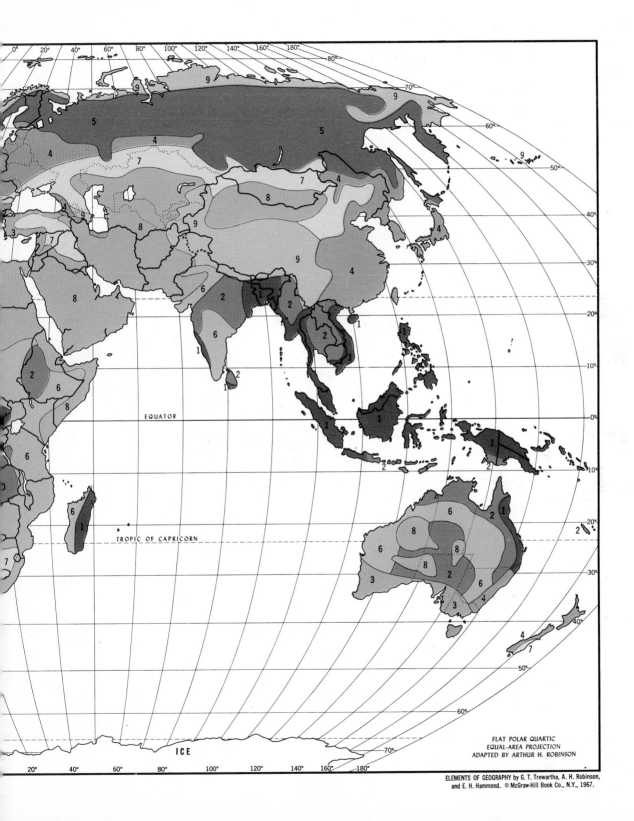

FLAT POLAR QUARTIC
EQUAL-AREA PROJECTION
ADAPTED BY ARTHUR H. ROBINSON

ELEMENTS OF GEOGRAPHY by G. T. Trewartha, A. H. Robinson, and E. H. Hammond. © McGraw-Hill Book Co., N.Y., 1967.

6 SOILS

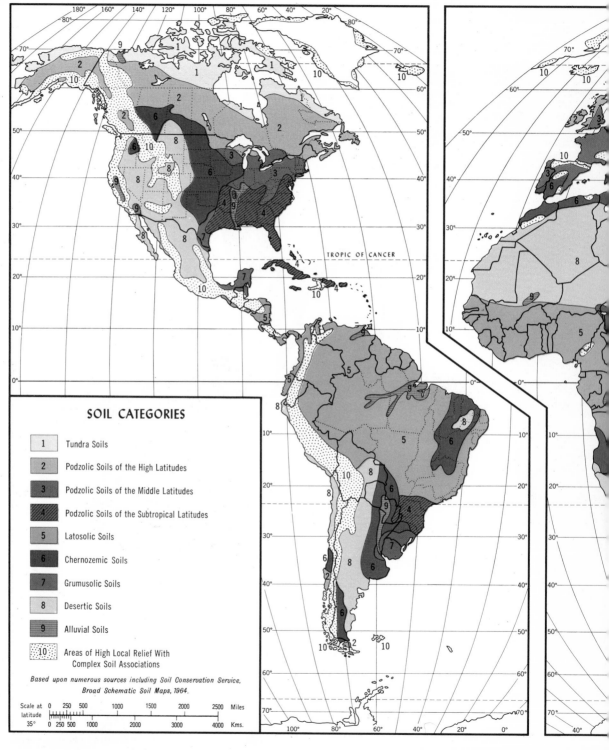

SOIL CATEGORIES

1	Tundra Soils
2	Podzolic Soils of the High Latitudes
3	Podzolic Soils of the Middle Latitudes
4	Podzolic Soils of the Subtropical Latitudes
5	Latosolic Soils
6	Chernozemic Soils
7	Grumusolic Soils
8	Desertic Soils
9	Alluvial Soils
10	Areas of High Local Relief With Complex Soil Associations

*Based upon numerous sources including Soil Conservation Service,
Broad Schematic Soil Maps, 1964.*

Scale at latitude 35°

0 250 500 1000 1500 2000 2500 Miles

0 250 500 1000 2000 3000 4000 Kms.

TROPIC OF CANCER

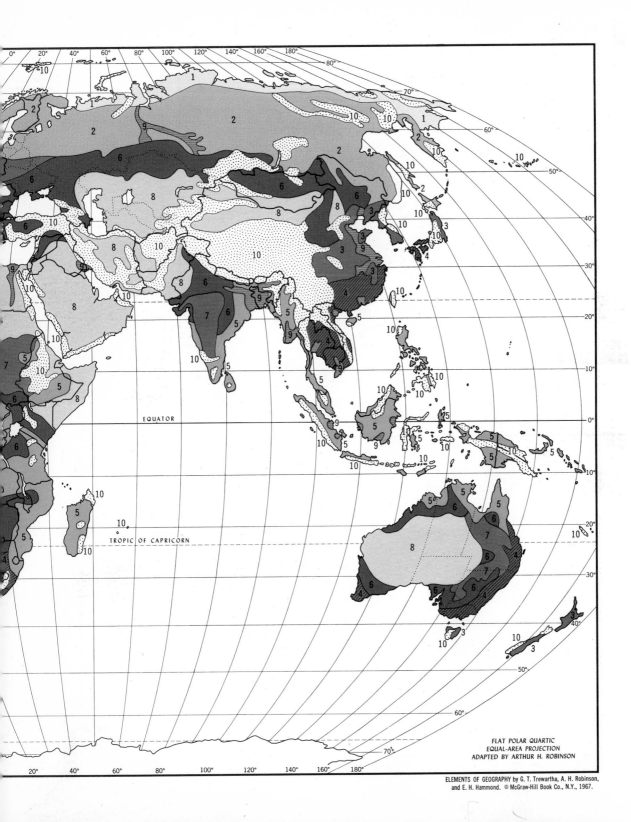

FLAT POLAR QUARTIC
EQUAL-AREA PROJECTION
ADAPTED BY ARTHUR H. ROBINSON

ELEMENTS OF GEOGRAPHY by G. T. Trewartha, A. H. Robinson,
and E. H. Hammond. © McGraw-Hill Book Co., N.Y., 1967.

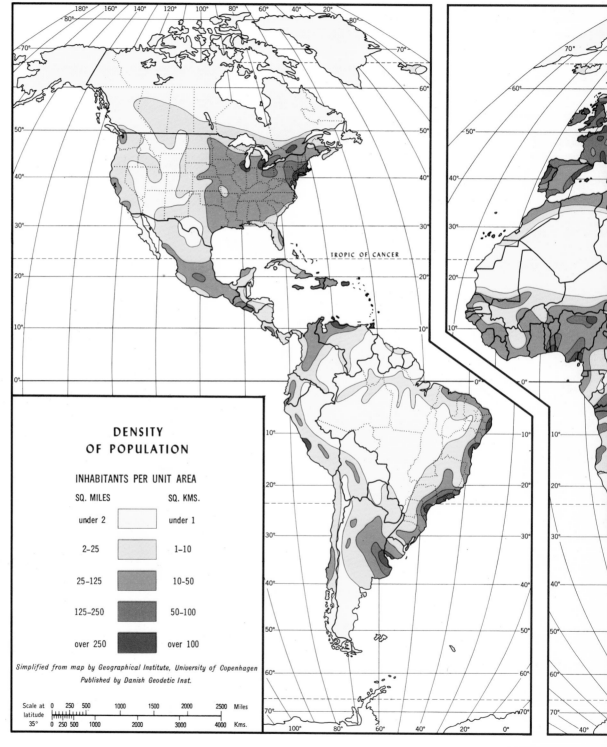

DENSITY
OF POPULATION

INHABITANTS PER UNIT AREA

SQ. MILES		SQ. KMS.
under 2		under 1
2–25		1–10
25–125		10–50
125–250		50–100
over 250		over 100

Simplified from map by Geographical Institute, University of Copenhagen
Published by Danish Geodetic Inst.

Scale at latitude 35°

0   250   500   1000   1500   2000   2500   Miles

0   250 500   1000   2000   3000   4000   Kms.

TROPIC OF CANCER

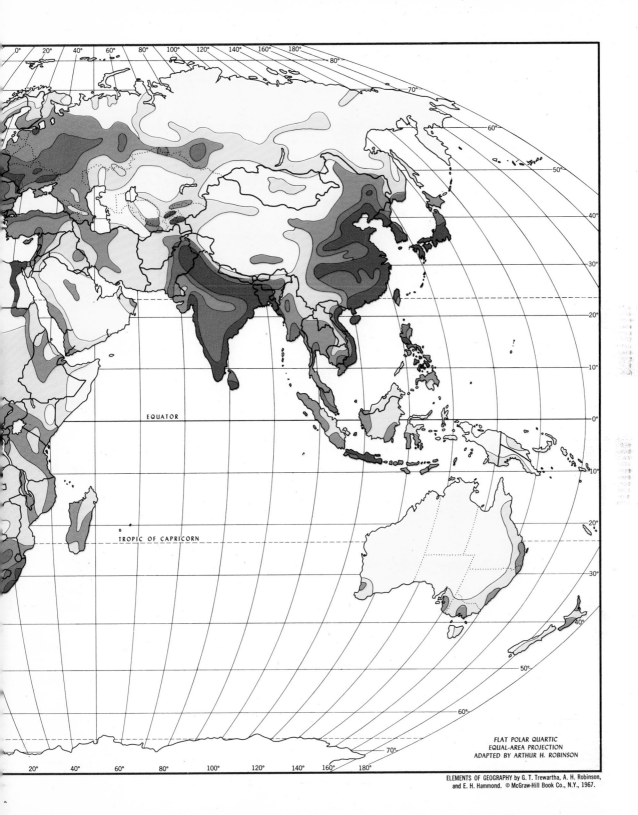

EQUATOR

TROPIC OF CAPRICORN

FLAT POLAR QUARTIC
EQUAL-AREA PROJECTION
ADAPTED BY ARTHUR H. ROBINSON

ELEMENTS OF GEOGRAPHY by G. T. Trewartha, A. H. Robinson,
and E. H. Hammond. © McGraw-Hill Book Co., N.Y., 1967.

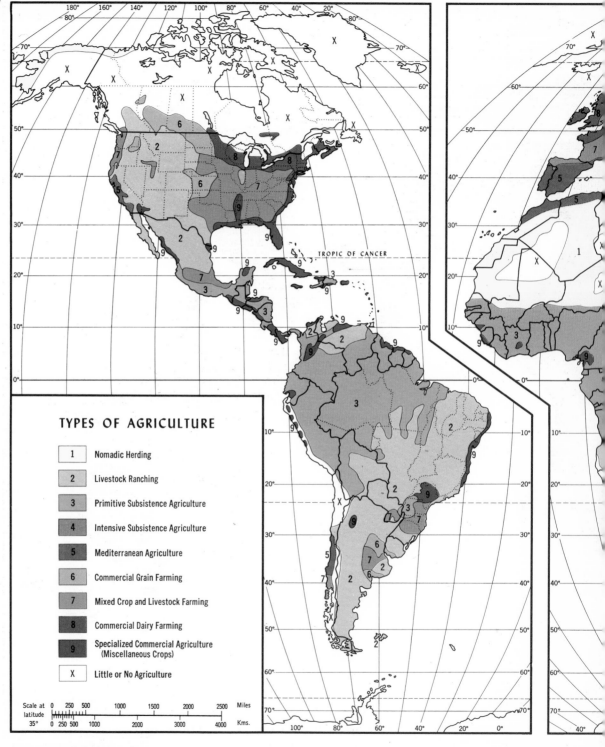

TYPES OF AGRICULTURE

1	Nomadic Herding
2	Livestock Ranching
3	Primitive Subsistence Agriculture
4	Intensive Subsistence Agriculture
5	Mediterranean Agriculture
6	Commercial Grain Farming
7	Mixed Crop and Livestock Farming
8	Commercial Dairy Farming
9	Specialized Commercial Agriculture (Miscellaneous Crops)
X	Little or No Agriculture

TROPIC OF CANCER

Scale at latitude 35°
0   250   500   1000   1500   2000   2500   Miles
0   250 500   1000   2000   3000   4000   Kms.

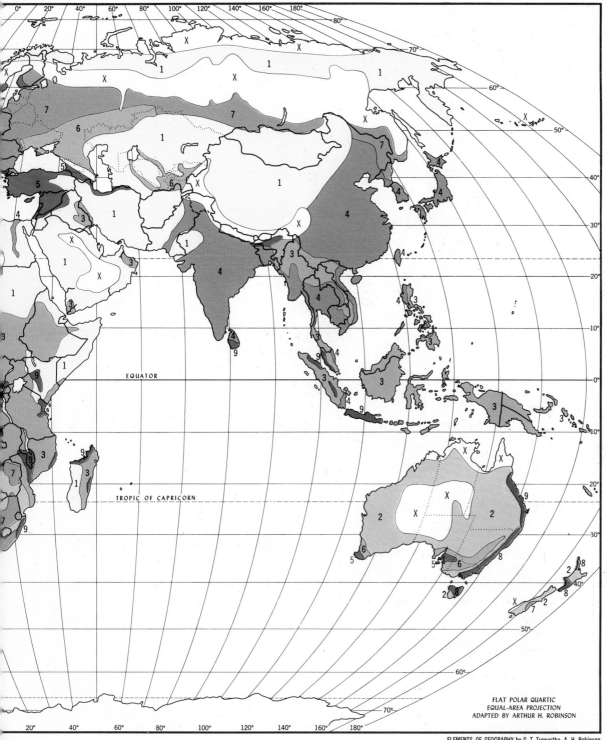

FLAT POLAR QUARTIC
EQUAL-AREA PROJECTION
ADAPTED BY ARTHUR H. ROBINSON

ELEMENTS OF GEOGRAPHY by G. T. Trewartha, A. H. Robinson, and E. H. Hammond. © McGraw-Hill Book Co., N.Y., 1967

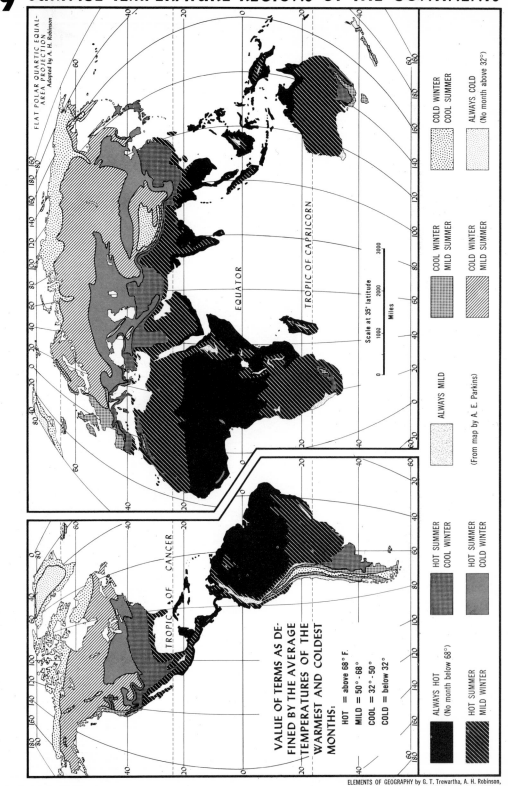

FLAT POLAR QUARTIC EQUAL-AREA PROJECTION
Adapted by A. H. Robinson

TROPIC OF CAPRICORN

EQUATOR

TROPIC OF CANCER

Scale at 35° latitude

Miles

0   1000   2000   3000

VALUE OF TERMS AS DE-FINED BY THE AVERAGE TEMPERATURES OF THE WARMEST AND COLDEST MONTHS:

HOT = above 68° F.

MILD = 50° - 68°

COOL = 32° - 50°

COLD = below 32°

ALWAYS HOT
(No month below 68°)

HOT SUMMER
MILD WINTER

HOT SUMMER
COOL WINTER

HOT SUMMER
COLD WINTER

ALWAYS MILD

(From map by A. E. Parkins)

COOL WINTER
MILD SUMMER

COLD WINTER
MILD SUMMER

COLD WINTER
COOL SUMMER

ALWAYS COLD
(No month above 32°)

ELEMENTS OF GEOGRAPHY by G. T. Trewartha, A. H. Robinson, and E. H. Hammond. © McGraw-Hill Book Co., N.Y., 1967.